ADVERTISING WORKS 13

Proving the effectiveness of marketing communications

ADVERTISING WORKS 13

Proving the effectiveness of marketing communications

Cases from the 2004 IPA Effectiveness Awards

Edited and introduced by

Alison Hoad

Convenor of Judges

First published 2005 by the World Advertising Research Center
Farm Road, Henley-on-Thames, Oxfordshire RG9 1EJ, United Kingdom
Telephone: 01491 411000
Fax: 01491 418600
E-mail: enquiries@warc.com

A CIP catalogue record for this book is available from the British Library

ISBN 1 84116 169 1

DVD of the 2004 IPA Effectiveness Awards winners produced by DigiReels.
Typeset by Godiva Publishing Services Ltd, Coventry
Printed and bound in Great Britain
by Cromwell Press, Trowbridge

Contents

SECTION 2: SILVER WINNERS

SECTION 3: BRONZE WINNERS (SUMMARIES)

CONTENTS

Foreword

The *Financial Times* has been involved in judging the prestigious IPA Effectiveness Awards since 1994 and has been overall sponsor since 1998. I was therefore delighted to be asked to write the foreword to this book (the 13th in the series) as the Awards celebrate 25 years of effectiveness.

Since their establishment in 1979, the Awards have gone from strength to strength – both in terms of the quality of the cases considered and the numbers of agencies and clients entering.

Just as the *FT*'s authoritative, accurate and incisive reporting and analysis make it an indispensable read for the international business community, the case histories published in the *Advertising Works* series are a vital reminder to businesses of the unique value of effective communication in building brands. They are of enormous value as examples of best practice for both agencies and clients alike.

This book brings together cases as diverse as O_2, Bounty paper towels, Volkswagen cars, Police Officer Recruitment, Marks & Spencer Lingerie and Tobacco Control. Each example demonstrates the effective use of marketing to deliver a real return on investment. Ingenuity, creativity and precise targeting are an essential part of the marketing mix.

We congratulate the authors, agencies and clients involved in the winning case histories, for the inspiration that their imaginative thinking provides.

Ben Hughes
Worldwide Advertising Director
Financial Times

IPA Effectiveness Awards 2004

THE STORY SO FAR

'There is nothing either good or bad but thinking makes it so'[1]

Or so said Hamlet in the play that carries his name. Anyone in search of proof of this supposition could do worse than read this book. It is full of case studies that show how powerful communication can be in changing the way customers think about products, services and brands.

Cast your eyes over the contents page of this book and you'll see an eclectic mix of organisations old and new, big and small. What unites them is that they are all better off financially as a result of investing in communication ideas that successfully influenced people's minds. All the case studies in this book are testament to this and all are worthy of reading. However, I doubt any of you will have the time or indeed inclination to read it cover to cover. So what I aim to do in this introduction is to highlight those case studies that offer particularly noteworthy learning. However, before we get to the case studies themselves, I have a guilty admission to make.

Before I was appointed as Convenor of these Awards I had never read an introduction to an IPA *Advertising Works* book. So, although I had been reading and entering papers for years and regarded this scheme as setting the gold standard in effectiveness, I didn't understand the broader remit of why they existed. I'm going to take a wild guess that I was not alone in this. I found it instructive to discover how controversial the scheme was at the time it launched and thought others might too.

It is indicative of how successful the Awards have been that, prior to their existence, it was intellectually respectable to claim that it was impossible to isolate and thus prove that advertising worked.[2] This was the context in which the Awards launched in 1979 with the headline shown below, which ran in management and trade publications.

Advertising works and we're going to prove it

The objective then was to create a collection of published case histories to prove that research, properly used, could *isolate* what advertising had contributed over and above other elements in the marketing mix, and that advertising was a contributor to profit not just cost.

---

1. Hamlet, act II scene ii. William Shakespeare, 1598.
2. As one of my predecessors, Tim Broadbent, noted in *Advertising Works 11*, a leading practitioner called R. Jones published a textbook called *The Business of Advertising* (Longman, 1973) in which he wrote 'the effects of advertising are largely immeasurable ... advertising makes an unknown contribution to selling goods'. His point was that many marketing activities other than advertising affect consumer demand for advertised brands and that separating advertising effects seemed impossible.

Nowadays the early case studies such as Krona, the first-ever Grand Prix winner in 1980, can seem naïve in their simplicity, dealing mainly with short-term sales effects. Yet within the climate of the time it was a tremendous achievement to isolate any effect of advertising at all. Later case studies identified the longer and broader effects of advertising. Landmark case studies such as BMW (1994) and Stella Artois (2000) demonstrated how advertising could maximise revenues, beyond temporary volume lifts, by building brands that people would desire not just in the short term, but also into the future and, importantly, were prepared, even happy, to pay a premium for. In turn, case studies such as Tesco (2000) and Orange (1998) isolated the manifold effects of advertising; its ability to maximise value by affecting not only customers but also other audiences such as staff and the City.

For the first 20 years of its life, although our understanding of 'effectiveness' evolved, the focus of the scheme remained on *isolating* the effect of advertising. Yet during this time the communications world had moved on and we had witnessed fundamental changes in the media landscape. In today's world of new channels and fragmented audiences it is now the norm for campaigns to be communicated in many different ways, in addition to or even instead of traditional above-the-line media advertising. Consequently, advertising now rarely works in isolation from other communication channels; indeed it is often consciously designed to work *with* them. And the number of channels a campaign is expected to work in is growing all the time (four on average for IPA winners), especially since, increasingly, it is essential that it works as hard for a company internally as it does externally. To look solely at advertising can actually devalue the impact of ideas because good ones live and have an effect beyond any one channel.

Therefore, in 2002 the Awards broadened to encourage entries from all communication channels. This change to the entry criteria was only possible because developments in evaluation techniques and ingenuity had demonstrated that we could look at complex communication techniques in a credible and convincing way. So a big hurrah to all those people involved in getting the Awards to this point. From here on in, the scheme was looking for papers to prove the commercial power of ideas, in whatever form they were communicated.

THE COMMERCIAL POWER OF IDEAS

Idea: Something, such as a thought or conception, that potentially or actually exists in the mind as a product of mental activity[3]

Ideas can be powerful. We all know that the most compelling ones make us think, and subsequently behave, differently. This year's crop of papers is bristling with ideas that have made people behave differently in relation to brands and issues. To be included in this book, the 'difference' in thought and action the idea has brought about must have translated favourably to an organisation's bottom line. Each case study tells its own story of how it transformed the fortunes of an organisation. Yet within this there are key learnings, as described below, about the ways in which a communications idea wields commercial power.

3. dictionary.com.

- **Ideas can create a brand**

The Virgin Mobile case study demonstrates how the idea 'See Red. Then see Virgin Mobile' quickly established the brand as a simple and human alternative to the 'Big Four'. The Virgin Mobile case study has an almost perfect control against which to assess its performance since it bought its airtime from One2One's existing network and sold it under the Virgin brand. It subsequently outperformed them, proving the power of an idea to add customer appeal not otherwise apparent in the product. The case study shows how an advertising idea built the brand and subsequently built the business.

- **Ideas can transform people's negative perceptions**

The Volkswagen Diesel case study shows how the idea 'Don't forget it's a diesel' transformed perceptions of diesel cars. Once seen as dull and sluggish this campaign 'helped to make diesel sexy'.[4] The Golf has become the UK's best-selling diesel and motorists are buying more powerful and expensive Volkswagen diesels than ever before.

- **Ideas can reposition the competition**

The British Airways case study shows how the carrier successfully reframed low-cost airlines. BA had dropped out of the FTSE 100, but rather than bail out of Europe, the airline believed it had to battle to survive. It took on the budget airlines at their own game, competing on price but also using its strong service heritage to its advantage. Its campaign exposed the false promises of budget airlines and simultaneously created awareness of BA's lower prices. This reset the value agenda and reframed the image of low-cost airlines. BA posted increased profits of £230m for year ending March 2004 and had re-established itself as a FTSE 100 company.

- **Ideas can rapidly make unknown brands salient**

The 118 118 case history describes how a hitherto unheard-of service usurped BT 192 ownership of the directory enquiries market. The launch of The Number 118 118 became a media event in its own right as the brand's iconic 70s runners and their catchphrase 'Got your number!' slipped into the public consciousness. The early launch was key as it ensured a free run of media space and 'first mover' advantage. By 'switch-off' not only had the 118 118 runners already clocked up 17 million customer calls, they had been referenced in 80% of all articles written about switch-off. No wonder 118 118 immediately became brand leader in the new deregulated market and managed to charge a price premium to BT while doing so.

- **Ideas can unite people behind a common cause**

The East of England Development Agency's 'Demand Broadband' case study describes how communication acted as a powerful lobbying tool. A lack of high-speed connections was stifling growth in the region so the development agency wanted to gain broadband access from telecoms companies that had refused to supply it to rural communities. So while most campaigns are designed to increase demand, the objective of this campaign was effectively to increase supply. Omobono's campaign idea, 'Demand Broadband', directed those without

4. Judges' comments.

broadband to an online brokerage system that grouped potential customers with other registrants in their area. It showed people that, while they had little influence on the situation individually, as a group they could have a strong voice. BT has now changed its policy and is in the process of enabling telephone exchanges throughout the region.

- **Ideas can transform social behaviour**

The 'Safer Travel at Night' case study submitted by Transport for London and Greater London Authority shows how an insightful idea led to a 22% reduction in rapes in London. By advising girls to 'Know what they were getting into' when using minicabs at night the ads succeeded in changing their attitudes and behaviour towards minicabs. These behavioural shifts took place at a time when people are at their least rational and most complacent – after a night out, when they just want to get home.

This shift to ideas per se and media neutrality seems to have been welcomed by agencies and clients alike, if this year's entries are anything to go by. In addition to the longstanding regulars (nine out of the top 10 creative agencies submitted case studies), over 20 new clients and agencies entered and, overall, the number of agencies entering was up by 50%.

Since, increasingly, we are all chasing ideas that are big enough to translate across all communication channels, this year we called for entries that investigated the power of integrated ideas. Our authors rose to the challenge with aplomb. The majority of submissions were integrated case studies and we saw a five-fold increase in jointly written papers to boot.

INTEGRATING AN IDEA TO MAXIMISE ITS COMMERCIAL VALUE

Indeed this year's entries demonstrate time and again that, the more integrated an idea, the more commercially powerful it becomes. The winners of the Grand Prix, the Charles Channon Award for Best New Learning and the prize for Best Integration (O_2, Cravendale and the Central London Congestion Charging Scheme for London respectively) demonstrate that integrated ideas can do the following.

- **Increase the efficiency of a campaign**

The astonishingly complete integration of O_2's campaign allowed it to punch above its media weight: despite an actual share of voice of 14%, O_2's effective share of voice was 33%. So had its advertising been more typical of the market O_2 would have needed to spend twice as much to achieve the same effect. This level of cut-through had broader benefits for the O_2 business. In just two years post-launch, despite being outspent by established competitors, O_2 became the most salient brand in the mobile telecoms market. This rapid advertising awareness translated into rapid brand awareness creating all-important scale for the new O_2 brand.

- **Build a brand long term while simultaneously delivering short-term revenue**

Beyond the obvious financial return of improving the efficiency of a campaign, one of the most interesting commercial benefits of integration lies in its power to fulfil long- and short-term objectives simultaneously. Again the Grand Prix is illuminating here: all of O_2's communications, regardless of their specific task, was visually and strategically consistent – having the brand idea of empowerment at its core. So although over 80% of O_2's marketing funds supported short-term sales-driving initiatives it has been unusually successful at securing longer-term sales too.

- **Make a whole marketing programme greater than the sum of its parts**

Cravendale, the UK's first premium milk brand, now worth £41m, accelerated the growth of its business by investing in an integrated idea. The creative concept was simple: cows as experts on great-tasting milk. The 'Cows' theme was established on TV to create awareness and then implemented through other trial-driving activity such as shelf barkers, door-drops and packaging. Integrating above and below the line was five times more effective at winning customers in the short term and three times more so in the long term than advertising alone.

- **Simplify complex communication tasks**

The Central London Congestion Charge case study shows how an integrated campaign simplified the complexity surrounding the launch of the largest traffic management system in the world. The campaign had to brief the whole of London on the new charge and how to act. The campaign had to speak to those people affected, ensuring they knew what to do, and inform those who would not be affected so they did not over-tax the system. Despite incredibly complex channel planning with discrete messages going to different targets at different points in time the campaign itself was seamless: a 'Q&A' approach combined with a large 'C' logo and visual of the road. By launch over 80% of Londoners were aware of the scheme and how it affected them. Consequently the scheme worked: it has reduced congestion by 30% and is generating net benefits of £50m a year.

So we now have concrete proof of what the agency sector has been saying for some time: that good ideas travel across media and they are more powerful as a result. And we don't just have proof; we have learning on how best to combine channels and quantify the extra power this can give an idea. Importantly, we also have a body of IPA case studies that can help to define what an integrated idea is.

WHAT IS AN INTEGRATED IDEA?

Most of us these days are in vigorous agreement that we want big ideas that can be integrated across media, across channels and even across entire organisations. Where disagreements most often occur is over what constitutes an integrated campaign. Who hasn't had the debate about whether *integrating* a campaign means *replicating* it or taking the core idea and executing it differently?

The simple answer is that for a campaign to be integrated successfully it can, but does not necessarily have to, look the same everywhere the consumer touches it. Integrating an idea does not just mean replicating it across channels. The only given is that the take-out of any part of an integrated campaign should be the same in order to meet the campaign's objectives, but that individual executions may be, and sometimes should be, different. It may be that a different execution of the core idea is needed to maximise the channel the advertising will appear in, or the discrete customer group it is targeting, or simply to keep the idea itself fresh through iteration in a new medium.

So there is no one-size-fits-all answer – just differing levels of consistency as the idea travels across media. All these approaches are equally valid depending on the task, brand and budget in hand. The broad approaches to integration adopted by the brands in this book are illustrated below.

Total strategic and executional consistency

Campaigns that have total strategic and execution consistency are rare but worth pursuing. As discussed, O_2 (Figure 1) and the launch of the Central London Congestion Charge both demonstrate this, and one could argue that the visual element of their campaigns became almost iconic.

Similarly case studies, such as 118 118 and Cravendale show how successful it can be to take one creative idea (a pair of geeky runners and some disgruntled cows respectively) and make it live across all channels. In these campaigns the idea looks the same in whatever channel it appears.

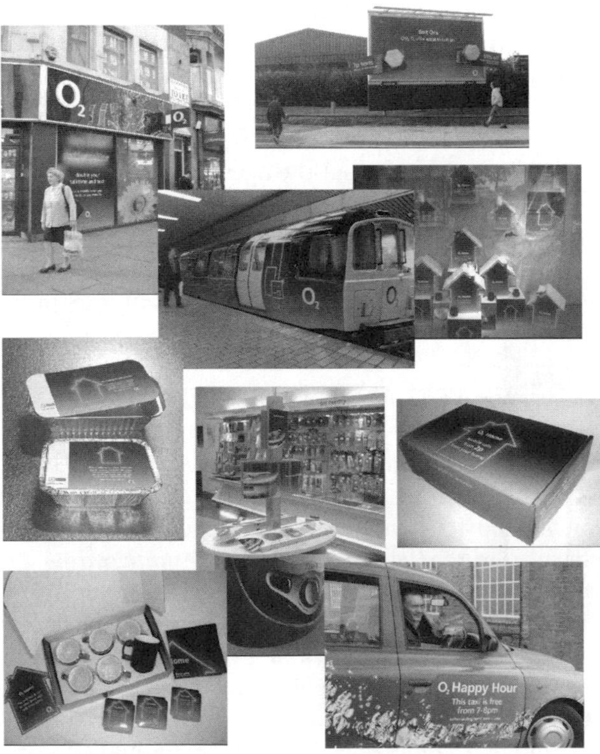

Figure 1: *Examples from the Grand Prix-winning O_2 case study 'It only works if it all works'*

Consistent creative idea executed differently

Many of this year's top prize winners describe campaigns where there was a strong core creative idea that was executed in different ways across channels.

Honda's Gold-winning case study shows how it inspired customers with the 'power of dreams' in television, in print, at the Motor Show, in dealerships, online, via direct mail and even in Selfridges where it hosted a week-long 'cog'-themed domino-toppling event. The core idea was always the power of dreams but it was executed in different ways across channels. Not only did the campaign work overall, leading to a 28% increase in sales, but it worked most effectively when drivers had seen it both above and below the line. (Figure 2)

The award for 'Best Idea' went to Volkswagen for its 'Don't forget it's a diesel' concept, which dramatised the difficulty that drivers of Volkswagen diesels had in remembering their car was not fuelled by petrol. This central idea was then executed in different forms in different channels. From a television commercial showing the ways in which people reminded themselves that their car was a diesel, to informative online banners, to posters of petrol pumps made to look like elephants' trunks, to the strategic use of petrol pumps at filling stations.

Figure 2: *The Honda case study, 'The power of dreams', won an IPA Gold Award and the John Bartle Award for Best New Agency*

Consistency of strategic intent, different creative ideas

Perhaps the point about integration not necessarily meaning replication is most dramatically shown in the Tobacco Control paper, which was awarded a Gold and won 'Best Dedication to Effectiveness'. This paper makes a powerful case for integrating multiple messages, and crucially shows the merit in different 'voices' delivering them. It demonstrates how the Government, via a coalition of related brands (NHS, Cancer Research UK and the British Heart Foundation), has successfully waged a war on tobacco. Each organisation offered up a different reason to give up, and did so in a way that did not victimise smokers. Since 2000, 1.1 million fewer people are smoking and 50% more people are calling the NHS Quit Smoking helpline.

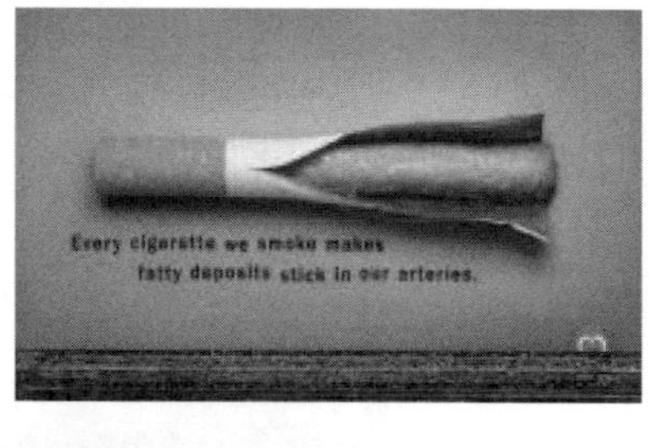

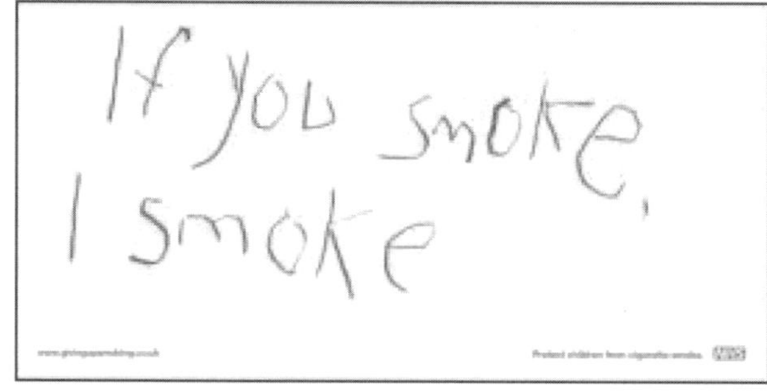

Figure 3: *The powerful Tobacco Control entry won an IPA Gold Award and Best Dedication to Effectiveness*

NEW WAYS OF COMMUNICATING

'You see things; and you say, "Why?" But I dream things that never were; and I say, 'Why not?'

George Bernard Shaw[5]

Lynx and BMW are both campaigns where people asked 'Why not', and subsequently developed new ways of talking to their consumers.

Lynx: Creating a phenomenon

The prize for 'Best Media' went to Lynx Pulse, which developed a new way of talking to, and ultimately *entertaining*, its customers. Lynx looked to the

5. *Back to Methuselah* (1921), part 1, act 1.

entertainment industry for inspiration and consequently generated incremental revenue of £20m. Lynx aimed to create a 'music and dance' phenomenon that would generate the buzz of entertainment properties like *Big Brother* and *Pop Idol*. It selected a relatively unheard-of track, 'Make Luv', and invented a series of simple dance moves to go with it. 'Make Luv' was made available to key opinion formers in bars and clubs. Merchandise followed, and then the dance was brought to life online prior to airing of the TV commercial, featuring a somewhat loveable geek. The track 'Make Luv' went straight to number one and, before long, the dance was being performed in clubs up and down the country and reported in all the tabloids.

BMW: turning product placement on its head

Do not be tempted to overlook the Bronze Award winning case studies, included as summaries in this book. The entry for BMW Films describes how they turned product placement on its head. Instead of paying to place its cars in a movie, BMW North America made its own films and ran them on the internet. This channel has tiny distribution costs and is a medium tied to the prospect's decision-making process. BMW directed prospects to the web by advertising 'The Hire' in the same way a feature film would be. These mini-movies attracted a large, tightly defined audience and boosted planned dealer visits four-fold. They generated $26m of free publicity and were more cost-efficient than their previous more traditional campaigns. This paper also explored 'annuity effects'. 'The Hire' has not had investment since 2002, yet is still working to build the brand. Driven by word-of-mouth, total film views continue to climb, DVDs of the series have traded on eBay and 'The Hire' now exists as a profit-producing venture in the form of a comic-book series.

The idea of 'branded entertainment' has been much written about and debated as the marketing industry's response to the decline of traditional media vehicles. Forward-thinking media owners, clients and agencies are trying to figure out new models of brand building. For these early adopters there's a certain amount of 'fame value' in being first with these new approaches, but there's also a lot of uncertainty and scepticism over whether these models yield any form of economic return on investment. Case studies such as those on Lynx and BMW are crucial in beginning to give us an understanding of how a different model can pay dividends.

If you are particularly interested in other new media learning I would refer you to the O_2 paper for its demonstration of the effects of sponsoring *Big Brother*, to the Imperial Leather summary, which looks at the value of event sponsorship, to Honda and 118 118 for their use of ambient media, Virgin Mobile Australia for its use of viral marketing within a textbook youth campaign and Hertfordshire Constabulary Police Officer Recruitment for its demonstration of the power of local media.

The East of England Development Agency's 'Demand Broadband' campaign brings new learning to the world of direct mail. It not only came up with the idea of mailing parish councils but also, given that no such database existed, painstakingly created one.

CLOSING WORDS

It seems to me that in every set of Effectiveness Awards there is one winning case study that demonstrates the financial value of a brand effortlessly, and the role a communications idea played in building it. This is the case study that you would give to the most hardened of sceptics, and the one you should reach for on those days when it's all going to hell in a handcart. In the case of such an emergency I would urge you to reach for O_2.

It tells the story of a corporate transformation driven by the idea of 'enablement'. In just two years, O_2's troubled predecessor, BT Cellnet, has been transformed into a vibrant brand and thriving business. Where it once trailed the market its share price has outperformed Vodafone, Orange and BT. It is a compelling example of the power of a brand and how re-engineering a flagging one can transform every facet of a business – not simply its sales performance, but the morale of its staff, the esteem of its customers, its ability to sustain competitive advantage and its potential to deliver future earnings. It won the Grand Prix for the sheer scale of its transformation and the totality of its integration. It is certainly an example that 'There is nothing either good or bad but thinking (and in this case a "cornucopia" of small blue bubbles) makes it so.'

The IPA Effectiveness Awards truly set the gold standard for measuring communication effectiveness, and it has been a privilege and a pleasure to have been involved in them. These Awards are only as respected and rigorous as their judges, so thank you to all of this year's, who ensured that each idea awarded had indeed delivered a return on investment. On a personal note, I am indebted to Niall FitzGerald, KBE, Chairman of Judges, whose commitment to his role made mine exceptionally easy to fulfil. And 'Thank you' to Laurence Green who was so much more than Deputy Convenor, especially while I was away on maternity leave.

Finally, a thank you, too, to the life-blood of these Awards, the authors and the clients that support them. Ideas are our business, they are what we create. It is imperative that we are able not only to prove their commercial power, but also understand how they work, in order to optimise their worth.

Alison Hoad
Convenor of Judges 2004

The Judges

STAGE 1: INDUSTRY SPECIALIST JURY

Alison Hoad
Convenor of Judges
Planning Partner
Campbell Doyle Dye

Laurence Green
Deputy Convenor of Judges
Planning Partner
Fallon

John Bartle
Founder
Bartle Bogle Hegarty

Will Collin
Partner
Naked

Wendy Gordon
Partner
Acacia Avenue

Glenn Granger
Associate Partner
Accenture

Mike Hall
Chief Executive
Hall & Partners

Roger Ingham
Managing Director
Data Alive

Iain Jacob
Chief Executive
Starcom MediaVest

Nigel Jones
Chief Executive
Claydon Heeley Jones Mason

Caroline Marshall
Executive Editor
Campaign

Mark Ritson
Associate Professor
London Business School

Roderick White
Editor
Admap

Bob Willott
Editor
Marketing Services Financial Intelligence

Joe Yasin
Partner
The Planning Business

STAGE 2: CLIENT JURY

Niall FitzGerald, KBE
Chairman of Judges
Chairman of Reuters
formerly Chairman of Unilever

Sly Bailey
Chief Executive
Trinity Mirror

Bernard Balderston
Associate Director UK Media
Procter & Gamble

Karen Crowshaw
Head of HR (Central)
HBOS

Adam Crozier
Chief Executive
Royal Mail

Jon Florsheim
Managing Director Sales, Marketing & Interactive
BSkyB

Ben Hughes
Worldwide Advertising Director
Financial Times

Tim Kaner
Director of Marketing
Communications Europe
Sony Europe

Amanda Mackenzie
Vice-President Marketing, EMEA
Hewlett Packard

Scott Morrison
Marketing Manager UK and Ireland
Levi Strauss (UK)

Andrew Nebel
UK Director of Marketing &
Communications
Barnardo's

Nick Ratcliffe
Marketing Director Mercedes Car
Group
Mercedes-Benz

Syl Saller
Director, Global Brand Innovation
Group
Diageo

Miles Templeman
Chairman
Eldridge Pope

Acknowledgements

The IPA Value of Advertising Executive Committee

Sven Olsen (Chairman)	FCB London
Martin Andersen	BDH\TBWA
Joanna Bamford	Consultant
Les Binet	DDB London
Jane Cunningham	Ogilvy & Mather
Neil Dawson	TBWA\London
David Golding	Rainey Kelly Campbell Roalfe/Y&R
Laurence Green	Fallon
Alison Hoad	Campbell Doyle Dye
Debbie Klein	WCRS
Sue Little	McCann-Erickson Manchester
Derek Morris	ZenithOptimedia Group
Hilde Oord	J Walter Thompson Co
Clare Rossi	Zalpha
Sue Unerman	MediaCom

Many people worked hard to make the Awards a success, especially the following: Sven Olsen, Chairman of the Value of Advertising Committee; Niall FitzGerald, KBE, Chairman of Judges; Alison Hoad, Convenor of Judges; and Laurence Green, Deputy Convenor of Judges, whose agency, Fallon, devised the advertising campaign.

At the IPA, the core team comprised Jill Bentley, Tessa Gooding, Emma Kane, Anna Foster, Hamish Pringle, Carey Quarrier and Alex Rogers.

Sponsors

The success of the 2004 IPA Effectiveness Awards owes a great debt to our sponsors. The IPA would like to thank the following companies, whose support made the presentation possible, especially the *Financial Times,* our overall sponsor, whose long-term commitment to the competition has been so important to the industry.

IN ASSOCIATION WITH

AND

campaign

Prizes

GRAND PRIX
Vallance Carruthers Coleman Priest for O_2 (UK) Ltd

CHARLES CHANNON AWARD (BEST NEW LEARNING)
DDB London for Arla Foods (Cravendale)

JOINT EFFECTIVENESS AGENCY OF THE YEAR (BILLINGS ABOVE £100M)
DDB London
Rainey Kelly Campbell Roalfe/Y&R

EFFECTIVENESS AGENCY OF THE YEAR (BILLINGS BELOW £100M)
Vallance Carruthers Coleman Priest

JOHN BARTLE AWARD (BEST NEW AGENCY)
Wieden & Kennedy for Honda (UK)

BEST DEDICATION TO EFFECTIVENESS
AMV.BBDO, Bartle Bogle Hegarty and Euro RSCG London for Department of Health (Tobacco Control)

BEST IDEA
DDB London for Volkswagen UK (Volkswagen Diesel)

BEST INTEGRATION
TBWA\London and Fishburn Hedges for Transport for London (Central London Congestion Charging Scheme)

BEST MEDIA
Bartle Bogle Hegarty for Lever Fabergé (Lynx Pulse)

BEST NEW CLIENT
Rainey Kelly Campbell Roalfe/Y&R, Manning Gottlieb OMD, OMD Metrics and Host for Virgin

BEST PRESENTATION
Rainey Kelly Campbell Roalfe/Y&R for Virgin Mobile Telecoms Ltd

BEST SMALL BUDGET
TBWA\London for Transport for London and Greater London Authority – Mayor's Office (Safer Travel at Night)

GOLD AWARDS

AMV.BBDO, Bartle Bogle Hegarty and Euro RSCG London for Department of Health (Tobacco Control)

DDB London for Arla Foods (Cravendale)

Rainey Kelly Campbell Roalfe/Y&R for Virgin Mobile Telecoms Ltd

TBWA|London and Fishburn Hedges for Transport for London (Central London Congestion Charging Scheme)

Vallance Carruthers Coleman Priest for O_2

WCRS and Naked Communications for The Number 118 118

Wieden & Kennedy for Honda (UK)

SILVER AWARDS

Bartle Bogle Hegarty for Lever Fabergé (Lynx Pulse)

Bernard Hodes Group for Hertfordshire Constabulary (Police Officer Recruitment)

DDB London for Volkswagen UK (Volkswagen Diesel)

DDB London and Claydon Heeley Jones Mason for Guardian Newspapers Ltd (the Guardian*)*

M&C Saatchi and ZenithOptimedia for British Airways

Mortimer Whittaker O'Sullivan and MediaCom for Direct Line

Omobono for East of England Development Agency (Demand Broadband)

Publicis for Procter & Gamble (Bounty)

Rainey Kelly Campbell Roalfe/Y&R, Manning Gottlieb OMD and OMD Metrics for Virgin Trains

Rainey Kelly Campbell Roalfe/Y&R and Walker Media for Marks & Spencer (Lingerie)

TBWA|London for Transport for London and Greater London Authority – Mayor's Office (Safer Travel at Night)

TBWA|London and Manning Gottlieb OMD for Eurostar Ltd

BRONZE AWARDS

Barkers for Scottish Executive (Children's Hearings)

Bartle Bogle Hegarty for Sony Ericsson (T610)

BDH\TBWA for PZ Cussons (Imperial Leather)

BMF Advertising (Australia) for Meat & Livestock Australia (Lamb)

Fallon for BMW (BMW Films)

FCB for Weetabix Ltd

Host for Virgin Mobile Australia

LyleBailie International for Department of the Environment Northern Ireland (Road Safety)

Publicis for The Army (Recruitment)

Rapier and Manning Gottlieb OMD for AA (Loans)

St Luke's for British Telecom (BT Broadband)

TDA DDB for Friesland Middle East (Rainbow)

WCRS for BUPA

Section 1

Gold Winners

GOLD

GRAND PRIX WINNER

1

O_2

It only works if it all works

How troubled BT Cellnet was transformed into thriving O_2

Principal authors: Sophie Maunder and Alex Harris, VCCP; Joanna Bamford, Consultant; Louise Cook, Holmes & Cook, and Andrew Cox, O_2 (UK) Ltd

EDITOR'S SUMMARY

This case study is the story of a corporate transformation. In just two years O_2's troubled predecessor, BT Cellnet, has been transformed into a vibrant brand and thriving business. Where it once trailed the market its share price has outperformed that of Vodafone, Orange and BT.

It is a compelling example of the power of the brand and how re-engineering a flagging one can transform every facet of a business: not simply its metrics, but the morale of its staff, the esteem of its public, its ability to sustain competitive advantage and its potential to deliver future earnings.

It describes how O_2's tightly integrated approach allowed it to build an attractive, long-term brand whilst at the same time delivering short-term revenue growth. Over 80% of O_2's marketing funds have supported sales-driving initiatives. Yet because these campaigns have been executed with a strong brand at their core, they have been unusually effective at winning long-term sales too. It has benefited enormously from the efficiencies of complete visual integration across all communication channels – from broadcast to retail level – and the paper quantifies the value of this.

O_2's investment in communications will pay for itself more than 60 times over, generating at least £4799m incremental margin over the long term.

INTRODUCTION

O_2 is the story of a corporate transformation.

In April 2002, BT Cellnet was a troubled business, losing ground consistently to competitors. A month later it was reborn as O_2: a vibrant, modern brand that has generated a turnaround that would have been inconceivable only weeks before.

Of course, O_2 has made on-going improvements to various structural facets of its business, but the most significant change has been the re-engineering of the brand. Hence this case study is emblematic of how brand engineering can transform not just the metrics of a business, but the morale of its staff, the esteem of its public, its ability to sustain competitive advantage and its potential to deliver future earnings.

The role of communications in this transformation is substantial. O_2's investment in communications will pay for itself more than 60 times over, generating at least £4799m (Holmes & Cook econometric analysis) incremental margin over the long term.

O_2's communications strategy has addressed one of the key challenges facing businesses operating in mature markets: how to build an attractive, long-term brand whilst at the same time delivering short-term revenue growth. Over 80% of O_2's marketing funds have supported sales-driving initiatives. Yet because of its brand-centric approach to communicating these initiatives, they have been unusually effective in securing long-term sales, akin to what might typically be expected of brand communications.

O_2 also provides an excellent example of the benefits of an integrated communications strategy. It has benefited enormously from the efficiencies of astonishingly complete visual integration across all communication channels. But more than that, it has maximised the effectiveness of its communications by employing strategic integration that starts with the brand idea, is carried through to product propositions and is fuelled and lubricated by communication.

THE NEED FOR TRANSFORMATION

On 19 November 2001, mmO_2 plc (formerly BT Wireless) was de-merged from BT plc in a one-for-one share offer, creating a wholly independent holding company.[1] The UK brand, BT Cellnet, was relaunched as O_2 in April 2002.

The new brand faced significant challenges – challenges that BT Cellnet had manifestly failed to tackle. The market had matured, making revenue growth increasingly hard to come by. And competition for that growth was intensifying.

Tougher trading conditions

For a number of years, mobile brands had recorded significant growth on the back of a growing market. But by 2002, as penetration plateaued, revenue growth had stalled (Figures 1 and 2).

1. mmO_2 plc is the holding company for operating mobile businesses in Germany, Ireland and the Isle of Man as well as the UK. This paper focuses on the fortunes of the UK business.

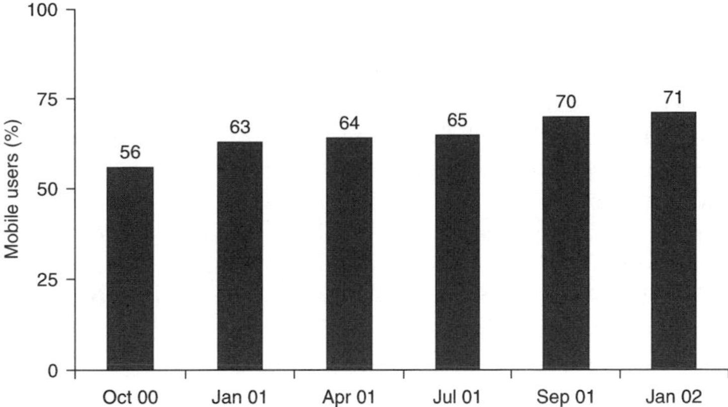

Figure 1: *Market penetration had plateaued*
Source: RSGB Omnibus (*c*.2000 adults per wave)

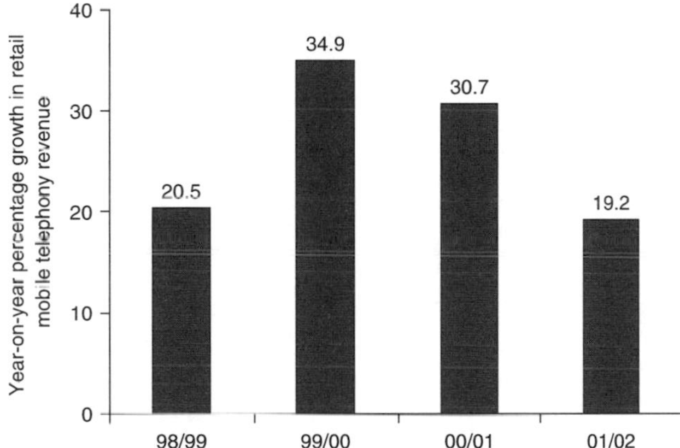

Figure 2: *Revenue growth had stalled*
Source: Oftel

This mature market presented new challenges. Success could no longer be guaranteed by a growing market. Instead, revenue growth had to be found either by enticing customers away from competitors and/or increasing average revenue per user (ARPU) – primarily by stimulating usage of non-voice services.

Growth was further hampered by the difficulty of securing technical advantage. In essence, all brands were working with the same technical raw material.[2] Real advantage had to be fought for on the marketing battlefield.

2. For example, in developing new tariffs (which have become one of the primary product battlegrounds), all brands are working with any combination of (a) monthly line rental, (b) inclusive minutes (peak/off-peak; to own or other networks), (c) subsequent cost per minute; (d) rate per minute and (e) charges for non-voice services. In the majority of cases, it is how these tariffs are marketed, rather than their technical content, that gives them differentiation.

Competition was intensifying

The new brand had to take on extremely well-established and well-supported competitors. Between 1994 and 2000, Orange and Vodafone had each spent *c.*£200m on advertising.[3] In 2001 alone, BT Cellnet's competitors jointly spent £118m.

In addition to these well-established competitors, O_2 would have to face the launch of two new brands.

One2One was being relaunched as T-Mobile.[4] This was sure to pose a significant threat: T-Mobile is a huge operator in Europe and the US, with a user base of over 60 million customers. Then there was the imminent launch of 3 (which proved to be the heaviest advertising launch the market had seen, offering a full range of 3G services via technology that was 18 months ahead of the market).

'The troubled legacy of BT'[5]

As a brand, BT Cellnet had neither the presence of Vodafone, nor the appealing image of Orange (Table 1). Although it was well known, it lacked a clear identity and had little sense of forward momentum.

TABLE 1: BT CELLNET'S IMAGE PROBLEM (INDEXED AGAINST THE MARKET LEADER)

	BT Cellnet indexed against market leader
Spontaneous brand awareness – all mentions	93
Total communications awareness – seen recently	71
Are refreshingly different	48
Make mobile phones simple	78
Lead the way in new ideas	58
Helpful and friendly	67

Source: Millward Brown, 4 weeks to 02/12/02; 300 16–65-year-olds

Significantly, it had been unable to make its market-leading technology[6] count with the consumer, failing to achieve market-leading growth in the expanding non-voice sector (Table 2).

TABLE 2: BT CELLNET HAD NOT CAPITALISED ON ITS MARKET-LEADING TECHNOLOGY: NON-VOICE GROWTH LAGGED BEHIND COMPETITORS

	Growth in non-voice revenue 6 months to Mar 2002 vs 6 months to Sept 2001
Orange	51%
Vodafone	36%
BT Cellnet	36%

Source: O_2 estimates/Oftel[7]

3. Source: MMS and spend figures published in previous IPA papers.
4. At the very same time as O_2 – in April 2002.
5. Paul Durman, *Sunday Times*, 29 February 2004.
6. For example, BT Cellnet pioneered the first texting service at the 2001 Brit Awards; in the same year it launched the UK's first ever consumer GPRS system; it launched Blackberry as early as June 2001.
7. One2One not reported. Non-voice revenue is officially reported as 'data as a percentage of service revenue'.

To compound the situation, public jadedness was mirrored by low internal morale:

> 'Cutting the apron strings will be a breath of fresh air as it will free us from the bureaucracy of BT.'
>
> Kelwyn Whittaker, Site Acquisition Manager

> 'BT Cellnet was not a great place to work. Everyone was depressed. It wasn't dynamic.'
>
> Will Harris, VP Marketing Director at launch (quoted in *Brand Strategy*, May 2002)

Only 20% of staff felt that the different parts of BT Cellnet worked well together in partnership and less than half believed that BT Cellnet management provided a clear sense of direction.[8]

As competitors appealed to consumers more effectively and staff morale flagged, BT Cellnet looked vulnerable. Despite some success in stimulating non-voice usage, any gains in revenue as a result of this were more than offset by a fall in subscribers.

In Table 3 we demonstrate BT Cellnet's position against the key metrics used to measure business performance in this market. (The metrics are explained in Figure 3.)[9]

TABLE 3: BT CELLNET LOOKED VULNERABLE

	BT January–March 2001	BT January–March 2002	Trend
New connections			
Millions	1.6	0.8	↓
Share (%)	27.9	22.8	
Total subscribers			
Millions	11.2	11.1	↓
Share (%) post-pay	25.1	24.8	
pre-pay	25.9	23.6	
Non-voice transactions			
Share of text and picture messages sent (%)	18.9	27.1	↑ [10]
Data as percentage of service revenue	8.1	13.8	
ARPU			
£ (blended, 12 month rolling)	269	231	↓
As a percentage of market average	91.7	87.7	
Revenue			
Share of retail revenue (%)	23.6	21.4	↓

Source: Oftel, BT Cellnet/O_2[11]

8. Source: BT Cellnet 'Care' Staff Survey, May 2001.
9. These measures are produced for Oftel by all mobile communications businesses and are used by City analysts in their assessments of performance.
10. We have seen in Table 2 that, although its non-voice transactions had grown, BT Cellnet's performance was not especially remarkable relative to the market.
11. January to March period selected to show the final quarter of BT Cellnet trading.

New connections – new connections within a defined period

Total subscribers – a business's overall revenue base – reflecting the balance between new connections and retention of existing customers. Share is expressed for different consumer groups: pre-pay (i.e. consumers paying for calls and other transactions up-front) and post-pay (i.e. consumers paying monthly)

Non-voice transactions – share of text and picture messaging sent and total non-voice activity (expressed as data as a percentage of service revenue – service revenue being that derived from all calls and non-voice transactions)

ARPU – average revenue per user

Revenue – it should be noted that, given the size of consumer base and a 'lifetime' of between three and five years for each user, small movements in share of new connections or subscribers and/or ARPU can have a significant impact on revenue

Figure 3: *Mobile communications: key performance indicators*

A poor prognosis

It was hardly surprising that neither pundits nor consumers were optimistic about O_2's chances of success:

> 'First impressions are difficult to shift. When mmO_2 de-merged from BT two years ago, few in the City expected anything but disappointment from the mobile phone group.'
>
> *Sunday Times*, February 2004

> 'Consumers are not that excited by yet another network. By the time of launch, consumers may know O_2 is ex-Cellnet, which brings reliability but constrains your ability to present O_2 as completely new. They may regard it as purely a cosmetic repackaging exercise.'
>
> Corr Research & Consultancy, December 2001

Summary

BT Cellnet was heading in the wrong direction. It was struggling on all the key metrics – new connections, total subscriber base, non-voice transactions, ARPU and revenue. To prove the cynics wrong, O_2 needed to build a strong brand – one that would be capable of turning around business performance, despite a maturing and more competitive market in which growth was far from guaranteed.

CREATING A TRANSFORMATORY BRAND

O_2 wasn't a new enterprise, but it would be a new brand. And the attractiveness of this brand would be fundamental to the future fortunes of the company.

Marketing principles

Two principles have driven O_2's approach, as described below.

1. *Custom-building the brand for its times*
   Unlike T-Mobile, which effectively retro-fitted onto its UK operations a brand that had been developed in a different market in a strikingly different era, O_2 sought to build an entirely new brand, deliberately designed to maximise growth in a mature market.

2. *Full integration*
   Market conditions dictated integration on two levels.

   - It was essential to build rapid brand awareness (to recoup the ground lost by switching from BT Cellnet to an entirely new brand). Given O_2's relative marketing budgets, this would only be achieved by complete *visual* integration across all of its channels.
     The level of visual integration O_2 has achieved is nothing short of an operational miracle: its iconography operates not just across individual campaigns, but across every type of communication (from promotional mugs to advertising) at all times. This approach is epitomised by the internal mantra: 'It only works if it all works'.
     As we shall see, this has been vital in rapidly building a presence in the market (and has delivered material financial efficiencies).
   - Market conditions also dictated that the bulk of O_2's marketing investment would need to be put behind revenue-driving products and tariffs. Yet at the same time it was essential to build a strong, attractive brand for the long term. The challenge for O_2 was how to be successful on both counts simultaneously.

The solution was to ensure complete *strategic* integration. The brand idea and attitude informs and shapes everything from product positioning to advertising and sponsorship, to staff conferences and trade launches. We will see how this has enabled the business to use what typically would be short-term initiatives to fuel long-term brand growth.

The brand idea

From the start, customers rather than products have been at the heart of O_2's approach. Through research, it became apparent that whilst consumers had moved on with mobile telephony, the brands operating in the sector had not.[12]

Where existing networks sought to offer a mobile vision, consumers were tiring of pretentious or empty promises. Where existing brands tried to force-feed technical innovation, consumers had grown adept at identifying only those aspects of technology that were actually of relevance.

So rather than being a provider of mobile technology or a mobile visionary, O_2 set out to become the most 'enabling' brand in the marketplace. The brand exists solely to provide more ways in which the customer can work, play, communicate. This central idea of 'enablement', and the 'fresh thinking' attitude that it has spawned, is epitomised by the brand's 'Can do' mantra and its values: bold, open, trusted and clear.

12. Source: Corr Research & Consultancy; H2 Research.

Strategic integration: the brand–product–communications continuum

Other brands in this market seemed to be rather remote from their day-to-day product offering. They established an image and a personality through their brand and, almost in isolation of the brand, used their product offering (such as bonus airtime, new tariffs, etc.) in a tactical way, to drive short-term sales (Figure 4).

O_2 had neither the time nor the resources to adopt this 'parallel' approach. Instead it has ensured that 'enablement' and 'fresh thinking' run from the brand, through its products into communications. Rather than treating products as technical gizmos, or tariffs as tactical one-offs, O_2's communications wrap them in the brand idea. This is intended not only to create consumer-focused propositions that are of genuine interest and relevance, but *also* to drive positive associations with the brand.

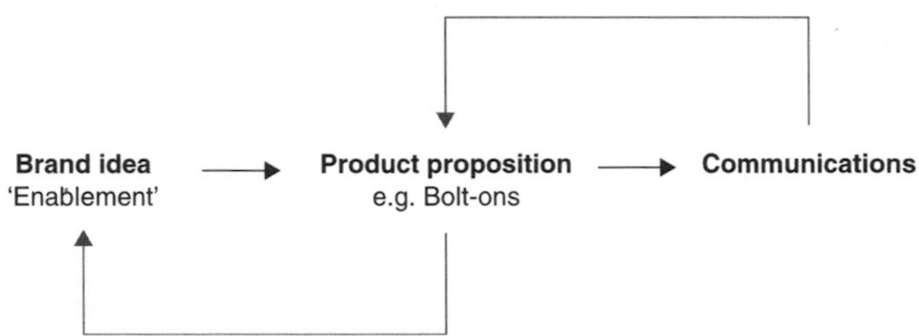

Figure 4: *Strategic integration: O_2's brand–product–communications continuum*

This 'brand–product–communications continuum' has generated a stream of fresh thinking from O_2 – Pay & Go Wild, Bolt-ons, Home, Happy Hour, Business Zones (Figure 5).

Figure 5: *Examples of O_2's fresh thinking*

The brand–product–communications continuum has also been adopted in O_2's sponsorship of *Big Brother*, which was designed to stimulate actual usage of non-voice services (e.g. *Big Brother* games, text alerts, text chat room) which, in turn, help build positive associations with the brand.

O_2's approach is in striking contrast to those of competitors and its predecessor. BT Cellnet products were just products (and were thus neither compelling in themselves nor exemplars of a bigger brand idea).

The striking difference between O_2 and BT Cellnet's communication approaches

A price discount

As the market for text messaging grew, so did the competition around the unit cost of each message. BT Cellnet adopted a conventional 'manufacturer' discount approach of 50% off over a given time span. In stark contrast, O_2 created a new vocabulary of value in text messaging with the concept of text 'Bolt-ons', which enabled regular text messagers to gain discounts of up to 60% by buying text bundles in advance (Figure 6).

Figure 6: *Different approaches by BT Cellnet and O_2*

This approach has pre-empted the three fundamental weaknesses of old-fashioned discounting; Bolt-ons are a proprietary idea that cannot readily be copied, they build in value over time rather than being rendered obsolete by the construct of a short-term deal – and they are self-defining in their appeal as opposed to being a blanket discount whether relevant or not.

A new capability

When promoting WAP, a significant new technology linking mobile phones to the internet, BT Cellnet again took a typical manufacturer-led approach, exhorting customers to 'Surf the net, surf the BT Cellnet' (Figure 7). Instead of leading with a customer benefit, it led with a technological capability – one that was largely rejected by customers.

In contrast, when O_2 launched MMS (picture messaging) the communication was benefit led. Picture messaging, like text messaging, was simply another means of human expression, another form of social interaction (Figure 8).

O_2 encouraged people to see the technology in these terms, inviting them into this new aspect of social culture, inviting them to 'invent their own language'.

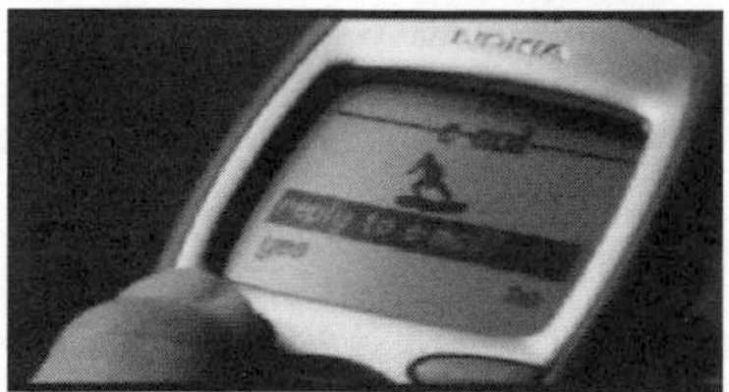
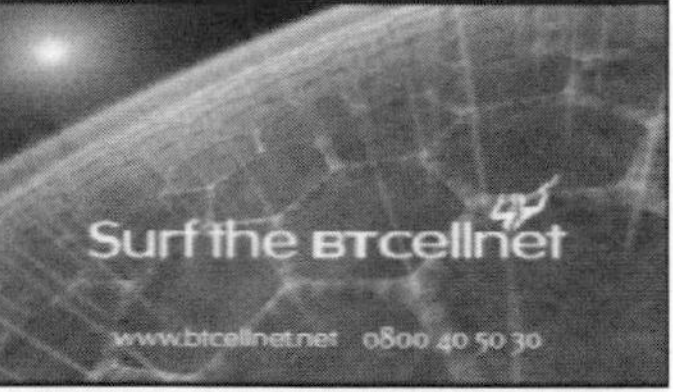

Figure 7: *Contrasting benefits of* O_2 *and BT Cellnet*

Figure 8: O_2*'s 'invent your own language'*

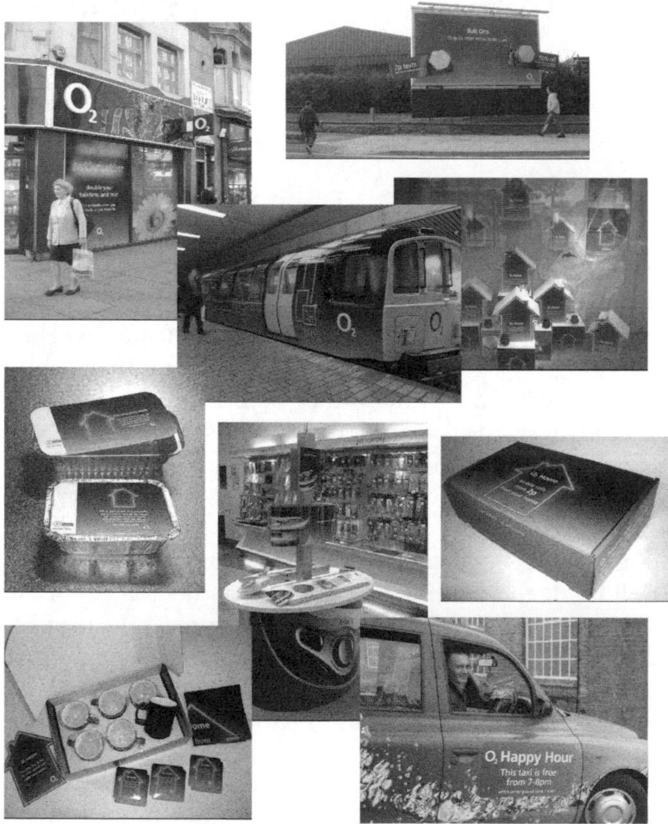

Figure 9: O_2*'s creative use across communication channels*

Each proposition is developed by advertising and carried into other areas – so the same idea and creative materials are used across the board. Of course, the blue and bubbles are present whatever the communication channel (Figure 9).

Summary

From its initiation, O_2 was devised to be more than simply a new look. The re-launch represented a radical departure from the fusty, technology-heavy days of BT Cellnet. By starting afresh, O_2 custom-built its brand and communications for today's market conditions. It adopted a fully integrated communications approach specifically designed to build rapid brand presence and pull off the all-important double-whammy: creating product and tariffs that would not only drive short-term sales, but also, at the same time, secure long-term, brand-led growth.

TRANSFORMATION

It is now two years since O_2 was launched. The pundits have eaten their words:

> 'Already O_2 is unimaginable from the scrappy wireless division that was de-merged from BT exactly one year ago.'
>
> *The Times*, 20 February 2003

> 'Not long ago mmO_2 was the ugly step-sister of Europe's mobile operators ... Now it's increasingly looking like Cinderella ... The main impetus behind the turnaround was mmO_2's business in the UK, where, despite increasing competition from the likes of new entrant 3, the company recorded a 16 per cent increase in revenues to £3.2bn on the back of a 10 per cent increase in new customers.'
>
> *Financial Times*, 19 May 2004

O_2 is an entirely different animal to its predecessor. It is a vibrant, healthy brand which drives consideration and growth; performance against every one of the key business metrics has been reversed.[13]

Transformation of the brand

Brand awareness: O_2 is on the map

One of O_2's most impressive achievements has been how rapidly it has established itself in the market. This is in contrast to both T-Mobile and 3.[14] O_2 is also more salient than its predecessor. Towards the end of its seventh year of trading, top-of-mind awareness of BT Cellnet stood at 20%.[15] After just two years, the level for

13. *A note about data sources*: Despite O_2's short life, three different tracking studies have been in operation at various stages. Unfortunately methodology changes have affected our ability to track various measures continually. The chronology is as follows: Taylor Nelson Sofres tracked BT Cellnet and covered O_2's launch to July 2002 amongst high-value consumers. NOP tracked O_2 and its competitors from May 2002 to April 2004, overlapping with TNS for three months. (NB: NOP only tracked advertising awareness and consideration from September 2002.) Finally, Millward Brown has run a multi-country tracker for mmO_2 since June 2003. In places we have had to show data from all three studies, but where possible we have tried to avoid data-overload.
14. Source: NOP. Unaided spontaneous awareness of O_2 is now 16 percentage points ahead of T-Mobile. In 11 months (on the back of £55m advertising support), 3 has achieved 18% total spontaneous brand awareness. In the same time frame, O_2 had reached 55%.
15. Source: TNS February 2002 – first mention spontaneous awareness.

O_2 is 28%,[16] making O_2 the most salient brand in the market. Figure 10(a) shows total spontaneous brand awareness (measured by NOP); Figure 10(b) shows more recent top-of-mind brand awareness (measured by Millward Brown).

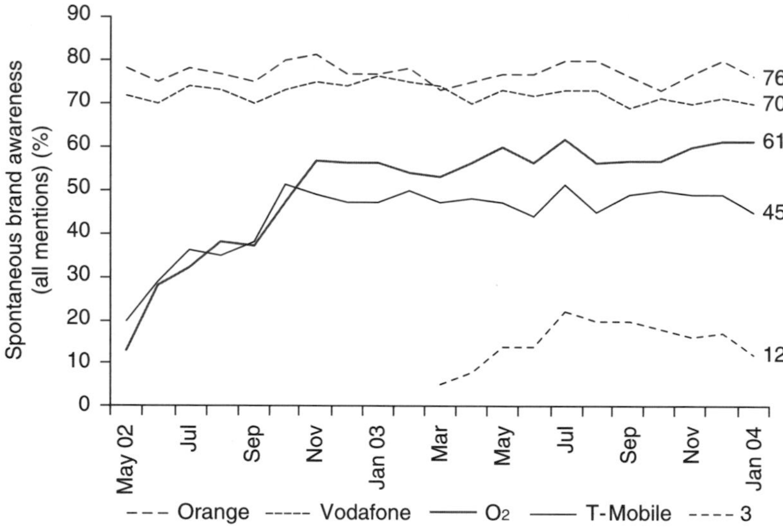

Source: NOP. Base: all mobile owners

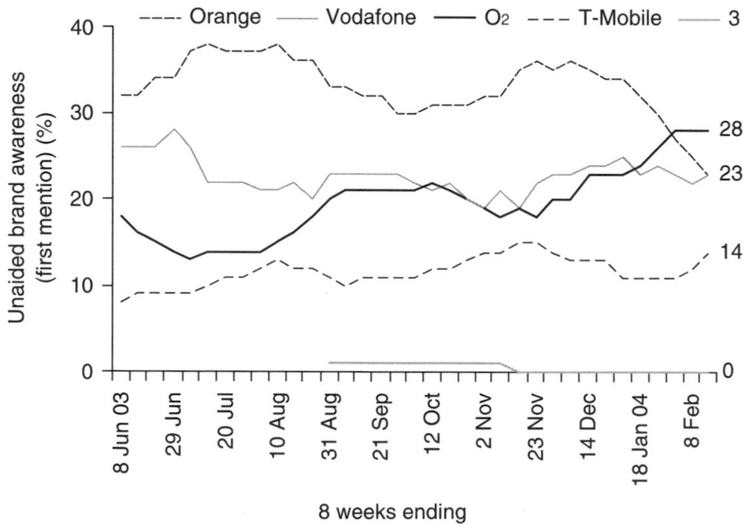

Figure 10: O_2 *is on the map*
Source: Millward Brown. Base: adults, 16–65, mobile phone owners/considerers

16. Source: Millward Brown, January 2004.

A relevant and compelling positioning

The consumer-led positioning of O_2's products has helped make them more compelling than they would have been under BT Cellnet's 'manufacturer-led' approach. It has also ensured that, simultaneously, O_2's products have a broader impact on positive impressions of the brand:

> 'Customer driven, not corporate force-feeding . . . In the words of one consumer, the brand appears both "high-tech" and "high-touch". In other words, softer, more empathetic, more real.'
>
> Corr Research & Consultancy, May 2002

> 'Since its launch, O_2 has been successful in positioning itself as a fresh, contemporary, youthful and innovative player (on its own terms and relative to the rather tired and muddled landscape that is mobile communications).'
>
> H2 Research, April 2004

This has been confirmed by tracking, which shows clear blue space between O_2 and its traditional rivals. Only 3, with its unique 3G technology, is seen as more 'refreshingly different' (Figure 11).

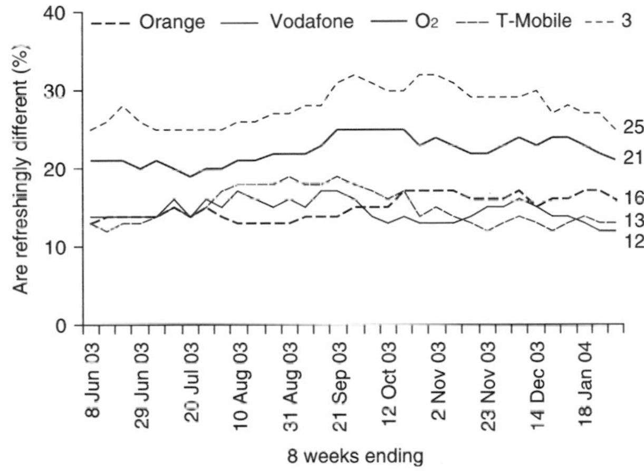

Figure 11: *O_2 has built a reputation for being 'refreshingly different'*
Source: Millward Brown. Base: adults, 16–65, mobile phone owners/considerers

Transformation in brand consideration

As salience and brand image have been transformed, there has been a parallel turnaround in consideration – which has grown consistently since its launch (Figure 12). Moreover, Millward Brown's 'network would choose tomorrow' measure of consideration shows that O_2 is now the most preferred brand – with a substantial advantage over T-Mobile (Figure 13).

The gap between O_2 and 3 is also telling. As we have seen, both brands have a reputation for being 'refreshingly different', but only O_2 has translated this into strong consideration – suggesting that O_2's 'difference' is more relevant to consumers.

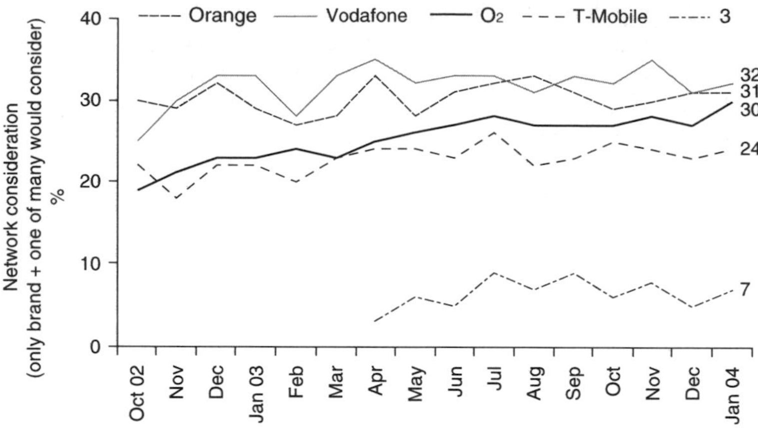

Figure 12: *Consistent growth in O_2 consideration*
Source: NOP. Base: all mobile owners

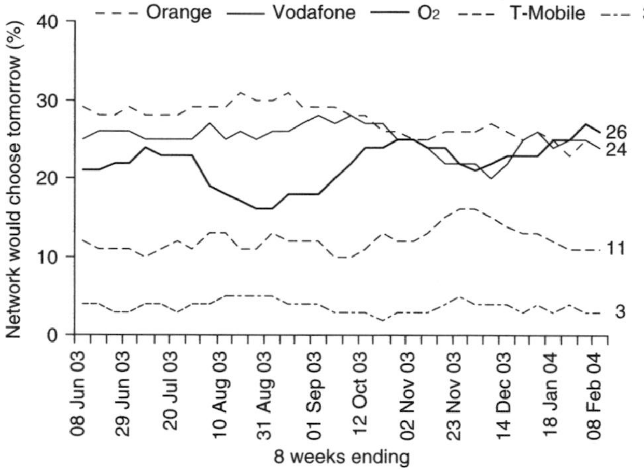

Figure 13: *O_2 is now the most preferred brand*
Source: Millward Brown. Base: adults, 16–65, mobile phone owners/considerers

Transformation of the business

Since rebranding as O_2, performance against every one of the key business metrics has been transformed. The consistent increase in consideration has translated into actual behaviour (Table 4).

It is worth noting that although O_2's non-voice growth looks less spectacular than BT Cellnet's, it is actually exceptional versus the market. Its benefit-led approach to non-voice services has paid off (Figure 14).

TABLE 4: KEY BUSINESS METRICS HAVE BEEN TRANSFORMED

	BT Jan–Mar 2001	BT Jan–Mar 2002	Trend	O_2 Jan–Mar 2003	O_2 Jun–Sep 2003	O_2 Jan–Mar 2004[17]	Trend
New connections							
Millions	1.6	0.8	↓	0.9	1.2	NA	↑
Share (%)	27.9	22.8		24.7	26.1	NA	
Total subscribers							
Millions	11.2	11.1	↓	12.1	12.6	13.3	↑
Share (%) post-pay	25.1	24.8		25.5	26.3	NA	
pre-pay	25.9	23.6		23.7	24.2	NA	
Non-voice transactions							
Percentage of text and picture messages sent	18.9	27.1	↑	33.1	33.4	NA	↑
Data as percentage of service revenue (12 monthly rolling)	8.1	13.8		19.4	19.4	22.3	
ARPU							
£ (blended, 12 monthly rolling)	269	231	↓	247	259	272	↑
As a percentage of market average	91.7	87.7		90.8	94.4	NA	
Revenue							
Share of retail revenue (%)	23.6	21.4	↓	21.9	23.3	NA	↑

Source: Oftel, BT Cellnet/O_2 (figures are for the three-month period shown)

Transformation of morale

Where BT Cellnet was hindered by low staff morale, O_2 is aided by the enthusiasm of its staff for the new brand and its consumer orientation.

> 'There is a real buzz about O_2 because people feel more alive.'
>
> Will Harris, VP Marketing Director at launch (quoted in *Brand Strategy*, May 2002)

> 'In the past there's often been a feeling that people were only worried about how their own area was doing and didn't care much about other parts of the business. Now there's much more emphasis on working together so we can do better in future.'
>
> Craig Dewhurst, O_2 telesales adviser

> 'In the past it's been quite disheartening to focus on quantity and not quality and as a result have lots of dissatisfied customers to deal with. Now the emphasis is on the customer and we are already seeing positive results.'
>
> Sue Dunn, DISE Upgrades, Sales

Belief in the brand is confirmed by O_2's internal staff survey, which shows particularly high morale among all-important retail staff (Table 5).

17. Latest Oftel figures are for June–September 2003, whereas the most recent O_2 figures are for January–March 2004. Since Oftel is the source of competitor information, we are able to show share figures up to June–September 2003 only.

(a) Text and picture messages

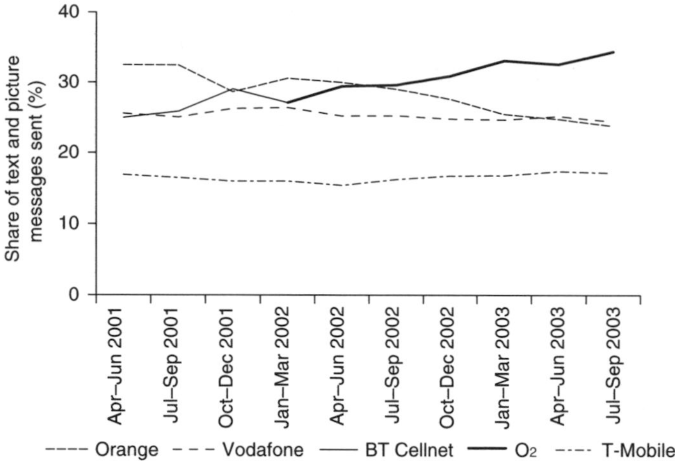

Source: Oftel

(b) Total non-voice

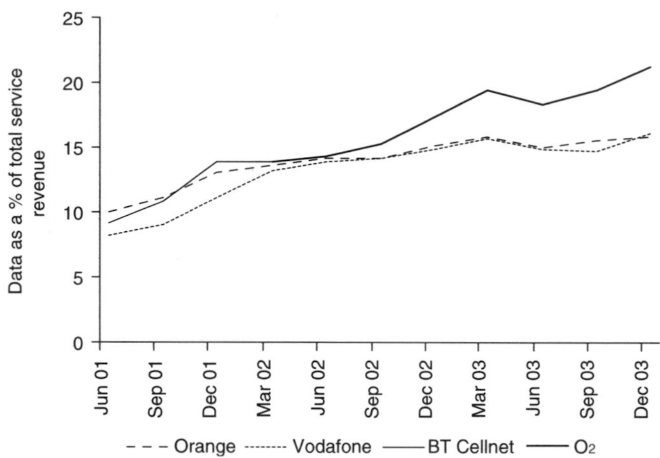

Figure 14: O_2*'s exceptional non-voice performance*
Source: Oftel

TABLE 5: POSITIVE MORALE

	Index vs benchmark	
	All O_2 staff	O_2 retail staff
'I am proud to work for O_2'	118	131

Source: O_2's internal Reflect Survey, conducted by Maritz Research, October 2003. The response rate is 73%. The benchmark is the average of 300,000 employee responses (including retail staff) from blue-chip organisations, including FTSE 100 companies, from a number of sectors including telecoms, finance, food, retailers, utilities and automotive.

Summary

In contrast to BT Cellnet, O_2 is a relevant and appealing brand (both internally and externally) with a strong presence in the market. It is a brand that has met the challenges presented by the market head on, resulting in a transformation of business performance on every measure. Where BT Cellnet suffered, O_2 has thrived.

THE ROLE OF COMMUNICATIONS IN TRANSFORMING THE BUSINESS: AN OVERVIEW OF HOW O_2'S INTEGRATED APPROACH WORKS

O_2's communications were designed to be integrated on two levels:

1. visually
2. strategically.

Both levels of integration have proved invaluable to the business in different ways: Visual integration has given O_2's communications exceptional cut-through. This has been instrumental in building rapid brand awareness. It also delivers financial efficiency. Strategic integration (across the brand–product–communications continuum) has delivered product propositions that are particularly compelling. As intended, they drive not only short-term consideration, but also longer-term *brand* consideration. As a result, despite a heavy emphasis on what would typically be classed short-term sales-driving initiatives, O_2's communications deliver the intended long-term sales effects normally expected of brand-level communication.

A similar effect has been seen internally and with trade partners.[18] Communications have driven belief in the brand alongside understanding of and enthusiasm for specific product propositions.

In the following sections, we explore these effects in four channels. Advertising and *Big Brother* sponsorship are examined in the next section, Internal and Trade Communications are reviewed in the following section and, finally, we demonstrate the financial value of this approach to O_2.

THE ROLE OF ADVERTISING AND SPONSORSHIP IN TRANSFORMING THE BUSINESS

Before we explore how advertising and sponsorship have worked, it is important to frame the findings in the context of share of voice and the balance of O_2's communication messages.

18. Carphone Warehouse, Phones4U, etc.

Share of voice

O_2 faced an onslaught of additional spend from competitors in both 2002 and 2003. As a result, O_2's share of voice has fallen versus the market and is lower than that for BT Cellnet.[19] Specifically, O_2 has consistently been outspent by both Orange and Vodafone, and its launch budget was well behind that of both T-Mobile and 3 (see Table 6).

TABLE 6: O_2'S DECLINING SHARE OF VOICE (SOV)

	April 2001–March 2002	April 2002–March 2003	April 2003–March 2004
Total market spend	£145m	£201m	£240m
SOV (%)			
BT Cellnet	21	–	–
O_2	–	17	15
Orange	25	24	26
Vodafone	27	29	21
One2One	17	–	–
T-Mobile	–	19	8
3	–	4	21
Virgin	10	7	6
BT Mobile	–	–	3

Source: MMS

O_2 invested significantly in the *Big Brother* sponsorship and also sponsored the England team at the Rugby World Cup. However, its competitors were also investing heavily in their own high-profile sponsorship activity. In particular, Vodafone spent £38m on sponsorship in 2003/04 alone.[20]

The balance of O_2's advertising and sponsorship messages

Table 7 outlines O_2's advertising and sponsorship programme from launch. The obvious point is that, apart from two 'brand manifesto' advertisements at the start of each year, the vast majority of investment has been placed behind product messages.

19. BT Cellnet's SOV in the three years prior to launch was 21% each year.
20. Source: Zenith estimates. In 2003/04, Vodafone spent *c.*£38m on its sponsorship of, amongst other things, Man Utd, David Beckham, Ferrari, the England cricket team and the Derby. Orange spent *c.*£3.6m on arts events including Glastonbury, the BAFTAs and the Edinburgh fringe. Virgin spent *c.*£2.98m behind various sponsorships including the Jordan F1 team. Finally, T-Mobile invested *c.*£2.25m in sponsoring *Charlie's Angels*, the Rolling Stones and ITV's *Record of the Year 2003*.

TABLE 7: THE FOCUS ON PRODUCT MESSAGES

	Q1 April–June	Q2 July–September	Q3 October–December	Q4 Jan–March
2002/03				
Brand manifesto	'Can do' launch			
Product propositions	Flat Rate Open Portal Email on Move Roaming Games	XDA Pay & Go Wild	MMS – Invent Your Own Language Bolt-ons (4p texts) Games Colour Handsets	
Interactive partnerships		*Big Brother* 3		
2003/04				
Brand manifesto	'Bubble Road'			
Product propositions	2 Minute Challenge XNET	Active No IVR	Bolt-ons (4p Texts) O_2 Home	XDA2
Interactive partnerships		*Big Brother* 4	Rugby World Cup	

Visual synergy has built rapid brand awareness[21]

O_2's advertising and sponsorship has been highly visible – especially when taken in the context of its share of voice.

Spontaneous awareness of O_2's advertising rose rapidly to a level enjoyed by its well-established competitors. It very quickly superseded memories of BT Cellnet advertising and is now well ahead of T-Mobile. We refer to Taylor Nelson (in Figure 15a) for the rapid growth of advertising awareness at launch before turning to NOP for the longer-term view (Figure 15b).

Sponsorship, too, has been highly visible. By the end of the third series of *Big Brother*, more people associated O_2 with TV sponsorship than *Coronation Street* sponsor, Cadbury's.[22] By the end of series four, 78% of 16–34 year olds spontaneously cited O_2 as the sponsor of *Big Brother*. This level of awareness will have been augmented by the high levels of PR coverage that the sponsorship generated. *Big Brother* 4, for example, triggered 126 pieces of free PR for O_2 (delivering an estimated 80 million impacts).[23]

21. A further note about data sources: we have already explained that O_2 has used three tracking studies over the course of its two-year life (see footnote 13). Aware of the limitations of tracking and the complexities of the market, O_2 has also used econometric analysis to inform its strategic and investment decisions from early on in the brand's life. There are three stages to this analysis. The first, which runs from May to December 2002, analyses the relationship between advertising and sponsorship and brand awareness. The second, which runs from September 2002 to September 2003, analyses consideration. More recently, as sufficient data has become available, it has been possible to analyse the relationship between advertising and sponsorship and gross connections (i.e. sales). This covers the entire period since launch to December 2003.
22. Source: NOP, July 2002: 30% of respondents spontaneously associated O_2 with TV sponsorship vs 25% for Cadbury's. It is estimated that Cadbury's has spent £10m a year over the last 10 years on its sponsorship of *Coronation Street*.
23. Source: Drum PHD.

(a) Rapid growth at launch (first three months)

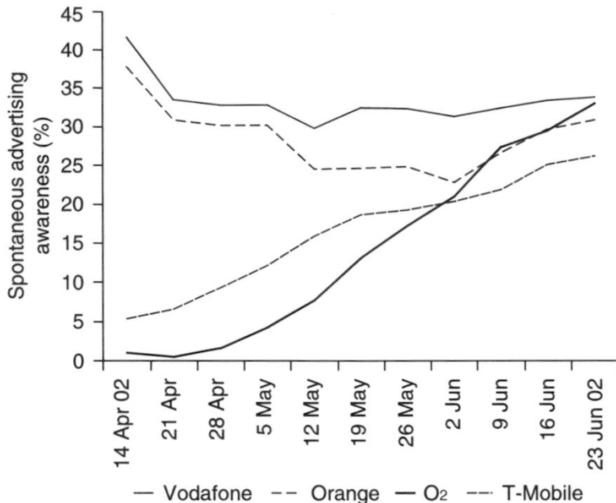

(b) Sustained awareness over time (since October 2002)

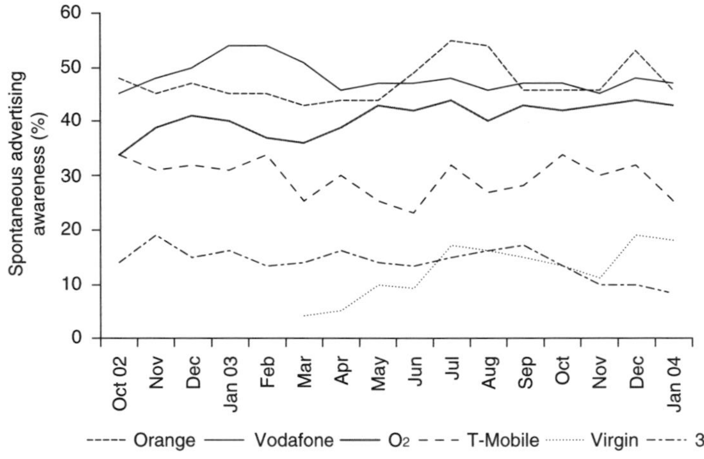

Figure 15: *O_2's highly memorable advertising*
Source: (a) TNS. Base: high-value mobile users. (b) NOP. Base: all mobile owners

Over time, O_2's combined communications have become the most memorable in the market (Table 8).

Importantly, O_2 has not simply been preaching to the converted. Getting on the radar of potential conquests is vital to share growth: 77% of those who are aware of any of O_2's combined communications are users of other networks.[24]

24. Source: Millward Brown; average from April 2003 to March 2004. Base: adults, 16–65, mobile phone owners/considerers.

TABLE 8: O_2'S COMBINED COMMUNICATIONS ARE THE MOST MEMORABLE IN THE MARKET

	Total communications awareness (seen anywhere recently) 8 weeks to end January 2004 (%)
O_2	66
Vodafone	59
Orange	50
T-Mobile	46
Virgin	43
3	32

Source: Millward Brown. Base: adults, 16–65, mobile phone owners/considerers

This level of cut-through has undoubtedly been driven by the consistent and instantly recognisable use of blue and bubbles across all O_2 activity.

> 'The brand has created its own iconography – blue, bubbles and natural space.'
>
> Corr Research & Consultancy, 2003

> 'Alone in this market, O_2 is synonymous with a distinctive creative device.'
>
> H2 Research, January 2003

But to what extent did this visibility affect brand awareness?

Tracking suggests that O_2's advertising played a vital role in building brand awareness in the launch period (Figure 16).

It is also clear that this brand awareness was generated in the minds of O_2's potential conquests (customers currently with other networks). As Figure 17 shows, among this key audience those who were aware of O_2's advertising at launch were twice as likely to be spontaneously aware of O_2.

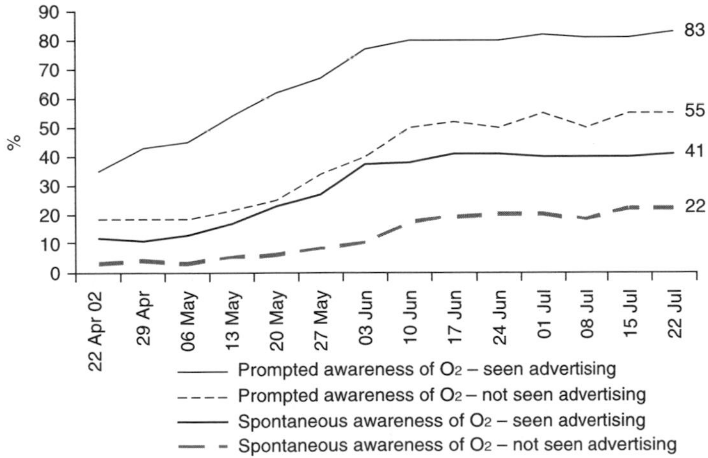

Figure 16: *Awareness of O_2 advertising drove awareness of the brand at launch (2002)*
Source: TNS. Base: high-value mobile phone users

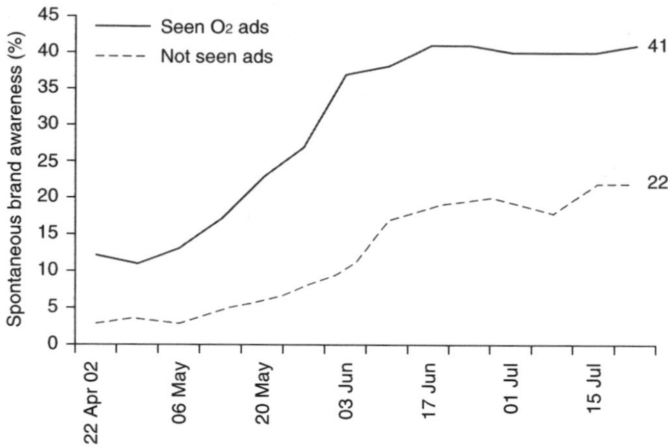

Figure 17: *The importance of communications in getting O_2 onto the radar of conquest consumers (2002)*
Source: TNS. Base: high-value mobile users using networks other than O_2

The econometric analysis of spontaneous brand awareness confirms the significant roles played by advertising and sponsorship in building brand awareness. By the end of *Big Brother* 3, for example, around three-quarters of O_2's rapid gains in awareness could be attributed to the combined effect of advertising and sponsorship.[25] The econometrics also show their effects are long-lasting. In Figure 18, the gap between actual awareness and awareness without advertising widens over time as the current advertising builds on the on-going effect of earlier advertising.

The brand–product–communications continuum has created a compelling brand

O_2's intention of communicating its products and tariffs as genuine consumer benefits, rather than just product or prices, is recognised and valued by consumers.

> 'In a near commodity market, any supplier may offer packages, but the way O_2 offers its packages through advertising (and *Big Brother*) is in keeping with its fresh and differentiated brand methodology.'
>
> H2 Research, Q2 2003

> 'The idea of better experiences as opposed to better gizmos is understood by consumers to be at the heart of the O_2 brand message,'
>
> H2 Research, January 2003 Bolt-ons Research

Importantly, advertising has also created the intended virtuous circle, whereby product messages feed back into consumers' understanding and appreciation of the brand.

> 'The advertising creates a distinctive, appealing and empathetic world for O_2 and its communications. It creates the impression of a brand that is both modern, progressive, vibrant and, crucially, believable, practical and useful.'
>
> Corr Research & Consultancy, 2002

25. Source: Holmes & Cook.

> 'The advertising serves to create differentiation between the O_2 way and that of other brands. Amidst the crudely tactical aspirations of the mobile telecoms market (epitomised by Vodafone) where product talk is all, the O_2 imagery is unexpected, fresh and distinctive.'
>
> H2 Research, January 2003

This relationship between communications and brand image is confirmed by tracking, which also suggests that O_2's communications have helped drive the impression that the brand is 'refreshingly different'. Again, this is the case amongst potential conquests (i.e. users of other networks) as well as existing customers (Figure 19). Note that we have seen in Figure 11 that O_2 is significantly ahead of all competitors (except 3) in terms of its 'refreshingly different' image. Figure 19

(a) O_2 spontaneous brand awareness. Model simulation showing where awareness would have been without advertising

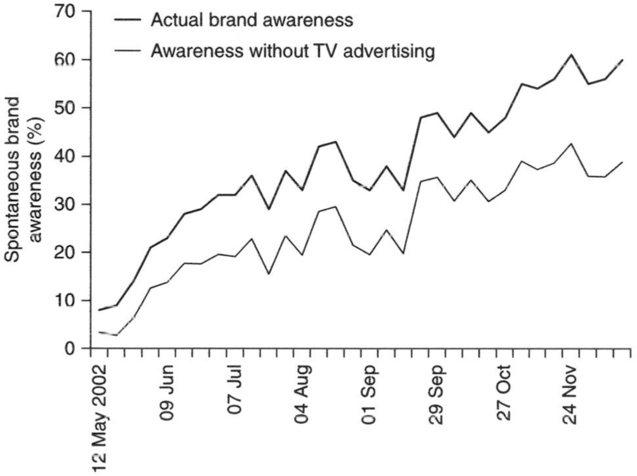

(b) O_2 spontaneous brand awareness. Model simulation showing where awareness would have been without *Big Brother* sponsorship

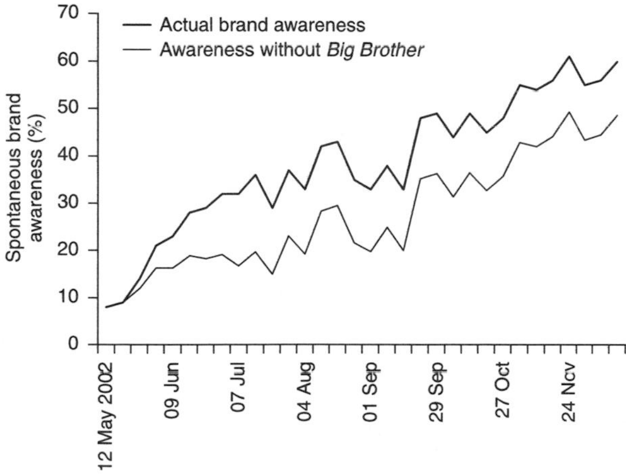

Figure 18: *The direct relationship between advertising and sponsorship and brand awareness (2002)*
Source: Holmes & Cook

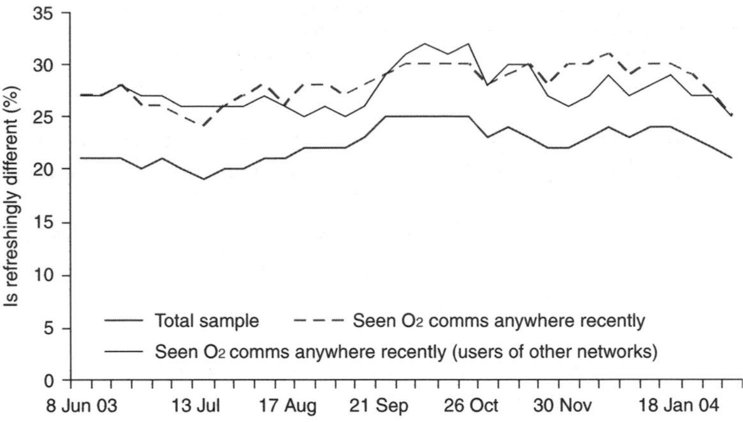

Figure 19: *O_2 communications drive brand image*
Source: Millward Brown. Base: adults, 16–65, mobile phone owners/considerers

simply shows the role of communications in driving this impression amongst its own customers and potential conquests.

The role played by *Big Brother* underlines the success of O_2's brand–product–communications continuum. Those aware of the *Big Brother* sponsorship have particularly favourable brand impressions on top of greater awareness of non-voice services (Table 9).

TABLE 9: *BIG BROTHER* DRIVES NON-VOICE AWARENESS AND POSITIVE IMPRESSIONS OF THE BRAND

	Percentage point difference between those aware of O_2's *Big Brother* sponsorship and those not aware
Brand impressions	
'Fresh'	+13
'Invigorating'	+11
Stands out	+10
Talks my language	+4
O_2's non-voice offer	
Offers more than just talk	+7
Helps me get the most from my mobile	+5

Source: TNS, high-value mobile users, July 2002. Base: 401 aware; 486 not aware

Advertising and sponsorship were instrumental in rapidly creating O_2's presence in the market and in building positive impressions of the brand. We shall now see that this translated into significantly higher consideration of the brand (Figure 20).

The brand–product–communications continuum drives brand consideration

As so many factors influence consideration, rather than rely on tracking, we have used econometric analysis. This allows us to isolate the contribution of communications and to understand the nature of their relationship with consideration. Again

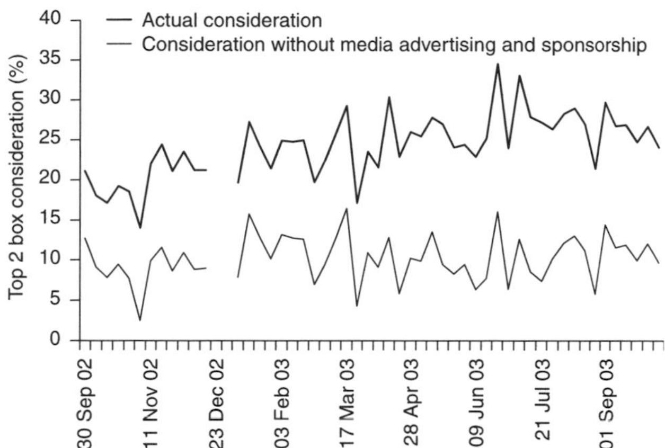

Figure 20: *The uplift in consideration generated by advertising and sponsorship. Consideration of O_2 (only company plus one of a few would consider)*
Source: Holmes & Cook. Base incorporates non-communication effects, competitive effects and sampling error

we see clear evidence not only of short term advertising effects, but also very persistent ones – and we see these coming from what are, intrinsically, product and tariff messages. The model attributes over half of O_2's consideration in the year to September 2003 to advertising and sponsorship; 90% of this additional consideration is attributable to product and tariff messages such as Bolt-ons or Pay & Go Wild.[26]

Brand consideration has converted into an unusually high level of long-term sales

The results of the econometric analysis of sales[27] have very direct parallels with the consideration findings (and support the tracking findings that O_2's communications have attracted conquest customers). Again, we see that both advertising and sponsorship have not only a short-term but also a very persistent effect on sales.

Since its launch in April 2002, O_2 has generated more than a million new connections per quarter. Clearly there are many factors that have influenced this, but the econometric analysis enables us to separate the contribution of communications from that of other sources.[28] It shows that advertising and sponsorship generated 4.1 million connections during the seven quarters from April 2002 to December 2003 (Figure 21).[29]

26. Holmes & Cook consideration model (see Figure 20).
27. The econometrics analyses gross connections. This is the total number of new connections occurring in any month and is the best overall measure of new business generated. It is important to note that the value of a new connection is not just revenue gained in the year of connection; it is revenue generated across the whole period that an individual stays with O_2.
28. In addition to advertising and sponsorship, the analysis investigated the contribution of market trends, seasonality, distribution (numbers of stores, quality of stores, etc.), staff training, staff productivity, incentives to trade partners, timing of the introduction of new technology (e.g. Blackberry, XDA), timing and nature of tariffs, PR, competitive activity and customer satisfaction.
29. Source: Holmes & Cook. 3.4 million to advertising; 646k to sponsorship.

(a) Gross connections: overall effects of O_2 advertising

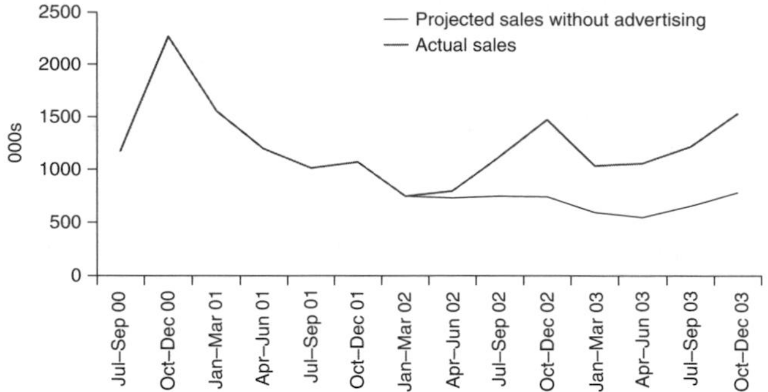

(b) Gross connections: overall effects of O_2's *Big Brother* sponsorship

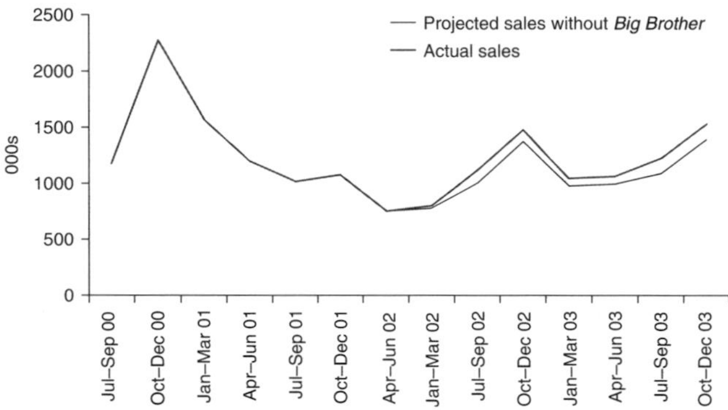

Figure 21: *Sales attributable to advertising and sponsorship*[30]
Source: Holmes & Cook

As with awareness and consideration, we see the effects on sales of advertising and sponsorship dying away only slowly (by 5% from month to month). This rate of decay implies that only 46% of their total effect on sales occurs within 12 months of airtime. Thus on top of the 4.1 million extra connections generated from launch to December 2003, a further 4.5 million will occur over the lifetime of the advertising.

The scale of effect

To establish whether the scale of these effects might simply be typical for the market, we have compared O_2's communications performance to that of both BT Cellnet and two competitors.

All things being equal, gross connections attributable to O_2's advertising are 1.5 million (or 24%) higher than they would have been had the same investment been put behind BT Cellnet advertising (Figure 22). Moreover, BT Cellnet's advertising decayed at a faster rate than O_2's – 10% or more per month compared to 5% for O_2.[31]

30. The models were constructed using monthly data but we have been asked to report only quarterly figures for gross connections.
31. Source: Holmes & Cook gross connections model.

GOLD GRAND PRIX

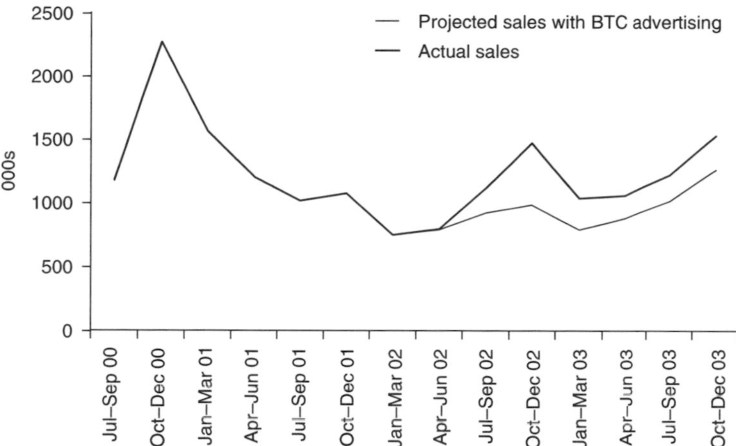

Figure 22: *O_2's advertising has been considerably more effective than BT Cellnet advertising*
Source: Holmes & Cook

O_2's sponsorship of *Big Brother* has also been considerably more effective in generating consumer sales than BT Cellnet's approach (which generated sales only amongst business users).[32] We have also compared O_2's advertising effects to effects previously reported for Orange and One2One.[33] Clearly comparisons need to be made sensitively, since these findings relate to the 1996–98 period, when the market was much smaller. However, if new connections are expressed as a percentage of each company's subscriber base at the time of the advertising, the scale of O_2's effect is still significantly larger. This is all the more remarkable since O_2 achieved this on a lower share of voice (Table 10).

TABLE 10: THE SCALE OF O_2'S ADVERTISING EFFECT

	New connections attributable to advertising (expressed as a percentage of the brand's subscriber base at the time of advertising)	SOV at time of advertising (%)[34]
Orange (1994–98)	+8.4	30+
One2One (1994–98)	+14	21
O_2 (2002–03)	+ 31	18

Source: *Advertising Works 10*; Oftel; Holmes & Cook

32. Source: Holmes & Cook.
33. We selected Orange and One2One simply because these are the two brands in this market whose advertising effects have been awarded by the IPA and are therefore published. See *Advertising Works 10*. We have compared advertising effects only, since both the Orange and One2One papers only measure the effect of advertising.
34. Orange's share of voice was 30%+ with one exception, 1998, when its SOV fell to 14.2%. One2One's share of voice was 21%+ with one exception, also 1998, when it fell to 18%.

Summary

The visual and strategic integration that runs through advertising and sponsorship has made a significant contribution to O_2's success. It was instrumental in getting the brand on the map. But more than that, it has driven sales to an extraordinary degree – as shown by the scale of effect vs BT Cellnet and vs Orange and One2One. The econometrics demonstrates that this is due to a combination of strong short-term uplifts (more typical of retailer price-led advertising) combined with a slow rate of decay that would more normally be expected of brand advertising.[35] All the evidence points to the virtuous circle created by the continuum that runs through O_2's brand, products and communications as the decisive factor in this remarkable effect.

THE ROLE OF COMMUNICATIONS IN DRIVING ATTITUDES OF STAFF AND TRADE PARTNERS

O_2 staff

An essential task of the relaunch has been to bring the brand to life for 5700 staff – to ensure they live and breathe the brand in what they do. Consumer-facing communications have been central to bringing about this change:

> 'Absolutely brilliant. The O_2 brand is the way forward. It's modern, fascinating, interesting. When I first saw the TV ad I was stunned – it wasn't what I expected as it's completely different to anything else we've ever done. Customer focus is the key. We all need to give 100% to that and to work together.'
>
> Hema Parekh, GPRS team

> 'I'm genuinely impressed by the feel and style of our ads. I'm also impressed by the way that the company is changing internally as well as externally.'
>
> Andy Horrocks, MIST team

> 'At last someone is thinking marketing, not technology.'
>
> Steve Williams, Building Manager

Moreover, the brand iconography and consumer-centric thinking, which has been carried through to in-store communications, has proved an effective sales tool:

> 'The store looks great. It's completely different to any other phone store. Customers particularly love the fact that everything is hands-on and that the explanations are clear, simple and non-techie. The new look is good for us too – it's much easier to sell if we can demonstrate live products. Overall I feel that we now have the tools to get the business in.'
>
> Helen Taylor, Kingston O_2 Retail Store Manager

> 'The new look and tariffs are outstanding and our figures are up on this time last year – and we were selling all four networks then!'
>
> Sarah Snelling, Assistant Manager, St Albans O_2 retail store

---

35. Holmes & Cook has compared the O_2 advertising effects with those for both tactical and brand advertising in a range of different markets.

A further selling effect of stores is also demonstrated by econometric analysis. An increase in O_2 store numbers delivers twice as many pre-pay customers (through a range of channels – not just the store) than might naturally be expected given the share of pre-pay business stores represent.[36] This suggests that a high-street presence triggers positive associations consumers have with the brand (producing a knock-on effect on sales). Clearly, visual synergy aids this effect.

Trade partners

Visual and strategic integration is also carried through into communications developed for use in non-O_2 stores (such as Carphone Warehouse, Phones4U and others).

Rather than creating separate creative work, visual integration is achieved by using images created for advertising and point-of-sale. As well as delivering financial efficiencies, this helps ensure that if trade partners use third-party agencies, they retain a synergistic look and feel.

Strategic integration is achieved through the way O_2 brief its trade partners. For example:

- 'Your Guides' (aka the 'O_2 Bible') are written in a 'see what you can do' style (as opposed to being product and technology driven).
- Advertising is used as briefing material which helps ensure trade partners fully understand the consumer-centric thinking behind O_2's product propositions.
- 'Fresh thinking' informs the way O_2 communicates new propositions to the trade; for example, to launch 'Happy Hour',[37] O_2 invited 1800 store sales staff to an extended happy hour at Fabric nightclub in London – which was fully branded O_2 for the night; invitations had a text response mechanic that encouraged active use of the Happy Hour proposition (Figure 23).

Figure 23: *Happy Hour venue*

36. Source: Holmes & Cook.
37. Happy Hour is O_2's latest product proposition, offering free texts in London between 7pm and 8pm.

TABLE 11: THE STRONG APPEAL AND SELLING EFFECT OF O_2'S TRADE PARTNER COMMUNICATIONS

	Rank			
	O_2	Vodafone	Orange	T-Mobile
'Their communications look and feel right for me'	1	2	3=	3=
'Communications I receive really help me to see the brand's products to prospective customers'	1	4	2	3
Overall satisfaction with field sales team	1	3	2	4

Source: ICM Channel Satisfaction Survey, February/March 2004. Base: 1000+ high-street store staff and in-depth interviews with key decision makers in trade partner head offices

Support by trade partners for these communications is strong (Table 11). Not only are they liked, but, more importantly, they are believed to be strong selling tools – more so than comparable competitor communications.

> 'I know they don't have a massive budget, so I think the way they spend their money is very good.'
>
> Carphone Warehouse

> 'The POS is lovely. The presentation of tariffs is superb. The booklets are absolutely fabulous. As a network, O_2 produces some of the most coherent business information.'
>
> Distribution stockist

> 'The best is the dealer bible. O_2 are the only ones who have this and it tells you everything you need to know about O_2. You couldn't improve on it.'
>
> High-street store staff

THE FINANCIAL VALUE OF O_2'S INTEGRATED APPROACH TO COMMUNICATIONS

O_2's integrated approach to communications has evidently been fundamental to the transformation of the business. We are able to place a value on both levels of integration and, more broadly, assess the overall effect of communications on shareholder value.

The value of visual integration

Savings generated by the visibility of O_2's advertising

Based on advertising awareness per TVR,[38] Millward Brown has calculated that despite an actual share of voice of 14%, O_2's *effective* share of voice is 33%. This

38. We have not included sponsorship spend since there are no reported figures for competitive spend – previous figures quoted are estimates only.

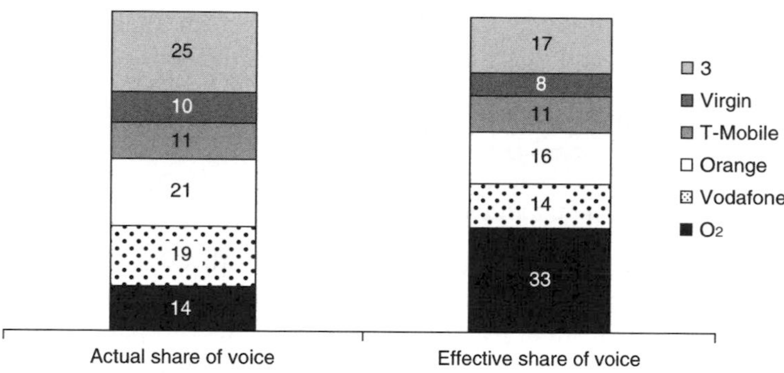

Figure 24: *The efficiency of O_2's advertising investment*
Source: Millward Brown April 2003–January 2004. Based on total TVRs of 21,654

implies that, had its advertising been more typical of the market, O_2 would have needed to spend more than twice as much on advertising as it actually did in order to achieve the same effect (Figure 24).

Savings generated by the rapidity with which O_2 established itself in the market

In 2002 Accenture reviewed the effectiveness of telecoms launches by assessing how long each brand took to reach its level of spontaneous brand awareness – and at what cost. No other brand achieved the same presence as rapidly or as cost effectively as O_2 (Figure 25).

> 'The O_2 launch has been the most successful mobile brand launch that Accenture's ROI group have seen. Based on numerous studies that we have conducted, the brand is rare in exceeding our most optimistic targets. The results are testament to the potency of the brand identity and advertising creative.'
>
> Accenture MROI group

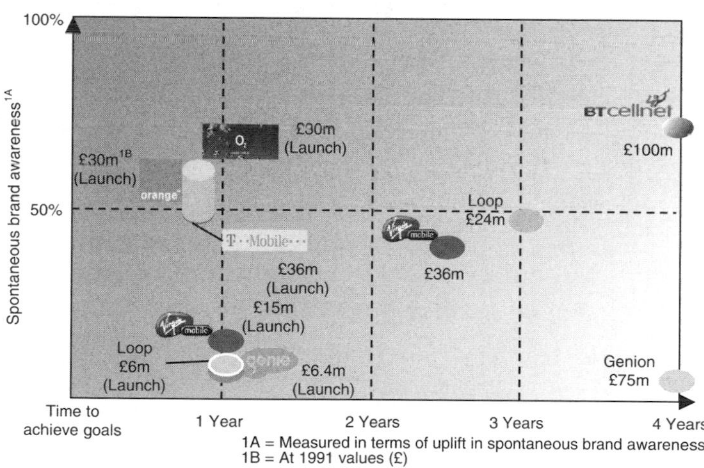

Figure 25: *The rapidity and cost effectiveness of O_2's launch*[39]
Source: Accenture MROI Group

39. This analysis was conducted in September 2002 (and therefore covers O_2's first nine months, by which time it had achieved spontaneous brand awareness of 59%).

Accenture's findings provide another perspective on the financial value of O_2's communications. If O_2 had run advertising of a similar nature to BT Cellnet, it would have needed to spend three times as much as it actually did to achieve its level of awareness (and it would have taken four times as long).[40]

The value of strategic integration

In this market because consumers generally remain with O_2 for a period of years, and because they generate revenue throughout their lifetime and not just at the point of purchase, only a small part of the benefit of the campaign has so far been realised. The activity that has taken place so far will continue to underpin revenue and margin for years to come.

The econometric analysis has assisted us in quantifying the relative scale of these effects. They are, first, those that have occurred from launch to December 2003 and, second, those that will come after December 2003 as a result of the advertising carryover and the average lifetime value of the consumers who have been attracted to O_2 as a result of the integrated campaign.

Factors included in the payback calculation are:

- the number of connections attributed directly to communications
- the average revenue generated by each connection in any given year (ARPU)[41]
- the average lifetime of each new connection (three to five years depending on consumer type)
- O_2's margin
- the cost of media, production and agency fees.

Up until December 2003 advertising and sponsorship combined generated £493m in additional margin for O_2 of which 84% was as a direct result of advertising, with the remaining 16% attributable to *Big Brother*. This is a return of 6.3:1 on the money invested.

But the best is yet to come.

Over the remainder of the lifetime of the advertising and sponsorship effects and new customers, a further £4.799bn in additional margin is expected. The ultimate payback is thus expected to be 62:1. Of course, this takes into account only the sales effects of the advertising and sponsorship. We have already seen, above, the further value gained through visual integration.

Shareholder value

The mmO_2 share price has outperformed the FTSE 100, Vodafone, Orange and BT (Figure 26).

---

40. Based on the figures quoted by Accenture in Figure 25.
41. As a measure of scale and as shown earlier in the paper. Blended ARPU is £272 (January–March 2004). We have actually used the rates appropriate to the individual consumer groups the econometrics analysed.

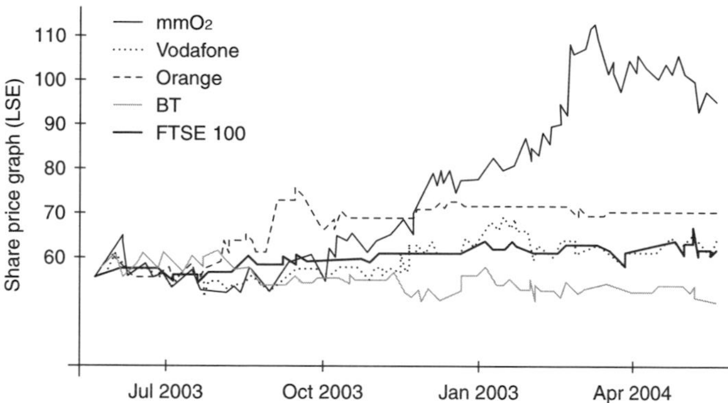

Figure 26: *The strong performance of mmO_2's share price relative to the market*
Source: mmO_2.com

The success of the O_2 brand in the UK has been fundamental to this performance, with industry experts agreeing with O_2 on the extent of its contribution:

> 'As services have become more or less interchangeable, it has been the skill of marketing and not the size of the operator that has made the difference. In the UK the market has gone – most of all and against the odds to O_2 which has shaken off its leaden Cellnet image and achieved a remarkable transformation. And the point is that they have not needed to be vastly big to do it. What they have had to do is understand the values that the young people in the market appreciate, deliver those and motivate the employees to live the brand. Being a faceless multinational – as Vodafone is finding out – is a positive handicap.'
>
> *Evening Standard*, 23 April 2004

> 'Not long ago mmO_2 was the ugly step-sister of Europe's mobile operators ... Now it's increasingly looking like Cinderella. The main impetus behind the turnaround was mmO_2's business in the UK, where, despite increasing competition from the likes of new entrant 3, the company recorded a 16 per cent increase in revenues to £3.2bn on the back of a 10 per cent increase in new customers.'
>
> *Financial Times*, 19 May 2004

> 'A fundamental part of the value O_2 now commands resides in the O_2 brand. This is now a key asset to the company, and significantly enhances our value to shareholders.'
>
> Sohail Qadri, Head of Strategy (and plc board member) mmO_2

In February 2004, mmO_2 became the target of a take-over bid from KPN, who valued the company at £9.5 billion or 110p a share. The offer was rejected. The turnaround in fortunes demonstrated by mmO_2's latest results has vindicated that decision. As the *FT* put it, mmO_2's 'miraculous turnaround' explains 'why KPN could barely contain its eagerness to capture the bride in February – and why mmO_2 refused the offer'.[42]

Perhaps the final word should go to Hans Snook, founder of Orange:

> 'They have done a superb job. They have done a superb job on branding.'
>
> *The Times*, February 2004

42. The results are shown in the January–March data in Figure 15; quote sourced from the *Financial Times* on 19 May 2004.

GOLD
BEST INTEGRATION

2

Central London Congestion Charging Scheme

Making sure it worked from day one

Principal authors: Chris Baker, TBWA\London and Sue Garrard, Fishburn Hedges
Media agency: PHD

EDITOR'S SUMMARY

This is the case of the launch of the largest traffic management system in the world, unique in scale, complexity and controversy. The brief was, in effect, to 'brief London'. There were only two scenarios for the day it launched, 17 February 2003 – London prepared and the system works or London not prepared leading to catastrophic failure and meltdown. If the widely predicted chaos and confusion had occurred the 30% decrease in congestion may never have materialised.

People had no pre-existing reference point and, as a virtual system, effective communication was a critical success factor. Of course, high awareness was important – everyone had to know what was coming. The solution was a 'Q&A' approach, combined with the now famous Congestion Charge 'C' visual identity. Awareness of the £5 charge grew to 91%, and 81% of Londoners could name the date of the launch.

But, more importantly, in order to avert a 'system meltdown' the campaign had to ensure that those drivers affected acted in time. The campaign prompted more than half a million pre-registrations for payment, discounts and exemptions by launch day – new channels such as the internet and texting accounted for almost half of payments. The London scheme has come to be regarded as a role model for other cities around the world.

This paper won the prize for Best Integration for its clarity of channel planning and its integrated creative approach. This campaign addressed a complex task and multiple audiences seamlessly.

INTRODUCTION

> 'It is a tax not a charge.'
>
> 'It is the work of Satan.'
>
> 'Lots of people won't pay, it will be complete chaos.'
>
> 'All the computers will crash.'
>
> TRBI/interviews with Congestion Charging Zone (CCZ) drivers pre-launch

The Central London Congestion Charging Scheme was launched on 17 February 2003 in the face of considerable antipathy and scepticism from the media, many drivers, and even Government:

> 'In relation to the Congestion Charge, I thought that wouldn't work ... and I was wrong, it has worked.'
>
> Tony Blair, *BBC News*, 6 January 2004

This raised the bar for what was anyway a daunting communications and implementation challenge – the launch of the largest traffic management system in the world – making it hard for us to get a fair hearing and stimulate the actions required.

Nothing like it had ever been tried before. London's road systems, the size of the zone, the scheme's virtual nature (no toll booths or physical barriers) and the requirement for social equity (via a large number of exemptions and discounts) all contributed to its complexity and scale.

People had no pre-existing reference point and, as a virtual system, effective communication was a critical success factor. Our nightmare was that six million Londoners would wake up on 17 February, read or hear the news reminding them that 'today is the day', and phone to find out whether and how they were affected, something no system could handle.

This risk of 'system meltdown', and the critical role of communications in avoiding it, kept the campaign at the top of the project's risk register for the three months before launch.

It would have been hard, if not impossible, for such a controversial scheme to survive a failed launch. As Table 1 shows, there were effectively only two scenarios for 17 February – the campaign did not just have to make sure the scheme worked, it had to 'make sure it worked from day one'.

We will show that success demanded a unique approach to communications, not conforming to traditional advertising and communications models. We will also show that it demanded a high degree of integration and the dependability of *paid for* communication channels to reach near 100% of Londoners, to cut through in a negative editorial environment, and lead those directly affected through a path of necessarily complex information delivery, *and then action*.

Creating awareness of the scheme was only a beginning. The real challenge was to translate this into understanding and then timely action by those affected. In this context the campaign's greatest contributions to making the scheme work from day one included:

- over 500,000 pre-registrations for payment channels, discounts and exemptions by launch day, entirely the result of the Public Information (PI) campaign

TABLE 1: LAUNCH SCENARIOS

A. 'London prepared'	B. 'London not prepared'
• High awareness and understanding amongst near 100% of Londoners	• Many people unaware or unsure how affected
• People know whether, and how, they are affected	• 'Last minute' psychology predominates – many don't pre-plan and decide to 'worry about it when and if it happens'
• People affected plan changed travel behaviour, or know how to pay	• Many affected don't change travel behaviour, or know how to pay
• Large numbers of CCZ drivers pre-register in good time to facilitate payment, for a channel that suits their needs (internet, telephone, SMS texting)	• Large numbers don't pre-register for easy/ automated payment channels and discounts/ exemptions
• CCZ residents, disabled and other groups eligible for discounts and exemptions (22 in all) aware and pre-register	• Traffic chaos on day one as drivers take last-minute avoiding action, make U-turns at Zone boundary, etc.
• Operational load for information and payment systems spread over several weeks (matching available capacity)	• Meltdown as information/payment systems are overloaded and crash – large numbers find it difficult or impossible to pay
• Know what to do from day one – no panic or chaos, or overloading of systems	• Revenues lost, fair enforcement impossible, operational crisis
• Non-payment levels (unconscious, deliberate or due to payment system failure) low	• Media and public uproar, payment strike, scheme suspended to stop London grinding to a halt
• **System works from day one**	• **Catastrophic failure and meltdown**

- promoting widespread adoption of new payment channels; 25% of payments via internet, 19% via SMS texting (pioneering its use as a transactional channel).

THE ESSENTIAL ROLE OF PAID-FOR COMMUNICATIONS

The controversy surrounding the scheme resulted in media coverage almost every day. Indeed this had already created general awareness of the scheme before the campaign commenced (and continued to help maintain this up to launch, although we could not depend on this). However, editorial coverage did little to support specific communications objectives:

- creating little understanding of the *details* of the scheme (information was patchy, the media tending to see the story more in terms of politics than as a transport initiative)
- offering little in terms of stimulating pre-registration and response
- largely hostile, critical, and negative, often predicting failure (creating the impression that the scheme would fail and quickly be suspended)
- specifically using the prolonged closure of the Central Line (from January 2003) to predict cancellation or postponement of the scheme.

Worse than this, coverage regularly included factual errors about the operation of the scheme – hours of operation stated incorrectly, eligibility criteria for discounts inaccurate, the prediction that systems would crash and the scheme would fail.

Even in the last week there were inaccuracies:

- the *Independent* (13 February) referred to 'buying a daily ticket' (there is no physical ticket)
- the *Daily Telegraph* (15 February) wrote that the payment had to be made on the day, discouraging pre-planning (you can pay up to three months in advance, and we were encouraging people to do so)
- the *Observer* (16 February) stated that Blue Badge holders pay nothing (they have to register, with a £10 fee, before they are exempt).

The campaign had to counter this and provide an authoritative source of accurate information. Further, to make people go against their natural inclination to 'wait and see', we had to create a sense of inevitability and encourage pre-planning, as well as get across a lot of information.

The dependability, accuracy and flexibility offered by paid-for media were essential to ensuring that London was prepared, and so avoid meltdown on 17 February.

BACKGROUND TO THE SCHEME

The scheme directly supports four of the Mayor's ten priorities for improving transport for London, set out in his Transport Strategy published in July 2001:

- reduce congestion
- make radical improvements to bus services
- improve journey time reliability for car users
- make the distribution of goods and services more reliable, sustainable and efficient.

The broader importance of its successful implementation cannot be overestimated. The scale and complexity of the implementation challenge in London meant that many major cities face gridlock equal to, or worse than, London. Many had considered congestion charging, but fought shy of being 'the first'. The London scheme was regarded as a test case for governments and cities around the world. In the UK alone over 30 local authorities have expressed interest, and in future years its success is likely to be seen as a 'tipping point' in national and global urban transport strategy.

> 'The world is a different place in terms of urban transport since 17 February.'
>
> Professor David Begg, Government Transport Adviser

Some aspects of scheme design were informed by the limited experience of congestion charging schemes elsewhere in the world: using the same camera technology as Melbourne, for example, and the same 'area' scheme concept as Singapore and Trondheim. But there was no parallel for the Central London scheme in terms of the scale of the infrastructure and communications challenge involved.

It was bound to be controversial, with widespread scepticism about whether it would work. From initial announcement of the scheme right up to launch, the media, political and stakeholder environment was consistently negative. Typical newspaper headlines included:

> 'Great congestion charge gamble: If it does not work the Mayor should have the courage to scrap it, say our transport experts.'
>
> 'THE TOLL TAX. Uproar at yet another plan to charge for driving a car.'
>
> 'Battle is on for drivers in the capital.'
>
> 'Chaos looms on London roads. Tomorrow is D-day for the capital's congestion charge and its foes fear the worst.'

Even the Mayor publicly accepted that the scale of the challenge meant that success could not be guaranteed.

Failure would have cost hundreds of millions in wasted investment, lost revenues and the broader economic benefits of the scheme to London. The world was watching and the stakes were high – in practice the scheme struggled to survive major financial and political problems.

Media coverage generated more heat than light, reinforcing the critical role for paid-for communications.

The TfL (Transport for London) PI (Public Information) Team was assembled, and agencies (TBWA\London, PHD Media, Triangle) appointed in early 2002. At this point the legal, contractual and operational framework was already finalised, with Capita contracted as service provider for the implementation, delivery and management of the scheme.

The scheme's complexity and timelines presented major challenges for campaign development. We had to fulfil the duty of TfL as a public body to inform Londoners (and visitors) about the scheme and how each individual would be affected by it (if at all). More crucially, we had to *match the behaviour of scheme users to its predetermined operational specification and capacity.* (For example, drivers would need to be encouraged not all to pay by phone, originally perceived by most as their likely payment method, and not all to call first thing in the morning, or the system would collapse.)

If we did not do this, *from day one*, the system would have crashed and chaos would ensue. Without effective communication, the scheme simply would not work.

From April 2002 until after launch we operated as a single integrated team, the only way we could deliver the coordination, flexibility and speed demanded by:

- timelines and the need to 'course correct' during the campaign
- the vast number of messages and materials required
- the need to present a totally *consistent message across the many different channels* used to effectively communicate with the *many audiences* concerned.

THE MARKETING COMMUNICATIONS TASK

The communications task mirrored the unique scale and nature of the scheme itself, with no precedent for the amount of information to be communicated, nor the breadth and complexity of the target audiences (and different responses required), nor the unpopularity of the message amongst the core 'behavioural change' target (drivers). Additionally there were no existing points of reference to help people understand how the system would work, or imagine where the boundary lay.

The task did not fit any of the standard communication models described below.

- The *Salience Model*: 'top of mind' came with the unique and bold nature of the scheme, and related media coverage, and was anyway only a small part of the task.
- The *Persuasion Model*: the legal requirement was for a public information campaign not a 'public persuasion' campaign, giving people the information they needed to make appropriate decisions about their behaviour when the scheme commenced, not try to garner support for it.
- The *Involvement Model*: similarly the task was not to popularise or develop emotional affinity with any particular target group.
- The *Familiarity/Favourability Model*: we were aiming to change behaviour not attitudes.
- The *Sales Model*: there were many possible responses, not a single 'offer', and anyway the charge was a legal requirement not a discretionary choice.

It demanded a new kind of model, which we term the *Action Briefing Model*. We were in effect briefing the London public (who already knew that this was something that may affect them) on what was going to happen and when; to help them 'self identify' (know whether and how they were affected, and what their options were); and then act in a timely way as the system could not cope with a last-minute rush.

In some respects, privatisations were a useful point of reference. The public would have to go through a steep learning curve, and there would be no second chance. The British Gas privatisation (well documented in the IPA Advertising Effectiveness database) was used as a model for the gradual unfurling of messages, using a broad mix of communications channels, and using tracking to monitor and adjust the campaign. It also provided a useful benchmark for budget setting.

It highlighted the importance of an extended campaign so that information could be delivered in bite-sized chunks. In this respect the October–March campaign period (with a break for Christmas), enforced by operational timings and the need to maximise pre-registration, was advantageous. It facilitated a 'rolling briefing', giving people time to digest and act upon the information provided. Figure 1 summarises the layers of the communications task.

Like it or not the scheme was going to happen. We had to make sure that people were prepared for 17 February and acted appropriately. And we had to cover several target audiences, some given special rights within the scheme's legal framework:

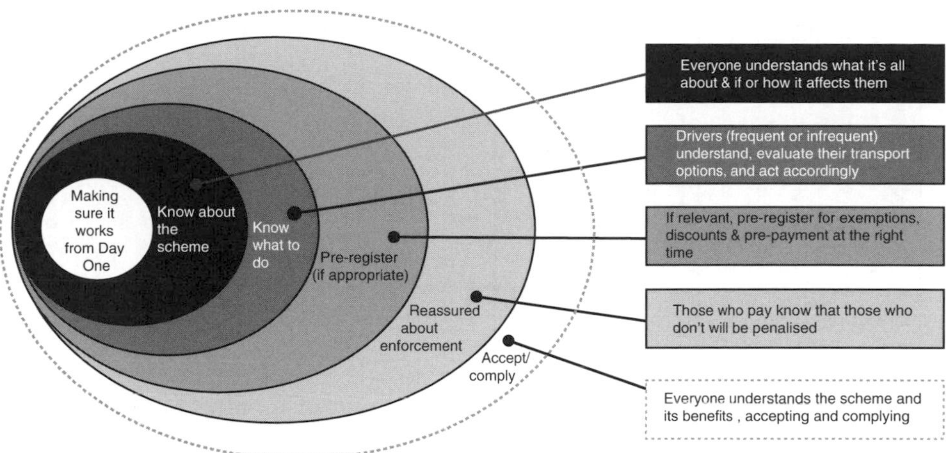

Figure 1: *Communications objectives hierarchy*

- all adults in the London area
- drivers (most but not all residing in Greater London)
  - frequent (driving into the CCZ more than once a month)
  - infrequent (driving into the zone less often)
- exemption and discount groups (22 in total), most notably Blue/Orange disabled badge holders, CCZ residents, alternative fuel vehicles, 9+ seater vehicles
- fleets with over 25 vehicles (eligible for a special scheme)
- ethnic minorities living on the boundaries and within the CCZ
- overseas visitors
- Central London businesses.

THE INTEGRATED COMMUNICATIONS STRATEGY DEVELOPED

We needed to encourage a peculiar combination of *inaction* (those not affected knowing this and not taxing the system) and *premature action* (those affected pre-registering or making other plans *well in advance*, managing the load on the system). The breadth of audiences involved, and the number of messages (both general and specific to individual groups), demanded a broad 'through-the-line' communications mix, summarised in Table 2.

The start date of 17 February was set for operational reasons. Once set, considerable cost – not to mention reputation – rode on meeting it.

Several factors – complex messaging, the need to maximise pre-registration, the need to stimulate a broad spread of channel choice for payment, and the evolving level of system functionality to process registrations – dictated a three-phase structure for the campaign: pre-Christmas (October–December), post-Christmas (January–17 February) and post-launch (17 February–March).

The complexity of messaging by phase is described below.

TABLE 2: COMMUNICATIONS TASKS BY CHANNEL

	1. Complement editorial coverage/ represent our desired CC message at 'Go Live' announcement (October 2002) in the national news environment	2. Ensure all London knows if/how they are affected – maximise coverage, raise profile and importance, communicate the top-line facts	3. Act democratically – ensure all Londoners understand the scheme	4. Deliver detailed information and, where necessary, stimulate the response/registration (in particular those qualifying for exemption or discounts)
National press	Primary		Secondary	
PR	Primary	Secondary	Secondary	Primary
TV (London)		Primary	Secondary	
Outdoor (London and arterial routes)		Primary	Primary	
London press		Secondary	Secondary	Primary
London radio		Secondary	Secondary	Primary
Ethnic and specialist press			Primary	Primary
Information booklets/leaflets/ packs, points of sale (retail sales channels), door drops, mailings, face to face, telesales, online			Secondary	Primary

Messaging overview

Pre-Christmas

- Raise awareness that the charge is 'on its way'.
- Raise knowledge of the start date.
- Deliver key facts, e.g. zone area, hours of operation, so that:
  - those who will not be affected will self-identify, reducing enquiry volumes dramatically, 'dial out' and not call us (the majority)
  - those affected will start to self-identify, 'dial in', creating engagement with future messages about the charge.
- Explain why the charge is being introduced, e.g.
  - slow-speed traffic in London at present, projected improved traffic speeds after the charge is launched
  - impact on London; social and financial costs of congestion
  - all profits raised will, by law, be ploughed back into improving transport.
- Inform people about the discounts and exemptions available, who is eligible, what the process is, and encourage people to start applying for them.
- Start communicating the basics of how to pay (more detailed information will be communicated in the post-Christmas campaign).

Post-Christmas

- Refresh general awareness and understanding.
- Detailed 'how to pay' messages, individually and together ('4 easy ways to pay').
- Encourage early registration for SMS texting payment, by positioning SMS as 'the easiest and quickest way to pay'.
- Encourage registration for Blue Badge, resident and alternative fuel discounts.
- Communicate more complex hours of payment message, i.e. £5 until 10pm; £10 from 10am until midnight; £80 penalty charge notice (PCN) if you have not paid by midnight.
- Communicate the enforcement message – what happens if you don't pay.
- Remind people that evenings, weekends and public holidays are free.
- Encourage people to pay in advance of 17 February, to avoid the rush.
- Encourage people to pay up until 10pm rather than in the morning.
- Embed the phone number, website address and ways to find a retailer to pay.
- Encourage regular drivers to pay for a week or month (one transaction vs up to 20).
- Reiterate key facts in the run-up to the launch ('boiling down' the many complex messages to a few simple key facts).

Post-launch

- Continue to direct customers to most convenient payment channels.
- Encourage further SMS registrations.
- Reiterate enforcement messages.
- Reiterate hours of operation and payment messages.
- Reiterate pay in advance messages.

The target of near 100% awareness amongst our various audiences, and the need to communicate detail to those directly affected, led to a media budget spread across all major channels:

- TV – 29%
- posters – 25%
- London press – 21%
- national press – 9%
- radio – 15%.

Total expenditure across the three campaign phases was approximately £12m (including all elements, including production and agency fees) – around 55% of this was spent on above-the-line media, with the overall split 45:55 pre- and post-Christmas.

THE CREATIVE APPROACH AND 'IDEA'

In communications terms an 'idea' is a means of capturing people's interest and imagination to sell a product, service or message. We quickly realised that the Congestion Charge itself was the 'idea' – a big bold plan that everyone instinctively knew would have a major impact on life in London, getting an instant, often very emotional response, whether positive, negative or simply inquisitive ('*How does it affect me?*').

We didn't need to create interest or emotional engagement – the Congestion Charge itself did that. Rather we had to deliver a clear and timely briefing on what was involved and how to act, in some cases detailed and tailored to the specific needs of diverse target groups. And do this in a way that calmed emotions rather than further inflaming them.

Anything promoting the scheme as a 'good thing' would be judged by the BACC/ITC as 'political advertising', excluding use of broadcast media. It was in any case immediately obvious that drivers were hostile towards messages attempting to sell the potential claimed benefits of the scheme. Indeed, hostility amongst drivers to any mention of the charge led to us abandoning use of group discussions amongst drivers for creative development (not least for the health and safety of the moderator), using paired depths instead.

So we made the scheme itself the 'idea' at the heart of communications, with the campaign approach deliberately very straightforward. What we needed was a simple means, and appropriate tone of voice, to present it to our various audiences.

A totally integrated 'visual language' was created with the congestion charge 'C' symbol and road background used to give all communications a consistent identity.

Print communications were based on the insight that people's first response to the scheme was almost invariably a series of questions: '*How does it affect me? How will it work? What will I need to do?*' and so on. This led to the 'Q&A' approach adopted.

TV and radio needed more character and a sense of dialogue to engage and communicate. The insight here was that, although many of those affected were very anti the scheme, there was broad acceptance that traffic congestion in London was no joke. Thus the use of comedian Bob Mills being uncharacteristically serious, to get across the message with an 'it's not desirable, but it is necessary' tone of voice for the initial phase.

TV

Posters and press

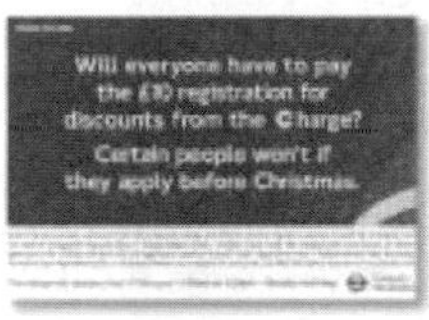

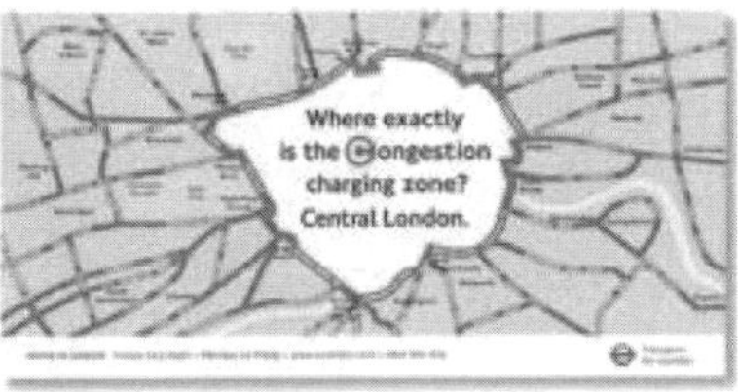

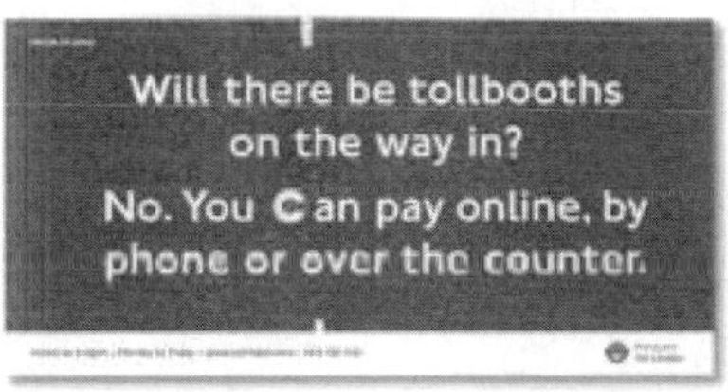

Figure 2: *Pre-Christmas campaign*

Figures 2 and 3 show a small selection of the 173 creative elements making up the campaign, comprising 42 poster executions, 42 radio, 37 press, 11 TV, 7 ambient, plus 34 BTL pieces.

THE OVERALL RESULT

The scheme itself has been highly successful in terms of the objectives set in the Mayor's transport strategy. Headline findings from TfL's *Congestion Charging 6 months on* report, published in October 2003, included the following.

- Traffic delays in the charging zone reduced by about 30% (high end of expectations).
- About 60,000 fewer car movements per day (a reduction of about 30%) now come into the charging zone. TfL estimates that 20–30% of these have diverted around the zone, 50–60% represent transfers to public transport and 15–25% other changes in travel patterns (car share, motorcycle, pedal cycle, travel outside charging hours).
- Journey times to, from and across the charging zone decreased by an average of 14%.

Door drops and retail

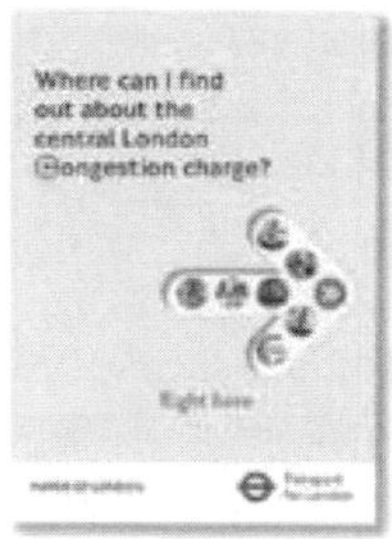

Face-to-face activity

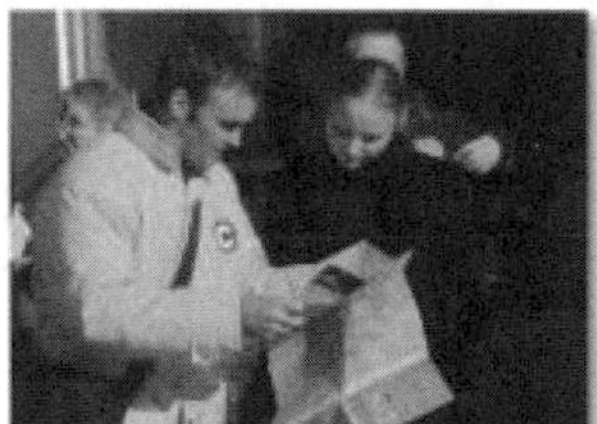

Print

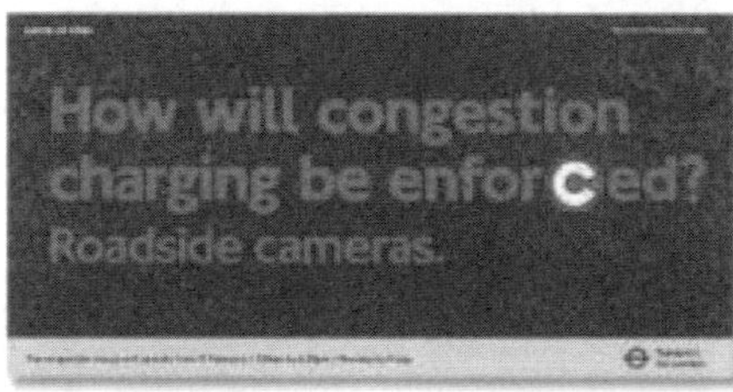

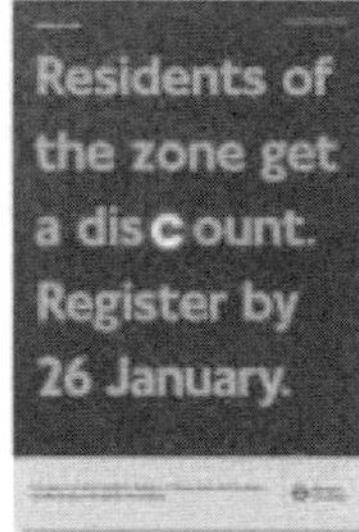

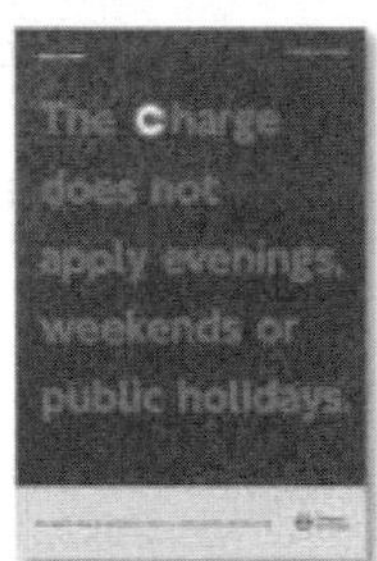

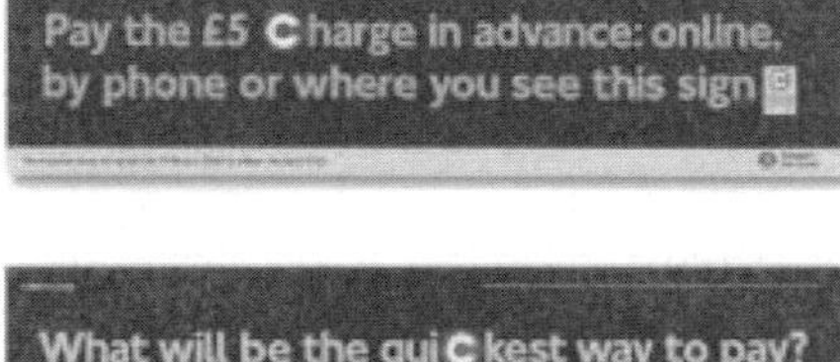

Figure 3: *Post-Christmas campaign*

- Journey time reliability improved by an average of 30%.
- Bus and coach movements in the zone have increased by around 15%, taxi movements by around 20%, motorcycle movements by around 20% and pedal cycle movements by around 30%.

TfL's subsequent update in February 2004 (www.tfl.gov.uk) reports a daily year-on-year increase of 29,000 bus passengers entering the zone within the morning peak

(7am to 10am). Comparing autumn 2003 with autumn 2002, an additional 560 buses were observed entering the charging zone within the morning peak. In the financial year 2003/04 congestion charging generated £78m for transport improvements, expected to rise to £80–100m in future years.

The Congestion Charge continues to arouse strong emotions amongst Londoners, politicians and the media, but there is broad acceptance based on objective evidence that the scheme has met its objectives.

> 'To a minority of people congestion charging is still seen as the worst disaster to hit London since the Great Plague. But if that's the case, why are so many city leaders from across the world rushing to London to infect themselves? Places as far apart as San Francisco, Stockholm, Barcelona, Milan, and Sao Paulo are starting to look at Ken Livingstone's triumph as an opportunity to rid themselves of congestion. A year to the day since charging was introduced in Central London, congestion is still down a third, traffic speeds are 10% faster and 50,000 fewer cars a day are clogging up the city centre.'
>
> Professor David Begg, Chairman of the Commission for Integrated Transport and Government Transport Adviser, writing in the *Evening Standard*, 17 February 2004

> 'Prior to the introduction of charging in August 2002 the Foundation measured traffic speeds of just 2.9mph on several key routes ... Now speeds are up to 7.4mph as the number of cars entering the zone has dropped by 50,000 a day (38%) ... The London scheme is working well in terms of traffic reduction in the centre without causing too many problems outside the zone.'
>
> RAC Foundation press release, 16 February 2004

The task of the campaign was 'to make sure it worked from day one', which it self-evidently did. Meltdown was avoided. People knew whether they were affected and what to do. The traffic chaos and systems failures widely predicted did not materialise, on day one or since. The call centre was not overloaded with enquiries, and payment was spread across the day and the various payment channels available.

> 'A historic day, but very much business as usual in London.'
>
> *BBC TV News*, 17 February 2003

In many ways this is the critical evidence of campaign effectiveness. The design of the scheme meant that effective communication to close to 100% of Londoners was as essential to success as the technology and infrastructure, in particular by matching response to the system's capacity to handle enquiries and payments. If the campaign had not been effective, then the whole scheme would have failed.

When looking more deeply at specific campaign contribution, none of the traditional means of isolating effect is available to us:

- no advertised and non-advertised periods to compare
- no test and control groups, or opportunity to experiment
- no basis for econometric analysis
- no competitive benchmarks (except in terms of budget setting where spend was modelled on privatisations such as British Gas, scaled down to London).

There is, however, plenty of evidence of the ways in which the integrated campaign contributed to the successful launch.

HOW THE CAMPAIGN CONTRIBUTED TO THIS SUCCESS

People knew what to do – London was prepared

As launch approached, our various audiences were fully briefed. The high level of knowledge achieved could only have been delivered by an effective communications campaign reaching all audiences across London.

London was prepared – pre-launch tactical research summary
By two weeks before launch, awareness of the scheme was at saturation levels at around 97% amongst Londoners. This was consistent across most groups, including key targets such as drivers in the Zone and residents.

Over 85% of Londoners knew they were not directly affected by the scheme (non-drivers, and those exempted and discounted) and this meant they would be unlikely to jam the call centre on day one of the scheme causing a systems crash.

Knowledge of the key facts was exceptional – most key measures were registering above the 80% mark:

- recall of the £5.00 charge was at 91%
- time of launch was well known at 88%
- over two-thirds of Londoners understood that it was a daily charge, and not per entry into the charging zone
- drivers had self-identified – they knew who they were and whether or not they were likely to be eligible for discount or exemption (85%), and this lessened the likelihood of the system crashing due to last-minute panics on day one
- 80% of drivers could name at least one payment channel
- awareness of the penalty charge was high at 80%, probably helped by the profusion of lead stories in the press
- two-thirds of Londoners did not think it would be easy to dodge the system, a good result given the level of negative media coverage just prior to launch
- 83% of Londoners knew that the funds raised from congestion charging would go towards improving transport in London.[1]

Speculation was replaced by information, reducing the 'temperature'

The high level of knowledge and preparation achieved contributed to a big change in the way that those most directly affected feel about the scheme. Some typical quotes from the several waves of qualitative research conducted with CCZ drivers illustrate this.

Pre-launch

> 'Lots of people won't pay, it will be complete chaos.'
>
> 'All the computers will crash.'
>
> 'It's only eight weeks and there's an awful lot we still don't know.'

---

1. Source: MORI, based on 1012 interviews weighted to be representative of London residents, conducted between 31 January and 6 February 2003.

Post-launch

'I hate to say it but it looks like it has worked.'

'It's been a breeze.'

'The Zone is really good to drive around in.'

'I begrudge paying the charge but I would begrudge paying the £80 even more.'

'You'd have had to be on the moon not to have seen the advertising.'

'The advertising has worked, they haven't just hit us with it, it's been here for a while now.'

'There are lots of ways to pay, they've made it easy for us.'

Source: TRBI/interviews with CCZ drivers

The campaign stimulated large-scale pre-registration

Most people are 'last-minute merchants', particularly when money is involved, and nobody had to pre-register to travel in the CCZ. But pre-registration for Fast Track payment (internet, phone, SMS), discounts and exemptions was a key objective.

This was not just for reasons of 'preparedness' and general efficiency, more critically operational capacity had been set on assumptions of good levels of pre-registration. Achieving the targets set for each payment, discount and eligibility group based on this was necessary to avoid system overload. We managed to beat every one, helped by stimulating early response so we could predict final outcomes, with time to take corrective communications action where necessary.

The high levels reached *before* launch – by encouraging people to go against their natural inclination and plan well in advance – were entirely the result of the campaign (Table 3).

TABLE 3: PRE-REGISTRATION

Registration for:	By w/c 17 February 2003	By end September 2003
Fast Track payments	303,649	453,300
SMS payments	84,127	177,300
Blue Badge discounts	95,404	113,800
CCZ resident discounts	19,741	26,800

Note: will include some not eligible or using CCZ at launch.

Source: TfL

We also needed to spread pre-registration over several weeks. A late rush in the last week or two could have crashed systems, and with registration taking up to two weeks to process it was in any case important to stimulate earlier response to maximise preparedness on 17 February. Figures 4–7 show our success in doing this.

The campaign effectively promoted payment choices

The development and promotion of a range of 'easy ways to pay' also contributed to high levels of payment and spreading the operational load. Table 4 shows the broad spread achieved, and how effective the campaign was at enabling drivers to pick the best channel for them.

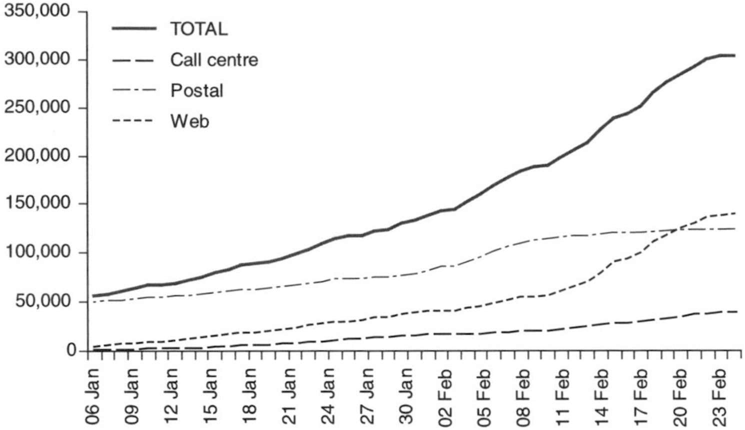

Figure 4: *Cumulative Fast Track cards*

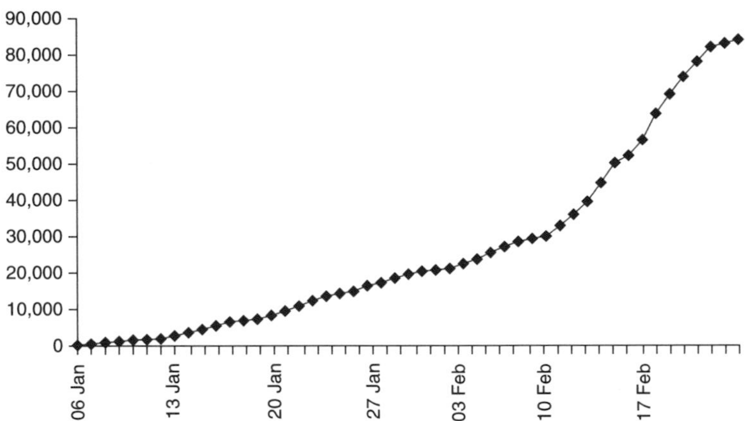

Figure 5: *SMS cumulative registrations*

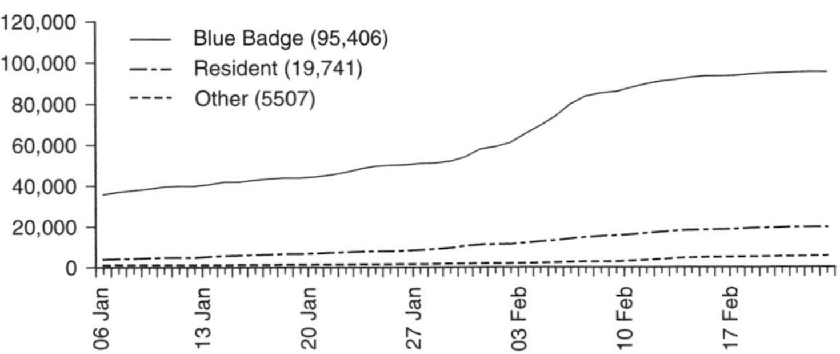

Figure 6: *Cumulative discount awards to date*

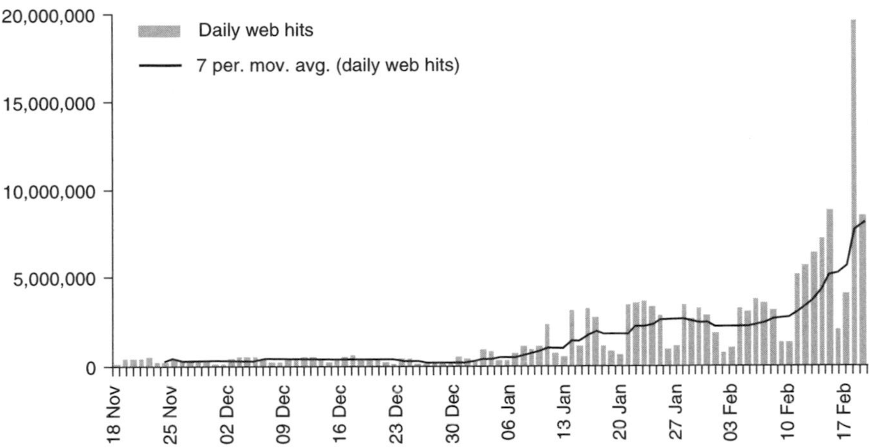

Figure 7: *Daily web hits to date*

TABLE 4: PAYMENT CHANNEL SPLIT

	w/c 17 February 2003 %	End September 2004 %
Retail payment points	37	35
Internet	16	25
Via call centre (including automated)	34	20
SMS (texting by mobile phone)	12	19
Post	1	<1

Source: TfL

New payment channels were pioneered

One of the most notable successes of the campaign was promoting the use of 'new payment channels', with 44% of all payments now made via internet or SMS.

The fact that 25% of all payments are now made via the internet is impressive – our early research showed that, while most of our driver population were 'internet savvy', their main use of it was for information not transactions.

Even more significantly, we pioneered wide-scale use of SMS as a transactional channel – 97% of those paying for the congestion charge by SMS had *never* previously used it to pay for goods or services (TfL research).

Penalty charges were minimised

Fewer than 10% of CCZ drivers incurred penalty charge notices (PCNs) in the first week of operation, despite this being a totally new system (without good awareness many people could inadvertently have entered the zone and/or failed to pay with no intent to evade, or been unaware of penalties). High levels of evasion would have put pressure on systems and brought the scheme into disrepute, as well being a sign of campaign ineffectiveness.

The operational load was spread across the day

Figure 8 shows how the timing of payments through the day was smoothed considerably versus that predicted by pre-campaign research. This is exceptional in two ways: first, breaking the mould of typical call centre load patterns, avoiding the 'early rush' (beneficial in terms of staffing and capacity); and, second, avoiding the 'late panic' and minimising those paying the 'late surcharge' after 10pm.

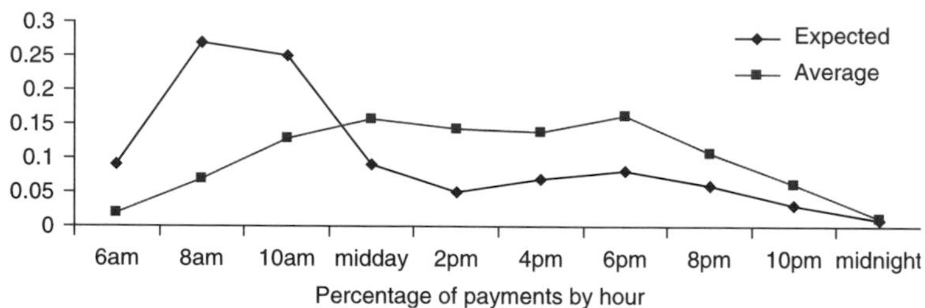

Figure 8: *Average payments per hour during first week of operation; expected figures based on consumer research before campaign started*
Source: TfL

Multiple channels contributed to meeting people's differing information needs

The campaign utilised multiple channels in an integrated way, first to push knowledge of key information to as near 100% as possible, second to provide detailed information to specific groups (e.g. for discounts and exemptions requiring pre-registration). Table 5 indicates how the multiple channels used contributed to informing the public, and so the overall success of the campaign. (Note: recall always tends to be over-attributed to TV, but the levels for other media are much higher than usually seen.)

TABLE 5: WHERE REMEMBER SEEING/HEARING INFORMATION (UNPROMPTED)

	Londoners (%)	Residents (%)	Drivers in CCZ (%)
• TV	68	53	62
• Newspapers	43	36	42
• Radio	33	24	39
• Poster/billboard	26	32	31
• Leaflet	17	26	18

Base: All seeing/hearing something about Congestion Charge
Source: MORI (February 2003)

Editorial coverage largely hindered rather than helped

Media monitoring by CARMA identified 371 articles about congestion charging in print media in October 2002 and 359 in November: 50% of these were negative, only 18% positive, and the remainder neutral. The main themes of coverage did little to advance the campaign: unfairness, lack of readiness, unworkable, negative impact on business, impact on the poor, and predictions that public transport would not cope. This persisted throughout the campaign. There were 273 articles (3898 column inches) in the seven days before 17 February alone, with a similar balance of themes.

Editorial coverage was the subject of a recent report from the Unit for Journalism Research at Goldsmiths College, University of London, based on a comprehensive analysis of national and London media coverage of the introduction of the scheme between 1 January 2002 and 31 May 2003.

> '[E]ven by British standards the reporting of congestion charging was seriously biased; most newspapers did a grave disservice to their readers who, on an important issue such as this, had a right to expect to receive information in a relatively straightforward manner. In this modest task, the majority of the press failed themselves, and, more importantly, failed their readers too.'
>
> Driven to distraction: an analysis of the media's coverage of the introduction of the London Congestion Charge by Professor Ivor Gaber

As already outlined, even when information was included in editorial it was generally sketchy at best, and at worst wrong or misleading.

Some help was provided by editorial – *non-paid-for* coverage via reader guides published by several newspapers (including the *Evening Standard*, *Metro*, *Daily Telegraph*, *FT*, *The Times*, *Mirror*, *Observer*). These were independent of our campaign, but drew on the information and materials we provided. Though positive, their contribution to 'making it work on day one' was small.

- They were only published in the last week, too late to influence pre registration by day one (applications take two weeks to process).
- High levels of knowledge were measured before their publication.
- Pre-registration built steadily over several weeks prior to launch.

So success was delivered almost entirely by the *paid-for* campaign, with little help and a lot of hindrance from editorial coverage.

COSTS AND BENEFITS

Return on the investment in marketing communications is demonstrated by the overall benefits of the scheme to London via the reduction in congestion versus its costs. Table 6 shows preliminarily estimates made in September 2003 that the scheme is generating net benefits of around £50m a year (including operating costs) – economic benefits are worth around £180m against total costs of £130m a year.

This estimated £50m net annual economic benefit *every year* compares with a one-off launch marketing communications investment of £12m (an investment that was in itself comparable to similar public information campaigns, such as British Gas privatisation, scaled down to London).

If the launch had failed, these benefits would have been postponed or, more probably, completely forgone. More than this, the overall costs of scheme failure or suspension (including operational costs written off) would have been several hundred-million pounds.

TABLE 6: PRELIMINARY ESTIMATES OF COSTS AND BENEFITS OF THE CENTRAL LONDON CONGESTION CHARGING SCHEME

	(£million per year, rounded)*
Annual costs	
TfL administrative and other costs	5
Scheme operation**	90
Additional bus costs	20
Charge payer compliance costs	15
Total	130
Annual benefits	
Time savings to car and taxi occupants, business use	75
Time savings to car and taxi occupants, private use	40
Time savings to commercial vehicle occupants	20
Time savings to bus passengers	20
Reliability benefits to car, taxi and commercial vehicle occupants	10
Reliability benefits to bus passengers	10
Vehicle fuel and operating savings	10
Accident savings	15
Disbenefit to car occupants transferring to public transport, etc.	–20
Total	180

*These are central values from the estimated range. The benefits are estimated by assigning economic values to time savings, reliability improvements, accident reductions and other effects of the scheme. This analysis excludes the revenues from the scheme, which help fund other improvements to London's transport systems, and additional bus fares, as in cost–benefit terms these are a 'transfer payment'.
**Including launch and set-up costs amortised over five years.
Source: TfL/*Congestion Charge 6 months on*

CONCLUSION

The Congestion Charge was by its nature unique and mould breaking; and without communication to ensure that London was fully prepared, it simply wouldn't have worked.

Based on its success it is likely to expand within the London area and encourage the adoption of similar schemes in other cities in the UK and worldwide. There are, of course, a long list of benefits that are difficult to quantify: to the environment; to city life, to businesses and residents; to the demand for (and use of) public transport systems; and, of course, to traffic flows in cities designed for chariots and stage coaches across the developed world.

The communications task was daunting. No previous campaign has so single-handedly borne the responsibility to introduce a new legal requirement, with so little support in the media or from stakeholders. Neither did the task fit conventional communication models identified in advertising literature – demanding a new approach we term the Action Briefing Model, based on information and action, not salience, attitude change or persuasion.

Millions of people were affected, but reading the media would lead them to believe that the scheme was flawed, doomed, and likely to result in chaos and suspension in its first days. Drivers could have been excused for discounting the campaign altogether. The fact that, despite this, it engaged, informed and ultimately delivered a compliant driver population so that the scheme worked from day one is a major achievement.

Communications objectives could only have been met through a truly integrated, closely coordinated, through-the-line campaign. By going the 'extra mile' that planning and delivering this requires, we created the most collegiate and coherent cross-agency team that those involved have ever experienced. The 'holy grail' of a single team delivering coherent plans, sharing creative ideas and planning together was achieved.

Overall this case reaffirms the power and dependability of paid-for communication channels to cut through, keep a message in front of people and lead them through a path of information delivery: sustain an extended campaign, giving people time to digest and act on information; counterbalance a negative editorial environment; ensure that people don't just have the necessary facts, but also act on them in a timely way.

Finally, it shows the power of an idea, in this case the Congestion Charge itself. Ultimately communications were just the servant of this idea, but played a vital role in making sure it became reality.

GOLD

CHARLES CHANNON AWARD (BEST NEW LEARNING)

3

Cravendale

Cash from cows

How integrated communications built a premium milk brand

Principal authors: Elisa Edmonds, DDB London, and Sara Donoghugh, DDB Matrix
Contributing authors: Les Binet and Sarah Carter, DDB London, and Justin Notley, BD-Ntwk/Scotland
Media agency: Carat

EDITOR'S SUMMARY

This case study demonstrates how an integrated campaign encouraged people to drink Cravendale, Britain's first branded milk, and to pay a premium for doing so. This created a milk brand worth £41m from a standing start.

Importantly, this paper proves the value of having integrated communications. It won the Charles Channon Award for Best New Learning for its thorough analysis of the long- and short-term benefits of integrated activity. It proves that the more integrated an idea is the more powerful it becomes, and highlights the importance of letting each channel plays to its strengths.

It makes the case for continuous evaluation in a refreshingly honest manner. The authors admit that getting it absolutely right first time isn't always possible when you're in virgin territory. Two years after launching, Cravendale sales had grown but were below target. Things had to change or the brand would be withdrawn. Building on what they knew thus far they developed a new campaign dramatising the taste benefit: because Cravendale tastes so good the cows want it back. New below-the-line activity was developed too, using the 'Cows want it back' theme, tonality and end-line, so for the first time Cravendale had a seamlessly integrated campaign. This integrated approach paid dividends. Within six months of the new activity, the brand was on track to hit sales targets and by the time the paper ends, sales had grown to the point that every drop of Cravendale that was produced was sold.

INTRODUCTION

How can you better milk? How can you break extraordinarily entrenched buying behaviour? How can you create interest in a category for which the term 'low interest' could have been invented? How can you persuade people to pay more for a version of something they feel perfectly happy with? This is the story of how Arla built a new premium milk brand worth £41m from a standing start.

The road to success wasn't an entirely smooth one however. IPA papers rarely disclose the lessons learnt from mistakes. But in this case, by outlining the vital role the process of evaluation played in two phases of communication (the 'Mr Hinchcliffe' campaign and the 'Cows' campaign), we show how we optimised communication strategy, execution and integration.

BACKGROUND

The British fresh milk market is massive – worth £1.5bn.[1] Household penetration of milk is practically universal, at 99%.[2]

The PurFiltre difference

In 1998, all milk available in Britain was the same. But in Canada – where our story really starts – the reverse was true.

The Canadian milk market is branded. Shoppers are accustomed to different types of milk. A brand called Lactantia[3] offers one such milk: PurFiltre. Milk is passed through a fine ceramic filter, which means it has far fewer bacteria than ordinary pasteurised milk. This means PurFiltre:

- tastes creamier and fresher
- stays fresher for longer, naturally without preservatives.

In Canada, Lactantia PurFiltre was positioned as pure, fresh-tasting milk that stays fresher for longer, and was sold at a 5% premium to standard milk. Two years after launch, it had built a 4% volume share of the total Canadian milk market and in Quebec, Lactantia's regional stronghold, PurFiltre had achieved a 15% share.

Arla Foods' investment in PurFiltre

Arla Foods[4] was one of Britain's major milk suppliers. PurFiltre attracted the interest of Arla's board, who saw great potential for it, and decided to launch PurFiltre in Britain. The financial implications were considerable:

1. Nielsen, 52 w/e Dec 2003.
2. Nielsen, 52 w/e Dec 2003.
3. Lactantia is a highly successful dairy brand based in Quebec, with a reputation for quality. Other dairy products (e.g. butter) are sold under this brand. In 1998 the brand was owned by Ault Foods. It was subsequently purchased by Parmalat, and it is with this company that Arla has the licensing agreement.
4. Although wholly owned by Arla (a major Danish dairy company), at that time the company was known as MD Foods in the UK.

- the licensing agreement meant royalties were to be paid to Lactantia (for the first five years), based on volume sold
- the dedicated PurFiltre production line cost £10m.

Milk is a low-margin business – these costs represented a significant extra overhead. To make PurFiltre profitable it would be necessary to command a price premium well above that achieved in Canada.

Further investment was needed, this time in building a new brand. Cravendale was born.[5]

MAKING A DIFFERENCE IN THE MILK AISLE – THE MAGNITUDE OF THE TASK

PurFiltre had proved a success in Canada. Nevertheless, Arla recognised the British market would be tough to crack.

- Milk was a low-interest, commodity category. Buying was done on auto-pilot.
- The market was unbranded; people were not used to making choices or paying a premium for milk.
- The product was undifferentiated.
- The basic quality of the product was high; consumer contentment with milk reflected this.
- Milk stands for 'natural goodness'. It is emotionally rich due to its role in early childhood. The notion of 'improved' milk raises suspicions of tampering:

> 'I can't see it as pure if they're messing about with it.'
>
> Roy Graham Marketing Research, October 1995

If that weren't enough, Cravendale, an unknown brand with no heritage or equity to leverage, needed to command a substantial price premium. At 50p for one litre and 90p for two litres, Cravendale would be about 28% more expensive than standard milk.

Business objectives

Arla's ongoing long-term sales objective is to establish Cravendale as a top 30 grocery brand by 2008. This means growing brand value to £60–65m[6] – in the same league as Nescafé Gold Blend and Whiskas.

In 1998, the short-term sales objective was to reach 2.6% volume share within two years. This target was based on PurFiltre's achievements in Canada, although around a third lower, to take account of Cravendale's higher price premium.

---

5. Arla did not use PurFiltre as the brand name, because it did not own the intellectual copyright. Arla already owned the Cravendale name – it had been used on some milk packs in the past but never as a brand.
6. From 'Biggest brands', *Marketing*, 23 August 2003, using IRI data.

Launching Cravendale – a regional approach

The scale of the task was such that Arla decided to take a 'test and learn' approach by rolling out Cravendale regionally, in four waves. Before each new roll-out, sales performance was reviewed and communication activity evaluated. We will describe these in turn.

COMMUNICATION PHASE 1: THE 'MR HINCHCLIFFE' CAMPAIGN, OCTOBER 1998–DECEMBER 2000

Cravendale was launched in the Meridian region in October 1998 (Figure 1).

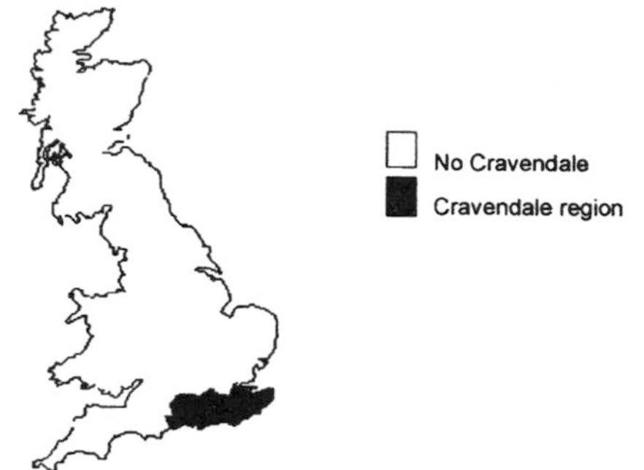

Figure 1: *Regional roll-out 1 (Meridian – October 1998)*

Communication strategy – 1998

Obviously, the main marketing objective was to gain trial for Cravendale. To this end, the key communication objectives were:

- create awareness
- generate belief that this is different milk
- create willingness to pay a premium for this.

A proportion of the budget was allocated to below-the-line (BTL) activity to incentivise people to try Cravendale. However, the emphasis at launch was on advertising, with DDB London commissioned to develop this.

We had two options to talk about to maximise trial:

1. It tastes cleaner and fresher than standard fresh milk.
2. It stays fresh longer.

We decided to follow the Canadian success model, which linked both benefits in its positioning. Our proposition was: 'Cravendale PurFiltre is so pure it will taste better than standard milk for longer'.

We had spread our net widely with the choice of message, and did the same with target audience. Our target was defined as all ABC1 adults aged 20–44. This group was considered more likely than older households to be open to a new type of milk, and prepared to pay for it.

The creative idea was: 'Cravendale tastes so good it's never around long enough to prove that it can stay fresh longer'.

The campaign centred around 'Mr Hinchcliffe': an enthusiastic Cravendale spokesman who keeps trying to prove that Cravendale PurFiltre stays fresher for longer, but is constantly foiled by people who can't resist their craving to drink the milk (Figure 2).

SFX: high-pitched microphone
Mr Hinchcliffe gives a speech:
That great man Louis Pasteur ...

Would have been astounded ... nay ... chuffed by what you are going to witness today

Ladies and Gentlemen I give you Cravendale PurFiltre fresh milk
SFX: clicking cameras

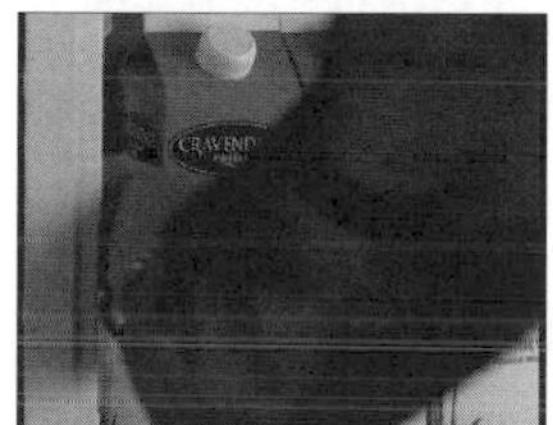

(*whispers to colleague to get the milk*: ... fridge! Fridge!) Cravendale PurFiltre is finely filtered to a greater level of purity so that it not only tastes great ...

... but it will stay fresh in your fridge for longer
SFX: last drops of milk fall into glass

Excuse me!

Scrambling sound as he grabs the colleague to hit him

FVO: Cravendale PurFiltre. Have you got the craving?

Figure 2: *Mr Hinchcliffe – Press Conference (40 secs)*

The campaign took a testimonial approach. Two 40-sec TV executions were developed (each with 10-sec cut-downs) for the Meridian launch region.

BTL activity was commissioned separately. A door-drop of a 25p-off coupon happened shortly after the TV, in late 1998. Like the advertising, the net was cast wide: nearly all households in the Meridian area received a coupon through their door. There was little executional integration between ATL and BTL, just the TV end-line (Figure 3).

		Total	Oct 98	Nov 98	Dec 98	Jan 99	Feb 99	Mar 99	Apr 99	May 99	Jun 99	Jul 99	Aug 99	Sep 99	Oct 99	Nov 99	Dec 99	Jan 00
Meridian	TV	£1.4m	■	■	■	■	■	■			■	■	■	■	■			
	BTL	£0.8m	░	░	░													

■ TV ░ Door-drop

Figure 3: *Roll-out 1 media plan (Mr Hinchcliffe, October 1998–January 2000)*

During the first roll-out there were some causes for concern. We tweaked the advertising and BTL for the second roll-out in February 2000, when other regions were added (Figure 4).

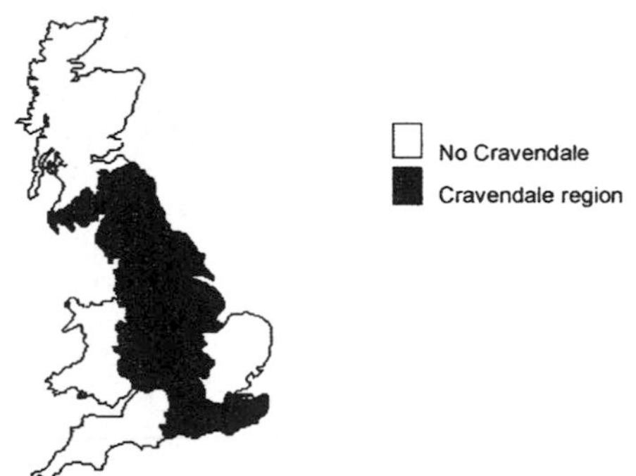

Figure 4: *Regional roll-out 2 (February 2000)*

There were two issues: first, 'The advertising raises the question for many of additive content or removal of nutrients ... the advertising lacks reassurance that this is real milk with nothing added or taken away'.[7]

In response to this, new TV executions were developed. Mr Hinchcliffe's testimonial was expanded, to give people rational reassurance that Cravendale was natural and unadulterated. The advertising – literally – ticked a checklist of product points (Figure 5).

Second, sales were growing but were not on track to hit targets. We needed to double the number of people trying Cravendale – only 11% of people in Meridian had done so. A new BTL agency was appointed: BD-Ntwk.

The focus of BTL activity was still on incentivising trial. But more tools were used: door-drops of coupons and free samples, with additional activity to disrupt

7. Source: JRA qual research summary, February 1999.

SFX: Jolly music playing
Mr Hinchcliffe: Martin me lad, it's time you learnt about the Cravendale PurFiltre checklist: fresh milk; whole.

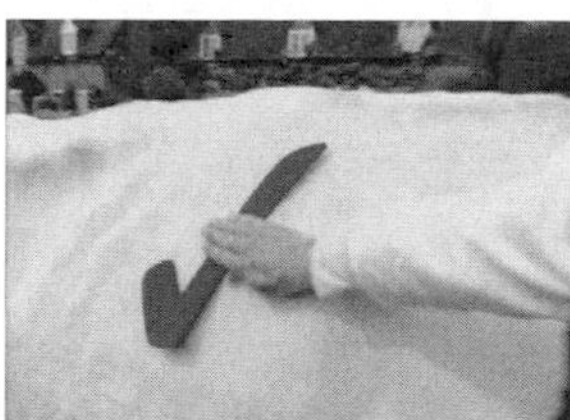

... semi and skimmed – tick!
SFX: ping sound

All the vitamins and minerals – tick!
SFX: ping sound

No additives or preservatives – tick!
SFX: ping sound

Fewer bacteria so it stays fresher longer – tick!
SFX: ping sound

... and great taste ...

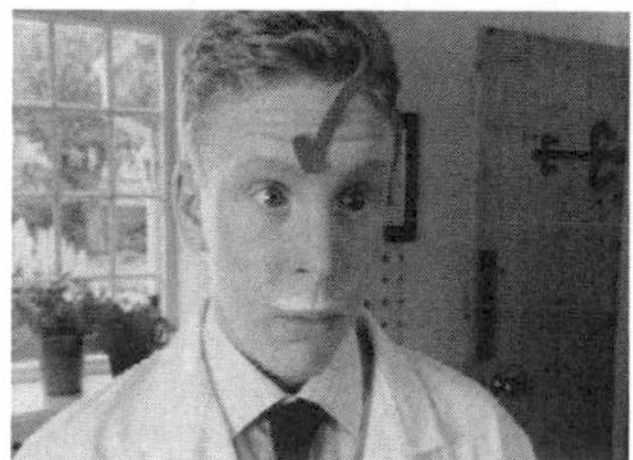

... tick!
SFX: ping sound

MVO: Cravendale PurFiltre. Have you got the craving?

Figure 5: *Mr Hinchcliffe – Checklist (30 secs)*

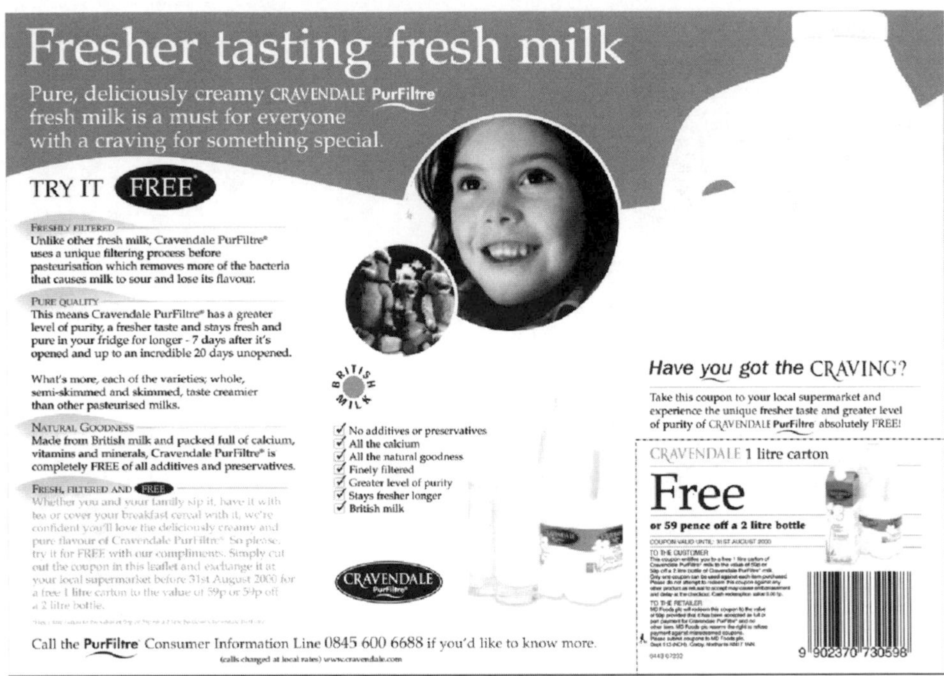

Figure 6: *Example of BTL activity during Mr Hinchcliffe communication phase*

the in-store auto-pilot, such as in-store tastings, on-pack competitions and POS material.

Below-the-line activity became more integrated with the advertising: door-drop activity used advertising elements (the checklist and tick) (Figure 6). MOSAIC profiling was used, to match the right message to the right people (e.g. door-drops talking about longevity to postcodes that had a high concentration of singles, who tend to buy milk infrequently).

RESULTS POST-'MR HINCHCLIFFE', DECEMBER 2000

By December 2000 (Figure 7), Cravendale sales had reached £10.6m – no mean feat given that people were not actively seeking a better milk. However these sales represented only 1.5% volume share of the regions where Cravendale was available. We had under-delivered on our objectives by nearly half (Table 1). Sales were not high enough by the end of the Mr Hinchcliffe campaign.

Brand awareness had grown, but 58% of people in the regions where Cravendale was available still hadn't heard of it. The campaign's awareness index (AI) (a measure that indicates the power of adverts to generate brand awareness) had grown from 2 to 5, but this was still below Millward Brown's AI norm of 6. Only about a quarter of people were aware of any communication, and fewer still had tried Cravendale (Table 2). Awareness and trial were low after the Mr Hinchcliffe campaign.

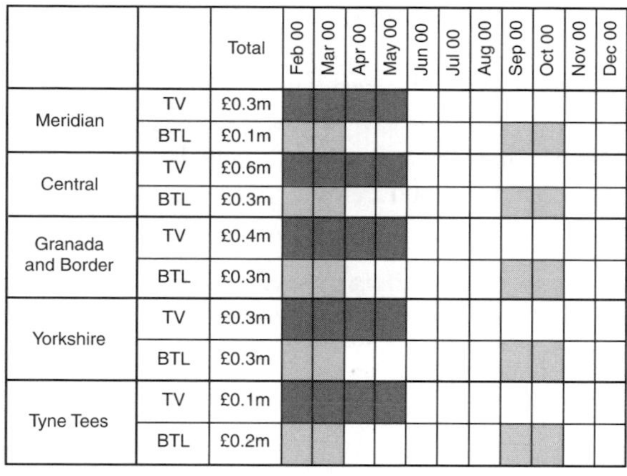

Figure 7: *Roll-out 2 media plan (Mr Hinchcliffe, February–December 2000)*

TABLE 1: ACTUAL SALES VS TARGET BY THE END OF THE MR HINCHCLIFFE CAMPAIGN

	Annual volume share (%)	Annual volume sales (million litres)	Annual value share (%)	Annual value sales (million litres)
Regions 1 and 2 actual post-Mr Hinchcliffe (2000)	1.5	21.1	1.8	10.6
Regions 1 and 2 target post-Mr Hinchcliffe (2000)	2.6	35.8	3.1	18.0

Annual multi-grocer sales results
Source: ACNielsen

TABLE 2: AWARENESS FIGURES AND TRIAL RATES BY THE END OF THE MR HINCHCLIFFE CAMPAIGN

	Brand awareness (%)	Awareness of any communication (%)	AI (Millward Brown)	Trial rate (%)
Regions 1 and 2 post-Mr Hinchcliffe (2000)	42	26	5	13

Source: INRA, Millward Brown

Sales *had* grown under Mr Hinchcliffe, but not enough. A loss of £1m was forecast for the next quarter. Things had to change. Arla's management gave Cravendale one last chance: Cravendale would have to generate profit in 2001 or it would be withdrawn. It was make or break time.

UNDERSTANDING WHERE THE PROBLEMS WERE

We took a step back to analyse why performance wasn't stronger. Repeat purchase rates were very good – we had a great product. But trial had barely improved over the course of the Mr Hinchcliffe campaign. Our evaluation showed that there were a number of problems, as described below.

The advertising lacked impact

Low advertising awareness testified to this, as did the campaign's AI, which was below norm. Cravendale, operating in a low-interest commodity category, needed advertising with higher impact than 'average'.

The message and targeting lacked focus

We were trying to be all things to all people – fatal when people were already happy with their milk. We had been misled by the Canadian precedent. The adverts were overloaded with messages, so shoppers didn't have a clear idea of what made Cravendale different.

BTL activity was suffering from this lack of focus too. Not enough people were acting on the door-dropped coupons. Redemption rates were just 8% and 11%. BD-Ntwk's experience suggested uptake should be better – milk was relevant to everyone and the saving offered was high enough to offset Cravendale's price premium. Furthermore, casting the net wide was proving costly. We estimated that in the Meridian area, 58% of door-drops were wasted.

The campaign lacked appeal

The tone of the advertising was too pushy and rational. We weren't winning people over, so they weren't giving us the benefit of the doubt and giving Cravendale a try:

> 'We don't want gimmicky advertising.'
>
> 'It's all rather cross.'
>
> Source: DDB Qualitative Research, November 1998

The pack was not cutting through in-store

After the first year in the Meridian area, 52% of people did not recognise the pack.[8]

A NEW PLAN WAS DEVISED

Understanding where the problems lay convinced us that we needed to re-focus nearly every aspect of the communications mix.

8. Source: INRA tracking, November 1999.

Focus the target

We sought to narrow our targeting, so we re-focused solely on families. They were potentially a lucrative bunch for Cravendale, consuming more than their fair share of milk volume.

Focus the proposition

The advertising was bogged down with multiple messages. But what should we talk about?

When we reviewed research amongst Cravendale buyers, the answer became clear – it was taste:

> 'Cravendale is typically used for the same purposes as other milks but there is a higher predisposition to use it on cereal and as a drink … the overwhelming reason for purchase of Cravendale is "Taste".'
>
> INRA Instore Research, August 1999

Tracking confirmed this (see Figure 8).

The taste benefit was especially important to families, as they consumed more milk in situations where the taste would be evident (e.g. drunk neat or with cereal), so we had a fit between message and target.

We decided to make taste core to Cravendale's positioning and to communicate it in a different way, using a more creative dramatisation of taste. This change proved to be our critical breakthrough, allowing us to start unlocking the potential of the brand.

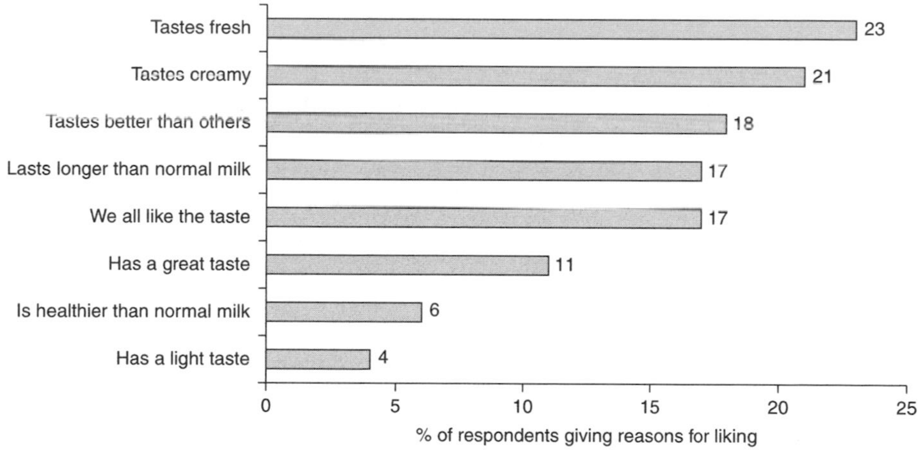

Figure 8: *Taste is the most important reason for liking Cravendale*
Source: Millward Brown, ATP, July 2000

Focus the roles of the different channels

We clarified the roles of advertising and BTL by identifying how each could challenge people's current milk buying habits.

- Advertising: drive awareness and create belief in Cravendale's superior taste, using dramatisation rather than explanation.
- BTL: work off advertising awareness – provide more detailed product information, incentivise trial, and grab their attention in-store.

In practice this meant that TV and BTL activity would run at the same time.

Make Cravendale stand out in-store

Cravendale wasn't getting noticed. People were on auto-pilot when shopping, so more emphasis would be put on point-of-sale (POS) material to grab their attention. A new pack design was also needed, to signal that Cravendale was milk with a difference with modern, premium values.

COMMUNICATION PHASE 2: THE COWS CAMPAIGN, JANUARY 2001 TO DATE

New TV advertising for the third regional roll-out

A new creative brief was written. The creative idea needed to be far more interesting and involving to generate greater awareness. In line with this, we needed to make a bold, superlative claim about the Cravendale taste, to make our family target audience sit up and take notice.

The proposition was: 'Cravendale – the *freshest*-tasting milk'. The tone was important to get right too. We needed to be far more engaging and less hectoring, so people would be more open to believing our superior taste claim.

The creative idea was simple but perfect: cows as experts on great-tasting milk. Because Cravendale tastes so good, the cows want it back. Out went the pushy salesman tone of Mr Hinchcliffe ... replaced instead by something dramatic and intriguing, a sort of bovine Hitchcock thriller.

Unlike the previous campaign, which was heavy on explanation, these executions *dramatised* the taste benefit – showing cows stalking Cravendale buyers, intent on getting their milk back. Of course, cows implicitly communicate naturalness, so the need to explicitly allay concerns on this front was eliminated. Two TV adverts were developed (Figures 9 and 10).

The new 'Cows' campaign began in January 2001, when London was added to the Cravendale regions, and was rolled out to the remaining regions in May 2002 (Figures 11 and 12).

New below-the-line activity for the third regional roll-out

Two weeks after the TV advertising, BTL activity started. Family households received a door-drop leaflet with a coupon and information about the Cravendale difference (Figure 13). Supermarkets in the same areas were contacted in advance to ensure they were well stocked.

The 'Cows want it back' theme, tonality and end-line was carried through to all BTL communication, so execution was consistent across channels. For the first time

Dramatic music throughout
SFX: Sound of milk pouring on cereal

Dramatic sound in music

SFX: Faint echoey 'moooing' sound

SFX: Door slamming

MVO: Cravendale

MVO: Tastes so good the cows want it back
SFX: loud 'mooooing'

Figure 9: *Cows – 'Security Guard' (20 secs)*

In the style of a Hitchcock thriller.
SFX: Suspense music, car trying to start up

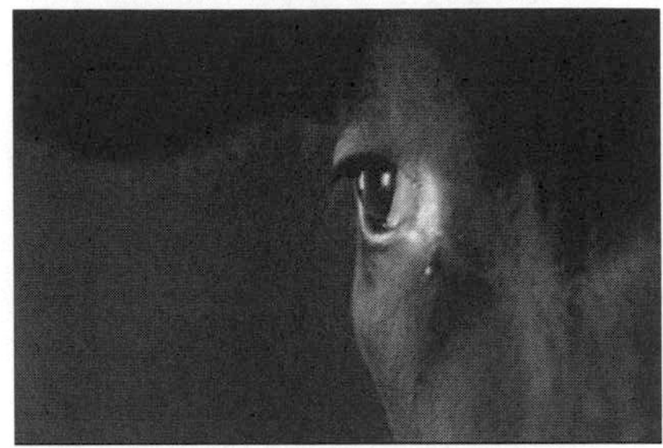

Music building up. Eerie sounds and unsettling camera angles

Man gets out of his car

Cracking sound as cow's hoof breaks the HT leads that start the car

Music building up the suspense

Sound of the cows' hooves as they follow the man, who leaves the car park to walk home

Figure 10: *Cows – 'Pursuit' (40 secs)*

The music gets louder as the tension builds
MVO: Cravendale is no ordinary milk

Cows in lift – SFX: Life muzak
MVO: It's filtered to make it purer

Mechanical sound as cow goes up in window lift

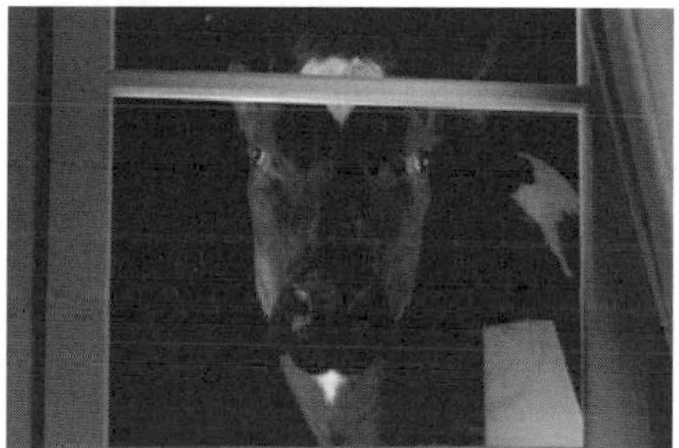

Dramatic sound in music as cow looks through window

MVO: Cravendale tastes so good
SFX: Doorbell ringing … and then loud knocking on the door

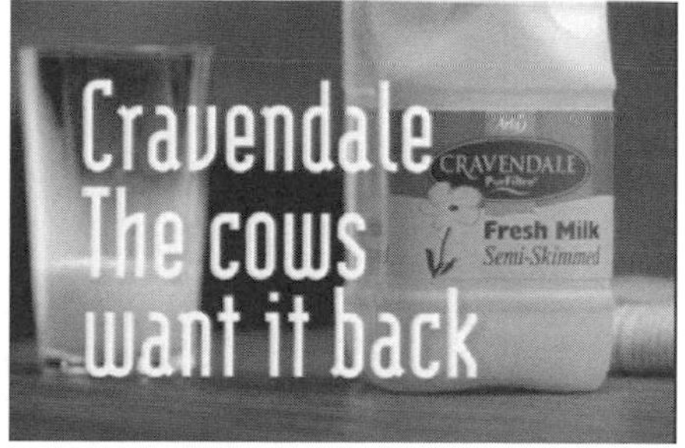

SFX: cows moo ominously
MVO: The cows want it back

Figure 10 (cont.): *Cows – 'Pursuit' (40 secs)*

Figure 11: *Regional roll-out 3 (January 2001)*

Figure 12: *Regional roll-out 4 (May 2002)*

Figure 13: *Example of Cows door-drop (front and inside of mailer)*

		Total	Jan 01	Feb 01	Mar 01	Apr 01	May 01	Jun 01	Jul 01	Aug 01	Sep 01	Oct 01	Nov 01	Dec 01	Jan 02	Feb 02	Mar 02	Apr 02	May 02	Jun 02	Jul 02	Aug 02	Sep 02	Oct 02	Nov 02	Dec 02	Jan 03	Feb 03	Mar 03	Apr 03	May 03	Jun 03	Jul 03	Aug 03	Sep 03	Oct 03	Nov 03	Dec 03
Meridian	TV	£0.5m																																		
	BTL	£0.09m																																		
Central	TV	£0.8m																																		
	BTL	£0.2m																																		
Granada and Border	TV	£0.5m																																		
	BTL	£0.1m																																		
Yorkshire	TV	£0.3m																																		
	BTL	£0.3m																																		
Tyne Tees	TV	£0.2m																																		
	BTL	£0.1m																																		
Carlton	TV	£1m																																		
	BTL	£1m																																		
Anglia	TV	£0.3m																																		
	BTL	£0.2m																																		
South West	TV	£0.3m																																		
	BTL	£0.1m																																		
Wales and West	TV	£0.2m																																		
	BTL	£0.4m																																		
Scotland	TV	£0.4m																																		
	BTL	£0.5m																																		

TV On pack Door-drop

Figure 14: *Roll-outs 3 and 4 – media plan*

we had a seamlessly integrated campaign that played to both channels' strengths (Figure 14).

Making Cravendale stand out in-store

Point-of-sale material was used more heavily than it had been before – in 1700 stores. Like the rest of the communication support, this used the Cows theme (Figure 15).

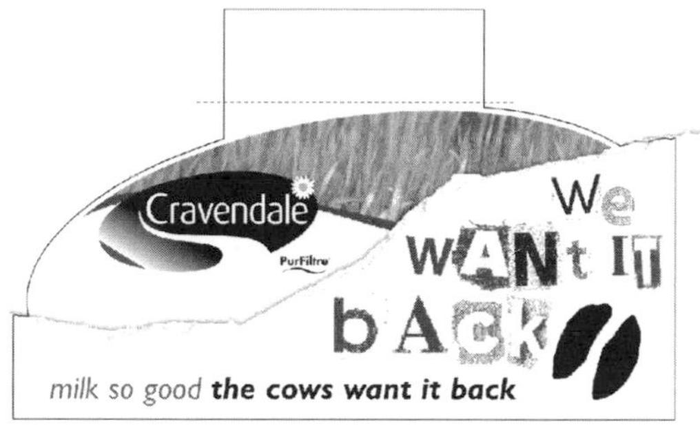

Cravendale
PurFiltre
We
WANt IT
bACK
milk so good the cows want it back

Figure 15: *Example of Cows POS – shelf barker*

To coincide with the final regional roll-out the pack design was tweaked. This new design aimed to make Cravendale look different to other milk on the shelf: more modern and bold (Figure 16). At the same time the 1-litre tetra-paks were withdrawn from supermarkets as this size wasn't suited to the needs of families, who typically consumed large volumes of milk.

Cravendale pack was tweaked in May 2002

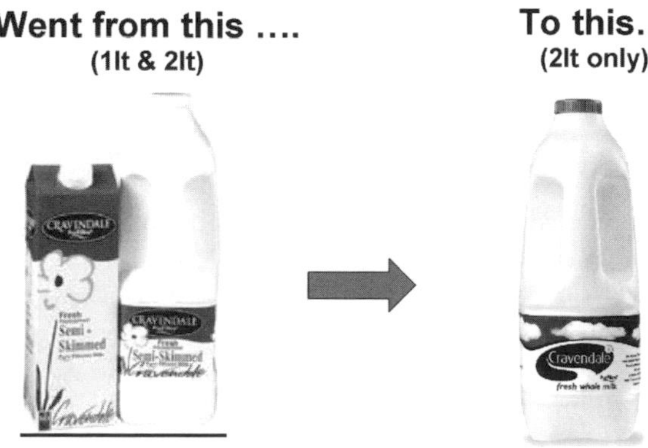

Figure 16: *Pack redesign for roll-out 4*

RESULTS POST-'COWS', DECEMBER 2003

The campaign saw improvement on every measure we had previously identified as needing change (Table 3). The Cows idea was far more powerful and efficient than Mr Hinchcliffe. Brand awareness jumped. The adverts were more impactful, as indicated by the campaign AI of 12 (double the UK norm and well above the drinks and fmcg norm of 7). Communication awareness improved greatly. Awareness and trial were much higher after the Cows campaign.

TABLE 3: AWARENESS AND TRIAL RATES POST-COWS CAMPAIGN

	Brand awareness (%)	Awareness of any communica-tion (%)	AI (Millward Brown)	Trial rate (%)
Regions 1 and 2				
post-Mr Hinchcliffe (2000)	42	26	5	13
Regions 1, 2, 3 and 4				
post-Cows (2000)	73	49	12	27

Source: Millward Brown

The campaign was also more engaging. Tracking showed that 60% of people thought the advertising was 'distinctive'.[9] Qualitative research confirmed the power of the Cows idea to signal that Cravendale was fundamentally different to standard milk:

> 'Communicates a different kind of milk ... Involving, compelling ... surreal wit ... iconoclastic dairy advertising.'
>
> Leapfrog, September 2001

BTL performance also improved with the Cows campaign: the number of people using door-dropped coupons had increased by 50% vs Mr Hinchcliffe.[10] So, the Cows communication had made more people aware that a different type of milk existed, it had engaged them with its distinctive approach and, crucially as a result, the number of people who had tried Cravendale had doubled.

After six months of Cows activity, it was clear that Cravendale was on track to meet the 'do or die' profit target set by management. We had cracked it.

The Cows activity was more effective than Mr Hinchcliffe

Cows communication proved to be more effective than Mr Hinchcliffe at launching Cravendale into new regions and generating sales from scratch (Table 4).

However, when we look at regions 1 and 2, which were supported by both Mr Hinchcliffe and Cows activity, a more remarkable picture emerges. We normally expect regions to grow fastest during launch. But when these mature regions were subsequently supported with Cows activity, growth *accelerated* (Table 5).

9. Source: Millward Brown Cravendale ATP, July 2003.
10. Source: BD-Ntwk using NCH coupon redemption data.

TABLE 4: LAUNCHES WERE MORE SUCCESSFUL WITH COWS

	Annual volume share (%)	Annual volume sales (million litres)	Annual value share (%)	Annual value sales (million litres)
Regions 1 and 2				
growth from Mr Hinchcliffe (Launch–2000)	1.5	21.1	1.8	10.6
Regions 3 and 4				
growth from Cows (2001–2003)	1.9	25.0	2.2	14.2

Annual multi-grocer sales results
Source: ACNielsen

TABLE 5: MATURE REGIONS EXPERIENCED ACCELERATED GROWTH WITH COWS

	Annual volume share (%)	Annual volume sales (million litres)	Annual value share (%)	Annual value sales (million litres)
Regions 1 and 2				
growth from Mr Hinchcliffe (Launch–2000)	1.5	21.1	1.8	10.6
Regions 3 and 4				
growth from Cows (2001–2003)	1.7	24.9	2.1	15.4

Annual multi-grocer sales results
Source: ACNielsen

The Cows idea was more efficient than Mr Hinchcliffe

The improvement in sales performance was not the result of extra communication spend. It was the result of a more powerful idea. We have clear evidence of this when we look at sales growth gained per additional £ spent on each campaign. The Cows communication was nearly four times more efficient at generating sales (Table 6).

TABLE 6: COWS CAMPAIGN WAS MORE EFFICIENT THAN MR HINCHCLIFFE

	Annual value sales (£ million)	Additional communication spend (£ million)	Growth per additional £ of communication spend (£ for £)	Efficiency of Cows vs Mr Hinchcliffe
Regions 1 and 2				
growth from Mr Hinchcliffe (Launch–2000)	10.6	4.3	2.4	—
Regions 3 and 4				
growth from Cows (2001–2003)	29.6	3.2	9.3	3.8

Source: ACNielsen, BD-Ntwk, DDS, BARB

Summary

As we have already seen, volume and value share grew in both phases of the campaign. In fact, sales have grown to the point where the factory is working to capacity: every drop of Cravendale that is produced is sold.

Cravendale is now a big brand, worth £41m. This puts it well on its way to making the Grocery Top 30 list; at current growth rates (+45% to end year to 2003), Cravendale looks set to hit the Top 30 list by the end of 2005, achieving the long-term target set for the brand three years ahead of schedule.

EVIDENCE THAT THE COMMUNICATION WAS RESPONSIBLE FOR THIS SUCCESS

So how can we tell that it was communication activity that was responsible for Cravendale's success? We will show five kinds of proof.

1. The communication channels worked in the way we'd intended.
2. Timing of communication spend and timing of share gains match.
3. Regional variations in communication spend and regional share uplifts match.
4. Elimination of other possible factors that could influence sales.
5. Econometrics to quantify the contribution of communication.

Along the way we will show that, while both campaigns worked, Cows clearly worked best. And we will reveal new evidence as to channel effects, individually and in combination.

The communication channels worked in the way we'd intended: advertising worked as planned

As planned, brand awareness grew after each burst of advertising in each region (Figure 17). More people were aware of Cravendale by the end of each roll-out.

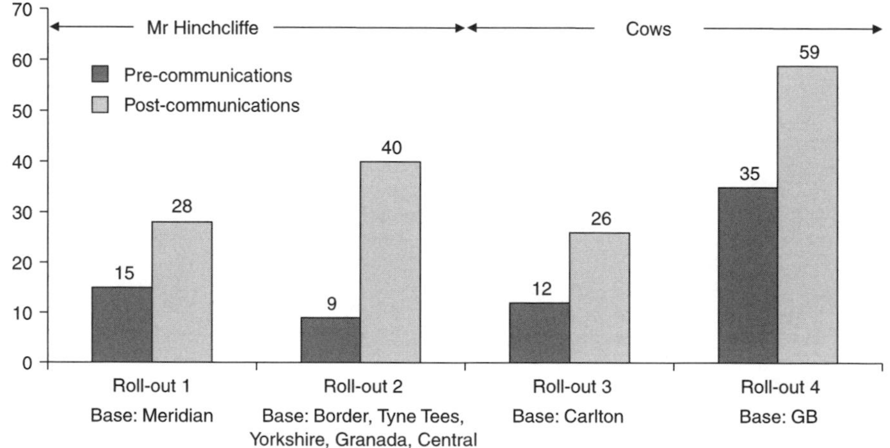

Figure 17: *Brand awareness grew after communication activity*

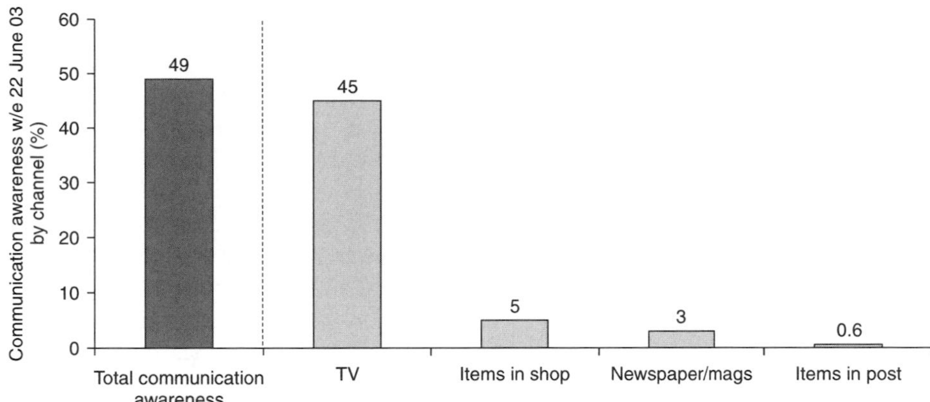

Figure 18: *Brand awareness grew after communication activity*

The primary source of awareness was advertising. Tracking data shows that, of the different communication channels, TV dominated recall. BTL activity (which targeted just as many households in the February–June burst of activity as TV did) had an effect, but it was far more muted (Figure 18). The primary source of communication awareness was TV.

Once we'd reached people, TV proved to be an impactful and memorable medium – the AI of 12 is one indication of this. Tracking provides further evidence: the ads were noticed, enjoyed and were well branded, all at rates well above UK norms (Table 7).

TABLE 7: ADVERTISING TRACKING MEASURES WERE ABOVE THE NORM

People agreeing	Cravendale (%)	UK norm (%)
Recognise the ad	66	49
'I enjoyed watching it a lot'	71	56
'I would definitely remember it was an ad for Cravendale'	72	56

Source: Millward Brown, ATP 2003

Furthermore, 81% of people agreed the Cows advertising was humorous.[11] Other research backs up the tracking:

> 'It made me laugh all the way through.'
>
> Qualitative Research, November 2003

> 'It has strong dark humour that appeals.'
>
> Millward Brown, December 2003

The other critical role for advertising was to create belief in Cravendale's superior taste. Here again the advertising succeeded: Millward Brown found that 78% of people agreed the advertising suggested Cravendale tastes better.

11. Source: Millward Brown Cravendale ATP, July 2003.

BTL worked as planned

The role for BTL activity was to break people out of their normal milk-buying routine, by giving them a coupon to try Cravendale. When BTL reached people with door-drop activity, it had a significant effect, as outlined below.

- **People acted on the coupons**
  Between February and June 2003, 6.3 million Cravendale coupons were door-dropped and 15% of these were redeemed. This compares favourably to average redemption rates for food products targeted at families (around 10%).[12] This 15% *excludes* mis-redemptions (when coupons are redeemed against another product in the same category). Mis-redemption is a useful indicator of how well BTL activity is working. Typical mis-redemptions of coupons for other dairy products are 23%.[13] In this case, mis-redemptions were only 13%. People were acting in the way we wanted.
- **People continued to buy Cravendale**
  Of the 15% of people who redeemed a Cravendale coupon, 20% went on to buy at least three more bottles of Cravendale within a six-week period – without needing an extra incentive to do so.[14]
- **BTL activity has generated sales**
  A total 4.4 million litres of Cravendale have been sold as a direct result of people receiving coupons since 2000.[15] Of course, this doesn't include subsequent sales, when people become loyal to Cravendale.
- **As a result, BTL increased penetration**
  We can see this clearly in Figure 19, where coupon redemption corresponds to increases in the number of households purchasing Cravendale.

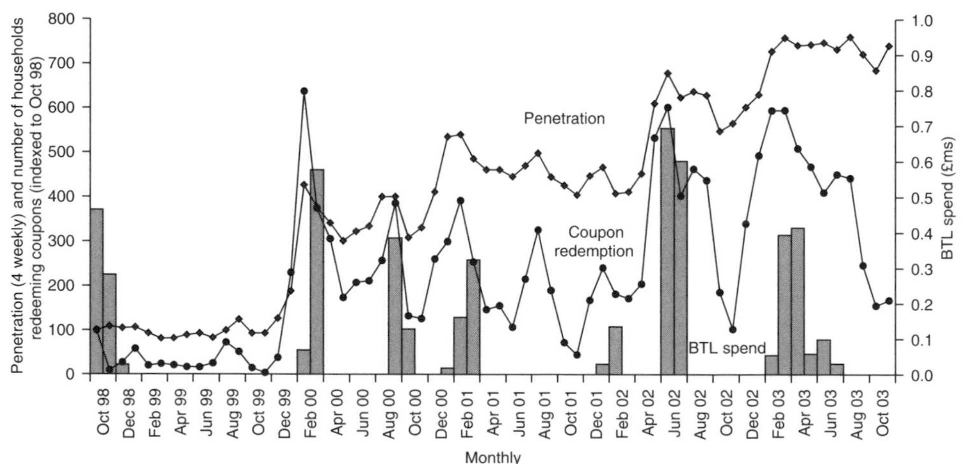

Figure 19: *Growth in penetration corresponds to coupon redemption*
Source: ACNielsen, BD-Ntwk

12. Source: BD-Ntwk, 2004.
13. Source: BD-Ntwk, NCH coupon redemption data.
14. Dunhumby Tesco Clubcard Transaction data; NCH coupon redemption data, September 2003.
15. Source: NCH coupon redemption data.

The timing of communication spend and timing of share gains match

A quick look at the sales data immediately reveals a strong correlation between market share and communication activity. Gains in market share coincide with each burst of activity, with the timing of the sales response generally matching the timing of the communications activity to the month (Figure 20).

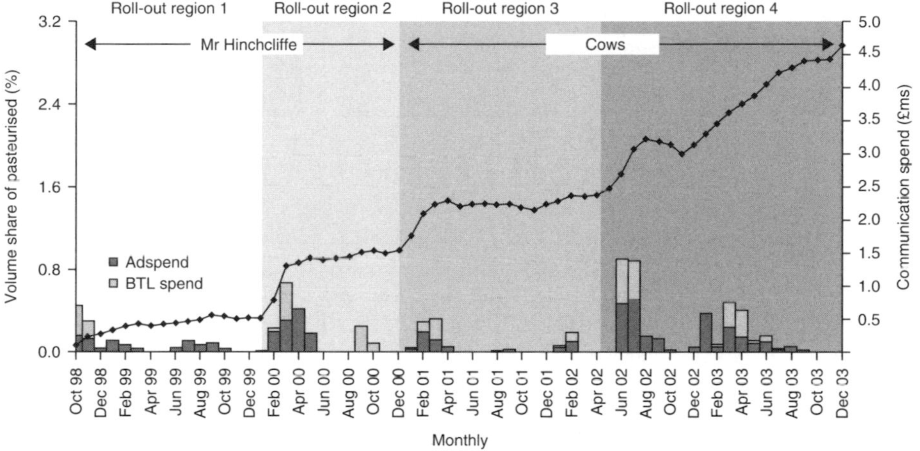

Figure 20: *Timing of share gains matched timing of communication activity*
Source: ACNielsen, BD Ntwk, DDS, BARB

However, we know that much of this growth was due to distribution gains, as Cravendale was progressively rolled out (Figure 21).

How can we separate out the effect of communication from the effect of distribution gains? The first thing to do is to look at rate of sale. We can see that rate of sale (ROS) in each region went up with each burst of communication (Figure 22).

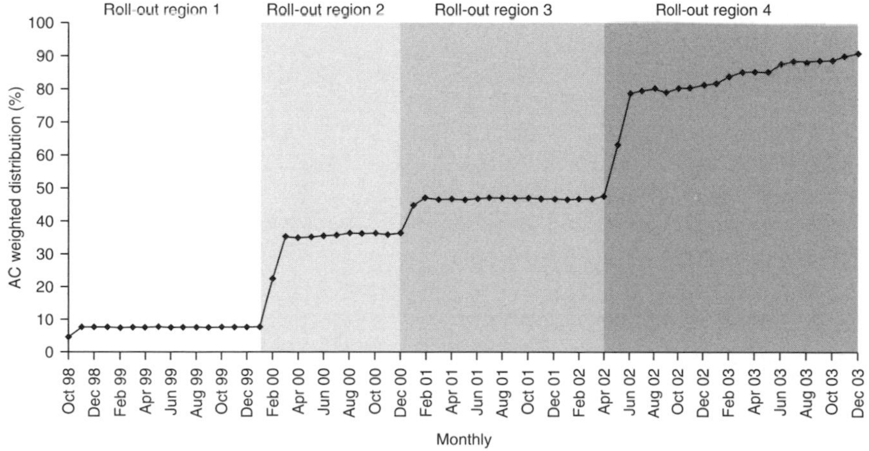

Figure 21: *Distribution grew with each roll-out*
Source: ACNielsen

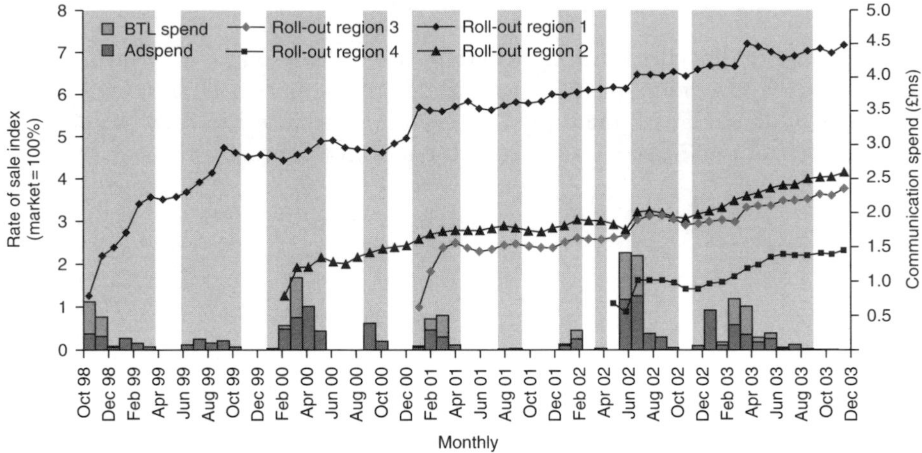

Figure 22: *ROS increased with each burst of activity in every region*
Source: ACNielsen, BD-Ntwk, DDS, BARB

Furthermore, when we compare the increase in ROS with variations in spend over time, a clear correlation can be seen in every region. When we look at the increase in ROS per £ spent per person, we can see that the return from Cows (regions 3 and 4) is greater than that from Mr Hinchcliffe (regions 1 and 2). (Figures 23 to 26). Communications spend matched rate of sale gains in each roll-out region.

Looking more closely at the regional data, we can see that share gains correspond to spend even when distribution is flat. In the Meridian area, when distribution and share are indexed, there is evidence of a clear relationship between market share and communication activity, even though distribution has been stable since January 1999. With each burst of activity there is a corresponding uplift in sales. In the absence of communication, sales flattened off and did not grow again until the Cows communication began (Figure 27).

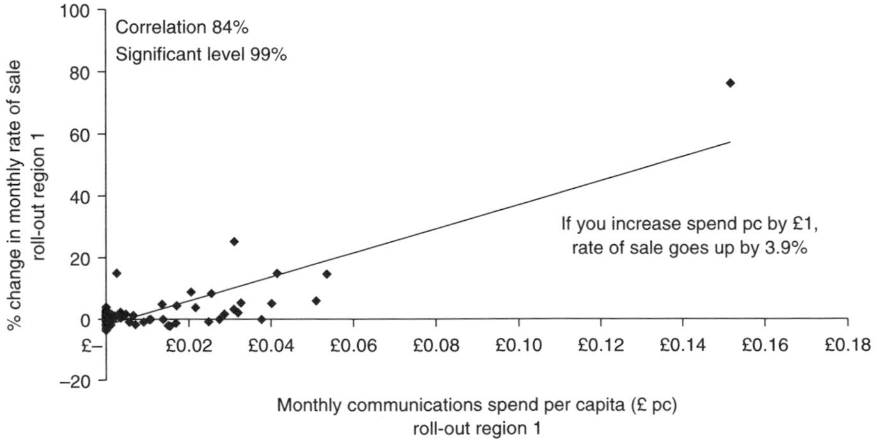

Figure 23: *Communication spend matched ROS gains in roll-out 1*
Source: ACNielsen, BD-Ntwk, DDS, BARB

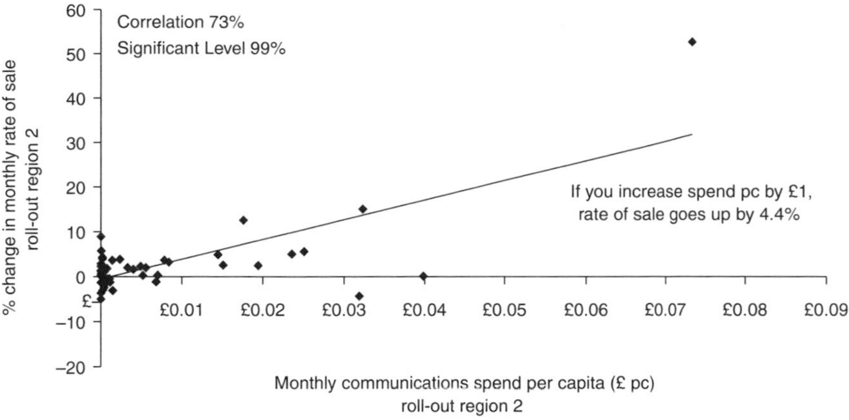

Figure 24: *Communication spend matched ROS gains in roll-out 2*
Source: ACNielsen, BD-Ntwk, DDS, BARB

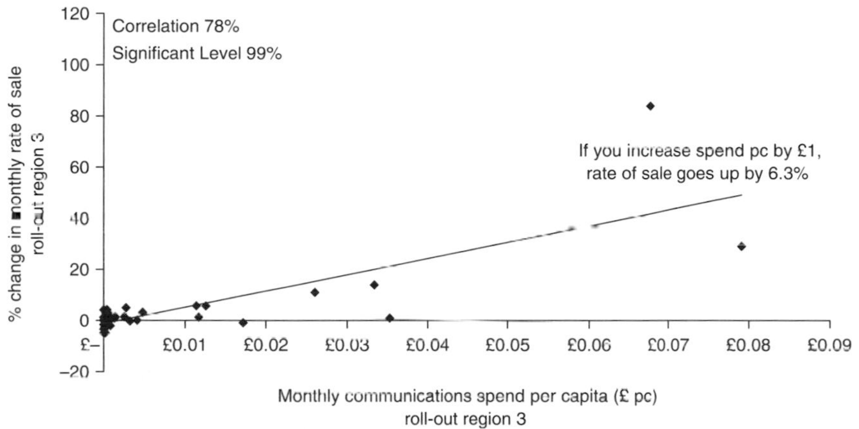

Figure 25: *Communication spend matched ROS gains in roll-out 3*
Source: ACNielsen, BD-Ntwk, DDS, BARB

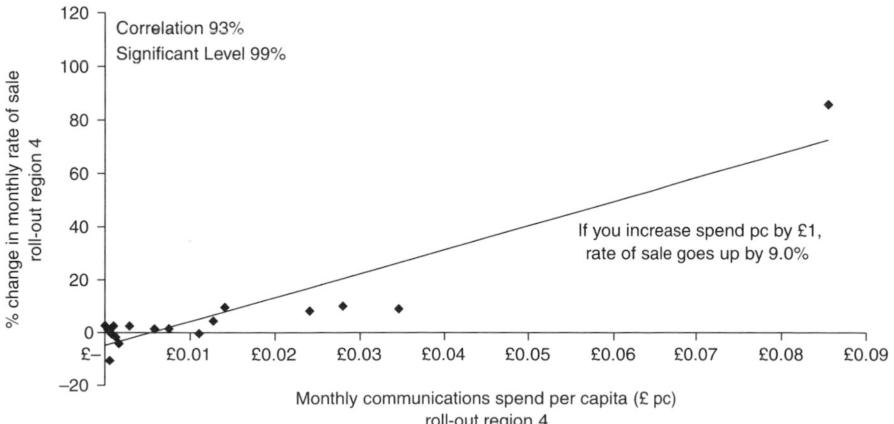

Figure 26: *Communication spend matched ROS gains in roll-out 4*
Source: ACNielsen, BD-Ntwk, DDS, BARB

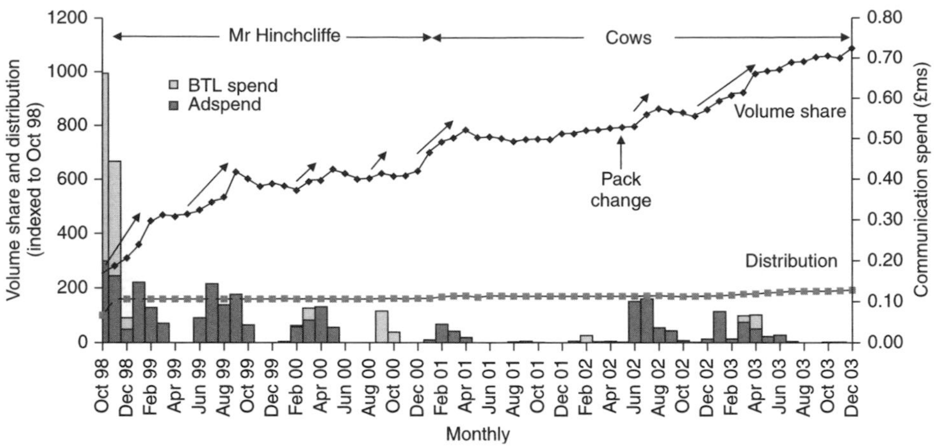

Figure 27: *Sales gains correspond to spend even when distribution is stable – roll-out region 1*
Source: ACNielsen, BD-Ntwk, DDS, BARB

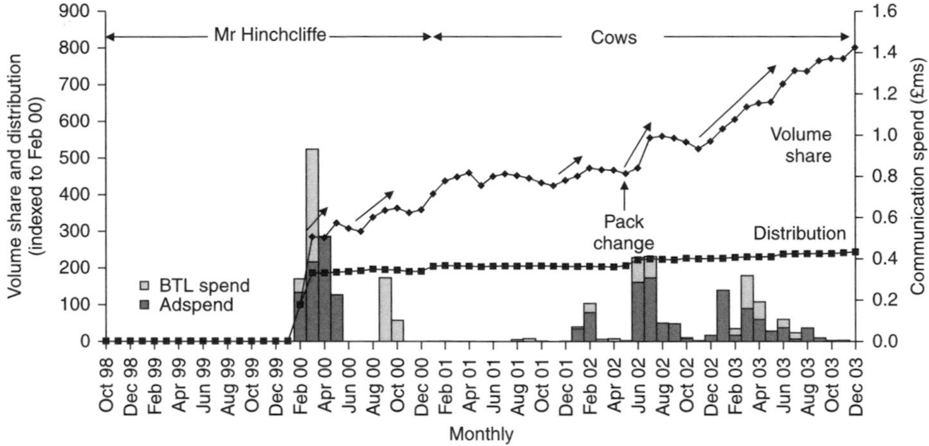

Figure 28: *Sales gains correspond to spend even when distribution is stable – roll-out region 2*
Source: ACNielsen, BD-Ntwk, DDS, BARB

The same pattern can be seen in the three other roll-out regions, where every phase of growth corresponded to communication activity (Figures 28–30).

Regional variations in communication spend and regional share uplifts match

We have further evidence that communication was responsible for growth when we look at the correlation between growth rate and communication spend (using a time period where distribution was stable). There is a strong positive relationship (Figure 31). Regions with high communication spend gained the most share.

To recap, we've shown that the timing of communication spend matches the timing of sales gains. Similarly we've shown that the regionality of spend matches regional gains. Could there be other variables that might have had some effect on sales? A review of these allows us to discount them, conclusively proving that communication was the key driver of Cravendale sales.

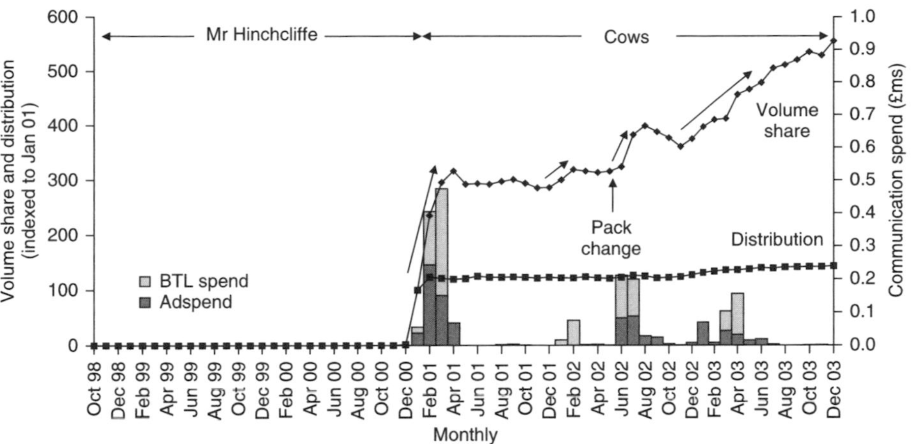

Figure 29: *Sales gains correspond to spend even when distribution is stable – roll-out region 3*
Source: ACNielsen, BD-Ntwk, DDS, BARB

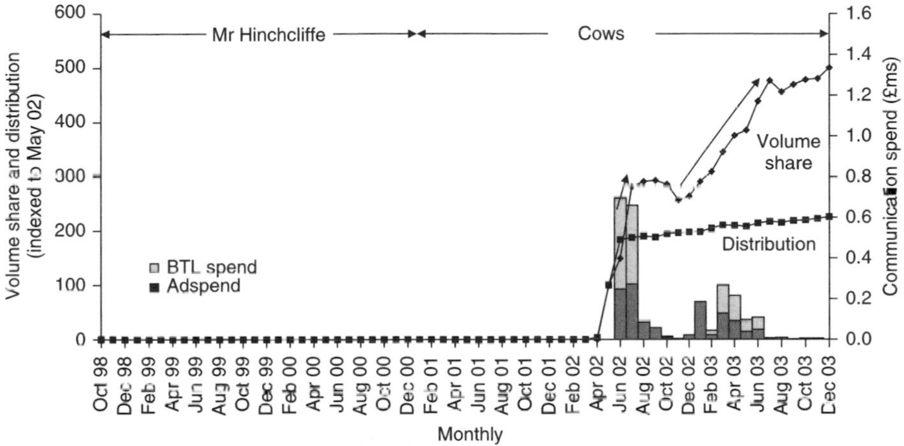

Figure 30: *Sales gains correspond to spend even when distribution is stable – roll-out region 4*
Source: ACNielsen, BD-Ntwk, DDS, BARB

Elimination of other possible factors that could influence sales

- It wasn't market growth: the milk market was static throughout the national roll-out. Moreover, we've already shown that Cravendale's market share increased (Figure 32).
- Distribution was an important driver of growth. But it couldn't all be distribution because ROS increased with each phase. We've also proved that the campaign increased sales even where distribution was stable.
- It wasn't changes in the product mix. Within stores that stocked Cravendale, the only significant changes were due to products being *withdrawn*. (The 1-litre size was largely withdrawn from supermarkets by the time of the Cows campaign.) This pack change was national, so can't explain the regional variation.

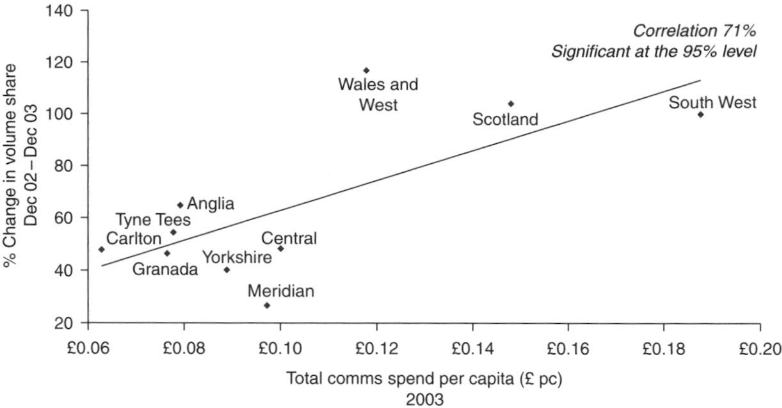

Figure 31: *Regional share gains match regionality of spend*
Source: ACNielsen, BD-Ntwk, DDS, BRB

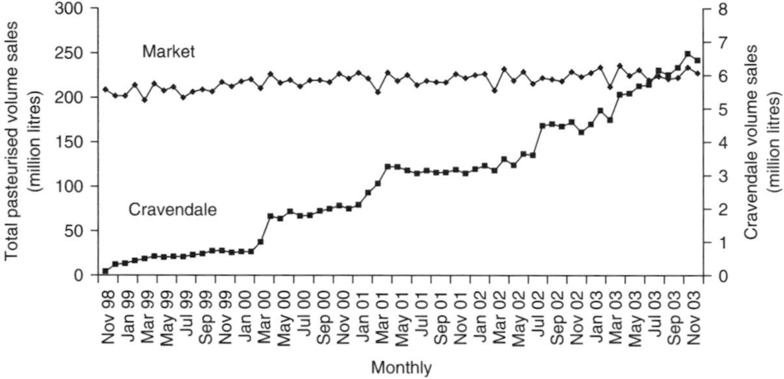

Figure 32: *Milk market was static while Cravendale grew*
Source: ACNielsen

- It wasn't due to price (which, again, was set nationally). Cravendale's price went up, both in absolute terms and relative to market. This is a significant achievement: in 1998 getting people to pay extra for milk – a humdrum staple they were perfectly happy with – seemed a huge task (Table 8).

TABLE 8: CRAVENDALE'S PRICE GREW

	Mr Hinchcliffe w/e 20 Nov 99	Cows w/e 13 July 02
Real price (at Jan 04 prices)	£0.51	£0.56
Relative price (market = 100)	120.8	124.4

Source: ACNielsen

- It wasn't due to in-store promotions, as the programme of price promotion was consistent over time (20p off, regularly rotated between retailers). Besides, it was national, so it can't explain the regional variations we have shown.

Final proof that it was the campaign that was responsible for growth comes from the econometrics.

Econometrics quantifies the contribution of communication

Econometrics proves that communication activity was highly effective. The model tells us that without the Cows communication, Cravendale's volume share would have been only about half what it actually was by December 2003 (Figure 33). The Cows campaign generated significant share gains.

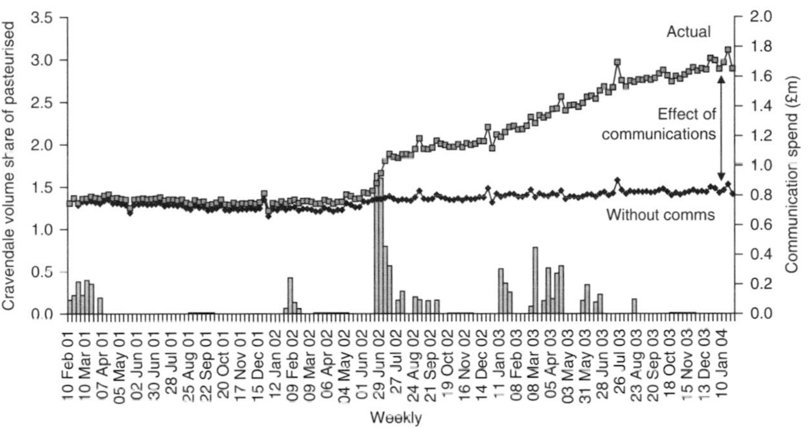

Figure 33: *The effect of Cows communication activity on volume share*
Source: BD-Ntwk, DDS, BARB, econometric model

DETERMINING THE CONTRIBUTION OF EACH COMMUNICATION CHANNEL

We've shown that the campaign as a whole worked, but what about the contribution of the different elements? We have a fascinating story to tell.

Advertising

There are a dozen examples of times and places where adverts ran without BTL, which allows us to look at the effect of adverts in isolation of BTL activity. Every single time, ROS increased significantly when TV aired (Figure 34). We can also demonstrate that regions that had heavier weights of TV also experienced higher ROS – there is a remarkably strong relationship here (Figure 35).

BTL

When BTL was the only communication activity running we can see that it too had the ability to increase ROS, although the effect was much smaller than that of TV support (Figure 36).

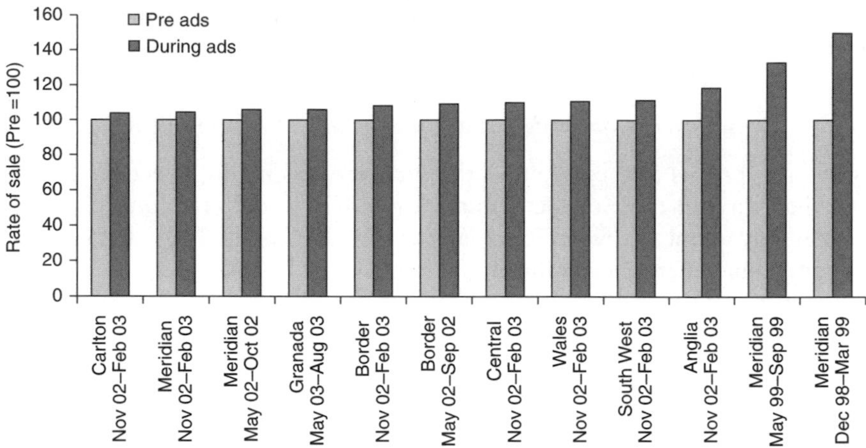

Figure 34: *ROS increases when TV is the only communication support*
Source: ACNielsen

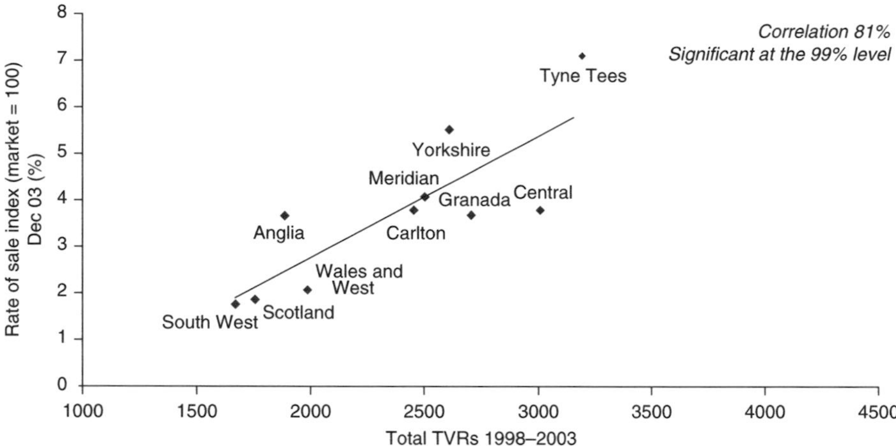

Figure 35: *Regions with higher TVRs had higher POS*
Source: ACNielsen, BARB

Interaction between advertising and BTL

The previous examples show that advertising and BTL are both able to increase sales. The *reason* for having both has already been made clear by our channel strategy – but what is the *value* of having both? Here we have exciting new learning to share.

Regional test activity was carried out in selected Asda stores in 2002, in a variety of regions. During the test, different combinations of communication activity ran (e.g. TV plus POS, no communication at all, door-drop only, etc.). The sales gained during the eight weeks of activity allow us to compare the effect of different channels.

When advertising and door-drops ran independently, they generated a similar sales response – around 10% each. Based on this, we would expect that if

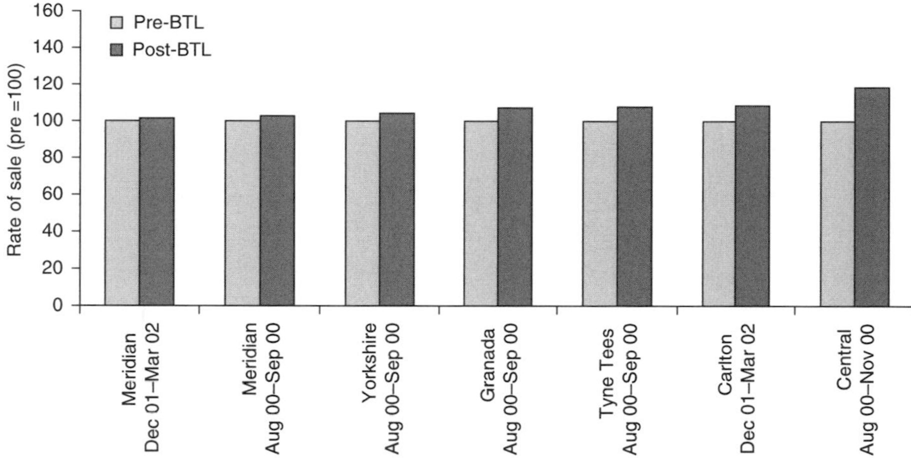

Figure 36: *ROS grows when BTL is the only communication support*
Source: ACNielsen

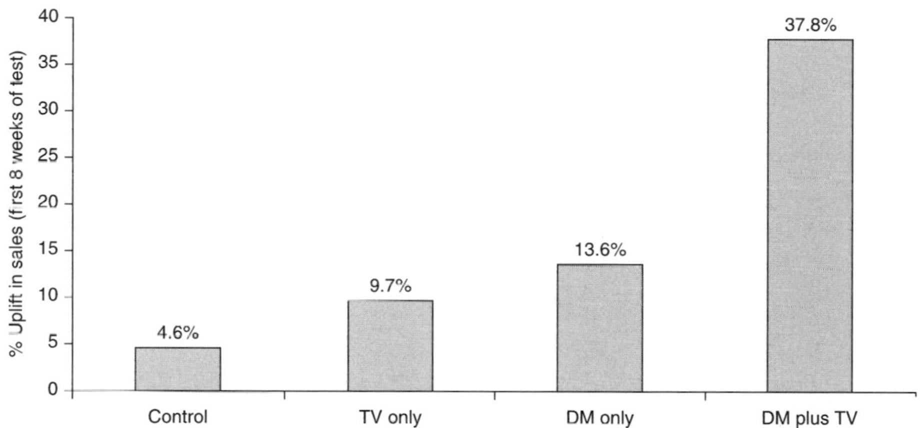

Figure 37: *TV and BTL enhance each other to create a bigger effect than individually*
Source: BD-Ntwk, Asda Retail Link, Jan–Mar 2002

advertising and BTL were running together, we could add the sales response together to get a sales gain of about 20%. However, this was not the case: in fact, a much greater uplift was seen – an extra 14.5% was gained. This proves that advertising and BTL enhance each other (Figure 37).

The same test activity also allows us to quantify the effect of in-store activity such as POS taste testing. On its own, in-store activity has only a tiny effect – little more than no communication at all. On the other hand, TV is about twice as effective at generating sales. But when in-store activity happens at the same time as advertising, the effect is, once again, greater than the two added together. This suggests that TV advertising enhances the effect of in-store activity and vice versa (Figure 38).

Another way of looking at the effect of interaction is by analysing postcode-level data, which allows us to see what happens to sales when households receive only

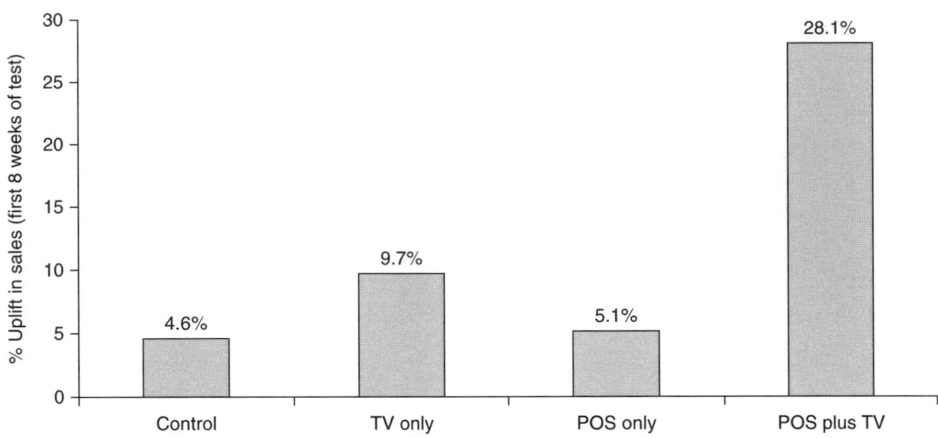

Figure 38: *TV and POS enhance each other to create a bigger effect than individually*
Source: BD-Ntwk, Asda Retail Link, Jan–Mar 2002

TV advertising vs households that received TV and BTL. We can see that in the short term, the overall effect of advertising and BTL is about five times more than just that of TV. Once again, this suggests that the channels enhance each other (Table 9).

TABLE 9: TV AND BTL ENHANCE EACH OTHER TO CREATE HIGHER LEVELS OF TRIAL

Activity received by households, Feb–Jun 2003:	ATL only (TV advertising)	ATL + BTL (TV and door-drop)
Households buying Cravendale	3%	16%

Source: Dunhumby Tesco Clubcard transaction data, NCH coupon redemption data

The effects can also be seen in the medium term, when we look at how many people continued to buy Cravendale after first trying it. Six weeks after the activity occurred, the combined effect of TV and BTL was three times greater than TV alone, which suggests that the ability of the channels to enhance each other works in the short and long term (Table 10).

TABLE 10: TV AND BTL ENHANCE EACH OTHER TO CREATE HIGHER LEVELS OF RETAINED CUSTOMERS

Activity received by households, Feb–Jun 2003:	ATL only (TV advertising)	ATL + BTL (TV and door-drop)
Households who went on to buy more Cravendale (3 x in 6 weeks)	1%	3%

Source: Dunhumby Tesco Clubcard transaction data, NCH coupon redemption data

Integrated communication makes intuitive sense: the aim being to amplify the effectiveness of a campaign, and so make the whole add up to more than the sum of its parts. These results prove that Cravendale has successfully put this theory into action, and reaped dividends as a result. We believe this is the first time the value of integrated communication has been quantified in this way.

Final proof of the effects of interaction of advertising and BTL comes from econometrics. The model shows that advertising is effective, but when advertising and BTL run together there is an even greater uplift in share. The econometrics supports the conclusions drawn from the previous examples: advertising and BTL enhance each other (Figure 39). BTL and advertising worker together to increase share.

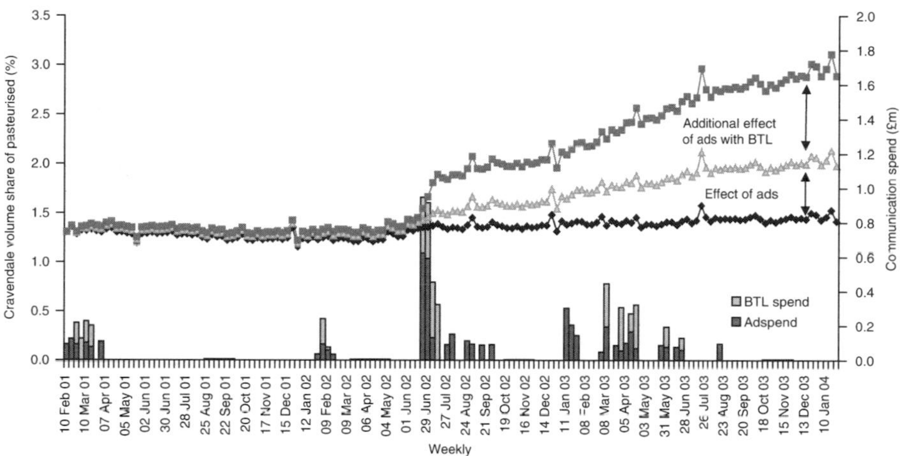

Figure 39: *Advertising and BTL work together to increase share*
Source: BD-Ntwk, DDS, BARB, econometric model

The pack change

In comparison to advertising and BTL activity, the effect of the pack change (which was made nationally), had a much smaller effect. Although there was a slight uplift, sales quickly settled at the new level, and didn't grow again until another burst of communication activity happened (Figure 40).

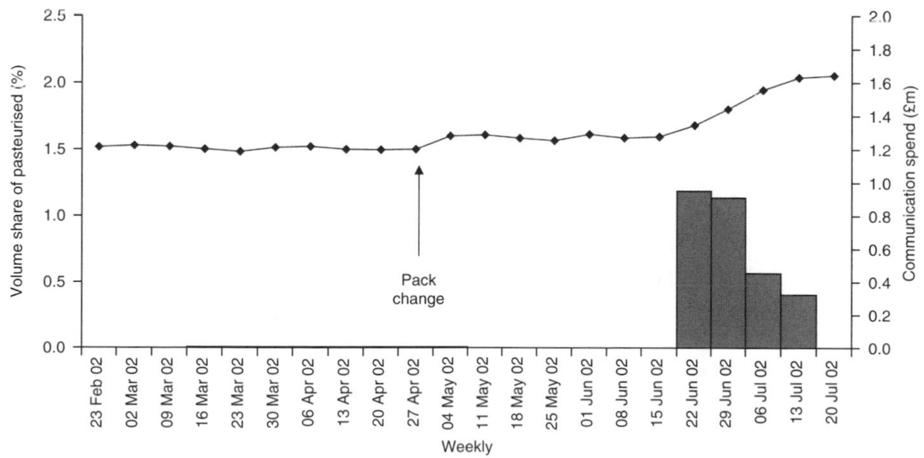

Figure 40: *Cravendale's pack change had little effect*
Source: ACNielsen, BD-Ntwk, DDS, BARB

PAYBACK

We have shown that communication activity was effective. We can also prove from econometrics that the activity paid for itself: every £1 spent on BTL activity delivered an additional £1.10 profit. Advertising's payback is even higher: every £1 spent on TV delivered £1.30 extra profit (Figure 41). Of course, these are short-term payback figures, and communication also has a longer-term effect – so there is even more profit to come.

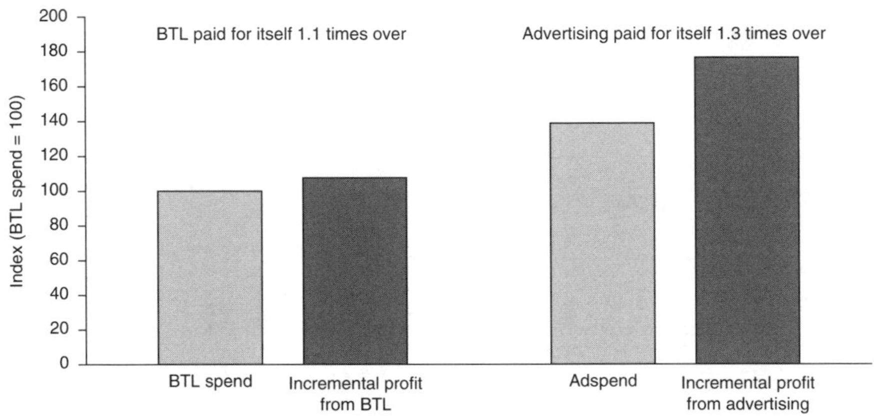

Figure 41: *The Cows campaign paid for itself*
Source: BD-Ntwk, DDS, BARB, econometric model

CONCLUSION

When Arla set out to shake up the milk market in 1998, everything was stacked against it. There was no British precedent for what it planned to do. The market was unbranded, it needed to command a big price premium in a commodity category and people had no need for, or interest in, a different kind of milk. Cravendale has successfully overcome all these hurdles. Indeed, Arla is now in the happy position of needing to invest again: £20m on a new factory to produce more Cravendale.

Cravendale's success boils down to three fundamental factors.

1. The value of a powerful idea: the 'Cows want it back' idea is an excellent example of a strong, focused idea that was able to work across channels in a highly efficient manner. The ultimate value of this idea is reflected in the incremental profit it generated.
2. The value of a robust channel strategy: creative consistency is vital, but the real value of integrated communications comes from clearly identifying how each channel can make a difference to people's attitudes and behaviour, and by playing each channel to its strengths.
3. The value of continuous evaluation: getting it right first time isn't always possible when you're in uncharted territory – and precedents from other markets do not always prove helpful. Sometimes it's necessary to learn along the way. Without this commitment to evaluation, Cravendale wouldn't be around today.

GOLD

JOHN BARTLE AWARD (BEST NEW AGENCY)

4

Honda

What happened when Honda started asking questions?

Principal author: Stuart Smith, Wieden & Kennedy

EDITOR'S SUMMARY

This entertainingly written case study describes how Honda's brave approach succeeded in increasing sales by 28% and delivering an incremental £84m in profit. The style of the paper is as original and brave as the campaign itself.

In a market littered with launches and product news, Honda decided to inspire people about their belief in 'The Power of Dreams'. This vision came directly from, and celebrated the values of, the company's creator Soichiro Honda.

The idea was channelled through a rich diversity of media, plus some new ones of their own. In addition to 120-second TV ads, posters, press and even an installation in Selfridges, Honda became the first advertiser to run a TV ad in the press by inserting DVDs there. The paper shows that the idea became more powerful when people were exposed to it both above and below the line.

The campaign changed the way people felt about Honda prompting more people to consider and actually purchase a Honda vehicle. Beyond incremental sales of more than 22,000 new cars, this paper looks at the positive impact the campaign has had on dealers, staff turnover, current owners and even used cars.

'Ever wondered what the most commonly used word in the world is? OK ... OK? Man's favourite word is one that means all right. Satisfactory ... Not bad ... So why invent the lightbulb when candles are OK? Why make lifts, if stairs are OK? Earth's OK, Why go to the moon? Clearly, not everybody believes OK is OK. We certainly don't. And we were wondering ... What would the world be like if its favourite word wasn't OK? What if we could change it? What if the word was ... What if?'

WHAT'S THIS PAPER ABOUT?

It's about belief in the power of dreams demonstrating belief in the commercial power of ideas.

What?

OK ... it's a study that shows how – and how much – Honda's communication has worked in the last two years. It answers a question about what happened to Honda when it started asking questions. It chronicles the journey of an integrated campaign; from conception through to record sales. Through bananas, cogs and leopard-skin traffic cones. Along the way, it states its case with a wealth of familiar measures, as well as introducing a few new ones. So where does the journey start?

WAS THERE A HAPPY ENDING?

You know those films where they start at the end of the story, then they go back and show the events leading up to that end point? Well, this study is going be a bit like that. Our equivalent of the dead body at the end is this fact:

'Communications generated £388m in revenue for Honda'

Which is a much happier ending than a dead body.

A new Honda campaign began in April 2002 (and is still going). Sales of new Honda cars since then have increased by 28% (Figure 1).

What would have happened to sales had the campaign not run? We can fit a trend to the sales pre-launch, project it forward, then compare that to what actually happened during the campaign (Figure 2).

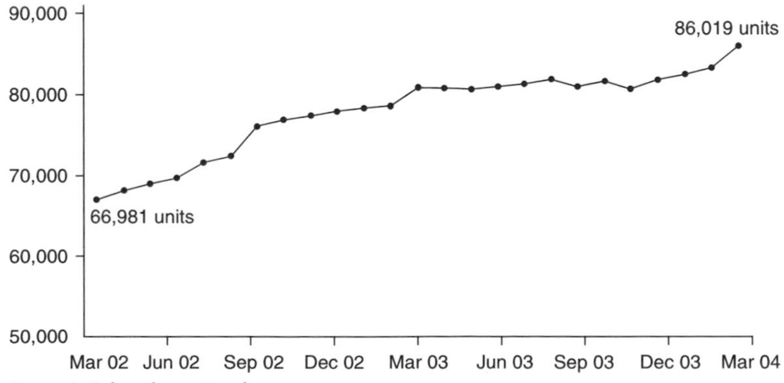

Figure 1: *Sales of new Hondas*
Source: Honda UK – 12-month rolling data

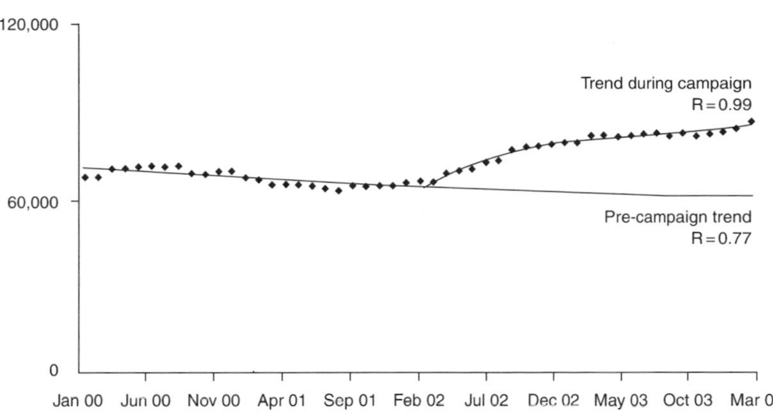

Figure 2: *Honda sales trends*
Source: Honda UK – 12-month rolling data

This uplift wasn't down to chucking more budget at the problem. Far from it. Media spend, share of voice and PR spend all went *down* (Figure 3).

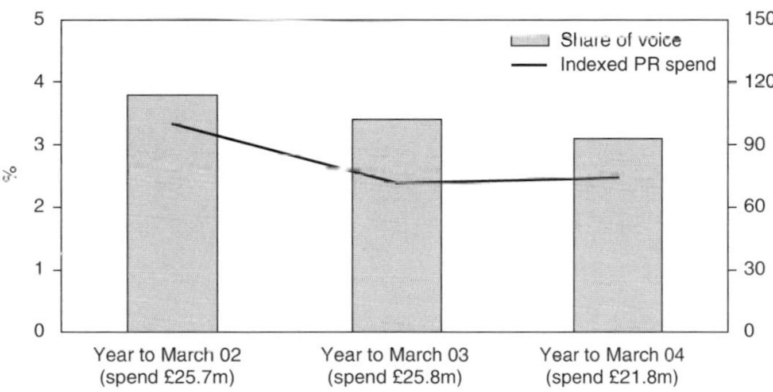

Figure 3: *Communication spends*
Sources: Starcom Mediavest, Honda UK

Nor was the sales increase a function of cheaper prices. On the contrary, prices went *up* across the range (Figure 4).

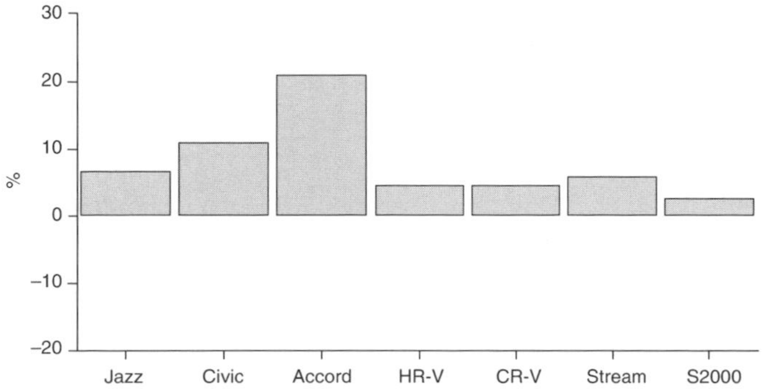

Figure 4: *Honda price inceases in the UK (index-linked change in on-the-road price, between April 2002 and April 2004*
Source: Honda UK

TABLE 1: HONDA DEALERSHIPS

Year before campaign	244
First year of campaign	217
Second year of campaign	226

Source: Honda UK

Improved distribution wasn't the reason either; throughout the campaign, the number of Honda dealerships was lower than before (Table 1).

Was the increase down to promotions? Not guilty. Less money went to dealerships to support finance deals, offers, and so on (Figure 5).

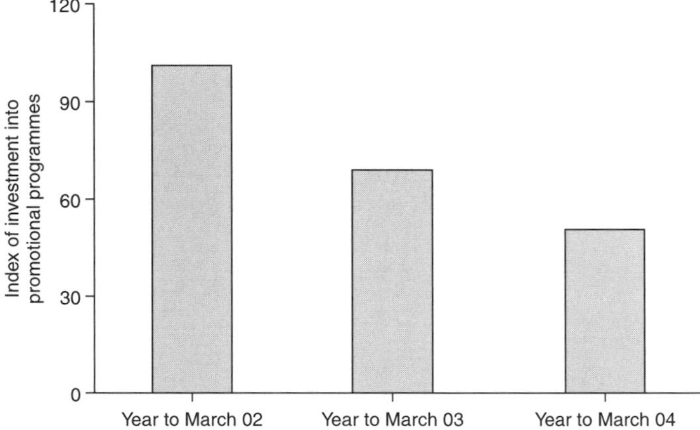

Figure 5: *Promotional activity*
Source: Honda UK

But wait – this still leaves one possible non-campaign reason behind the sales increase. Cars. As in new Honda models. We can't discount that factor, and we wouldn't want to. New models and upgrades had been successful, which was brilliant. To measure the contribution of *communications alone*, we can use either modelling or control region analysis. Or why not both? No harm in proving the same thing from two different directions.

Independent modelling work (non-linear regression, not full econometrics) found a strong link between advertising and sales (Figure 6).

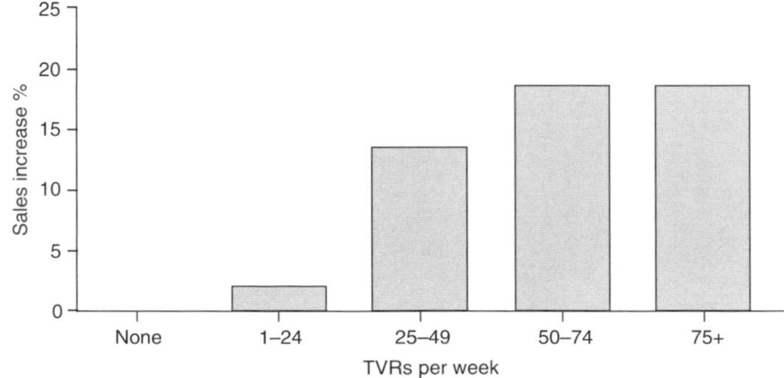

Figure 6: *Sales model*
Source: Simpson Carpenter modelling

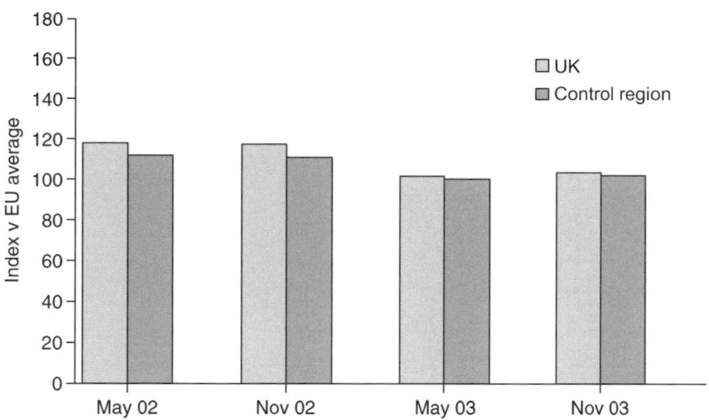

Figure 7: *Honda retail prices*
Source: European Commission

Building in decay rates, the modelling concluded that the sales contribution from communications was 13.6%. This works through to 22,708 extra units being down to the communications.

Now for a control region. We need somewhere where all the important variables were the same, except one – they didn't run the campaign.

For this, we can use other comparable European markets. Germany, France, Spain, Italy and the UK are by far the biggest car markets in Europe, as they are for Honda (totalling 79% of Honda's European sales). Germany, France, Spain and Italy combined provide a robust control group for the UK. All had the same model launches and upgrades. Combined, their distribution changes were similar to the UK, as was spontaneous Honda awareness (18%) at the time of launch.

Finally, there was negligible Honda price difference between the UK and the control region (Figure 7).

By looking at the pattern of control region share, we can calculate what we would expect UK share to be, had the campaign not run (Figure 8).

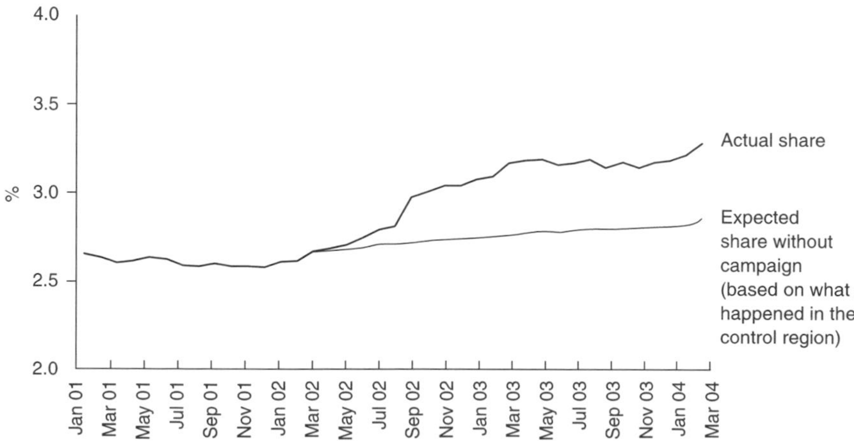

Figure 8: *Campaign contribution to sales*
Source: Honda UK – 12-month rolling data

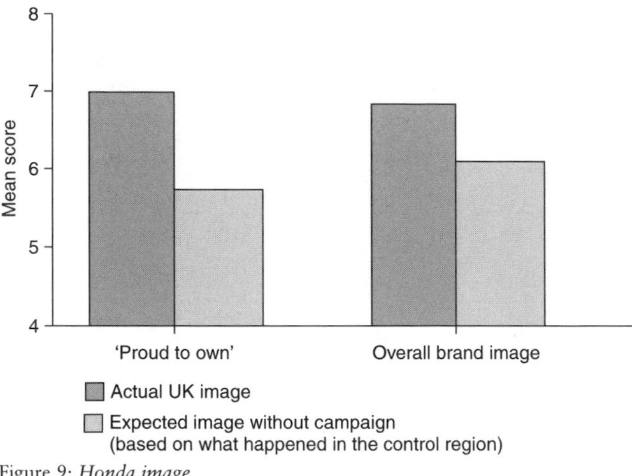

Figure 9: *Honda image*
Source: Simpson Carpenter

When you do the sums, this represents 23,570 extra units to Honda, down to the communications. Reassuringly, this is very close to the figure from modelling (22,708). Figuring out how many of each model that splits into, then multiplying each by average price-per-model, you get £352m in extra revenue. To this, we can add after-sales value. Of the 23,570 extra units, an estimated 11,785 would go through Honda for their parts and servicing, each yielding an average of £3048 to Honda over the car's lifetime. This increases the total revenue, from communications alone, to £388m. Not a bad return on a £47m budget (over the two years).

We can apply the same principles to tracking data for the UK vs the control region. This gives further evidence that the sales difference was down to communications shifting Honda's image (Figure 9).

So *revenue* far exceeded spend, but what about profit? Cost-per-unit data isn't available, but we can calculate an (extremely conservative) estimate of the campaign's profit contribution.

The difference between retail and trade price represents some of the unit profit to Honda – a conservative estimate of margin. As before, we can take the 23,570 extra units sold from communications, and work out how many of each model that splits into. Multiplying those figures by our conservative margins-per-model, tells us that the campaign generated £84m of extra profit for Honda. This underestimates the true figure, but serves to show that the campaign easily paid for itself.

So communications were a big part of Honda's success in the UK. As the UK is Honda's biggest market in Europe (42% of it), the UK achievements were a significant contributor to the financial success of Honda in Europe (Table 2).

TABLE 2: HONDA'S OPERATIONAL PERFORMANCE
(YEAR TO MARCH 2002–YEAR TO MARCH 2004)

	Year to March 2002	Year to March 2003	Year to March 2004
Operating revenue (€m)	4538	6200	7132
Operating income (€m)	–266	107	194

Source: Honda Motor Co. Ltd

All of this till-kerchinging shows that the campaign worked. We now want to explore *how* it worked. That's probably the more interesting bit, to be honest. Or at least the bit with some new stuff to think about.

So where does the story start?

WHAT'S THE BACKGROUND?

> 'My Mum's friend drives a Civic ... and raves about it. So much so that my Mum is thinking about buying one too. The other day she asked me if Civic did a Honda version.'
>
> Research quote, early 2002

This tells you something about that person's Mum (apologies to that person's Mum), but also points to something deeper about the issue for Honda. The quality of the cars was no problem – it was the brand's image and familiarity.

For many, Honda has always meant 'quality motorbikes', which gave the brand a bit of vroom cred. In fact, Honda is really an engine company. It builds engines then looks for things to put them in. Everything from generators to jets.

Honda has been selling cars in the UK for 29 years. Not many knew. Or cared. Even Honda owners felt compelled to justify their choice, with 'I drive a Honda because ...' instead of the proudly simpler 'I drive a Honda'. They were buying them for the perfectly rational reason that the cars are excellent. Trouble is, 'rational' is in the same neighbourhood as 'sensible', which is only a few doors away from 'dull'. Although Jeremy Clarkson might disagree, it's hard to buy a *bad* car these days, so emotional pull really matters. On that score, Hondas were a bit low-fat vanilla.

Also, Hondas were seen to be for drivers who didn't want to use their free bus passes. Nothing against the more mature generation, you understand, but a brand with big ambition needed to have bigger appeal.

And just how big *was* Honda's ambition?

WHAT WERE THE OBJECTIVES?

The business goals were simple, but challenging. The plan was, and still is, to grow annual sales to 100,000 units by the end of 2005. Simple to understand, maybe, but not so simple to achieve; in March 2002 the figure stood at less than 67,000.

From a marketing objectives perspective, this meant growing Honda awareness and consideration enough to increase showroom visits, and ultimately conversion to dotted-line signing.

To make the brand a business asset, communications were needed to make people feel better about owning a Honda. This demanded making them radically revalue the brand. It called for long-term commitment.

The task was tough.

- Car customers are decreasingly loyal and increasingly discerning. This is escalating the cost of retaining owners and acquiring new ones.
- Car communications have to bellow through ever-growing noise, to be heard by audiences whose willingness to listen is ever-waning. Consequently, the quality

of car communications has progressed greatly in recent years. In the old days it used to be rubbish. It's not now.

- All the objectives had to be achieved with a planned reduction each year in communications spend.

Blimey. What could Honda do to get itself spotted across the crowded room?

WHAT WAS THE STRATEGY?

'The Power of Dreams'. Sounds like a cheesy self-help book. Or worse; a global corporation's empty slogan. In fact, this *was* a global corporation's slogan – for Honda. Yeucchh. Come on – let's put our fingers in our ears. If we ignored it for long enough, it might go away.

Guess what? It was never going to go away. And guess what else? That turned out to be a brilliant thing.

In rummaging around for insights down at Honda, a crucial breakthrough was made. At first you couldn't see it for looking. The breakthrough came with the realisation that something internal could be used as the external solution. The Power of Dreams was true to the spirit of how the corporation thought and acted. And how?

The values of the company's creator were still coursing through the veins of its culture. Soichiro Honda was relentlessly passionate about engines, optimistically imaginative, socially responsible and just a little bit bonkers (see Figure 10). In a nice way.

Figure 10: *Soichiro Honda*

He bequeathed such attributes to the company in a legacy that still walks the Honda corridors today. Honda had never before thought to fashion this into a weapon for brand communications. And so the marketing strategy was born: to expose the inner truth about Honda.

No need to invent or exaggerate – just build familiarity with previously unknown aspects of the brand. It was about having the bravery to believe that telling people the truth about 'Hondaness' would do the job; the job being, to make them feel better about owning one. In other words, to make them want a Honda. Actually, not in other words – those are the *exact* words.

That's all fine and dandy, but *how* would this Hondaness be expressed?

WHAT WAS THE IDEA?

Sounds simple. Just tell people the truth about Honda. Only, it wasn't. It was very unsimple. Honda's culture is one of rich diversity and nuance. It would be doing it a disservice to boil it down to a couple of adjectives in the centre of a brand onion. The multidimensionality of Honda is what makes it what it is. It would have been wrong to ignore some of those shades, just for the sake of marketing simplicity. Honda needed to adopt an unconventional approach. To build a brand with scale and emotional depth required embracing and then communicating the whole king-sized onion.

A new tool was needed to paint a full portrait of Honda. Traditional tools would only allow for the capture of some of the parts, rather than the sum of the parts. This tool was 'The Book of Dreams'.

The Book of Dreams merged creative strategy with execution. The integration of 'what we say' and 'how we say it', early in the process, was fundamental to its value. It was fashioned around Honda reality, and defined a unique voice for the brand. It illuminated Honda's philosophy and way of behaving, whilst creating a distinctive look, feel and even vocabulary. Handy. Here's a flavour (Figures 11a and 11b).

Much of the uniqueness of this voice came from its absence of complacency or boastfulness. Instead, it was crafted as a voice that asks plain-speaking questions,

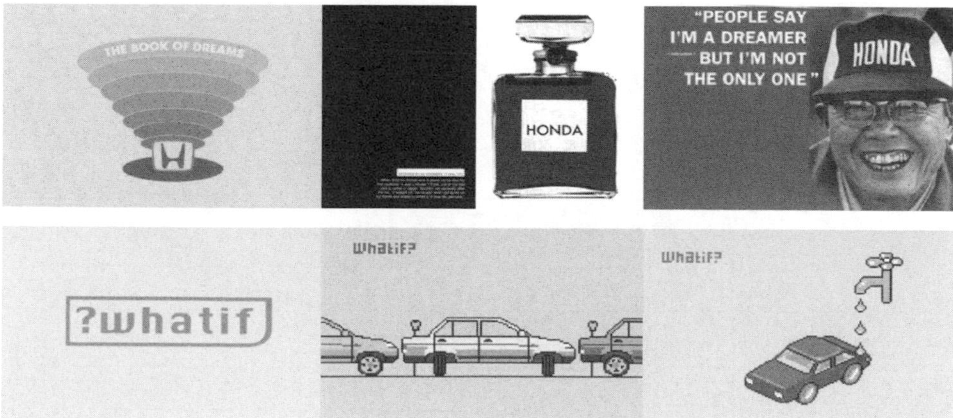

Figure 11(a)

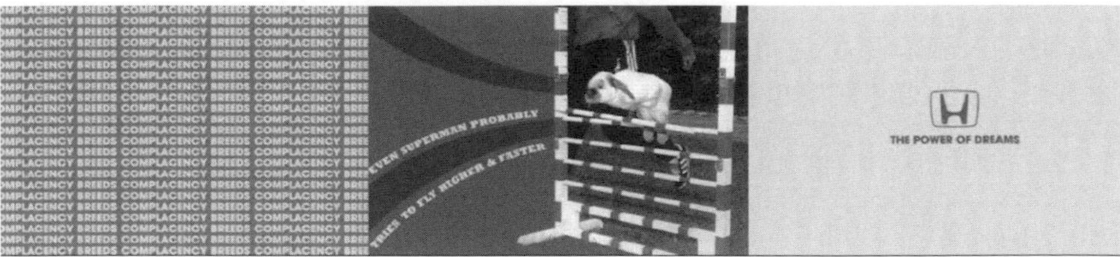

Figure 11(b)

with imagination and optimism. Crucially, it was much much more than just a tone-of-voice to shove at the end of communications briefs. The book *was the brief itself*, and getting the voice of the book out there *was the idea*.

So what did the 'out there' look like?

WHAT WAS THE CAMPAIGN?

Smaller budget, more competitive noise than ever, yada yada yada. A familiar complaint, but true in this case, so everything had to collaborate to maximise the idea's power. Appreciating the importance of this, 'The Dream Factory' was created. Nothing to do with Willy Wonka, but instead a collective of Honda representatives and its agencies (they had chocolate biscuits though). This ensemble worked together to ensure every piece of marketing collateral conveyed the same voice of Hondaness.

The diversity of Honda demanded a diversity of creative approaches. There were a number of integrated mini-campaigns, each of which was glued together with the same inquisitive voice.

The work went right through the line; TV, direct mail, radio, posters, press, interactive television, cinema, magazines, motorshows, press launches, dealerships, postcards and beermats. Oh, and traffic cones. Here's a selection, starting with some of the print work (Figures 12–22).

Figure 12

Figure 13

Figure 14

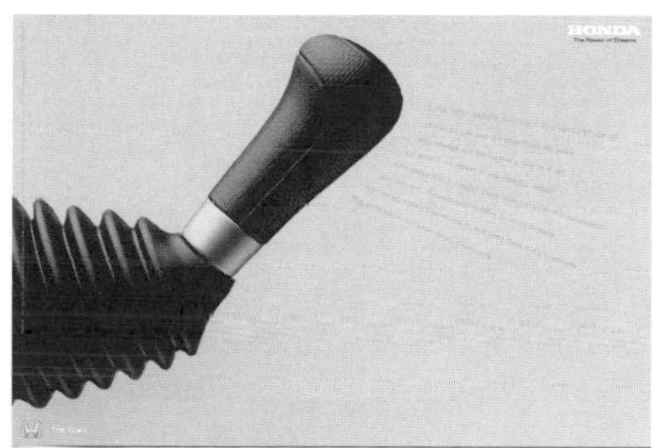

Figure 15

Figure 16

Figure 17

Figure 18

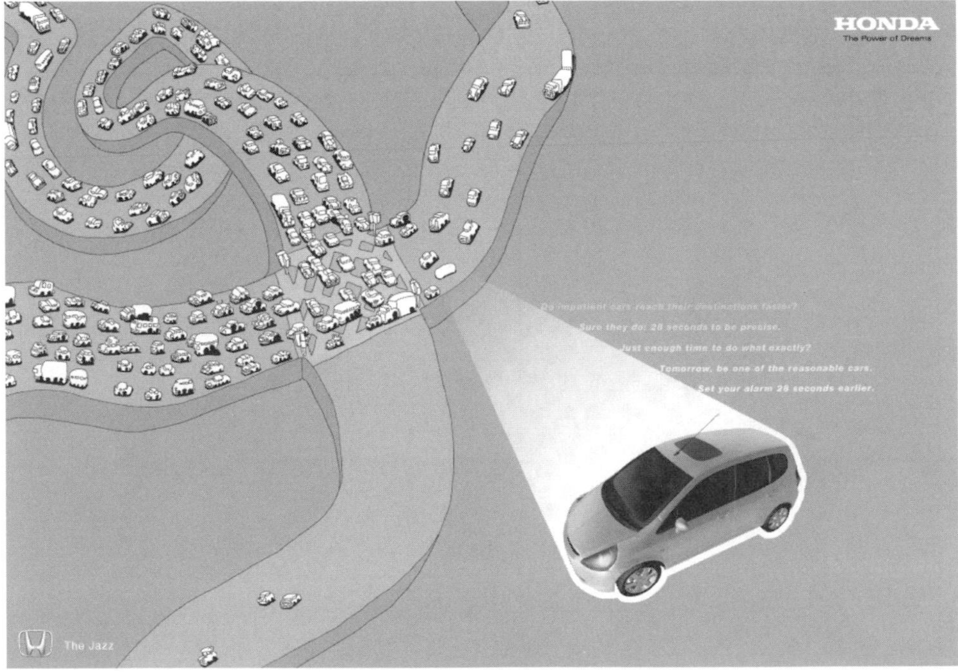

Figure 19

Figure 20

Figure 21

Figure 22

Above-the-line communications were augmented with online campaigns and microsites. For Honda IMA, as just one example, people got to appreciate the technology by having a little play with it. Virtually (Figure 23). By direct mail (Figure 24). Through dealership materials (Figure 25). Or at motorshows (Figure 26).

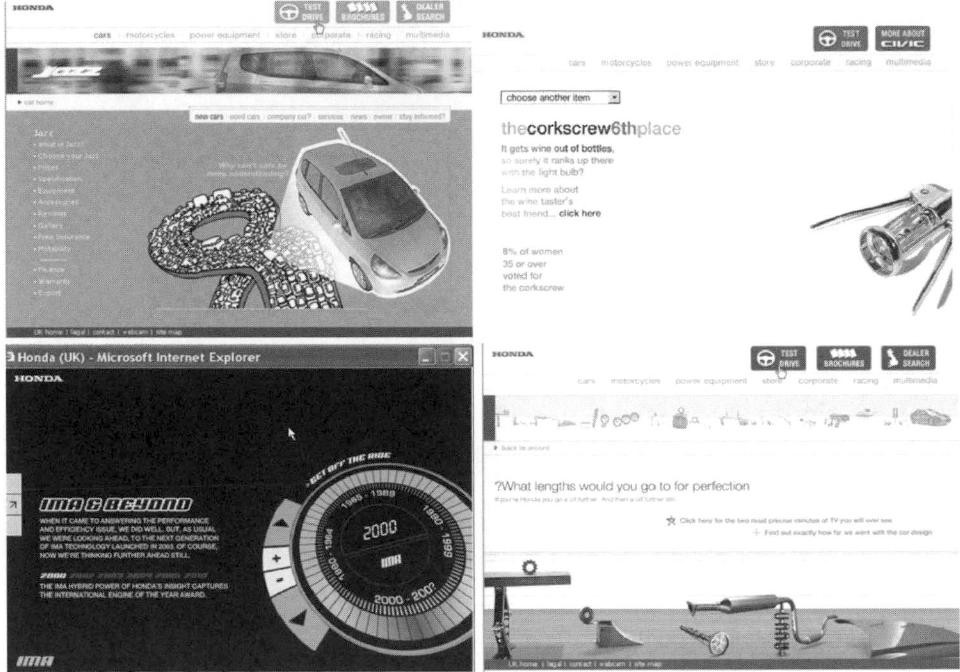

Figure 23: *Virtual experience*

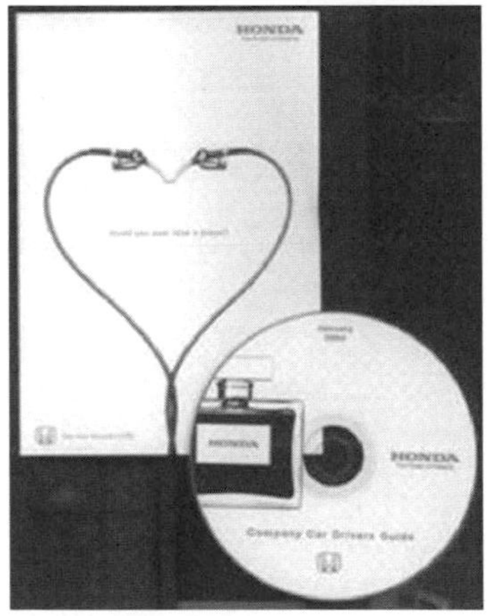

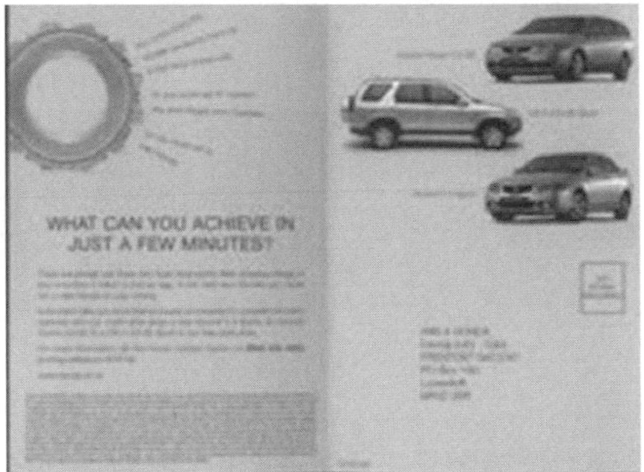

Figure 24: *Direct mail*

Waiting in receptions often means reading the only bit of the newspaper that hasn't been nicked. Not down at Honda HQ. Reception was given a makeover into a new 'World of Honda'. Displays showcased 'power of dreams' stories and screens showed films about the campaign (Figure 27).

Innovative media-neutral planning was required. One example of this was the strategic thinking behind 'Cog'. It was not a TV advert, in the conventional sense,

GOLD

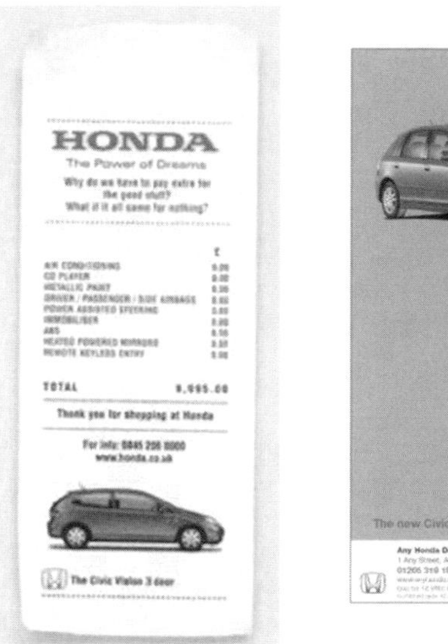

Figure 25: *Dealership materials*

Figure 26: *Motorshow*

Figure 27: *Reception area*

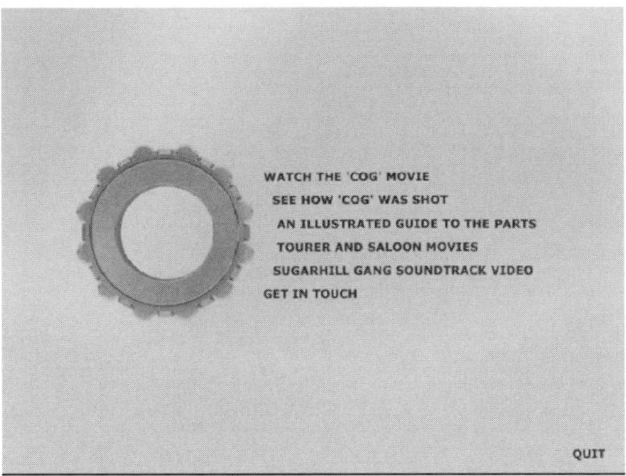

Figure 28: *'Cog'*

but instead was planned and created as a piece of film to be used in a new integrated way.

In its entirety, it ran only a handful of times on TV. The hope was that this would generate enough cultural interest to create *demand* for it through other channels in the mix. Not just the film, but even the *making* of the film. It was hoped that people would come to honda.co.uk to download it, learn about it, and pass it on virally to their friends.

Part of the media solution was to make Honda the first advertiser to run its TV campaign in the press. Sort of. A DVD was created containing the advert, plus a whole bunch of other stuff (Figure 28).

Nothing had ever been done like it on that scale – 1.3 million DVDs were distributed with magazines and papers.

The integration even included live events. In Selfridges, a Cog-themed domino-toppling-athon was held for a week – precision, reliability, chain reactions and all that. A bit barking, but loads of people went to see it (Figure 29).

Anyway, enough of the fluffy stuff and pretty pictures. Did any of it actually do anything for Honda?

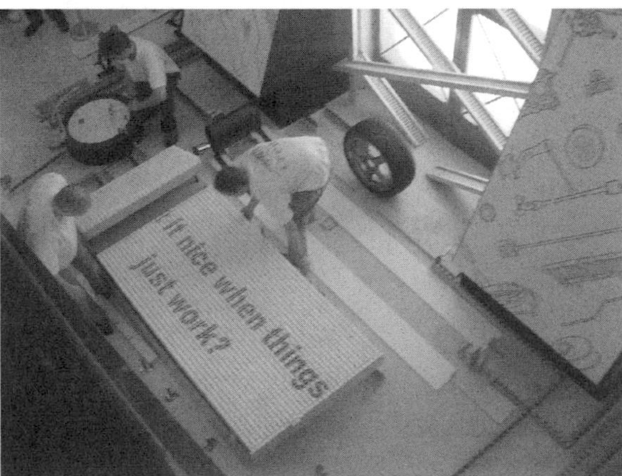

Figure 29

DID PEOPLE NOTICE IT?

Yes. Unprompted recall of Honda communications averaged 35% in 2003 (reaching 48% during the IMA campaign). Pound for pound, it was pretty efficient (Figure 30). Tremendous media momentum was generated (Figure 31). National print coverage alone represented £1.74 million-worth of free media value (Figure 32). CNN ran two features on the campaign (totalling 13 minutes) and Discovery ran a documentary on it. It featured in Channel 4's *100 Greatest TV Moments 2003* and Channel 5's *The Ads that Changed the World*. That's a healthy old slug of unpaid-for exposure.

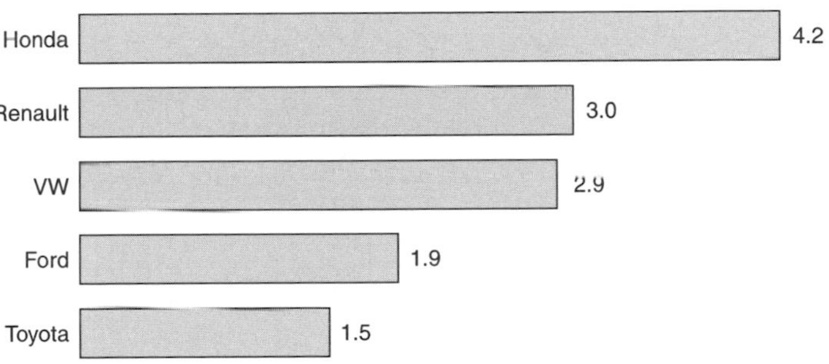

Figure 30: *Advertising efficiency (average ad recall/average TVR intensity)*
Base: all adults
Source: Simpson Carpenter Ad Tracker

Figure 31

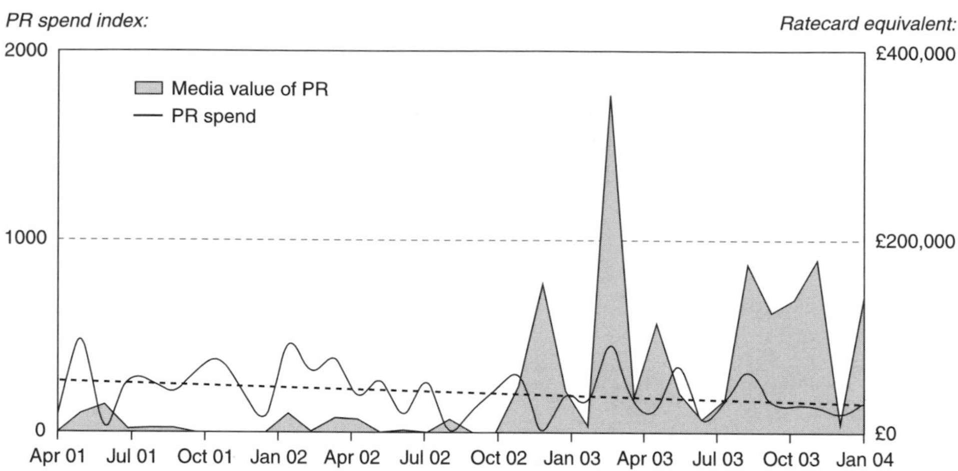

Figure 32: *PR about the communications*
Source: Millward Brown Precis

Encouragingly, Honda advertising was getting noticed by younger audiences (Table 3).

TABLE 3: MOST-TALKED-ABOUT ADVERTS OF THE YEAR

Rank	Company	%
1	Honda	24
2	X-Cite	20
3	John Smiths	15

Base: 18–30-year-olds
Source: Research International

Potential new buyers were the broad target, which varied from project to project (Jazz was younger, Accord was upmarket, etc.). Across it all, from a media-buying point of view, the TV advertising certainly delivered against the intended audiences (Table 4).

TABLE 4: INDEX OF ACHIEVED MEDIA VS PLANNED MEDIA

TVRs	99
1+ cover	100
2+ cover	103

Base: DDS BARB

That's just TV. As we'll soon see, this was just one of the places doing the job.

So far so good. The activity did the 'Hey ... look at me' thing very well. But did people care about the 'me' that they were looking at?

DID THEY ENGAGE WITH IT?

In fact, they went out of their way to engage with it: 500,000 DVDs went to people who contacted Honda requesting one; tens of thousands pressed to find out more on interactive TV adverts; Cog was downloaded 2.3 million times from honda.co.uk (that's a media equivalent value of £1.2m, though this was much higher-quality 'airtime' than normal, as people had come to Honda's world to view it).

The Civic 'Everyday' campaign integrated an online element, in which people were invited to vote for the best everyday object; 94,070 took part. The light bulb won, by the way, narrowly beating the toilet.

People found the adverts cool, which was cool (Table 5).

TABLE 5: 'COOLEST ADVERTS OF THE YEAR'

Rank	Company	%
1	Honda	78
2	John Smiths	57
3	Nike	54

Base: 18–30-year-olds
Source: Research International

But a much more interesting demonstration of their power to engage comes in looking at a *new* measurement approach. Or at the least the first thoughts on an approach that, with time and sophistication, could become an established weapon in the armoury of advertising effectiveness evaluators. And it's *free*. Well, at least for now. That weapon is Google.

Where the *intent* is to create noise about the communication, search engines could become barometers of cultural interest. For starters, just typing in 'new Honda ad' (and date-fixing the search to the year since Cog launched), returns a million website matches (Table 6).

TABLE 6: GOOGLE MATCHES

Honda ad	1,850,000
New Honda ad	1,000,000
New Accord ad	725,000

Source: Google, year from March 2003

OK, fair cop, at the moment this method has flaws. For instance, not all matches necessarily reference *exactly* what you're searching for (though in this case almost all seemed to be), but that's just a question of developing more accurate search software. With more time and more cases, benchmarks could be established.

What about search engines measuring the *international* appeal of communications? You could look at Google hits by country. Or, if it only appeared in one market (as in Honda's case), you could measure how far communications have *spread* beyond their official borders, giving a gauge of viral effectiveness.

What we've called the 'global spread factor' (which sounds a bit scary) looks at the ratio of worldwide matches to UK matches. The bigger the number, the further the spread in relation to its UK popularity (Figure 33).

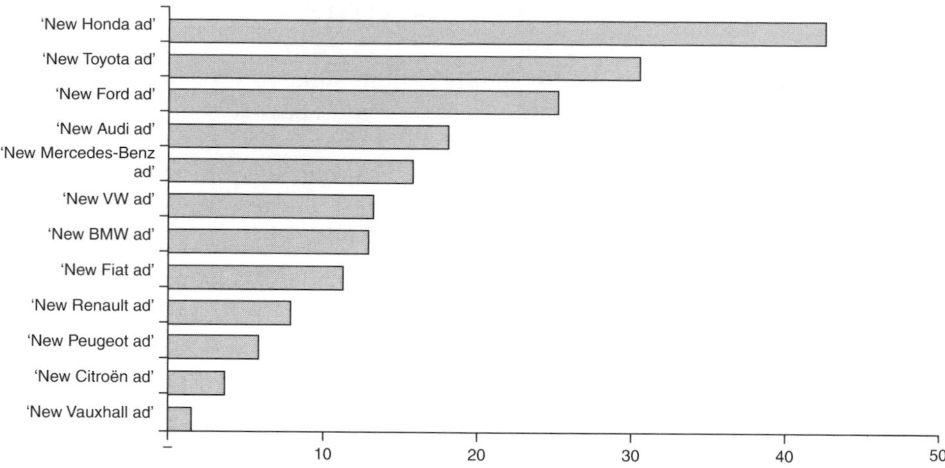

Figure 33: *'Global spread' factor*
Source: Google, world matches/UK matches, year from March 2003

There's another use of search engines to measure cultural interest you've generated. Since the whole Honda campaign began, 3110 Google newsgroups have discussed the 'new Honda ad'. That's impressive enough, but it's even more interesting to look at the composition of a random sample of those newsgroups (see Table 7).

TABLE 7: RANDOM SAMPLE OF NEWSGROUPS DISCUSSING THE 'NEW HONDA AD'

alt.pro-wrestling.wwf	talk-religion.buddhism
rec.music.artists.springsteen	ba.mountain-folk
rec.models.rc.air	uk.local.cumbria
rec.sport.soccer	rec.arts.sf.fandom
rec.crafts.textiles.needlework	alt.sports.basketball.nba
rec.arts.mystery	rec.games.chess.analysis
rec.crafts.metalworking	rec.music.classical.guitar
soc.culture.china	rec.arts.movies.production
alt.fan.british-accent	alt.conspiracy.jfk
alt.gossip.celebrities	misc.writing
alt.music.dave-matthews	sci.physics
alt.movies.cinematography	soc.subculture.bondage-bdsm

Source: Google Groups

This is a clear (if vaguely weird) demonstration of the variety of cultures that Honda communications touched. We'll leave the reader to discover the campaign's relevance to bondage subculture.

People certainly engaged with the communications. Someone even sent Honda their CV – written on a banana. The campaign created a dialogue between Honda and its audience, but what was Honda saying about itself in that dialogue?

DID IT SAY THE RIGHT THINGS TO THEM?

Well, they remembered that it was for Honda, which was a start. It also increased familiarity, which was vital, given the strategy of exposing them to the truth about Honda (Table 8). The campaign increased familiarity with key dimensions of 'Hondaness' (Figure 34), which led to improved perceptions of brand and models (Figure 35).

TABLE 8: HONDA BRAND TRACKING
Change: average since campaign start vs pre-campaign average (%)

Spontaneous brand awareness	+29%
'Know very well'	+21%

Base: all adults
Source: Simpson Carpenter Ad Tracker

Figure 34: *Brand image from advertising*
Base: all adults
Source: Simpson Carpenter Ad Tracker

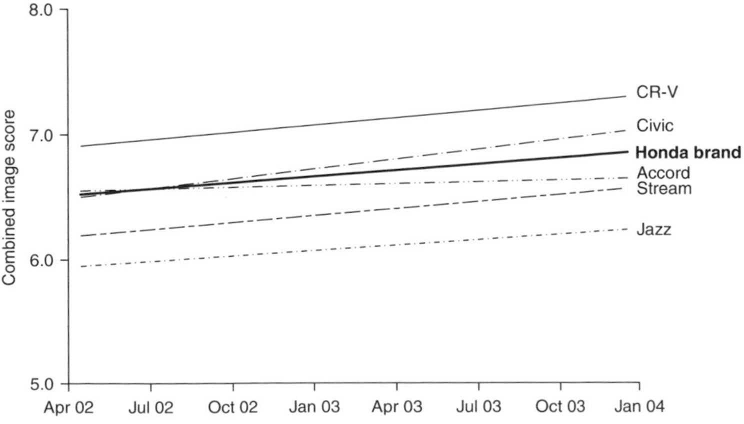

Figure 35: *Honda image trends*
Base: all adults
Source: Simpson Carpenter Brand Monitor

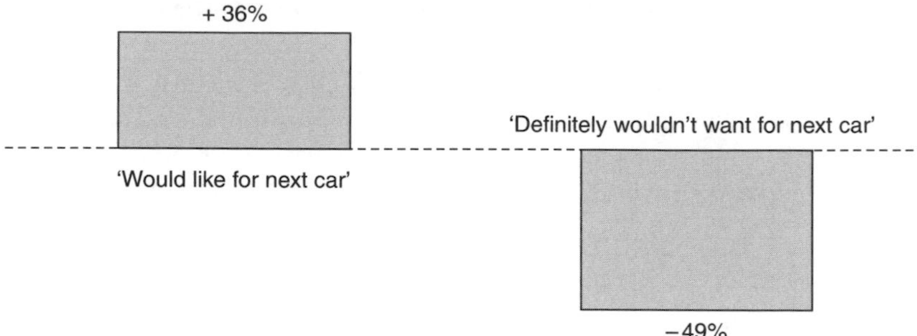

Figure 36: *Honda brand tracking; change: average since campaign start vs pre-campaign average (%)*
Base: all adults
Source: Simpson Carpenter Ad Tracker

People knew more about Honda, knew the *right things* about Honda, which increased desire to own one (Figure 36). These pre- and post-campaign shifts compellingly evidenced that the *communications* should take a bow for improved brand desire. There was more proof that pushed it beyond doubt (Table 9).

TABLE 9: 'WOULD LIKE FOR NEXT CAR' (HONDA)

Unaware of the communications	19%
Aware of the communications	39%

Base: all adults
Source: Simpson Carpenter Ad Tracker

The modelling work showed that TV advertising played a key role (Figure 37).

But it was by no means just the stuff on the box that was doing the business. The integrated approach was working. A cumulative benefit was recorded, amongst people familiar with both above- and below-the-line activity (Table 10).

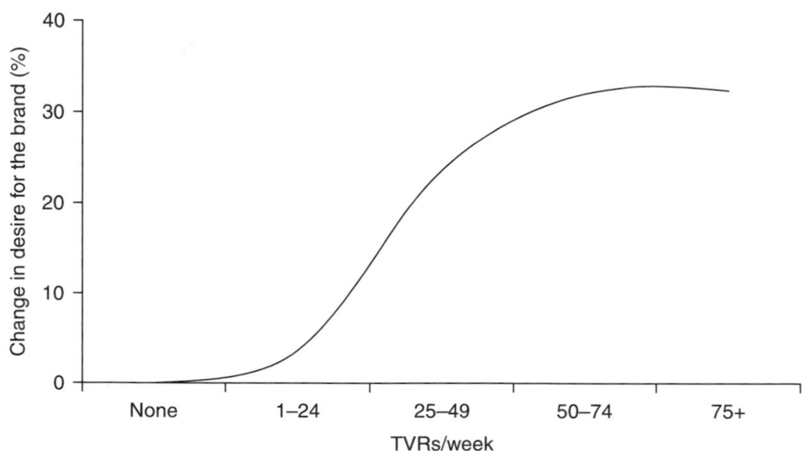

Figure 37: *Desire to own a Honda*
Source: Simpson Carpenter modelling

TABLE 10: 'WOULD LIKE FOR NEXT CAR' (HONDA)

Unaware of the communications	19%
Recall above the line only	38%
Recall above *and* below the line	43%

Base: all adults
Source: Simpson Carpenter Ad Tracker.

Direct mail, in particular, was successful. It must have been saying something right to its audience (Figure 38).

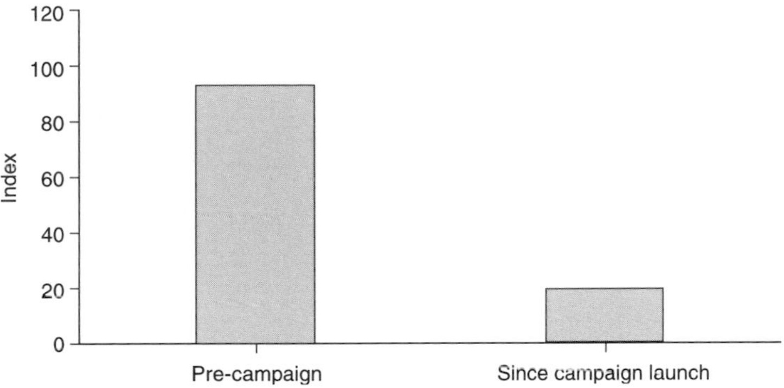

Figure 38: *Direct mail – average cost per sale*
Source: Hicklin Slade & Partners

PR was another important part of the whole communications mix. During the campaign, there was considerable improvement in PR results for Honda as a whole (beyond the communications PR). There was a very positive impact on 'very positive impact' scores (a calculation that factors in everything from circulation to page location) (Figure 39).

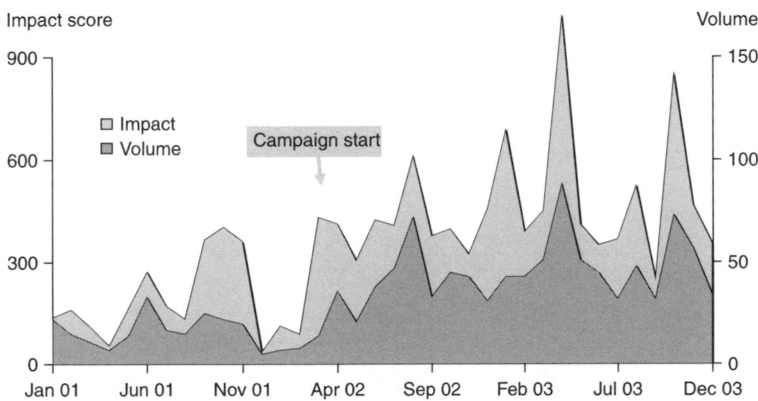

Figure 39: *'Very positive' Honda PR*
Source: Millward Brown Precis

So people were hearing more about Honda and hearing the right things. Honda was becoming 'less boring' (Figure 40).

Figure 40

They fancied Honda a bit more. But did they want to go out with it?

DID IT MAKE THEM DO ANYTHING?

Knowing more about Honda led to people wanting to know more about Honda. First port of call – the website (Figure 41). Honda was achieving thought leadership well beyond its share of voice. By December 2003, honda.co.uk was welcoming more visitors than most of the bigger boys (Figure 42).

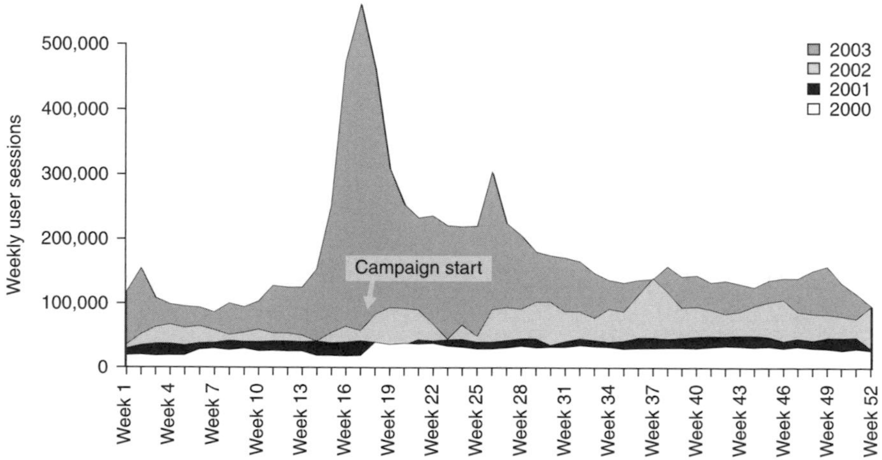

Figure 41: *Visits to honda.co.uk*
Source: Honda UK

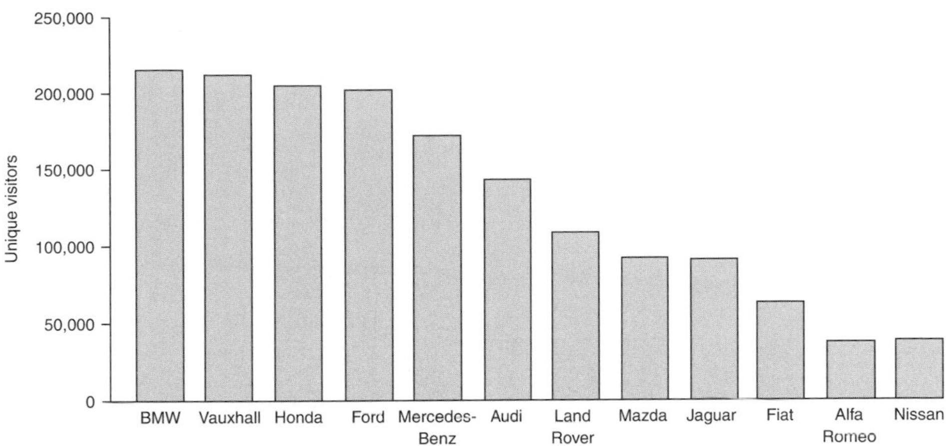

Figure 42: *Unique UK website visitors – December 2003*
Source: Honda UK

They weren't just going there for a laugh either; searches for Honda dealer information increased by 302% (Table 11).

TABLE 11: WEB SEARCHES FOR HONDA DEALERS (MONTHLY AVERAGE)

Pre-campaign	18,359
Since campaign launch	55,495

Source: Honda UK

Nor was it just the web. From interactive TV, 10,368 people requested a test drive, ordered a DVD or viewed the full commercial. Plus, Cog generated a trebling of calls to Honda – mainly for brochure requests (Figure 43).

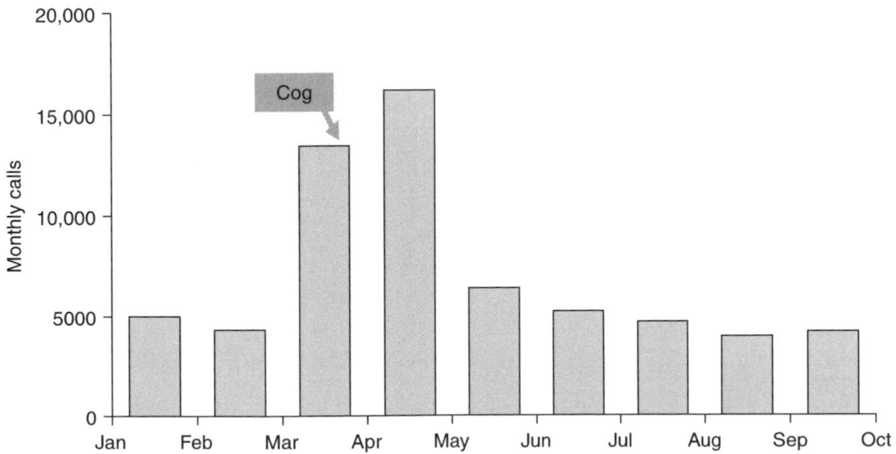

Figure 43: *Honda call centre*
Source: Honda Call Centre

Getting people to visit your website or call you is tough enough, but getting them to cart themselves to your showrooms is another thing. The campaign persuaded more people to do just that (Figure 44).

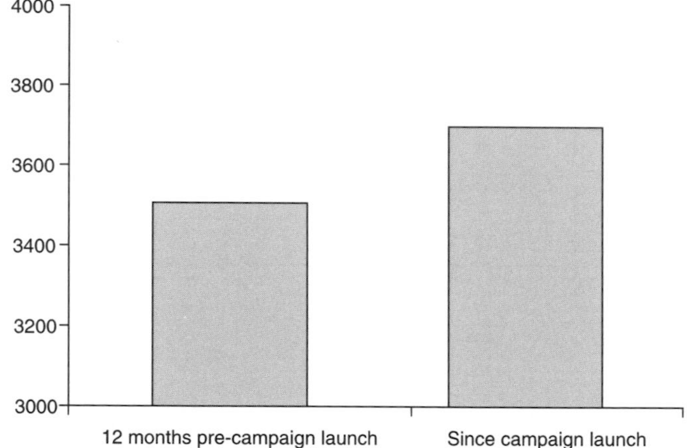

Figure 44: *Showroom visitors*
Source: Honda UK

What happened when there were more people in showrooms, and those people thought more of Honda? More people bought Hondas (Figure 45).

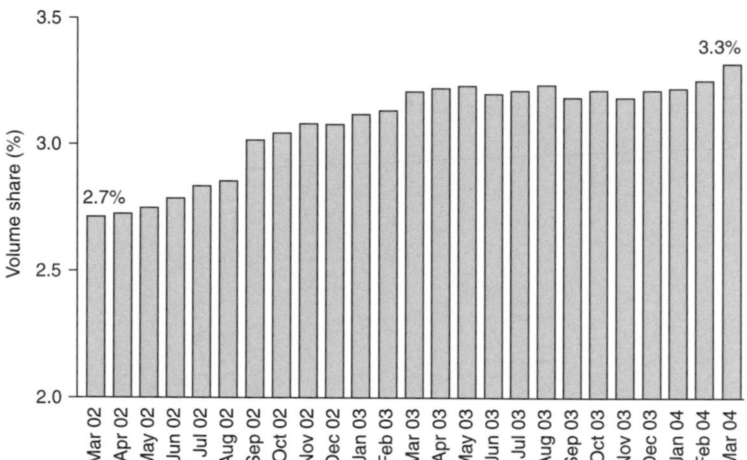

Figure 45: *Honda market share*
Source: Honda UK

So from researching Honda, right through to handing over their cash, people were demonstrably acting on what they'd seen. In volume terms, this picture was as in Figure 46. Which is where we started the story, lots of pages ago. And was there a subplot to the story?

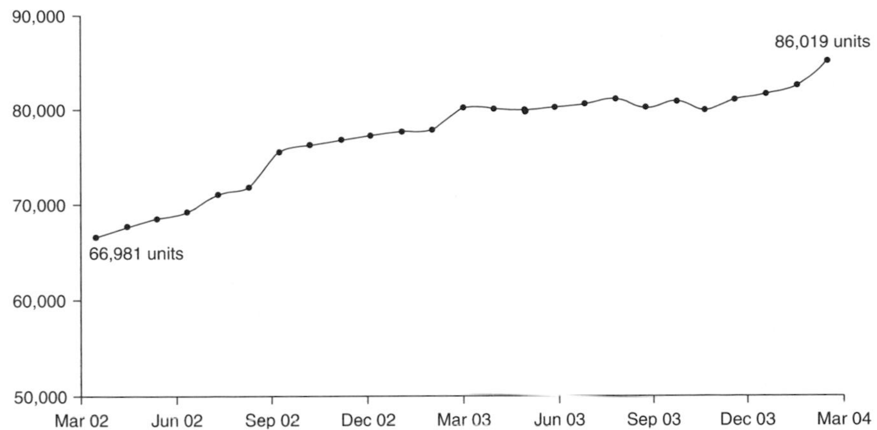

Figure 46: *Sales of new Hondas*
Source: Honda UK – 12-month rolling data

DID IT HAVE BROADER BENEFITS?

The campaign had put lots of new bums in Honda driving seats, but what had it done for existing stakeholders in the business? First up, Honda owners. They'd always been a relatively loyal bunch, but the communications made them feel even more likely to choose Honda next time around (Figure 47).

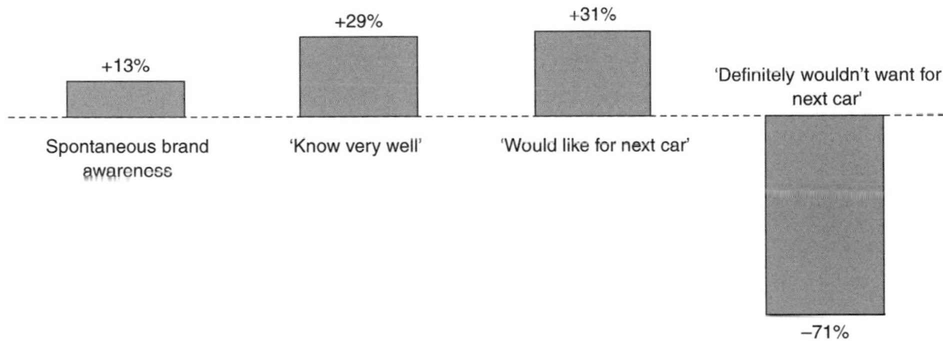

Figure 47: *Honda brand tracking among owners. Change: average since campaign start vs pre-campaign average (%)*
Base: Honda owners
Source: Simpson Carpenter Ad Tracker

What about the dealers? It's not *completely* unheard of for car dealers to be a tad cynical about big and glossy brand advertising. Not so in the case of the Honda campaign. Category-wide dealer surveys showed that the Honda guys were getting it, and getting behind it (Figure 48).

No wonder the dealers started to welcome what Honda were up to. We showed earlier that people visited showrooms with more regard for Honda, so it was easier to get them to leave with the keys to one (Figure 49). It wasn't just motivating dealers to sell more *new* Hondas, either. Sales of Honda used cars also showed a steady increase (Figure 50).

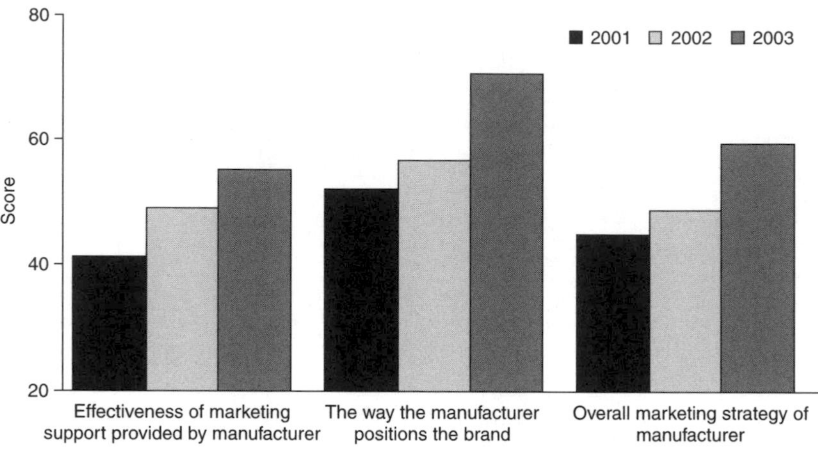

Figure 48: *Honda dealer attitudes*
Source: Sewells Dealer Attitude Survey

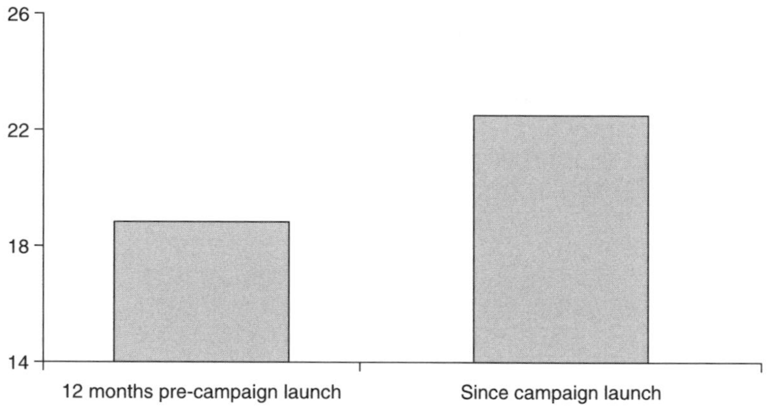

Figure 49: *Conversion rate; showroom visitors who bought (%)*
Source: Honda UK

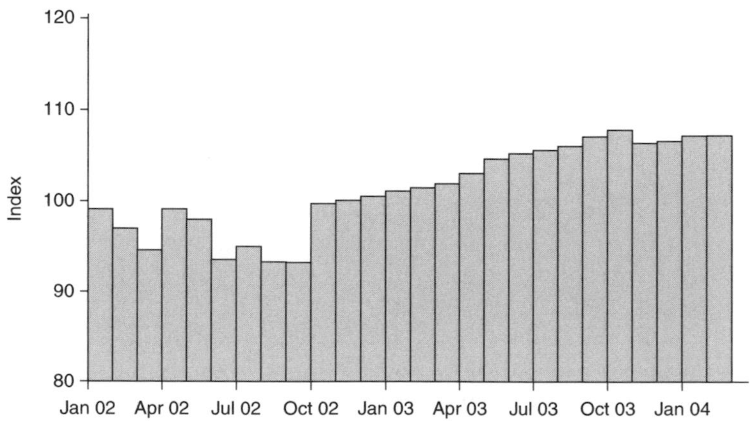

Figure 50: *Honda used car sales*
Source: Honda UK

Then there was the Honda staff. For the first time, in 2003, Honda made it into '*The Sunday Times* Best Companies to Work For' list. Entry is based on surveys measuring staff satisfaction and pride in working for the company. Honda made number 18. In 2004, it climbed the charts to 16, when 89% of staff said they were proud to work for Honda. Staff turnover was down to 11% by early 2003, and then just 7% by early 2004.

Comparisons can also be made between Honda UK staff and their European counterparts (based on the control region from before) (Figure 51).

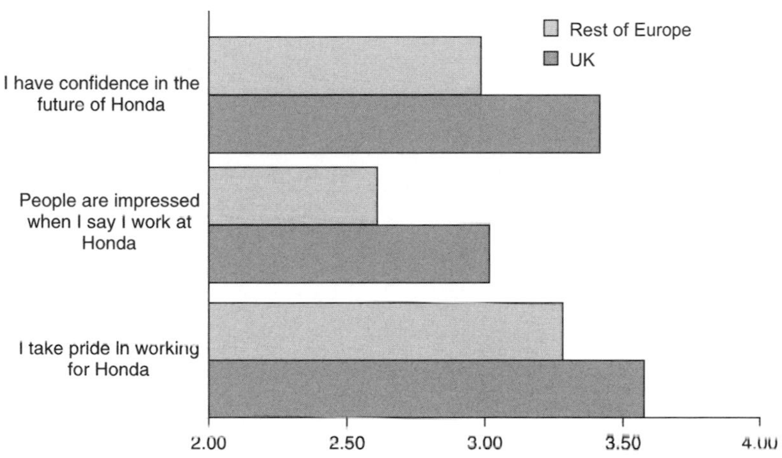

Figure 51
Source: Spirited Independence 2003, Honda Europe

OK, the communications can't take the credit for all of that, but they must have helped.

The activity seemed to be marshalling all kinds of troops. Not all the benefits of this will have trickled their way down to the balance sheet yet, but they will. Perhaps there were other, unknown beneficiaries from the campaign. Banana sellers, perhaps?

HOW WOULD WE SUM IT ALL UP?

'Less is more.' Isn't that what they say? But is that always true? Rather than simplifying the brand, Honda wondered what would happen if it embraced its diversity. What if it simply told the truth about Honda? Nothing but the whole truth? It did – by crafting a consistent voice to communicate the brand's many beliefs and shades. Less wasn't more for Honda.

Ah, but what about 'more for less'? Surely that's a different matter? Isn't that something we all want, whether we're buying Brillo pads or building a business? It's what Honda wanted. It's what Honda achieved. Less media spend, less PR spend and less promotional spend. More effective integrated communications and more types of measurement to judge them. More motivated stakeholders. More brand preference, more sales and more profit; 28% more sales, in fact, and £388m more revenue – £388m, just by telling the truth. Makes you think.

The most commonly used word in the world is 'OK'. A word that means all right. Satisfactory. Not bad. Not everybody believes that OK is OK. Honda certainly doesn't, as this story has shown. And what if it's not the end of the story?

5

The Number 118 118

They came, they saw, they conquered

Principal authors: Cameron Saunders, WCRS, and Yusuf Chuku, Naked Communications

EDITOR'S SUMMARY

This paper shows how advertising created a phenomenon in the dull world of directory enquiries, propelling an unknown brand to market leader within a matter of months.

It was a brave decision to advertise several months ahead of switch-off but one that paid off, since by then the 118 118 runners had already clocked up 17 million calls. Another key tactic was spending £2m of the advertising budget on buying the 118 118 number sequence.

Post switch-off 118 118 dominated the deregulated market whilst charging people a premium for it. At the time of this paper's submission 118 118 had 44% of the directory enquiries market. Next with 34% was BT, which has the luxury of a 47-year relationship with the British public.

This highly original communication idea was transformed into a cult-like phenomenon by equally inventive media thinking. The brand's iconic 70s runners and their catchphrase 'Got Your Number' has slipped into the public consciousness. So prolific was this campaign that the majority of all articles written about deregulation were accompanied by imagery provided by 118 118.

By focusing on the period when consumers still had a choice of calling 192 or the new 118 number, this paper provides a straightforward advertising effect: £11.5m communications spend delivered £45m in revenue.

INTRODUCTION

This study shows how advertising launched a branded phenomenon in the dull world of directory enquiries, which in a matter of months enabled a relative upstart to take on and ultimately destroy BT's market dominance despite its 47-year head start.

It aims to be a relatively straightforward effectiveness case study, proving in no uncertain terms that advertising created a profound brand and business success which went from nowhere to established market leader within a matter of months – they came, they saw, they conquered. The study aims to show a straightforward, common-sense return-on-investment case without the need for elaborate models. In the spirit of the IPA Awards, it's simply about advertising that works.

The Number 118 118 was created by US-based InfoNXX in 2002. InfoNXX is the leading US provider of directory enquiries for mobile users, but prior to its entry in the UK market it had provided services purely on a 'white label' business-to-business basis. The UK entry was the first time it had sought to create a consumer-facing brand, and it found itself up against BT, which had been delivering directories for over 40 years, and also against a range of European competitors, which had been successful in markets such as Ireland, Germany and Austria.

This study will show how an advertising campaign, brand idea and brand name and number were packaged together for InfoNXX in order to create a 'meme' – an idea that took on a life of its own and spread like wildfire, driving recognition and memorability in the most memorable campaign in recent advertising history.[1]

It will show how the campaign drove The Number's spontaneous brand awareness head and shoulders above its rivals, and how this awareness was directly related to which number consumers would call. It will show how an audacious strategy of brand and number memorability saw off both BT and another new entrant that sought to compete aggressively on price ('half the price of BT 192').

The post-192 switch-off period remains largely outside the scope of this paper due to concerns regarding the sensitivity of data during what remains the early stages of the company's development. The post switch-off situation is also complicated by the fact that people were forced overnight to choose a new number and at this point a manifold number of other factors beyond advertising response affected that decision. Whilst the front-of-mind awareness generated by advertising was the primary factor, for the sake of simplicity this paper focuses on quantifying the measurable value of the advertising and communications investment prior to 192 switch-off only.

It will show how the campaign established The Number as market leader and generated almost 17m calls in the eight months prior to the switch-off of 192. It will also show the longer-term effect of the launch activity will have been to generate at least a further 53.4m calls subsequent to 192 switch-off. In terms of revenues this is equivalent to a total return on investment of at least £45.4m, on an investment of £13.5m (an investment that includes the cost of buying the number 118 118).

1. Source: *Marketing* 'Adwatch' October 2003 – at 90% this was the most recalled campaign in any week of any advertiser on any budget since 1997.

Whilst commercial confidentiality means that this study cannot reveal margins, it is important to note that the margin received comfortably exceeded the advertising investment. As a result of the ROI generated, The Number 118 118 continues to invest in advertising as a key driver to sustained growth – and at the time of writing is the only 118 provider to do so.

Subsequent to switch-off the brand has moved from strength to strength, and at the time of writing holds 44% market share vs BT 118 500's 34% market share.[2] The Number 118 118 is currently taking up to half a million calls per day and still growing, and on current projections by year end it will be a £100–110m a year brand – broadly equivalent in size to brands such as Müllerlite or PG Tips (Table 1).

TABLE 1: TOP 20 UK BRANDS

Rank	Brand	Sales to June 2003 (£m)	Percentage change year on year	Manufacturer
1	Walkers Crisps	240–245	–3.8	Walkers
2	Persil main wash	210–215	2.7	Lever Fabergé
3	Diet Coke	195–200	20.3	Coca-Cola
4	Hovis pre-packaged bread	190–195	11.9	British Bakeries
5	Coke	185–190	0.3	Coca-Cola
6	Kingsmill pre-packaged bread	180–185	10.6	Allied Bakeries
7	Warburtons pre-packaged bread	160–165	10.9	Warburtons
8	Ariel main wash	150–155	9.2	Procter & Gamble
9	Nescafé Original	135–140	–4.9	Nestlé
10	Pampers Baby Dry	110–115	6.1	Procter & Gamble
11	Müllerlite	100–105	–0.8	Muller
12	PG Tips Pyramid bags	95–100	–7.6	Unilever Bestfoods
13	Bold main wash	90–95	3.7	Procter & Gamble
14	Heinz Soup (ready to serve)	90–95	9.3	HJ Heinz
15	Colgate dental cream	90–95	2.2	Colgate Palmolive
16	Nestlé Kit Kat chocolate	90–95	–7.3	Nestlé Rowntree
17	Comfort	85–90	7.3	Lever Fabergé
18	Cadbury Dairy Milk	85–90	20.9	Cadbury Trebor Bassett
19	Tetley tea bags	80–85	0.2	Tetley GB
20	Silver Spoon white sugar	80–85	4.6	Silver Spoon

Source: *Marketing* Annual Survey of Top 50 UK Brands, 2003

MARKET ENTRY CONTEXT

Oftel, the telecoms regulator, announced the deregulation of the UK directory enquiries market in 2001, with '192' due to be switched off in August 2003 and replaced with a range of competing services all beginning with 118 followed by three further digits to be allocated by lottery.

At the beginning of 2003 there were over 80 companies and 300 '118' numbers set to contest the race to take over the provision of directory enquiries services, with over 20 companies having already launched services. Experience from other markets suggested only two would profitably survive – the incumbent provider

2. Source: TNS Omnibus study May 2004, sample size 2100 UK adults.

(BT) and one new entrant. InfoNXX was determined to be the single new entrant that would take on BT, and set about creating a new brand from scratch.

The key business issue facing InfoNXX was how to launch and grow a new brand that successfully captured the public imagination and drove usage ahead of up to 20 competitors with similar numbers, without the ability to undercut on price or over-invest.

In brief, the success of InfoNXX in the UK rested entirely on its ability to deliver a superior brand solution at the same or lower cost than its competitors.

THE MARKETING SOLUTION

We knew from Oftel that there would be no 'official' communication of the range of new numbers available, as it sought to leave the new entrants (and BT) to bear the expense of educating the market.

We also knew this to be a low-interest category for consumers, and that they would only 'want' to remember one new number. When asked in consumer research what they wanted from the deregulated '192', consumers said they were simply looking for lower prices (Figure 1).

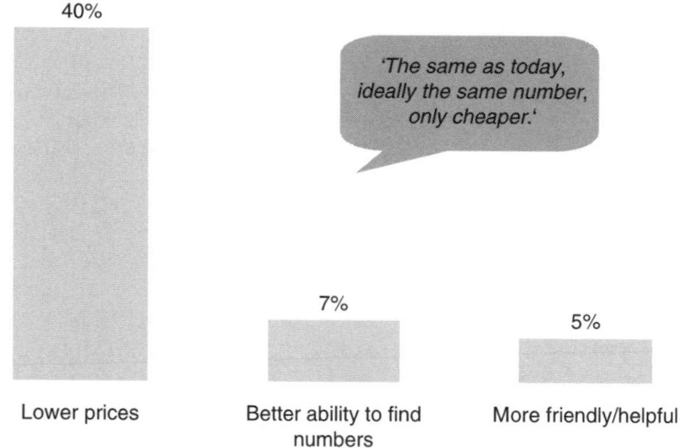

Figure 1: *Suggested improvements for directory enquiries*
Source: Oftel/Ipsos-RSL, November 2000

This was not an economically viable option for InfoNXX to pursue – to offer lower prices meant that there would be no money available for marketing! We had to 'think different'.

The strategy put forward was an audacious one – to be the new number for directory enquiries. We would act and behave as the new market leader, and advertise early on the principle that first to mind would be first in market. This led to the development of the brand name and initial logo (Figure 2).

Whilst this strategy and logo was being presented, CEO of InfoNXX, Robert Pines took a phone call where he was informed that the number '118 118' was available for £2m. Robert asked the brand team whether it was worth purchasing this number given the cost of it would be deducted from the advertising budget.

The Number™

118 811

Figure 2: *The original logo concept*

There was much debate amongst all the 118 providers as to the value of '118 118'. In other markets such as Germany and Austria the 'Golden Numbers' had revolved around 'doubles' – e.g. 11 88 88 ('double one, double eight, double eight') and 11 88 66 ('double one, double eight, double six'). In Ireland the winning number had turned out to be 11 850 ('eleven, eight fifty').

The former two numbers were owned by leading rivals in the UK. Orange owned 11 8000 ('eleven eight thousand'). InfoNXX already owned '118 811' which could also have been presented as '11 88 11'.

For these reasons, none of our competitors took up the opportunity to purchase the number. Experience in other markets suggested that a range of different numbers could be equally effective and the magic was in how the number was communicated. It was InfoNXX's strategic and creative vision that enabled it to see the true potential value of the number 118 118.

> 'Any of the new entrants to market could have bought the number 118 118, but given our strategic intent only we recognised its true potential value. Whilst buying 118 118 resulted in the advertising budget being reduced by £2m, it paid back for itself many times over in terms of the results it enabled the advertising to deliver.'
>
> Chris Moss, CEO, The Number 118 118

The rest is history. The Number now owned the definitive number, which enabled the brand to own the market generic ('118').

However, the brand remained a mere number – one of many contenders for space in the mind of our target audience. In order to capture the popular imagination in a low-interest category and establish The Number as the leading

Figure 3: *The final logo*

brand, we set about building a powerful brand personality to accompany our rather attractive six-digit number.

The brand essence was defined as 'going the extra mile', with core values of passion, dedication, helpfulness and focus. The creative challenge was to find a way of executing this brand in a way that resonated with our core target audience.

Quantitative research identified a clear target audience of high directory users – the 25% of the market who accounted for 89% of all directory calls. Further quantitative and qualitative research identified the core of our target as:

- 25–44
- urban, primarily London and the south-east but also Manchester, Birmingham, Leeds, etc.
- professionals
- hectic work and/or social lives
- advertising literate.

Having sat in on just a handful of focus groups amongst our core target consumer, it was clear that the advertising clichés used successfully in other markets – dancing numbers, jingles, and so on – wouldn't really cut it.

Whilst we needed to make number memorability absolutely central to communications, it was equally important that we communicated both the essence and the personality of the brand, using a fresh creative vehicle that uniquely resonated with our target audience.

The advertising idea: the 118 118 runners

Our unique 'twin' number clearly pointed to a pair of twins, who represented the brand. After weeks of character development the agency were inspired by a picture of US runner Steve 'Pre' Prefontaine (not, for the record, David Bedford). His image was duplicated and doctored to use as a source of inspiration, and the DNA for the 118 118 runners was born (Figure 4).

Figure 4: *The original creative concept*

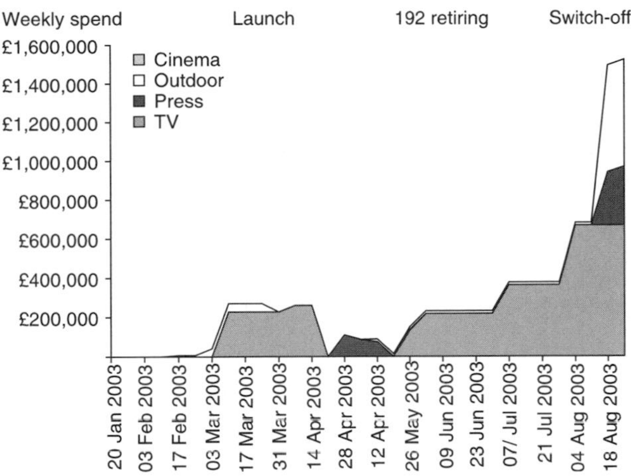

Figure 5: *2003 media schematic (January–August)*

The campaign was developed and tested qualitatively and quantitatively, where it elicited a strong 'love it or hate it' reaction. The 1970s theme resonated strongly with our target audience, who had grown up during that period, and the honest British slapstick humour appealed to ad-literate consumers who were tired of irony and dark humour. The creative idea was then developed into a clearly phased campaign (Figure 5).

Pre-launch campaign

The runners first appeared in February 2002 on their own dedicated website – www.mysteryrunners.com. This contained photos, videos and interviews with a pair of 'powerful, powerfully moustached men who quite literally refuse to stop'. Links to this site were seeded in key internet locations and weblogs, and in a matter of days the site had generated hundreds of thousands of hits. Discussion sites suggested that many people thought this was a 'serious' fan website, whilst others smelt a marketing scam going on but appreciated the sophistication of it (Figure 6).

Figure 6: *www.mysteryrunners.com*

Launch campaign

The next phase of the campaign was to create mass awareness of the 118 118 runners. An integrated multimedia campaign was launched across TV, outdoor and radio featuring the runners and their soon to be famous catchphrase – 'Got Your Number' (Figures 7–9).

Figure 7: *48-sheet poster*

Figure 8: *Launch TV advert*

The launch had the desired effect of generating manageable levels of call volumes and also drew out Conduit – though with a higher media spend than anticipated (with 75% more ratings than ourselves), and a powerful price-led message ('Half the price of BT'). This sent out a clear signal to other would-be players that this would be a tough market to enter.

The gloves were now off, and it was time for us to play our trump card.

192 retirement

Our 118 118 number placed us in the unique position to own the market generic – '192 is about to become 118'. Having established the icon and personality of the runners, we now introduced a new character for 192 who was handing over to a more sprightly and energetic pair of runners – 118 and 118 (Figures 9 and 10).

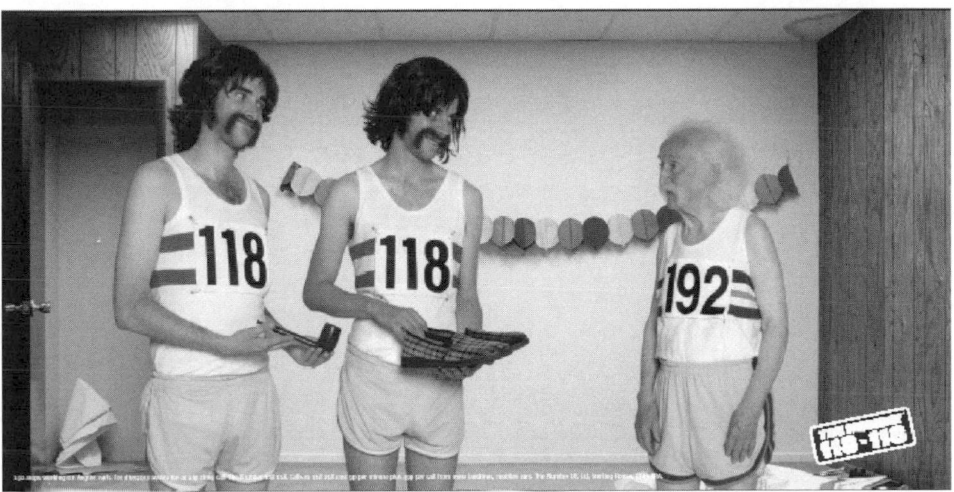

Figure 9: *192 retirement poster*

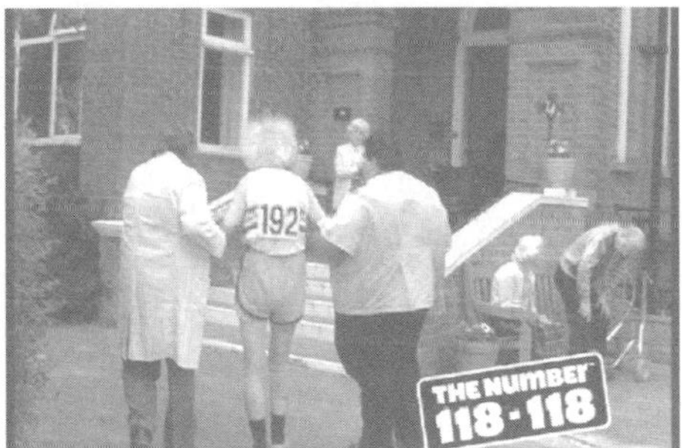

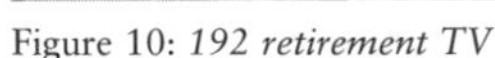

Figure 10: *192 retirement TV*

Creating a cult campaign

In addition to mainstream media, we set about truly embedding the image of the 118 118 runners into people's heads by building upon their nascent 'cult' characteristics. This included an investment of approximately £200k in a range of activities (Figures 11–17).

The 118 runners were also cleverly placed at key events such as Wimbledon, where they were viewed as genuine British eccentrics rather than a marketing ploy (a key part of the magic of the creative vehicle).

Figure 11: *Real-life runners*

Figure 12: *The 118 118 boys appear as mystery guests on* Question of Sport

Figure 13: *The 118 118 boys appear live on stage at the opening of the Millennium Place stadium in Coventry promoting their new single (along with Atomic Kitten and the Fast Food Rockers)*

Figure 14: *Ice-cream vans*

Figure 15: *Barber shop windows*

Figure 16: *Special-build advans*

Figure 17: *Viral and online*

Placement of tens of thousands of vests in Cancer Research shop windows[3] and vest 'giveaways' by cleverly placed 'street hawkers' (in fact actors paid by 118 118) also created a sense of people actually choosing to dress up as runners, which then led to genuine spontaneous imitation (Figure 18).

Figure 18: *Genuine stag party: Newquay, August 2003*

3. Over 20,000 vests were sold through Cancer Research, raising over £100,000 for the charity.

Figure 19: *Rocky TV*

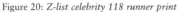

Figure 20: *Z-list celebrity 118 runner print*

The 118 118 costume also became the fancy dress of choice at the Test Match, with up to 30 or 50 people spontaneously coming as runners.

This tide of enthusiasm for the 118 runners was then fanned by the 'Rocky' TV ad and a press campaign featuring 'z-list' celebrity 118 runners, which celebrated the popularity of both the runners and the service, which by this point had taken millions of calls (Figures 19 and 20).

By August 2003 the runners had become a national icon and the brand had developed significant status amongst opinion formers – particularly in media and marketing circles. This provided us with a crucial point of leverage amongst journalists in the run-up to switch-off.

Journalists had to write about the 192 switch-off as part of their service to readers. Given this was hardly a thrilling subject and taking up valuable column inches, they inevitably wanted to write about the 118 runners, and over 80% of articles written about the switch-off were accompanied by imagery provided by 118 118 (source: 118 118 press research).

To consumers this was now the only brand.

HOW THE ADVERTISING WORKED

The campaign consistently delivered advertising awareness more efficiently than those of its competitors, with rapid acceleration from June onwards as the activity moved from an advertising campaign to a national phenomenon (Figure 21).

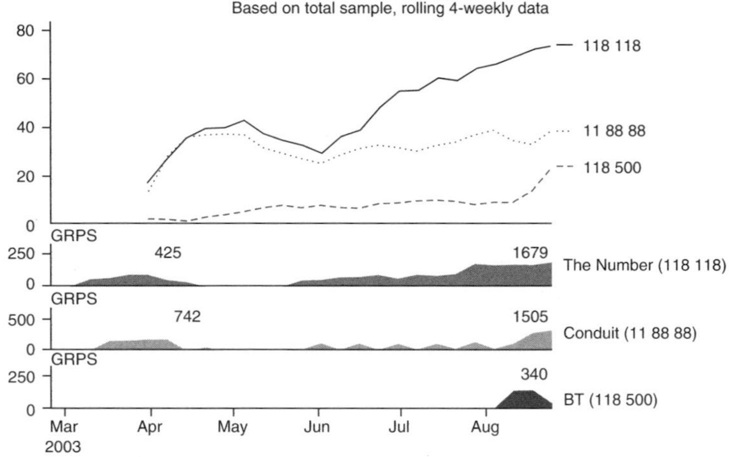

Figure 21: *Total communications awareness*

It is worth noting that in the early months of the campaign, awareness of 118 118 was neck and neck with Conduit's 11 88 88 (albeit on a lower advertising spend). It was only when the campaign became a phenomenon that the advertising really began to pay off – a result of the creative device in the advertising rather than the 'superiority' of the number.

The campaign worked three times as efficiently as 11 88 88's, and double the UK average (Figure 22).

The campaign consistently ranked as the most recalled in any week in the *Marketing* Adwatch tables, with the campaign generating the highest level of awareness of any campaign on any budget in the past six years (Figure 23).

It was by far the most talked about and imitated campaign during the crucial period of June to August 2003, creating a huge volume of 'free' advertising (Figure 24 and 25).

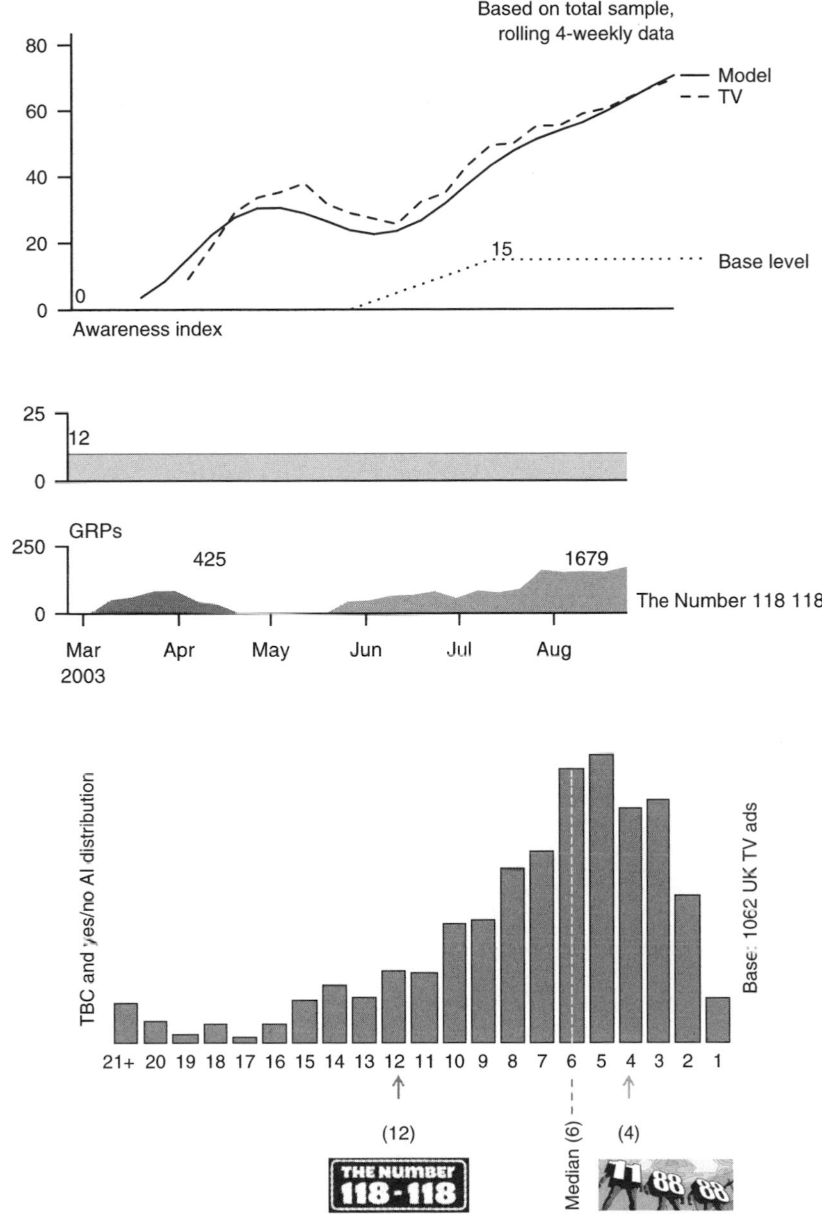

Figure 22: *Millward Brown Awareness Indices*

This communications awareness led directly to extremely high front-of-mind spontaneous brand awareness (Figure 26).

This was a critical indicator that there was a clear correlation between saliency of number and the number people were most likely to call (Figure 27).

This meant that the direct effect of the advertising was consumers were twice as likely to call 118 118 over the nearest competitor (Figure 28).

Highest recall in any single week

	02	Brand	Agency/TV buyer	Score	Issue	Budget* (£m)
1	-	**118 118**	WCRS/OMD UK	**90**	16.10.03	15.24

POSTERWATCH

The monthly analysis of outdoor recall in association with CONCORD EFFECTIVE OUTDOOR

Q: Which of the following poster campaigns do you remember seeing recently?

Back two weeks of August

Rank	Format	Brand	Planning agency	Specialist	Recall (%)
1	48-sheet and 96-sheet	**118 118**	Manning Gottlieb OMD	Posterscope	75
2	Buses	**11 88 88**	Media Planning Group	Posterscope	70
3	48-sheet and 6-sheet	**BT 118 500**	Rocket	Outdoor Connection	67
4	96-sheet and buses	**Lord of the Rings 2 DVD**	ZenithOptimedia	Concord	64
5	48-sheet and 96-sheet	**AA Insurance**	Manning Gottlieb OMD	Posterscope	54
6	6-sheet, 48-sheet, 96-sheet	**Ford Ka**	MindShare	MindShare Outdoor	43
7	6-sheet	**Tomb Raider: Cradle of Life**	Mediaedge:cia	Portland	43
8	6-sheet	**Guinness**	Carat	Posterscope	39
9	48-sheet and 96-sheet	**Land Rover Freelander**	MindShare	Portland	36
10	6-sheet	**Lucozade**	Mediacom	Mediacom Outdoor	32

Posterwatch research was conducted from August 8 to 10 and August 22 to 24 by **NOP Research Group** (020 7890 9000) as part of a fortnightly telephone omnibus survey among more than 1000 British adults. Advertisements were selected on size of campaign by **Concord** (020 7543 4444) www.concord.co.uk

1. 118 118

Figure 23: Marketing *Adwatch tables*
Source: *Marketing*, August 2003

Brand Republic 09-09-2003
The 118 118 runners top Ads That Make News survey
Gordon MacMillan

LONDON - WCRS seems to have hardly put a foot wrong in the battle to succeed 192 and its 118 118 ads for The Number have again come out on top in the latest Ads That Make News survey.

August saw the 118 118 ads, featuring the two Seventies-style long-distance runners, beat out the latest Abbott Mead Vickers BBDO spot for Walkers Crisps in the survey, which measures the most famous ads of the moment.

The 118 118 ads seem to have easily risen above the clutter, beating rivals such as 11 88 88 and BT's own replacement service BT Directories 118 500, which both failed to make the top 10.

The 118 118 has gained widespread word-of-mouth and more column inches with the Seventies vests worn by the two runners gaining a cult status in the summer as they went on sale in Cancer Research charity stores.

Figure 24: *Brand Republic*

www.mysteryrunners.co.uk

SITE OF THE DAY

A WEBSITE dedicated to two extraordinary men who can't stop running.

You may have seen these hirsute nutters on a TV ad for a new directory enquiries.

But who are they?

If you've got a net story contact AMY VICKERS at amysl@mirror.co.uk or phone 020 7293 2413

Daily Mirror, 03.04.03

Ad of the week

Advertiser/agency The Number/WCRS

Background Got an ad that won't get past the watchdogs? Put it on the internet and before you can say "www" it's whizzing around on e-mails. That was the solution for directory inquiries service The Number, with two runners promoting its 118 118 service, when Honda said it couldn't film a parody of the car manufacturer's famous "cogs" chain reaction ad.

What happens The runners roll wheels, bounce on space hoppers, slide Chinese takeaways down ramps ... The Honda ad ended with Garrison Keillor saying: "Isn't it nice when things just work." This time one of the runners says: "Isn't it nice when a directory inquiries service just works. 118!" Given Honda had a legal spat with two Swiss artists who claim it copied their film, refusing a parody seems a bit rich. Word has it Honda has already allowed another parody and this would be one too many.

Where to see it www.the118118experience.com

Daily Telegraph, 07.06.03

Pick of the week

Mark Sweney finds WCRS's 118 118 viral homage to "cog" (at www.the118118experience.com) amusing: "The moustachioed runners are an incongruous contrast to the technical perfection of 'cog'. Seeing them bumble through a series of events deflates the original idea and makes this spoof work beautifully." A copy of Campaign Screen goes to the copywriter Anson Harris and the art director Per Kvalvaag.

Pick of the Week, *Campaign*, 19.06.03

We've got directory enquiries' number

GOOD ADVERTISING works. So far the only confirmed winner from the grand plan to bring competition into directory enquiries has been WCRS, the ad agency that created a national talking point with its £16 million campaign for the new 118 118 service. Only true creativity could have brought this peculiarly obscure piece of regulatory meddling into the forefront of public consciousness.

The Times, September 2003

WCRS's 118 118 ads are doing their job

Now that the 192 Directory Enquiries Service is no more, confusion still reigns over the new 118 marketplace. Product differentiation between the services is almost impossible to gauge but it's one of the purest marketing scenarios in which to judge the saliency of advertising: all of the service providers are operating on a relatively level playing field. But WCRS's 118 118 campaign is the only one that's come close to the goal so far.

Campaign, August 2003

Figure 25: *Small selection of press coverage of the campaign*

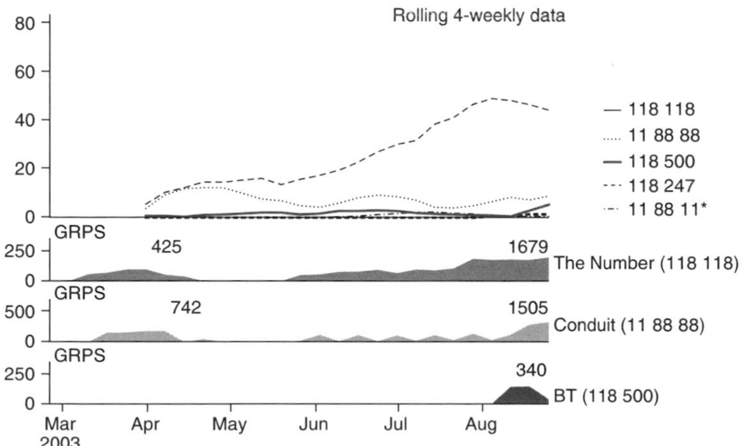

Figure 26: *Unaided awareness – first mention*
Source: Millward Brown, October 2003

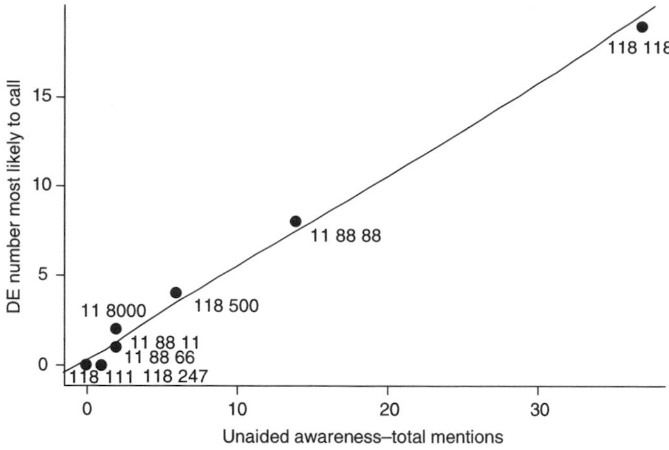

Figure 27: *Brand usage profile analysis*
Source: Millward Brown, October 2003

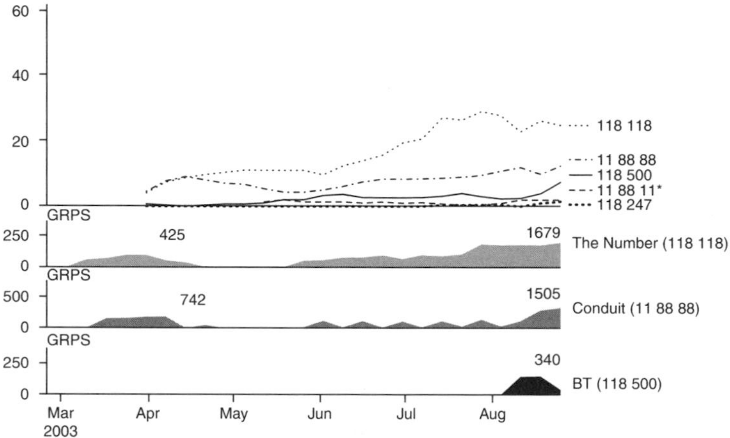

Figure 28: *Number most likely to call for directories*

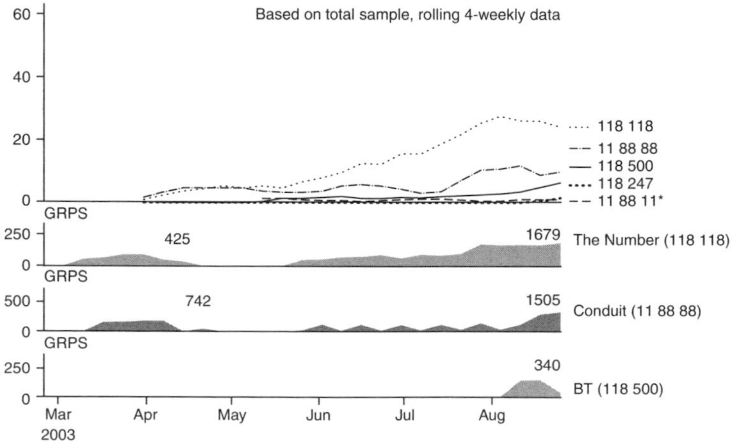

Figure 29: *Ever used*

A very similar pattern was observed in terms of the impact of the campaign upon claimed usage (Figure 29).

THE BUSINESS RESULTS

The Millward Brown data above was reflected in the call volumes being driven to 118 118 well ahead of 192 switch-off, and ahead of any competing new entrants.

Figure 30 shows a seven-day rolling average of daily calls to 118 118 since the beginning of 2003, and demonstrates the momentum generated ahead of 192 switch-off with upwards of 200,000 calls per day.[4]

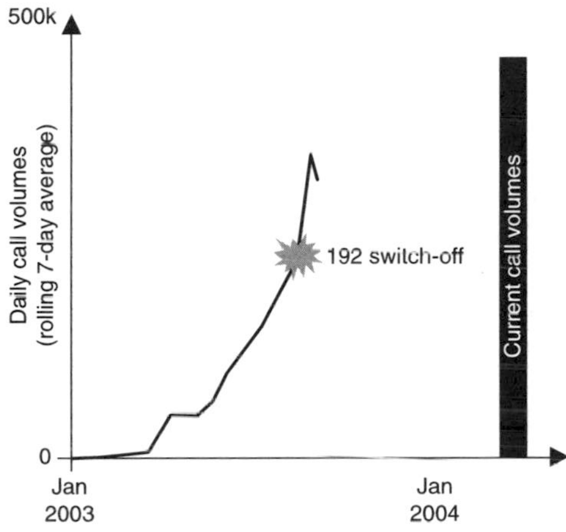

Figure 30: *118 118 call volumes*
Source: Company data

Before switch-off there was no reason to call 118 118 except as a response to the advertising and associated activity. The Number offered a similar service to that offered by 192 and other 118 providers, but at a significant price premium (Table 2).

TABLE 2: 118 PRICE COMPARISON FOR TYPICAL 40-SECOND BASIC ENQUIRY

	192	118 118	11 88 88	118 500	11 88 11[5]
Cost of 40-second call	40p	55p	13p	45p	40p

Except for 118 118 advertising, there was little communication of the service to the general public. Oftel provided details of the new providers via the internet and via a basic leaflet – but given the price comparison outlined in Table 2 this would, if anything, have been detrimental to the likelihood of people calling based on a rational decision.

4. For reasons of client confidentiality the call volumes from post-switch-off are not shown on the chart, except for the current seven-day average call volume from April 2004.
5. InfoNXX also launched a 'basic' service using its 11 88 11 number, which offered callers only one number per call, as opposed to as many numbers as you wanted via 118 118.

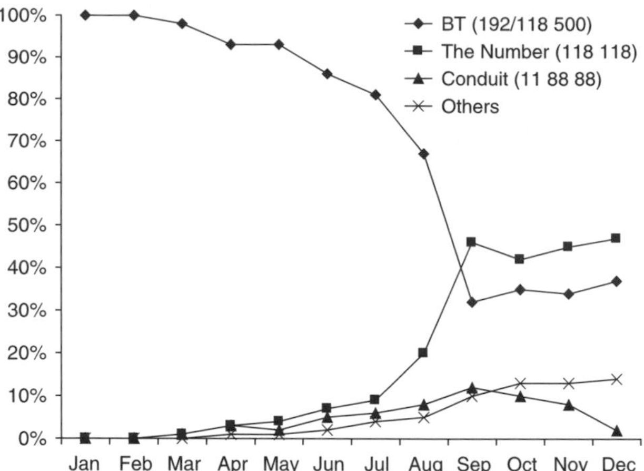

Figure 31: *Market share by provider, 2003*
Source: Millward Brown/TNS Omnibus

As such, this study argues that all calls made to 118 118 prior to switch-off can be attributed to the advertising investment. Following switch-off the situation becomes considerably more complicated as consumers had to choose one provider and would have referred to various materials to make a decision.

In order to make the most straightforward case and in order not to rely on sensitive client data, this study limits itself to the return on investment for the activity before switch-off. However, it is worth noting the extraordinary market share performance of 118 118 following switch-off and the clear role the campaign played in building momentum (Figure 31).

The collection of smaller 'others' consists entirely of 118 providers with less than 1% market share, and is made up of smaller network or paper directory-owned providers such as Orange, Telewest, OneTel and Yell, who communicate their number direct to their customer base through customer communications.

THE RETURN ON INVESTMENT MODEL

Before switch-off the campaign generated a total of 16.9m calls, with a significant and growing customer base making regular calls. For the reasons detailed above all these call volumes have been attributed to advertising because:

- throughout the launch period consumers still had the option of calling 192; there was no reason to call 118 118 except as a response to the advertising
- 118 118 did not have a price advantage vs 192 and it had a significant price disadvantage vs other providers
- other forms of information about 118 providers highlighted the various service prices and placed 118 118 as part of a list of providers including pricing
- the 'advantage' of owning the number has been included in the campaign costs
- the publicity surrounding the switch-off of 192 was accompanied by the high-profile use of 118 118 campaign images – this was part of the communications strategy with press relations playing a key role in the success of the brand.

Had switch-off not occurred, and had 118 118 ceased advertising at that date, call volumes would have been maintained as a result of the customers the brand had attracted. By switch-off, millions of people had tried 118 118 and many of these would go on to call again. The nature of the competitive post-switch-off market means that this customer base would gradually decay without advertising due to:

- competitive communications activity – particularly BT promoting its number on its phone books and vans
- customers switching to other ways of finding numbers such as the internet, the phone book, etc.

In order to quantify the 'lag' effect of the campaign, we have looked at the first three months of 2004 where we had ceased advertising. This period suggests a linear 7% per month 'decay' rate in call volumes once seasonality has been taken into account (Figure 32).

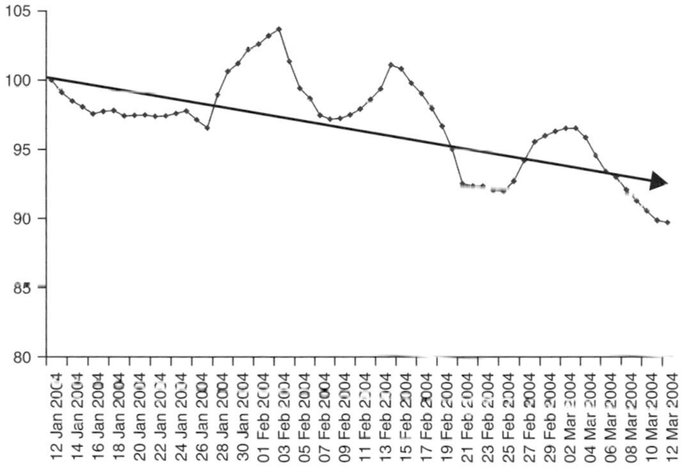

Figure 32: *118 118 call volume decay rate without advertising support (Indexed Jan 12 = 100)*

Assuming this relationship would have applied from the end of August onwards, and had switch-off actually not occurred (i.e. if 192 was still around today), Figure 33 projects the total call volumes that could reasonably be attributed to the customers attracted to the brand before switch-off occurred. This model provides the most conservative estimate of total calls generated by the advertising campaign, with an additional 53.4m calls to the 16.9m generated prior to switch-off.

With average call duration since launch of 104 seconds, this is equivalent in revenue generation terms to 70.3m × £0.646, or £45.4m.

The total advertising spend prior to switch-off was £11.5m, plus the 'campaign' cost of buying the number of £2m.

Thus, even with the most conservative assumptions the campaign clearly delivered real financial results. The true value of the campaign is therefore much

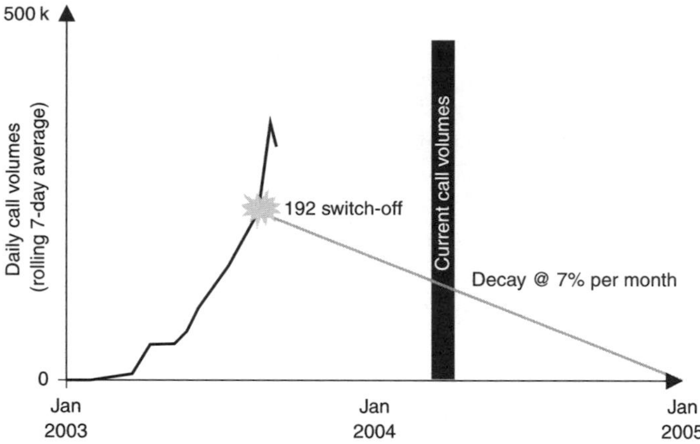

Figure 33: *Total call volumes attributable to pre-switch-off campaign*

higher and will doubtless be a case in a future IPA study, but in the meantime it is worth noting that The Number continues to lead the directory enquiries market in 2004 and is the only remaining player to continue to invest heavily in advertising.

GOLD
BEST DEDICATION TO EFFECTIVENESS

6

Tobacco Control

WARNING: advertising can seriously improve your health

How the integration of advertisers made advertising more powerful than word of mouth

Principal authors: Clare Hutchinson, Jane Dorsett and Annabelle Watson, AMV.BBDO, Ann Marie Kilpatrick and Frank Reitgassl, Bartle Bogle Hegarty, and Kate Waters, Euro RSCG London
Media agency: PHD

EDITOR'S SUMMARY

This paper shows how the Government, via a coalition of related brands (NHS, Cancer Research UK and British Heart Foundation), has successfully waged a war on tobacco. Since 2000, 1.1 million fewer people are smoking and 50 per cent more people are calling the NHS Smoking Helpline. During this time anti-smoking advertising has quadrupled in effectiveness to become the most powerful trigger to smokers kicking the habit.

It makes a powerful case for integrating multiple messages and crucially shows the merit in different 'voices' delivering them. Each organisation offered up a different reason to give up, and did so in a way that did not victimise smokers: the damage inflicted by each cigarette; an assault on the tobacco industry; the effects of smoking on loved ones.

Tobacco kills 120,000 people every year in the UK, costing the NHS £1.5 billion. In this context the paper looks at how efficient the campaign has been in achieving its ends. To have paid for itself the campaign needs to have accounted for 7661 of the 1.1 million people who have given up.

Perhaps most powerfully, judges told anecdotes of people they knew personally who had given up as a result of these campaigns.

INTRODUCTION

In the last five years, anti-smoking advertising has quadrupled in effectiveness to become the most powerful trigger to smokers kicking the habit: more important even than word of mouth or doctor's advice, growing the number of prompts to quit (Figure 1).

At its heart this case is proof that integration works. However, this is not the usual story of integration. This is the story of how sometimes the best, most powerful form of integration involves not just different channels, different products or different brands, but actually *different advertisers*.

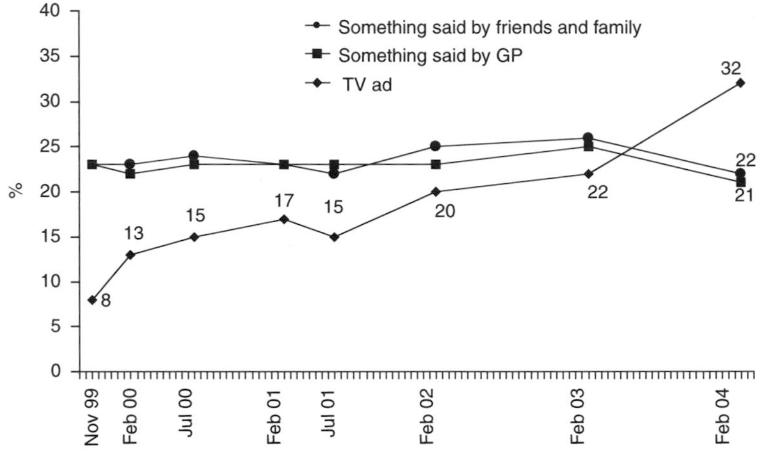

Figure 1: *Prompts for quit attempts (prompted)*
Base: Ever tried, currently trying or gave up in past six months – base varies by wave (n = *c*.900)
Source: BMRB Tobacco Education Campaign Tracking Study

It's the story of how in today's integrated world we must never confuse the means with the end, or the execution with the purpose. To do so is to ignore the opportunity to create even better, more effective forms of integrated communications.

Specifically, we shall show how a purpose-led rather than an execution-led approach to integration made communication a more powerful weapon in the war on smoking than it has ever been. Playing its part in helping Tobacco Control reduce the number of smokers by over a million, exceeding the 2005 target three years early.

THE SMOKING ADDICTION

Tobacco kills 120,000 people a year in the UK. More than five times the number of deaths collectively caused by road accidents, drug or drink abuse, accidents, murder, suicide and AIDS.[1]

1. Source: ASH factsheet based on 2002 data.

Figure 2(a): *1950s cigarette advertising*

When tobacco first came to these shores it was a health product, a cure for cancer and halitosis.[2] In the 1950s it was advertised for its health benefits (Figure 2a). It wasn't long before smoking was cool, sexy and 'grown up'. By this time it had become the biggest cause of preventable death in England. When people found out, they tried to give up.

Smoking peaked in the 1950s and 1960s and fell steadily in the 1970s and 1980s. But the downward trend levelled out. In 1996 smoking rates rose for the first time since 1972 (Figure 2b). Sporadic health education advertising campaigns did little to turn the tide.

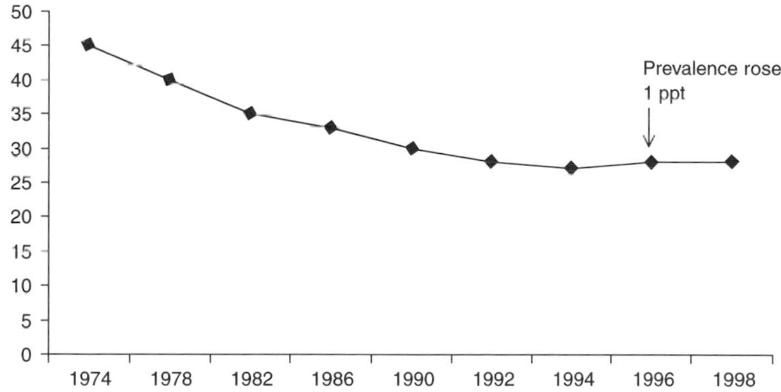

Figure 2(b): *Prevalence of cigarette smoking 1974–98*
Source: GHS

Worryingly, British smokers were consuming roughly 25% more than the EU average.[3] Smoking was killing one in two smokers.[4] It was costing the NHS £1.5 billion every year.[5]

---

2. Introduced by Drake into the court of Elizabeth I in 1572 it was recommended as a treatment for toothache, worms, halitosis, lockjaw and cancer.
3. Smoking Kills (Government White Paper, 1998), p. 6.
4. Smoking Kills (Government White Paper, 1998), p. 7.
5. Buck, D., Godfrey, C., Parrott, S. and Raw, M. (1997) *Cost Effectiveness of Smoking Cessation Interventions*. London. Health Education Authority.

In 1998, Labour released a new assault on tobacco in the White Paper 'Smoking Kills'. The key objective of the paper was to help existing smokers to quit. A target was set to reduce adult smoking from 28% to 24% by 2010; with a fall to 26% by 2005.

A KINGSIZE PROBLEM

Achieving these targets would not be easy.

- *We needed to fight the power of addiction*

Whilst 69% of smokers claimed 'I want to give up smoking',[6] and 83% wished they had never started,[7] 44% of smokers agreed 'I don't think I could give up smoking because I am addicted.'[8] Getting people to take action was not going to be easy. Smokers had developed barriers and denials to avoid having to give up:

> 'You might as well smoke, because you've got as much chance as being run over by a bus, as dying from smoking.'
>
> 'My gran smoked like a chimney 'til she was 93.'[9]

- *We needed to get people to give up for good*

To reach our 2005 targets would mean encouraging almost a million smokers to give up.[10] It takes the average smoker five or six attempts before they give up for good.[11] This would mean that we would need to create over one million quit attempts a year, 5.6 million by 2005.

- *We needed to out-shout the competition*

Before tobacco advertising was banned in 2003 the industry was spending an estimated £25m on advertising a year (almost four times our budget) plus an estimated £7.5m on sponsorship.[12]

- *But we couldn't afford to be heavy handed*

The Government didn't want to bully smokers into submission. We would need to increase the media spend to create enough momentum, but we needed to do it in a way that was not oppressive.

We wanted to bring smokers with us rather than turn them against us.

---

6. BMRB Tracking Study Benchmark 1999.
7. Source: ASH.
8. BMRB Tracking Study Benchmark 1999.
9. CRD qualitative research.
10. Based on White Paper estimate of 13 million smokers in UK and prevalence of 28%.
11. Prochaska and Di Clemente, *The Stages of Change Model*, 1983.
12. ASH factsheet.

STRATEGY

Support strategy – from public information to public service

Information was not enough – people needed help. Before smokers could be motivated to give up, there needed to be an infrastructure of support in place to help them quit and stay quit.

For the first time the strategy was to move beyond being an information provider and become a 'service provider'. Previously, anti-smoking messages had come from the Health Education Authority. This time they would come from a brand that people trusted and associated with health and service: the NHS. Communications would be supported with a comprehensive range of NHS 'products' and 'services' to increase quitters' success rates. Tobacco control was acting like a service brand.

A range of products was developed in line with the NHS strategy to supply 'personalised' healthcare to suit people's needs (Figure 3).

With a support structure in place we now faced the formidable challenge of stimulating more smokers to make a serious attempt to quit.

NHS Local Stop Smoking Services
Local face-to-face support network. Choice of group sessions or one-to-one offering expert advice and free Nicotine Replacement Therapy (NRT) on prescription.

Together Programme
A tailored personal step-by-step programme, using multiple interventions to guide smokers through giving up.

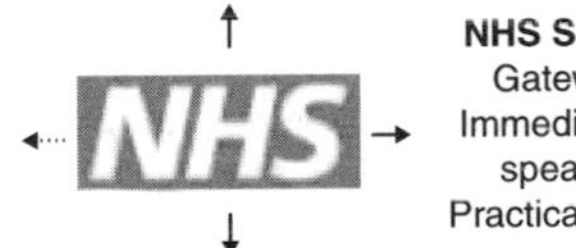

NHS Smoking Helpline
Gateway to services. Immediate opportunity to speak to counsellor. Practical self-help booklet.

www.givingupsmoking.co.uk
Private and instant advice and information. Gateway to services.

Figure 3: *'Personalised' healthcare products*

Two-stage communications strategy

There was no silver bullet; 76% of smokers claimed they wanted to give up for more than one reason.[13] We needed a multi-faceted approach that appealed to a wide range of smokers, and gave individual smokers more than one reason to quit. To outweigh the strong stimuli that nurtured the habit – addiction, tobacco advertising, social pressure, get-out clauses – with a multiple offensive. In short, our job was to create a series of 'triggers' to stimulate smokers to take action. We rolled this out in two stages.

13. ONS Smoking Related Behaviour & Attitudes, 2000.

Stage 1 – Foundation health reasons

To establish the campaign, we focused on the primary trigger that stimulates almost 90% of quit attempts:[14] the key principle at the heart of the NHS: health. The strategy was to focus on health issues and their emotional and physical consequences, to encourage smokers to seek support. This would act as the backbone to all ongoing communications, adding new triggers when and where appropriate.

Stage 2 – Building new reasons

In 2000 and 2003 the Department of Health (DH) hosted two international meetings. Australia, Canada and the United States had all seen dramatic reductions in prevalence partly driven by a multi-message approach.

In particular, we discovered three additional triggers that would help push smokers to the services (see Figure 4).

1. *SHOCK – damage you are doing now*. Australia had created a very successful controversial campaign – 'Every cigarette is doing you damage' – a hard-hitting campaign that connected the cigarette to internal organ damage.
2. *INDUSTRY – exposing the truth*. California had successfully disabused smokers of some of their beliefs about smoking, which had been fostered by the industry.
3. *KIDS – damage your smoking does to your loved ones*. Second-hand or 'passive' smoke messages had had a powerful effect in California and Massachusetts.

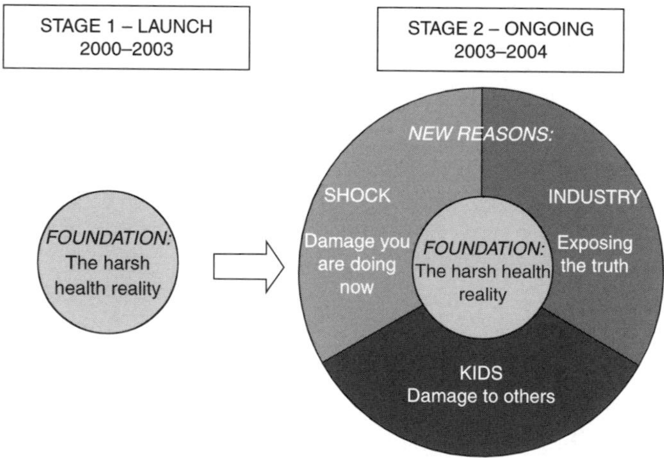

Figure 4: *Two-stage communication strategy*

14. ONS Smoking Related Behaviour & Attitudes, 2000.

Then something brilliant happened …

These were new and powerful messages that researched well. However, there was a problem. The graphic visual style of the Australian campaign was too hard-hitting for the NHS brand. Government messages exposing the industry were counterproductive and viewed as hypocritical.[15] We also couldn't afford to make smokers feel 'victimised' by too many 'Government warnings'. Conscious of these issues, the decision was made to do something very radical – *build a partnership of advertisers*.

In November 2002, the DH committed to provide £15m over three years to fund tobacco control campaigns from charities:

> 'Over the last few months my department has been discussing with some of our key health charities how we could learn lessons from abroad and apply them here at home.'
>
> Alan Milburn, Secretary of State[16]

Put simply, two of the three secondary messages would be more powerful if they came from different brands.

Cancer Research UK agreed to reveal the truth about the tobacco industry's 'light & mild' cigarette deception, and the British Heart Foundation (BHF) brought its authority to the link between smoking and the heart in a new and graphic way. In doing this we effectively created a new type of integration: an *integration of advertisers* that would be compelling but not oppressive.

This brand coalition would help to grow the 'noise cloud' around smoking. We wanted to stimulate discussion in the media, in the pub and in the home: to increase Tobacco Control's share of voice. And yet, by spreading the load, there was less chance that smokers would feel victimised.

The third piece of 'new news', damage to loved ones caused by smoking, was felt to be a suitable NHS message, as it focused on protecting children.

CREATIVE

Stage 1 – Foundation health reasons: testimonials

The first way that we exposed smokers to the many realities of smoking was through the testimonial campaign. Real smokers, telling it like it is. Conversations that lay bare the terrible consequences of smoking.

They worked by confronting smokers with their potential future in an empathetic way. We presented a series of mirrors: a broad range of smokers with different stories to tell, creating new news and a kaleidoscope of reasons to quit (see Figure 5).

15. CRD qualitative, 2001. People think that because the Government makes money from the tax on cigarettes, it is hypocritical for it to criticise the tobacco industry.
16. Speech by Alan Milburn, Secretary of State, to the Faculty of Public Health Medicine, 20 November 2002.

If you smoke you can get a range of different diseases …

Byron who can only slur his words after his stroke

Janice who suffers from chronic obstructive pulmonary disease, and is reliant on oxygen

Smoking can affect you earlier than you thought …

Steve who got lung cancer from 'little white sticks' aged 34

Your life and the life of those you love may be changed for ever …

Rebecca who was scared her dad was going to die

Colleen who felt she had sacrificed the chance of grandchildren, because she knew she was dying

Figure 5: *Stage 1 – Foundation health reasons*

Stage 2 – Building new reasons: kids, shock and industry

For the second stage, three creative campaigns were developed by AMV.BBDO, Bartle Bogle Hegarty and Euro RSCG London, the respective agencies of DH, CRUK and BHF (Figure 6).

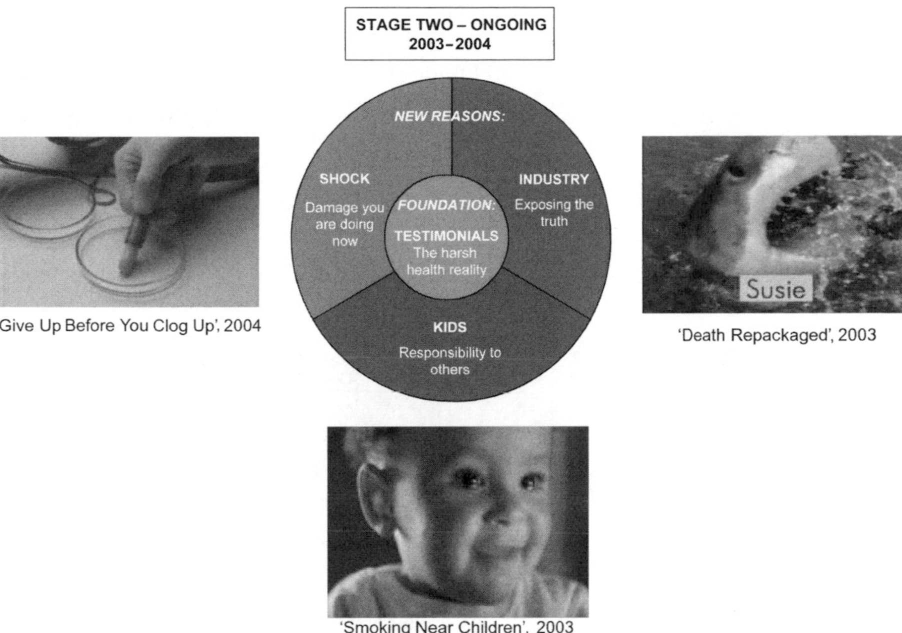

Figure 6: *Stage 2 – Building new reasons*

NHS – 'Smoking near children'

AMV set up the very simple idea that if you smoke, those around you smoke too, by showing small children 'naturally' exhaling cigarette smoke. This was backed up with evidence: every year thousands of children go to hospital because of breathing their parents' cigarette smoke.[17]

The campaign was extended into print, 'If you smoke, I smoke', which was also distributed on bibs to new-born babies (Figure 7).

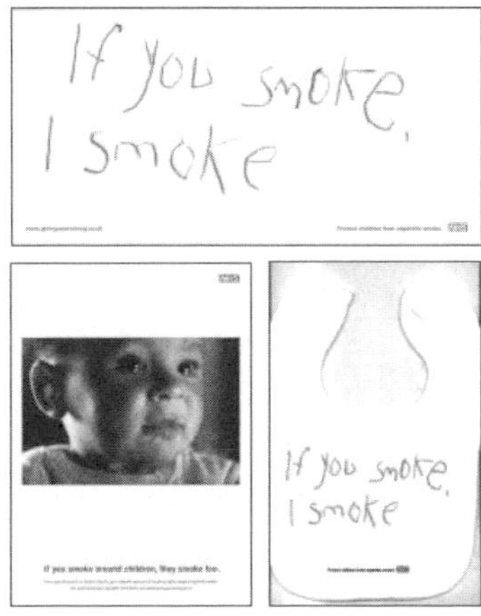

Figure 7

17. Cook, D.G. and Strachan, D.P., Summary of effects of parental smoking on the respiratory health of children and implications for research. *Thorax* 1999: 54, pp. 357–66.

Cancer Research UK – 'Death repackaged'

In December 2002 the Department of Health announced new tobacco legislation, which meant that from September 2003 cigarette companies would be banned from using *misleading descriptors such as 'Light' or 'Mild'*[18] on their packs.[19] BBH embraced the powerful motivation behind the legislation; consumers were being '*misled*'. From this developed the idea that just because 'low tar' cigarettes have nice names such as 'lights' or 'mild' doesn't mean they are any less dangerous. 'Low tar cigarettes. Death repackaged'.

The campaign used dangerous animals with nice names to bring this thought to life (Figure 8).

Figure 8

BHF – 'Artery'

The campaign targets C2DE multiquitters[20] and sets out to be anti-cigarette rather than anti-smoker or anti-smoking. It does this by inextricably linking cigarettes with the damage they cause to arteries, using the similarity in shape between the two to graphically portray the build up of fatty deposits caused by smoking (Figure 9). In doing this we intended the campaign to be 'portable', such that every time a smoker

18. *Consultation on Regulations implementing EU Directive 2001/37/EC – The Labelling Directive*. Department of Health, p. 7, para. 14.
19. The introduction of 'low tar' cigarettes resulted in fewer smokers giving up (*Factors influencing choice of low-tar cigarettes*, Martin Jarvis, Alan Marsh, Jil Matheson, 2000). 'Low tar' cigarettes are perceived to be less dangerous than regular cigarettes (38% of light and mild (L&M) smokers believe that L&Ms are healthier for them than regular cigarettes, BMRB International Research, July 2003, total sample: smokers, pre-stage (480)) and as such offer a way for smokers to continue their habit whilst reducing the risks associated with smoking. In reality 'low tar' cigarettes offer no significant health benefit. Tests of L&M cigarettes show that smokers are as likely to inhale as much tar and nicotine from 'low tar' cigarettes as they would if they smoked regular cigarettes (*Nicotine yield from machine-smoked cigarettes and nicotine intakes in smokers: Evidence from a representative population survey*, Martin Jarvis, Richard Boreham, Paola Primatesta, Colin Feyerabend and Andrew Bryant).
20. Multiquitters are defined as smokers who have tried but failed to give up three or more times.

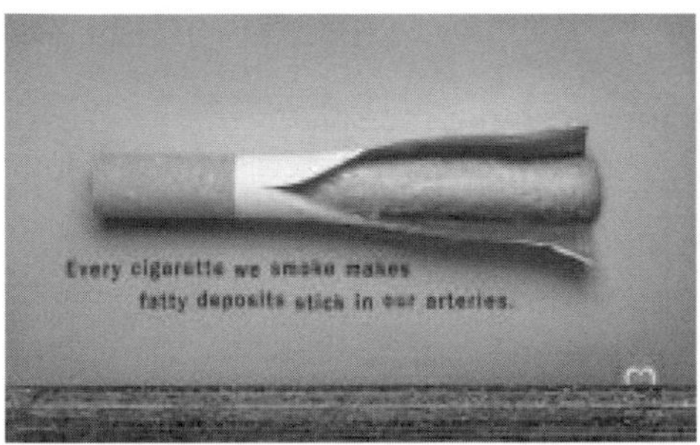

Figure 9

sees a cigarette they can't help but think of the fat collecting in their arteries – a so-called 'Pavlovian' response.

COMMUNICATION ACTIVITY

Stage 1 – The importance of constant presence

Learning from international campaigns demonstrates the importance of a constant media presence to continually motivate smokers to give up and stay given up.[21] Since its launch in December 1999, the campaign has had a consistent presence. By the end of March 2003 a total of £28m had been deployed and the campaign had been active across 44 of 53 months.

Stage 2 – Amplifying additional triggers

In 2003, the budget was broadened to support the additional triggers (Figure 10).

But the strategy had to deliver more than just presence. We had to communicate to smokers in fresh and challenging ways. There were two main imperatives:

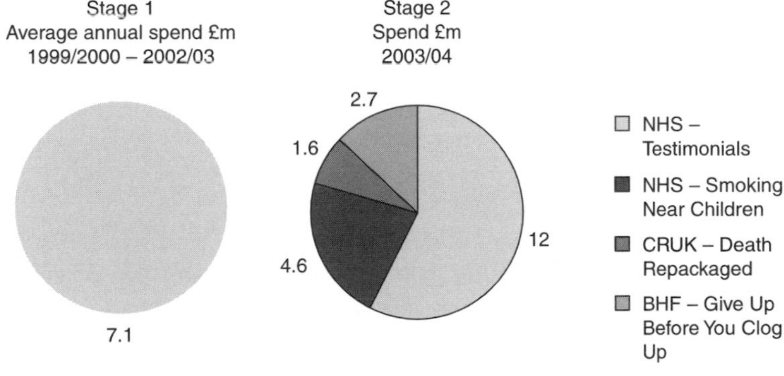

Figure 10: *Advertising spend 1999–2004*
Source: PHD/COI Communications

21. WHO Report 2001: Smoking Cessation Media Campaigns From Around The World: Recommendations from lessons learned 'A strong, ongoing media presence should be maintained. Asking an individual to change behaviour requires repeated conversations and support.'

1. Get the campaign issues talked about, whilst maximising visibility through integration across all channels.
2. Hothouse key 'launch' periods through up-weighting the spend levels.

RESULTS

Section A – Success of individual strands

In this section we will look at the performance of each individual strand of communication, demonstrating how they all achieved excellent levels of awareness and communication that have changed behaviour.

Foundation Health Reasons – Testimonials (2002–2003)[22]

Awareness

The testimonial campaign has built up incredible awareness over time with almost total penetration at 93% recognition (3% of households don't have television) – (Figure 11).

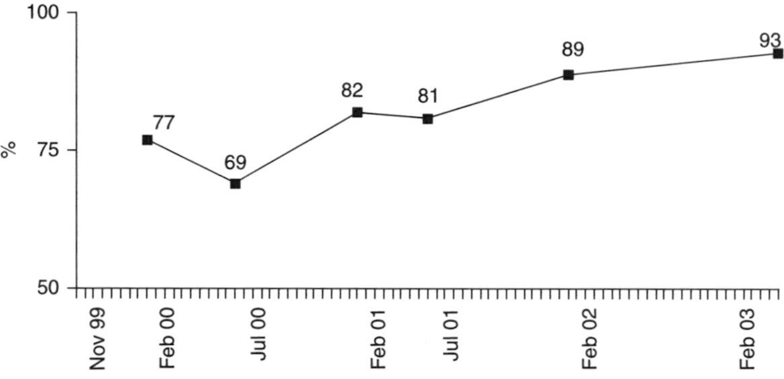

Figure 11: *Recognition of testimonial campaign*
Base: Smokers – sample varies by wave (n = *c*.1500) per wave
Source: BMRB Tobacco Education Campaign Tracking Study

Communication

Over the course of the campaign, testimonials have shifted a wide range of attitudes[23] (Figure 12).

22. Effectiveness data in this section is based on the period 1999–2003, because during this time testimonials ran exclusively so all the tracking data relates to the 'pure' effect of testimonials. The latest tracking (February 2004) reports the combined effect of the testimonials and other strands.
23. Key communication questions only added to tracking study from February 2001.

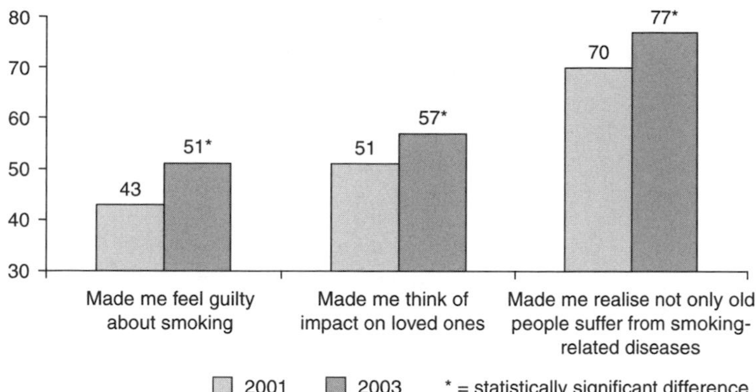

Figure 12: *Key communication – testimonials*
Base: Smokers 2001 (n = 480), 2003 (n = 1275)
Source: BMRB Tobacco Education Campaign Tracking Study

Outcome

The number of smokers who claim to have taken action as a result of seeing the advertising has almost doubled from 33% in 2000[24] to 50% in 2003, with the majority of smokers claiming to have discussed giving up with friends, family, their GP or having cut down (Figure 13).[25]

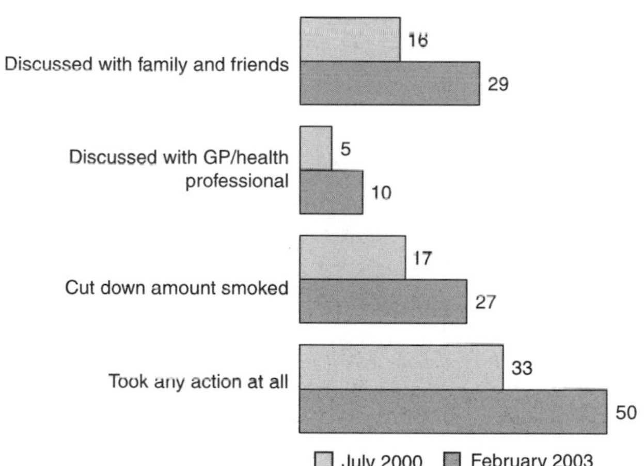

Figure 13: *Percentage taking each action as a result of seeing advertising*
Base: Smokers who saw adverts July 2000 (n = 992) *vs* February 2003 (n = 1113)
Source: BMRB Tobacco Education Campaign Tracking Study

During the campaign period there has also been a statistically significant shift in the number of smokers moving out of pre-contemplation (where they have no plan to give up, down by 7 ppts to 64%) and into action (where they are giving up, up by 4 ppts to 8%), effectively doubling the number of 'giver-uppers' (Figure 14).

24. 'Action taken as a result of advertising' only added to the tracking study in July 2000.
25. The Prochaska model is a psychological behavioural change model based on the premise that giving up smoking is a 'process' that smokers need to move through.

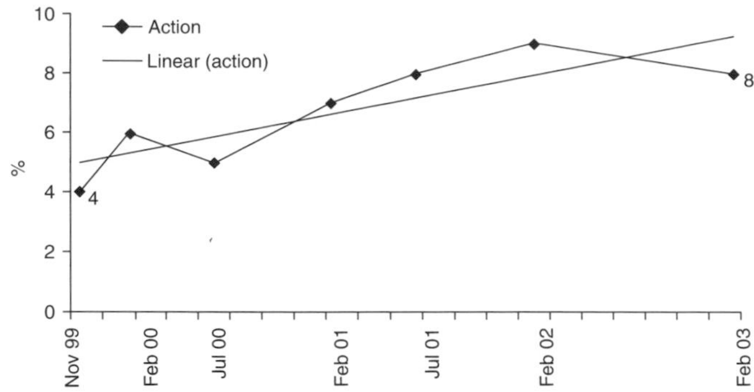

Figure 14: *Percentage of smokers in 'action' phase*
Base: Smokers – sample varies by wave (n = *c.*1500) per wave
Source: BMRB Tobacco Education Campaign Tracking Study

New reason 1 – NHS Smoking Near Children campaign (2003)

Awareness

After the first burst of advertising, total campaign recognition was a remarkable 83%, this rose to near universal recognition of 90% following the second burst of advertising.[26]

Communication

Tracking data shows that the ads worked by educating people about the dangers of second-hand smoke to children's health, and then made smokers and non-smokers alike alert to their duty to protect children (Table 1).

TABLE 1: KEY COMMUNICATION – SMOKING NEAR CHILDREN

	Peak score (%)
Made me realise kids can be affected by SHS*	80
Made me feel guilty smoking around kids†	62
Made me feel I should encourage partner/friends not to smoke around kids‡	69

Base: Varies – some asked to all (*n = c.1600), others current smokers only (†n = c.675), others non-smokers only (‡n = c.925)
Source: BMRB Smoking Kids Campaign evaluation (pre-advertising and two post-advertising waves conducted)

Outcome

Prior to the campaign launch only 28% of people saw second-hand smoke as a health risk to children – far behind traffic fumes and pollution. Following the advertising, second-hand smoke was seen as the number one danger with over half of respondents (56%) mentioning it spontaneously (Figure 15).

There has also been a significant uplift in the number of people banning smoking in the home from 45% to 49% (Figure 16).[27]

26. Source: BMRB Smoking Kids Campaign Evaluation (pre-advertising and two post-advertising waves conducted). Base: all respondents: July 2003 (n = 1546), September 2003 (n = 1608), January 2004 (n = 1591).
27. The shift in absolute number terms may appear small but it is statistically significant and to see an actual behaviour shift after such a short period of advertising is remarkable.

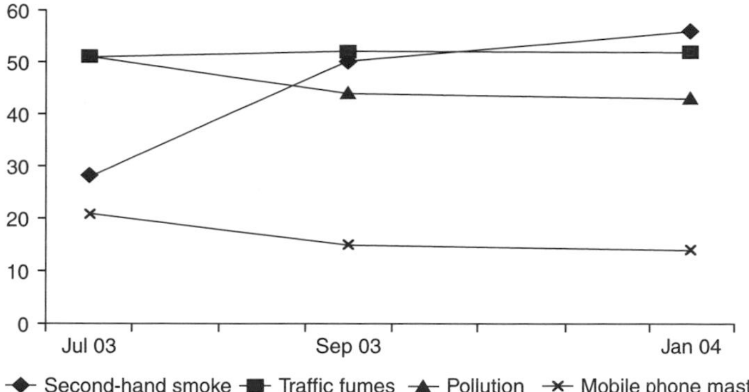

Figure 15: *Spontaneous awareness of risks to children's health*
Base: all respondents: July 2003 (n = 1546), September 2003 (n = 1608), January 2004 (n = 1591)
Source: BMRB Smoking Kids Campaign evaluation (pre-advertising and two post-advertising waves conducted)

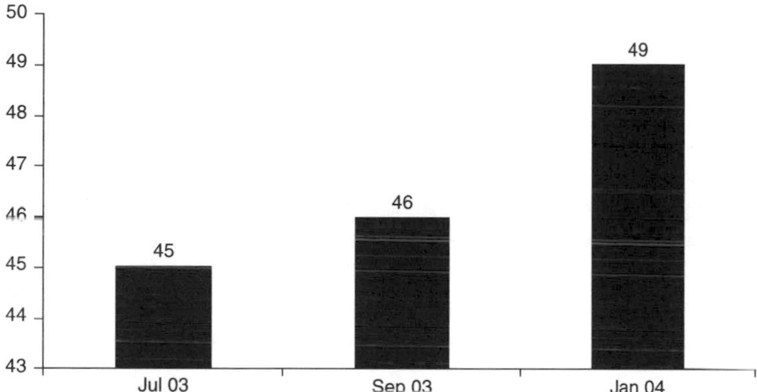

Figure 16: *Percentage of respondents banning smoking in the home*
Base: all respondents: July 2003 (n = 1546), September 2003 (n = 1608), January 2004 (n = 1591)
Source: BMRB Smoking Kids Campaign evaluation (pre-advertising and two post-advertising waves conducted)

New reason 2: Cancer Research UK Death Repackaged (2003)

Awareness

Following the first burst of advertising, total campaign recognition hit 76% and spontaneous awareness of advertising or publicity about the dangers of smoking low-tar/light cigarettes rose from 42% pre-advertising to 71% post-advertising, 19 percentage points above the target of 52%.[28]

Communication

Smokers had to believe the message before they would act on it. After less than a month of Cancer Research UK's campaign the number of believers had more than doubled, smashing their targets (Figure 17).

28. Source: BMRB Cancer Research UK Campaign Evaluation post-advertising wave (pre- and post-advertising waves conducted). Base: smokers: pre-stage (n = 480), post-stage (n = 526).

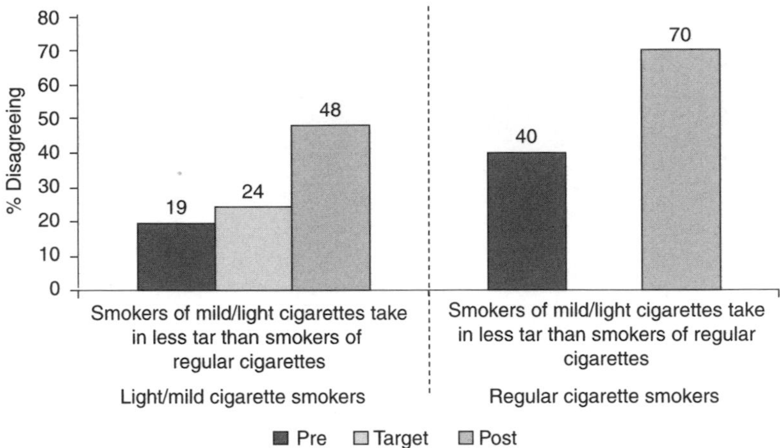

Figure 17: *Attitudes towards smoking mild/light cigarettes*
Base: smokers: pre-stage (n = 480), post-stage (n = 526)
Source: BMRB Cancer Research UK Campaign evaluation (pre- and post-advertising waves conducted)

Impact

Cancer Research UK branding increased the impact of communication; 67% of smokers agreed that the advertising 'really caught' my attention; but if smokers were aware it was from Cancer Research UK, 84% found it attention grabbing (Figure 18). This clearly shows the strength of using charities as an independent credible voice.

Cancer Research UK's 'Death Repackaged' created a PR explosion. MediaCom estimates that the PR was worth £1.5m, almost doubling our effective spend.

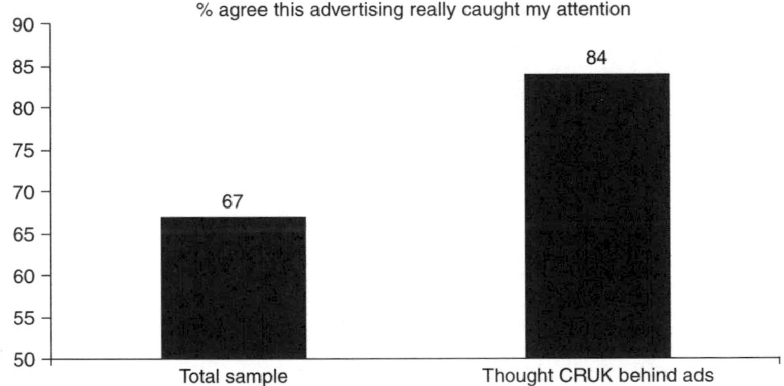

Figure 18: *Cancer Research UK branding drives impact*
Base: smokers post-wave (n = 526), smokers who think Cancer Research UK were behind ads (n = 89)
Source: BMRB Cancer Research UK Campaign evaluation post-advertising wave (pre- and post-advertising waves conducted)

Outcome

Over half of smokers took some form of action as a result of seeing the advertising (Figure 19).

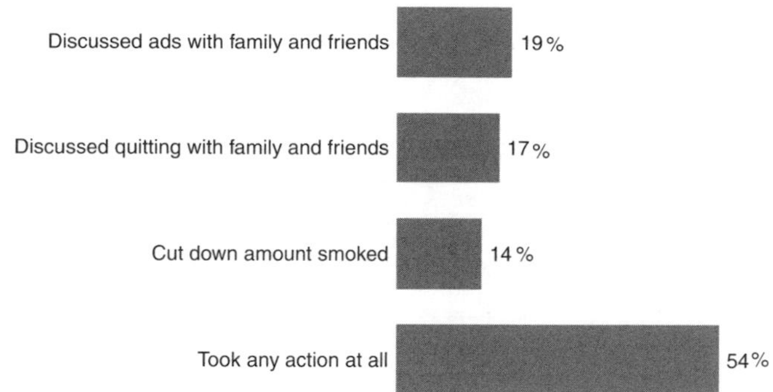

Figure 19: *Main action taken as a result of seeing advertising*
Base: smokers who saw adverts post-wave (n = 398)
Source: BMRB Cancer Research UK Campaign evaluation post-advertising wave (pre- and post-advertising waves conducted)

New Reason 3: BHF 'Artery' (January 2004)

Awareness

After only four weeks, total campaign recognition reached 94%.[29] The research agency concluded 'in our history, we have never seen any advert cut through so strongly. When you consider the TV ran for only one month it is all the more amazing.'[30]

The campaign cut through so strongly, the *Observer* was able to run a cartoon only 18 days into the campaign referencing 'fatty cigarettes' (Figure 20).[31]

Figure 20: Observer *cartoon, 18 January 2004*

Communication

A total of 43% of respondents spontaneously mentioned 'smoking clogs/makes fat stick in your arteries' as the main message of the campaign, with 98% agreeing that 'your heart can't work properly with clogged arteries' on prompting.[32] This

29. BHF tracking study, February 2004. Base: all respondents (508).
30. Helen Westwell, Hall & Partners, quoted in BHF press release, 30 March 2004.
31. This cartoon was one of over 250 articles in the press mentioning the campaign. The advertising was also discussed widely on TV and radio, gaining a mention on the Brits and receiving the second 'bong' on the ITV *News at 10* on New Year's Day. Total estimated value of the PR generated by the campaign is £895,000 (source: Metrica, MG OMD).
32. BHF Tracking Study, February 2004. Base: all respondents (150,508).

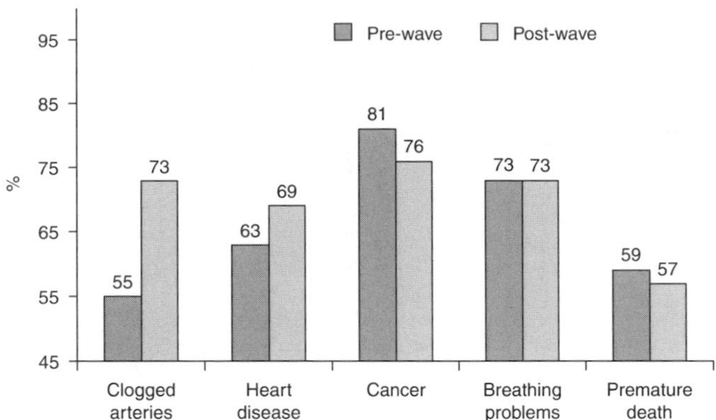

Figure 21: *Pre- vs post-comparison in awareness of the link between smoking and various health concerns*
Base: respondents (n = 150,508)
Source: BHF tracking study, February 2004

translated into increased knowledge of the link between smoking and heart disease, establishing how and why smoking causes heart disease by clogging arteries (Figure 21).

Outcomes[33]

- Over the course of the campaign, spontaneous concern about heart disease among smokers doubled from 10% to 21% (Figure 22).[34]

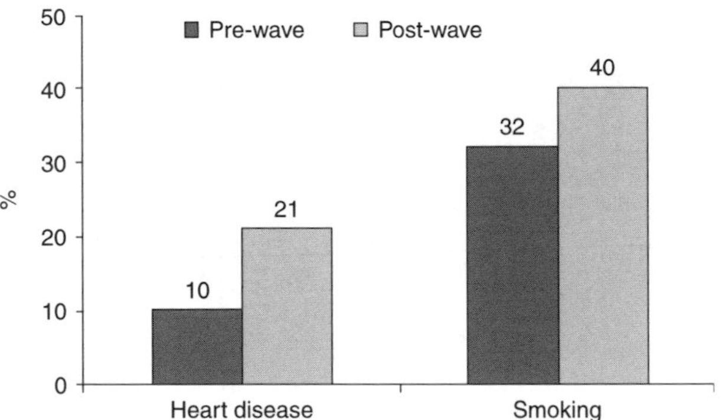

Figure 22: *Spontaneous health concerns of smokers pre- and post-campaign*
Base: all respondents (n = 150,508)
Source: BHF tracking study, February 2004

33. The campaign generated an extraordinarily rich and varied set of outcomes in addition to those described here, including: requests from teachers and health professionals for campaign materials that could be used as health education resources; playing a role in smoking prevention (65% of 11–15 year olds claimed they were less likely to start smoking as a result of the campaign – source BHF omnibus May 2004, base (100)); stimulating discussion about smoking between friends and family (95% of BHF staff and 40% of 11–15 year olds said they'd discussed the campaign with friends or family); being used by smokers as an aid to quitting to help overcome cravings ('every time I crave a cigarette I visualise the ad'); significantly enhancing perceptions of the BHF brand (source: BHF tracking study); strengthening relationships between the BHF and its corporate supporters (source: BHF head of corporate fundraising, Dez Timmiss, Marketing Director Cereal Partners); improving motivation among 80% of BHF staff (source: BHF internal staff survey); and increasing the perceived authority and salience of the BHF among journalists and MPs (source: BHF head of press and PR). As Peter Hollins, Director General of the BHF, concluded, 'marketing doesn't get any better or any more rewarding than this'.
34. Source: BHF Tracking Study, February 2004. Base: all respondents (150,508).

- Extreme concern about clogged arteries also increased significantly from 29% to 45% post-campaign.[35]
- 12,762 calls were made to the BHF helpline,[36] 83,650 visits were made to the BHF smoking microsite,[37] and 28,093 'Smoking and how to give up' booklets were distributed.[38]
- 46% of those who called the helpline claimed to have quit smoking at the time of calling. 34% of callers had still quit a month after the end of the campaign.[39]
- Some NHS primary care trusts reported up to a 25% increase in referrals to smoking cessation clinics as a direct result of the campaign.[40]
- Pavlovian responders[41] to the campaign were 42% (15 ppts) more likely than the total sample to claim to have quit, providing strong evidence that the campaign was responsible for triggering the claimed quit attempts (Figure 23).

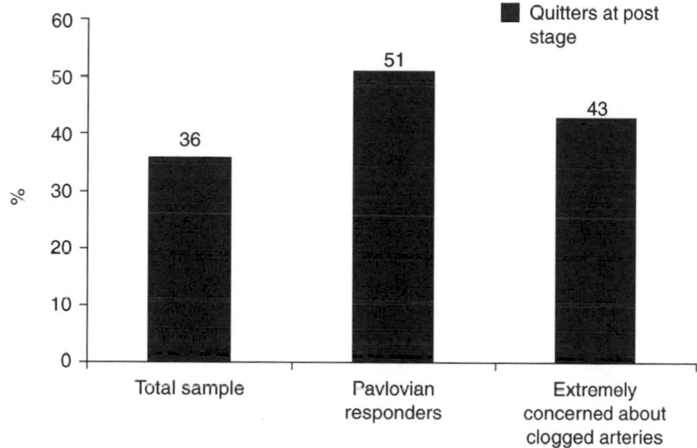

Figure 23: *Percentage of claimed quitters by sub-group*
Base: all respondents (n = 508), Pavlovian respondents (n = 150)
Source: BHF Tracking Study, February 2004

Section B – The total advertising effect

We have looked at the strands in isolation; we will now look at the multiple effect of integrating advertisers.

In this section we will show how advertising has grown to become the most important influence on smokers: how parallel strands have had a complementary but also additive effect, so that the whole is even greater than the sum of its parts.

35. Source: BHF Tracking Study, February 2004.
36. The helpline number was only publicised via the campaign, so virtually all the calls were a direct result of the campaign; 90% of calls to the helpline were from multiquitters and 60% were from C2DEs, indicating that the campaign worked hardest among its bullseye target.
37. In January 2004, traffic to the main BHF website doubled year on year, making bhf.org.uk the second most visited healthcare website in the UK after breastcancer.org.uk.
38. Source for all statistics is BHF internal data.
39. BHF helpline evaluation, March 2004.
40. North Birmingham PCT reported a 25% uplift attributable to the campaign; Fylde PCT saw a 20% increase with 60% of smokers specifically mentioning the campaign as a trigger. Swindon PCT even issued a press release (3/2/04) stating that 98% of smokers contacting their cessation service cited the campaign.
41. This is the group identified in the tracking that on being shown an image of a cigarette and asked what it brings to mind, responded with 'fatty cigarettes', 'clogged arteries', etc. In other words, the group amongst whom the campaign has worked hardest and literally created a 'Pavlovian response'.

Finally we will look at how this strategy has driven behaviour change.

Multiple strands have made advertising the most important influence

Advertising is now the biggest prompt for smokers to give up smoking
A total of 32% of smokers claim it prompted them to quit (uplift of 10 ppts from 22% in 2003 – five times greater than uplift of the previous year).

Previously 'something said by GP' or by 'friends and family' have always outperformed advertising. Now advertising is the biggest trigger, more powerful than personal or professional advice (Figure 24).

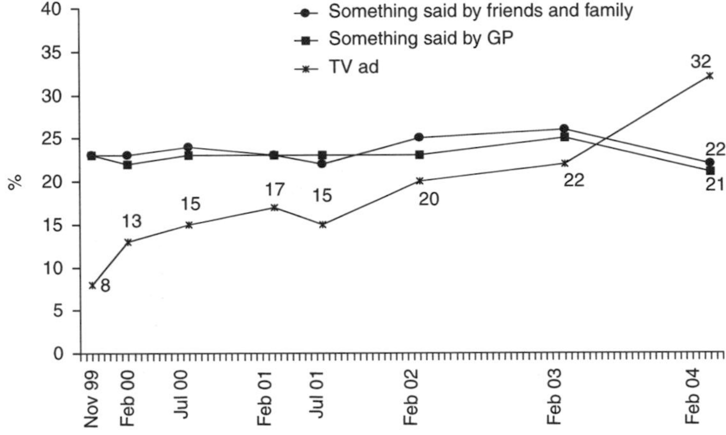

Figure 24: *Prompts for quit attempts (prompted)*
Base: ever tried, currently trying or gave up in past six months – base varies by wave (n = *c*.900)
Source: BMRB Tobacco Education Campaign Tracking Study

Multiple strands have broadened and deepened the reach of advertising

Broadening the reach of advertising
Spontaneous awareness of anti-smoking advertising is the highest it has ever been (Figure 25). Importantly, spontaneous awareness of advertising has improved significantly amongst harder-to-reach manual smokers (DEs) where prevalence is highest.[42] In February 2004 spontaneous awareness amongst DEs rose 32%, against 20% uplift among ABs (Figure 26). Previously they had grown at a similar rate.

We believe this broader reach has been achieved because individual strands have significantly greater empathy and impact among specific discrete groups, so collectively we have reached more smokers (Table 2).[43]

---

42. Prevalence amongst manual groups is 31% versus 20% for non-manual groups (source: GHS, 2002).
43. Absolute scores for each advert are not directly comparable because the timing of the February 2004 (wave 8) tracking favours some campaigns over others – BHF ran directly prior to this wave of tracking whereas, for instance, CRUK ran four months prior.

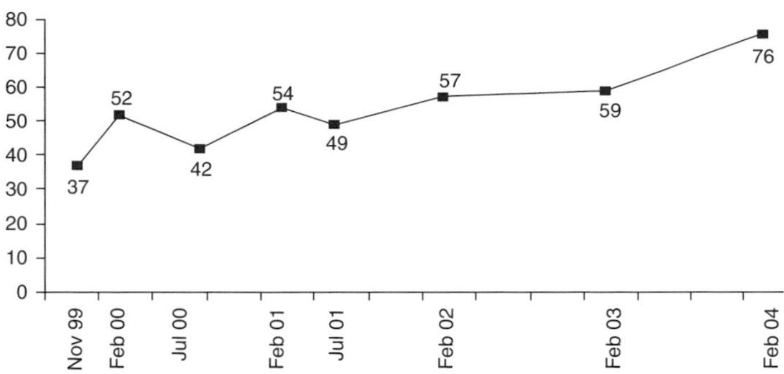

Figure 25: *Spontaneous awareness of anti-smoking advertising*
Base: smokers, sample varies by wave (n = *c*.1500) per wave
Source: BMRB Tobacco Education Campaign Tracking Study

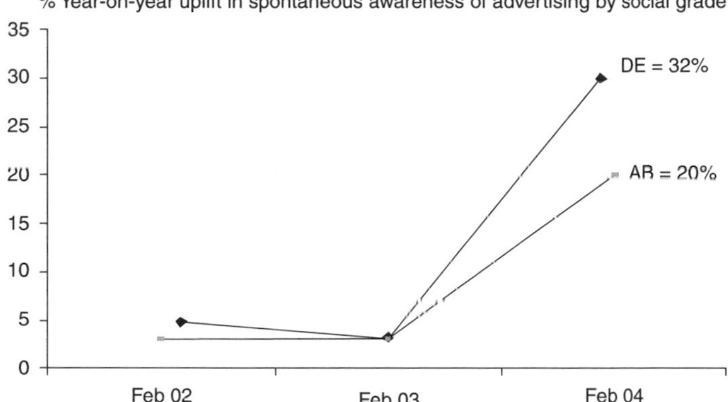

Figure 26: *Advertising has been particularly salient amongst hard-to-reach groups*
Base: smokers: February 2002 (n = 1252), February 2003 (n = 1275), February 2004 (n = 1078)
Source: BMRB Tobacco Education Campaign Tracking Study

TABLE 2: RECOGNITION AND COMMUNICATION OF THE DIFFERENT STRANDS

	Percentage agree total sample	Percentage agree discrete group	
Recognition			
Testimonial (Janice)	79	88	F 45+ years*
Cancer Research UK	44	53	F 16–24 years
Smoking Near Children	80	89	F 25–44 years*
Aimed at people like me			
Testimonial (Janice)	64	76	45–54 years*
Smoking Near Children	56	65	F 16–24 years*
		66	F 25–44 years*
Made me think about own health			
Testimonial (Jak)	29	43	Non-white*
BHF	64	73	25–34 years*

* Stat. sig. difference
Base: smokers shown adverts, February 2004: Janice (n = 572), Jak (n = 506), SHS Kids/CRUK/BHF (n = 1078)
Source: BMRB Tobacco Education Campaign Tracking Study, February 2004

Deepening reach of advertising
Integrating advertisers allows us to reach more smokers with more messages, increasing the number of reasons to give up.

For example, Janice and BHF make smokers think about their own health and body, whereas Smoking Near Children makes smokers feel guilty (Table 3). *Importantly all this has been achieved without victimising smokers.*

TABLE 3: DIAGNOSTIC SCORES INDEXED AGAINST AVERAGE FOR ALL CAMPAIGNS

Campaign strand	Made me think about own health	Made me feel guilty
Janice	132	101
BHF	193	108
Smoking Near Children	51	192

Base: smokers shown adverts, February 2004: Janice (n = 572), SHS Kids/BHF (n= 1078)
Source: BMRB Tobacco Education Campaign Tracking Study, February 2004

Using other 'voices' has helped us to deliver more messages without victimising smokers. This was supported qualitatively in a review of advertising messages in 2004:

> 'Perhaps surprisingly, very few smokers seem resistant to the broadcasting of anti-smoking advertising, and almost all feel such advertising is on the increase.'[44]

It is also supported quantitatively. Agreement with the statement, 'These days smokers are under too much pressure to give up', has remained static since the beginning of the campaign, despite increased media spend (Figure 27).

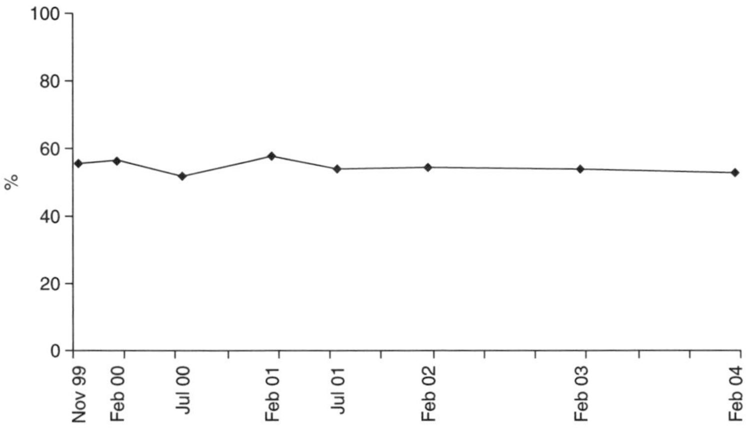

Figure 27: *Percentage agreeing 'These days smokers are under too much pressure to give up'*
Base: smokers, sample varies by wave (n = *c*.1500) per wave
Source: BMRB Tobacco Education Campaign Tracking Study

44. CRD Qualitative, 2004.

Integrating advertisers creates a greater manifold effect
Multiple voices are not only complementary, but additive. They build momentum and word of mouth, fuelling intention to give up smoking. We can prove that the multiplier effect works harder than single campaign strands by looking at how smokers' attitudes are affected by advertising according to the number of strands they have seen.[45] Analysis shows that the profile of smokers who have seen one or two strands versus all strands is statistically the same, so we are not seeing a 'usage pull' effect of 'giver-uppers' recognising more strands.[46] Smokers who have seen more strands have significantly higher awareness of smoking-related diseases (Figure 28).

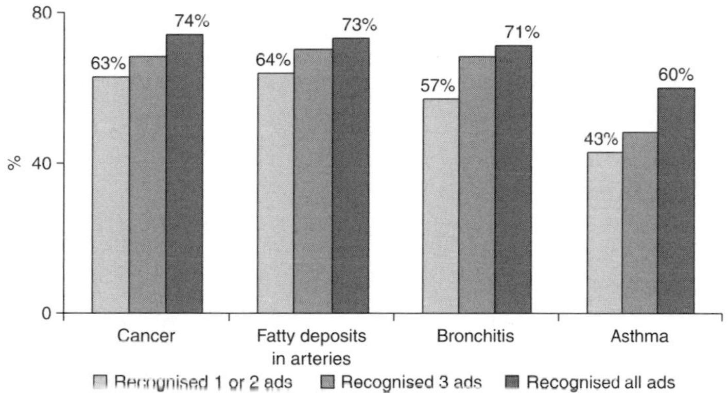

Figure 28: *Diseases smokers think can be caused by smoking (prompted)*
Base: smokers (n = 1078): seen one or two adverts (n = 380), seen three (n = 289), seen all (n = 341)
Source: BMRB Tobacco Education Campaign Tracking Study, February 2004

They are also more likely to think that 'more and more people are giving up smoking these days' and to have a stronger desire to quit (Figure 29).

The *integration of advertisers* also appears to fuel the smoking debate. Smokers who have seen multiple strands are more likely to discuss advertising with their family and friends (a key prompt to quitting). They are also more likely to take action (Figure 30). They are more likely to have heard of the NHS Smoking

45. In February 2004, five adverts were tested as part of a BMRB tracking study: testimonials (Janice and Jak), BHF, CRUK and Smoking Near Children – multiplier effect is determined by comparing the scores of those smokers who have seen only one or two of these ads (380 = 35% of smokers) versus those who have seen all of them (341 = 31%) or three of them (289 = 27%). Campaigns are distributed evenly throughout the three groups.
46. We have split the sample according to smoking status and have cross-tabulated this against seen one or two/seen three/seen all and there is no statistically significant difference between the groups. This suggests that the multiplier effect we are seeing is genuine, rather than a result of more 'keen to quit' smokers recognising all strands of advertising. There is no 'usage pull' effect.

	Total sample	Seen 1 or 2	Seen 3	Seen All
Unweighted total	1078	272	402	347
Weighted total	1078	289	380	341
Currently trying to give up	10%	8%	11%	10%
Tried to give up in the past	61%	62%	61°/a	65%
Have never tried to give up	20%	22%	16%	19%
Recent ex-smokers	9%	8%	13%	7%

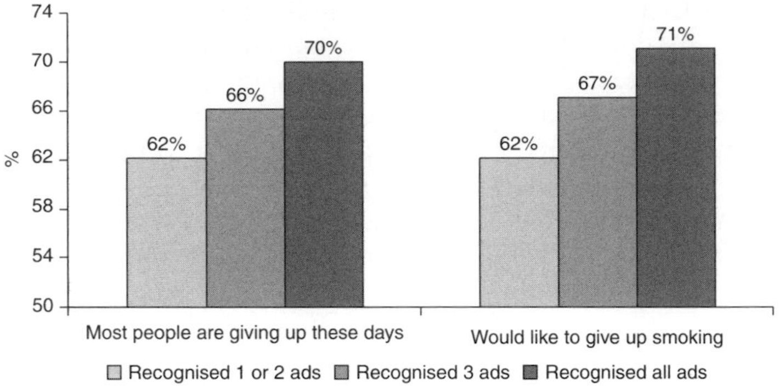

Figure 29: *Attitudes to smoking*
Base: smokers (n = 1078): seen one or two adverts (n = 380), seen three (n = 289), seen all (n = 341)
Source: BMRB Tobacco Education Campaign Tracking Study, February 2004

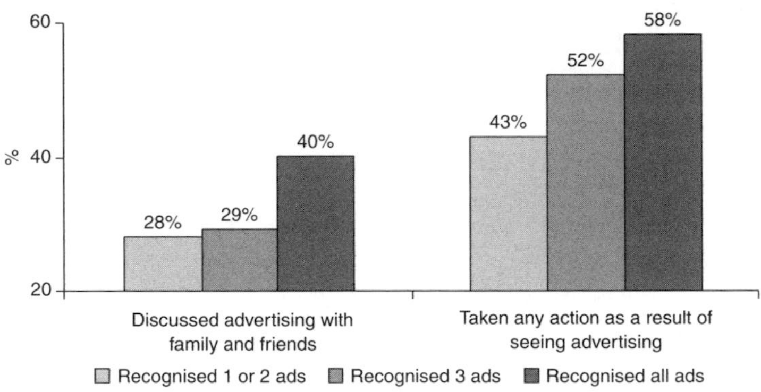

Figure 30: *Impact of advertising*
Base: smokers (n = 1078): seen one or two adverts (n = 380), seen three (n = 289), seen all (n = 341)
Source: BMRB Tobacco Education Campaign Tracking Study, February 2004

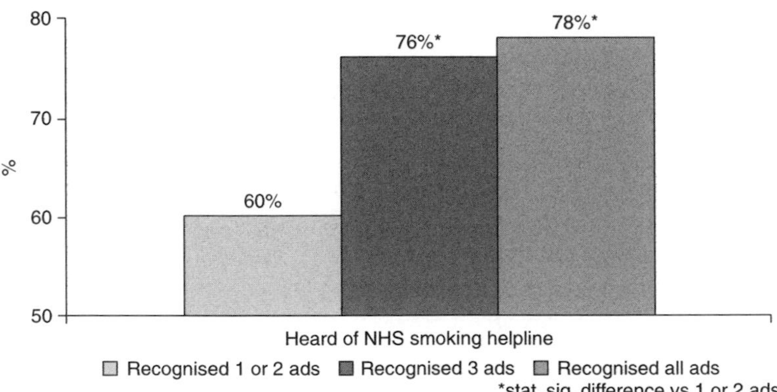

Figure 31: *Awareness of the NHS Smoking Helpline*
Base: smokers (n = 1078): seen one or two adverts (n = 380), seen three (n = 289), seen all (n = 341)
Source: BMRB Tobacco Education Campaign Tracking Study, February 2004

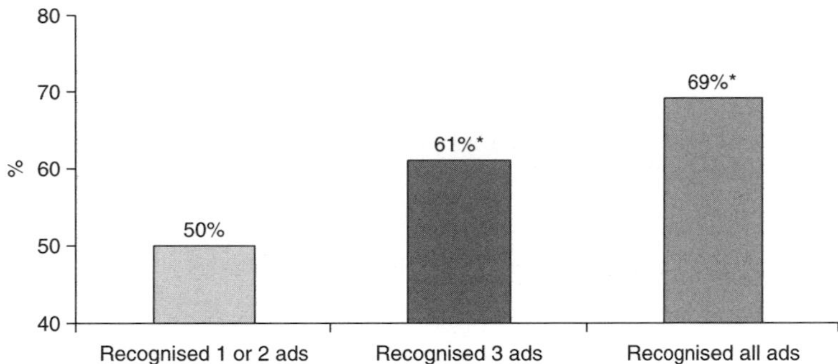

Figure 32: *Consideration for NHS Stop Smoking services*
Base: smokers (n = 1078): seen one or two adverts (n = 380), seen three (n = 289), seen all (n = 341)
Source: BMRB Tobacco Education Campaign Tracking Study, February 2004

Helpline (Figure 31), and are more likely to consider using the NHS Stop Smoking Services (Figure 32).

Advertising is driving strong behavioural change
There is strong evidence that the Government's long-term commitment to tobacco control advertising is working. We have two key pieces of behavioural change evidence.

1. Advertising is driving smokers to call the helpline to seek support.
2. Fewer people are smoking.

Advertising is driving more smokers to call the helpline
Calls to the helpline are hugely advertising-responsive – when we are on-air calls rise dramatically and decline in line with media spend (Figure 33).

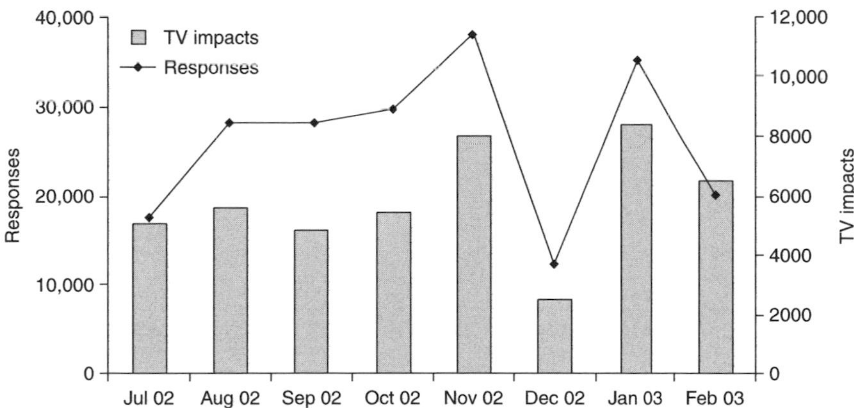

Figure 33: *Calls to the NHS smoking helpline vs TV impacts*
Source: COI Communications

Research among helpline callers also evidences advertising as the primary driver for calls:[47]

- 84% of those who called the helpline heard of it through TV advertising
- 52% claimed that TV advertising was the main reason they called
- 37% claimed it was the secondary reason.

The helpline received 369,583 calls in 2003/04, a year-on-year uplift of 54% (Figure 34). There have also been 320,000 website hits over the past two years.

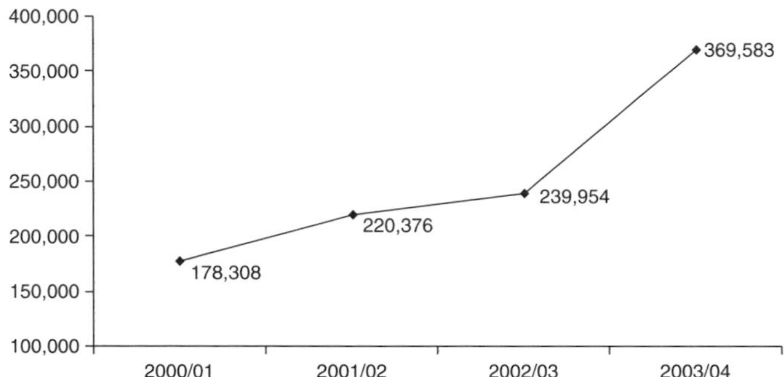

Figure 34: *Total calls to NHS smoking helpline*
Source: COI Communications

Fewer people in England smoke[48]

We have beaten the 2005 target set in 'Smoking Kills' three years early. Prevalence has dropped 2% since the start of the campaign, and was last measured at 26% in 2002,[49] an average fall of 0.4% per year.

We only have prevalence data prior to the new brand partnership. Rather than predicting that prevalence will mirror the exponential effect seen in other measures, we assume a further 0.4% fall as a conservative estimate. Predicted prevalence for 2003/04 is 25.6% (Figure 35).

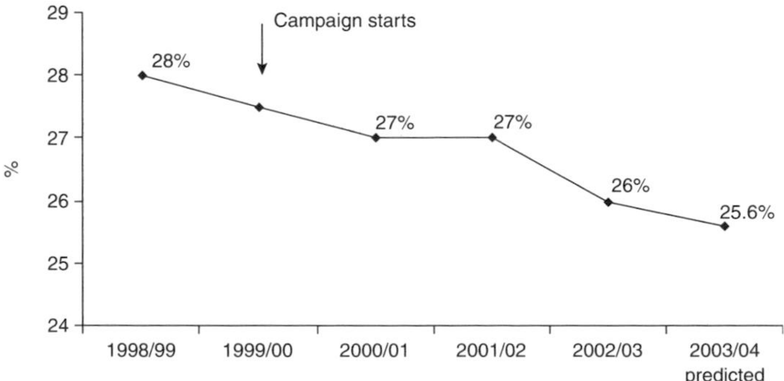

Figure 35: *Smoking prevalence*
Source: GHS

47. Source: Network Research, May 2003.
48. Smoking prevalence, which is the number of people who claim to smoke cigarettes nowadays, is measured annually in England via the General Household Survey; prior to 2000 the survey ran every two years.
49. Source: GHS. Target has been beaten as original 28% target was unweighted. GHS prevalence is now weighted (26% in 2002), equivalent unweighted prevalence would be 25%.

There are now 1.1 million fewer smokers in England.

In line with this drop in prevalence, there is also evidence that fewer cigarettes are being smoked. Sales of cigarettes are down year on year (Table 4).

- Consumption rates are in decline, down 6% from 105 billion cigarettes in 1999 to around 99 billion in 2003.[50]
- A further decline to 96 billion cigarettes is estimated for 2004.

TABLE 4: CIGARETTE CONSUMPTION RATES

Cigarette consumption (billion sticks)	1999	2003	Difference 1999–2003
UK duty-paid cigarettes	63	53.5	-15%
Non-UK duty-paid cigarettes	21	20	-5%
HRT cigarette equivalent	21	25	19%
Total consumption	105	98.5	-6%

Source: TMA/Mintel/National Statistics

WHAT ELSE CONTRIBUTED TO THE REDUCED NUMBER OF SMOKERS?

Since the start of the campaign, the greatest shift in prompts to give up smoking has been from advertising. Other factors act as prompts to giving up smoking (e.g. pack warnings, restrictions in the workplace and TV programmes/magazines), however their impact appears to have remained fairly static relative to the advertising effect (Figure 36). We shall now explore these and other factors in more detail.

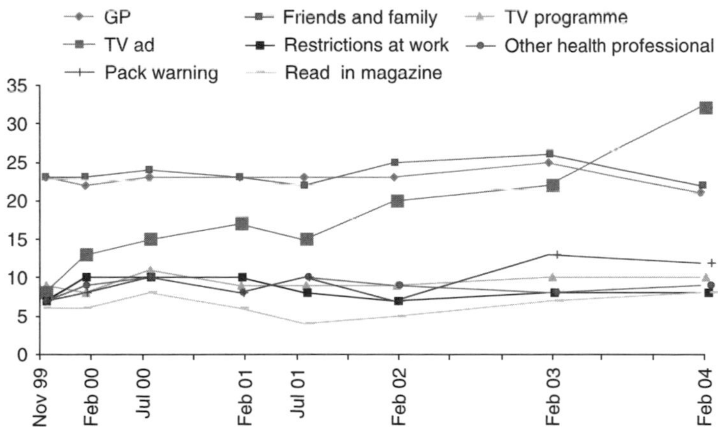

Figure 36: *Prompts to giving up smoking (prompted)*
Base: ever tried, currently trying or gave up in past six months – base varies by wave (n = *c.*900)
Source: BMRB Tobacco Education Campaign Tracking Study

50. Source: TMA/Mintel/National Statistics. This includes non-duty-paid cigarettes (smuggled and cross-border shopping) and hand-rolling tobacco (HRT).

Other DH Tobacco Control policy action designed to work in conjunction with communications

Advertising ban on secondary media

This was introduced in February 2003 and is expected to reduce prevalence in the long term by decreasing uptake, so we can exclude this as a likely factor in reducing smoking prevalence over the period in question. Tobacco companies are still active in some sports sponsorship.[51]

NHS Stop Smoking Services

Services have generated over half a million quit dates and 300,000 successful quit attempts (Table 5).[52] As we have seen above (Figure 32), advertising plays an important role in driving consideration for the services.

TABLE 5: SMOKERS USING NHS STOP SMOKING SERVICES

	2000/01	2001/02	2002/03	2003/04
Number of people setting a quit date through NHS Stop Smoking services	132,544	227,335	234,855	–
Number of people successfully quitting after four weeks (self-report)	64,554	119,834	124,082	–
Success rate	49%	53%	53%	–

– = results not yet available

Source: DH Statistical Bulletin on Smoking Cessation Services in England

The increased size of cigarette packet warnings

From December 2002 manufacturers have been required to produce new packaging with larger labelling.[53] Our campaign is designed to complement this activity. The strapline for 'Smoking Near Children' echoes the label warning 'Protect children. Don't make them breathe your smoke' and the label featuring the helpline number acts as another call to action. Currently 12% of smokers claim that the labels were a prompt to quitting – an uplift of 70% over the campaign period versus a 400% uplift for advertising (Figure 37).[54]

An increase in workplace bans

The introduction of workplace bans does drive intentions to quit. However, over the campaign period the number of smokers citing restrictions at work as a prompt to quitting has remained static at around 8% versus a 400% uplift for advertising (8% to 32%) (Figure 38).[55]

51. Sponsorship for exceptional global events will only be allowed until July 2005.
52. Source: DH Statistical Bulletin, 'Statistics on smoking cessation services in the England, April 2002 to March 2003' – successful quit attempt is at four-week stage; 75% of those setting a quit date received NRT, which was made available free on prescription in April 2001. Source: National Statistics Statistical Bulletin, 2003.
53. All old labelled cigarette packs were phased out by October 2003.
54. BMRB Tracking Study, February 2004.
55. BMRB Tracking Study.

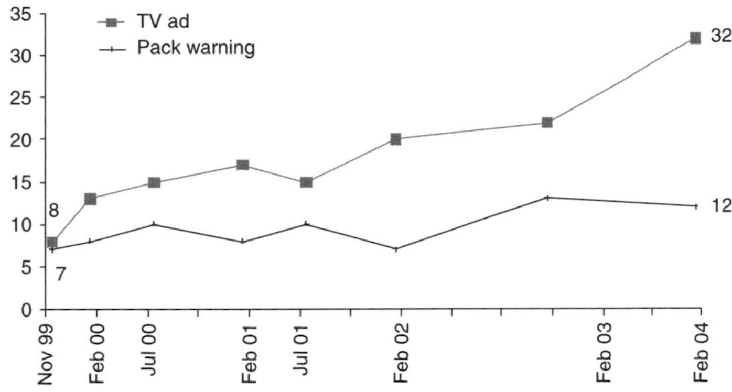

Figure 37: *Prompts to giving up smoking (prompted)*
Base: ever tried, currently trying or gave up in past six months – base varies by wave (n = *c*.900)
Source: BMRB Tobacco Education Campaign Tracking Study

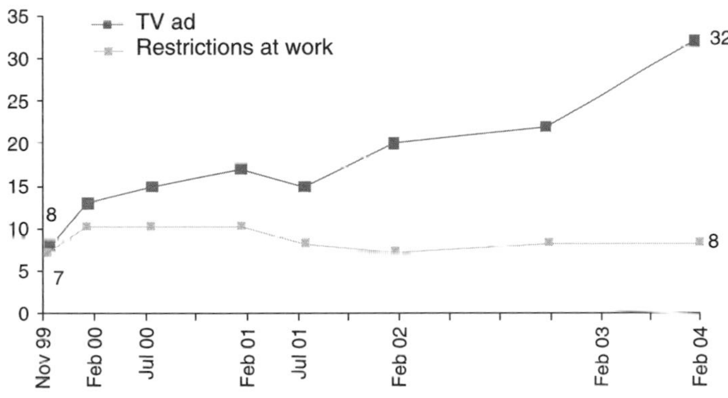

Figure 38: *Prompts to giving up smoking (prompted)*
Base: ever tried, currently trying or gave up in past six months – base varies by wave (n = *c*.900)
Source: BMRB Tobacco Education Campaign Tracking Study

NRT available on prescription

NRT was made available on prescription in April 2001. The following year saw an uplift in NHS costs from £15.6m in 2000/01 to £28.9m in 2001/02.[56] NRT has been shown to double the chances of a smoker quitting successfully. We assume this has been a factor in reducing prevalence.

Other factors

The rising cost of smoking

Over the past five years there has been an increase in the cost of smoking in both cash (18%) and real terms (11%). However, relative to households' real disposable income, the increase in the cost of smoking has been more modest. The Affordability of Tobacco Index shows a 1.8% increase from 1999 to 2002.[57] Cost

56. DH Statistical Bulletin, November 2003.
57. Source: DH Statistical Bulletin, November 2003.

has also become a less motivating reason to quit: falling from 41% in 2000 to 28% in 2002 (when last measured).[58]

Effect of PR coverage

There has been extensive coverage of tobacco issues in the press over the past year but it does not appear to have been picked up more strongly by smokers. In 2003, 26% of smokers said they had seen/read/heard recent news stories about smoking and cigarettes, and this rose by only 2 ppts to 28% in 2004.[59]

There is also no evidence that coverage of other issues (for example, bans in Ireland and New York) has changed behaviour. Looking at prompts for quitting, 'TV programme' and 'article in magazine' have remained fairly static versus the 400% uplift in advertising (Figure 39).

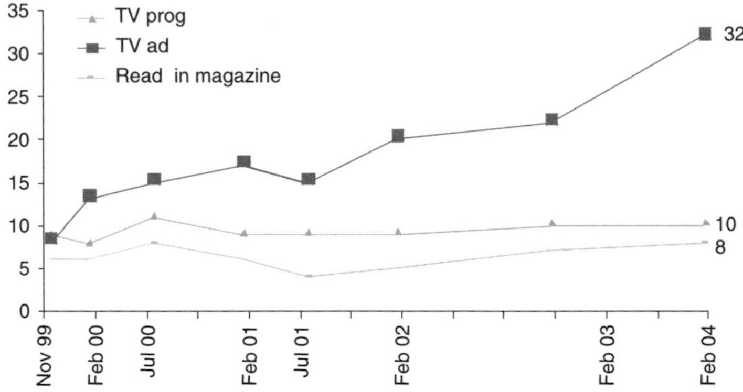

Figure 39: *Prompts to giving up smoking (prompted)*
Base: ever tried, currently trying or gave up in past six months – base varies by wave (n = *c*.900)
Source: BMRB Tobacco Education Campaign Tracking Study

NRT advertising

Advertising spend behind NRT has fluctuated across the five-year period but the overall trend has been downwards from £14.6m in 1999 to £7.9m in 2003.[60]

TOBACCO CONTROL ADVERTISING HAS MORE THAN PAID FOR ITSELF

- Advertising is now the biggest prompt to giving up smoking.
- Advertising is driving smokers to seek help giving up.
- Since the start of the campaign there has been a 2.4 ppt fall in smoking prevalence – an 8.6% reduction.

The intention of the Tobacco Control campaign is to save lives rather than create revenue, so traditional return on investment calculations are not appropriate.

58. Smoking Related Behaviour and Attitudes, ONS.
59. Source: BMRB Tobacco Education Campaign Tracking Study – question only asked for first time in 2003.
60. ACNielsen MMS.

However, the cost of smoking to individuals, the healthcare system and society is high. Any reduction in the number of smokers will deliver huge savings.

As we have seen, there are a multitude of factors that impact on a smoker's decision to quit. While advertising is now the biggest prompt to giving up smoking, and has shown a 45%[61] uplift in 2003/04, we cannot isolate its impact. Rather we consider the savings to society made as a result of the entire Tobacco Control effort and determine:

- whether these savings cover the cost of DH advertising
- the proportion of smokers advertising would have had to influence in order to cover the costs.

Since the start of the DH campaign, there are 1.1 million fewer smokers:

- saving the NHS £129m[62]
- saving £13m by decreasing domestic risk of fire[63]
- saving 3.2 million working 'sick' days at a value of over £28m.[64]

These three points save the nation £170m.

'Nicotine Addiction in Britain'[65] points out the importance of understanding long-term savings by considering the 'human cost' of a life.[66]

- 120,000 people die each year from smoking-related illnesses.
- A 2.4% fall in prevalence is 10,284 lives saved.
- The human cost of saving of these lives is £6.9bn.[67]

In total over £7.1bn has been saved.

- £7.1bn savings clearly cover advertising costs.[68]

Given that advertising is now the biggest prompt for quitting, we could make lofty claims that advertising alone has been responsible for the savings, giving an ROI of 145:1.

---

61. Source: BMRB Tobacco Education Campaign Tracking Study, February 2004. Increase of 10 percentage points from 22% in 2003 to 32% in 2004 represents an uplift of 45%.
62. Source: Parrott, S., Godfrey, C., Raw, M., West, R. and McNeill, A. Guidance for commissioners on the cost-effectiveness of smoking cessation interventions. *Thorax* 1998; 53 (Suppl 5, Part 2). It is estimated that smoking-related illness costs the NHS £1.5 billion every year. An 8.6% reduction in prevalence gives savings of £129m.
63. Source: Buck, D. and Godfrey, C. Helping smokers give up: guidance for purchasers on cost effectiveness. Health Education Authority. It is estimated that fires caused by smoking cost £150m a year (excluding cost of human life). An 8.6% reduction is a saving of £12.8m.
64. Source: Buck and Godfrey, *op. cit.*, note 63. It is estimated that 34 million working days are lost due to smoking-related illness costing £328m. An 8.6% reduction saves 2.9 million working days and £28.1m.
65. Royal College of Physicians, 2000.
66. Source: Department of Transport, Highways Economic Note No 1, 1997. Human cost represents the pain, grief and suffering to the casualty, relatives and friends, and, ... the intrinsic loss of enjoyment of life over and above the consumption of goods. This reflects the non-resource element of the total cost of the casualty and is calculated by subtracting the value of lost output and medical costs from the overall value for a fatality.
67. The human cost of a life saved is £680,590.
68. £7.1bn saved more than covers the £49.3m advertising spend.

However, we cannot categorically isolate the effect of advertising from the other tobacco control initiatives discussed above. But we can consider how many smokers advertising would have had to influence in order to cover costs.

Advertising would need to save 71 lives to cover costs[69]

The minimum advertising would have had to achieve to cover our costs would be to save 71 lives out of the 10,284 lives saved or to have been responsible for 7661 of the total 1.1 million fewer smokers.

SUMMARY

In today's world of ever expanding communication channels and media options, received wisdom tends to suggest that advertising is no longer as potent a force as it once was. Although there is clearly much to be said for this assertion, this case study is a good reminder that received wisdom is there to be challenged. The unique issues facing anti-smoking communications have required us not only to convert their role from information provider to service provider, but to consider advertising in an entirely new way; to integrate the advertisers, not just the advertising.

The complementary voices of Cancer Research UK, BHF and the NHS have created an additive effect: reaching more smokers, targeting them more closely, and giving them harder-hitting reasons to quit. We have found a new way to grow the smoking noise cloud without overwhelming smokers.

This study represents an unprecedented way of working together. An integrated partnership of advertisers that has collectively quadrupled effectiveness, making advertising the biggest prompt to giving up smoking.

69. The average 'cost' of a life is £697,000; 71 × £697,000 = £49.4m. This covers the £49.3m advertising spend.

GOLD

BEST PRESENTATION AND BEST NEW CLIENT

7

Virgin Mobile

In the red corner

How Virgin Mobile challenged the mobile phone establishment on behalf of the public

Principal authors: Tom Morton and Sherree Halliwell, Rainey Kelley Campbell Roalfe/Y&R
Media agencies: Good Stuff; Manning Gottlieb OMD

EDITOR'S SUMMARY

Virgin's launch into the mobile phone market is testament to two things: that even the most mature category can be disrupted by what we have come to describe as a challenger brand, and that positioning and branding alone are powerful commercial weapons.

Virgin was late to the mobile party, but delighted to find that the incumbent operators presided over a complex jungle of a market, one already offering the consumer over a million possible tariff options. Piggybacking One2One's existing network and selling its airtime under the Virgin brand, Virgin Mobile not only entered the market as a 'white knight' but as one that had only to focus on consumers and communications, rather than network issues.

Virgin Mobile's communication quickly established it as a simple and human alternative to the 'Big Four' networks, and the brand recruited two million customers in less than three years. Virgin's growth demonstrably outstripped the market, with share growing to 6.8% and revenue to £458m by end 2003.

Discounting other variables that could have grown the brand (price, distribution, etc.) the Virgin Mobile paper emphatically makes the case that it is advertising that has built the brand, and the brand that has built the business.

Indexing Virgin Mobile's performance against that of T-Mobile (the rebranded One2One), Virgin claims two million incremental brand-generated customers for its business. A textbook case of the commercial return from a challenger mentality.

INTRODUCTION

Challenger branding is a much discussed but little measured idea.[1] The notion that ambitious second-tier brands can achieve rapid growth by pursuing a radically different strategy from established brands is appealing (Morgan, 1999). Brands that pursue a challenger strategy, such as Absolut and Swatch, are sexier than defensive, dependable market leaders. And it's often more fun for marketers to work for the brand equivalent of the pirates than the navy.[2]

But can a challenger strategy ever take a brand beyond a fashionable niche? Are challenger advertising campaigns anything more than opportunist propaganda? And can a challenger brand create real commercial value? This study answers yes to all three questions.

It tells the story of Virgin Mobile's growth from a standing start into a £458m business,[3] with four million customers,[4] in just four years. It demonstrates how a challenger positioning, bought to life through advertising, can overcome the advantages of larger established competitors. It demonstrates how advertising can build a brand by mounting a challenge to an established market. It demonstrates how advertising kept Virgin Mobile growing as its market was slowing. And it quantifies the return from a challenger strategy by comparing Virgin Mobile's performance with the performance of a technically identical but differently branded rival. It is easy to talk about: 'Zigging where others zag'. This study puts a value on it.

MARKET OUTLINE: THE RISE AND RISE OF MOBILE TELEPHONY

Virgin companies work by challenging established industries on behalf of the consumer. So it is necessary to understand the mobile telephony establishment to appreciate Virgin Mobile's strategy and subsequent growth.

Mobile telephony is a big business dominated by big brands. Originally it was a business-focused duopoly, split between Cellnet and Vodafone. But the launch of new networks One2One (1993) and Orange (1994) began the democratisation of the market.[5] Initiatives such as per-second billing (1994), where networks stopped rounding up call charges to the nearest minute, and 'pre-pay' packages (1997), where customers bought airtime with vouchers rather than with monthly contracts, brought the cost of mobile ownership within the reach of the general public.

Networks began to see themselves as brands, building a name and a value around their otherwise intangible services. They invested heavily in brand advertising – £144m in 1999.[6] The endlines 'The Future's Bright, The Future's Orange' and 'Who Would You Like To Have A One2One With?' entered everyday

1. The WARC database of brand case studies contains 38 references to challenger branding.
2. Adam Morgan came up with this superb analogy to compare working for an ambitious challenger brand with working for a monolithic market leader.
3. Virgin Mobile's turnover was £458.3m in 2003. It recruited its four-millionth customer on 29 April 2004.
4. Virgin Mobile's customer base hit the four million mark on 29 April 2004.
5. This paper will refer to mobile networks by their names at the time. Cellnet became BT Cellnet in 1999 and O_2 in 2002; One2One rebranded as T-Mobile in 2002.
6. Source: MMS.

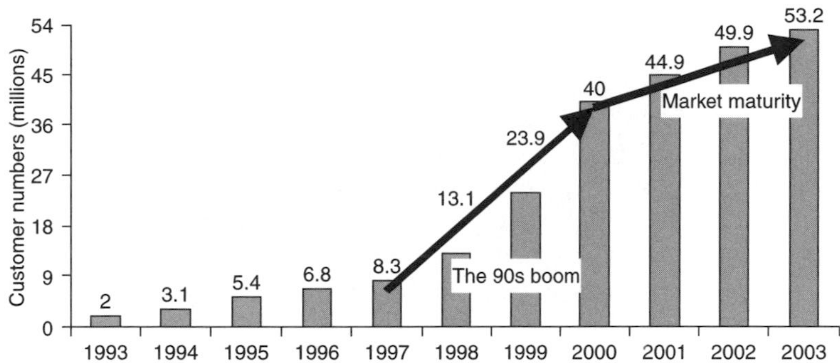

Figure 1: *The growth of mobile telephony in the UK*
Source: Oftel, company press releases

language.[7] The result was breathtaking growth, averaging 55% a year between 1994 and 2000.

More recently, market growth has slowed as the market approaches saturation. Latest estimates are that there are 53.2 million mobile phone accounts in Britain, equivalent to 90% of the population (Figure 1). Networks that once relied on market growth now concentrate on poaching high-spending customers from other networks, and developing new revenue streams such as text messaging.

IN AT THE DEEP END: VIRGIN ENTERS THE MOBILE MARKET

Virgin Mobile launched on 11 November 1999.

The logistical challenge

As a new entrant, Virgin faced a logistical challenge. How to acquire network capacity? Established players had built their networks over several years, at a cost of billions. Virgin answered the logistical challenge with a new business model.

Instead of building a physical mobile network, Virgin would piggyback One2One's existing network and sell its airtime under the Virgin brand. This virtual-network model enabled Virgin to avoid the capital commitment of building a network, and to focus on its core competence of packaging, marketing and servicing the end product.

The strategic challenge

How could Virgin carve a viable place out of an already competitive market? Again, Virgin's solution was to challenge convention. The growth and excitement of the market were marred by confusion and bad practice.

Southampton University estimated that Britain's four networks offered over one million possible tariff options. The market had evolved from a duopoly to what Scott Adams dubbed a 'confusopoly' (Adams, 1998). The jungle of prices and

7. Source: 'One2Many: How advertising affected a brand's stakeholders', IPA Effectiveness Awards Paper, 1998.

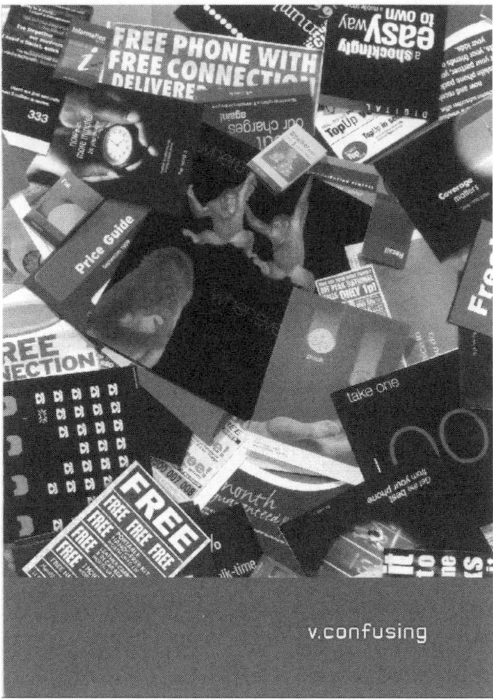

Figure 2: *The Confusopoly – myriad competitive offers, 1999*

promotions was so tangled that consumers could not see what they were paying or whether they were getting value (Figure 2).

Customers suffered from:

- endless different tariffs
- peak rates, so calls were dearer when customers wanted to make them
- line rental fees, unrelated to how many calls customers made
- contracts that tied customers in for 12 months, and
- extra charges for listening to voicemail.

Behind the corporate slogans, the future looked a lot less bright from a customer's point of view.

Send for the people's champion!

Virgin Mobile's opportunity was to enter the market as a white knight, bringing simplicity and humanity to a telephony market that had forgotten the poor customer during its relentless expansion. Virgin offered:

- one tariff
- no peak rates
- no line rental
- no contracts to tie customers in, and
- no hidden charges.

Sir Richard Branson encapsulated the offer at the brand launch:

> 'No catches. No line rental. No rip off. Virgin Mobile ... aims to bring its reputation as the consumer champion to this needlessly complex sector. However you look at it, mobile phone users have been bamboozled and short-changed.'
>
> Sir Richard Branson, 11 November 1999

THE MARKETING CHALLENGE: DAVID VERSUS FOUR GOLIATHS

Though the market was growing rapidly, there was no guarantee that a new entrant would succeed. Barriers to entry were high. Established operators had big budgets, tied-in customer bases and owned their own networks.

Virgin Mobile's £4.3m launch budget represented less than 3% of market spend. Since then, Virgin Mobile's annual share of voice has never exceeded 11.1% (Figure 3). Virgin could never hope to match the financial clout of its rivals, with their wealthy, publicly listed parent companies.[8]

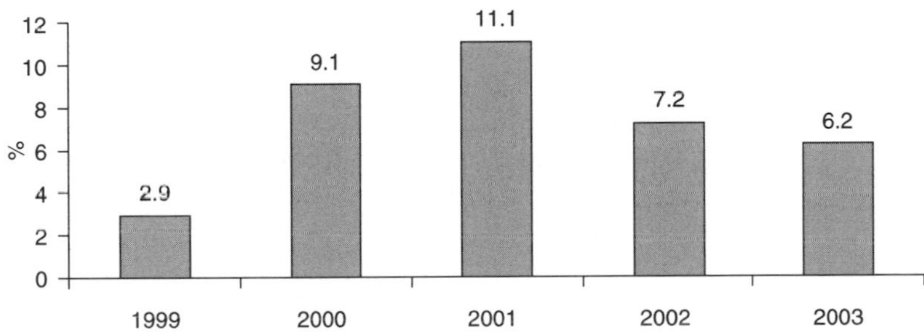

Figure 3: *Virgin Mobile's share of voice*
Source: MMS

Virgin Mobile had none of the distribution advantages of the established networks. They had all developed their own branded high-street outlets and were available through specialist mobile chains such as Carphone Warehouse (Table 1).

By contrast, Virgin had to rely on small concessions within Virgin Megastores and other Virgin retailers. It did not secure distribution in specialist chains until September 2001. A customer looking for a network would not have seen Virgin Mobile in a mobile phone store for the first two years of the brand's life.

Virgin Mobile lacked the product range of its rivals. This made Virgin easy for customers to understand, but equally easy for competitors to copy, which they all did. Orange even referred to its equivalent tariff as 'The Virgin Tariff'.[9]

If ever there was a case of out-thinking rather than out-spending the competition, this was it.

8. And those pockets were indeed deep. When Vodafone's share value peaked in March 2000, the company accounted for one-quarter of the value of the entire FTSE 100 (source: MSN Money).
9. Virgin successfully challenged this plagiarism through the Advertising Standards Authority.

TABLE 1: VIRGIN MOBILE MEASURES UP TO THE ESTABLISHMENT

1999	Establishment networks	Virgin Mobile
Customer base	23.9 million	None
Brand awareness	Average 98%	9% at launch
Advertising budgets	£144m	£4m at launch
Advertising approach	Generic, universal targeting, corporate-led	Spiky, young, customer-led
Distribution	Branded outlets, specialist retailers, independent dealers, direct sales to corporate accounts	Concessions in Virgin Megastores and Our Price
Customer relationships	Monthly contracts, pre-pay	No contracts
Tariffs	Multiple, ever-changing	One
Networks	Owned	None: airtime bought from One2One

VIRGIN MOBILE'S MARKETING OBJECTIVES

Virgin Mobile's overarching objective was to build its customer base. The company had to build a critical mass of customers if it was to be viable as a business. Indeed, the financiers of Virgin Mobile's launch made customer base size a condition of their loan covenants. The key measure of success was net new customer acquisitions.

As a challenger brand, Virgin Mobile had more particular marketing objectives. It had to establish why it was different to the other networks. Virgin Mobile's purpose was to rectify the shortcomings of the mobile market on behalf of the customer.

The brand launch brief stated the role for advertising was:

- to assert and evidence Virgin Mobile's differentness
- to provoke people to respond and find out more.

Four years later, the same role still applied.

VIRGIN'S STRATEGIC SOLUTION

Virgin Mobile developed its offer as a challenger to the market. It would develop its brand communication in the same way. The communications strategy was to leverage the conventions of the market on behalf of the public in order to demonstrate how it was appealingly different from the competition. This could mean:

- using communication to wake up the market
- highlighting bad practice and absurdities in the mobile market, or
- communicating an offer differently from the competition.

This strategy places a greater responsibility on advertising. It has to be more than a messenger for product news. Advertising has to:

- make room for Virgin Mobile in an already crowded market
- find a role for Virgin Mobile's one product in an ever-changing market
- draw the public's attention away
- offer a customer-friendly alternative, and
- be a shopfront for the brand.

When competitor advertising was often generic and soporific – Vodafone asking 'How Are You?' and O_2's blue-bubbled livery – Virgin advertising would be spiky and engaging.

And when rivals copied Virgin's tariff, advertising would keep it relevant and distinct.

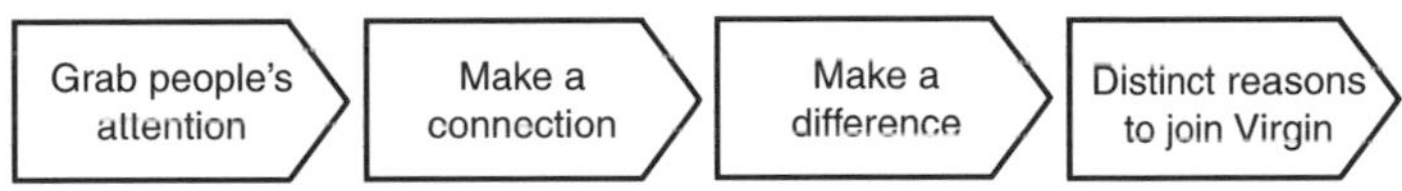

Figure 4: *Virgin Mobile's advertising model*

VIRGIN'S VS DIFFERENT ADVERTISING

Virgin Mobile advertised consistently from its launch. The highlights of Virgin's advertising history indicate how it challenged the establishment on behalf of the consumer (Figure 4).

Highlighting difference: the brand launch (November–December 1999)

The launch campaign proposition was: Virgin Mobile is reinventing everything you thought was fixed about mobile phones. The campaign consisted of a series of short films, each dramatising a different aspect of what made Virgin Mobile different. Endlines such as V. Different and V. Overdue created a cumulative sense that Virgin Mobile was taking on the market.

Stirring up the market: the Divorce campaign (2000)

Recruiting customers from other networks was a growth opportunity. But mobile users were either unaware that they could switch networks, or saw the process as a hassle. Consumers' ignorance benefited established networks. Virgin could enlighten them.

Virgin launched a campaign to educate the public about the ease of switching networks, in which a white-suited evangelist toured the country on a flatbed truck, encouraging customers to divorce their mobile networks by getting a Virgin Mobile SIM card. Virgin Mobile even took the Divorce roadshow to shopping centres and events around the country.

Stirring up the consumer: the See Red campaign (April–August 2001)

Virgin had always recognised customers' latent dissatisfaction with mobile networks. Virgin used advertising to convert latent dissatisfaction into active willingness to switch networks, with a TV and press campaign that dramatised people's anger at the bad practices of mobile networks. This challenge to the market resolved with the endline: 'See Red. Then See Virgin Mobile' (Figure 5).

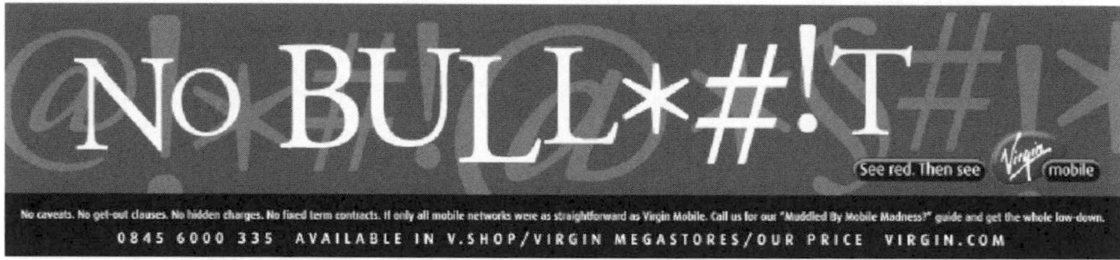

Figure 5: *This poster needs no explanation*

The campaign extended into a press insert of a poison pen letter from an irate customer to his network. In true challenger style, the insert was both one of the most complained about and most responded to advertisements of 2001.[10]

A people-driven strategy: targeting younger users (September 2001–present)

As market growth slowed, Virgin saw an opportunity to target younger mobile users in order to grow its business. Younger people made more calls and were more open to Virgin's no-contract, sold-in-record-stores proposition. Virgin switched its advertising and media budget to target people aged 16–24 in September 2001, thus becoming the first network for young people. Advertising would have to weave the brand into Britain's youth culture (Figure 6).

Figure 6: *Virgin Mobile enters youth culture – this campaign mimics celebrity gossip magazines*

10. Source: Advertising Standards Authority.

Challenging market convention: be careful what you sign (May 2002–March 2003)

Research showed that many younger customers reluctantly signed up to a contract package in order to get free minutes.[11] Virgin Mobile highlighted this dilemma with a TV campaign in which American rapper Wyclef Jean committed himself to a nightmarish trailer park marriage after absent-mindedly signing a contract. 'Be careful what you sign' warned the endline. 'With Virgin Mobile you can earn free minutes without signing your life away' (see Figure 7).

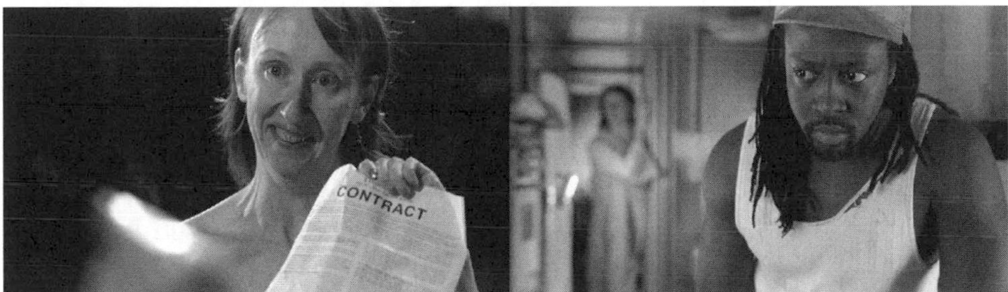

Figure 7: *Be careful what you sign – Wyclef Jean signs up to a trailer park marriage*

Using a rapper in a comedy role struck a chord with Virgin's younger audience. It contrasted the brand with establishment rivals, especially T-Mobile, which was using Andre Agassi and Steffi Graf to front a corporate rebranding campaign at the time.

Breaking communication convention: the Idle Thumbs campaign (May 2000 –present)

By 2003, text messaging had become the mobile market's competitive battleground. Networks attracted customers with spectacular headline rates. Virgin's own text proposition – text another Virgin Mobile for 3p[12] – was modest by market standards. But Virgin's insight was that rival networks created a blur of forgettable figures with their numbers-driven promotions. As the offers became more spectacular, the networks' reputation for good-value texts actually fell.[13] The customer-friendly solution was to make the offer memorable, rather than hammering home the price. Advertising would magnify it by making it resonate with people.

TABLE 2: TYPICAL TEXT MESSAGE OFFERS, 2003

Orange	6000 free texts when you buy direct; 1825 free texts
T-Mobile	500 texts a month
O_2	400 texts a month for just £16
Vodafone	50 free text messages a month

Source: company websites

11. Source: focus groups with young mobile users, 2CV Research, February 2002.
12. The typical cost of a text message on a pre-pay package is 10p.
13. The average score for rival networks on the brand measure 'Good value for texts' was 28% in August 2002 and 25% in April 2003.

Figure 8: *Busta Rhymes presses all the wrong buttons in the Idle Thumbs campaign*

The campaign idea was: 'The Devil Makes Work For Idle Thumbs. Keep Yours Busy. Text Another Virgin Mobile For 3p.' Virgin entertained its audience with executions across all media carrying the cautionary tale that your thumbs would get up to mischief if they were not occupied by Virgin's text offer. TV executions showed humorous scenarios where idle thumbs created mayhem. Most famously, American rapper Busta Rhymes almost flushes himself away when his thumb presses one button too many in the toilet of his LearJet, and he accidentally exposes himself when his thumbs head for the console controlling his hotel curtains (Figure 8).

Viral versions of each TV advert were distributed on the internet, and an interactive version of the Busta Rhymes adverts attracted 435,000 click-throughs on Sky Digital.

A summary of Virgin Mobile's advertising evolution is given in Table 3.

TABLE 3: VIRGIN MOBILE'S ADVERTISING EVOLUTION

Phase	The consumer challenge to the establishment	Creative solution	Annual spend[14]
1999 Brand launch	Changing what you think about the mobile market	V. Different	£4.3m
2000 Recruiting from other networks	It's actually easy to switch networks	Divorce	£15.7m
2001 Recruiting from other networks	You don't have to put up with the other networks' bad practices	See Red. Then See Virgin Mobile	£14.3m
2002 Attracting young people	Don't sign a contract if you want to earn free airtime	Be Careful What You Sign	£12.8m
2003 Attracting young people with text	No more blinding the public with figures	Idle Thumbs	£13.6m

Before looking at the commercial contribution of this advertising, we need to establish Virgin Mobile's commercial performance.

14. All media data is from MMS and is at ratecard.

VIRGIN MOBILE'S COMMERCIAL PERFORMANCE

Virgin Mobile enjoyed spectacular commercial growth.

Rapid business growth

Virgin Mobile achieved its objective of building a viable customer base. It recruited a million customers by June 2001 and two million by September 2002. So while it took Virgin Mobile 34 months to recruit two million customers, it took Orange 56 months, T-Mobile five years, and Vodafone and O_2 over ten years (Figure 9).[15]

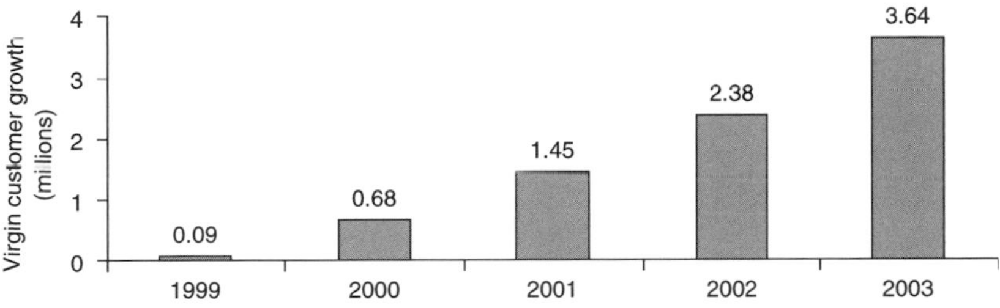

Figure 9: *Virgin Mobile customer growth*
Source: Virgin Mobile

Growth beyond market rates

Virgin's customer growth was not merely the result of market growth. Virgin's market share increased steadily, from 1.7% at the end of 2000 to 6.8% at the end of 2003 (Figure 10).

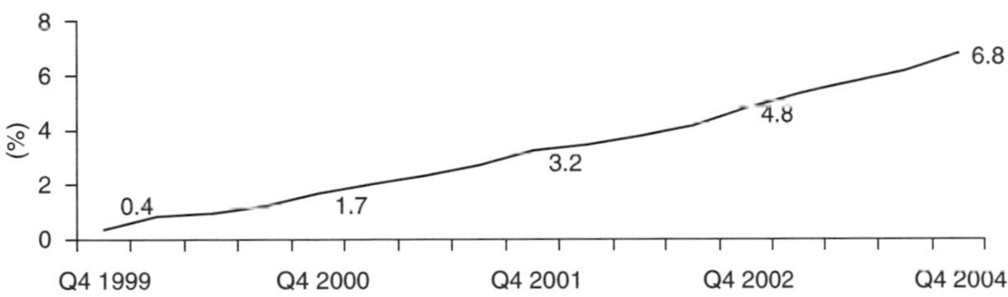

Figure 10: *Virgin Mobile's share growth*
Source: Oftel, company market press releases

Faster growth as competitor growth slowed

The most dramatic illustration of Virgin's market-beating success is the key net new customers metric. Virgin managed to increase the rate of net customer acquisitions, at a time when growth was slowing for other networks (Figure 11).

15. Source: Virgin Mobile, company estimates.

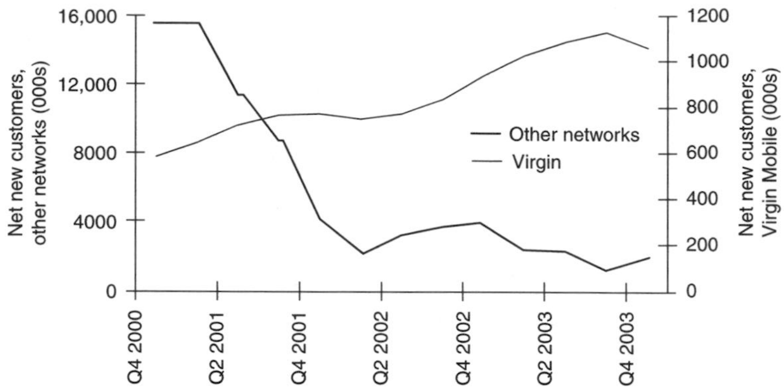

Figure 11: *Virgin Mobile customer growth vs rival networks' customer growth*
Source: Oftel, company press releases

Growth in turnover as well as volume

Volume growth did not come at the expense of value growth. Virgin Mobile's turnover increased six-fold from £76m in 2000 to £458m in 2003 (Figure 12).

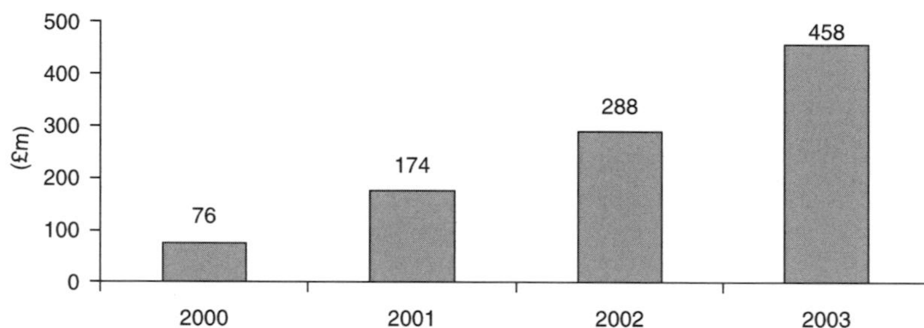

Figure 12: *Virgin Mobile turnover growth*
Source: Virgin Mobile

Virgin Mobile's growth was brand-led growth

Significantly, Virgin Mobile grew as a brand as it grew as a business. Market observers recognised this brand-led growth.

> 'In terms of scale, brand and customer awareness, Virgin Mobile has established itself as a serious challenger to the traditional four UK networks.'
>
> Chris Godsmark, telecoms analyst, Investec

> 'Virgin Mobile is a comparatively new kid on the block compared with the other networks and is signing up new users at a faster rate than its rivals by virtue of clever marketing.'
>
> *Guardian Unlimited*, 4 January 2002

> 'From a virtually standing start, Virgin Mobile has gained almost 4 million customers by focusing on pay-as-you-go and younger customers.'
>
> *Guardian*, 19 April 2004

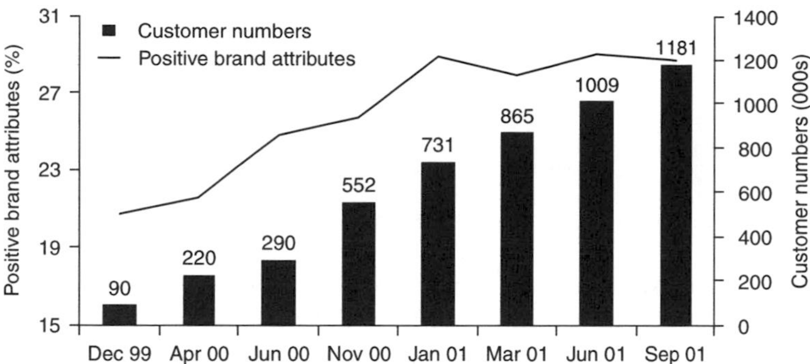

Figure 13: *Virgin Mobile sales growth and brand growth*
Source: *Consumer Insight*, Virgin Mobile

Virgin's brand image growth[16] mirrored its sales growth (Figure 13).

HOW ADVERTISING CONTRIBUTED TO VIRGIN MOBILE'S SUCCESS

Advertising played a bigger-than-average role in Virgin's strategy. It therefore played a bigger-than-average role in Virgin's success.

Creating a presence for Virgin Mobile

First, the advertising generated a presence for the brand (Figure 14). Other networks had their mature customer bases and their high street presence: Virgin had its advertising.

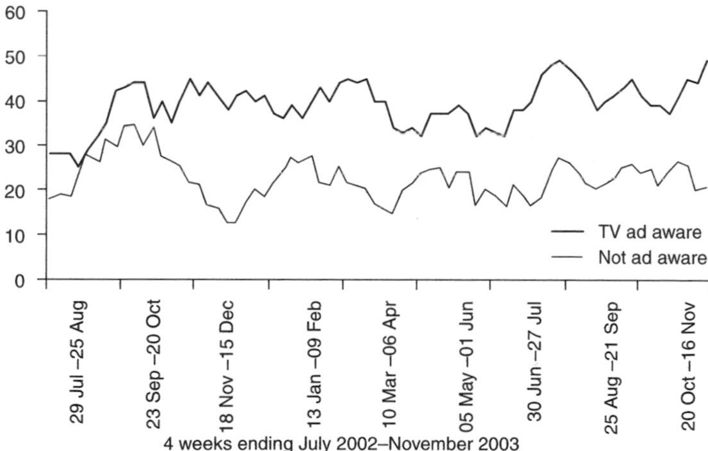

Figure 14: *Virgin Mobile brand awareness*
Source: *Consumer Insight*

16. We measured Virgin Mobile's brand image as an average score of the following brand attribute statements: forward thinking; not afraid to be different; changing the mobile phone market; a brand which people like and admire; a leader; a trustworthy company; becoming more popular nowadays; most economical mobile phone packages and has no hidden charges. The dates relate to waves of brand tracking.

Between July 2002 and December 2003,[17] Virgin's brand awareness was 73% higher amongst people aware of its TV advertising.

Connecting with the public

Virgin's advertising was not simply high-profile propaganda. It struck a chord with the public.

> 'Virgin Mobile's goals are clear and the strategy equally so. No-one is attempting to strike up a real relationship with the people who are most addicted to mobiles – the young ... The brand has staked out its ground and if I don't want the same phone service as my large uncle then Virgin is now my natural choice.'
>
> Tim Delaney, *Campaign*, 11 January 2002

Contestant Kate Lawler gave an impromptu performance of a Be Careful What You Sign advert during *Big Brother* 3.[18] The campaign was one of the top ten adverts of 2002 in *The Face* (Figure 15). DJs discussed it on Radio 1. Journalists wrote about it in the *Sun* and the *Star*. An actress from the campaign became a pin-up in *Maxim*.

As one teenage customer explained:

> 'I love that Wyclef and "Oh Wyclef, come to momma" idea. Virgin understands us, not like Vodafone who look down on me 'cos I ain't a businessman.'
>
> *Consumer Insight* customer interviews, 2003

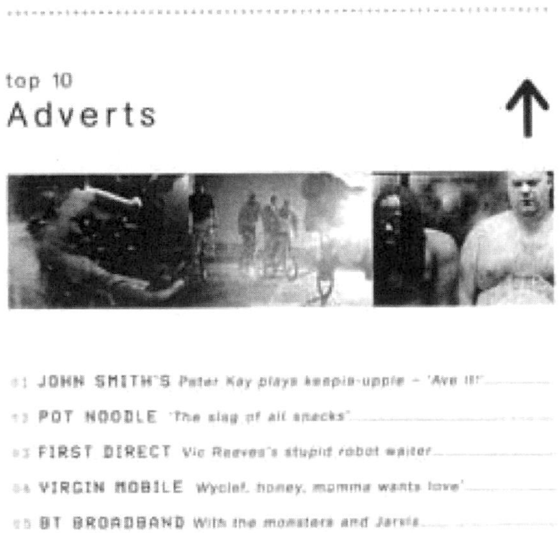

Figure 15: *High praise for the Wyclef advertising in* The Face's *review of the year, January 2003*

17. Virgin Mobile began continuous brand tracking in July 2002. Previously the brand had tracked consumer awareness and attitudes in occasional waves to coincide with marketing activity.
18. Source: *Big Brother* 24-hour coverage on E4, July 2002.

The Idle Thumbs campaign struck a similar chord:

> 'The Busta commercials went down very well. They were considered to fit well with the Virgin brand – young, cheeky, provocative and playful. The message is very clear ... and was seen as a neat and logical extension of previous Virgin Mobile work – combining the use of a celebrity with the "Idle Thumbs" idea.'
>
> Decision Point research debrief, November 2003

Viewers actively sought out Virgin's advertising. Viral versions of Virgin Mobile TV adverts topped the Lycos chart of most-watched viral films on the internet five times in 2003.[19]

Maximising Virgin's marketing investment

Challenging, customer-friendly advertising bought Virgin a disproportionate share of awareness. Virgin calculates success as 'bangs per buck': its share of advertising awareness over its share of advertising spend. This ratio shows that £1 of Virgin spend generates as much advertising awareness as £1.87 of competitor spend (Figure 16). This made Virgin Mobile's customer acquisition more efficient than any other network's. Virgin's advert spend per net new customer was 19% lower than its nearest competitor (Table 4).

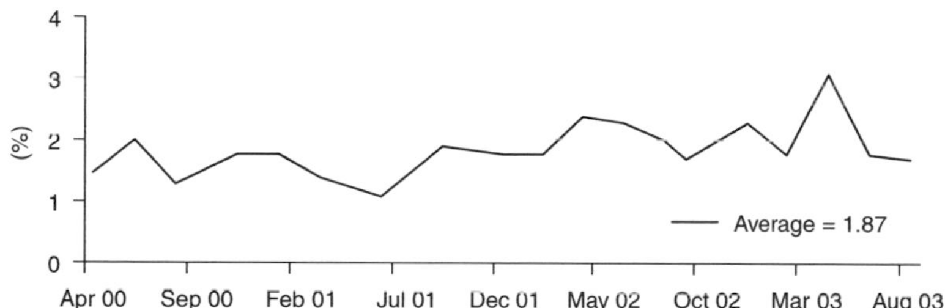

Figure 16: *Bangs per buck – Virgin Mobile's share of awareness versus its share of voice*
Source: *Consumer Insight*, MMS

TABLE 4: AD SPEND PER NEW CUSTOMER

2000–03	Advertising spend	Net new customers	Ad spend per net new customer
Virgin Mobile	£56.4m	3.56m	£15.85
T-Mobile	£114.9m	5.89m	£19.51
Orange	£186.6m	8.75m	£21.33
O_2	£133.5m	6.1m	£21.89
Vodafone	£159.6m	4.99m	£31.98

Source: MMS, Oftel, company press releases

Shaping the image of Virgin Mobile

Advertising shaped people's perception and knowledge of the brand (Tables 5 and 6). Virgin gained a strong competitive reputation around its two recent advertising messages – having no contracts and being good value for texts (Figures 17 and 18).

19. Source: DMC.

TABLE 5: BRAND IMAGE AMONGST AD-AWARE PEOPLE

Virgin Mobile's brand image amongst ad-aware people	Index: non-aware = 100
Changing the mobile phone market	148
Becoming more popular nowadays	142
A brand people like and admire	142
Not afraid to be different	141
Treat customers fairly	135

Source: *Consumer Insight*, 1999–2003

TABLE 6: PRODUCT KNOWLEDGE AMONGST AD-AWARE PEOPLE

Virgin Mobile's product knowledge amongst ad-aware people	Index: non-aware = 100
Cheap texts even if no contract	200
Has no contracts	156
Good value for money	153
Good value for texts	150
Free minutes without signing a contract	131

Source: *Consumer Insight*, 1999–2003

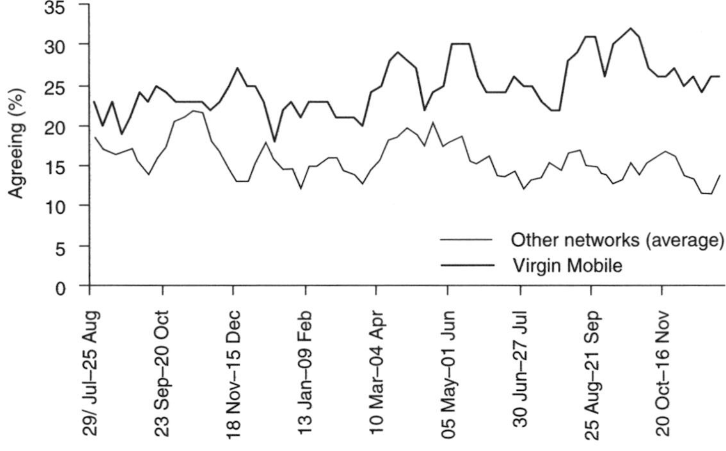

Figure 17: *Competitive brand image – has no contracts (July 2002–December 2003)*

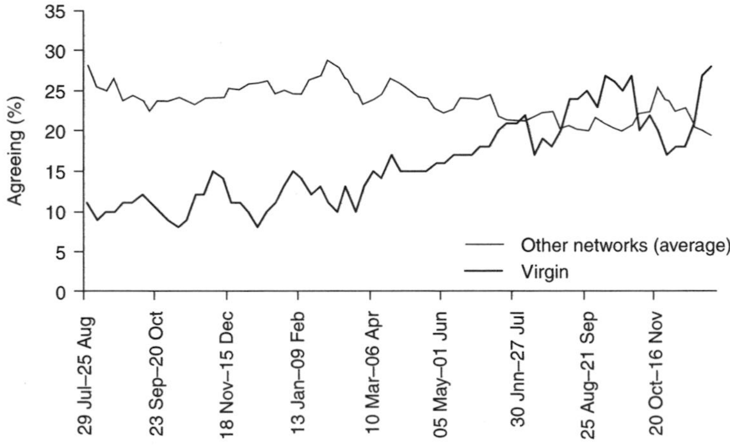

Figure 18: *Competitive brand image – good value for texts (July 2002–December 2003)*

Each individual campaign built a clear impression of Virgin Mobile amongst the public (Table 7).

TABLE 7: MAIN MESSAGES TAKEN OUT OF VIRGIN MOBILE ADVERTISING

Campaign	Main prompted communications	% agreeing
Launch campaign	(1) Good value for money	36
	(2) Cheaper calls the longer you talk	35
	(3) Cheaper than many packages	22
Divorce	(1) Is changing the mobile phone market	41
	(2) Good value for money	41
	(3) Enables you to switch without changing your phone	39
See Red	(1) Good value for money	38
	(2) Cheaper than many packages	26
	(3) Has no line rental/service charges	21
Be Careful What You Sign	(1) Has no contracts	36
	(2) Is a fun company to be with	26
	(3) Won't treat you badly like other networks	16
Idle Thumbs	(1) Is a fun company to be with	36
	(2) Offers 3p texts to people on the same network	34
	(3) Offers cheap texts	32

Source: *Consumer Insight*

Driving consideration of Virgin Mobile

Importantly, advertising did encourage people to find out more. Brand consideration was 73% higher amongst people who were aware of Virgin Mobile advertising (Figure 19).[20]

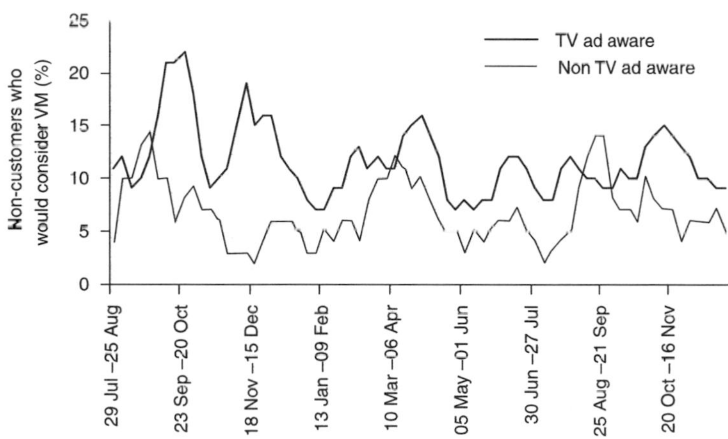

Figure 19: *Virgin Mobile brand consideration (July 2002–December 2003)*
Source: *Consumer Insight*

Driving customer acquisition

Virgin's advertising also struck a chord with the buying public. The reasons that customers give for joining Virgin Mobile closely mirror the brand's advertising messages (Table 8).

20. Source: *Consumer Insight* surveys of non-customers. Between July 2002 and December 2003, average brand consideration for Virgin Mobile was 10%. It was 17% for Orange and T-Mobile, 18% for O_2 and 19% for Vodafone. So Virgin Mobile enjoyed an average 12% share of brand consideration compared to a 5.2% share of market during this period.

TABLE 8: NEW CUSTOMERS' MAIN REASONS FOR JOINING VIRGIN MOBILE

Year	Main reasons for joining Virgin Mobile	% citing
2000	(1) No rip-off line rental	72
	(2) No contract to tie you down	69
	(3) Cheap calls	56
2001	(1) No contract to tie you down	69
	(2) No rip-off line rental	64
	(3) Cheap calls	55
2002	(1) No contract to tie you down	82
	(2) No rip-off line rental	70
	(3) Offer straightforward/no catches	65
2003	(1) No contract to tie you down	76
	(2) No rip-off line rental	65
	(3) It only costs 3p to text another Virgin Mobile	40

Source: *Consumer Insight* surveys of new Virgin Mobile customers

In fact, Virgin Mobile's new customer profile closely mirrored the changes in communications strategy. The proportion of new customers joining Virgin Mobile from other networks rose from 40% in December 1999 to 48% in July 2000 following the Divorce campaign.[21] (Yes, Virgin was recruiting fewer virgins.) And the proportion of new customers aged 16–24 rose from 34% to 47% between the first and last quarters of 2001, after Virgin Mobile changed its media buying audience from all adults to 16–24 adults in September of that year.[22] Finally, when customers joined Virgin Mobile from other networks, they cited brand image and communications as its biggest advantages over their previous networks (Figure 20).

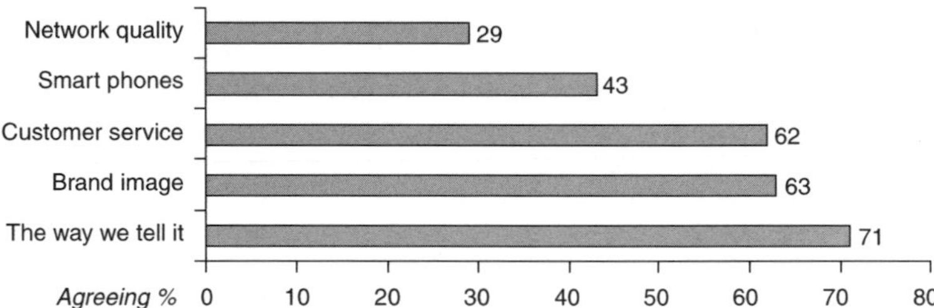

Figure 20: *New customers compare Virgin to their previous networks: 'Where are we better than your previous network?'*
Source: *Consumer Insight* surveys of customers switching to Virgin, 2000–2003[23]

This market-challenging advertising strategy therefore generated a growing stream of new customers, many of whom joined Virgin for communications-driven reasons, at a time when the market was changing and rival networks' growth was slowing.

21. Source: Virgin Mobile customer registrations.
22. Source: Virgin Mobile customer registrations, Manning Gottlieb OMD.
23. Brand image was only added to the questionnaire in June 2002.

WHY ADVERTISING MADE THE DIFFERENCE

We can demonstrate the contribution of advertising to Virgin commercial success more emphatically by discounting other variables that could have grown the brand.

Seasonality – every network gets a Christmas bonus

Seasonality has a big impact on retail mobile sales. Mobile phones are a popular Christmas present, and Virgin enjoys a seasonal uplift.[24] Yet Virgin Mobile's sales have grown across the years, not just at Christmas time. And all networks benefit from seasonality. The fact that Virgin Mobile's share has grown every quarter indicates that Virgin's sales success is not due to seasonality.

Discounting discounting

Virgin Mobile did not discount its way to success. The clearest indication is its average handset price. Over 80% of people join pre-pay networks by buying a handset from the network. Handset prices therefore reflect joining costs and promotional activity. Virgin's average handset price is dearer than any other network (Table 9).

TABLE 9: AVERAGE HANDSET PRICES

	Average pre-pay handset price, 2001–2003 (£)[25]
Vodafone	88
T-Mobile	89
Orange	91
O_2	94
Virgin	102

Source: GfK

Sales accelerated without distribution

Virgin did secure distribution through specialist retailers in November 2001, but this extra distribution did not accelerate Virgin Mobile's growth.

Virgin's net customer growth rate[26] increased less in the 12 months after securing specialist distribution than at any other time. Virgin Mobile's sales grew faster in the following year, with no additional distribution (Table 10).

TABLE 10: VIRGIN MOBILE'S RATE OF CUSTOMER GROWTH

Year to November	2000	2001	2002	2003
Net additions (000s)	496	742	854	1183
Increase vs previous year (000s)		246	112	329

Source: Virgin Mobile sales data

24. 23% of Virgin Mobile net sales in 2000–2003 occurred in the month of December.
25. No handset sales data is available before May 2001.
26. Rate of growth is fairest measure of distribution's impact. We do not have comprehensive sales data per outlet, and it is likely that distribution in specialist stores cannibalised customers who would have previously bought from Virgin stores. Rate of sale per outlet would not take account of this.

Even if we assume that distribution gained Virgin Mobile all those extra 112,000 net customers a year from November 2001 (as we will in the final calculation) Virgin Mobile's overall growth was not distribution-based.

No Virgin brand halo for Virgin Mobile

Virgin Mobile did not merely owe its success to its parent brand. Though Virgin is a successful brand, the Virgin name isn't always a guarantee of resounding growth, as Virgin Clothes, Cola and Vodka have found. Virgin Mobile did not simply recruit customers from sister companies; it bought new people into Virgin. By 2003, 96% of Virgin Mobile customers were not users of Virgin's other major service companies (Table 11).

TABLE 11: VIRGIN MOBILE CUSTOMERS WHO USE OTHER VIRGIN SERVICES

	2000	2001	2002	2003
Virgin Mobile users who also use Virgin Atlantic or Virgin Money	10.9%	4.2%	3.9%	3.9%

Source: TGI

Virgin's unique offers were relatively niche

What if Virgin Mobile's offer was so strong that it would have succeeded without advertising? Although the core tariff was simple and fair, it was not unique. All other networks copied it. Virgin's unique offerings are the ability for customers spending over £30 to earn free minutes and the ability to text another Virgin Mobile for just 3p (until O_2 copied it in 2004).

In practice these offers have limited reach. The mean monthly spend on Virgin Mobile is £12.94.[27] And 3p texting only applies to messages sent to the three million people on Virgin Mobile, not to the 47 million people on other networks.[28] Virgin Mobile's unique offers would have remained niche propositions if brand communications had not magnified them.

A TALE OF TWO NETWORKS: VIRGIN MOBILE'S RETURN ON INVESTMENT

What would have been the ultimate consequence for Virgin Mobile of pursuing a different advertising strategy? We have unique evidence of what could have been.

Virgin Mobile is a virtual network. It packages and markets T-Mobile airtime on the T-Mobile network. The two networks share the same back end. They share the same market, with its promotions, competitors and seasonality. What is different is the front end of the networks – the positioning and branding. So we can

27. Source: Virgin Mobile. Virgin Mobile's average revenue per user was £143 in 2000, £157 in 2001, £160 in 2002 and £161 in 2003, which averages out at £155.25 per year or £12.94 per month.
28. Numbers relate to the market as at May 2003. Even in the first three months of 3p texting, Virgin carried 51 million Virgin-to-Virgin texts, and 197 million texts to other networks. So the offer did not apply to 79% of Virgin's text traffic.

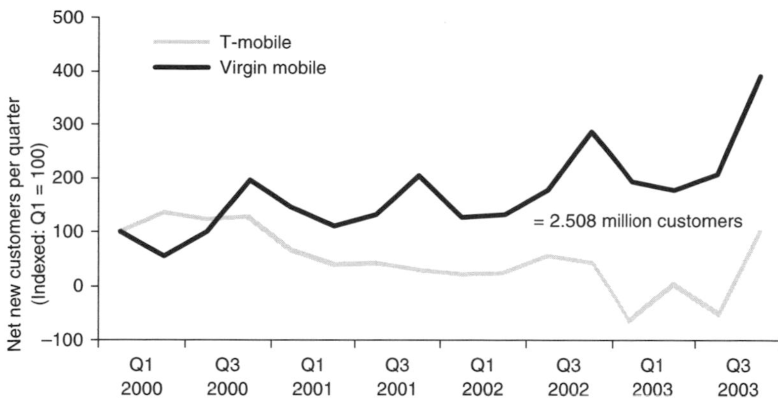

Figure 21: *Virgin Mobile outpaces the technically identical but differently-branded T-Mobile*
Source: Oftel, company press releases

see what would have happened to the company without its branding activity by looking at the performance of T-Mobile.

Indexing the net customer acquisitions of T-Mobile since the launch of Virgin Mobile gives us a base level for how Virgin Mobile would have performed without its brand activity. This comparison also removes the effects of seasonality, word of mouth and promotion, as these affected both networks.

The gap between Virgin Mobile and T-Mobile's growth rates is equal to 2.508 million additional customers between 2000 and 2003. Subtracting the contribution from distribution[29] and 3p texting[30] gives Virgin Mobile 2.043 million additional brand-generated customers. The value of these additional customers comes from the following calculation.

Additional net customers	×	Annual revenue per user	×	Customer lifetime	×	Gross margin	−	Cost of advertising	=	Return on investment

The annual revenue per user is shown in Table 12.

TABLE 12: VIRGIN MOBILE'S AVERAGE REVENUE PER USER

	2000	2001	2002	2003
Virgin Mobile average revenue per user	£143	£157	£160	£161

A conservative estimate is that a customer's spend remains static. The value calculation will assume that a customer recruited in, say, 2001 will continue to spend £157 a year. The true value of a customer is measured in the customer lifetime.

29. This assumes that extra distribution gave Virgin an additional 111,833 customers a year from November 2001.
30. Virgin Mobile year-on-year connections were 212,227 higher in the eight months since the launch of 3p texting.

Virgin Mobile's churn rate is 15.8%, so its average customer lifetime is 1/0.158, or 6.33 years. This compares with the market's average customer lifetime of 3.83 years, from a churn rate of 26.1%.[31] This additional customer lifetime is primarily due to Virgin's products and its customer service. The calculation will therefore err on the side of caution and use the market average. Virgin Mobile's gross margin, after cost of sales, averages 37.8%,[32] and Virgin Mobile invested £56.42m in advertising between 2000 and 2003. Therefore the total gross profit that Virgin Mobile will recoup from new customers generated by the brand between 2000 and 2003 is £427.6m. Every pound that Virgin Mobile invests in advertising returns £8.58 of gross profit.

Further returns for Virgin Mobile

Virgin Mobile's advertising was an efficient investment. We have seen how Virgin Mobile spent £15.85 on advertising for every customer it recruited. The average spend for rival networks is £23.11. If Virgin's advertising was only as efficient as its rivals, it would have to spend a further £25.85m on advertising to recruit the same number of customers.[33]

Virgin Mobile has introduced millions of new customers to the Virgin brand. Virgin Mobile is increasingly becoming the flagship Virgin brand for young people.[34] The brand strategy for Virgin Mobile in the UK has created a template for successful international brand expansion. Virgin Mobile USA launched a no-contract network for young people, under the campaign line 'Live Life Without A Plan.' The brand now has 1.8 million US customers.[35]

It is interesting to speculate how the ultimate return on investment from Virgin Mobile's advertising could be an increase in shareholder value.

At the time of writing, the City press is speculating on a flotation for Virgin Mobile that would value the company at £1bn.[36] The company has no physical network: its main asset is its customer base. Our calculation shows that the brand is responsible for 2.043 million of the 3.555 million customers the brand recruited between January 2000 and December 2003, or 57.5% of that base. The brand would therefore be responsible for £575m of the predicted value of Virgin Mobile plc.

---

31. Source: Gartner Dataquest, March 2004.
32. Gross margin is turnover minus the variable cost of sales that are related to additional customers. It is therefore the fairest measure of the commercial contribution of additional customers. Virgin Mobile's gross margin has increased from 26% in 2001 to 39% in 2002 to 48% in 2003.
33. Rival networks spent £594.6m to recruit 25.73 million net new customers between 2000 and 2003, which is equal to £23.11 per customer. £23.11 × 3.56 million new customers = £82.27m, a full £25.85m above Virgin Mobile's ad spend.
34. Source: Virgin Group brand tracking study, HPI Research, December 2003.
35. Source: *Information Week*, 12 April 2004.
36. 'There are signs that the pipeline of initial public offerings headed for the main market is filling up once more ... Virgin Mobile will follow', *The Times*, 2 May 2004; 'Sources ... told Reuters earlier this month that Virgin was lining up ... advisers for a flotation, expected to value the company at more than a billion pounds', *Reuters*, 29 April 2004; 'Expectations rise that the cellphone group will push for a £1billion-plus flotation this year', *Telegraph*, 26 April 2004.

SUMMARY

Virgin Mobile's brand story demonstrates the sheer leverage that convention-busting, customer-championing advertising can provide for a business. It proved stronger than competitors' budgets, technology and incumbency.

A brand-led David can successfully challenge a corporate Goliath.

Archimedes said: 'Give me a lever and a place to stand, and I will move the earth.' Virgin Mobile's challenger position was a place to stand. Advertising was the lever.

REFERENCES

Adams, S. (1998) *The Dilbert Future: Thriving On Business Stupidity*. London, Boxtree Books.

Morgan, A. (1991) *Eating The Big Fish: How Challenger Brands Can Compete Against Market Leaders*. Winchester, John Wiley.

Section 2

Silver Winners

SILVER

8

Bounty

How advertising caused a seismic change in the UK's use of paper towels

Principal authors: Fiona Keyte, Publicis, and Sam Dias, Publicis Commetrix

EDITOR'S SUMMARY

This is a case where advertising not only led to success for Procter & Gamble's Bounty paper towels brand but is also responsible for changing seemingly entrenched consumer behaviour. The achievement is all the more impressive because it succeeded in building a brand in a market where other household names had failed.

The 'Strong Housewives' campaign set out to convince people that paper towels are not just for mopping up spills. Because Bounty stays strong when wet, the campaign argues, they can be used for tougher chores such as scrubbing sticky surfaces. The 'Strong Housewives' campaign has led to more people using paper towels wet to tackle kitchen mess – something that was unthinkable prior to the advertising – and a significant increase in paper towel usage.

Within the first year of the campaign Bounty value share increased by 50%. To date it has generated additional sales of £37m from slightly more than £10m worth of TV advertising: an estimated ROI of 10%. This paper contains a particularly useful discussion of future value. Based on the assumption that this behavioural shift is permanent it highlights the potential of a £167m opportunity going forward.

A couple of judges were so impressed by this case that they bought some to try at home and have been convinced!

BACKGROUND

In the US Bounty is a mega-brand. Having been around for over 40 years with 35% of the market volume it is synonymous with the paper towel market. So, in 1999, it was understandable that Procter & Gamble (P&G) should look at the UK and see an opportunity for Bounty lurking in an affluent country with an underdeveloped paper towel market.

Signs of this underdevelopment were:

- a market dominated by private-label products – 70% volume, 65% value
- volume sales growing faster than value sales, implying market commoditisation
- despite market penetration into over 80% of UK households (almost as high as the US), the number of sheets used per day is half the number used in the US.[1]

Whilst these characteristics presented an opportunity, they also represented a risk. In 1993 another paper manufacturing giant, Andrex, introduced a range of premium paper towel products to the UK under the name Andrex Ultra. Despite supporting this range until 1996 Andrex subsequently withdrew from the paper towel market.

Undaunted, P&G launched Bounty in 1999. By the end of its first year it had invested over £7m in advertising; sent trial-generating coupons to 43% of UK homes; rapidly built distribution to over 90% of sterling-weighted grocery multiples and achieved a value share of 14%.[2]

So far, so good. Well, not quite. Whilst superficially a promising start, cracks were beginning to emerge by mid-2001.

1. As Figure 1 shows, growth to date had been driven by price decreases, a situation that was neither desirable nor sustainable.[3]

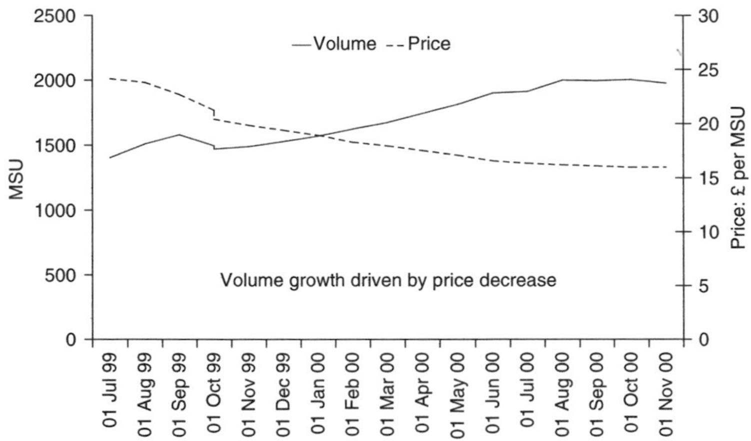

Figure 1: *Bounty MAT volume sales vs MAT price*

1. Calculated by comparing per capita volume consumption in the UK vs US.
2. Source: ETPD audit data.
3. MSU is a volume metric that represents 1000 sales units where a sales unit is 30 rolls.

2. The long-term sales trend was not looking favourable. Moving annual total (MAT) value sales were in decline for three consecutive months from June to August 2001, with an average decline of 9.4%.
3. Although a respectable value share, to have achieved 14% was not sufficient to overcome the significant fixed costs associated with paper towel manufacture.

By the autumn of 2001 a tough decision had to be taken. Should P&G cut its losses, assume the UK paper towel market was one where consumers could not be persuaded to pay for a quality product and exit? Or should it fight on, despite the unfavourable outlook? P&G and its agency went on the offensive. This was not a fight that they were going to give up easily.

THE CHALLENGE

To get consumers to experience the unique properties of Bounty they first have to change the way they use paper towels. That is, rather than only using paper towels for mopping up spills and liquid as they normally do, they need to start using them to do things they might never have thought paper towels could do.

The magic thing about Bounty is that it stays strong when wet. This is a counter-intuitive property of paper, since paper is meant to disintegrate on contact with water. But Bounty doesn't. Bounty is manufactured in a different way to other paper towels. This manufacturing process means that Bounty does not fall apart when it is wet. In fact, it stays so strong you can actually scrub with it and successfully clean sticky surfaces, messy floors, even stained carpets.

In 2001 the decision was taken to grow the Bounty business by changing (and growing) the market. That is, to encourage people to use Bounty in ways they hadn't thought were possible with a paper towel.

The only marketing tool capable of generating such a seismic change in consumer behaviour, quickly, was advertising. None of the other tools (such as pricing, distribution or product) creates fundamental changes in category behaviour. Furthermore, it was not commercially feasible to reduce prices, distribution was already good and in fact the weight of advertising was already at a healthy level. Only a change in the content of the advertising stood any chance of creating the sort of behaviour change that the brand needed. Furthermore, this was not about just any sort of advertising. It was decided very early on that 30-second TV advertising would be the most effective way to reach a large mainstream housewife audience, quickly.

Creative work of new campaign

The brief was to find a creative vehicle that would teach the British housewife how she could use Bounty. The proposition:

'Bounty works when wet allowing you to handle daily cleaning tasks you never thought a kitchen roll could do.'[4]

4. Source: Partners BDDH creative brief.

Two incredibly demanding (and somewhat unusual) housewives were created to put Bounty to the test. The idea being that if Bounty is the strongest kitchen roll available then it takes the strongest housewives to put it to the test. And so our particular variety of housewife began bringing something truly mind-opening to the attention of the consumer. It encouraged them to take a product they were familiar with (a paper towel) and begin to use it in a very unfamiliar way.

Six 30-second executions have since been aired: 'Strong Housewives', 'Burly Housewives', 'Spring Cleaning', 'Cooking Show', 'Roadshow' and 'Rajput' Additionally, four 10-second executions supported the launch of Fat Rolls. For the remainder of this study we will refer to the 'Strong Housewives' campaign as a collective term covering all executions.

TABLE 1: STRONG HOUSEWIVES ACTIVITY FROM THE CAMPAIGN'S LAUNCH[5]

	October–December 2001	2002	2003	Total
TVRs[6]	738	2967	2840	6545
Spend on TV £(m)	1.3	4.7	4.1	10.1

This advertising had two key ingredients for success. First it was strategically focused – as encapsulated by the endline, 'Have you tried it wet yet?' Second, the ads were creatively entertaining and rewarding. They are colourful, loud and yet informative. The female target audience enjoyed the spectacle of these outrageous pseudo-housewives putting their backs (hairy though they may be) into the tasks they faced.

> 'I love those adverts with the men dressed up as women. I can imagine that they had a lot of fun making them.'[7]

WHAT HAPPENED?

There are four areas in which we will demonstrate advertising effectiveness.

1. Advertising awareness and message recalled.
2. Paper towel usage.
3. The sales effect.
4. Comparing Bounty's performance in UK vs Germany.

Advertising awareness and message recalled

P&G conducts periodical surveys of its brands' awareness and image. To provide a longitudinal perspective, Table 2 compares three of these snapshots. Autumn 2001 represents the last researched period for the 'Cathy' campaign; winter 2002 comes

5. Source: Nielsen MMS.
6. Housewives with children.
7. Source: Publicis qualitative research, June 2003.

after 'Strong Housewives' had been running for 12 months; and autumn 2003 provides the most recent data.

Advertising awareness is measured via the combination of executional cut-through (ECT) and branded cut-through (BCT). ECT is the percentage of respondents who can describe an advert well enough for it to be tied directly to a specific execution, regardless of whether they are able to remember the correct brand or not. BCT is the proportion of respondents able to describe the execution and correctly identify the brand.

TABLE 2: P&G PERIODICAL SURVEYS

	Autumn 2001 'Cathy'	Winter 2002 'Strong Housewives'	Autumn 2003 'Strong Housewives'
Branded cut-through	100%	141%	141%
Executional cut-through	100%	471%	471%

This data suggests that the new advertising was over four times as effective vs the previous campaign at generating advertising awareness for Bounty. Furthermore, the executions were over five times as memorable in the first place.

But what about the clarity of the message within the adverts themselves? Evidence that the clarity of the intended message was replicated once the adverts went on air is again provided by P&G's periodic snapshot of its brands.

Table 3 compares what people knew about the Bounty brand over the same three periods. Knowledge of the brand's attributes – particularly in relation to its ability to remain strong when wet – improved dramatically.

TABLE 3: ATTRIBUTES ASSIGNED TO BOUNTY

	Autumn 2001 'Cathy'	Winter 2002 'Strong Housewives'	Autumn 2003 'Strong Housewives'
Can be used to tackle tough cleaning tasks	100%	113%	115%
Doesn't disintegrate when wet	100%	171%	171%
Is strong enough for tougher tasks like dried-on messes	100%	112%	114%

Base: all respondents
Notes: data movements between autumn 2001 and winter 2002 are statistically significant; data movements between winter 2002 and autumn 2003 are not

Paper towel usage

This story's real potency rests on the fundamental and permanent change to the UK paper towel market that this advertising provoked. We believe it has begun to change the way people use paper towels and that this, in the long term, will leave the UK with a bigger paper towel market from which Bounty can continue to benefit into the future.

P&G conducted a major study of behaviour within the UK paper towel market in 1995, prior to the launch of Bounty. It was a comprehensive study requiring a large, nationally representative sample, keeping a diary of both their paper towel habits and their entire household cleaning habits. It was repeated in 2003. These two UK studies (1995 and 2003) provide the data for all of the tables in this section.[8]

We intend to prove that paper towel habits have changed significantly between these two studies. The introduction of Bounty in 1999 would have resulted in some of these changes without the 'Strong Housewives' advertising. However, we will contend that the brand's experience and difficulties between 1999 and 2001 illustrate that the product alone would not have effected such a fundamental change in product habits. It was totally counter-intuitive before the 'Strong Housewives' advertising to use a paper towel in the way millions of consumers now do.

Table 4 shows the key changes in the dynamics of this market between the two studies:

- more tasks were described in the respondent diaries for 2003 vs 1995
- more sheets of paper were being used each day
- the number of sheets being used per task had grown.

TABLE 4: DIARY DATA – NUMBER OF SHEETS USED PER DAY

Index 1995 = 100	1995	2003
Number of tasks mentioned	100	128
Number of sheets per day	100	143
Number of sheets per task	100	148

Table 5 demonstrates that the degree to which certain tasks were being performed by a paper towel had changed dramatically: cleaning the inside of the oven (something that is featured in several of the executions) saw a particularly impressive shift. We cannot reveal the actual numbers but for each of the tasks below paper towels are now used for at least 40% of the occasions on which that task is performed.

TABLE 5: PERCENTAGE OF THE TASK PERFORMED BY A PAPER TOWEL

Index 1995 = 100	1995	2003
Cleaning appliance surfaces	100	163
Cleaning windows	100	176
Cleaning inside oven or stove	100	385

As people began to use paper towels more confidently to perform these tasks (rather than just finishing the job off with them or for the less demanding occasions) so the number of sheets used for each task grew significantly, as illustrated in Table 6.

8. For all of the data for Tables 4–6 the shifts between 1995 and 2003 are statistically significant unless otherwise stated.

TABLE 6: NUMBER OF SHEETS OF PAPER TOWEL USED PER TASK

Index 1995 = 100	1995	2003
Cleaning appliance surfaces	100	185
Cleaning windows	100	184
Cleaning inside oven or stove	100	164

Of the paper towel tasks described in the diaries of the two surveys not only was the list longer in 2003 but it also included several applications that would have been totally unforeseen of a paper towel back in 1995. For example, cleaning the kitchen floor, cleaning greasy messes, cleaning stuck-on dried-on messes, cleaning the shower/bathtub, cleaning around the toilet, washing dishes by hand and scrubbing carpet stains.

These are tasks that required a major change in the way paper towels are used. These tasks have an above-average tendency to require the paper to be self-consciously wet before it is used (either with water or with a cleaning agent) and they are more likely to consume an above-average number of sheets (Table 7).

TABLE 7: PERCENTAGE OF TIMES A TASK IS PERFORMED WITH A PRE-WET PAPER TOWEL (OR WITH CLEANING AGENT) AND THE AVERAGE NUMBER OF SHEETS USED PER TASK (2003)

	Pre-wetting or using cleansers	Number of sheets used per task
Cleaning the kitchen floor	101	103
Cleaning greasy messes	132	132
Cleaning stuck-on dried-on messes	312	113
Cleaning the shower/bathtub	152	200
Cleaning around the toilet	210	116
Washing dishes by hand	129	100
Scrubbing carpet stains	160	145

Indexed against the average for all tasks

The sales effect

The short-term sales response was instant. Figure 2 shows four-weekly value share for Bounty. The four-week period ending 6 October 2001 was the last period before this advertising broke and Bounty had dropped to a value share of 9.9%. Six months later, in the four-week period ending 23 March 2002, the share had hit 16.8% – more than 50% greater than the October level.

Comparing Bounty's performance in GB vs Germany

Germany is the largest of the other European countries to have launched Bounty and it provides an interesting comparison for the British data. Prior to 'Strong Housewives' the two countries were employing the same advertising creative strategies. The new campaign disrupted this similarity, and the effects it had upon the fortunes of the UK value share, relative to Germany, are illustrated in Figure 3.

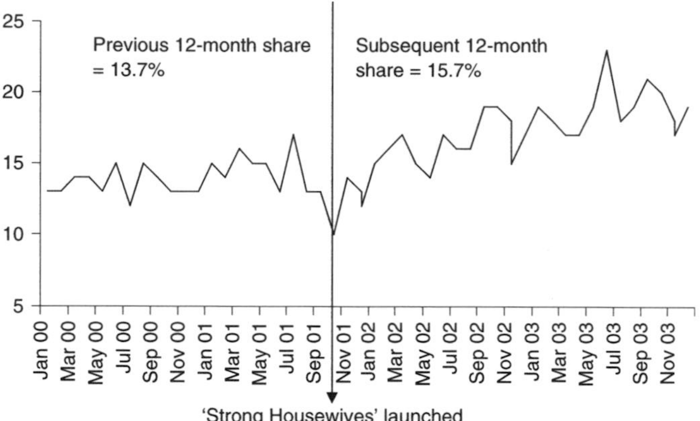

Figure 2: *Bounty value share*

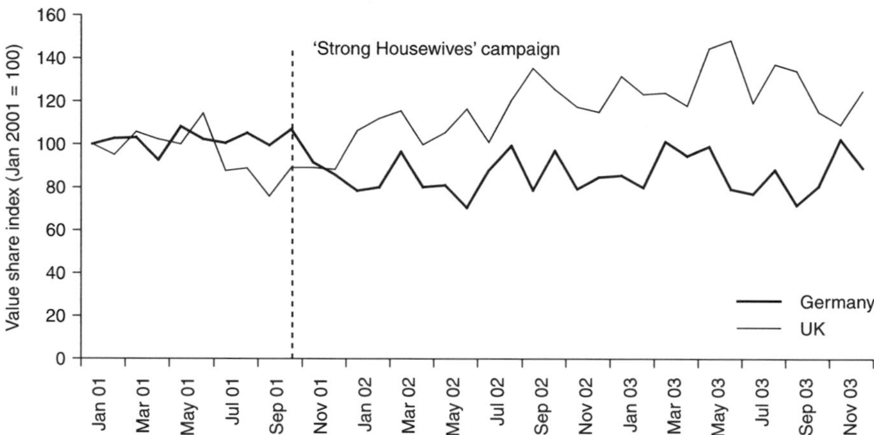

Figure 3: *Indexed value share: UK vs Germany*

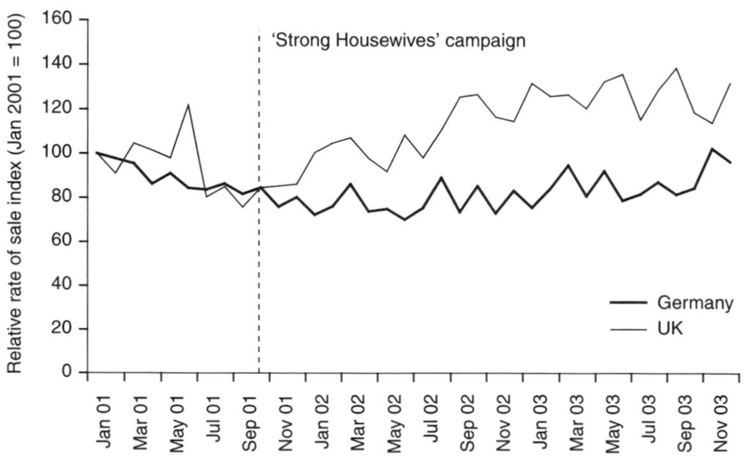

Figure 4: *Index of relative rate of sale: UK vs Germany*

Relative rate of sale[9] eliminates sales increases that could be driven by sector growth and aggregate distribution growth. Figure 4 shows that prior to the launch of 'Strong Housewives', Germany and GB were at parity in terms of RROS. This changed after the launch of the new campaign.

The team in Germany is now using the 'Strong Housewives' campaign.

WHAT ELSE COULD HAVE CAUSED THESE CHANGES?

The coincident timing of the new advertising and the almost immediate improvement in sales performance suggests that the advertising was responsible for the changes described. But could any other factors have had an influence? We will demonstrate that there were no other changes in the marketing mix towards the latter part of 2001 that could explain the improved fortunes of the Bounty brand into 2002 and beyond.

Price

Figure 5 shows that Bounty's average price declined for the first two years from launch. However since August 2001 (and throughout the duration of the 'Strong Housewives' campaign) average price has actually increased. Therefore, price was in fact working against the 'Strong Housewives' campaign rather than for it, and could not explain the uplift in sales. Furthermore, Bounty's price relative to that of competitors shows the same picture (Figure 6).

The full effect of Bounty's price, promotions and competitor pricing are explicitly accounted for in the econometric model. As such, our return-on-investment calculations isolate the effect of advertising exclusive of pricing variations.

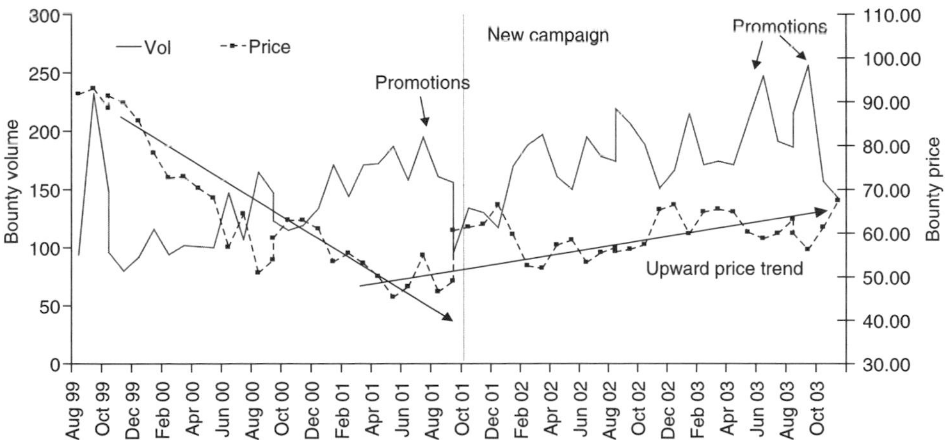

Figure 5: *Bounty volume sales vs average price*

9. Relative rate of sale (RROS) = market share/sterling weighted aggregate distribution. RROS is market share per point of aggregate distribution. Aggregate distribution is the sum of each stock-keeping unit's sterling weighted distribution. It is a measure of the breadth and depth of distribution for a brand.

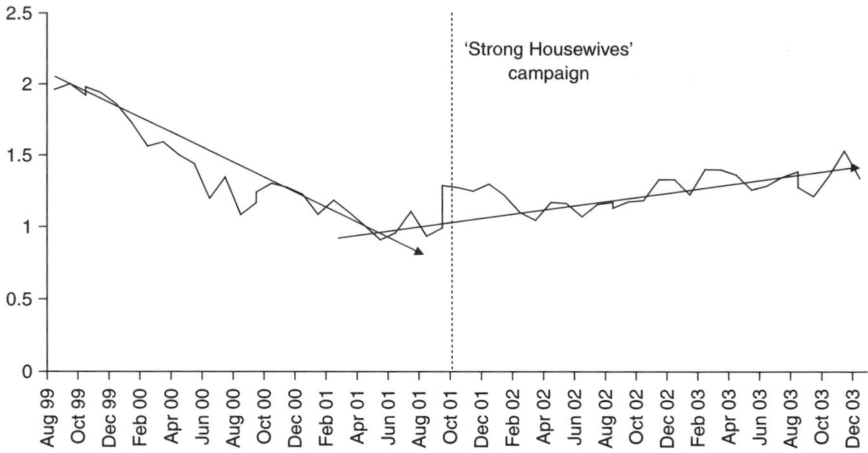

Figure 6: *Bounty price relative to competitor price*

Distribution

Sterling-weighted distribution of the Bounty brand was constant during the period under review and aggregate sterling weighted distribution[10] slightly declined. Therefore, sales growth could not be because of gains in either overall brand distribution or improved availability of new variants (Figure 7). Furthermore, distribution of competitive brands either increased (as with Kittensoft's aggregate distribution) or did not change. So the growth of Bounty was not the result of either improvements in its distribution or the decline in competitive distribution.

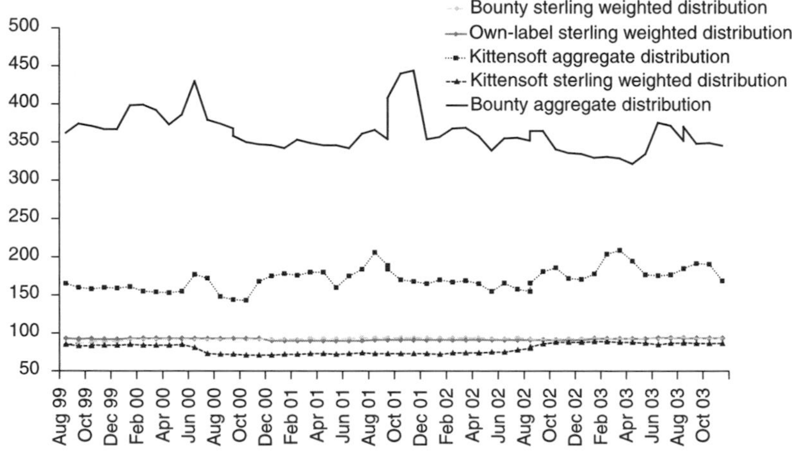

Figure 7: *Sterling weighted distribution*

10. Aggregate sterling weighted distribution is defined as the sum of each SKU's distribution. It is a measure of the breadth and depth of distribution for a brand.

Sector growth

The paper towel sector grew by 15% in volume between October 2001 and December 2003, whilst Bounty grew by 28.8%. It is clear that far from being driven by growth in the market, Bounty was actually doing the driving.

Media weight

Table 8 shows that 'Strong Housewives' received less media pressure than 'Cathy' had in its first 12 and 24 months. In other words, this brand did not spend its way out of trouble.

TABLE 8: MEDIA SPEND £(M)[11]

	'Cathy'	'Strong Housewives'
First 12 months	8.2	5.1
First 24 months	10.8	9.3

Competitive advertising

When Bounty launched, competitive advertising was virtually non-existent. Andrex had not advertised since it had given Ultra one final push in 1996.

Figure 8 shows how competitive activity increased in 2003. This was due to Kittensoft resuming advertising following its relaunch as Thirstpockets. Therefore, if anything, the competitive landscape got hotter only after the introduction of our 'Strong Housewives'.

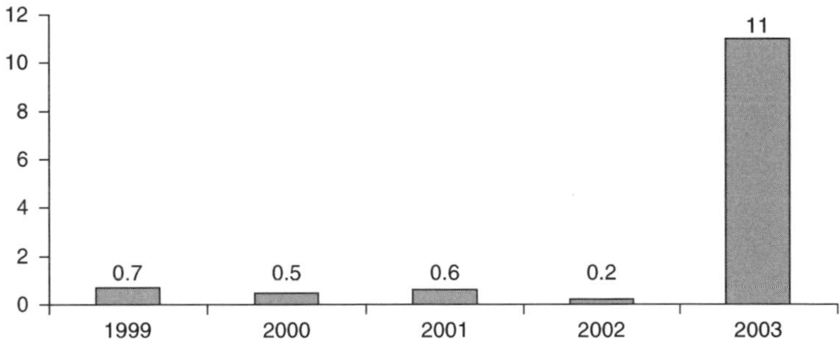

Figure 8: *Competitor share of voice (%)*

Product

Since launch, Bounty has been a product that stays strong when wet. Moderate improvements were made, however, to its wet-strength properties in early 2002. These improvements were never highlighted on-pack, nor did they feature in any consumer communication. It is therefore highly unlikely that this product improvement was responsible for the sales growth Bounty has enjoyed.

11. Source: Nielsen MMS.

Any other explanations for the change in paper towel behaviour?

By all accounts such a change in category behaviour was unforeseen by market commentators. Mintel, for example, published a report in July 1997. Its experts provided forecasts for the size of the market up to 2001. They predicted that volume growth would be minimal between 1997 and 2001. We assume this to also mean that at the time they also envisaged a flat volume scenario for subsequent years.[12] By contrast, the market volume has actually grown by 33% since 1997.

RETURN ON INVESTMENT

Having ruled out or accounted for the impact of other variables, we have employed an econometric model to calculate advertising return on investment to the end of December 2003.

We have then applied the findings of this model to two different perspectives on the financial return generated by the advertising investment to date.

1. We will extract the value of incremental sales already directly attributable to the advertising. We are not permitted to reveal any details relating to P&G's financial structures, therefore we have applied an estimate for the additional profit and return on investment these incremental sales are likely to represent.
2. We will provide estimates for the value of future incremental sales that the advertising may have created. That is, thanks to the permanent change in the way people now use paper towels, what can Bounty still expect to enjoy?

Incremental sales

Figure 9 provides the modelled paths for sales with and without the 'Cathy' campaign. 'Cathy' generated £15.5m[13] of incremental sales on media spend of £10.8m. Figure 10 shows the modelled sales with and without the 'Strong Housewives' campaign.

When 'Strong Housewives' started, Bounty was a £32m business (per annum). By December 2003, it had grown to £47.3m. This is consistent with the level of change witnessed in the diary-based sheets-per-day usage (which moved from an index of 100 in 1995 to an index of 143). Relevant, consumer-centric advertising has been the key engine of this growth.

Since the start of 'Strong Housewives', Bounty has enjoyed £95m of sales. Our model suggests that advertising generated £37m (35%) of these sales.[14] This has been achieved on a budget of £10.1m to the end of 2003. Applying a typical fmcg average margin of 30%, the profit generated on the incremental sales generated by the advertising amounts to £11.1m. Therefore the financial contribution of the

12. Else they would have stated otherwise.
13. This number is based on an analysis of market figures incorporated in the econometric model that has been built by Publicis. They are not derived from P&G financial statements.
14. This number is based on an analysis of market figures incorporated in an econometric model that has been built by Publicis. They are not derived from P&G financial statements.

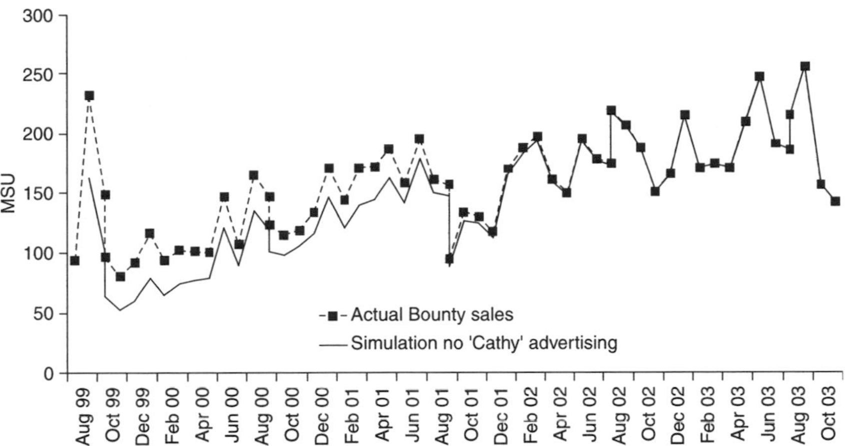

Figure 9: *Effect of 'Cathy' advertising*

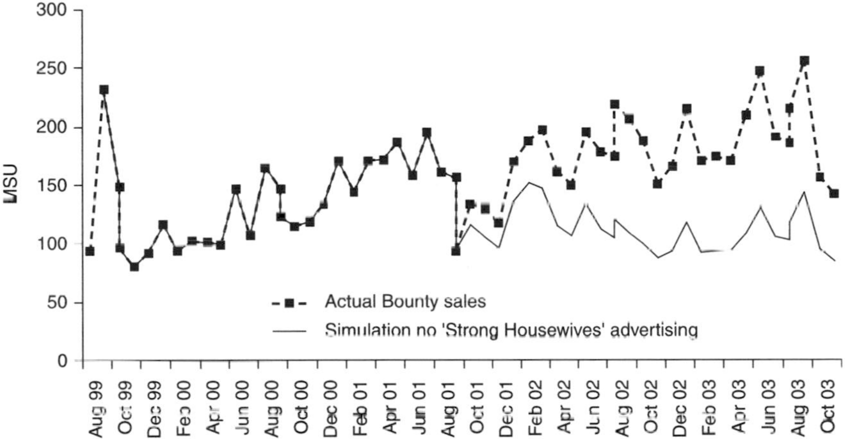

Figure 10: *Effect of 'Strong Housewives' advertising*

advertising (incremental profit less investment) comes to £1m (1/10.1 = 10% return on investment).

Clearly this advertising has already been a worthwhile endeavour.

Future value creation

The grid overleaf defines four different scenarios that could describe the future dynamics of this market. It is built from two axes.

1. Market sheet usage – assuming that the rate of increase continues at the current rate.[15]
2. Bounty volume share – comparing the US to the UK.

15. Given there remains a significant gap in paper towel usage between the UK and US this not an unrealistic assumption.

Current UK sheet usage (Index 100) Current UK MAT volume share (14.2%) Current sales = £47.3m	Future UK sheet usage (Index 143) Current UK MAT volume share (14.2%) Opportunity = £47.3m x 143/100
Current UK sheet usage (Index 100) Current US MAT volume share (35%) Opportunity = £47.3m x 35/14.2	Current UK sheet usage (Index 143) Current US MAT volume share (35%) Opportunity = £47.3m x 35/14.2 x 143/100

The quadrant in the top left-hand corner describes the current situation in terms of consumer sheet consumption and Bounty volume share being maintained into the future. As such, this is the least ambitious of these future scenarios. The bottom right-hand corner describes the most ambitious scenario where consumer sheet consumption continues to grow at the same rate as it did between our two studies of 1995 and 2003, whilst volume share reaches US levels (see Figure 11).

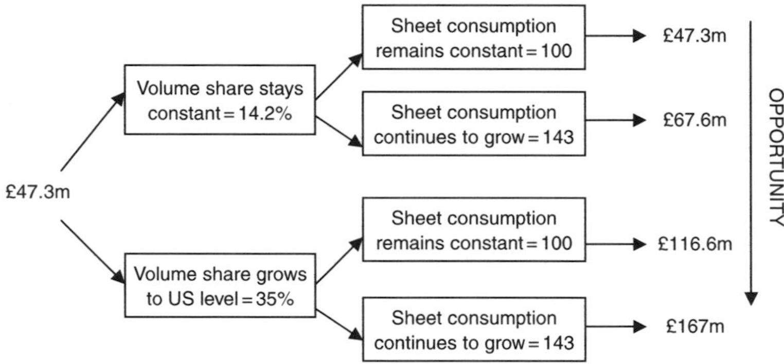

Figure 11: *Scenarios for future dynamics of the market*

CONCLUSIONS

This study is a good example of advertising paying back in the short term. However, whilst ROI is an important indicator of the wisdom of the original media investment it describes what has happened in the past. Yet it is in the prospect for future growth for Bounty where this case differs to others, and where the true value of this activity will pay back.

9

British Airways

Climbing above the turbulence

How British Airways countered the budget airline threat

Principal authors: Rob Day, ZenithOptimedia;
Richard Storey and Andy Edwards, M&C Saatchi

EDITOR'S SUMMARY

This case study tells the story of how BA faced up to new competition using communications to drive through a fundamentally restructured business model.

BA was facing huge threats from low-cost airlines that were jeopardising its long-term position in Europe. The airline had dropped out of the FTSE 100, but rather than bail out of Europe, BA believed it had to battle to survive. If it turned its back on its short-haul service, the company figured its premium long-haul operation would be next to suffer.

BA took on the budget airlines at their own game by competing on price, but also using its strong service heritage to its advantage. Research showed that consumers wanted 'services that matter' such as centrally located airports and allocated seating, as long as the price wasn't out of their reach.

BA launched its communication strategy, exposing the false promise of 'no frills' and creating awareness of BA's lower prices. At the core of BA's communications strategy was the element of surprise. It bought typically un-BA media such as street projections and ATM machines to supplement its commercials.

This campaign re-set the value agenda and began to reframe the competition. In doing so, it has played a crucial role in safeguarding BA's standing amongst the public, its staff and the City. BA posted increased profits of £230m for year ending March 2004 and has re-established itself as a FTSE 100 company. Its European position looks secure.

TROUBLED TIMES

The twenty-first century has not exactly been kind to British Airways.

Serious threats to BA's business have followed one after another: the bursting of the dotcom bubble and subsequent recession; SARS; the hideous events of 9/11 and the continuing threat of terrorist strikes against passenger aircraft; wars in Afghanistan and Iraq, and their surrounding uncertainty; associated spiralling insurance and fuel costs; the strength of sterling versus the dollar, inhibiting inbound US tourism.

On top of all this, BA faced a massive competitive threat: a vigorous, aggressive and worryingly effective assault by the budget airlines on its domestic and European routes.

The financial impact of this new world on BA was stark. The airline dropped out of the FTSE 100, and post-9/11 was viewed by some observers to have its very existence counted in months rather than years.

Airlines such as Sabena, Swissair, KLM and Buzz did not survive the period and were sold, merged or financially restructured. Other airlines relied on injections of state funding (a luxury unavailable to BA plc) or on complex bankruptcy protection legislation. And yet, as we go to press, BA posted increased profits of £230m (April 2003–March 2004) and has re-established itself as a FTSE 100 company. The company took some tough decisions in effecting such a robust turnaround. Out-thinking the budget airlines was one of the most vital.

This study tells the story of how BA faced up to new competition, using communications to drive through a fundamentally restructured business model. By committing to an unprecedented communications assault, BA shifted apparently unshakeable attitudes, directly grew its passenger volumes and decreased its overall selling costs.

'NO FRILLS'

The very phrase 'no frills' encapsulates the potency of the budget airline proposition. If you're travelling short haul – so goes the sales pitch – you don't need elaborate meals, allocated seats, free drinks and other 'bolt-ons'. You want an airborne bus. And you want it cheap.

The public's appetite for low-cost flying proved so strong that even the fears stoked by war and terrorist outrage couldn't stifle it. Fares advertised on the internet for sometimes less than the cost of a taxi ride proved irresistible.

The consumer was being virtually bombarded by the budget airlines with attractive offers to destinations previously unknown. In the first half of 2002 the budget airlines accounted for no less than 73% of the mushrooming advertising spend in short haul. The traditional carriers were being out-shouted 3:1 (Figure 1). BA was barely in the game.

And budget airlines shouted one thing, day in day out (Figure 2).

As a result, the short-haul economy sector of the airline market was unique in showing spectacular growth. BA, in contrast, suffered the dual indignity of being portrayed as both long on 'frills' and short on value.

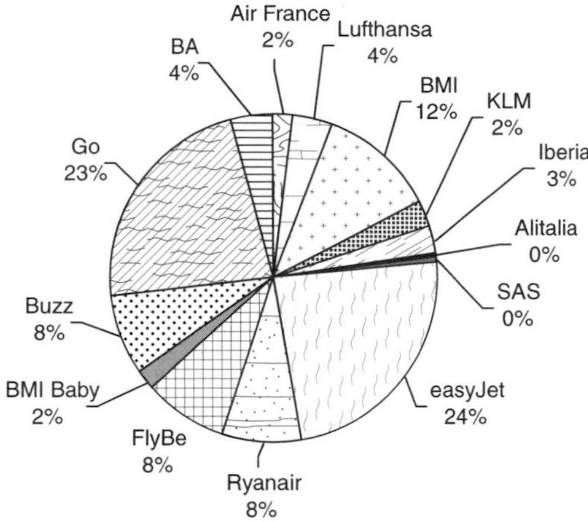

Figure 1: *BA out-shouted*
Source: NMR, January–August 2002

Figure 2: *Budget airline advertising shouted one thing – price*

BA's range of passenger benefits and services was sneeringly dismissed by the competition as mere frills. And a large proportion of the public seemed to agree. Consideration scores versus low-cost alternatives declined alarmingly (Figure 3).

BA's market share followed suit and losses mounted.[1] City analysts were clear about the implications of further market share loss:

> 'It's make or break time for British Airways in Europe now. It can barely afford to haemorrhage cash at its present rate. If they [the budget airlines] keep making gains it will take BA over the edge. BA has two choices. Either stem the decline and begin to stem the losses. Otherwise it has to make a strategic withdrawal from short-haul services. I personally don't believe there's much of a middle ground between the two options.'
>
> High yield analyst, August 2002

1. BA declared a loss on European services of £244m in 2002, £72m up on the already disastrous 2001.

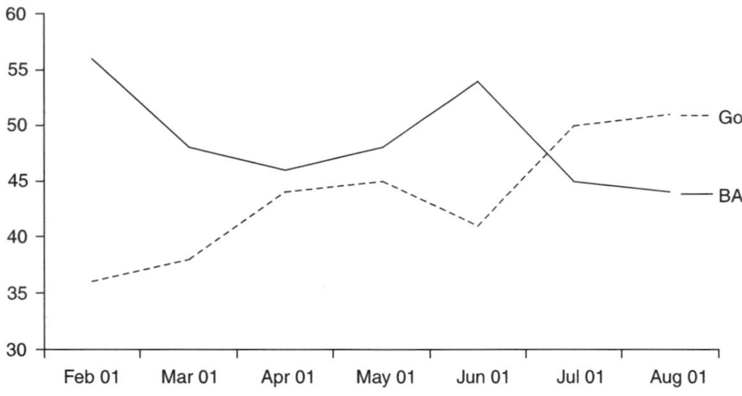

Figure 3: *Declining consideration vs budget airlines*
Source: BA tracking/RI

JOIN THE FRAY – OR BACK AWAY?

BA's response to the macro-economic threats to its total business was to embark on an aggressive business restructuring, its 'Future Size & Shape' initiative. This would completely overhaul the organisation and business operations. It would pare down costs, rationalise the fleet, cut uneconomic routes and introduce rigorous efficiencies.

However, it faced a choice as to whether to fight the budget airlines toe to toe in Europe, or just focus on its premium and long-haul business. On the face of it, taking on the budget airlines on their terms seemed least likely to succeed.

BA's strength historically had been the long-haul business market. However, this could no longer be solely relied on, with business flyers downgrading from premium cabins in the tough economic climate or not flying at all due to security concerns.

The reality up in the skies was that the short-haul, 'back of the plane', market was showing the most vigorous growth prospects. More fundamentally, BA needed to preserve its short-haul routes to 'feed' long-haul traffic. As a major player BA could not afford to abandon Europe – however tough.

The problem remained that the budget airlines had the bit between their teeth and the consumer in their grasp. Ever-confident Ryanair boss Michael O'Leary declared that 'price is the only service that matters'. Superficially the consumer seemed inclined to agree and was voting with its seat (Figure 4).

CRUCIAL INSIGHTS

At this point BA commissioned a vital piece of research into short-haul leisure flyers' expectations. The research confirmed that budget flyers disliked paying for what they perceived as 'frills'. However, they were passionate about what they regarded as 'essentials'.

> 'Let's face it. If they don't even get you there in reasonable time and in reasonable shape it doesn't matter how little you paid.'
>
> Hall & Partners qualitative research

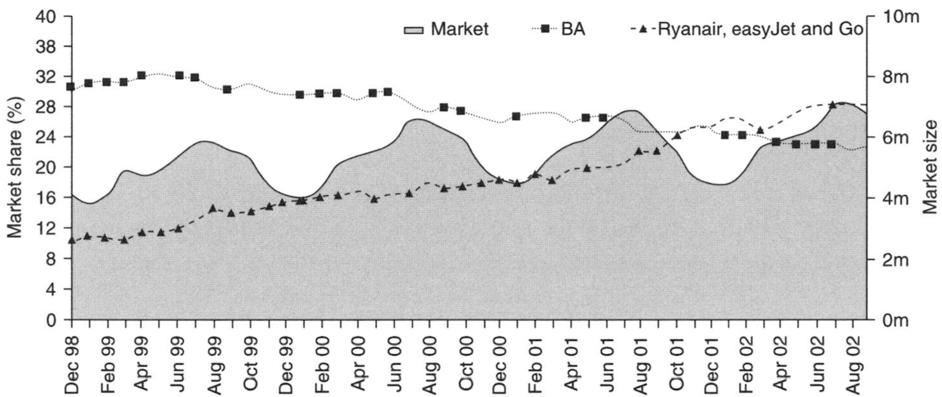

Figure 4: *Declining market share*
Note: this chart includes routes that BA does not fly on – hence it is not a direct comparison of the competitive threat to BA. It does, however, highlight the magnitude of the competitive presence in Europe

Research revealed that flyers valued things like centrally located airports, allocated seating, availability of professional staff, ability to handle problems, back-up aircraft in the event of delays and cancellations, good punctuality, and so on. On the back of these, they also voted for some of the things that make a difference to the quality of the flying experience like food, and goody bags for children. Furthermore, research indicated that passengers trusted BA rather than the budget airlines to provide this kind of service (Figure 5).

Indeed there was increasing evidence in BA's mail bag as well as in qualitative research, that there was real dissatisfaction with the lack of service on budget airlines, particularly when it compromised fundamental aspects of the journey.

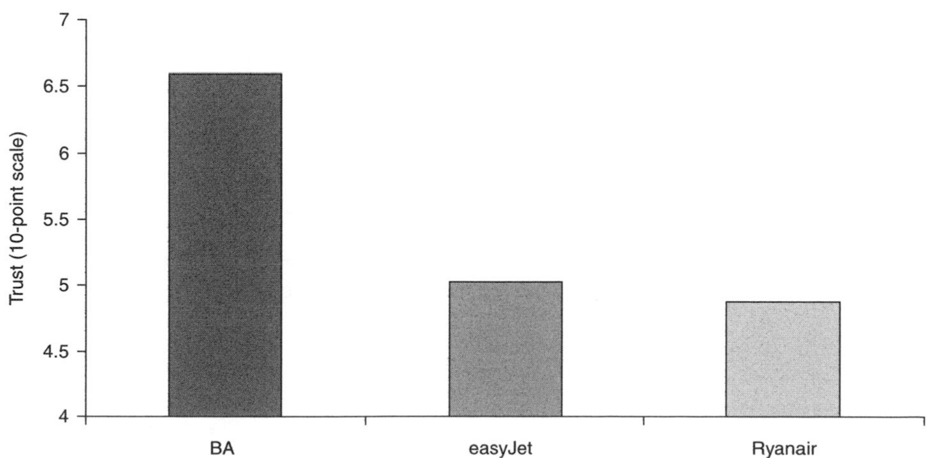

Figure 5: *BA uniquely trusted to deliver*

> 'I was supposed to be going to Toulouse for a wedding, but Sleasyjet [sic] landed me seven hours' drive away, with my bags still on the tarmac at Gatwick.'
>
> Letter to BA

In short, they wanted service that mattered, as long as price did not act as a deterrent.

This showed that BA, with many other more fundamental drivers to purchase, had a clear opportunity to beat the competition if it could address the issue of price.

FIGHTING BACK

BA could do the seemingly impossible: appeal to the budget airline customer whilst not actually being a budget airline.

The over-riding goal was to achieve sustainable volume in the short-haul market. The City saw this as vital to the airline's future with Chris Avery at JP Morgan commenting that

> 'all BA needed to do was stabilise volumes at the back of the plane and break even'.

Profitability, at this point, did not enter the equation. Sustainability was the word.

So BA chose, in spite of intense cost-cutting across the whole business, to invest more, rather than less, heavily in communications. The strategy was to respond to the consumer's desire to have its cake and eat it, and provide the service standards associated with BA at prices no longer out of sight from those of easyJet or Ryanair.

This approach made financial sense if, and only if, BA changed its business model to reduce its selling costs. This meant advertising would become directly responsible for making the sale, rather than merely offering costly incentives to travel agents to sell.

Specifically, driving those sales online, rather than via the telephone would eliminate further costs, by automating the booking process.

And driving sales quickly was imperative. The new revenue model made it advantageous for BA to sell out its cheapest seats on any given flight as early as possible in order to best manage its yields.

THE BIG CONUNDRUM

Driving these sales would prove to be doubly difficult for British Airways because the concept of 'frills' positioned it as the polar opposite of the budget airlines (Figure 6).

BA needed to challenge the very concept of 'frills' to reverse price and service perceptions. This would mean taking on two seemingly contradictory tasks.

Budget airlines	= No frills	∴ Low cost
British Airways	= Frills	∴ High cost

Figure 6: *Opposite perceptions*

'No frills' operators had created a widespread belief that the only way to offer low prices would be to cut back on service levels. BA had to destroy the myth that 'if you have service, it will cost you'.

Conversely, BA loyalists enjoyed the premium nature of the brand. And they didn't like the 'no frills' operators, regarding them as cheap but not exactly cheerful. It would be important to ensure that price competitiveness did not undermine perceptions of BA's world-renowned service delivery.[2]

ELICITING VALUE REAPPRAISAL

The solution to this conundrum was to address both issues with interrelated strands of activity.

The first sought to reposition 'frills' as 'service that matters', service that customers regarded as essential, service that customers perceived BA naturally would deliver and that budget airlines would not. The second was to create surprise at how low British Airways prices actually were. This achieved two things. It made a drama out of the smallness of the price whilst excusing the audience for not having noticed such low prices from BA before.

The value reappraisal strategy was therefore that BA offered service that matters at a surprisingly low cost, offering real competitive advantage (Figure 7).

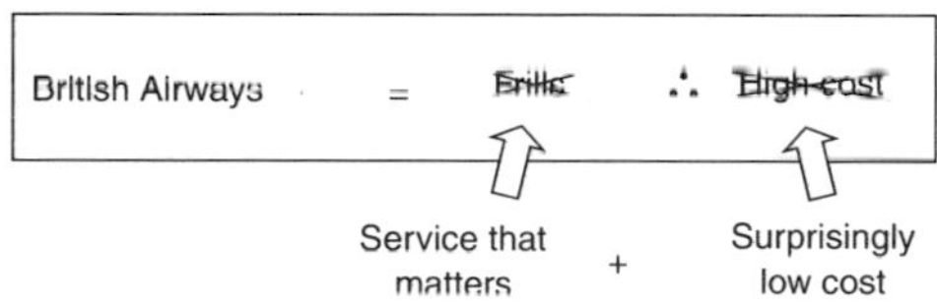

Figure 7: *Value reappraisal*

TWIN-TRACK CAMPAIGN

Two communications campaigns were developed to run simultaneously and achieve value reappraisal (Figure 8).

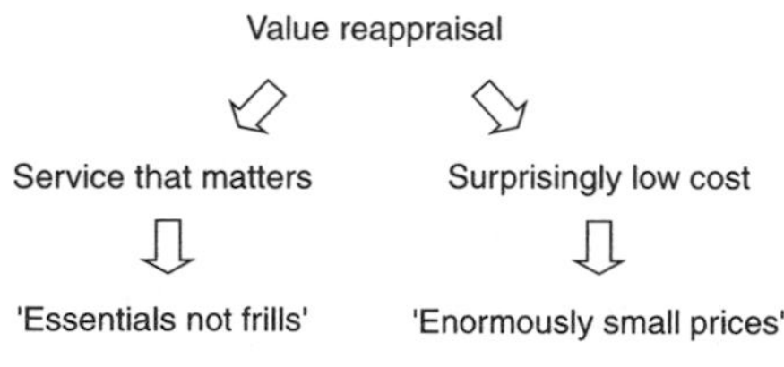

Figure 8: *Twin-track campaign*

2. This was particularly important to customers in other added-value segments in which BA operated – long haul, business, holidays, etc. – where service is a key driver of preference (not to mention a justification for a price premium).

Essentials not frills

This used P.J. O'Rourke (a familiar BA spokesperson) commentating on the shortcomings customers experience with budget airlines; musing on the importance of staff, back-up, 'planes that land somewhere near the city centre', etc. P.J. asked – 'Now where would you find an airline that gives you all that?', whilst seated in a BA lounge (Figure 9).

Music: 'We're all going on a summer holiday' (piano instrumental)

P.J. O'Rourke: The whole world and his wife wants to fly low cost these days …

But what we also want are airlines with, you know, more flights and more back-up when things go wrong …

A few more staff would be nice …

Planes that land somewhere near the city centre …

Reserved seats perhaps …

And food, all included in the price.

[As music turns into 'Lakme']
Now where would you find an airline that gives you all that?

You got it.

Figure 9: *Essentials not frills*

Enormously small prices

This showed small prices (in monetary terms) displayed in an un-missably large format. The campaign cheekily asked 'Have *you* seen how small our prices are?' (Figure 10).

The campaign's heavy use of large posters was even made the subject of the TV execution, with scenes of people going about their everyday lives not noticing the BA posters around them.

Music: 'Lakme' (piano instrumental)

[Woman sneezes and misses poster]

[Train passengers miss poster]

[Truck driver misses poster]

[Lady hanging out washing misses poster]

MVO: Have you seen how small our prices are?

Figure 10: *Enormously small prices*

INTEGRATED MEDIA

Stelios Hajiioannou of easyJet has said:

> 'You can't save souls in empty churches. Very quickly I realised that unless you make a big bang in advertising and make a big noise, you just die with lack of passengers.'[3]

To combat this, BA's media approach was stepped up to both out-shout and out-think the relentless visibility of the competition (Figure 11).

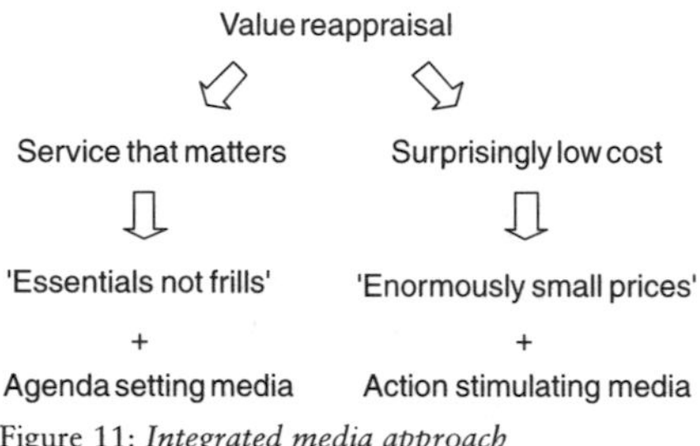

Figure 11: *Integrated media approach*

BA's spend was increased way above its short-haul market share. Frequency of communication was pumped up to convey that BA was committed to everyday low pricing, not just offering a one-off cheap-seats deal, with a small-space national press campaign running for 40 weeks out of 52 (Figure 12). The competition were effectively engaged on their own media territory, using national press, posters and radio.

THE SUNDAY TIMES

UK jets to get sky marshals

£59

Figure 12: *Regular use of high-traffic sites – national press and travel magazines*

In addition, however, 'surprise media' were used to echo the surprising prices theme. Poster projection images were placed on large buildings in key cities (Figure 13). The new medium of bank ATM screens was used for the first time ever as a way of interrupting people's daily lives with the BA message. BA 'camped out' in a previously very un-BA medium, *Time Out*, on its travel page. Finally, BA worked with *Sky News* to produce the BA Destinations Report, a bulletin running three times daily on *Sky News* for a whole year (Figure 14). The effect was a sense of ubiquity, un-missability and numerous triggers to action.

---

3. Quoted in Simon Calder, *No Frills*. Virgin Books.

Figure 13: *'Surprise media': Bank ATM screens and street projections*

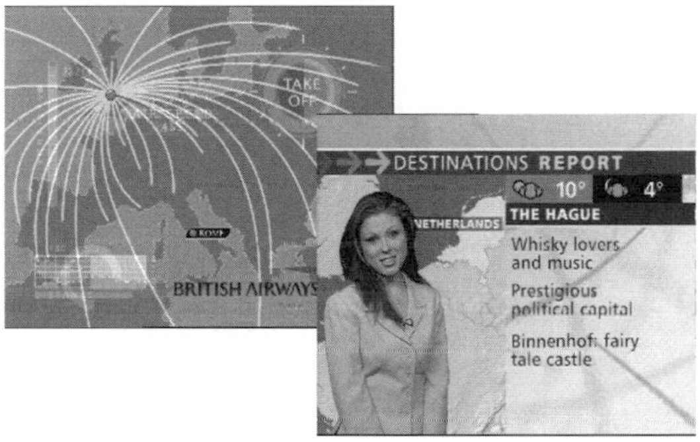

Figure 14: *BA Destinations Report on* Sky News

Additionally, television – hitherto not used by anyone in the budget sector – was introduced by BA as a powerful media differentiator.

Television played a role in both of the twin-track campaigns. The medium's power as an agenda setter was harnessed for the emotive service messaging. Its power as a media multiplier was used to spread the surprising prices messaging seen in the other media. Crucially, the two TV commercials were aired together as a top and tail, so that BA's competitive advantage was evident in every break.

Regional weightings of the campaign majored on BA's airport strengths around the country, highlighting a key competitive advantage of flying from convenient well-known airports such as London Heathrow, Gatwick, Birmingham and Manchester.

This was a short-haul campaign like no other in BA's history (Table 1). Scale and pattern of deployment were changed to match consumer behaviour and beat the budget airlines.

The campaign launched in September 2002, the initial phase running through to December. With a further roll-out over the next 18 months, the presence was deliberately long term (Figure 15).

TABLE 1: SHORT-HAUL CAMPAIGN

	Typical BA leisure campaign	Value reappraisal campaign	Strategic rationale
Unique channel ownership	None	TV	Achieve high cut-through
Budget	£0.5m	£10.5m at launch £21m to Mar 04	
Share of voice	10%	48% over launch	
Campaign length	3 weeks	Launch – 4 months Ongoing	Match flat purchase cycles
Number of channels deployed	3 (national press, radio, online)	10 (see Figure 15)	Become ubiquitous
Regional media usage	Radio	Regional press, radio, outdoor	Reflect BA's regional offering
Channel territories	None	Transport media	Take on the budget airlines
Channel up-weights	None	Posters, online, radio	

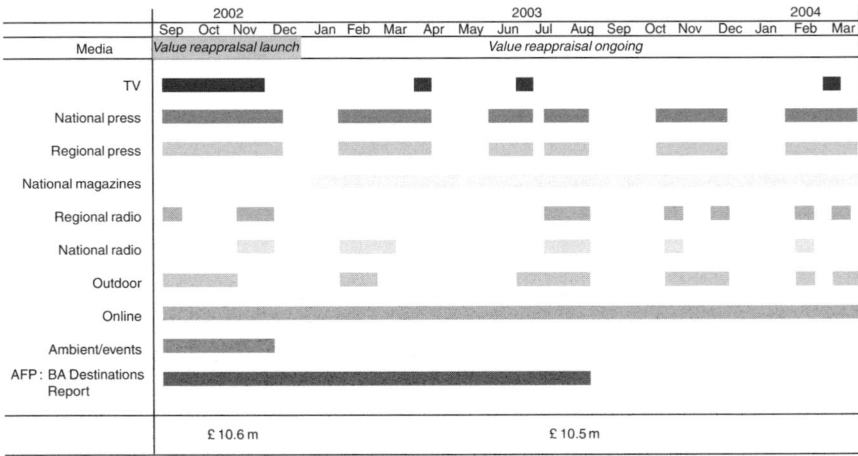

Figure 15: *Media schematic*

TURNING THE TIDE

Whereas the initial aim of the campaign was commercial stability, the campaign's impact first halted and then reversed the decline in BA's sales.

In overall terms, budget airlines appear to have squeezed yet more growth from the European market by opening up new routes. However, it is possible to analyse market share specifically on those routes operated by BA and budget airlines. Due to commercial sensitivity, we are unable to show this data. What this analysis does show, though, is a reversal of the long-term share losses and indeed a recovery to the extent that BA had regained share leadership of these key routes.

A number of factors strongly suggest that this sales response was directly caused by the advertising, starting with the clear effect it had on the mindset of the target audience.

SHIFTING PERCEPTIONS

The campaign sought to prompt more budget flyers to consider BA as a viable and preferable option to the budget airlines, by getting them to see the good value now on offer and 'bookmark' BA in their minds as better value (as opposed to just cheaper).

Looking specifically at short-haul leisure flyers, tracking data shows that the campaign achieved significant shifts in consideration to fly BA (Figure 16). What's more, these gains were clearly achieved at the expense of budget airline preference.

Tracking also shows us exactly how the campaign achieved this switch in loyalties.

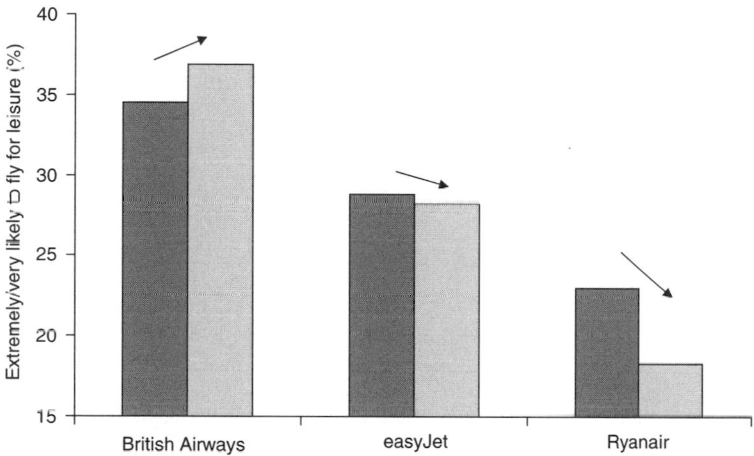

Figure 16: *Improved consideration*
Base: all short-haul leisure flyers, time period; pre-mid-June to mid-September, post-mid-September to mid-December
Source: IPSOS

Advertising recognition was enormous

British Airways advertising heritage ensures that awareness is always high. However, a strong uplift above BA's highest historical level demonstrates this particular campaign's powerful recognition amongst short-haul leisure flyers (Figure 17).

Consumers admitted the adverts were persuasive

It is relatively rare for consumers to admit that advertising persuades them of anything. However, when shown the BA advertising in qualitative research, leisure flyers not only correctly fed back the key price and service messages, but admitted these might influence their future flying choices.

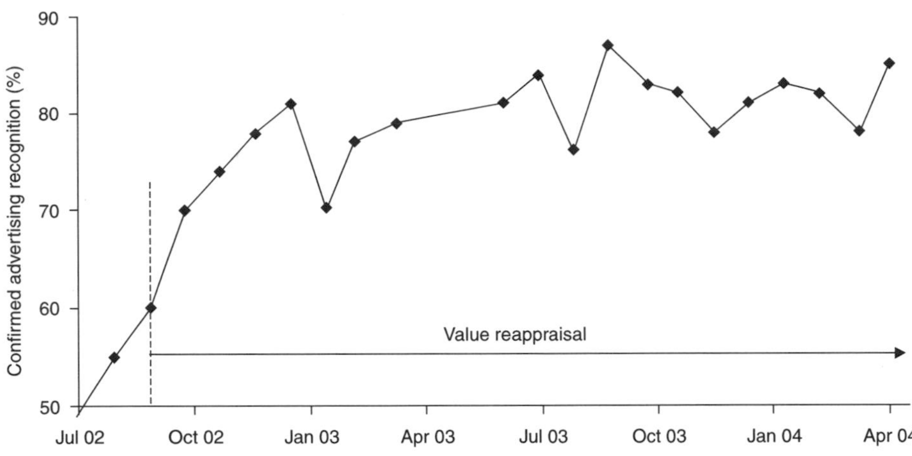

Figure 17: *Recognition of BA advertising*
Source: IPSOS

Quantitative research backs this up, with both price and service messages seen to be persuasive. Significantly this pattern is repeated amongst budget airline flyers who haven't recently flown BA, as well as BA regulars (Table 2).

TABLE 2: CONSUMER PERSUASION

	This advert makes me more likely to fly BA for leisure	
	Essentials not frills	Enormously small prices
BA flyers	37	45
Budget airline, non-BA flyers	32	50

Base: All short-haul leisure flyers, time period – mid-September to mid-March
Source: IPSOS

Price perceptions improved

Those aware of BA advertising have shown improving opinions of BA's prices over the course of the campaign (Figure 18).

Significantly the same people have shown a worsened perception of the budget airlines' prices (Figure 19).

Quality perceptions bolstered

Far from diminishing service perceptions as feared, the price campaign appears to have strengthened them.

Leisure flyers recalling BA's advertising have better perceptions of BA's quality of service (Figure 20). The increase in quality perceptions occurs in the early stages of the campaign, coinciding with the bulk of the media spend behind the 'Essentials not frills' element of the campaign.

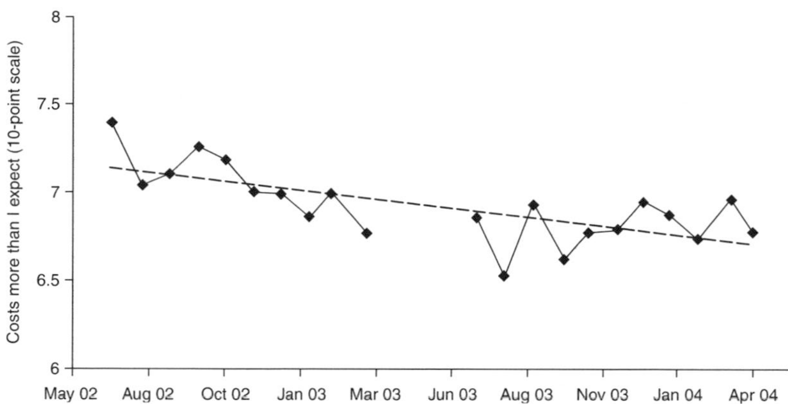

Figure 18: *Reduced price perceptions*
Note: Spring 2003 points missing owing to data error
Source: IPSOS

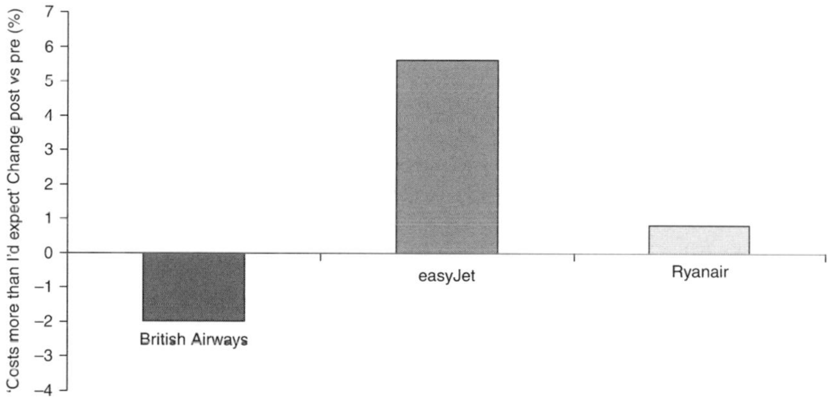

Figure 19: *Worsened competitor price perceptions*
Base: all short-haul leisure flyers aware of BA campaign – time period pre-mid-June to mid-September
Source: IPSOS

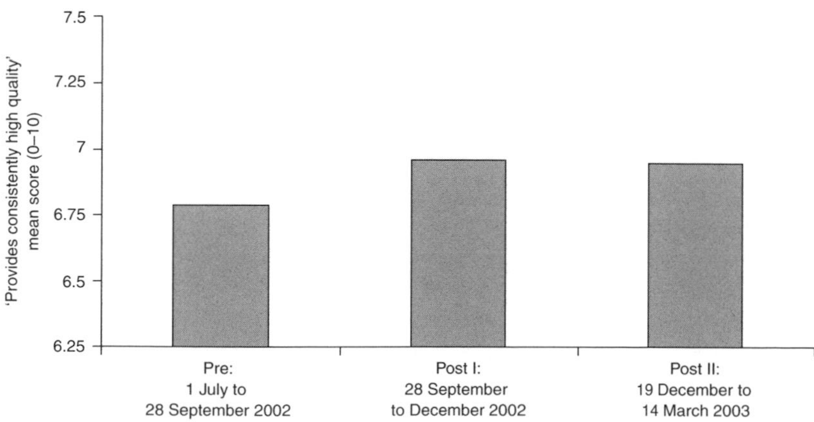

Figure 20: *Improved service perceptions*
Source: IPSOS-ASI Tracking Study

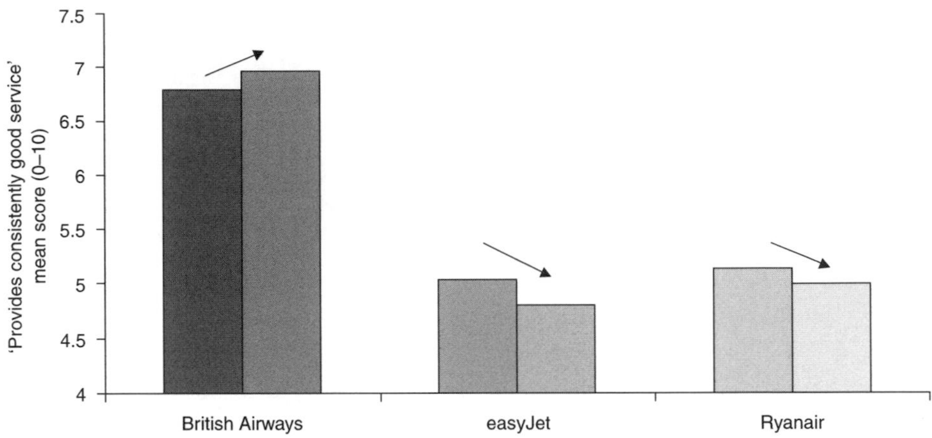

Figure 21: *Worsened competitor service perceptions*
Source: IPSOS

Once again, this increase is at the expense of perceptions of competitors' quality – something the service element of the strategy was clearly intent on doing (Figure 21).

It is also useful to note that the campaign did not prejudice the perception of BA's other important customers (e.g. business flyers and long-haul customers). Indeed it positively reinforced their perception of BA's quality of service (Figure 22).

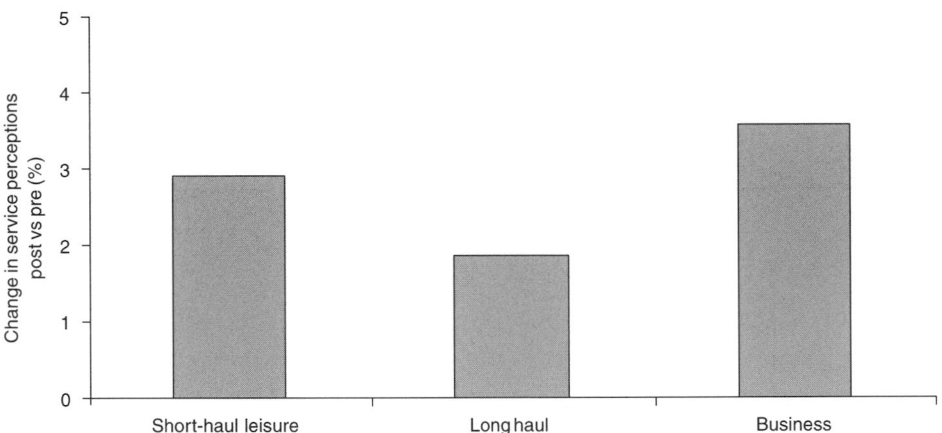

Figure 22: *Across the board improvements*
Source: BA Tracking Study

Leading to increased consideration

The shifts in consideration amongst short-haul leisure flyers can be apportioned to advertising by illustrating a decline in consideration for those not aware of BA's advertising versus an increase in consideration amongst those aware (Figure 23).

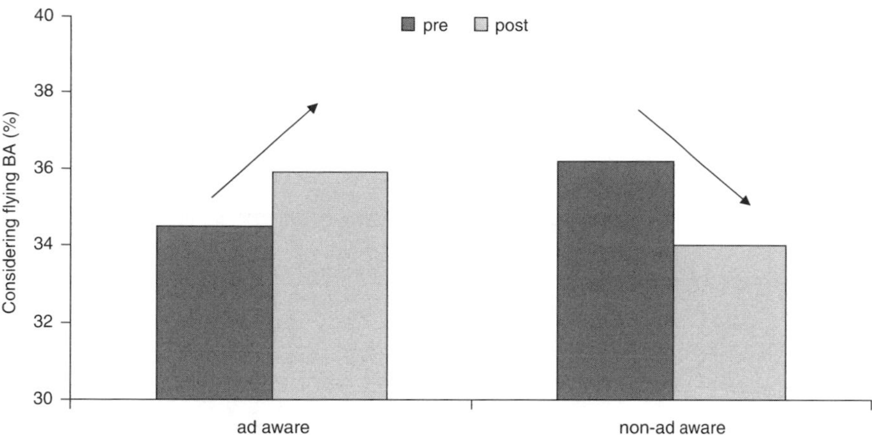

Figure 23: *Advertising influences consideration*
Base: all short haul leisure flyers, time period – pre-mid-June to mid-September
Source: IPSOS-ASI Tracking Study

SHIFTING BEHAVIOUR

These shifts in consideration scores converted directly into changes in behaviour, hence an improvement in BA's bookings. One simple analysis allows us to attribute the behavioural response directly to the campaign. A key plank in the strategy was not only to encourage consumers to book with BA, but specifically to book online. Consequently the advertising only featured ba.com and never a telephone number as point of access (Figure 24).

Figure 24: *Detail from press and TV advertisements*

This was a radical and significant change for BA. It had been possible (albeit not that easy) to book fares on the site for some time. However this had never been a priority channel for the airline, attracting less than 5% of all bookings. Consequently it had never been prominently or exclusively featured as a call to action in marketing. It is hugely significant therefore to look at the trend of bookings made at ba.com following the campaign (Figure 25).

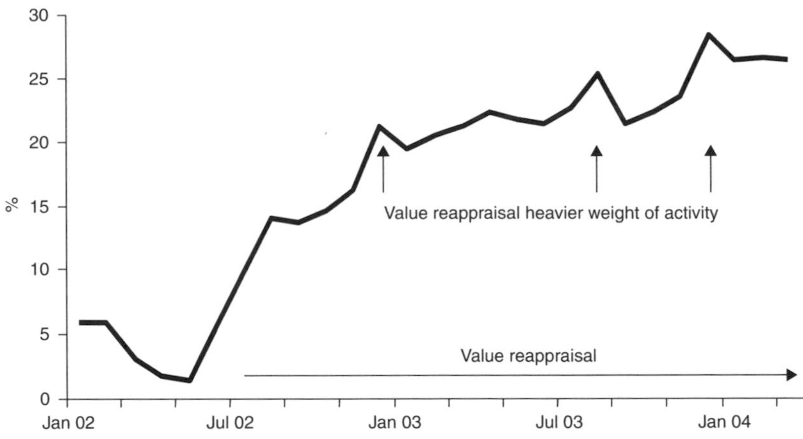

Figure 25: *Shift to online booking*

BA did improve its fare-booking engine to make booking online easier in spring 2002, before significant advertising support. Without any activity driving site visits, the initial impact of this change was modest. Online bookings growth really took off around the time of the value reappraisal campaign.

There has undoubtedly been a trend towards booking airfares online; consumers had tended to use travel sites (such as Expedia or Travelocity) or indeed the budget airlines' own sites. This campaign, however, saw the first significant upturn in BA's own *direct* online bookings.

We also note the response in online bookings specifically to heavier weights of value reappraisal activity.

RETURN ON INVESTMENT

Two sets of analyses were carried out to determine the campaign's effect on sales:

1. an econometric analysis
2. a route analysis.

Econometric analysis

This allowed us to quantify the power of TV (see Table 3), and account for the impact of 9/11 (–9.7%), seasonality and competitive activity (–4%).

TABLE 3: MODELLED MEDIA EFFECTS

	Volume (%)*	Revenue (£m)	Coefficient	T-statistic	Confidence (%)
TV effect	7.8	£13	1.27	5.0	100
Other media	1.4	£4.7	0.0139	0.9	80.1
Total	9.2	£17.7			

R squared = 83%, Durbin-Watson = 1.17
* Average weekly percentage uplift in volume year on year
Source: Ninah Consulting

On an advertising investment of £10.6m across September–December 2002, this represents a revenue ROI figure of 1.7.

Additionally, we have projected that the uplift over the campaign's life (had there been no competitive activity, e.g. Ryanair's '500,000 Free Flights' or easyJet's '50% Off' offers), would have generated an additional £29.4m.

If BA had not advertised, the model shows it would have lost over £11.7m in sales.

Without being privy to detailed actual price tracking,[4] we have constructed another analysis to tease out the direct effects of price.

Route analysis

To isolate the effects of price from communications, advertised routes vs non-advertised routes were compared (Figure 26). The basis for this is that no significant price differentials existed between destinations that were advertised and those that were not advertised. Routes were then allocated into different sets, depending on whether fares to that specific destination were featured in advertising or not. Passenger data could then be analysed according to whether routes had received advertising or not, and with which media specifically.

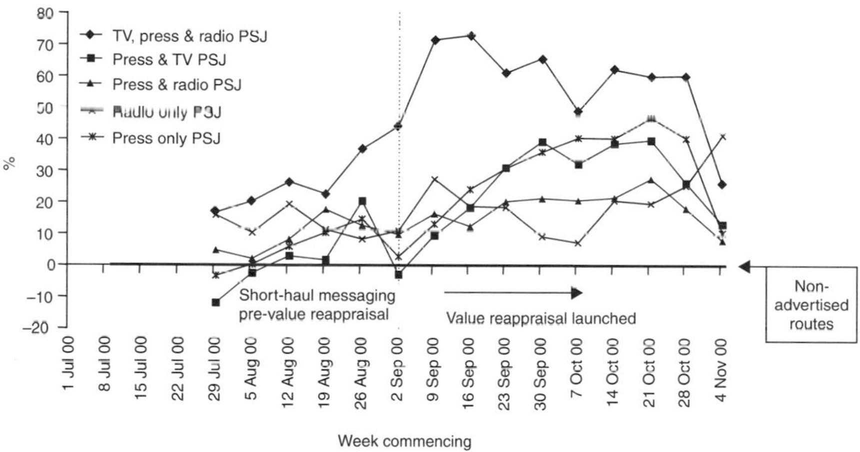

Figure 26: *Multi-media effects*

Two key learnings arise from the data.

1. The sheer power of pure advertising and the effects of combinability across media. This clearly (and reassuringly) shows that a combination of television, press and radio is the most effective media mix, although all media mixes out-perform the non-advertised routes (Table 4).[5]
2. Perhaps the most potent conclusion was the fact that the value reappraisal campaign accounted for a greater uplift in bookings than the effect of the price

4. Owing to client confidentiality we were unable to gain access to this data.
5. Owing to confidentiality we were unable to disclose the exact detail for how these media interact.

reductions themselves. In other words, telling people about the low prices generated more sales than lowering the prices alone.

TABLE 4: THE POWER OF ADVERTISING

	Volume (%)*	Revenue (£m)
Pure advertising effect	7.3	£11.9
Price reduction effect	1.7	£5.8

Table 4 shows the pure effect of communications having accounted for price; and that the three main advertised media drove revenue generated by the campaign by a factor of more than double that of price.

BROADER INFLUENCES

BA's value reappraisal campaign not only had crucially invigorating effects on BA's commercial performance, it also had a host of other positive repercussions for the company.

Influence on competitors

Foremost of these was the impact on the budget airlines themselves. Simon Calder stated that:

> 'The low-cost carriers have been genuinely surprised by how robust and sustained BA's response to them has been.'

easyJet, Go and Ryanair had enjoyed an almost unchallenged position. They were clearly rattled by BA's sudden competitiveness. They responded with a flurry of new price initiatives rushed to market at great cost to their profit margins. These offers were heavily promoted in the autumn of 2002 (Figure 27).

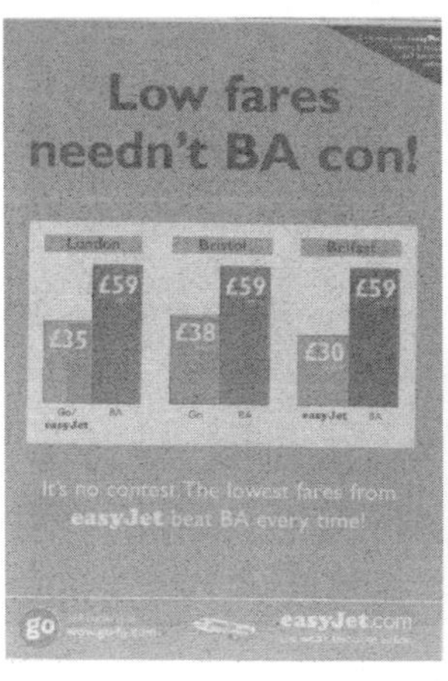

Figure 27: *BA's competitors' offers*

Influence on the media

The campaign also encouraged the media to change their tune. Prior to BA's activity, the media had supported the budget airlines as champions of customer value. During the period of activity (in direct contrast to their previous portrayal of BA) there were no less than 109 positive articles in the national press on BA's value reappraisal initiative. More generally, a shift in reporting became evident. With BA now seen to be offering good value and with the news agenda shift to 'service that matters', the media began to be openly supportive of BA and increasingly critical of the budget airlines' shortcomings (Figure 28).

Before

Low-cost carriers take off but BA still in a tailspin
'The continued and rapid expansion of low-cost airlines such as easyJet and Rayanair has become a far greater threat to British Airways than the loss of passengers resulting from the terrorist attacks on the United States.'
The Business, 13 January 2002

BA loses to no-frill carriers
'Airline travellers are more likely to fly with one of the low fare carriers than with British Airways, figures today show for the first time.'
Evening Standard, 8 April 2002

BA persists with sky-high fares on domestic flights
'BA seems intent on pricing itself out of the market.'
The Times, 11 April 2002

'Expensive BA**ds'**
'British Airways executives rattled by the low-cost airline's advertising ... it's time they started worrying about the prices they charge their passengers.'
Sun, June 2002

At these prices you'd have to BA mug
'... you'd have to be off your airline trolley to choose British Airways at the moment.'
Daily Mirror, March 2002

After

We're cheap ... so fly us – BA is taking on the low-cost airlines
'The airline that once proudly proclaimed it was the 'world's favourite airline' has changed tack and is now fighting for its life with advertising asking 'have you seen how small our prices are?'
'The company has never before advertised itself so widely: on primetime television and in newspapers; even at cash point machines and on Tube trains.'
Daily Mail, 21 September 2002

Happy landings – Looking to make your money go further?
'Many scheduled airlines are offering deals that rival the no-frills operators ... BA is worth a look.'
Guardian, 19 April 2003

Which is the low-cost airline?
'The no-frills airlines are beginning to lose their monopoly of cheap fares. Our latest survey shows that you often have as good a chance of finding the cheapest fare on British Airways.'
Daily Telegraph, 11 January 2003

The five gripes that irritate you the most
'Cut-price airlines – their flights are often cheap, but not always cheerful – that is the message from our postbag.'
Mail on Sunday, 15 December 2002

My low-cost journey from hell
'How a journey that should have taken two hours took me over 24 ... Next time, I'll take the easy option, BA!'
Daily Express, January 2002

Figure 28: *Examples of press reporting before and after value reappraisal*
Source: Reuters

Confirmation of this perceptual shift amongst travel journalists came when *Time Out* took the significant step of retitling its publication *European breaks by budget airlines* to *Europe by air*, because it now included BA flights and prices in its pages for the first time.

Perhaps the biggest recognition of the perceptual shift came in June 2003 when BA won a reader poll in the *Guardian* and *Observer*, being named 'Best Low-cost

Best low-cost airline

In a year when the line between the budget, charter and scheduled airlines grew increasingly blurred, and — in advertising and strategy — airlines challenged their rivals' claims to be the cheapest, one company seems to have emerged as a clear winner in the minds of our readers. British Airways' price cuts seem to have propelled them to the top of this particular league. Meanwhile, the two best scoring no-frills brands, Buzz and Go, no longer exist.

	%score
Totals	*66.8*
1 **British Airways** (-)	76.6
2 British Midland (8)	74.1
3 Buzz* (6)	71.2
4 Go* (1)	70.7
5 easyJet* (2)	67.2
6 Britannia (-)	65.4
7 Monarch (7)	62.7
8 My Travel Lite (-)	62.6
9 Aer Lingus (-)	62.1
10 Ryanair* (3)	61.4
11 JMC (4)	61.2
12 Airtours (-)	60.8
13 Air 2000 (5)	58.1

Figure 29: *'Best low-cost airline'*

Airline'. To have even been considered for a sector that less than a year earlier it was not even regarded as in, is an astonishing achievement (Figure 29).

Other influencers picked up on the transformation in a positive light too. The Air Transport Users Council Study (September 2003) reported that BA was often the cheapest short-haul airline, and it further underlined the value to passengers in time and money of centrally located airports and service elements such as greater leg-room, the provision of back-up aircraft, and complimentary food and drink. The *Daily Telegraph* picked up on the report, headlining: 'BA often better value than Ryanair, says fares watchdog'.

INFLUENCE ON THE CITY

We examined earlier how seriously the City regarded the issues with BA's European network. A change of heart is now apparent there too.

Chris Avery (JP Morgan) elaborates:

> 'The [value reappraisal] initiative is an important part of the fight for volume in short haul. A way had to be found for dealing with the low-cost carriers, to reduce erosion in economy class – which BA has succeeded in doing. The campaign need not turn a profit; the strategy is about breaking even – which it is now doing.'

The success of the campaign is seen to have helped in stabilising the European network, effectively giving the company a blood transfusion.

Recent analyst reports have become much more favourable on the airline's fortunes

> '...The airline has transformed its heavily loss-making European operations and addressed its cost of sale position .... Buy.'
>
> UBS report

Consequently BA's share price has improved markedly since its low point in March 2002, securing BA's return to the FTSE 100 (Figures 30 and 31).

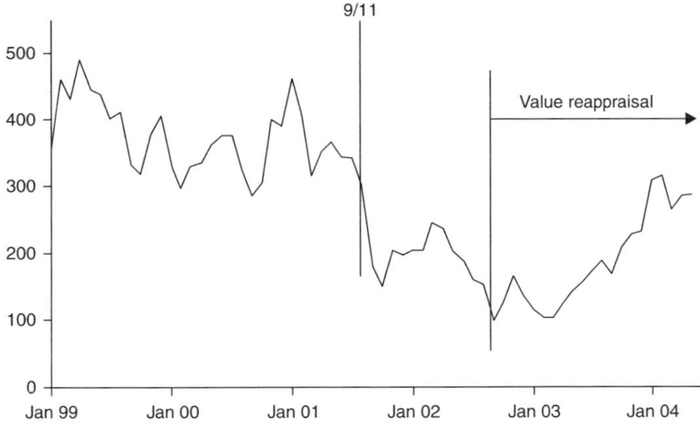

Figure 30: *Share price recovery*

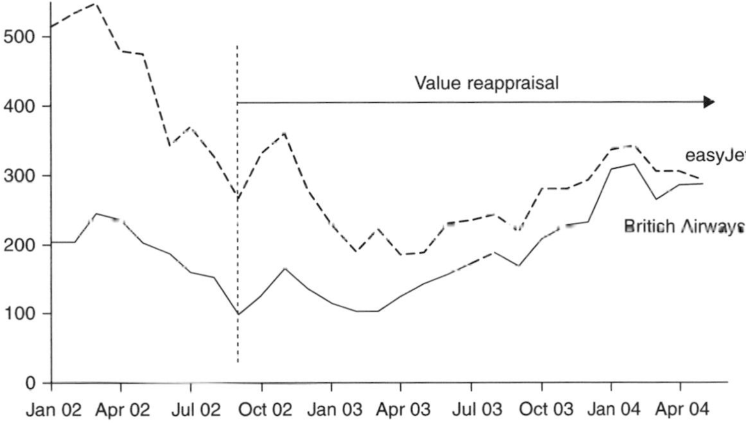

Figure 31: *Share price outperforms budget airlines*

Influence internally

Not least, the value reappraisal campaign has changed attitudes within BA. Two quotes from front-line BA staff sum up the change of attitude perfectly:

> 'We do things differently now because we know the company is selling itself as a low-cost-option airline – it changes the way we do things.'
>
> 'We've come back fighting. I can't tell you how good that makes you feel when you're wearing the uniform.'

BROADER RETURNS

As we have shown, there was much more than just a few points of market share at stake here. Indeed, options considered in the airline's 'Future Size and Shape' review included withdrawal of all or most services in Europe. The BA board rejected these options because of the following implications.

- *Loss of feeder traffic for long haul.* 35% of passengers carried on BA's long-haul routes are transfer passengers making journeys to or from Europe, via Heathrow or Gatwick. It is reasonable to assume that most of this revenue would be lost if British Airways withdrew such a service.
- *Loss of revenue covering fixed costs.* Whilst European services were not profitable at a net level. Their revenue does nevertheless contribute towards offsetting overheads. Large chunks of the airline's fixed cost base (e.g. property costs) would remain, even without a European network to service.
- *Loss of strategic position.* With consolidation forecast for the European market, there is great value to the British Airways board of having a viable and substantial network. It opens up options to make proactive and strategic moves, rather than being dictated by reactive tactics. As the CEO put it:

> 'We're either a player in Europe or we're not. When consolidation comes, we want to be in the position of consolidator, not consolidatee in Europe.'
>
> Rod Eddington, press release

- *Loss of reputation.* Withdrawal from Europe would have been seen as a regrettable move many times more significant than the retirement of Concorde. The impact on brand reputation at both consumer and corporate level would have been considerable.

It is disingenuous and commercially sensitive to reveal here the financial magnitude of all these consequences. Nevertheless, on the first point alone, it is interesting to note that 35% of the airline's long-haul business is worth some £2.9bn annually. That revenue has been safeguarded by the value reappraisal campaign. Even if one took a deeply sceptical view and apportioned the campaign only a 1% influence in the safeguarding of this business, it would have more than paid for itself on this measure alone, in one year alone.

Cost of sale reductions

Perhaps the most interesting learning to emerge from this case is the effect of increased advertising on selling costs. As we saw, the campaign effectively drove consumers to book direct and to make that booking online. This has a double saving for BA – both agents' commission and the costs of running telephone booking are eliminated.

So the overall cost of selling went down, even though advertising spend went up. Unfortunately commercial sensitivities prevent us from revealing the exact value of this move. However, in its latest results, BA lists selling costs reduced from £706m to £554m. A saving of some £152m and certainly worth investing in advertising to achieve.

Shareholder value

Immediately before the value reappraisal campaign, British Airways was valued on the stock market at a historical low of £1.07bn. At the time of going to press, the airline was valued at £3.11bn, a growth in shareholder value of over £2bn. Even as a modest factor in this turnaround, the value generated by the campaign is considerable.

ON THE HORIZON

Horizons in the airline market are short and getting shorter. So many factors, many of them way beyond the control of the airlines themselves, impact on the size and dynamics of the market, and BA – above all – has had to learn to adapt fast, effectively and radically to the travelling public's needs.

But BA has proved that it can weather some pretty inclement competitive conditions, and that it has the resource and will to win. The budget airlines have not all fared so well. Duo has gone bust and neither Go nor Buzz exist any longer.

Simon Calder believes that there is more to come in the next few months (winter 2004–05):

> 'There is likely to be a bloodbath in the low-cost sector this winter. From their perspective the last people the low-costs should be fighting is each other, but that's what they're doing by competing on routes and bringing too much capacity into the market.'

He adds a positive footnote for BA:

> 'BA is well positioned through this period given its entire network – with business traffic more buoyant than leisure in the winter and the ability to match capacity to demand.'

Importantly, BA has proved the positive contribution that a coherent, aggressive communications campaign can make to the sort of competitive struggle it had on its hands in the short-haul sector. It has learnt that promotion can drive volume, and it has seen the power of a multimedia approach. It has also demonstrated the enduring effectiveness of television. It has been able to evaluate the effect on sales of strong promotion, and it has learnt how to borrow some of its competitors' communications clothes without abandoning its core brand values.

BA's value reappraisal campaign is a dramatic example of the almost instant business effectiveness a well-engineered communications programme can have. When times are very tough the temptation to withdraw from advertising investment is strong. BA's experience, however, will serve to remind us all of the potential of the communications tools at our disposal.

ACKNOWLEDGEMENTS

The authors would like to thank the following for their valued advice and sterling efforts: Simon Marquis, Mark Waugh and Emma Robertson at ZenithOptimedia; Rohini Varughese at M&C Saatchi; Mike Campbell and Mike Cross at Ninah Consulting and Sam Dias.

10

Demand Broadband

Making supply match demand

Principal authors: Francesca Brosan, Ben Dansie and Chris Butterworth, Omobono
Media agency: John Ayling Associates

EDITOR'S SUMMARY

This is a textbook regional and small-budget marketing case study covering a unique range of media and reporting a broad series of effects.

In 2002, the East of England Development Agency decided to promote broadband in the region because a lack of high-speed connection had been stifling growth there. The objective was to gain broadband access from telecoms companies that had refused to supply it to rural communities.

Cambridge-based agency, Omobono, developed an integrated campaign to drive those without broadband to an online brokerage system that grouped people with other registrants in their area. The idea was to show people that, while they had little influence on the situation individually, as a group they could have a strong voice on the future of broadband in the region. The 'Demand Broadband' pressure group was born. The campaign involved outdoor, radio, sales promotion and pioneering direct mail; Omobono was the first agency to use parish council records to create a direct mail database.

Before the campaign launched, the availability of broadband in the East of England was 53%. Afterwards this figure had risen to 98%. Of the 16,699 registrants who could not get broadband, 93% will be broadband-enabled by the end of next year. BT has now changed its policy and is in the process of enabling telephone exchanges throughout the region.

This campaign, costing £413,000, has created £4m of value for its client.

INTRODUCTION

Most communications campaigns aim to make demand match supply. The Demand Broadband campaign had the opposite objective. Plenty of people in the East of England wanted broadband, but the telecoms companies weren't supplying it.

The East of England Development Agency (EEDA) identified this as a major barrier to economic growth in the region. The Demand Broadband campaign by Omobono had a direct effect on removing that restraint. Through an integrated communications campaign it drove the broadband bereft to an online brokerage that grouped people with other registrants in their area. The results were dramatic.

- Online registration targets were surpassed by 800%.[1]
- Of the 16,699 registrants who previously could not get broadband, 93% will be broadband enabled by the end of 2005.[2]
- Availability of broadband in the region increased from 53% pre-campaign[3] to 98% post campaign.[4]
- Overwhelming response to EEDA's Connecting Communities competition. From an original desired target of 70,[5] 2850 communities requested entry forms; 192 got through to the final stage.
- BT changed its tune, initially supplying broadband in eight rural locations of EEDA's choice, subsequently establishing trigger levels in all but 12 exchanges.[6]

But don't take our word for it – for what the client said, see Figure 1.[7]

---

1. All statistics on registrants to the brokerage are downloaded directly from the database contained on www.broadbandbrokerage.co.uk.
2. Memo from Laurence Ramsey to Omobono, May 2004, based on Masons Communications report to EEDA, April 2004:

   '93% of registrants are connected to exchanges that are enabled, or that Mason forecasts will be enabled by BT before the end of 2005, or are in areas covered by EEDA funded projects and thus should receive broadband by the end of 2005.'

   'The figures were based upon those in the Masons report on the number of registrants on the database receiving broadband. To quote: "From the EEDA sample, Mason predicts that some 11% (1748) of registrants will not have a BT Broadband service before the end of 2005. However, 50% of this number (8711) currently resides within an area that has received funding from the EEDA Competition, and should have alternative service availability in the coming months.'

   'This gives us about 5.5%. The other 4.5% is derived from the effect of our advertising on the number of registrations on the BT website reflecting increased takeup of broadband across the region and thus exchange enablement.'

   'We know that BT's figures show that the region is in third place in terms of broadband takeup whereas we are in the middle area of ICT adoption as seen in the Regional ICT Benchmarking survey. This would indicate an increased demand effect of 5–6%. I am translating that into the 4.5% extra coverage due to an increase of exchanges reaching their trigger levels due to this demand.'
3. Pre-campaign coverage figures for broadband in the eastern region and the UK supplied by Analysys Consulting Ltd (April 2002).

   'Analysys estimates that 53% of the population of the East of England currently has access to a 'mass market' broadband solution – that is one targeted at residential or small business consumers. This compares with a national figure of 62%. In rural communities in the East of England this figure falls to 5%.'
4. Masons Communications, April 2004:

   'With the growing number of local initiatives, particularly those with direct support from EEDA through the Connecting Communities Competition and Broadband Brokerage Service, this figure will near 98% by the end of 2005.'
5. Campaign target of 2000 registrations and 70 competition entries by March 2004 agreed with EEDA at tender stage – September 2002.
6. Masons Communications presentation at the EEDA Broadband Summit, 7 May 2004.
7. Memo from Laurence Ramsey to EEDA Board, 16 April 2004.

This is a summary of a report compiled by Masons Communications to assess the impact of EEDA and BT initiatives on the registrants in our Demand Broadband website.

I think a number of positives come out of the work:

- 49% of registrants now have ADSL available on their local exchange
- 71% of registrants either have ADSL available now, or are on an exchange that has exceeded the BT pre-registration threshold
- 88% of registrants are connected to exchanges that are enabled, or that Masons forecast will be enabled by BT before the end of 2005
- 93% of registrants are connected to exchanges that are enabled, or that Mason forecasts will be enabled by BT before the end of 2005, or are in areas covered by EEDA funded projects and thus should receive broadband by the end of 2005

Bearing in mind that our registrations are heavily biased towards rural areas (unlike BT's figures), I think that this is a great result. I would estimate that the effect of our activities has been to increase the probable availability to our population by at least 10%: 5% by direct action with the Connecting Communities Competition in the areas least likely to get broadband and another 5% by a combination of advertising (which put the region third in the country in terms of registration rates with BT and subsequent take-up levels), by initiating pilot projects and provoking BT into taking action in some areas and responding energetically to threats in the market.

Figure 1: *Memo from Laurence Ramsey – EEDA Broadband Fund Manager, 16 April 2004*

BACKGROUND

Every day, we use the web more – in our homes, for our children, in our business lives. The strain being placed on old 56K modems is just too much. Long waits are the norm, frustration mounts. So why not switch to broadband, you may ask? Well, in 2002 this was easier said than done. In the more rural areas of Britain, broadband coverage was almost non-existent. It cost at least £45,000 to enable one telephone exchange and unless demand for the service was high enough, the telecoms companies weren't interested in supplying it.

This was the problem faced by the East of England Development Agency (EEDA). In 1999 it had identified lack of broadband internet access as one of the major constraints to the region's economic growth. Even in early 2002, only half the population in the region had access to broadband, compared to 62% of the UK as a whole. And the telecoms companies, under huge financial pressures, were only interested in supplying areas with high-density populations. This ruled out most of the eastern region. The UK Government target, 'to have the most extensive and competitive broadband market in the G7 by 2005',[8] seemed a long way off.

8. UK National Broadband Strategy quoted in EEDA Broadband Fund Action Plan: Final version/Background 1.1/April 2002.

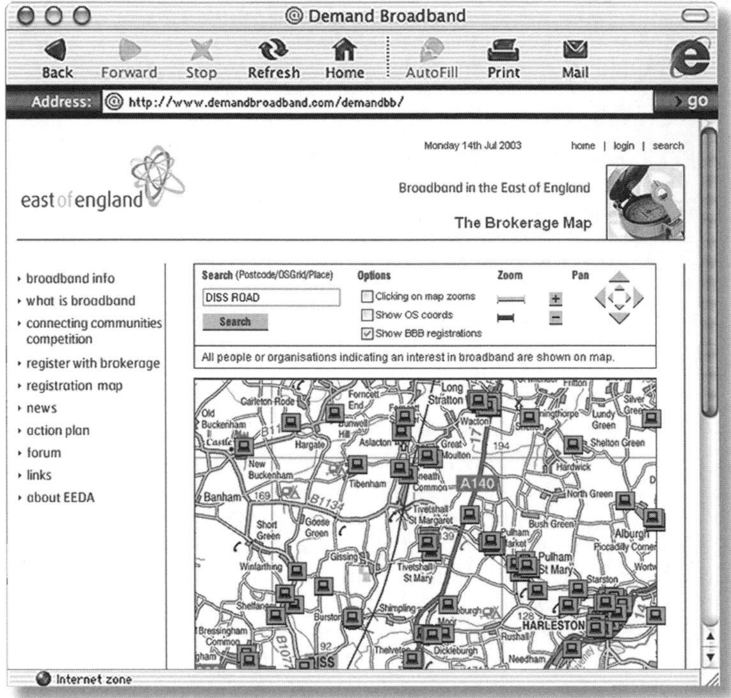

Figure 2: *Map showing individual registrations around Diss, Norfolk. Diss was one of the first two clusters to be identified and broadband enabled as a direct result of the campaign*

EEDA's solution was two-fold. First it set up an online brokerage where people could register their interest in getting broadband (Figure 2). Registrations from the same areas could then be clustered together to prove to the telecoms companies that there were potentially profitable pockets of demand.

The second strand of EEDA's plan was a competition for communities in the region to win connection to broadband; £3m was set aside to fund it. To win, communities had to make a convincing case for the need for broadband in areas where it wasn't commercially available.

COMMUNICATIONS PLANNING

So the initiative was in place. Now EEDA had to tell people about it. Lots of people. In fact, anyone in the East of England who used a computer. And, not least, they had to get businesses interested in the initiative, as it would be their custom that would really whet the appetite of the broadband suppliers.

In April 2002, EEDA appointed the Cambridge-based agency Omobono to plan a communications campaign to stimulate awareness, drive registrants to the brokerage and get entries to the competition. The targets set were seemingly simple: 2000 registrants on the broadband brokerage and 70 communities to register interest in entering the competition.

But there was a problem. In mid-2002, broadband was not well understood by either the consumer or business audiences. Education was therefore going to be required, education of the entire adult population. But, with a total communications budget of £500k, the perfect medium for reaching them – regional TV – was beyond EEDA's means. Luckily, this was about to be resolved without it lifting a finger.

As part of its pre-campaign research, Omobono discovered that BT was planning a major advertising campaign that would explain the benefits of broadband to the public. This meant that EEDA's money could be put directly into helping the region get more access to it.

Power to the people

It became clear that for the campaign to achieve its objectives (registration of interest and competition entries) it had to do more than just raise people's awareness, it had to get people to act. And it had to get them to act without there actually being a product to buy.

Omobono also realised it could show people that, whilst they had no influence on the situation individually, as a group they could have a strong voice on the future of broadband in the region. The inspiration was to infer that there was already a group out there that people could join up with. The Demand Broadband pressure group was born.

By creating an online presence at www.demandbroadband.com, Omobono offered broadband malcontents a home. The objective of the communications campaign therefore became to drive people to the brokerage, where their details could be captured and where they could learn about all the aspects of the competition (Figure 3).

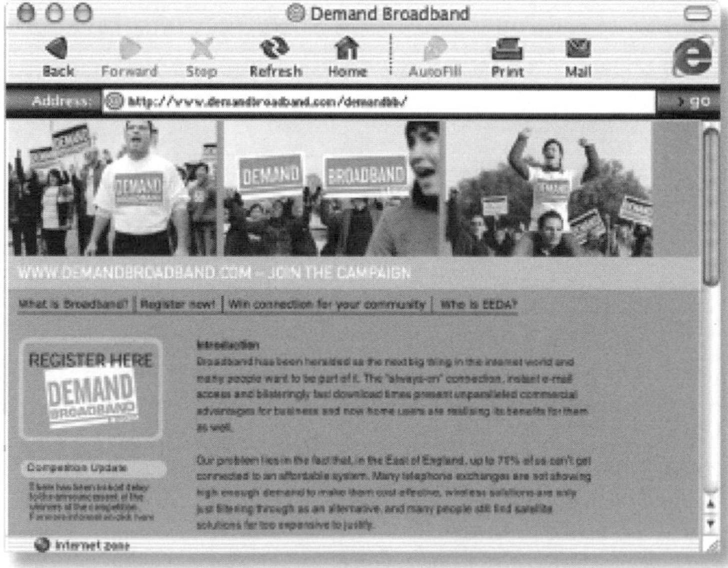

Figure 3: *Demand Broadband home page*

Omobono also realised that advertising alone could not achieve what was needed. A strong creative theme was required not just to create the necessary impact in advertising, but to pull all the communications together, and to allow the campaign to run over a continued period. Its first inspiration again provided the answer. The Demand Broadband pressure group had a strong visual presence, showing campaigners rising up in protest. Black and white reportage-style photography was used to accentuate the grittiness of the subject matter and this was offset with a striking use of colour to emphasise the call to action. But the theme also allowed the campaign to run not just in traditional advertising media, but to act in the manner of the word, thereby permeating the consciousness of residents and businesses in the eastern regions.

MEDIA PLANNING

Omobono's media buying partner, John Ayling Associates, put together a cost-effective media plan that addressed the problems of advertising in a rural area by using radio (Figure 4), supplemented by bus sides and the imaginatively titled 'mega-rears' (Figures 5 and 6).

Omobono suspected, however, that communities would need more than advertising to get them to enter the competition. So, it came up with the idea of mailing every one of the 1653 parish councils in the region (Figure 7).

Unbelievably there was no database of the parishes in existence, so the agency undertook the task of building one. This involved spending days in libraries around the region where only hard copy was available, searching the myriad websites that local government generates and spending hours on the telephone tracking down the various individuals involved. In many cases the process was so difficult that data entry had to be done line by line.

Radio Script

Client East of England Development Agency

Title What the.....???

Length 30 seconds **Air Date** TBC

Male radio presenter:
Right, I think we've just got time to go over for the weather...

SFX: *Muffled banging and shouting. Door opens – shouting gets clearer*

Protester 1: *(shouting)*
Demand broadband now

Presenter:
Well, we seem to be...

Protester 2:
Demand broadband. Almost half the East of England can't get hi-speed internet access. We're waiting too long for stuff to download, businesses are losing money 'cause they can't make the most of e-commerce...

SFX: *Microphone ruffle*

Presenter:
OK. You've made your.....

Protester 1:
Rise up. Click onto www.demandbroadband.com. Join the campaign from the East of England Development Agency.

Protester 2:
yeah, join up... www.demandbroadband.com

SFX: *More microphone ruffle and sudden cut-out. A few seconds silence....*

omobono The Elim Building, 27 Montague Road, Cambridge CB4 1BU, UK
Tel +44 (0)1223 307000 Web omobono.co.uk

Radio Script

Client East of England Development Agency

Title Faulty

Length 30 seconds **Air Date** TBC

SFX: *Sounds of meeting in a community centre*

Chairman *(stuffy & slightly officious)*:
Thank you. And now to Item 6 on the agenda, the faulty connection on the light outside the community centre...

Protester 1: *(middle class female, interjecting)*
I must protest. This whole community is not connected properly because we can't get broadband internet access. I asked the Chairman to put this on the agenda but he just fudged the issue. Now look, there's a competition from the East of England Development Agency to win broadband connection for communities in this region. We must get a group of people together to enter it.

Chairman:
Thank you Mrs Brown, you've made your point...

Protester 1:
No, I haven't finished yet. All the information about the competition is on the website www.demandbroadband.com

Chairman:
Thank you Mrs Brown

Protester 1:
I say again, www.demandbroadband.com

SFX: *Muttering in the crowd, fade out*

omobono The Elim Building, 27 Montague Road, Cambridge CB4 1BU, UK
Tel +44 (0)1223 307000 Web omobono.co.uk

Figure 4: *Scripts for the radio adverts: 'What the ...?' promoted registration on the brokerage, whilst 'Faulty' drove entries to the competition*

Figure 5: *Bus sides took the message across the East of England*

Figure 6: *Mega-rears*

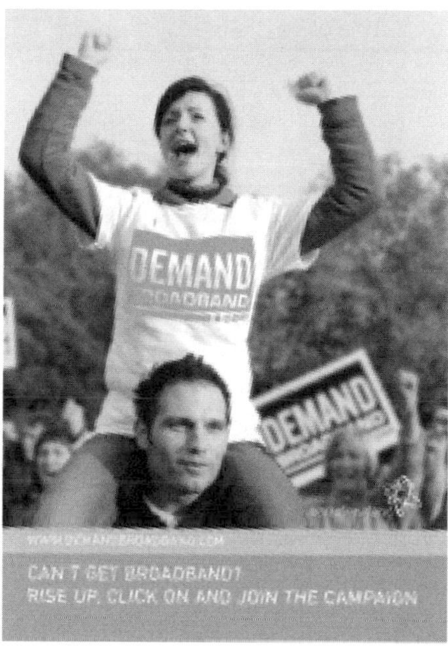

Figure 7: *One of the parish packs sent to each of the 1653 parishes in the East of England*

Once the database was complete a parish pack was assembled containing information about the competition and how to enter. It also included publicity material, which the parish could personalise to promote the initiative locally.

Business overload

A major issue affecting the campaign was the amount of brain-space the subject could command with business people. Business revenue would be key to driving supplier interest, but business managers already suffer from a barrage of mailings about seminars, events and networking sessions. To get a business audience to attend yet another event about a subject peripheral to revenue generation would be an uphill struggle.

It was a thorny problem, until Omobono realised that the number of events and seminars already happening in the region wasn't a hindrance, it was a solution. Piggybacking was what was required.

First, a list of all the professional networks and special interest groups in the region was compiled, and their planned activities over the next 18 months mapped. Second, a range of tools was developed that could be used to raise awareness at

Figure 8 (above): *Tools to use at third-party events included a large display stand and an interactive kiosk*

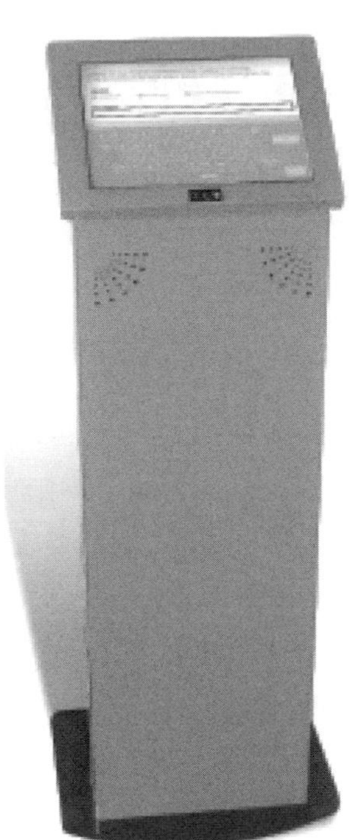

Figure 9 (right): *A Demand Broadband kiosk used at events throughout the region to enable people to register without the need to be online*

events. These included Demand Broadband 'kiosks' so that registrations for the brokerage or interest in the competition could be gathered, even when internet connection was not available (Figures 8 and 9).

Third, the Demand Broadband campaign infiltrated mailings being undertaken by other groups (from the Royal Institute of Chartered Surveyors to the Institute of Management). In one example, the CBI sent information about the campaign to its members (Figure 10).

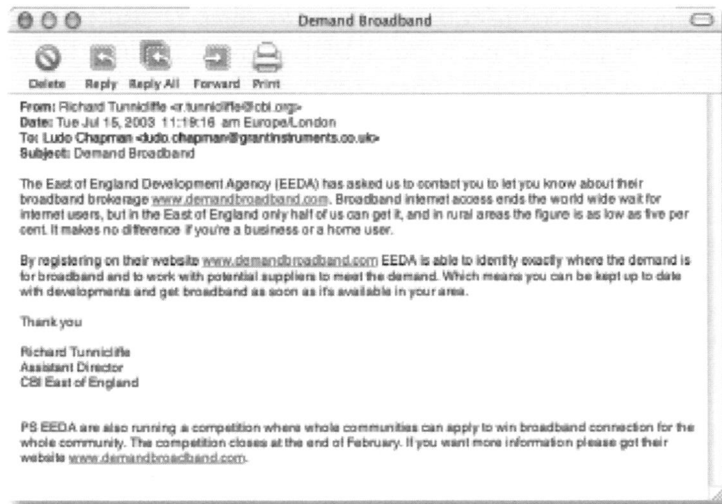

Demand Broadband

Delete Reply Reply All Forward Print

From: Richard Tunnicliffe <r.tunnicliffe@cbi.org>
Date: Tue Jul 15, 2003 11:19:16 am Europe/London
To: Ludo Chapman <ludo.chapman@grantinstruments.co.uk>
Subject: Demand Broadband

The East of England Development Agency (EEDA) has asked us to contact you to let you know about their broadband brokerage www.demandbroadband.com. Broadband internet access ends the world wide wait for internet users, but in the East of England only half of us can get it, and in rural areas the figure is as low as five per cent. It makes no difference if you're a business or a home user.

By registering on their website www.demandbroadband.com EEDA is able to identify exactly where the demand is for broadband and to work with potential suppliers to meet the demand. Which means you can be kept up to date with developments and get broadband as soon as it's available in your area.

Thank you

Richard Tunnicliffe
Assistant Director
CBI East of England

PS EEDA are also running a competition where whole communities can apply to win broadband connection for the whole community. The competition closes at the end of February. If you want more information please got their website www.demandbroadband.com.

Figure 10: *One of the emails sent out via the CBI to its members, promoting the Demand Broadband campaign*

GETTING THE SHOW ON THE ROAD

Now Omobono knew how it would deliver the campaign. The next step was to get this intricate piece of machinery on the road. The campaign launched to the press on 15 October 2002. Speakers from EEDA outlined the importance of the initiative to a group of 50 journalists and opinion formers. In the spirit of the campaign concept, the press launch was hijacked by a group of broadband protesters chanting slogans and waving placards.

Internal launch

These protesters then reappeared at EEDA's offices, where they repeated their antics as a way of raising the profile of the campaign amongst the internal audience (Figures 11 and 12).

Broadband pressure triggers BT reaction

Join our battle for broadband!

'Join drive for broadband' plea

Figure 11: *Thanks to Omobono's media relations campaign, broadband was adopted as a key issue by the region's press. In addition, features ran frequently on the region's radio and TV stations*

Figure 12: *The Demand Broadband group that protested at the launch event*

The campaign then rolled out on radio and buses, and the media relations programme began in earnest. The dedicated URL went live and the parish pack was sent out to every parish in the region. In October, Omobono also began piggy-backing on other people's events in the region. Arriving with a kiosk for offline registrations, a pop-up display stand, giveaways including mousemats, T-shirts, bookmarks and stickers, Demand Broadband spread its message to the business audience. By the end of the campaign the Demand Broadband group had gatecrashed 30 events and provided collateral material to a host of others, including those held by UK Online for Business, the regional Chambers of Commerce and the East of England Show.

The go-between

Part of the campaign's success also lay in Omobono's ability to act as a proactive information channel for the various interested parties. The agency became the go-between for the broadband suppliers and other regional and national initiatives such as the DTI Online for Business. Omobono also managed a series of briefings to EEDA's public-sector partners and has kept all parties informed via a regular e-mail bulletin that told them how the campaign was progressing (Figure 13).

By ensuring that these groups were talking to each other and discussing their needs openly, the likelihood of increasing broadband penetration in the region was brought one step closer.

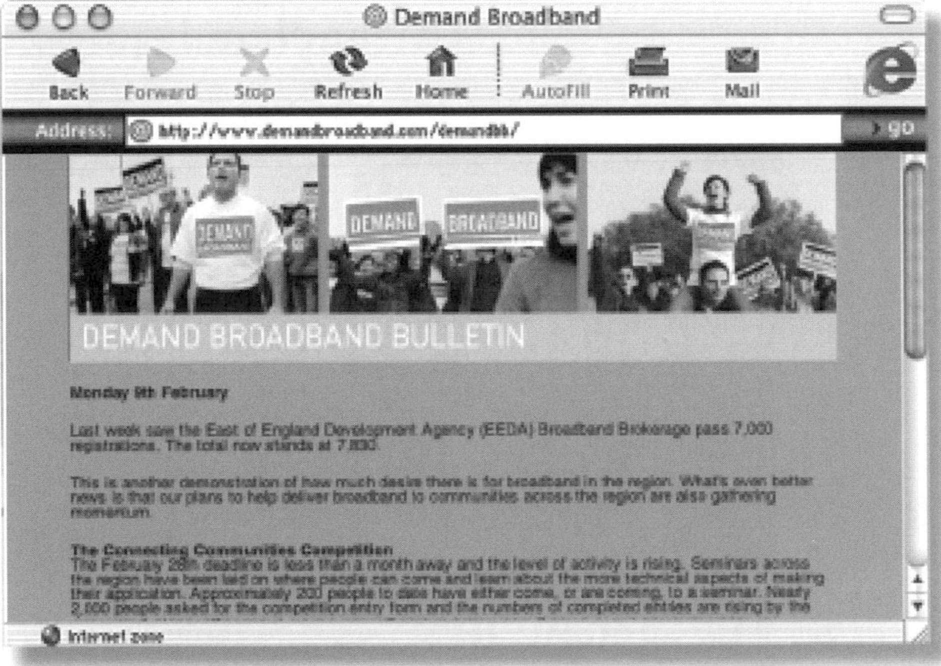

Figure 13: *One of the regular e-mails sent out to registrants and stakeholders to keep them informed of the campaign's progress*

The final act of dedication

As a final contribution to closing the gap between demand and supply, Omobono set up a Broadband Helpline in its office, for people to garner more information on the competition or find out about broadband availability in their area. This quickly began ringing as the message was driven throughout the region. During the campaign period Omobono handled over 1000 calls to this line.

DRAMATIC EFFECTS

So it was a campaign with intensive management, diverse activities and a strong creative theme. But what effect did it have?

Registrations

The original target for the brokerage was 2000 registrations by March 2004. By March 2004, we had achieved 16,699 registrations, 835% over target (Figure 14).

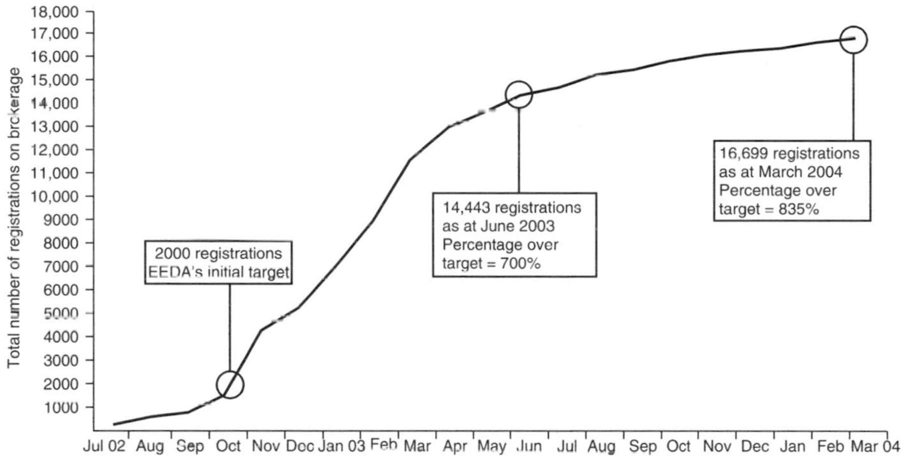

Figure 14: *How registrations on the brokerage rose over the course of the campaign*

The advertising has been the major contributor to this level of overachievement and the registration peaks correlate exactly with the radio bursts. Radio was responsible for 26% of all registrants on the brokerage.[9] The next largest section of registrants was informed by word of mouth, a testimony to the time taken to drive the campaign at a grassroots level and engage with businesses face to face (Figure 15).

9. Radio as a percentage of all registrations – July 2003. Interestingly, but understandably, this decreased to 20% by the end of the campaign (March 2004). In contrast 'other' grew from 13.46% in July 2003 to 17.3% by March 2004, as people became less sure where they had heard the message.

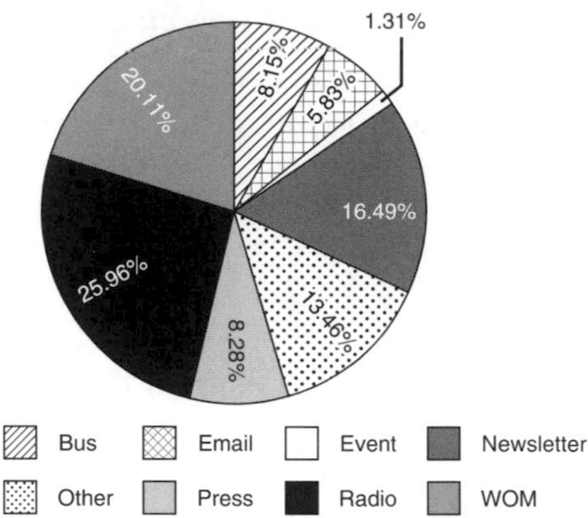

Figure 15: *How people registered on the brokerage heard about the Demand Broadband campaign (July 2003)*

Entries to the competition

The campaign also generated an overwhelming response for the competition. The targets were based on the number of entries.[10] More than 40 would count as success, with more than 80 being a 'great success'. The number of communities requesting entry forms was 2850, of which 192 prepared a business case that got them through to the final stage.

Influencing opinion formers

Getting opinion formers to support the Demand Broadband initiative was also a key objective. It was agreed at the outset that Omobono would deliver 30 opinion formers to the launch event. Over 50 attended, including journalists, business leaders and local government officials.

In May 2004 Omobono organised a Broadband Summit to examine 'What next for Broadband'. This event was attended by 67 people including representatives of the DTI, MPs and MEPs (Figure 16).

Six MPs signed an early day motion in support of the campaign and in March 2003, Stephen Timms MP, the DTI's e-minister declared:

> 'The number of registrations on the Demand Broadband website shows the level of enthusiasm among both businesses and consumers. EEDA's project is bolstering the competitive environment driving forward broadband in the UK.'

---

10. Campaign targets from EEDA Broadband Fund Action Plan: Final version/Targets for Broadband initiatives/April 2002.
'Wired Up Communities Competition'
(a) Target: Encourage the formulation of Local Partnerships which will enter the competition. Scoring based on number of entries, an indication of the success in encouraging local demand and the formation of Local Partnerships: (i) Under 20 entries: failure, (ii) 21–40 entries: partial success, (iii) 41–80 entries: success, (iv) 81+ entries: great success. (b) By when: March 2003. (c) How to measure: All entries will be filed by the competition committee. Auditors will count the entries and do a random sampling by contacting the Local Partnerships who have submitted the entries to ensure their validity.

Figure 16: *Richard Howitt MEP (left) and Chris Mole, MP for Ipswich at the Broadband Summit*

PROVING THAT ADVERTISING WORKS

Overall, the campaign had some dramatic effects. But how far can these be attributed to communications? Did the fact that £3m was on offer from EEDA mean that they could have achieved this result anyway? Was it just the inevitable result of the general swing to broadband, or BT's inexorable drive to connect the UK? And what was the ultimate value of the campaign?

Was the advertising effective or did the world beat a path to EEDA's door?

In hindsight it is easy to believe that broadband coverage was inevitable. But in mid-2002 things looked very different. Omobono's pre-campaign qualitative research (face to face and telephone depths) indicated a number of factors that meant times were hard for broadband. First of all people didn't really know what to do with it. Awareness was not high, and understanding was even lower.

In addition, the telephone companies were in trouble. Having spent vast amounts on 3G licences in early 2000, they were having to spend heavily to maintain the conditions of those licences, so they weren't cash rich. And the cable companies, who had the infrastructure in place, had actually got it wrong. They'd installed cable into downmarket homes, believing that their future revenue was in games and movies. In fact the market was in upmarket homes (to shop online and have faster and more secure access to business applications), and in businesses themselves.

But, pre-advertising research revealed that businesses themselves were unsure of the benefits of broadband, beyond being able to access the internet faster. In 2002, without a killer application, broadband was a 'nice to have', not a service with a demonstrable cost benefit. In other words, the business world had not yet beaten a path to broadband's door.

Advertising works – on its own and to maximise the power of other media

Yes, arguably the advertising campaign was successful because the product was good. A £3m fund for broadband was a powerful incentive. But advertising works best when it has good product to sell. How often as an industry do we emphasise to clients that advertising cannot make people buy a bad product?

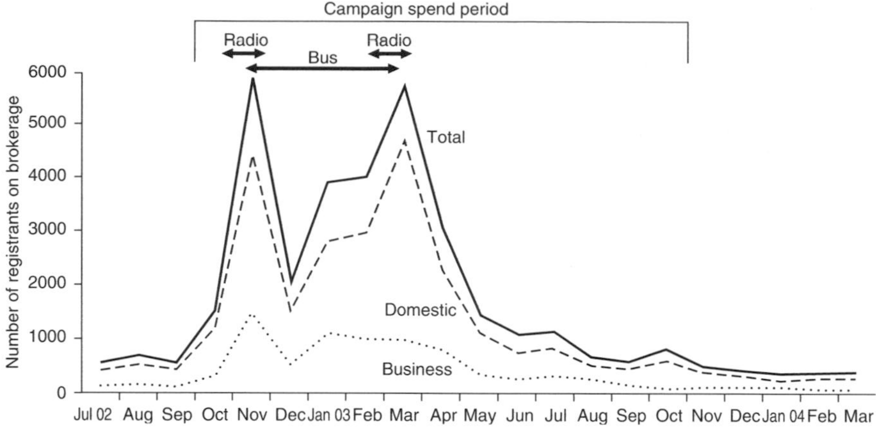

Figure 17: *Registrations by month plotted against advertising spend*

The crucial factor was that the campaign drove people to act when there wasn't a product to sell. There was no guarantee that people would get broadband, but they still signed up. The campaign was specifically designed to do this – to create, and demand, interaction. The fact that there are still currently 35 live links to the Demand Broadband website from people who are linking their local campaigns to EEDA's, is testament to this.

More simply, when the advertising ran, people acted. The advertising, particularly the radio, drove people to the site. When Omobono stopped advertising, registrations dropped off (Figure 17). Whilst it's clear that advertising was powerful in its own right, the effectiveness of other communications mechanisms is also visible, as the responses on the website revealed (Figure 18).

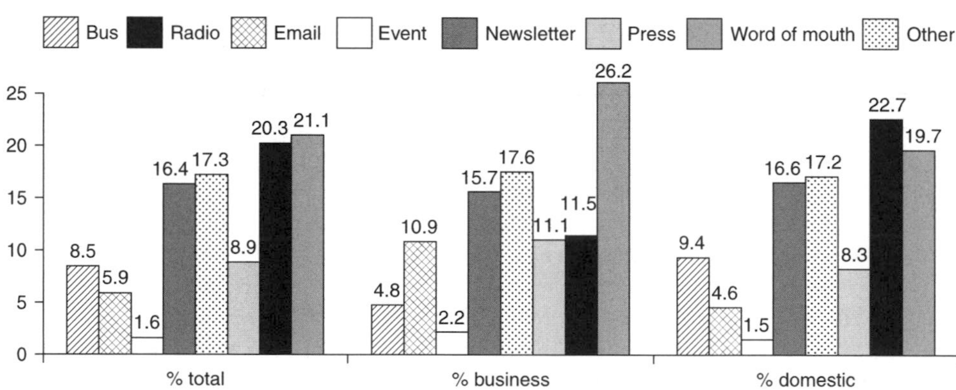

Figure 18: *Registrations plotted against communications channels (March 2004)*

Results

A total of 75% of all registrations happened in the campaign period (October 2002–April 2003). A quarter of all registrations happened in the remaining 50 weeks. So advertising can be said to have had twice the effect of other communications.

Advertising also had the greatest effect in its own right. Over the full campaign period, 29% of all registrants cited radio or bus advertising as the way they had heard about the campaign, the next nearest being word of mouth at 21%.[11] Monthly registration rates dropped at the end of the advertising period, from 2667 in March to 675 by mid-May. However, other campaign elements (events, PR and online communications) between May and September 2003 continued the momentum. It was not until PR activity had dropped to an ad hoc rather than structured process and all other activities had ceased (December 2003) that registrations finally tailed off.

Whilst advertising drove 16.5% of business registrations, the complexity of the campaign delivery undoubtedly increased its effectiveness with this audience. Events, e-mail and newsletters (all aimed at business) accounted for a further 29% of responses. We would therefore suggest that the effect of the multi-approach campaign was to double the number of businesses that registered.

The corresponding effect on domestic registrations of these activities was 22.7%, less than that produced by the advertising, but nevertheless important.

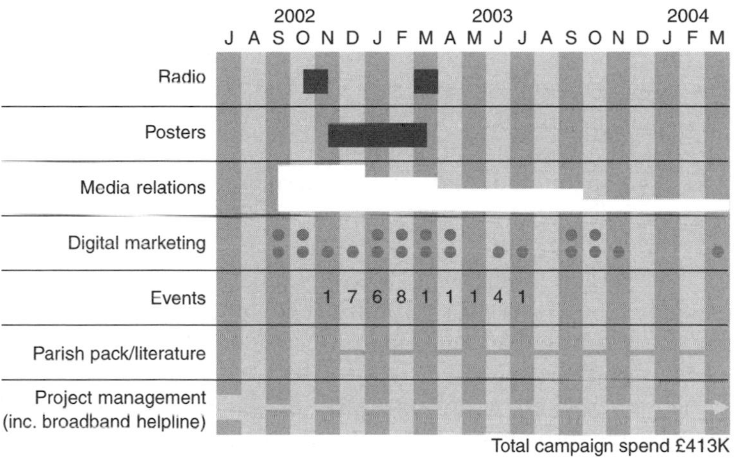

Figure 19: *Communications plan showing activities by month*

WAS BT RESPONSIBLE FOR THE SUCCESS OF EEDA'S CAMPAIGN?

What about BT's own efforts? Between September 2002 and March 2004 it spent £38m on a nationwide advertising campaign.[12] Whilst it was advertising throughout the campaign period, registrations on the Demand Broadband site declined after EEDA's campaign finished in March 2003. When BT upped its spend again in August 2003, registrations on the Demand Broadband site didn't fluctuate (Figure 20).[13]

11. Calculations, based on registrations from the website March 2004, excluding word of mouth, press and other, which resulted from overall campaign activities and cannot be said to have been aimed at one or other audience.
12. Source: John Ayling Associates/Nielsen MMS.
13. The slight rise in registration rates in October 2003 was, we believe, due to the effect of a meeting with the losing communities, to encourage them to continue the clustering process.

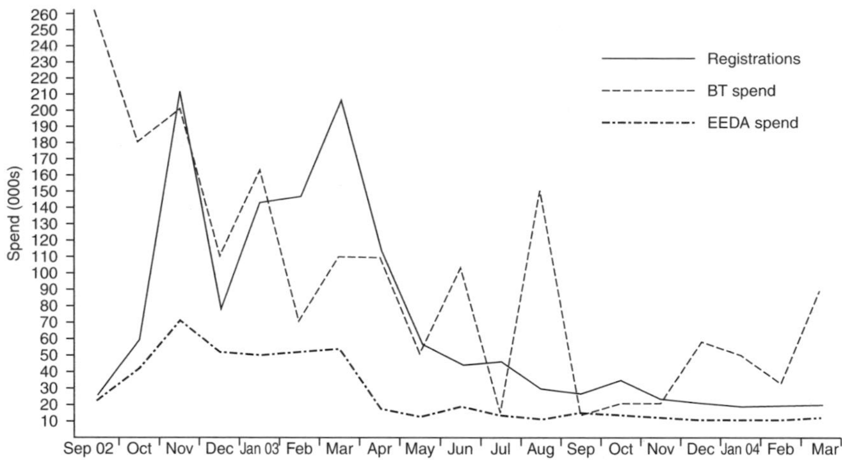

Figure 20: *Registrations vs EEDA campaign vs BT activity*

BT spent 4.3% of its budget in the region (£1.6m).[14] Anglia, however, accounts for 7.9% of the population (source: BARB), whilst just over 9% of the population live in the East of England (source: EEDA). Despite the absolute, and relative, underspend (the region received the fifth largest media spend in BT's campaign), registrations on BT's own site and subsequent take-up rates were third in the country, after London and the south-east. So perhaps the contribution was actually the other way round?

Research in mid-2002 with senior executives at BT revealed, unsurprisingly, that it was more interested in urban areas, where populations are concentrated, than in rural areas where cost to serve was prohibitively high.

During the period of the campaign this attitude changed. This was first in evidence as early as February 2003, when EEDA held its first suppliers' briefing. Fifty potential broadband suppliers were given information on clusters of registrants from the brokerage. As a result of this information-sharing, two exchanges in Norfolk (Diss) and Suffolk (Belstead) were enabled. They were actually enabled by BT (which had previously deemed the trigger levels unreachable). In July 2003 it offered to enable eight remote rural exchanges of EEDA's choosing. Subsequently it has demonstrated an active commitment to working in partnership with EEDA, consistently lowering triggers for the majority of exchanges in the region.

> 'Campaigns like "Demand Broadband" have succeeded in raising public awareness and in driving the registrations which have helped BT optimise and accelerate its deployment of broadband in the East of England.'
>
> Peter McCarthy Ward, Regional Director, BT

This is confirmed by the Masons report, which shows that broadband penetration has grown particularly in non-urban areas, at odds with BT's corporate strategy (Figure 21).

14. Source: John Ayling Associates/Nielsen MMS.

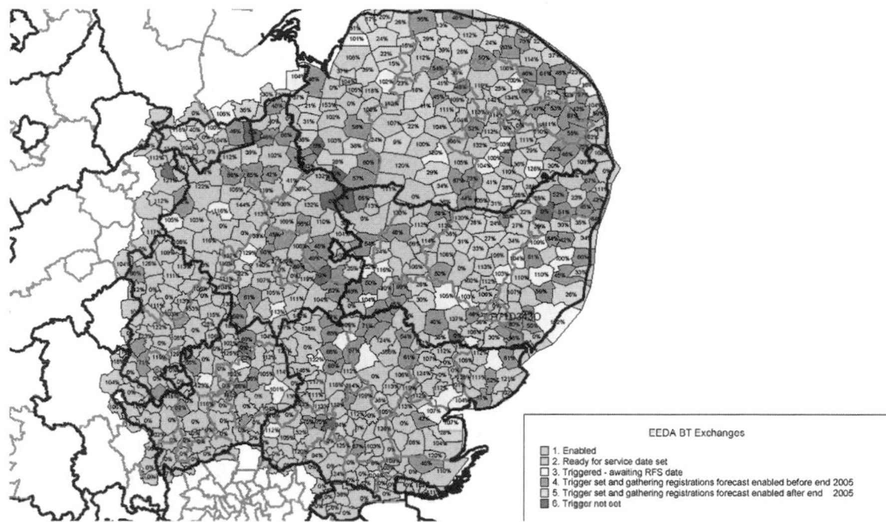

Figure 21: *Regional coverage post-campaign*

This is reinforced by Laurence Ramsey, Broadband Fund Manager at EEDA, who states that 'the effect of our activities has been ... provoking BT into taking action' and who reacted, as Laurence continues, 'by responding energetically to threats in the market'.

WHAT IS THE REAL VALUE OF THE INVESTMENT MADE?

The communications campaign drove registrations to the site. Registrations were then used to encourage suppliers (not just BT) to provide broadband solutions to high-registration areas. Masons Communications, which has been providing the coverage analysis to EEDA since mid-2002, estimated that by the end of 2005, 98% of people in the eastern region will have access to broadband, up from 53% prior to the campaign. But what does this mean in revenue terms?

For the telephone companies

If EEDA were a company, we would be looking at evidence of additional revenue generation. But the revenue generated by the campaign went not to EEDA but to the broadband suppliers, principally of course BT. However, it is still possible to estimate this.

By March 2004, 16,699 people had registered on the campaign website. These were people who did not have access to BT or any other broadband service at the time they registered. EEDA estimates that by the end of 2005, 93% of them will be able to get broadband (either from BT or other suppliers). So the income generated from them connecting to broadband can be directly attributed to the effect of the campaign.

A total of 3104 registrations were business users. Based on business rental income alone (at a minimum monthly cost of £29.99) this is equivalent to additional revenue to BT and other suppliers of just over £1m per annum.[15] And of course business broadband line rental can go as high as £41.99 or £99.99 per month which, using the same calculation, would produce revenue-generation figures of £1.45m and £3.46m, respectively.

Revenue from the domestic registrants on the site, at a monthly rental income of £19.99, would add just over £3m minimum pa.[16] So, in total, revenue generation from the site has been over £4m.[17]

For business

According to research published by ntl[18] those 3104 businesses will gain 52 days of lost productivity as a result of accessing broadband. The GDP of the average business in the East of England is £333,000 pa, according to figures supplied by EEDA.[19] They achieve this in 260 working days, at a rate of just over £1280 per day. The average headcount in those companies is 10.5. So arguably each of these people is responsible for reclaiming £122 of GDP per day; 52 days of increased productivity could increase their contribution to GDP by £6344 per business. Therefore the campaign could be said to be generating an additional £18m of revenue for the regional economy.[20]

Government estimates are more cautious. Recalculated on a £3.5bn cost saving for the UK as a whole,[21] a £4.3m productivity increase could be generated by the 2887 firms who will be broadband enabled as a result of this campaign.

For the Government

Laurence Ramsey, EEDA Broadband Fund manager estimates that the absolute result of the campaign is an additional 5% of broadband coverage in the region. Applied to business, with 245,800 companies in the region overall (and 98% of them able to get broadband by the end of 2005) the additional revenue translates into a further £18m+ going into the economy as a result of increased productivity stemming from broadband access.[22]

---

15. Telephone company revenue generation from business rental income on the site; £29.99 × 12 months × 2887 (93% of 3104 registered business users) = £1,038,973.
16. Telephone company revenue generation from domestic rental income on the site; £19.99 × 12 months × 12,643 (93% of 13,595 registered domestic users) = £3,032,803.
17. Combined revenue of 93% of all on website; £1,038,973 + £3,032,803 = £4,071776.
18. Source: www.theregister.co.uk/2004/05/12/broadband_productivity_increase/.
19. Figures taken from EEDA website.
20. Additional revenue figure for the region based on registrations; 2887 (number of additional businesses now able to receive broadband) (3104 x 93%) × £122 lost revenue per day × 52 days = £18,315,128.
21. Government figures based on 2001 survey of small businesses estimated that 'by 2005, broadband will be making £3.5bn of productivity savings and £1.2bn cost savings a year for the UK Small and Medium Sized Enterprise (SME) sector'. Source: SME broadband user research (May 2001) Fletcher Advisory for BTopenworld. East of England share of productivity savings would be £367.5m (the region produces 10.59% of national GDP, which is created by 245,800 business sites) or £1495 per firm. The 2887 business users enabled as a result of the campaign would therefore create £4,316,405 of additional productivity.
22. The additional revenue figure for the region based on number of businesses in region (245,800) able to get broadband by end 2005 (98%) by 5% (increase in broadband penetration for region as a whole as a result of the campaign) = 12,044 x increased productivity of £1495 per firm = £18,006,079.

LONG-TERM EFFECT

Of course, although difficult to quantify, broadband penetration has other benefits too. Greater lifestyle choices for people as home-working possibilities increase. Improved public service delivery through transformation of the public sector, and increased access for citizens to online education and health services. New opportunities for digital content providers to commercialise new products in the ever expanding digital space (in which the UK stands particularly to benefit due to its strong media and computer games industries). More support for rural communities. Fewer cars on the road. Less global warming. Fewer stressed executives. The list is a long one. Which is why the Government was keen to pursue the penetration of broadband in the first place.

Penetration in rural areas

All of the above benefits of broadband are particularly important for rural economies, and one of the major successes of the campaign has been to drive broadband penetration in these areas (Figure 22).

> '11% of registrants will not have a BT broadband service before the end of 2005. However, 50% of this number currently resides within an area that has received funding from the EEDA competition and should have alternative service availability in the coming months.'
>
> Masons Communications, April 2004

Laurence Ramsey concurs: 'Bearing in mind our registrations are heavily biased towards rural areas (unlike BT's figures), I think that this is a great result'.

Figure 22: *There is now a clear understanding of how important broadband is to businesses*

Public acknowledgement

At the broadband summit in May 2004 Nigel Heriz Smith, Head of Rural Broadband at the DTI, offered this view of the initiative, and the contribution of the campaign: 'EEDA's Demand Broadband communication campaign is the exemplar for how RDAs should be driving the demand for and take-up of broadband across the UK.'

SILVER

11

Direct Line

How a Red Phone grew a super product into a superbrand

Principal authors: Dom Boyd, Mortimer Whittaker O'Sullivan and Nigel Robinson, MediaCom

EDITOR'S SUMMARY

It's not often that communications can credibly claim the credit for £1bn of incremental profit. But such is the potency of Direct Line's business and the iconic red phone device it has pressed into service for 15 years now – a device and business model that have both spawned a long list of copycats and generated a truly extraordinary return on investment for the brand leader.

In the low-cost insurance sector, salient advertising is not just an efficient way to drive sales (by their nature, direct insurers have few alternative sales channels). It is also a critical part of the business model: increasing operating efficiencies, which are then passed back to the consumer via low premiums and enhanced service.

Direct Line's advertising has not just given the brand a critical advantage in terms of awareness, consideration, cost of sales and market share; it has also broadened the brand footprint beyond price and towards a service proposition. Moreover, the campaign is judged to have dramatically reduced the cost and risk of entering new markets or establishing new channels: be it pet insurance on the one hand or internet presence for Direct Line on the other.

This paper claims a return on investment of £4 profit to every £1 spent, and overwhelmingly makes the case for branding and communications in even this most price-sensitive and price-led of markets.

INTRODUCTION

An extraordinary story

This is a story about a remarkable transformation, against significant odds. It is about how a company that sold a single product – motor insurance – more cheaply through cutting out brokers, has become big enough to join the FTSE 100,[1] selling over nine different products to 10 million customers, with profits increasing from £26m in 1996 to £355m in 2003.[2]

In a commoditised price-driven market characterised by promiscuity, Direct Line commands increasing loyalty that outstrips competitors.[3] It has literally grown from a super product into a superbrand, loved by consumers and the City alike.[4] Moreover, it has played a part in helping the Royal Bank of Scotland become one of the fastest-growing financial institutions in the world.

Summary of what advertising has added to Direct Line

We will demonstrate how advertising has been the central catalyst in this extraordinary business performance, through achieving the following:

- creating outstanding advertising 'cut-through', via the Red Phone device (Figure 1)

Figure 1: *The 'Red Phone'*

- making the brand more 'front of mind' than competitors
- building superior perceptions of price, service and innovation
- increasing brand disposition and share in a market with declining loyalty
- generating cheaper cost per policy sale, through preference from new customers
- creating disproportional loyalty and extra business from existing customers

---

1. *Superbrands.*
2. Royal Bank of Scotland Reports and Accounts.
3. NOP Financial Research Survey 2003.
4. Taylor Nelson Brand Health Tracking; MORI Financial Services Survey.

- creating stronger operating margins than any competitor
- enabling cheaper underwriting prices, which can undercut the competition
- building disproportionate profits in unprofitable market conditions.

Success not guaranteed in a risky business

Of course, it would be easy to assume that success was automatic and Direct Line has simply ridden on the back of an increasingly profitable market with flabby competitors. In fact, nothing could be further from the truth.

The level of competition in the insurance market is cut-throat – none more so than in private motor insurance where Direct Line specialises.[5] Of the 300+ insurance companies in the UK, more than 20 were 'direct' operators by 1995,[6] causing a sustained and costly price war in which the motor market lost over £2bn.[7] In addition, Direct Line has had to contend with the huge potential threat of the internet, bringing new business challenges and competition.[8]

Direct Line's success has been no fluke.

No place to hide for advertising

As a 'direct' business with no retail outlets or salesforce, advertising is the lifeline driving Direct Line's business:

> 'Direct Line is hugely driven by its advertising because it is our only shop window. It is absolutely fundamental to the success of the business.'
>
> Jim Wallace, Group Marketing Director

In addition to 'hard' tracking and sales data, the use of econometric modelling analysis is a central component in Direct Line's communication planning armoury, helping to quantify accurately the effect of every piece of communication.

A unique commitment to building an insurance superbrand

Direct Line has demonstrated a clear commitment to advertising since 1990 when it first went on TV with the 'Red Phone' (Figure 2).

However, Direct Line is no typical 'direct response' advertiser. What sets it apart is its belief in the power of its brand. It doesn't just set out to acquire sales at lowest-cost media (although it does use lots of this), but consistently invests a higher proportion of its budget in more expensive brand-building communications than competitors (Figure 3).[9]

The reasoning behind this belief in the brand is simple – it delivers back far more strongly over the longer term.

> 'Because the brand impacts so fundamentally on how our business performs, everyone in the company is committed to making it even stronger.'
>
> Ian Chippendale, Chairman

5. Direct Line – approximately two-thirds of Direct Line's revenue comes from motor insurance business.
6. Association of British Insurers.
7. Mintel Motor Report, 2003.
8. Datamonitor Motor Report, 2004.
9. All channels against ABC1 adult impacts: peak 17:30–22:59; off peak 06:00–17:29, 23:00–05:59.

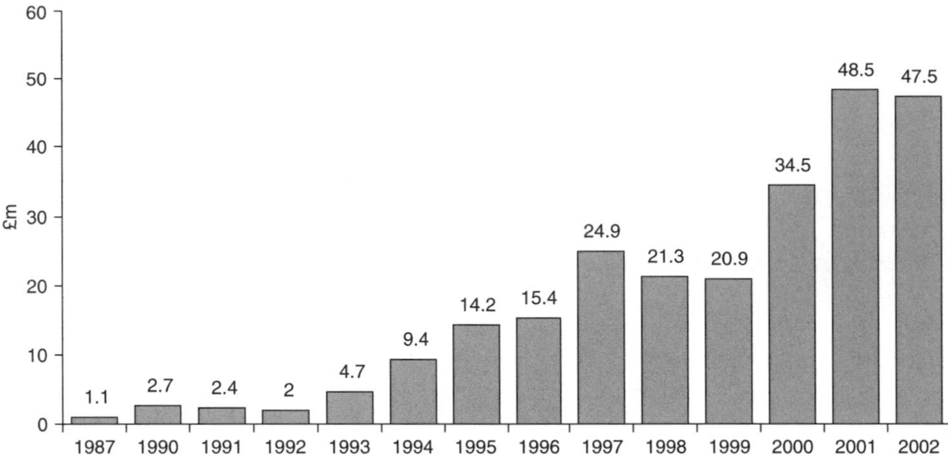

Figure 2: *Direct Line has increased its investment in advertising over time*
Source: MMS/MediaCom

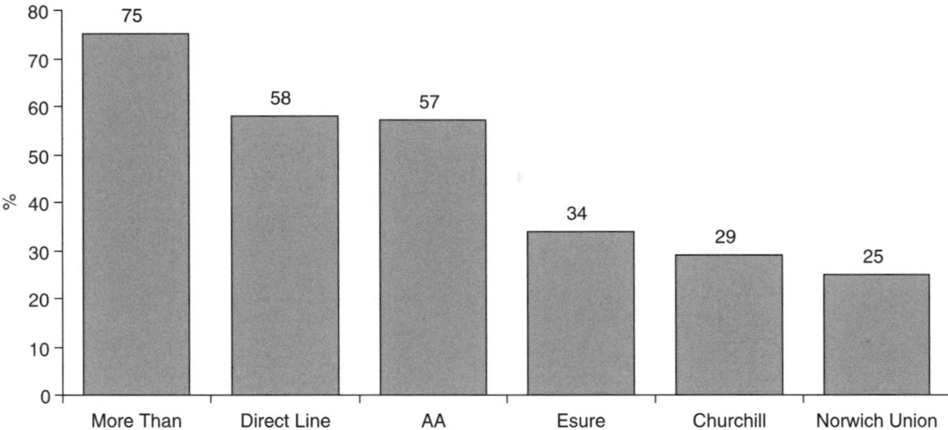

Figure 3: *Direct Line spends a higher proportion of its TV budget on peak-time TV than competitors*
Source: BARB/MediaCom

We will demonstrate that it is the power of Direct Line's brand, built through its advertising, that has driven the business's success.

HOW ADVERTISING BUILT A SUPERBRAND THAT DELIVERS BUSINESS SUCCESS

Advertising acts as the high-performance oil in Direct Line's business machine. It is the essential catalyst in a model that has driven Direct Line's success.

In this model, the first step has been to create high advertising cut-through. This is achieved through the Red Phone device, which keeps the brand front of mind, constantly adding messages to create superior brand perceptions over time.

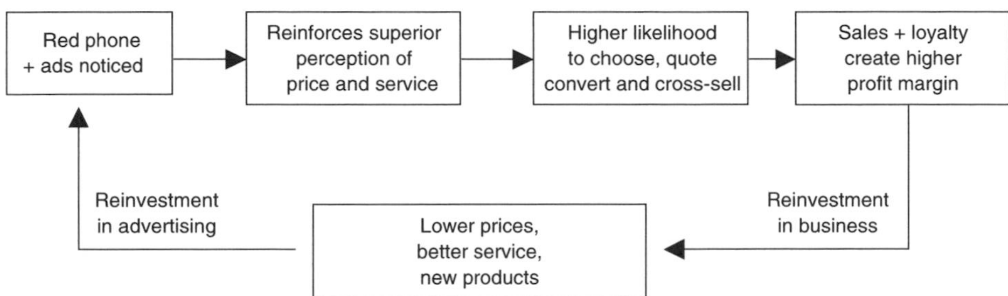

Figure 4: *How advertising creates a competitive advantage for Direct Line*

These create a competitive advantage for Direct Line by attracting and converting more 'good risk' customers, making them more resistant to leaving and cross-selling them more products than competitors.[10]

Through higher sales and lower costs, the business can operate at a higher profit margin than competitors.[11] In turn these economies are passed back to consumers via cheaper prices and superior services,[12] reinforcing the brand's competitive advantage in a virtuous cycle (Figure 4).

In fact, while price has clearly been a component in Direct Line's success, we will demonstrate that advertising has actually played a critical role in helping Direct Line maintain their price advantage through boosting its core operating margin.

Making the little Red Phone the hero

Since its introduction in 1990, Direct Line's Red Phone device has been used in every single piece of advertising communication across many thousands of press adverts, hundreds of posters and direct mail (DM) pieces, over 25 TV ads and even on radio.

However, as the needs of the business and the brand have evolved, so has Direct Line's advertising. This has meant a number of different phases rather than a single 'campaign'. What binds them together is the glue of the Red Phone device (Figure 5).

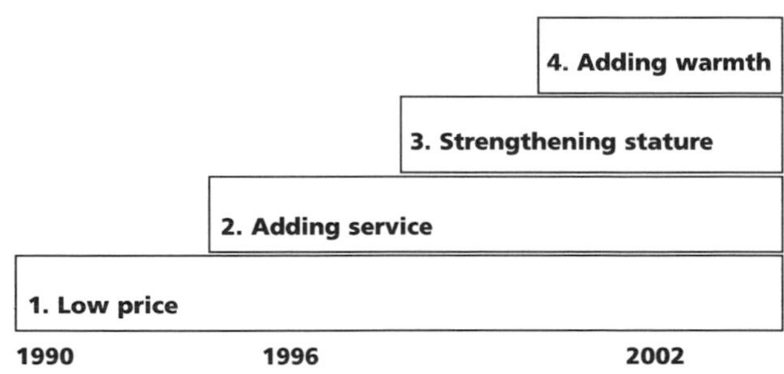

Figure 5: *Communications strategy*

10. NOP Financial Research Survey 2003 – see later evidence.
11. Datamonitor Motor Report 2004 – 'Direct Line has the lowest expense ratio of any insurer.'
12. Datamonitor Motor Report 2004 – Direct Line is still about 3% cheaper than the market ('AA index'), but not as cheap as it used to be. At launch it was almost 20% cheaper.

Owning low price

Although the Red Phone and sonic device were created to give the Direct Line brand presence and identity, nobody imagined quite how successful it would ultimately become.[13]

On TV for the first time in 1990, it took centre-stage as the 'hero' coming to motorist's rescue. It was a symbol of a new dawn of cheaper, more convenient 'direct' insurance, with an irrepressible, loud character and jingle that literally leapt out from the screen, appearing out of nowhere to cut out the middleman. Everything about the communication was designed to be unmissable.

This not only built advertising and brand awareness quickly,[14] it captured the public imagination in way a few brands ever manage. Like Richard Branson, it was a maverick 'champion of the people', mingling with the man on the street with its carnival street call, in-your-face attitude and bargain prices (Figures 6–9).[15]

'Sorry mate, the phone rolled out in front of me'

Figure 6: Punch *cartoon by Martin Ross*

This attitude was no accident, but a genuine ethos permeating Direct Line,[16] which proved a highly successful advertising recipe, outperforming other direct competitors[17] and growing share and policies significantly (Table 1).[18]

TABLE 1: DIRECT LINE PROFIT INCREASES POST-RED PHONE LAUNCH

	1990	1991	1992	1993	1994
Motor share (%)	1	2	3.1	5.7	7.9
Motor policies (000s)	293	411	670	1200	1903

In turn, combined with an efficient IT infrastructure the campaign generated strong profit through lower marginal costs (Table 2).[19]

13. 'Ten years ago no-one would have dreamt we'd be where we are today', *Hotline* staff magazine, spring 1995.
14. Datamonitor, 'the Direct Line product was launched with a highly effective and recognisable advertising campaign which succeeded in placing its brand at the forefront of the consumer's mind.'
15. Semiotic Solutions Research Debrief, 1997.
16. 'I want us to be a company of the highest quality, dominating our markets but not exploiting them. We'll be No 1, but we'll also be something more. We'll still be the best', Chief Executive, Staff *Hotline* magazine, spring 1995.
17. Datamonitor Direct Line indexes 800 vs Total Direct sector 600 between 1990 and 1994.
18. Datamonitor Motor Report, 1998; private motor share and policies.
19. *Hotline* staff magazine, 1995.

Salesman: Here's the key, sir, now what about insurance?

SFX: Direct Line jingle

Salesman: May I draw your attention to our whizzo megaplan?
SFX: Direct Line jingle

VO: If you want to save time and money on motor insurance, call Direct Line where you deal with a human being, not a blank form, and a computerised system that already provides low-cost insurance to over a quarter of a million motorists.

VO: You're covered
Man: Thanks.

VO: For cheaper insurance with a human voice, call Direct Line.
SFX: Direct Line jingle

Figure 7: *Car showroom*

VO: In order to save money on his motor insurance this man relies on his broker.

VO: But his broker won't be calling every company for a quote.
SFX: Direct Line jingle

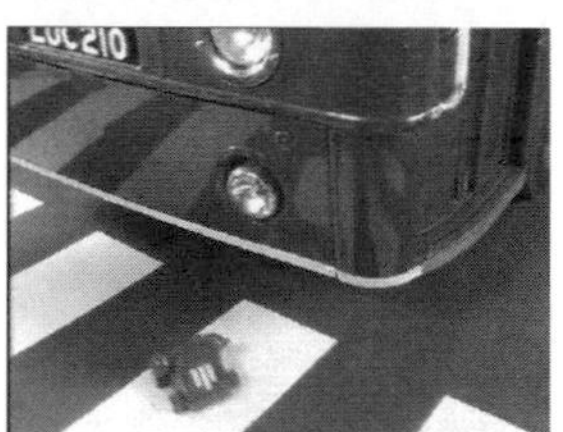

VO: Because Direct Line don't pay commission to brokers, we can pass the savings on to you.
SFX: Direct Line jingle

VO: So why not let Direct Line cut out the middleman ...

VO: ... and you might just find out we're the cheapest of the lot.

VO: For cheaper insurance with a human voice, call Direct Line.
SFX: Direct Line jingle

Figure 8: *Saw*

VO: Would you recommend your insurance company to a friend?
Man: Is that what you're paying? You know who you should call ...
Da-da-da-da-da-de-de-de-da-da (hums jingle)

VO: Well each year, hundreds of thousands of satisfied customers recommend Direct Line.

Passer-by: Da-da-da-da-da-de-de-de-da-da (hums jingle)

Judge: As to your claims that you cannot afford motor insurance, I can only say Da-da-da-da-da-de-de-de-da-da (hums jingle)

VO: Direct Line insurance. We come highly recommended.
SFX: Direct Line jingle

Figure 9: *Highlife*

TABLE 2: DIRECT LINE PROFIT INCREASES POST-RED PHONE LAUNCH

	1991	1992	1993	1994	1995
Costs per in-force policy	63	57	53	53	47
Profits (millions)	12.2	15	50	100	112

Evolving our communications strategy – adding service

By 1995 a huge increase in competition from traditional and direct competitors all chasing the same pool of switchers led to a market price war, causing a significant drop in Direct Line's performance as policy growth and share stalled (Table 3).[20]

TABLE 3: DIRECT LINE GROWTH STALLS WITH INCREASED COMPETITION

	1995	1996
Direct Line motor share (%)	8.9	8.7
Direct Line's share of 'direct' motor channel (%)	40.2	34.7
Direct Line motor policies (000s)	2180	2100

Indeed, City observers were hawkish about its future prospects:

> 'For direct [brands] the future is uncertain ... there are now 20 direct insurers in the UK and competition between them has become so intense Direct Line is suffering – rapid growth has been thrown into reverse.'
>
> *Financial Times*, 31 January 1997

Direct Line realised it needed to break its brand away from the pack once again by repositioning itself 'from Kwiksave to Tesco', broadening its reputation for service. This would distance it from competitors and provide a platform to extend into new markets.[21]

A new role for the Red Phone

Creating a genuine shift in brand strategy from low-cost to service meant we needed a step-change in communications approach. The Red Phone would continue to feature in the ads as a powerful brand sign-off, but – bravely – would no longer take centre-stage (Figures 10 and 11).[22]

A new campaign was developed featuring conversations between customers and Direct Line operators, highlighting the multiple service benefits of being a Direct Line customer. This not only continued to build advertising awareness measures, it successfully boosted broader image perceptions.[23]

---

20. Datamonitor Motor Report, 1998; private motor share.
21. Marketing Strategy Report, 1995/96: 'We need to accelerate the repositioning of the brand from "cheap and cheerful" ... to an all rounder offering great value and first class service. The pay off for this will permeate all areas of the business from new business to retention to new products.'
22. Ian Chippendale, Chief Executive, 'In spite of rumours to the contrary, the Red Phone will be staying!'; *Hotline* staff magazine, 1997.
23. Millward Brown Brand Tracking, July 1996 to July 1997; appeals from 43% to 52%; higher opinion than others from 28% to 33%; a company you would trust from 38% to 40%; better value for money from 41% to 44%.

SFX: crashing cars

Man: Oh no. How am I going to sort this lot out?
Staff: Don't worry, Mr Jones.

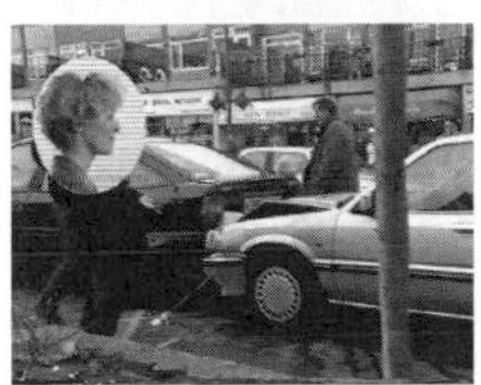

Man: All those other insurance companies.
Staff: We'll do all that.
Man: I'll have to take a day off going round garages getting estimates.
Staff: Leave that to us.

Woman: But we'll still have to get it picked up.
Staff: No, we'll get it picked up.

Man: When do we have to come and get it?
Staff: We'll deliver it back to you.
Woman: I wonder if it will be ....
Staff: .... cleaned inside and out and looking like new. Absolutely.

Man: It looks good.
Staff: It's better than that, Mr Jones. All the work is covered by a three-year guarantee.

VO: For easy, low-cost motor insurance, better call direct – Direct Line.
SFX: Direct Line jingle

Figure 10: *Bump*

Woman: I mean I was so surprised – £25

Other woman: Your building society are going to charge you £25?

Woman: Yes, to cancel my buildings insurance they're going to charge me £25.

Other woman: I hope you haven't paid it yet?
Woman: Well, I suppose it was my fault. It was in the small print so what else can I do?

Other woman: I tell you what you could do. You could let us pay it.
Woman: Hang on … and I could still save 30% of my premium on the same cover?
Woman: Absolutely!

VO: If your mortgage provider charges you £25 to move your buildings insurance to Direct Line, we'll refund it.
For home insurance, better go direct – to Direct Line.
SFX: Direct Line jingle

Figure 11: *Face to Face*

Strengthening stature – extending products

The new service strategy, in combination with the Red Phone's low-cost heritage provided a stronger stature from which to launch new products cheaply, broadening the revenue base (Figure 12).

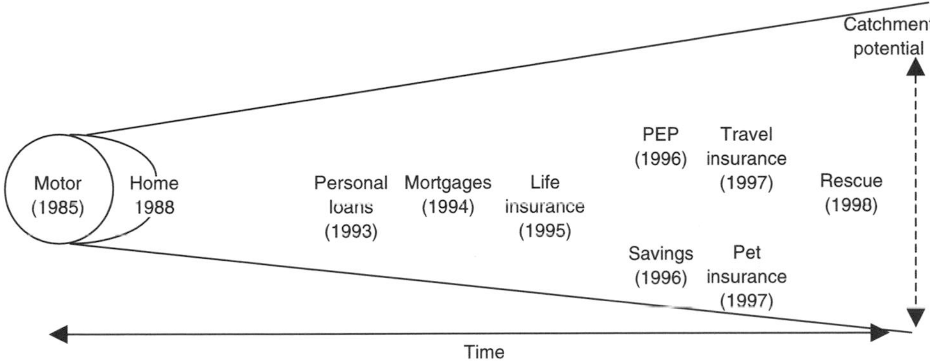

Figure 12: *Direct Line product launch timeline*

Typically, these products were launched on direct channels such as direct response television (DRTV) (Figures 13–15) and specialist titles. In addition, Direct Line promoted its internet credentials using a unique media strategy that used the top and tail of the advert break itself to demonstrate the ease and speed of Direct Line's online service. This stature strategy boosted Direct Line's revenue and share to new levels (Table 4).

TABLE 4: DIRECT LINE BUSINESS GROWING AND BROADENING IN SCOPE[24]

	1999	2001
Direct Line motor share (%)	7.7	10.5
Direct Line non-motor gross written premium (£m)	214	427

Amazingly, in a market still rife with undercutting, and losing £2bn in 1998,[25] Direct Line improved its profits to a new high (Table 5).[26]

TABLE 5: INCREASING DIRECT LINE PROFITABILITY IN A NEGATIVE MOTOR MARKET

	1996	1997	1998	1999	2000	2001
Direct Line profit (£m)	+26	+36	+64	+101	+201	+261
Market underwriting loss (£m)	–522	–878	–959	–876	–638	–455

24. Datamonitor Motor Report, 2004; private motor share.
25. Association of British Insurers/Mintel.
26. Royal Bank of Scotland Reports & Accounts; profits before tax amortisation.

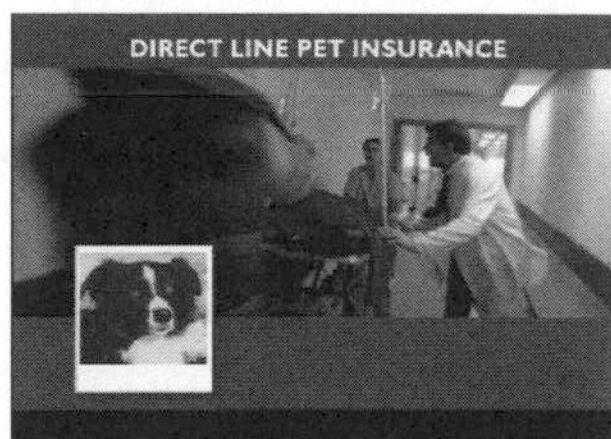

VO: Misty was four when she was run over and seriously injured.

VO: Because she was covered by Direct Line pet insurance, the decision to operate was immediate.

VO: … otherwise Misty's owners would have faced agonising choices on where to find the £3000 to save Misty's life.

VO: You can cover your dog or cat from just a few pounds a month.

VO: Just call. … Call or buy online. It's a small price to pay.
SFX: Direct Line jingle

Figure 13: *ER – pet DRTV*

(We see money falling from the sky.)
Man: Crazy, isn't it? But how many of you all over the country are doing this, every year?

Man: When you pay your buildings insurance along with your mortgage, you could literally be throwing money away, until you do this.

SFX: Red Phone jingle

Man: Switching your buildings insurance from your mortgage provider to Direct Line could save you up to 30%. So stop throwing your money away, and go to Direct Line instead. Go on, try them and see for yourself.

Figure 14: *Rooftop – home DRTV*

(Part 1)
Man: Don't move. Whatever you do before the programme starts again …

Man: Sit tight and don't go away …

Man: … all right? …

(Part 2)
Man: Right, come in, come in. Sorry about the mess – it's my son's room.

Man: While you've been away, I've been on the internet – great, isn't it? Now I've logged on to directline.com, I sent them my details and now my car's insured. It only took two minutes. Simple …

Man: Saved me a few quid, though. Could save you a bit of money, too. It's easy.
SFX Direct Line jingle
Man: Directline.com. Motor insurance in under two minutes. Next time you've got a couple of minutes to spare, give it a try.

Figure 15: *The Den – .com launch*

Adding warmth

Supporting new products resulted in an increase in Direct Line spending[27] and we were worried consumers would get irritated. In 2002 we therefore set out to adopt a warmer communication style, showing people in everyday situations benefiting from Direct Line's great service and value. Brand TV focused on service, DRTV on price.

Media strategy built on this by identifying new high-engagement consumer 'touchpoints' we could use to exploit brand presence, and to give the Red Phone more prominence. In 2004 this included a deal to sponsor Channel 4 weeknight home programmes – Direct Line's biggest ever sponsorship (Figure 16).

Figure 16: *Channel 4 sponsorship*

Despite a sharp decline in share of voice, this strategy increased share profits to new records (Table 6; Figure 17).[28]

TABLE 6: FURTHER INCREASES IN DIRECT LINE SHARE[29]

	2001	2002
Direct Line motor share (%)	10.5	12.4

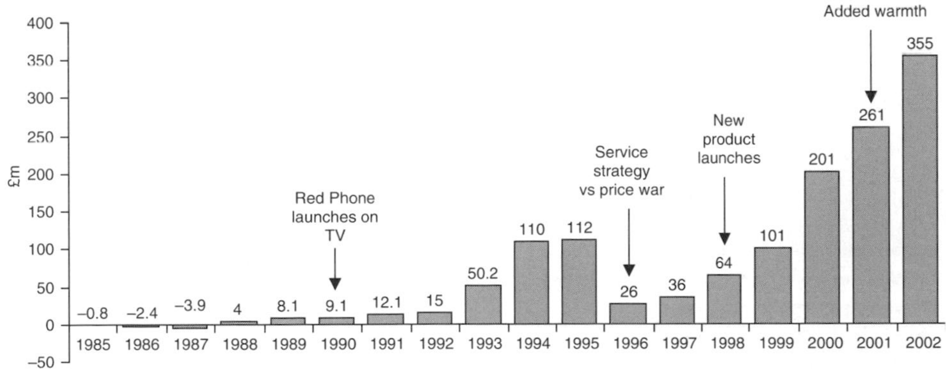

Figure 17: *Direct Line's profits over time*

27. MediaCom/MMS. From £20m in 1998 to £48m in 2001; Direct Line's share of voice in motor declined from 24% in 1998 to 9% in 2002.
28. Royal Bank of Scotland Reports and Accounts.
29. Datamonitor Motor Report, 2004; private motor share.

Woman 1: Hello, Betty. I heard about the burglary, so I brought this. I know how much you loved your own stereogram.

Woman 2: Direct Line have replaced my old one with a brand new one.

Woman 2: It does this (flicks on to play loud music)

Woman 2: ... and this (plays loud dance music)

Woman 2: ... and this comes in very handy.

(Laughs)

VO: Direct Line's new-for-old home insurance delivers a replacement right to your door. Call or buy online.
SFX: Direct Line jingle

Figure 18: *Grannies – home brand*

Woman: Hi. Missed me?

Man: Of course.
Woman: Are you all right? You said you had a crash.
Man: I'm fine. The car was worse. Direct Line sorted it all out, though. You wouldn't know, would you?

Woman: Not bad, seeing as you only went with them because they're cheap.

Woman: They've cleaned in here as well!
Man: What makes you think I didn't do it? (as cup falls over)

VO: Direct Line. Unbelievably good motor insurance that could save you up to 20%. Call or buy online.
SFX: Direct Line jingle

Figure 19: *New man – motor brand*

Woman: How much did you save again with this Direct Line car insurance?
Man: 20%.

Woman: Mmm. That's quite a lot.
VO: Call Direct Line today and see how much you could save, too.

Woman: So you've got a bit more spare cash than you had before, then?
Man: Loaded!

Woman: Well, stop here and you can buy me lunch (looking at swanky restaurant).
Man: Absolutely. (heads for cheap café across the street)

Figure 20: *Restaurant – motor DRTV*

VO: Switch now and you could save up to 20%. Call now.
SFX: Direct Line jingle

ITV Better Homes sponsorship

Radio programme sponsorship

Sponsorship of Good Homes Show

Door-drops

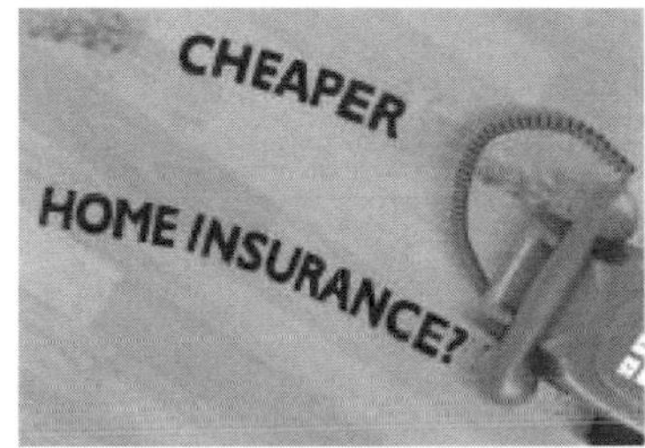

Home interest magazine activity

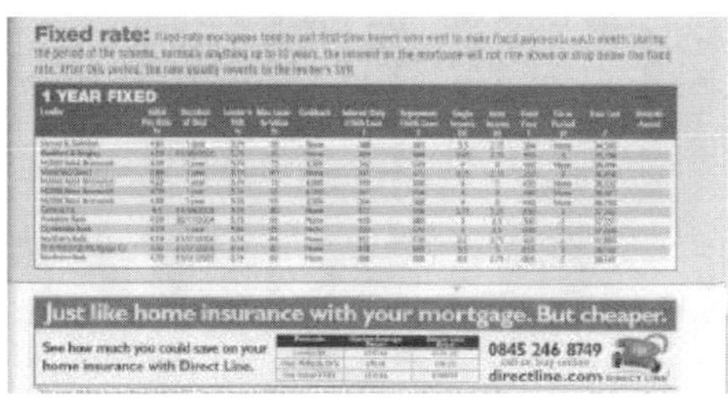

Ideal Home Show Exhibition

Figure 21: *Home insurance brand touchpoints 2002–2003, beyond TV*

Evolution of media

It would be tempting to think that Direct Line media planning has revolved solely around a number of very big spreadsheets – however, while there is certainly an element of pride in checking and re-checking critical cost and response numbers, media has been restless at identifying and exploring new opportunities to drive brand effectiveness and accountability.

As a result, media now has much more multi-dimensional laydown compared to only a few years ago, reflecting both the emerging needs of Direct Line to keep growing new product businesses, and the broadening scope of media to maximise total communications impact (Figures 18–23).

Although Direct Line is famous for its TV advertising, it has spent an increasing proportion of its budget in other areas – some to drive 'direct' sales, some to supplement the brand (Figure 24).

The use of econometric modelling accurately quantifies the effect for each separate piece of media and explores its long-term contribution on brand quoting behaviour. This has enabled Direct Line to significantly increase its optimisation of

Posters

National bus backs

Specialist motor press

National roadside 6-sheets

Figure 22: *Motor insurance brand touchpoints beyond TV, 2002–2003*

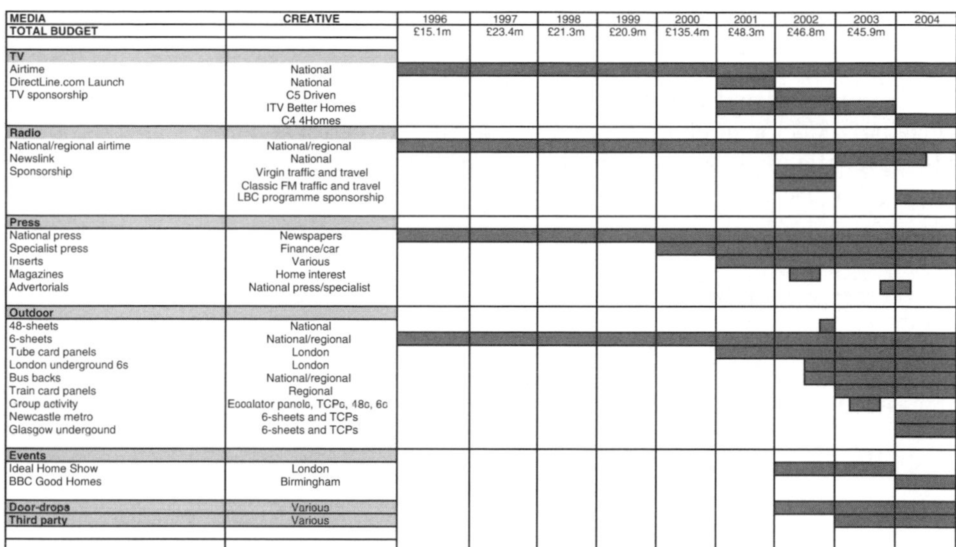

MEDIA
CREATIVE
1996
1997
1998
1999
2000
2001
2002
2003
2004
TOTAL BUDGET
£15.1m
£23.4m
£21.3m
£20.9m
£135.4m
£48.3m
£46.8m
£45.9m
TV
Airtime
DirectLine.com Launch
TV sponsorship
National
National
C5 Driven
ITV Better Homes
C4 4Homes
Radio
National/regional airtime
Newslink
Sponsorship
National/regional
National
Virgin traffic and travel
Classic FM traffic and travel
LBC programme sponsorship
Press
National press
Specialist press
Inserts
Magazines
Advertorials
Newspapers
Finance/car
Various
Home interest
National press/specialist
Outdoor
48-sheets
6-sheets
Tube card panels
London underground 6s
Bus backs
Train card panels
Group activity
Newcastle metro
Glasgow undergound
National
National/regional
London
London
National/regional
Regional
Escalator panels, TCPs, 48s, 6s
6-sheets and TCPs
6-sheets and TCPs
Events
Ideal Home Show
BBC Good Homes
London
Birmingham
Door-drops
Third party
Various
Various

Figure 23: *Change in communications laydown*

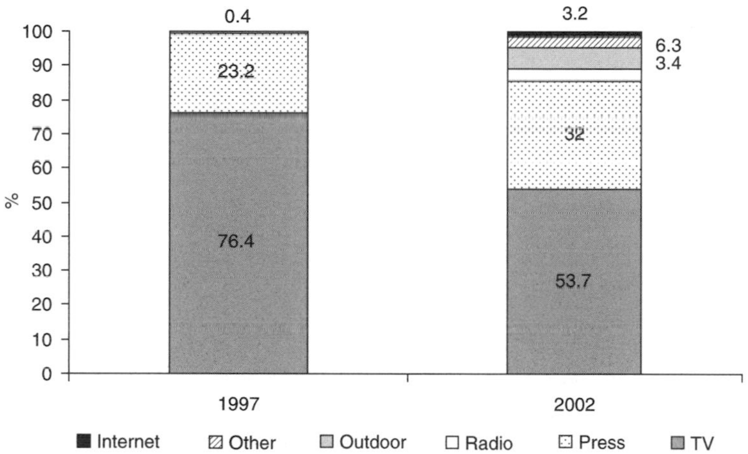

Figure 24: *Broadening of Direct Line media channels*

direct channels while experimenting with branding activity beyond 30-second TV adverts. As we shall see, this has been a central component in achieving superbrand status, helping Direct Line increase profit margins.

HOW ADVERTISING HAS MADE THE DIFFERENCE

So far we have demonstrated how advertising has caused the shift from a super product into a super-profitable business. Now we will demonstrate that this shift has been created through what can only be described as superbrand traits, using our model (see Figure 4).

The Red Phone device creates higher advertising and brand cut-through

Through ingenuity and media profile, the Red Phone device has become a branding icon as powerful and well recognised in the UK as the Nike swoosh. In a survey, an amazing 98% of adults correctly identified the Red Phone as Direct Line's.[30] Moreover the jingle has higher recognition than some of the most famous brands around (Figure 25).[31]

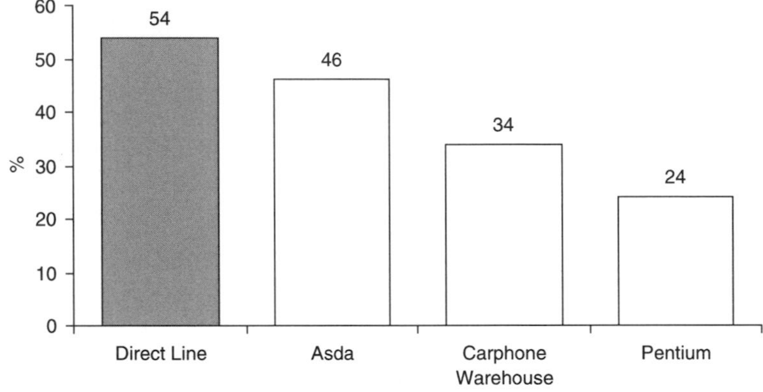

Figure 25: *Adults correctly identifying sonic logo*

This visual and sonic combination has been very effective in creating advertising you cannot ignore, especially once amplified by a peak-heavy TV media strategy. In turn, this advertising awareness has driven a huge increase in brand awareness (Figure 26).[32]

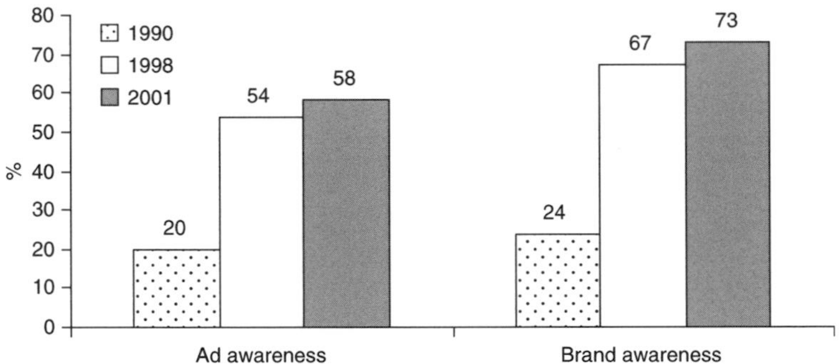

Figure 26: *Increasing advert awareness has driven brand awareness*

In fact, the Red Phone device has not only created a brand that is increasingly recognised, it has created a brand that is increasingly front of mind and at the top of recall polls (Figures 27 and 28).[33]

Front-of-mind measures are now ahead of any competitor (Figure 29).[34]

30. Direct Line research, 1998.
31. NOP Research, Capital Radio (500 adults).
32. 1990 Millward Brown Tracking; Taylor Nelson Brand Health Study.
33. Taylor Nelson Brand Health Study, 2002 (motor).
34. Taylor Nelson Brand Health Study, 2002 (motor).

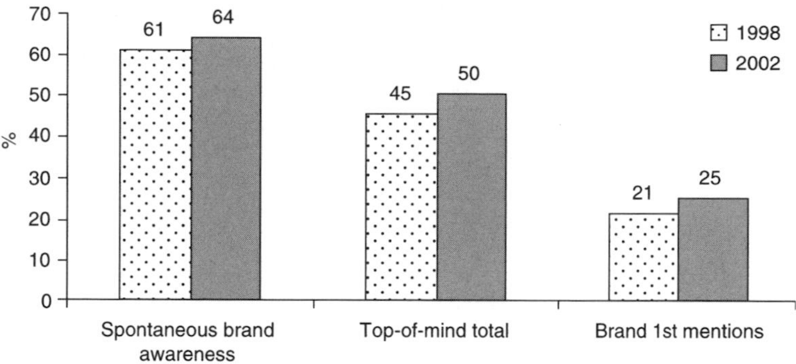

Figure 27: *Direct Line increasingly front of mind*

ADWATCH

The weekly analysis of advertisement recall

Q: Which of the following TV commercials do you remember seeing recently?

	Last week	Account	Agency/TV buyer	%
1	(1)	**Direct Line**	Faulds Advertising/MediaCom TMB	75
2	(3)	**Asda**	Publicis/Carat	72
3	(4)	**B&Q**	Bates UK/Zenith Media	70
4	(2)	**Specsavers**	In-house/CIA Medianetwork	60
5	(5)	**McDonald's**	Leo Burnett/Starcom Motive	63

Adwatch research was conducted from September 22 to September 23 by **NOP Research Group** (020 7890 [illegible]) as part of a weekly telephone omnibus survey among more than 500 adults. Copies of the Adwatch data and analysis are available from Victoria Blake at NOP. Advertisements were selected by [illegible]

ADWATCH

The weekly analysis of advertisement recall

Q: Which of the following TV commercials do you remember seeing recently?

	Last week	Account	Agency/TV buyer	%
1	(2=)	**Direct Line**	Mortimer Whittaker O'Sullivan/MediaCom	81
2	(2=)	**B&Q**	J Walter Thompson/ZenithOptimedia	78
3	(1)	**Churchill**	EBP/MediaCom	77
4	(5)	**McDonald's**	Leo Burnett/OMD UK	75
5	(4)	**DFS**	Phillipson Ward Longworth Camponi/Brilliant Media	67

Adwatch research was conducted from March 5 to March 7 by **NOP Research Group** as part of a weekly telephone omnibus survey among 495 adults. Copies of the Adwatch data and analysis are available from Jane Hosker at NOP (020 7890 9712). Advertisements were selected by **Xtreme Information** (020 7575 1800) and Mediaedge:cia UK (020 7803 2000).

Figure 28: *Direct Line top of the recall polls, 2000 and 2004 (left: Marketing Adwatch Poll, September 2000; right: Marketing Adwatch Poll, March 2004)*

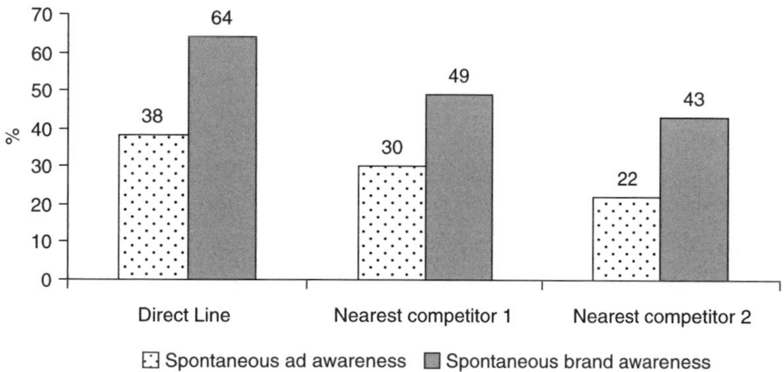

Figure 29: *Direct Line has a big front-of-mind advantage*

Advertising reinforces superior perceptions of Direct Line

Direct Line has certainly achieved its ambition of transforming itself 'from Kwiksave to Tesco'.[35] Its brand 'footprint' shows it has successfully grown beyond just 'cheap' – it is now equally strong for value and service, way ahead of any other player in its category (Figure 30).[36]

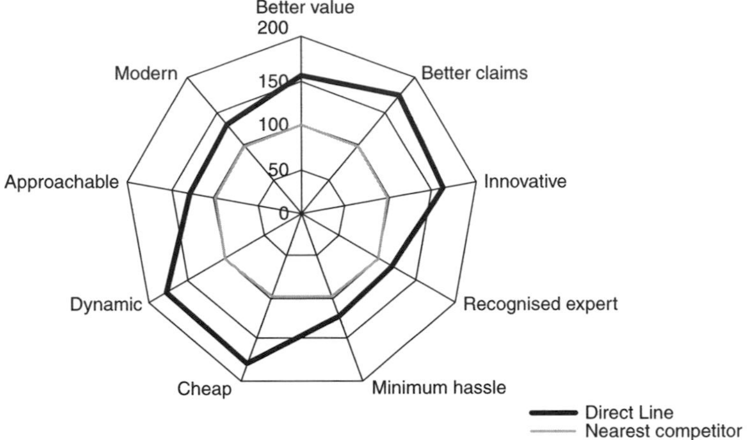

Figure 30: *Direct Line has a stronger brand imprint than nearest competitor (competitor index 100)*

Moreover, it is becoming stronger in personality over time (Figure 31).[37]

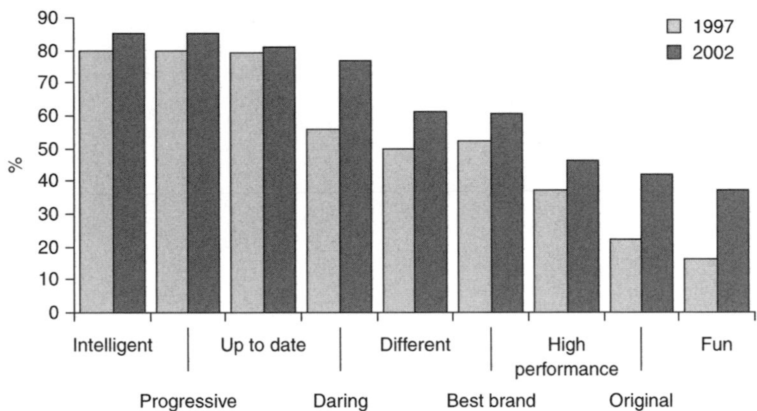

Figure 31: *Direct Line personality traits are growing stronger*

As a result Direct Line comes top of class in brand strength on every measure, according to the Brandz Voltage study. Its sector 'bonding' score is seven times higher than the score for the average brand (Figure 32).[38]

35. Marketing Strategy documentation, 1995/6.
36. Taylor Nelson Brand Health Study, 2002.
37. MediaedgeCIA/WPP Brandz Asset Valuator, 2003.
38. MediaedgeCIA/WPP Brandz Asset Valuator, 2003.

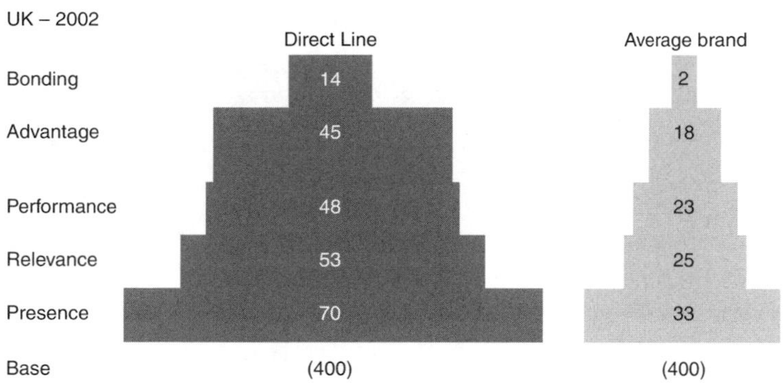

Figure 32: *Direct Line top of the Brandz Voltage study (UK, 2002)*

We can prove this strength comes from the advertising by comparing Direct Line's image strength among those who saw its brand TV advertising in 2003 against those who did not see any. The results clearly show Direct Line's brand image strength is very strongly determined by its advertising (Figure 33).[39]

Recent brand sponsorship activity reinforces this argument.

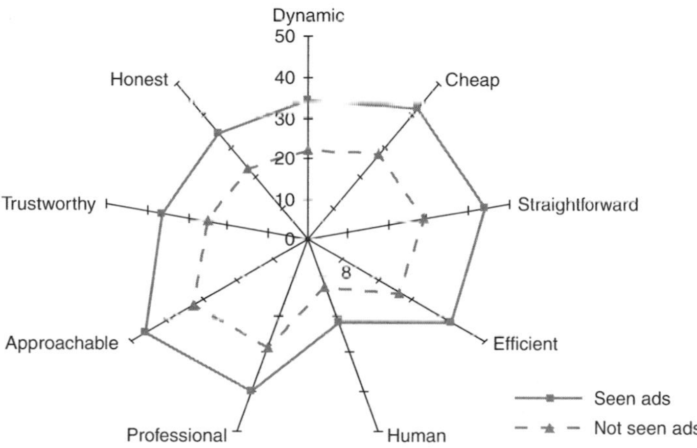

Figure 33: *Direct Line recallers have a stronger image of the brand*

People who have seen Direct Line's home sponsorship on Channel 4 also have stronger perceptions of the brand than those who have not seen any idents – testimony to the fact that it is brand communications that are driving brand perceptions (Figure 34).[40]

39. Taylor Nelson Brand Health Study, 2003; annual data. Recall ads: cut-through (proven recall) of any Direct Line motor or home TV ads (base size 714). No recall ads (base size 2993).
40. SPA Research Wave 1 C4 sponsorship research, 2004.

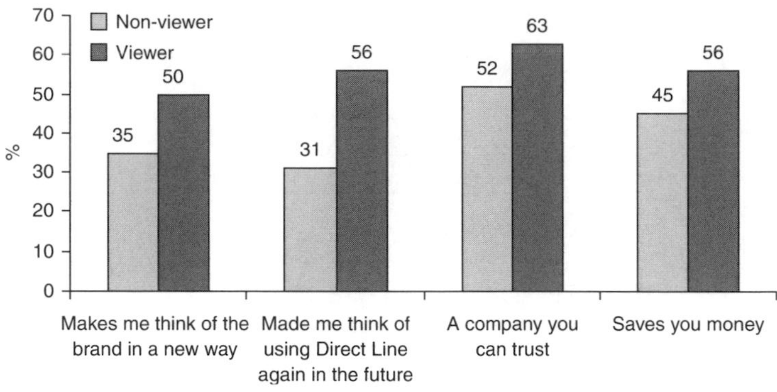

Figure 34: *Effect on Direct Line brand of C4 home sponsorship activity*

Direct Line has superbrand strength perceptions

In fact, this image goes beyond 'top of sector' class. According to the Brandz study, Direct Line has grown to be in a super-league alongside Sony, Nokia, Vodafone and Virgin Atlantic as a brand of 'Olympic' stature (Figures 35 and 36).[41]

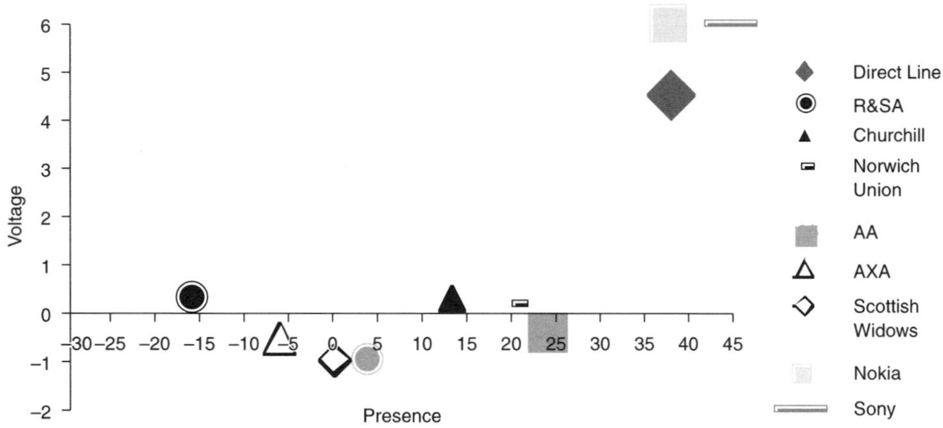

Figure 35: *High Direct Line superbrand voltage*

Superior brand perceptions create stronger attraction

Through perceptions created by advertising, Direct Line is now the number one preferred brand on people's home or motor insurance shopping list, significantly ahead of competitors (Figure 37).[42]

In fact, uniquely, more people claim it is the advertising that drove them to get a quote from Direct Line than any with other competitor (Figure 38).[43]

41. MediaedgeCIA/Brandz Brandz Voltage study.
42. NOP Financial Research Survey, 2003.
43. NOP Financial Research Survey, 2003.

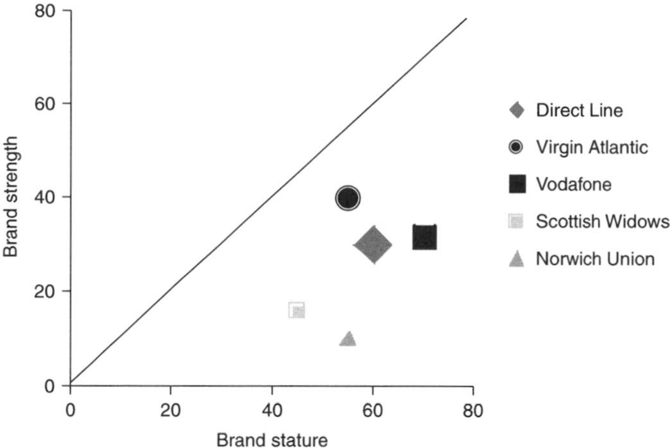

Figure 36: *Direct Line superbrand performance*

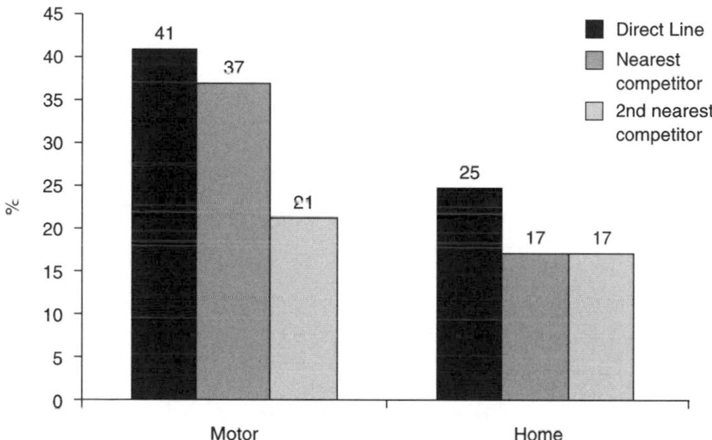

Figure 37: *Direct Line advantage via consideration*

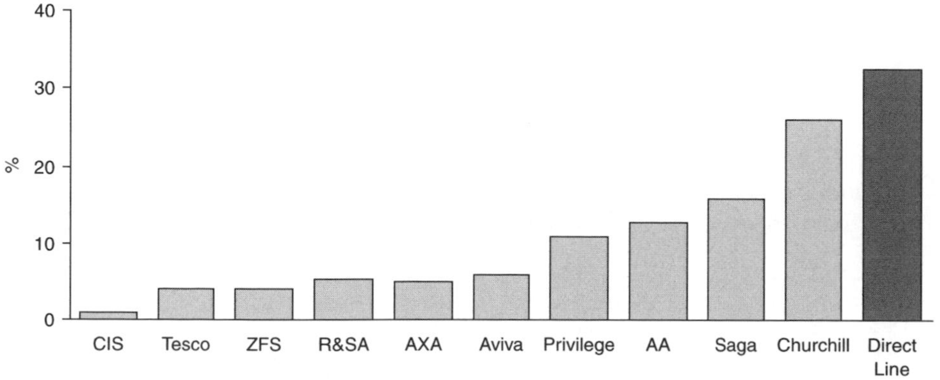

Figure 38: *More people claim Direct Line's advertising prompted them to arrange a quote than any competitor*

Superior brand perceptions create stronger conversion and loyalty

Significantly, Direct Line not only gets to the top of the shopping list, it is also able to convert call quotes into sales with far greater success than competitors amongst both new users (cold/warm prospects) and current users (Figure 39).[44]

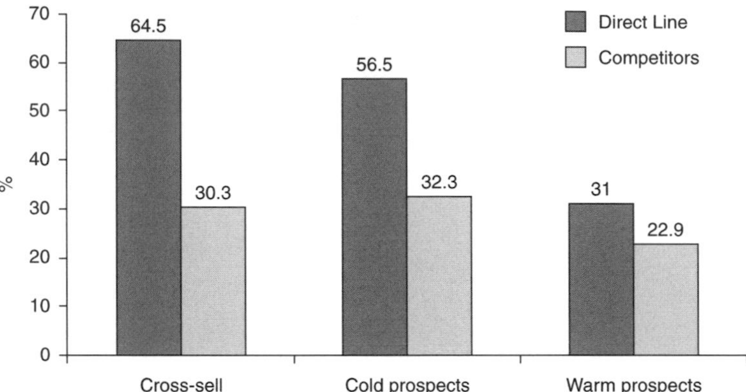

Figure 39: *Higher Direct Line conversion rate*

Moreover, no other brand has a higher level of cross-holding loyalty between home and motor insurance (Figure 40).[45]

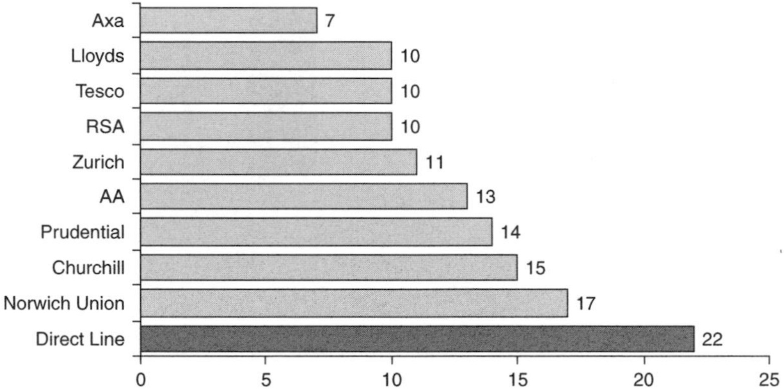

Figure 40: *More customers have joint home and motor policies with Direct Line than competitors*

This is more than effective call-centre sales technique – in an increasingly promiscuous market, Direct Line's users seek fewer quotes than competitors[46] and are less likely to switch away from it than almost any other competitor (Figure 41).[47]

44. Tank Analysis of Direct Mail; competitors include Norwich Union, Lloyds TSB, Tesco, Sainsbury's, HFC, Insure Direct, Abbey National, Marks & Spencer, HboS, Nationwide.
45. NOP Financial Research Survey, 2003.
46. NOP Financial Research Survey, 2003 – Direct Line customers (motor) seek 3.17 quotes vs 3.62 Churchill customers, 4.13 Tesco customers, 4.39 Privilege customers.
47. NOP Financial Research Survey, 2003.

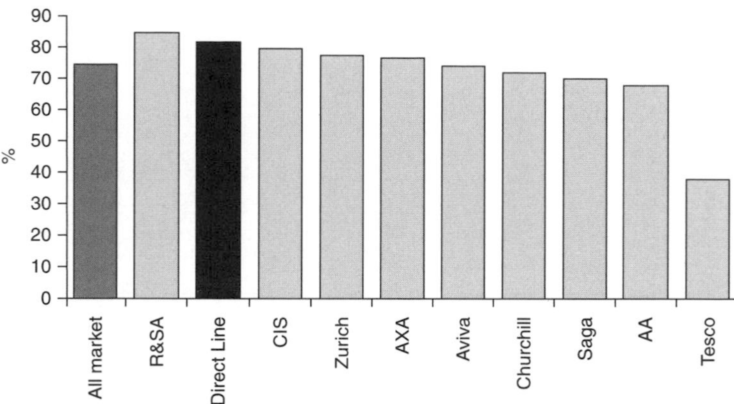

Figure 41: *Motor renewals versus competition, 2002*

These examples demonstrate Direct Line's users are actually more loyal than competitors. We can prove advertising has created this extraordinary brand loyalty in two ways. First, people who have seen Direct Line advertising insist or prefer the brand at higher levels than those who have not (Figure 42).[48]

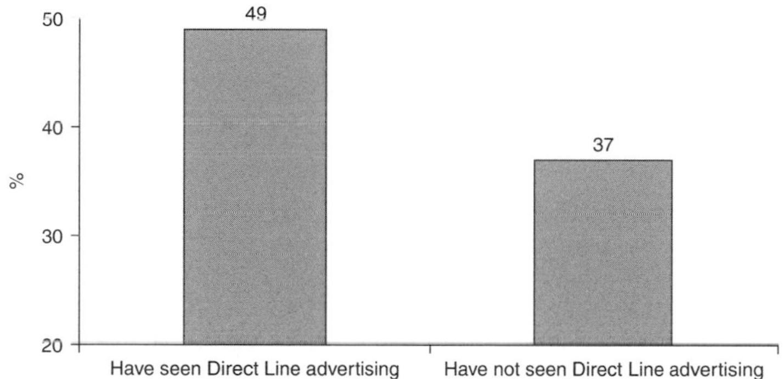

Figure 42: *People who see Direct Line adverts are more likely to insist or prefer the brand*

Second, our econometric analysis can examine the effect of withdrawing brand advertising on quotes, through isolating Granada as a test region (Figure 43).[49]

This analysis shows brand advertising has a significant long-term-effect factor on business – despite reintroducing brand advertising to matching levels, Granada has remained behind the rest of the country in achieving its fair level of quotes, despite spending an equivalent sum (Figure 44).[50]

This is irrefutable evidence that the advertising has both a short- and long-term effect on business. Critically, the value of brand TV has been calculated to deliver response at 2.5 times the level of direct responses, over a 24-month period. In our

48. Taylor Nelson Brand Health Study; annual data, 2003. Recall ads: cut-through (proven recall) of any Direct Line motor or home TV ads (base size 714). No recall ads (base size 2993).
49. MediaCom 'Economiser' Econometrics.
50. Brand advertising remained constant in the rest of the country but was withdrawn from Granada in 1999 and 2000 for business reasons. Don't recall ads (base size 2993).

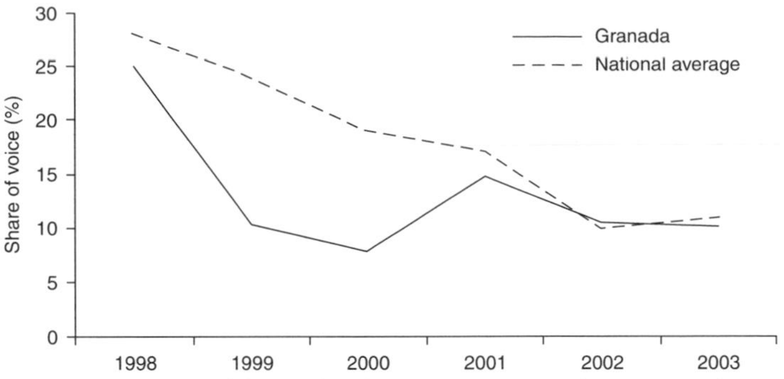

Figure 43: *Impact of withdrawing brand TV support on Granada versus rest of network*

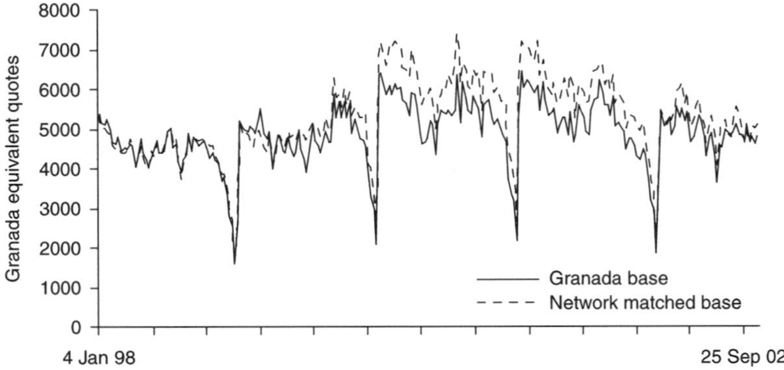

Figure 44: *Granada quotes have not returned to network levels, even over the longer term*

model, this proves brand advertising is the biggest single factor in creating growth through longer-term loyalty.[51]

Strong sales and loyalty enhance the operating efficiency of the business

Creating a brand means nothing unless it brings value to the bottom line. As we have demonstrated, advertising has generated disproportionate preference and loyalty towards Direct Line, enabling further economies of scale to Direct Line's (already efficient) model.

> 'Direct Line is the most efficient company in the market. This is partly due to their historic focus on cost-reduction, but probably owes much more to their established brand image which has been assiduously built up.'
>
> Datamonitor

This has given Direct Line the lowest overall operating ratio in the market, creating a significant advantage through higher profit margins (Figure 45).[52]

51. MediaCom 'Economiser' econometric model; the model also demonstrates an incredible 80% of quotes now come independent of advertising activity, such is the strength of the Direct Line brand. In fact, motor quotes would only decline by 17% a year without advertising support (excluding directories)!
52. Datamonitor/Direct Line.

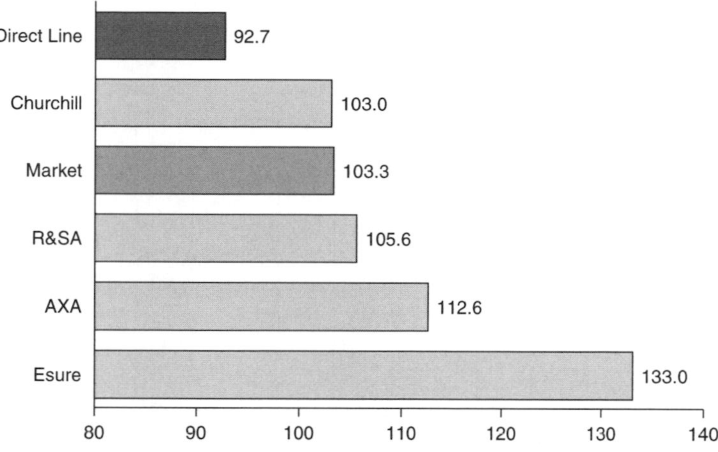

Figure 45: *Direct Line has a lower operating ratio than competitors*

> 'Direct Line's efficiency has increased ... through economies of scale – our outstanding operating efficiency is one of the key areas that makes us so much stronger than the competition.'
>
> Ian Chippendale, Chief Executive 1995, post-Red Phone TV launch advertising

Media has played a central role in enabling and sustaining this efficiency, both through ensuring that Red Phone brand communications have maximum visibility and cut through, but also though exploiting econometrics tools to refine direct channel plans, managing down the average cost per quote while driving volumes. For instance, on motor there has been a consistent decline in cost per quote and increase in overall responsiveness, despite a constant spend (Figure 46).[53]

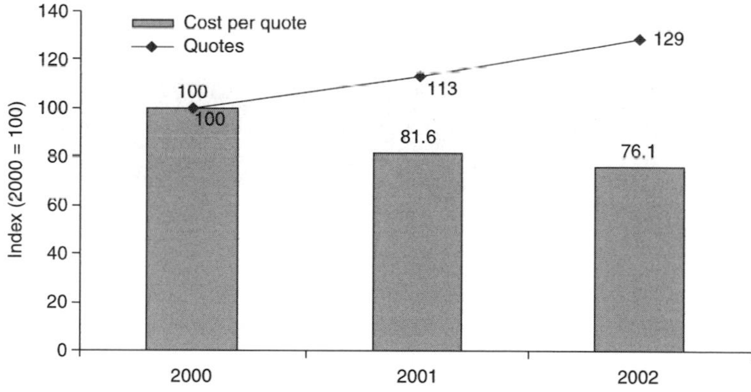

Figure 46: *Reduction in costs per quote, but increase in responsiveness for direct channels*

This has been achieved through a combination of expanding specialist press and door-drops and making press work harder, using smaller press sizes and increasing the frequency of insertions (Figure 47).

53. MediaCom.

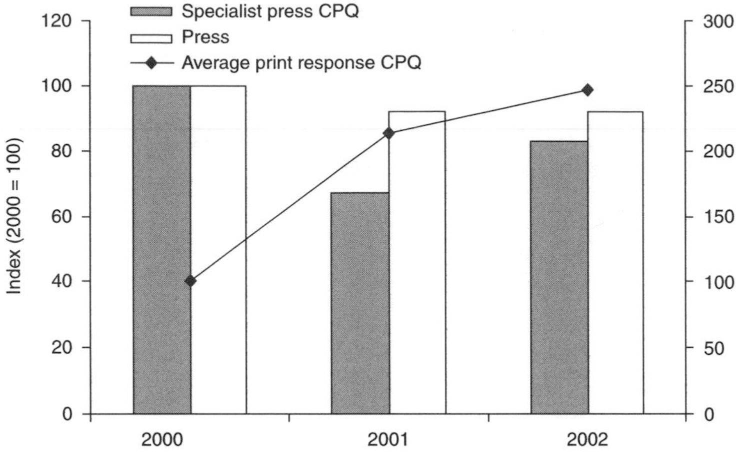

Figure 47: *Direct Line increasing print performance*

Through strategic and tactical communications, advertising has enabled Direct Line to run at better margins than competitors, enabling it to sustain underwriting profitability as it expanded in tough market conditions.

In addition, advertising has created a brand strong enough to withstand the potentially huge threat of the internet. This has enabled Direct Line to successfully replicate its number one status in awareness, consideration and conversion online,[54] while continuing to acquire customers at almost three times lower cost than competitors (Figure 48).[55]

'No other direct insurer converts traffic into sales, with the same success as Direct Line.'

ebenchmarkers, 2003

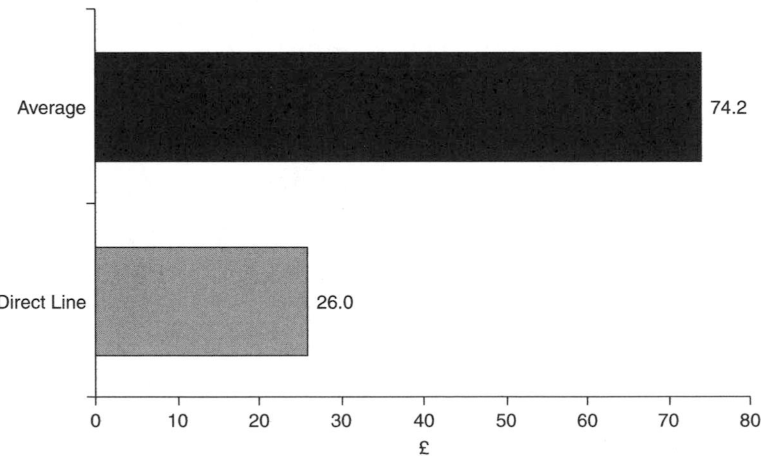

Figure 48: *Direct Line has lower online marketing cost per sale*

54. NOP Financial Research Survey.
55. ebenchmarkers, 2003; Direct Line is the most visited insurance site in the UK, used by over 50% of researchers; number one online market share in home and motor, more than double any competitor.

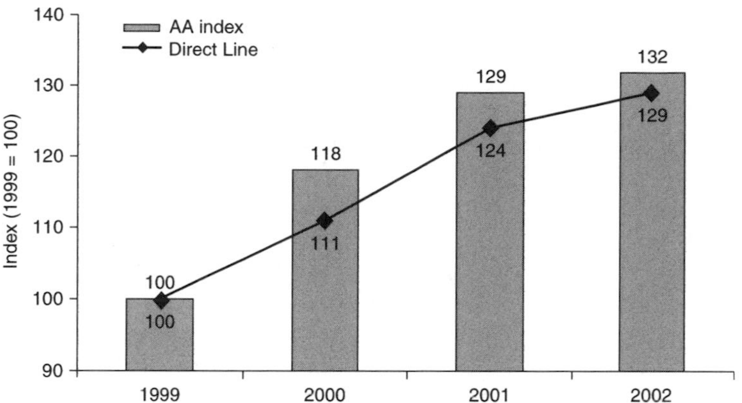

Figure 49: *Consistently cheaper Direct Line pricing versus competitors ('AA index' = market average)*

Success has enabled Direct Line to further improve its prices, product and services

Significantly, Direct Line has invested profits back into the business, allowing it to create further competitive advantage, undercutting competitor prices (Figure 49),[56] while creating a reputation for excellent service.[57]

In addition it has enabled Direct Line to launch internationally,[58] and launch genuinely new products such as Home Response 24 and Jamjar.

> 'Direct Line is the sort of company that I would expect to implement something that everybody started copying.'
>
> TRBI Brand Health Qualitative Research, 2003

DISCOUNTING OTHER FACTORS

Direct Line undoubtedly has a strong business model. Nethertheless, as the 'only shop window', advertising has played a critical role as the fuel that ignites the business – there really are no other factors that could have accounted for driving Direct Line's business so strongly.

- *Not price:* while price is clearly an important part of Direct Line's brand promise, we have demonstrated how advertising has actually underpinned this underwriting advantage. However, even if we wanted to argue that price is a factor, then this is decreasingly valid – Direct Line's pricing margin is now far less than it was relative to the competition versus when it launched.
- *Not product differences:* the products on offer were not significantly different to the competition. While Direct Line was keen to innovate and offer better added

56. Datamonitor Motor Report, 2004 – it is important to note this is now is less than at launch, when there was a 20% difference.
57. Taylor Nelson Brand Health Study, 2002.
58. Direct Line has launched in France, Italy, Spain, Germany and Japan, providing a further platform for growth.

value to customers, any new initiatives have quickly been followed and initial advantage lost.

- *Not market growth:* Direct Line's core market – motor insurance – was in massive negative underwriting profit from 1995 to 2002 – Direct Line has grown its profits despite the market, by increasing its share.
- *Not other communications:* the financial worth of additional variables is accurately accounted for and evaluated within our econometric model, and is insignificant.
- *Not a decline in competitive spending:* Direct Line has invested consistently in brand communications because it pays back handsomely. However, while total spend has increased, this has not kept pace with the market – its share of voice in the motor market has fallen year on year from 24% in 1998 to 9% in 2002 as market spending increased from £27.6m to £113m. It has not 'spent its way to success' – it has performed it.

This demonstrates that Direct Line's extraordinary success really has been a direct result of its Red Phone advertising, not other factors.

FINANCIAL PAYBACK

> 'The results are so good it looks like I'm making it up!'
>
> Jim Wallace, Direct Line Group Marketing Director

Return on investment has been calculated for a minimum case scenario.

Direct Line had 1988 and 1989 profits of £12.1m over two years (pre-TV Red Phone). This can be used as a 'base' profit level that would have occurred regardless. Between 1990 and 2002, this would have added up to £78.65m. In this period, total advertising investment was £249m (our 'investment'). In this period, pre-tax profits were £1352.4m (our 'return').

Therefore our total return in advertising investment (1990 to 2002 inclusive) is: £1024.75m. So every £1 spent on advertising generated £4.11 return. This excludes significant further financial value we have demonstrated exists from econometrics and impact in RBS revenue:

1. The continued value of *new* business.[59]
2. The continued value from *existing* customers.[60]
3. The added financial value Direct Line may have contributed to RBS's market capitalisation.[61]

These cannot be included for reasons of confidentiality.

59. Econometrics from the Granada region show, without advertising support, motor would decline at 17% quotes per year, and home at 11% a year. This calculation is based on withdrawing brand advertising, but would apply the same ratio to direct activity. Over only four years this would equate to at least 2,290,149 *additional* motor and home policies. Given in 2002 Direct Line made profits of £355m and had 4.6 million motor and home policies, this would create an additional £88.37m.
60. Direct Line internal figures give an average lifetime customer value of four years (over 80% of customers automatically renew their motor quotes). If we apply the above profit-to-policy calculation to only four million of its customers, over their four-year 'lifetime', this would equate to £1.23bn.

SUMMARY OF WHAT ADVERTISING ACHIEVED

We have demonstrated how advertising has achieved the following:

- created outstanding advertising 'cut-through', via the Red Phone device
- made the brand more front of mind than competitors
- built superior perceptions of price, service and innovation
- increased brand disposition and share in a market with declining loyalty
- generated cheaper cost-per-policy sale, through preference from new customers
- created disproportional loyalty and extra business from existing customers
- created stronger operating margins than any competitor
- enabled cheaper underwriting prices that can undercut the competition
- built disproportionate profits in unprofitable market conditions
- created a minimum additional profit of £1bn since 1990; every £1 spent delivers over £4 return.

As a result, Direct Line's Red Phone advertising has enabled it to grow from a low-cost motor insurer in a highly promiscuous market into a super-profitable superbrand.

61. It is worth noting that RBS share price increased from £1.66 in 1990 to £16.82 in 2002. Given RBS's 2002 market capitalisation (pre-NatWest merger figures) of £51bn, this would hypothetically value Direct Line at £6.9bn – a hypothetical increase of £5.2bn if taken as a proportion to RBS's profits, based on increases in RBS's share value from 1990 to 2002.

12

Eurostar

Learning to Fly

The difference an idea made to the relaunch of Eurostar in 2003

Principal authors: Neil Dawson, TBWA\London, and Jon Gittings, Manning Gottlieb OMD
Contributing author: Greg Nugent, Eurostar Ltd

EDITOR'S SUMMARY

This novel case study demonstrates how communication capitalised on Eurostar's 20-minute reduction in journey time to reposition the brand.

For six years after it launched in 1994 Eurostar enjoyed growth in sales and volume. It then expanded its services and by 2000 was carrying seven million passengers a year under the Channel. But between 2000 and 2003 its performance and position weakened. Low-cost airlines were inflicting considerable damage and Eurostar was suddenly no longer the exciting new way to travel. However with the Channel Tunnel rail link complete in 2003, Eurostar trains in the UK could now run faster on a high-speed track designed for them rather than relying on the already congested rail system designed for UK snail-speed trains.

The 'Fly Eurostar' idea for the first time positioned Eurostar as better than, as opposed to an alternative to, the plane. It was a distinctive, aggressive and well-integrated campaign, which used the 20-minute reduction in journey time to hit back at the airlines.

The relaunch transformed the business in the UK. Between September and March 2004 Eurostar enjoyed two record quarters in terms of volume and sales and the year-on-year revenue increases more than covered the cost of the entire campaign. Its success has caused major competitors to withdraw from competing routes in the skies.

The difficulty in judging this case study was teasing out the effect of communication from the product improvement itself, and the paper isolates the effect very comprehensively.

INTRODUCTION

This study will demonstrate how a disruptive idea can maximise the opportunity afforded by a product improvement; by flying in the face of the accepted wisdom about its position in the travel marketplace, Eurostar learned to fly. It will illustrate how a powerful integrated communications idea can transform the fortunes of a business and revitalise a brand. It will show how this idea cut through in the competitive, price-driven travel market to deliver a step-change in volumes and revenues. Launched in late September 2003, the campaign had immediate effect, delivering best ever Q4 and Q1 volumes for Eurostar. It will also show how the re-launched Eurostar achieved this by growing the market for trips to Paris and Brussels, as well as growing share from both established and low-cost airlines. Its success has driven major competitors to withdraw from both London–Paris and London–Belgium routes.

The evaluative challenge is that the Eurostar product improvement – a 20-minute reduction in journey time – occurred at the same time as the campaign broke (and indeed was the springboard for the campaign). Communication had a role in rapidly building awareness of the improvement, but we will demonstrate how it had a broader impact on the Eurostar brand. The power of the idea was to deliver results well beyond those that can be explained by the product improvement alone.

EUROSTAR AS A BUSINESS

Eurostar is a unique business in terms of structure and ownership. It is a private company run by a joint board comprising directors of Eurostar (UK) Ltd, Eurostar Group Ltd, and SNCF and SNCB representatives (Figure 1).

Its structure and ownership present clear constraints on what Eurostar is and what it can do.

- It is a fixed-route operation operating on high-speed lines in France, Belgium and the UK – and through the Channel Tunnel.
- It operates a fleet of specialist trains with potentially very large capacity.[1]
- Through its shareholders Eurostar has exclusive rights to operate passenger trains through the Channel Tunnel.
- Its shareholders invested in excess of £1bn in the high-speed lines and the trains, with the investment structured to produce a long-term return (i.e. over 25–50 years).
- There is a strong public interest in Eurostar's operation because of UK Government grants for investment and public ownership of SNCF and SNCB.
- The key fixed costs of the business include tunnel and track charges to Eurotunnel and SNCF/SNCB respectively. Hence Eurostar provides revenue for its shareholders.

1. Theoretically Eurostar in the UK could carry 14 million passengers per annum. It currently operates at an average 46% of maximum capacity.

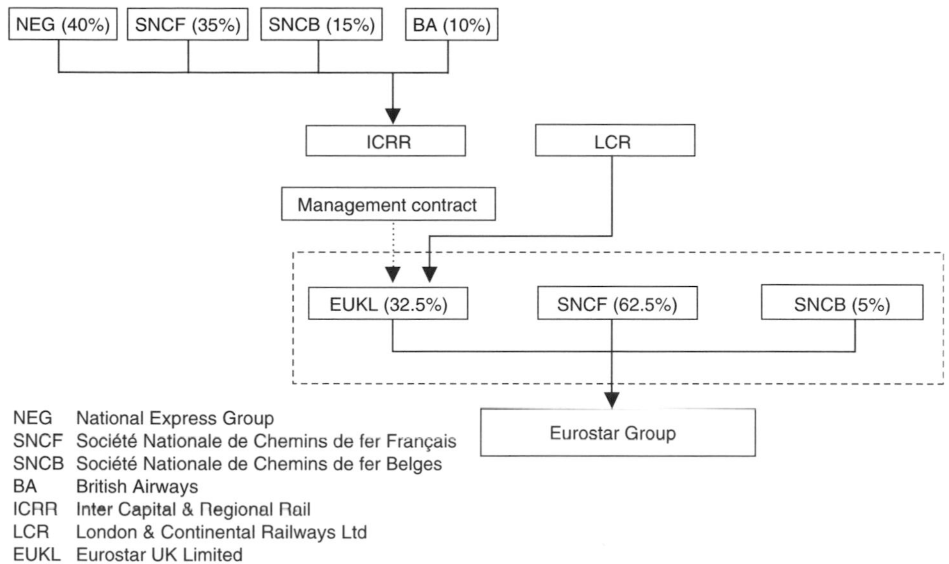

Figure 1: *Eurostar ownership structure*

The stated business objective for Eurostar is to maximise the return to its shareholders on their investment in both the high-speed lines and the trains.[2] Given that the business is so strongly a fixed-cost operation, this will be achieved by growing revenue over and above any variable costs (e.g. ticket distribution, service, train operation and maintenance).

In order to achieve significant revenue growth, Eurostar must pursue two key strategies:

1. Grow share of the existing market (defined as the air/rail market in the Paris/Brussels corridor).
2. Expand its markets by creating new reasons or desire to travel.

This pertains to each of the markets in which Eurostar operates: the UK, France and Belgium. From this point on, this study tells the story of the relaunch of Eurostar in the UK, although from time to time reference will be made to the French and Belgian markets (where different campaigns ran), as points of comparison.[3]

The structure and ownership of Eurostar also dictates that Eurostar has to satisfy a range of audiences (Figure 2).

The definition of success for each of these audiences is different.

- Passengers are looking for quality and value for money. Specifically in the business sector, they want to be associated with successful brands.[4]

---

2. Eurostar Corporate Strategy Document, 2003.
3. The terms ex-London, ex-Paris and ex-Brussels are used to differentiate the markets ('ex-' means running out of). Where no ex-London data is available 'Total' Eurostar data is shown. Ex-London is approximately 70% of total sales.
4. Source: Research International.

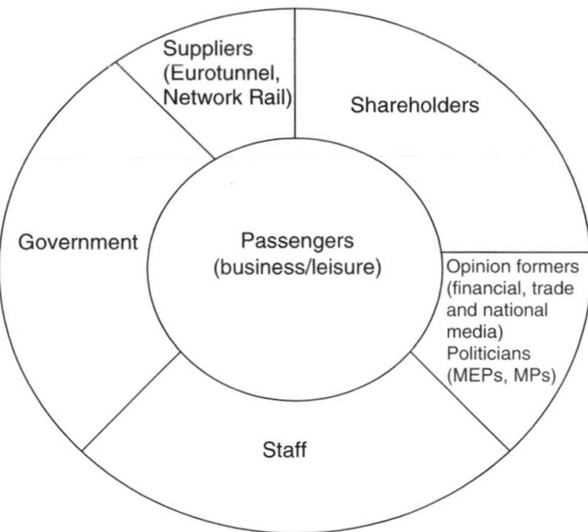

Figure 2: *Eurostar's key audiences*

- The UK Government and Department of Transport want Eurostar to be (and be seen as) both a worthwhile investment and a much-needed positive story in the British railway network.
- Shareholders want to see evidence of return on investment in the long term.[5] Growth in revenue and volume are their key indicators of success.
- Opinion formers such as journalists in business, trade and national news media create a climate of opinion for Eurostar. Positive endorsement from this audience is therefore key.
- Staff are the critical factor in delivering the Eurostar experience. They need to feel proud and motivated to work for Eurostar.
- Suppliers benefit financially from delivering an efficient service.

Value for Eurostar is created by satisfying each of these audiences.

FROM LAUNCH TO RELAUNCH

For the first six years after launch in 1994, Eurostar experienced sales and volume growth. A unique product, which brought Belgium and France closer to Britain, it grew the market five-fold. Eurostar expanded its services to include Lille, Disneyland Paris, ski trains to the French Alps and Avignon, and by 2000 was carrying seven million passengers through the Channel Tunnel every year.

But between 2000 and September 2003, Eurostar's performance and position weakened (Figures 3 and 4). A number of factors contributed to the decline.

Consumer

- The rise of a pick 'n' mix generation who liked to mix their lifestyles and personal attributes.[6] In the travel market this led to increased demand for a

5. It should be emphasised that long term means 25–50 years from launch.
6. Source: Henley Centre.

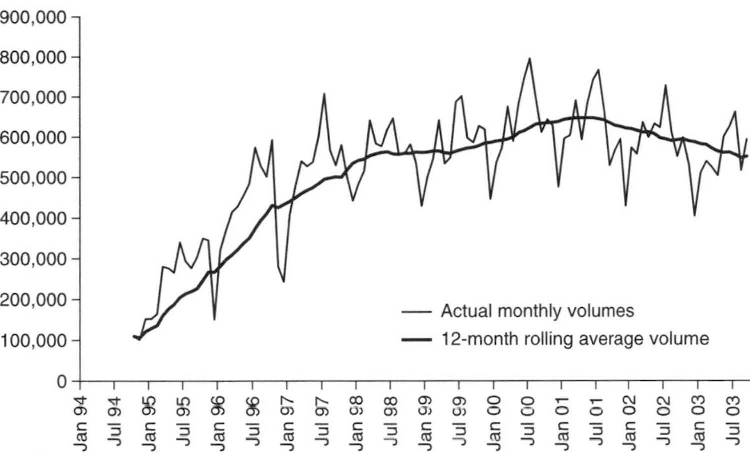

Figure 3: *Total Eurostar volumes – by month (October 1994–September 2003)*
Source: Eurostar

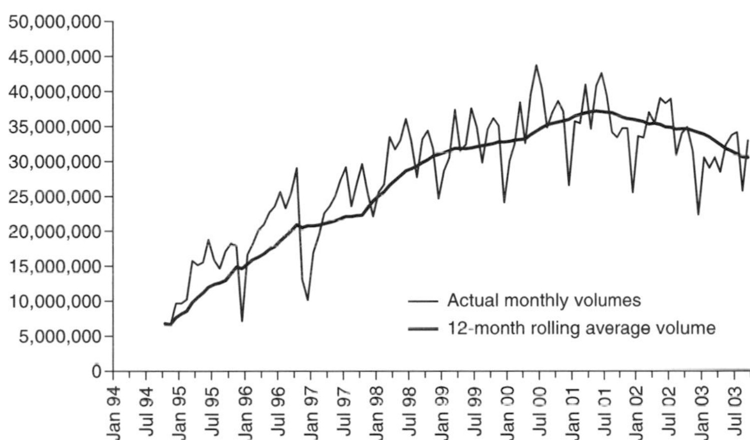

Figure 4: *Total Eurostar revenue (£) – by month (October 1994–September 2003)*
Source: Eurostar

wider range of experiences, and increasingly unpredictable consumer behaviour, Eurostar, with its necessarily limited offering, found it hard to compete.

Low-cost airlines

- A permanent shift downwards in price expectations as a result of the emergence of the low-cost airlines.
- A trend towards short-haul air travel becoming a commodity as a result of competitive forces pushing price and costs down.
- Shift towards internet distribution and e-ticketing, to cut costs.
- An explosion in new short city break destinations opened up by the low-cost airlines.[7] This created significant competition for the established leisure destinations of Paris and Brussels served by Eurostar.

7. By 2003 easyJet alone was flying to 70 destinations in Europe (Source: *Sunday Times*, March 2003).

- Aggressive price competition from low-cost airlines on the Paris/Brussels routes themselves. Eurostar was increasingly perceived as less affordable than its competitors.

Eurostar specific

- Several changes of management led to a loss of confidence and business direction.
- The trains themselves had not changed significantly since launch.
- The 'novelty' factor declined as the initial wave of one-off travellers had satisfied their curiosity about Eurostar.
- Adverse publicity surrounding delays due to bad weather and strikes reinforced negative associations with British trains. This created specific barriers for business travellers who want to be associated with success, as well as demanding reliability.
- An over-emphasis on the leisure market to Paris undermined the business market performance and left the Brussels route weak.

Added to all of the above, international terrorism (11 September 2001) and the wars in Afghanistan (2002) and Iraq (2003) made the travel market worldwide increasingly volatile and unpredictable.[8]

In summary, by 2003 Eurostar was in decline as a business and the brand was suffering. This was both an economic and political problem given the size of the organisation and the money invested in it. The improvement to the product provided a much needed opportunity to establish new momentum and confidence.

An opportunity to turn the tide – Channel Tunnel Rail Link (CTRL)

The CTRL was part of the original plan put together by the UK and French governments. It was critical to delivering the high volumes anticipated for Eurostar. It also meant that Eurostar trains in the UK would run at 186mph on a high-speed track designed for them, rather than relying on the already congested rail system designed for lower-speed trains. Dedicated Eurostar links meant reduced journey times, increased punctuality and reliability. CTRL was to be introduced in two stages.

The first was the £1.9bn public–private partnership project CTRL 1, extending 46 miles from the tunnel entrance near Folkestone to Fawkham Junction near Gravesend. At this point the trains return to the slower 'classic' lines into London, which terminate at Waterloo Station. The journey time reduction was to be 20 minutes (from 2 hours 55 minutes to Paris to 2 hours 35 minutes).[9]

Opening on 28 September 2003, CTRL 1 was much needed new news for Eurostar. Given the state of the Eurostar business and the brand, it was clear that this had to seek to do more than simply communicate an approximate 10% reduction in journey time. CTRL 1 was an opportunity to revitalise the fortunes of both the business and the brand.

8. There is little or no evidence of any consumer shift from planes to trains for safety reasons as a result of any of these events. They simply depressed the travel market as a whole.
9. CTRL 2 is due to open in 2007, and will continue from Gravesend, pass under the Thames and approach London from the East, terminating at St Pancras Station, which is currently being redeveloped as a major travel centre. The expected journey time reduction is a further 15 minutes.

MARKETING OBJECTIVES

- *Overall*: to relaunch the Eurostar brand and revitalise the business.
- *Consumer*: to increase revenues and volumes in business and leisure. Specifically to encourage switching from air travel among core business travellers.
- *Additional audiences*: to show success and positive momentum to Government, shareholders, suppliers and opinion formers in the media. To galvanise the Eurostar staff.

Developing the strategic solution

At a straightforward level, the CTRL 1 project improvement meant a faster train and a journey time reduction of 20 minutes. However, consumer research indicated that, while the time reduction was an important attribute, it would not be enough in itself to encourage fundamental appraisal and the desired relaunch effects. Quantitative research indicated that speed or journey times were ranked low on the list of drivers of preference for both audiences (Figures 5 and 6).

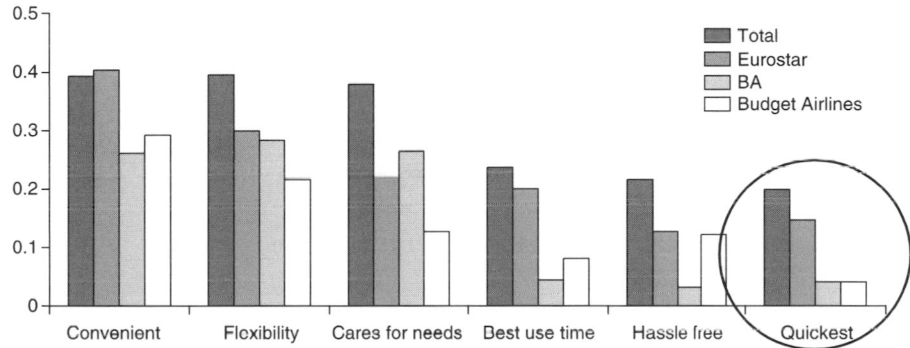

Figure 5: *Eurostar key drivers of brand preference (business)*
Base: business travellers, sample: 400
Source: NFO WorldGroup, 2003

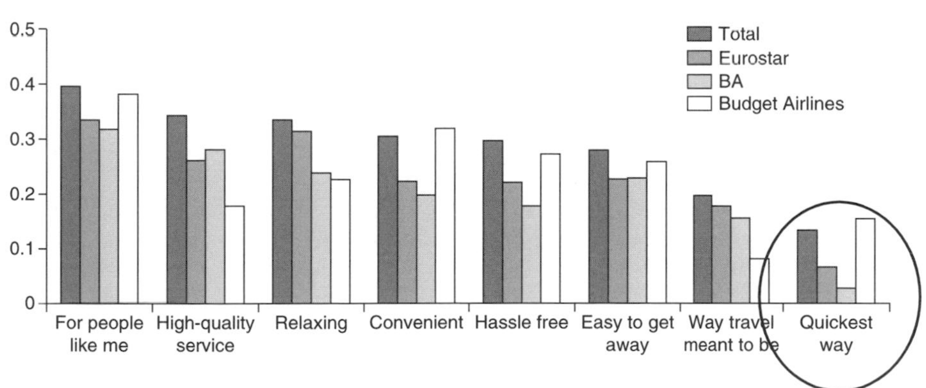

Figure 6: *Eurostar key drivers of brand preference (leisure)*
Base: business travellers, sample: 865
Source: NFO WorldGroup, 2003

Qualitative research confirmed this:

> 'It is apparent that a creative territory based on time saved has more potential than speed … although there are indications that focusing on time as the central message will not meet all the objectives of the company.'
>
> Source: CSR Eurostar CTRL Creative Development Research

The research also confirmed that while reduced journey time was relevant to the core business traveller, it was unlikely to motivate the leisure market, for whom time was not a major factor and certainly not enough to stimulate a trip.

It was evident that while CTRL 1 represented a platform for new news and some important messages about speed and ease of journey, this alone would not be sufficient to revitalise the brand.

The challenge was to increase the emotional connection with Eurostar via the relaunch, while still allowing room to communicate the rational product improvement.

The communications brief

The brief was as follows.

- Objectives
  - invite widespread and fundamental reappraisal of Eurostar
  - communicate the improved Eurostar service due to CTRL 1
- Target audiences
  - leisure travellers
  - business travellers and specifically core business flyers who we want to switch
  - Eurostar staff
- Communications proposition
  - Eurostar – the train is now better than the plane
- Support
  - now 20 minutes off the journey time
  - faster than ever from the heart of London to the heart of Paris/Brussels
- Requirements
  - an idea that feels confident and says Eurostar is changing for the better to the wider audiences of government, stakeholders, suppliers and opinion formers such as journalists
  - an integrated idea that is flexible enough to communicate brand, product and tactical messages, and that works in a wide range of media.

The communications idea – flying in the face of the airlines

The idea had to deliver a fundamental reappraisal of Eurostar. To do this, it had to break with the conventions that had surrounded Eurostar's marketing communications since launch. Rather than positioning Eurostar as *different* from airlines, it had to assert its *superiority*.

It also had to be a vehicle for the CTRL 1 product improvement messages, while also encouraging broader reappraisal by making Eurostar special and relevant to its key business and leisure audiences.

The creative solution was 'Fly Eurostar'. A disruptive thought, which invited direct comparison with airlines, demonstrated Eurostar's benefits and also delivered a call to action. We were quite literally flying in the face of our competition.

Consumer qualitative research endorsed the idea:

> 'The comparison with air travel (which is the fastest mode of travel to the centre of Paris/Brussels) is very effective ... it encourages reappraisal ... thought-provoking.'
>
> 'It also works hard at a brand level ... Eurostar is a confident brand:
> - confidence in the product
> - confidence vs air travel.'
>
> Source: CSR Eurostar CTRL Creative Development

The value of an idea is that it informs all forms of communications; in order to maximise its potential 'Fly Eurostar' had to work against key audiences across a range of channels.

Communications strategy

Figure 7 shows the integrated plan that was developed. Let us consider each element in turn.

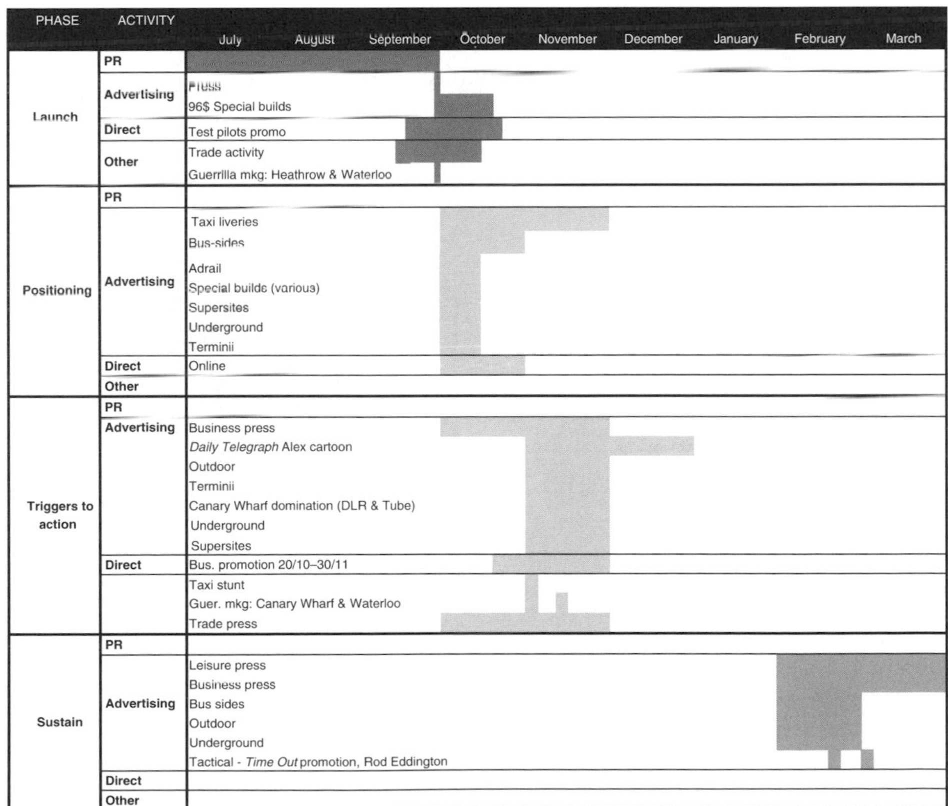

Figure 7: *Eurostar CTRL communications plan*

PR

The pre-launch had to make CTRL news throughout the summer of 2003 and right up to the day of launch on 28 September 2003.

Various events were delivered:

- breaking UK rail speed record (30 July 2003)
- the offical opening of the line by PM Tony Blair and Transport Secretary Alistair Darling (16 September 2003) and simultaneous launch event at Leeds Castle with key business people and journalists (Figures 8 and 9)

Figure 8: *Official opening*

Figure 9: *Launch event at Leeds Castle*

- second launch celebration event at Leeds Castle held on 17 September for trade partners and Eurostar staff
- party at Waterloo station and a chartered trip that broke the rail speed record from Brussels to London and London to Paris on 27 September carrying celebrities, journalists, trade partners and other opinion formers (Figures 10 and 11)
- 28 September, services open to the public.

Figure 10: *Party and chartered trip*

Figure 11: *Party and chartered trip*

Advertising

The communication goals for consumers demanded a strategy that could combine both a celebratory launch of the universal 'Fly Eurostar' message with specific media triggers that would turn the business audience away from the airlines.

The campaign was initially built around these two principal needs.

1. *Celebration*: Phase 1 *The launch of 'Fly Eurostar' to the wider public* (Figures 12 and 13). To embed the idea into the public consciousness we had to be single-

Figure 12: *Phase 1 posters*

Figure 13: *Phase 1 posters*

minded, innovative, impactful. This meant building fast, effective and impression-forming awareness through flagship media formats and innovative techniques that leveraged and amplified the 'Fly Eurostar' message.

2. *Challenge*: Phase 2 *Aggressive and disruptive targeting of hard-nosed business flyers*. To break the ingrained habits of the business flyer demanded we take a precise, confident, persuasive and challenging stance. Media selection had to be personal, immediate and direct (Figure 14).

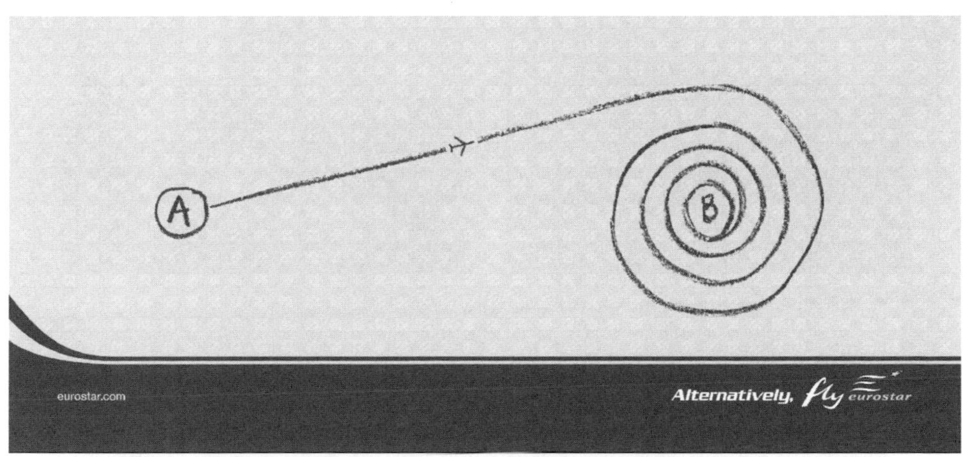

LDN Heathrow, LDN Gatwick, LDN Luton.
And now LDN London.
eurostar.com
Central Paris 2h35. central Brussels 2h20. fly eurostar

Figure 14: *Phase 2 posters*

Figure 15

Figure 16

Figure 17

Media formats and messages were highly tailored to business roles and business environments. Four key techniques were identified through which to disrupt.

1. Target rail and road routes to London's airports (Figure 15).
2. Infiltrate London's airports through creative or non-traditional methods. BAA does not allow Eurostar to advertise within the boundaries of its airports (Figure 16).[10]
3. Target 'switching zones' around London where the 20-minute reduction in journey time would be enough to make Eurostar a valid choice vs the airlines (Figure 17).
4. Take ownership and cement presence in business properties, from the City and Canary Wharf to *The Sunday Times* business section (Figure 18).

10. Note, the use of tactics at airports to circumvent this, shown in Figure 16. This involved promotions teams holding banners near airport entrances advocating Eurostar.

Figure 18

This included briefing *Daily Telegraph* cartoonists Peattie and Taylor to create a series of 11 one-off 'Alex' cartoons based on the theme of 'Fly Eurostar', selling the benefits of Eurostar's journey experience whilst lampooning the airlines (Figure 19). The 'Fly Eurostar' idea evolved in 2004 (Figure 20).

Direct activity targeting the business traveller

- Prospect database gathering – 'Fly Eurostar, it's only Eurostar that flies' (Figure 21).
- Increase sales of business tickets – 'Fly Eurostar Free' (Figure 22). Customers were encouraged to 'Buy a business ticket' to get two leisure tickets free.

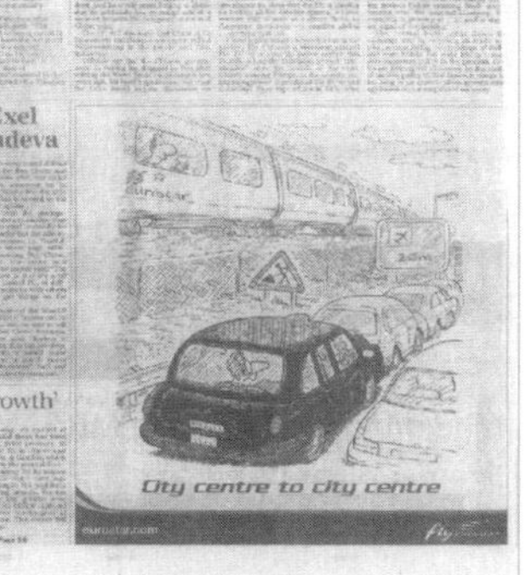

Figure 19: *Alex cartoons*

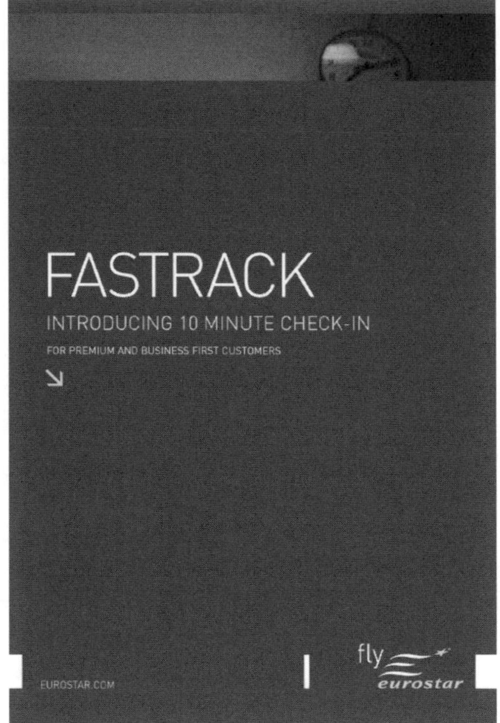

Figure 20

Total spend on the relaunch campaign between July 2003 and 31 March 2004 is shown in Table 1. This was similar to investment levels in previous years (Table 2).

TABLE 1: COMMUNICATIONS SPEND

Advertising	£5.5m
PR	£300k
Direct	£500k
TOTAL	£6.3m

Source: OMD/Proximity

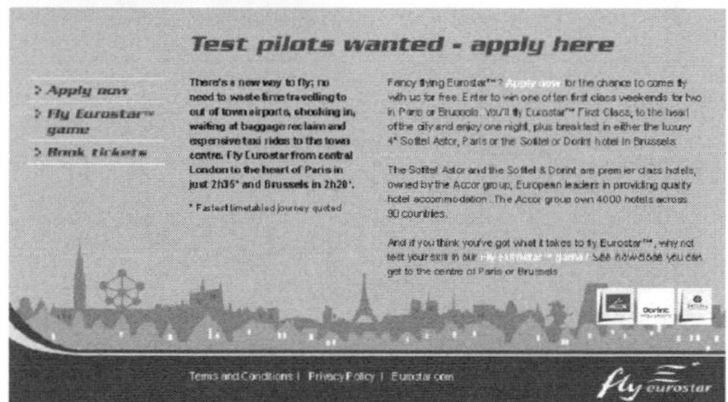

Figure 21

Figure 22

TABLE 2: HISTORIC COMMUNICATIONS SPEND,[11] EUROSTAR (EX-LONDON)

Year	Spend ($m)
2000	9.5
2001	7.5
2002	7.2
Jan–28 September 2003 (non-CTRL)	4.8
September 2003–March 2004 (CTRL)	6.0

Source: OMD/Proximity

11. Figures are for advertising and direct spend only.

THE RESULTS

The overall story

The relaunch of Eurostar in the UK has transformed its business. In the ensuing period of 28 September 2003 to 31 March 2004, Eurostar enjoyed two record quarters in terms of volume. There has been a significant and growing impact on revenues in business and leisure from launch up to the time of writing (Figure 23).

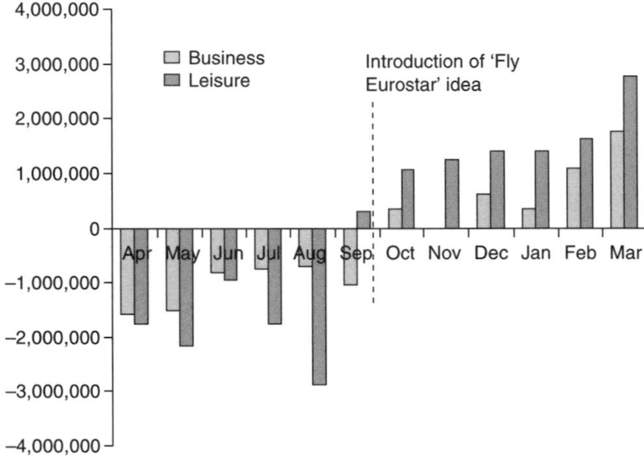

Figure 23: *Eurostar (ex-London) year-on-year revenue changes 2003–2004 vs 2002–2003, business and leisure*
Source: Eurostar

There was a small decrease in average yield from £63.3 to £59.9 over the period. This is reflected in the fact that volumes rose by 18% and revenues by 13% overall. The impact of price is taken into account in the econometric model shown later.[12]

The effect was such that the year-on-year revenue increases (net of the variable costs of carrying the additional passenger volume) had more than covered the cost of the entire launch campaign within the first six months. This is calculated as follows:

Total increase in revenues	= £13.6m
Cost to Eurostar of handling additional passengers (additional volume × average cost per passenger (331,276 × £14[13]))	= £4.6m
Total campaign spend	= £6.3m
Cost of promotion[14]	= £0.2m

The total increase minus cost to Eurostar of handling additional passengers minus campaign spend and promotional cost equates to incremental revenue to Eurostar of £2.5m within six months.

12. And furthermore all payback/value of idea calculations are based on revenue.
13. Source: *Evening Standard* interview with Richard Brown, CEO of Eurostar, *Evening Standard*, April 2004.
14. The promotion resulted in 5960 tickets being given away. On average each ticket resulted in £21 yield through upgrades and cost of entering. Average yield for this period is £59.9. This means that the promotion cost Eurostar 5960 x £38.9 = £230k. Obviously this is the maximum estimate of the cost; it assumes that none of the promotion travellers would have travelled without the promotion.

There is evidence of a sustained and broader effect on the business

Demand increased and has continued to grow. All the indications are that the new level of demand created will be sustained. Indeed there has been continued growth over the whole period (Figure 24).

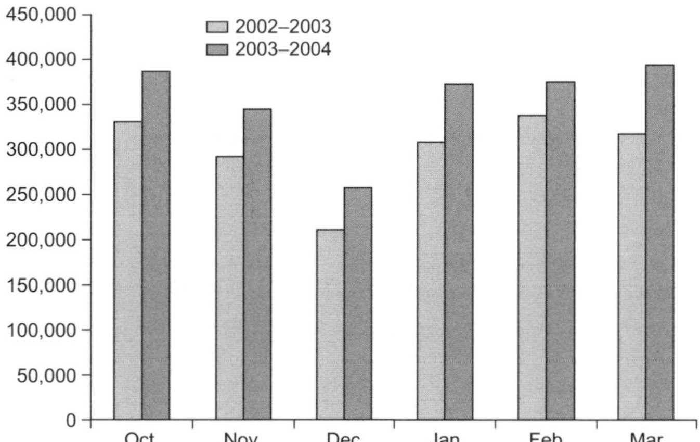

Figure 24: *Total monthly volumes (ex-UK) for period October 2003–March 2004 vs October 2002–March 2003*
Source: Eurostar

Market share and market growth objectives were achieved. On the Paris route no other operators have shown growth (Table 3 and Figure 25). Eurostar's volumes grew during the period, while established and low-cost competitors' volumes declined. On the Brussels route Eurostar grew faster than any competitor (Table 4 and Figure 26). This is in the context of overall market growth of flights/rail journeys to Paris/Brussels.

TABLE 3: PARIS ROUTE EX-LONDON ABSOLUTE CHANGE (OCTOBER 2002–MARCH 2003 VS OCTOBER 2003–MARCH 2004)

	October 2002–March 2003	October 2003–March 2004	Absolute change
Eurostar	2,039,000	2,389,000	+350,000
British Airways	536,000	487,000	–49,000
Air France	461,000	424,000	–37,000
easyJet	226,000	222,000	–4,000
British Midland	173,000	171,000	–2,000
Buzz/KLM	78,000	0	Withdrew route
Other	12,000	7,000	–5,000
Total	3,491,000	3,665,000	+174,000

Source: Civil Aviation Authority (CAA)

It is worth adding that during the campaign period there was no significant growth in other potential modes of transport to the Paris/Brussels corridor. During the period October 2003–March 2004, Eurotunnel volumes dropped 8.2% and total ferry volumes dropped 9% on the France/Belgium routes, compared with the period October 2002–March 2003.[15]

15. Source: IRN Research.

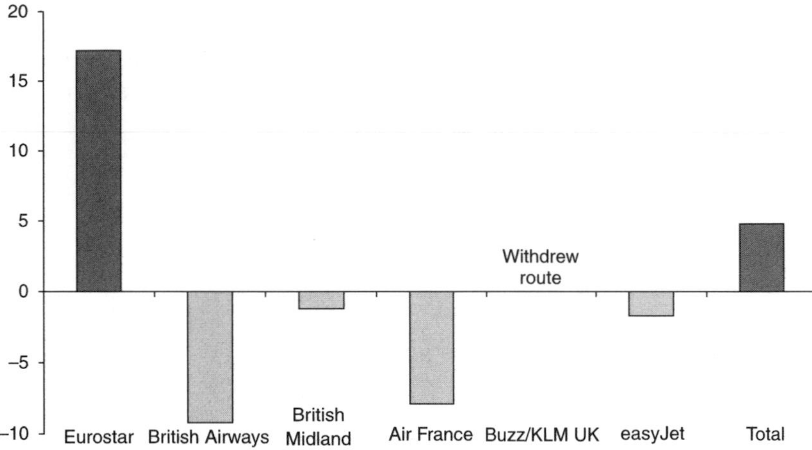

Figure 25: *Total Paris route percentage change (October 2002–March 2003 vs October 2003–March 2004)*
Source: CAA

TABLE 4: BRUSSELS ROUTE ABSOLUTE CHANGE (OCTOBER 2002–MARCH 2003 VS OCTOBER 2003–MARCH 2004)

	October 2002–March 2003	October 2003–March 2004	Absolute change
Eurostar	475,000	612,000	+137,000
British Airways	315,000	265,000	–50,000
British Midland	147,000	172,000	+25,000
Ryanair	153,000	144,000	–9,000
VLM	33,000	36,000	+3,000
Other	10,000	3,000	–7,000
Total	1,133,000	1,232,000	+99,000

Source: CAA

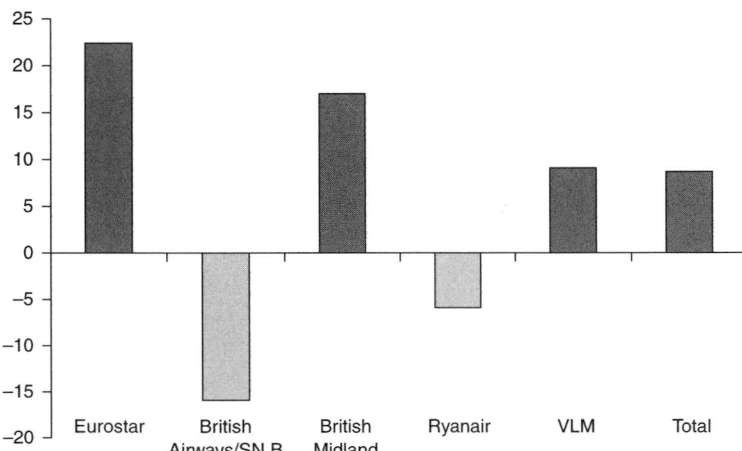

Figure 26: *Total Brussels route percentage change (October 2002–March 2003 vs October 2003–March 2004)*
Source: CAA

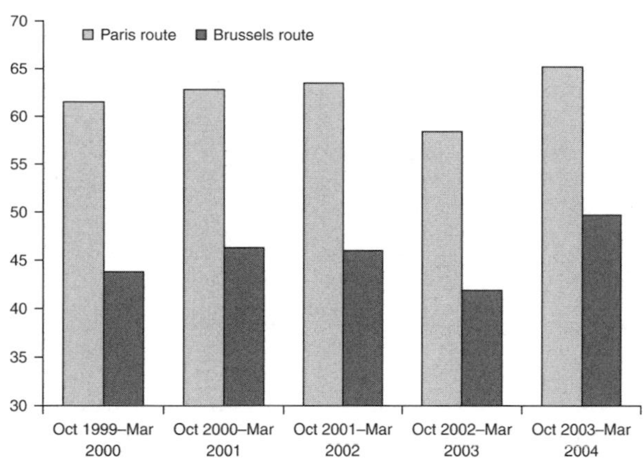

Figure 27: *Eurostar's average market share per period (October–March) for Brussels and Paris routes*
Source: Eurostar/CAA

So it was Eurostar rather than broader trends or competitor activity that was driving the market.

Eurostar's share of passengers on both the Paris and Brussels routes has risen to its highest levels for five years (Figure 27). Recent withdrawals and reductions of capacity by airline competitors indicate the market-changing nature of the relaunch and increase the likelihood of a sustained effect (Table 5).

TABLE 5: WITHDRAWN/REDUCED SERVICE ON LONDON–PARIS AND LONDON–BRUSSELS ROUTES

	Paris route	Brussels route
Routes axed	BA (London City – Charles de Gaulle) – 28 February 2004	BA (Gatwick – Charleroi) Ryanair (Stansted – Charleroi) – 29 April 2004
Reduced frequency	BMI (Heathrow – Charles de Gaulle) six flights – down to five per week – March 2004	VLM (London City – Brussels National) increased flights from five to eight per week – 12 January 2004 But put it back down to five again – April 2004

Source: Eurostar

There have been fundamental shifts in perceptions of Eurostar among key audiences, which indicate increased specialness and relevance (Tables 6 and 7).

TABLE 6: PRE-/POST-SHIFT SEPTEMBER VS NOVEMBER 2003

	Business (%)
Brand awareness	+17
For people like me	+13
Really special	+6

Base: business travellers. Sample: 150/150
Source: NFO WorldGroup, 2003

TABLE 7: PRE-/POST-SHIFT
SEPTEMBER VS NOVEMBER 2003

	Leisure (%)
Brand awareness	+10
Brand preference	+25
For people like me	+17
Enriching experience	+7
Really special	+23

Base: leisure travellers. Sample: 46/94
Source: NFO WorldGroup, 2003

Owing to the change in tracking research suppliers during the course of the campaign, there are two data sources quoted in the study.[16]

Government ministers and opinion formers alike helped revitalise the organisation through their endorsement.

> 'Congratulations to Eurostar, one million passengers in less than two months is a remarkable achievement for the Channel Tunnel Rail Link.'
>
> Tony McNulty, Transport Minister, November 2003

> 'Eurostar seems an attractive alternative to air travel.'
>
> Andrew Main Wilson, Chief Operating Officer IoD, April 2004

> 'The whole experience was infinitely better than flying, with no hanging around for delays and no charmless secuity staff. So if you're planning a trip to France, forget planes and boats. Take the Eurostar.'
>
> Quentin Wilson, columnist in *Sunday Mirror*, 4 April 2004

Staff were motivated by the relaunch and feel it was well communicated (Table 8). Eurostar staff turnover rates have declined over the six-month period since the relaunch and this is believed to have delivered savings in recruitment and training costs.[17]

TABLE 8: STAFF SURVEY RESULTS

	Agreeing November 2003 (%)
I know what is happening at Eurostar	90
I feel confident in the future of the company	91
I enjoy working at Eurostar	97
I think the opening of CTRL was communicated well	95

Base: Eurostar staff. Sample: 197
Source: Voyage Staff Survey (November 2003)[18]

16. (a) a 'pre' and 'post' tracking study conducted by NFO between September and November 2003; (b) an ongoing brand and advertising tracking study conducted by Millward Brown, first wave March 2004.
17. Source: Eurostar HR department. Work is still under way to determine the financial value of the savings.
18. Unfortunately we do not have comparative data for 2001 but key scores of over 90% are considered high for the service industry, according to Eurostar HR department.

WHAT ROLE DID COMMUNICATIONS PLAY?

The success of the relaunch is clear, but wouldn't this have happened anyway given that the product had improved? And regarding the campaign, did it do anything more than accelerate awareness of a product improvement, which is a valid but hardly exceptional role for communications.

We will consider in turn the effect of the communications on the brand and the business.

Impact on the brand – consumer communications were seen by the intended audiences and the right messages were taken out

Levels of awareness were driven by a wide variety of media, indicating the power of the integrated campaign.[19]

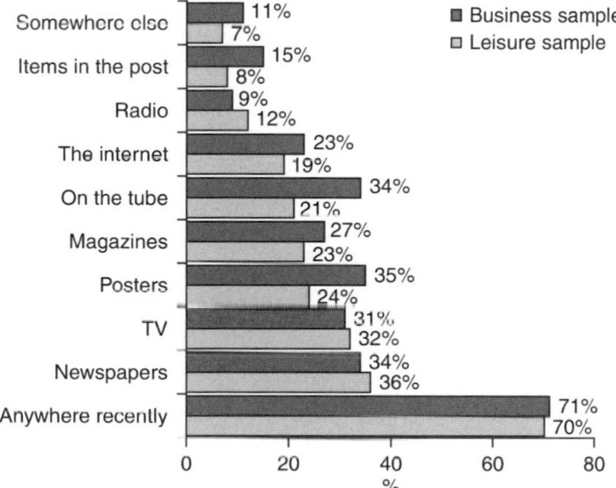

Figure 28: *Awareness of Eurostar by media*
Base: business/leisure travellers who have seen, heard or read anything about Eurostar recently
Sample: business: 145; leisure: 178
Source: Millward Brown, 2004

For the two press executions tracked, recognition was above average and branding high. Key messages were delivered (Table 9). For the two poster executions tracked, recognition was high and branding high. Key messages were delivered (Table 10). There is evidence of an integrated effect among those who claim to have seen both advertising and direct activity. Not only are those who claim to have seen both more likely to agree with key rational attributes, but there is evidence of increase in emotional attributes such as specialness and relevance. On average the integrated effect is +8% on each of the statements (Figure 29).

There are clear differences in perception between those who saw and those who didn't see the campaign in the business audience (Table 11).[20]

---

19. The misattribution to TV is likely to be a combined effect of historic TV advertising and the coverage of CTRL on TV from the PR launch.
20. For the leisure audiences the shifts were as per the overall brand shifts shown earlier because nearly all the leisure travellers claimed to have seen the adverts.

TABLE 9: PRESS TRACKING RESULTS

	Louvre (Leisure)	FastTrack (Business)		MB Norm
Recognition	24%	24%		21%
Branding	86%	86%		54%
Communication strongly suggests ...		Communication strongly suggests ...		
– Takes you to centre of destination	42%	– Taking Eurostar is more convenient than the plane	33%	
– Closer to the attractions of your destination	41%	– Eurostar is a better way to travel to your destination	27%	
– Most stylish way to travel to your destination	24%	– Eurostar takes you from centre of London to centre of destination	28%	

Base: business/leisure travellers. Recognition base: relevant readers. Branding base: relevant readers and recognise ad
Sample: Louvre/FastTrack recognition: 103/104, Louvre/FastTrack branding: 58/51, Louvre/FastTrack statements: 178/145
Source: Millward Brown, 2004

TABLE 10: POSTER TRACKING RESULTS

	Eiffel Tower	Brussels	MB Norm
Recognition	41%	35%	21%
Branding	79%	not available	54%
Takes you to centre of town	59%	56%	n/a
Is more direct to your destination than plane	54%	45%	n/a
Is fastest way to centre of your destination	45%	34%	n/a
Is most stylish way to travel to Paris/Brussels	32%	25%	n/a

Base: all travellers. Recognition base: travelled past poster sites. Branding base: travelled past poster sites and recognised ad
Sample: Eiffel Tower/Brussels recognition: 323/323, Eiffel Tower/Brussels branding: 131/too small, Eiffel Tower/Brussels statements: 165/158
Source: Millward Brown, 2004

TABLE 11: PRE-/POST-SHIFT SEPTEMBER VS NOVEMBER 2003

	Business (%)	Business + seen any ads (%)
Brand awareness	+17	+25
Brand preference	0	+9
Quickest way	–8	+8
Hassle free	–3	+8
Quality time	+5	+8
For people like me	+13	+24
Enriching experience	–6	+9
Reliable	+7	+18
Really special	+6	+19

Base: business travellers. Sample: 150/150, 42/56
Source: NFO WorldGroup, 2003

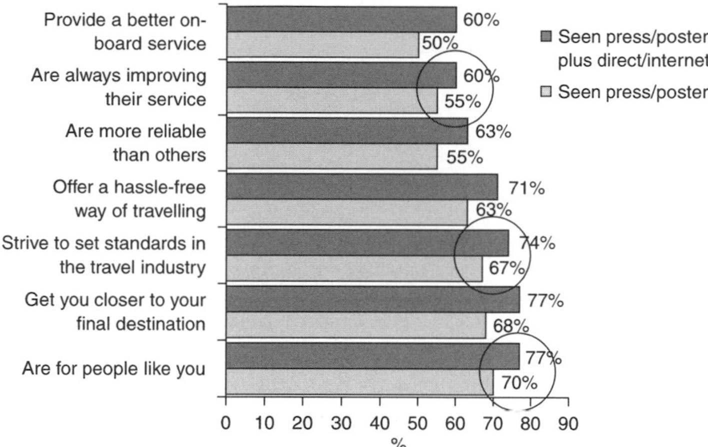

Figure 29
Base: all travellers. Sample size: 35/60
Source: Millward Brown, 2004

PR created positive momentum for the brand. The high-speed record run generated the equivalent of over £14m worth of advertising coverage.[21] The official opening events of 16 and 27 September also generated positive coverage. According to Presswatch, Eurostar's image has changed for the better. In June 2003, Eurostar rated in the bottom quartile for positive coverage in a study of 1100 companies. By November 2003, Eurostar ratings had risen to the top quartile.[22]

The Fly Eurostar idea had a galvanising effect on the organisation:

> 'The confidence of the integrated marketing and PR communication gave Eurostar a new lease of life. The idea and the messaging were designed to show we could get passengers to their destination quickly, on time and in a less stressful way – this boosted the whole business behaviour.'
>
> Paul Charles, Director of Corporate Communications, Eurostar

Impact on the business

Obviously, the product improvement and the 'Fly Eurostar' campaign (which used the product improvement as a strategic platform) are inextricably linked in terms of their impact on consumer demand (Table 12). However, we have a number of pieces of evidence that indicate a significant added value for the 'Fly Eurostar' idea and its communication over and above the impact of the product improvement.

We have three ways of benchmarking the predicted impact of the product improvement and its communications:

1. Independent modelling conducted on behalf of Eurotunnel and Eurostar to understand the likely impact of the high-speed links on market share, based on examples from around the world.

21. Source: Freud Communications.
22. Source: Presswatch.

TABLE 12: THE ABILITY OF EACH BENCHMARK TO ALLOW FOR THE KEY FACTORS OF PRODUCT IMPROVEMENT AND CAMPAIGN EFFECT

Benchmark	Product improvement	Campaign effect
High-speed link model (Paris/Brussels)	✓	✓ (Overall)
France/Belgium comparison (Paris/Brussels)	✓	✓ ('Fly Eurostar')
Econometric model (Paris only)	Only estimates joint impact of product improvement and 'Fly Eurostar', but enables us to discount impact of other factors during the campaign period	

2. Comparisons drawn with France and Belgium over the same period with the same product improvement but different communications.
3. Eurostar's own econometric model.

We will now take each in turn. In 2000, independent modelling was conducted on behalf of Eurotunnel by UIC[23] to understand the likely impact on market share of high-speed rail links. It was built on experience of high-speed trains around the world. The model is based on a long-term impact and allows for wear-in (effectively assuming 100% awareness of the improvement and a static market) (Figure 30).

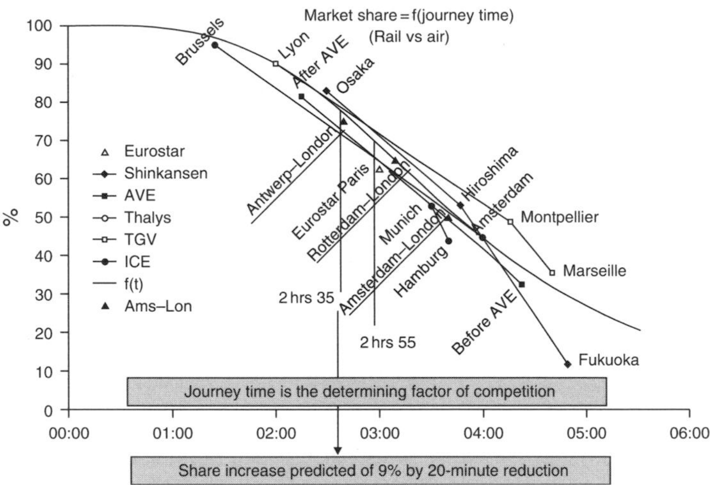

Figure 30: *High-speed rail product attractiveness vs airlines*

The curve predicted that a 20-minute journey time reduction would generate a market share increase of 9% in a static market and with 100% awareness of the improvement. Given the low average frequency of usage (the average Eurostar user travels 1.2 times per annum) it would have taken actual levels well over a year to reach the predicted levels.

23. International Union of Railways (UIC) is a worldwide organisation for railway cooperation. It is active in all fields of railway transport. Its High Speed Task Force ran a seminar in 2002 entitled 'Reduced journey times on conventional lines'. See UIC website for details.

TABLE 13: PREDICTED VOLUME UPLIFT FROM THE BASE PERIOD OF OCTOBER 2002–MARCH 2003 ON PARIS/BRUSSELS ROUTE

Predicted	Actual	Actual higher by
13%	21.7%	+8.7%

A 9% share increase from 71% to 80% in a static market equates to a 13% volume increase. Hence Eurostar significantly outperformed the forecast (Table 13).

A total of 8.7% of volumes on the Paris and Brussels routes for the period equates to 143,558 extra passengers. Average yield on the route was £59.9.

The following equation enables us to calculate the incremental revenue to Eurostar:

Additional volume × (Average yield – average variable costs per passenger)
= Incremental revenue to Eurostar
= 143,558 × (£59.9 – £14) = £6.6m

So the Fly Eurostar campaign generated £6.6m incremental net revenue above that predicted for the product improvement alone.

A comparison of the total revenue growth in each market provides an interesting benchmark. This shows a significantly better performance in the UK. The product improvement is the same, and communications budget to sales ratios were actually relatively higher in both France (ex-Paris) and Belgium (ex-Brussels).[24] Only the UK used the 'Fly Eurostar' idea, the other markets had separate campaigns based on the reduced journey times. In order to compare like with like, we have compared ex-London, Paris and Brussels with the ex-Paris and ex-Brussels routes (Table 14).

TABLE 14: COUNTRY-BY-COUNTRY COMPARISON OF REVENUES AND COMMUNICATIONS INVESTMENTS, 28 SEPTEMBER 2003–MARCH 2004

	Ex-London (P and B)	Ex-Paris	Ex-Brussels
Total revenues	£98.8m	£58m	£13m
Communications investment	£6.3m	£6m	£1.7m
Revenue increase, year on year	+15.3%	+10.3%	+3.9%

Media spend source: OMD Europe

Both the French and Belgian performance are more in line with the share curve model predictions. Taking the average overall increase of France and Belgium together (9%), the UK outperformed this by 6.3%.[25] This is the equivalent of £6.2m additional revenue, from which must be subtracted the figure of £1.4m, which is the cost to Eurostar of carrying the additional passengers through the Tunnel. So we arrive at £4.8m incremental revenue over and above the product improvement and a generic communications campaign.

24. Analysis by OMD suggests that the UK and French spends are roughly equivalent taking into account exchange rates, the channels used and the relative cost of channels in each country.
25. On the assumption that, with a similar type of campaign, Eurostar's UK performance would have been the average of France and Belgium.

Obviously factors other than advertising influenced the sales performance. Using the econometric model, it is possible to identify the factors that were having a positive or negative effect on the business and their commercial impact, and thereby more accurately estimate the value of the Eurostar idea (Table 15).

TABLE 15: POSITIVE AND NEGATIVE FACTORS WITHIN THE ECONOMETRIC MODEL (OCTOBER 2002–MARCH 2003 VS OCTOBER 2003–MARCH 2004)

	Factors	Effect on revenue (£m)
Leisure	Prices and competitor advertising	–4.4
	Rugby internationals in Paris, fewer train strikes and perceptions of value for money	+3.2
Business	ATC strikes, Euro:£ exchange rate and competitor activity	–4,5
	Increasing business confidence and rugby internationals in Paris	+5.9
Difference in impact		+0.2

This means that the overall net effect of price and non-campaign-related factors on the business is £0.2m. So the estimated 'value' of the idea can be adjusted down by just £0.2m. This applies to both the high-speed link model and the France/Belgium comparisons (Table 16).

TABLE 16: BENCHMARK ESTIMATES OF INCREMENTAL NET REVENUE ADJUSTED FOR NON-ADVERTISING FACTORS

	Predicted (£m)	Revised (£m)
High-speed link model (Paris/Brussels)	6.6	6.4
France/Belgium comparison	4.8	4.6

Added to this, the econometric model shows an advertising carry-over rate from month to month of 90%. Thus Eurostar has only had 35% of the total likely effect of the campaign in the long term. Eurostar, then, has so far only benefited from around one-third of the total value of the idea.

CONCLUSION

To recap, in the six months since the relaunch of Eurostar, the total impact of the campaign is a net increase in revenues of £13.6m, from which must be subtracted the cost to Eurostar of £4.6m for carrying the additional passengers, giving a total increase of £9m. This compares to a campaign and promotional cost of £6.5m.

So what's the difference an idea makes? On this evidence, between £4.6m and £6.4m incremental net revenue in the first six months alone, depending on the benchmark used, and three times this in the long term (so between £14m and £19m). And at what cost? In practice, nothing. All of the above estimates are based on the results achieved over and above predicted levels, which already included campaign cost (explicitly in the econometric model and the comparison with France/Belgium, implicitly for the high-speed rail link model, which assumes 100% awareness).

SILVER
BEST MEDIA

13

Lynx Pulse

Proving the value of integration

Principal authors: Gwen Raillard and Will Nicholls, Bartle Bogle Hegarty

EDITOR'S SUMMARY

This unconventional campaign, which won the prize for Best Media, describes how Lynx created a 'music and dance' phenomenon to launch Lynx Pulse.

Rather than behave as an fmcg brand, Lynx and its agency, Bartle Bogle Hegarty, looked to the entertainment industry for inspiration. The brief was to create a phenomenon that would generate the levels of buzz, talkability and intrusiveness of entertainment properties like *Big Brother* and *Pop Idol.*

Taking inspiration from the product's name, 'Pulse', and its iconic green dot packaging, the idea was to focus on music and dance. The relatively unheard-of track 'Make Luv', by DJ Room 5, was selected, plus a series of simple dance moves that would, it was hoped, be aped on British dance floors. 'Make Luv' was made available to key opinion formers in bars and clubs. Pulse merchandise followed, and then the dance was brought to life online before the TV commercial, featuring your typical lovable geek, hit TV screens.

The track 'Make Luv' went straight to number one and, before long, the dance moves were being performed on dance floors up and down the country and reported in all the tabloids.

A triumph for popular culture, this paper offers up new industry learning on communication as brand entertainment. It shows that by finding a new way of talking to, and ultimately entertaining, its consumers Lynx generated incremental revenue of €20m. This paper also indicates that integrated communications are twice as effective at getting a return on investment as traditional advertising-only campaigns.

INTRODUCTION

For the last two years, one topic has dominated the UK advertising industry. Call it media-neutral thinking, joined-up communications solutions or engagement planning, the subject of integrated communications has never been far from the headlines.

Integrated, multi-channel communication has been hailed as the solution to reaching increasingly time-poor and attention-short consumers with an increasing willingness to opt out of conventional advertising. However, the superior effect of this approach has never been quantified.

In this study we will demonstrate that integrated communications are more effective than traditional advertising alone, and calculate how much more efficient an integrated campaign can be, showing the financial value of this new way of thinking. We will do this by looking at the launch of Lynx Pulse, one of the best loved and most talked about integrated campaigns of the last 18 months.

We will start by outlining our communications strategy and how we developed a new model for our launch to enable us to get the scarce attention of young male consumers. We will then describe the development of the campaign and the impact it had on sales. Most importantly we show how by creating integrated communications, our campaign was far more efficient at generating a return on investment than had we simply spent money on TV advertising. We will conclude by demonstrating how the value of integrated multi-channel communication is more than twice that of advertising alone.

CREATING INTEGRATED COMMUNICATIONS

The Lynx effect

Lynx is the number one deodorant brand in the UK.[1] It is an aerosol deodorant which kills body odour and has a fragrance that leaves you smelling great. Owned by Lever Faberge, it is positioned for 16–24-year-old guys and is available across Europe where it goes by the name 'Axe'.[2]

Lynx owes its success to its ability to own the emotional high ground in a formulaic category. When the Lynx campaign was developed the deodorant market was characterised by functional communications that focused on odour control. We realised that the benefit was actually confidence and that this was most relevant in the context of getting girls. Lynx helps young guys to get the girl, it's their best first move, and communications have dramatised this using the line 'The Lynx Effect' for 10 years of famous advertising.

The rational foundation for this emotional promise is Lynx's range of fragrances. Smelling great gives guys the confidence to seduce. Each year a new fragrance is launched in order to refresh the brand. This new fragrance replaces the weakest fragrance (in terms of sales) of the current portfolio. The new fragrance for

1. Total deodorant value sales in the UK: 1. Lynx €120m; 2. Sure for Women €76.6m; 3. Sure for Men €43m. Source: ACNielsen Europanel.
2. For simplicity we will refer to both the UK product and products from other countries as 'Lynx' throughout this study.

2003 was designed with a citrus, fresh smell and was named Lynx Pulse, replacing Lynx Atlantis.

The need for a new approach

New variants had traditionally been launched by borrowing the advertising codes and media strategy of fine fragrance marketing. However, the continuing explosion of media channels and the growing competition from new forms of entertainment meant that it was becoming more and more difficult to get people's attention.

This meant that the solution was not simply to do a better advert or to spend more money to buy attention. We were going to need to work harder to compete with the attraction of popular youth culture.

Rather than simply needing to launch a new product, we needed to create a phenomenon. Our challenge was to compete head on with *Big Brother*, *Pop Idol* and *I'm A Celebrity Get Me Out Of Here* in terms of buzz, talkability and intrusiveness. The phenomenon would command attention in its own right as it would engage our audience in a completely new way and give the new fragrance a level of salience a deodorant had no right to expect (Figure 1).

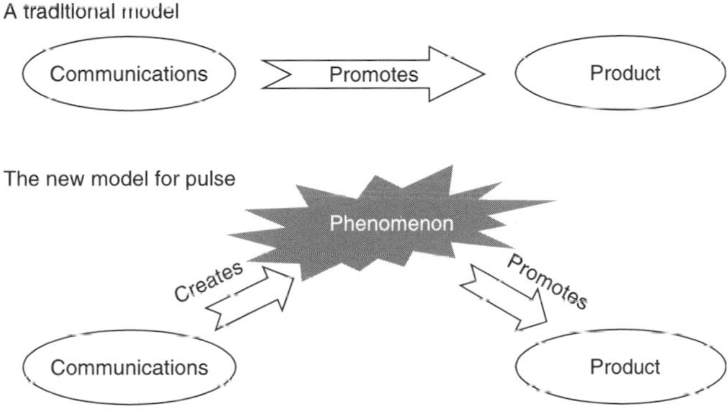

Figure 1: *Changing the model for launch*

CREATING A PHENOMENON

It is much easier to talk about wanting to create a phenomenon than to actually make sure one happens. Looking at other cultural phenomena we could see that we needed an idea that was infectious and simple. The idea created was 'music and dance', the inspiration for which came from the product name 'Pulse'. This was the right answer for three reasons. First, music is an area that our target are interested in, which makes the task of getting their attention easier.[3] Second, it's linked to our brand territory of seduction; as dance goes hand in hand with getting girls. Finally, it had the potential to be simple and infectious (Figure 2).

3. Men Aged 16–24 (UK, Germany, France and Spain) 'Music is an important part of my life' – index of 137 vs all adults. 'Visit a nightclub more than once a week' – index of 517 vs all adults. Source: TGI.

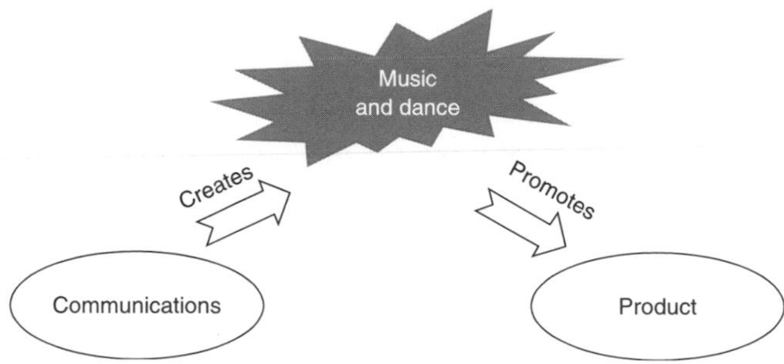

Figure 2: *A music and dance phenomenon*

Before thinking about specific executions, we needed to identify the right kind of music, the right kind of dance and the right kind of graphic look. Our graphic look came from the Lynx 'Pulse' packaging – an iconic image using green dots (Figure 3).

To find the right music track we developed a brief that would help us evaluate the thousands of music tracks we would have to listen to (Table 1).

Using this brief to guide us, and after an extensive global search, we discovered an unknown music track, 'Make Luv', by DJ Room 5, which combined all the criteria we had defined (Figure 4).

Next, we needed to create the dance element. The essential requirement in developing the dance was to define a series of very simple movements that everyone could copy and reproduce in clubs and bars on Friday nights – 'dance bites' rather than a complicated dance routine. Richmond Talauega, a choreographer famous for working with Madonna and Christina Aguilera helped us develop them (Figure 5).

These three elements – the music, the dance, the graphic look – were used in different combinations across all media to create a truly integrated campaign that

Figure 3: *The Lynx Pulse logo in situ*

TABLE 1: SELECTING THE MUSIC TRACK

Must haves	Why
Inclusivity	To be unmissable, the track needs to generate broad and mass appeal. A niche track limited to specific music and dance tastes would be too exclusive.
Musical 'hook'	We need a musical 'hook': either a memorable lyric or moment to help recall and playback.
Infectious	Makes you want to get up and dance.
Positive/ feel good	No weird, dark dance anthems.
Non-famous artist	The track needs to come from a relative unknown – so it can be owned by 'Pulse' and not be famous because of artist who performs it.

Source: BBH

Figure 4: *The music track*

nevertheless allowed us to play to the strengths of media channels. We were confident that we had content that had all the core elements necessary to become a phenomenon. The key question was how to deploy them in such a way as to ensure the desired result.

Figure 5: *Planning the dance routine*

THE COMMUNICATIONS CAMPAIGN

We knew that if we wanted to create a real phenomenon our campaign needed to make consumers feel they were experiencing a piece of popular culture – something big and interesting.

Rather than use a traditional fast moving consumer goods (fmcg) launch model, we looked to the entertainment industry – which is adept at creating phenomena – for a way to create the anticipation and excitement that we would need. The entertainment model concentrates in the early stages on opinion formers and teaser strategies, which grow in scale and noise, before mainstream marketing kicks in. Only then is the product itself launched. PR and online channels are also used extensively before the main activity starts (Figure 6).

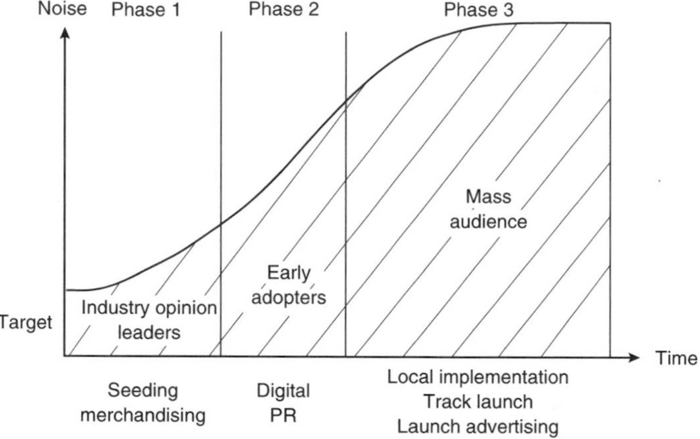

Figure 6: *The entertainment industry launch model*
Source: BBH

The model informed both our choice of channel and the way in which the communications were phased. We will now look at the channels that were selected using this model.

Phase 1

Seeding
The music track got exposed to the right people at the start of the campaign. It was sent as a white label to key opinion formers such as DJs ensuring that the track was heard in all the right places. This activity was led by PIAS/Positiva, who had responsibility for launching the music track (Figure 7).

Merchandising
Merchandise was developed by below-the-line agency Out of the Blue. T-shirts, DJ slipmats and record bags went out to key opinion formers. Other elements were later distributed to a wider target audience (Figure 8).

Figure 7: *'White label' sent to opinion formers such as DJs*

Figure 8: *The Lynx Pulse merchandise*

Phase 2

Digital

Dare Digital created 'The Dotman', an animated online character, made of the same graphic elements as the Lynx Pulse logo and available as a screen saver. Its main function was to do the Lynx Pulse dance on the nation's computer screens (Figure 9).

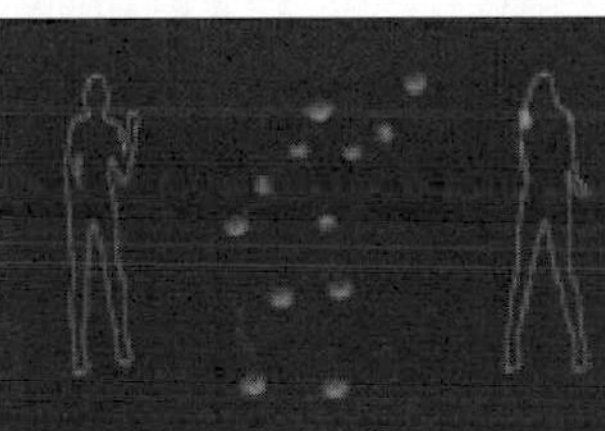
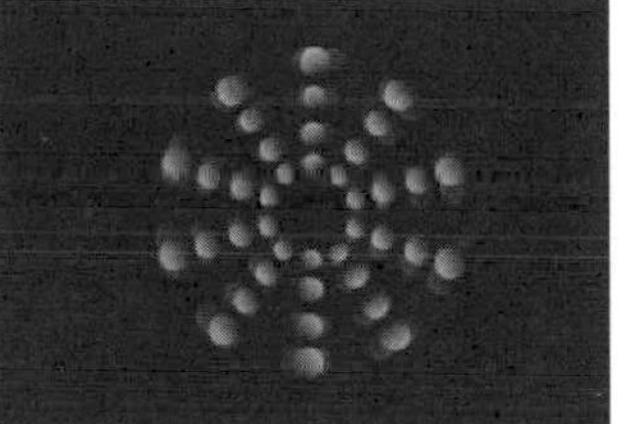

Figure 9: *The Dotman doing the Lynx Pulse dance*

Phase 3

Advertising

Having seeded the music and dance elements, a TV advert brought them to life in one piece of communication and took the campaign to a mass audience (Figure 10).

Advertising engaged consumers in style press where consumers look to see what's cool at the moment, and posters when they were out and about (Figures 11 and 12).

PR

PR led by Freud Communications was used as a key tool in amplifying the excitement around the campaign. Several TV appearances were planned for Tom, the main character from the advert, and features in the *Evening Standard* had already been prepared.

Local implementation

Out of the Blue also arranged tours by dancers such as the Cuban Brothers in the UK, bringing the dance to people when they were out and about (Figure 13).

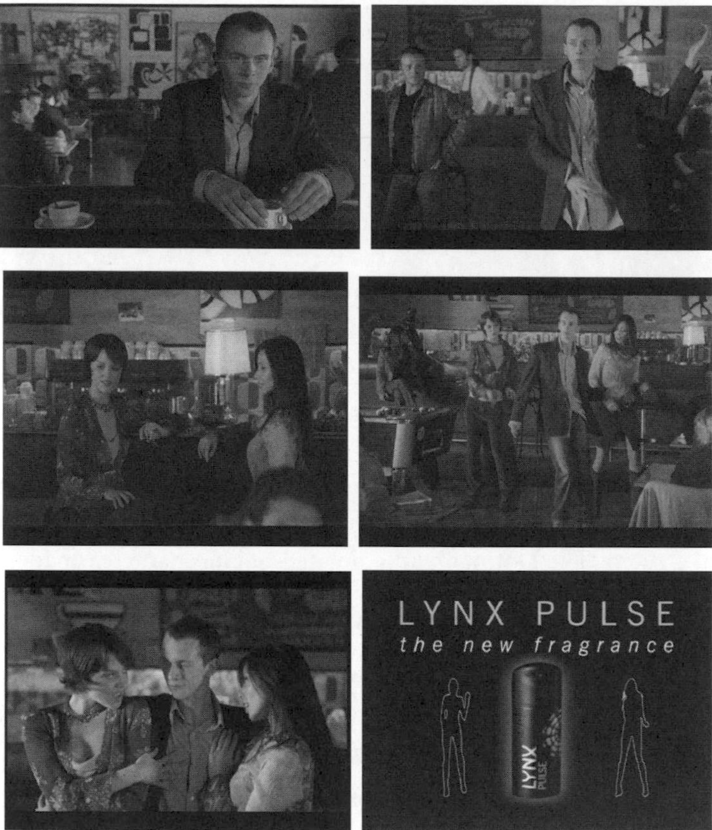

Figure 10: *The TV commercial*

Figure 11: *Poster*

Figure 12: *Press advert in situ* – FHM

Throughout the country, our student brand managers went to clubs on Friday nights to do the dance. In this way we helped people to learn the dance themselves (Figure 14).

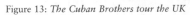

Figure 13: *The Cuban Brothers tour the UK*

Figure 14: *The student brand managers promoting the dance throughout the country*

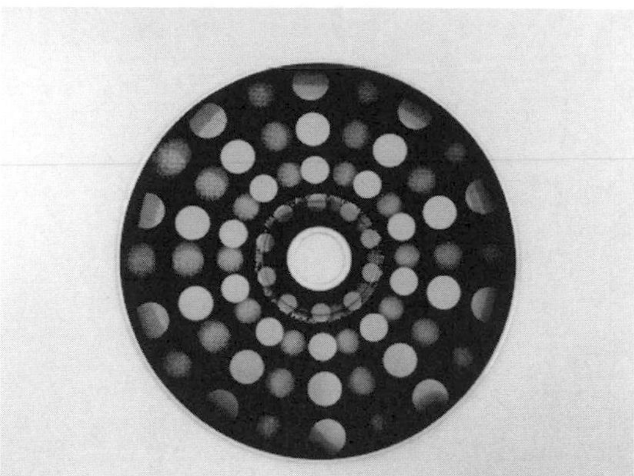

Figure 15: *The CD*

Music track launch

After all the build-up, the music track itself was finally launched in March. The CD artwork used the same design elements as the Lynx Pulse logo (Figure 15).

Summary

Close collaboration between the large number of specialist agencies was key. Working towards a shared goal with the same core music, dance and visual elements meant that the agencies could create a campaign that was truly integrated, rather than simply interpreting an advertising idea into other channels.

The campaign kicked off in February 2003, with the activity outlined above. Availability of Lynx Pulse was building during phase 1 and 2, nearing full distribution in time for the music launch.

DID WE CREATE A PHENOMENON?

We will now demonstrate that each element was successful in its own right, and that in combination they created an unmissable pop culture phenomenon.

The music track was a hit

As soon as it was launched into the mainstream, 'Make Luv' rocketed straight to number one in the official charts, outselling the number two song by 20,000 copies in a week. It stayed there for a total of four consecutive weeks! Gareth Gates, the *Pop Idol* sensation, was pushed off the number one slot and Westlife were prevented from reaching number one.

'Make Luv' sold over 325,000 copies, turning silver in the UK (Figure 16). It outsold releases by artists such as Eminem, 50 Cent, Christina Aguilera, J-Lo and Justin Timberlake in 2003. At the *Music Week* Awards 2004, 'Make Luv' won the prize for 'Best music exploitation in an ad'.

The success of the music track also ensured very strong presence and visibility in record stores (Figure 17).

Figure 16: *Silver disc awarded to 'Make Luv', Room 5*

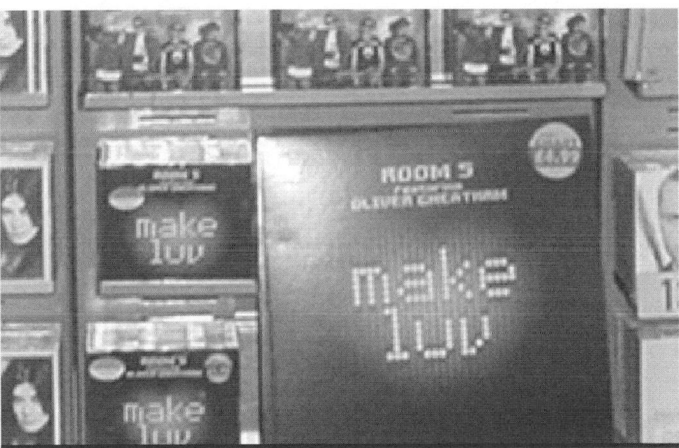

Figure 17: *A strong presence in music stores*

The Lynx Pulse dance became a craze

The dance routine played a crucial role in the success of the launch. The dance caught on in the UK, encouraged by the 'student brand managers' from Get Real, and by a number of newspapers and magazines that taught the public the moves (Figures 18 and 19).

We even received a strange request from a young lady that speaks for itself (Figure 20).

Lynx song is smash hit in the clubs

NIFF-TY FOOTWORK

How to do TV ad dance

Figure 18: *The press teaches the Lynx Pulse dance (whole page in the* Sun, *Saturday 29 March 2003)*

1 STEP AND SLIDE

A simple diagonal slide to your right then left

2 AIR GUITAR

3 DISCO SHUFFLE

Let's all do the Lynx!

LEARN AD GEEK'S SEXY MOVES

By EMMA BUSSEY

GEEKY Tom Godwin has girls swooning at his fancy footwork in the Lynx TV ad – and you can do the same.

Just follow the smooth moves on this page, add a splash of aftershave and you'll soon be in business.

the Lynx Pulse role. A third of the moves in the ad are his own.

5 BACK AND FORTH

6 ELECTRIC SLIDE

7 BOX MIME

8 MOONWALK TO LEFT

9 FRONT SHUFFLE

10 HOLD YOUR GIRLS

Figure 19: *The press teaches the Lynx Pulse dance (*People, *16 March 2003)*

@hotmail.com>
26/02/2003 11:30

To @bbh.co.uk
cc
Subject Lynx Ad

Dear
A strange request for you - I really hope you can help. My fiance and I are getting married in afew months. We, and all our friends and family, are massive fans of the fab new Lynx ad with the guy dancing in the bar to Room 5's Make Love. Big congrats to BBH. Believe it or not, we are going to attempt to copy the dance for our 'first dance' at our wedding, as a surprise to everyone. Only one problem - we need to learn the moves and can't do so without a video recording. Any chance you can send us one, or perhaps easier, tell us when it is scheduled to be aired on sky or terrestrial - then we can record it ourselves?
We would be forever in your debt - and we'll send you the wedding video in return!
Kind regards

It's fast, it's easy and it's free. Get MSN Messenger today!

Figure 20: *Email received by BBH PR department, 26 February 2003*

In addition the PR effort even helped deliver some celebrities who got involved in the dance. Tom and two girls got Vernon Kay, the rest of the crew and the entire audience to do the dance on TV in front of the whole nation on *Boys and Girls* on Channel 4 (Figure 21).

Figure 21: Boys and Girls, *Channel 4, Saturday 8 March 2003*

Figure 22: The Salon, *Thursday 13 March 2003, and* Richard & Judy, *Monday 23 March 2003*

'The best ad on TV at the moment.'

Vernon Kay

Tom and the girls were also invited to other TV shows (Figure 22).

Finally, Kate Ford, who plays temptress Tracy Barlow in *Coronation Street*, was spotted giving it a go at the BAFTA dinner party (Figure 23).

Tom also became an overnight microphenomenon. His geeky look made him liked by both men and women (Figure 24).

20 THE SUN, Tuesday, April 15, 2003 3G

Doing the Bafta boogie

HERE's proof there is nothing dafter than a Bafta after-show party dancer.

Telly stars were up for some weird late night prancing at London's Grosvenor House following Sunday's awards ceremony.

First on the floor was chat show host TRISHA GODDARD who performed a unique interpretation of the Little

Teapot dance. Hollyoaks beauty **ELIZE DU TOIT** seemed hellbent on showing off her knickers as she did an exotic flamenco.

Ever at the cutting edge of the latest dance crazes, Coronation Street's **KATE FORD** – she plays temptress Tracy Barlow – showed she has mastered the dance from the Lynx advert.

Not to be outdone, her Street mate **SAMIA GHADIE** broke into a spontaneous version of Staying Alive. John Travolta eat your heart out.

But it was roly-poly comic **JOHNNY VEGAS** who stole the show outside the bash with his own unique pole dance.

Very sexy.

Figure 23: *The* Sun, *Tuesday 15 April 2003*

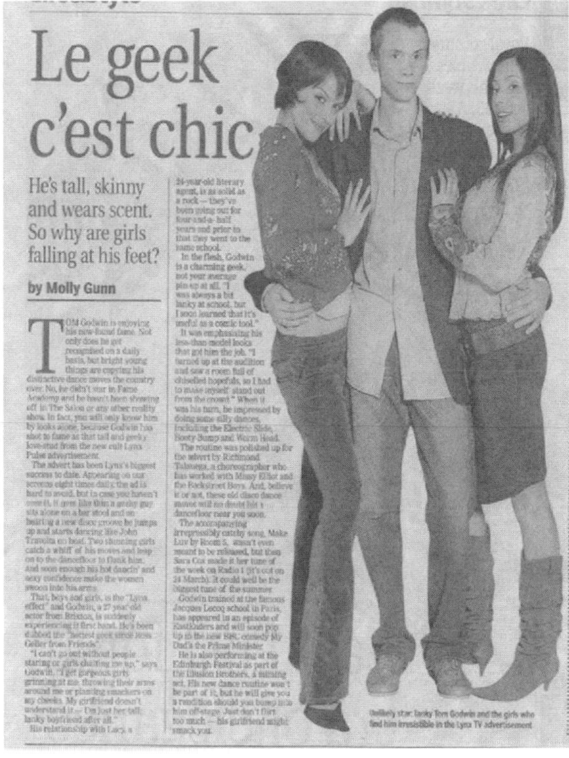

Le geek c'est chic

He's tall, skinny and wears scent. So why are girls falling at his feet?

by Molly Gunn

THE GEEK ADONIS!

Tom is lanky Lynx sex-god

Figure 24: *Tom becomes a national hero*
Source: *Evening Standard* and *Daily Star*, March 2003

The advert was loved

We needed the TV commercial to work harder than a normal ad if it was going to help create a phenomenon. Not only would we need high awareness and enjoyment of the advert, but we wanted people to talk about it.

Awareness

Spontaneous awareness of Lynx TV advertising rose 18 points from 72% to 90% within a month of the launch (Figure 25). The advert was also well branded and drove specific awareness of the new fragrance (Table 2).

TABLE 2: MILLWARD BROWN BRAND RECALL MEASURE

I would definitely remember the ad was for Lynx Pulse	87%
UK average	45–64%

Base: Male 16–55
Source: Millward Brown

Enjoyment

The advert was extremely enjoyable and well liked by our target (Table 3).

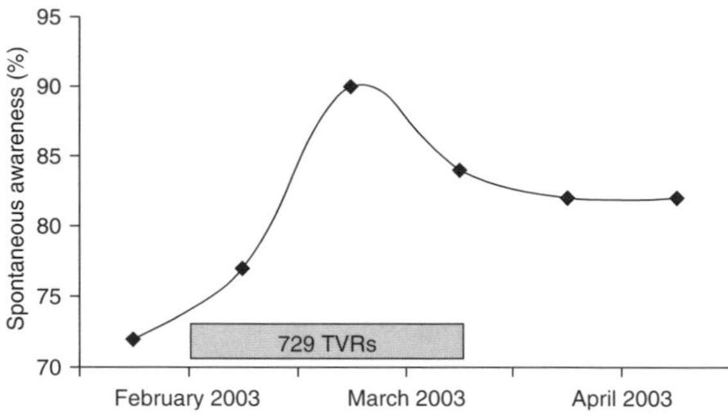

Figure 25: *TV ad awareness*
Source: Millward Brown

TABLE 3: MILLWARD BROWN ENJOYMENT MEASURE

I enjoy watching it a lot	84%
UK average	50–64%

Base: Male 16–55
Source: Millward Brown

It was also highly involving and distinctive versus the UK advertising norm (Figure 26).

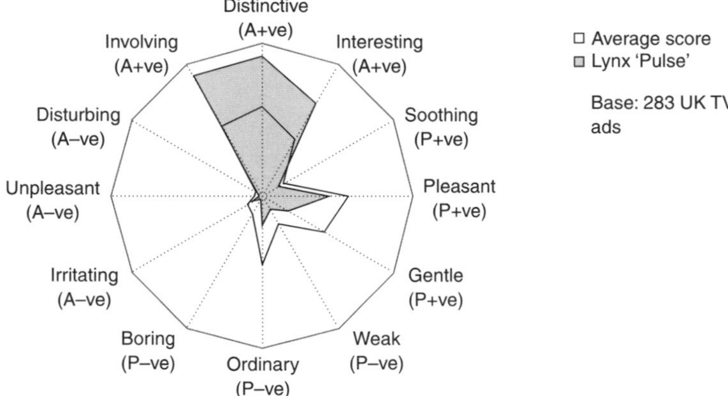

Figure 26: *An involving and distinctive advert*
Base: Male 16–55
Source: Millward Brown

Word of mouth

Most importantly, the advert had an exceptional capacity to generate word of mouth; 73% of people said they would talk about the advert with friends – more than double the UK average (Table 4).

TABLE 4: MILLWARD BROWN ENJOYMENT MEASURE

The sort of ad I'd talk about with friends	73%
UK average	25–39%

Base: male 16–55
Source: Millward Brown

PR coverage was extensive

The work we had done to make the campaign newsworthy and worth talking about had paid off. The campaign attracted a lot of attention from the media. Figure 27 shows some of the cuttings.

hot CLUBBING WITH RADIO ONE'S DAVE PEARCE

It must be Luv

DANCE IS A SMASH

TOP 5 NIGHTS

hot WONDER what the tune is off that Lynx Pulse ad with the bloke dancing? It's called Make Luv by Room 5 featuring Oliver Cheatham and it's out on March 24. hit

Ad Of The Week

TOP 10 GETTIN' LASHED

HOT

LYNX AD: It's wordless, classy and ever so slightly sexy. When that boy gently funks his two-step stuff, it's quite the most irresistible ad on TV at the moment. He could make his disco moves on me any time.

ADVERTISING » Peter York

Armpit spectators must see this

laughing all the way to

what's new

Ad lad

We reckon Tom Godwin, who shakes his thang in the hilarious new Lynx ad, is a real cutie. Bet he smells nice too!

Jacko to pay for gig snub

A STUDENT from Bath is hoping that first impressions last as she stars in a TV deodorant advertisement.

Former Oldfield School pupil Sophie Walker, *pictured right*, helps to illustrate the power of Lynx's new Pulse fragrance in the commercial, which is now being shown.

She appears in the advert with actress Rachel Grant, who was also in the latest James Bond movie, Die Another Day.

Sophie, who also studied at the sixth-form of Beechen Cliff School, and Rachel play customers at a bar who are transfixed by a man who suddenly starts dancing to a song playing in the background.

The pair join him in the dance – entranced by the sweet smell of his deodorant.

Sophie, who lives in the city centre, is now studying history of art at University College, London.

The 21-year-old signed up with a modelling agency while working as a waitress at the Beaujolais restaurant in Bath.

After moving to London, she started working as a temp at an advertising agency and was soon auditioning for promotional work.

ingredients, including basil (for a bit of stimulation), lavender (well known for its relaxing properties), jasmine (the girlie-magnet floral note to show your feminine side) and a spot of sandalwood (for a touch of blokiness). This new scent should send her pulse racing. Prices start from £1.99 for Pulse Roll-on (50ml).

Ad of the week

WE'D be surprised if the new Lynx TV ad for its fragrance Pulse doesn't get you in the mood for dancing. It depicts the amazing transformation of a lonely man at a bar into a wild party animal. The ad kicks off with a clubby beat and a posse of beautiful ladies – clearly intended to raise the pulse of male viewers!

THE GEEK ADONIS!

Tom is lanky Lynx sex-god

7

Lynx uses dance for Pulse launch

Le geek c'est chic

He's tall, skinny and wears scent. So why are girls falling at his feet?

smart it hurts!

Listen Up! to Heather Suttie

Figure 27(a): *Some examples of the PR coverage*

Figure 27(b): *Some examples of the PR coverage*

It was estimated that the 85 pieces of PR coverage were worth £2,065,011.[4] All this from a PR budget of £16,150.

4. Source: Freud Communications.

The cumulative effect – a phenomenon

In the previous sections we established that the individual elements of the campaign were highly successful. Of course, other brands have had success in some of these areas; brands have had number ones before, or loved and talked about advertising. The significant difference in our case is that these waves of activity were carefully engineered to peak in rapid succession, generating a sense of growing excitement. This culminated in the music track reaching number one as the advertising awareness peaked and there was the most PR coverage (Figure 28).

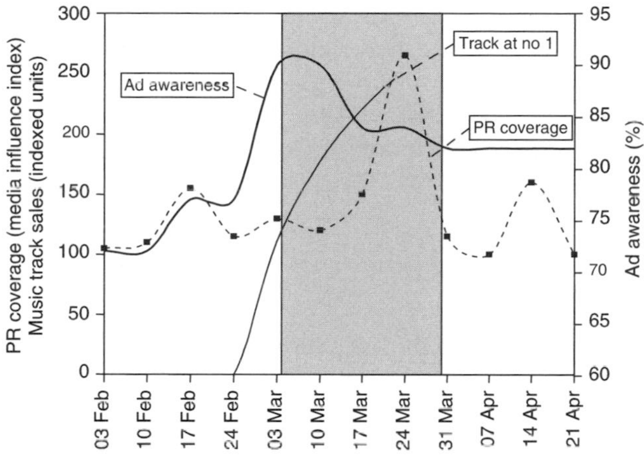

Figure 28: *The campaign peaks in March*
Source: Millward Brown and Positiva/EMI

We have clearly demonstrated that the Lynx Pulse campaign achieved our objective of creating a genuine phenomenon, by using key elements to tie all activity together and by coordinating the phasing of these channels so as to generate maximum public awareness.

DEMONSTRATING THE EFFECTIVENESS OF INTEGRATED MULTI-CHANNEL COMMUNICATION

In the remainder of this study we will identify the effectiveness of our integrated approach versus a traditional advertising campaign and will quantify the benefits of integration.

What we will cover in this section

The objective of this paper is to establish the superior effectiveness of integrated communications over advertising on its own.

A traditional approach to evaluating effectiveness is to identify and isolate the effects of individual elements of a campaign. However, we believe that the virtue of integrated communications lies in the holistic effect of the overall media mix. Our campaign was specifically designed such that every channel helped multiply the effects of all the others. Pulling these multiple, overlapping effects apart would therefore be entirely inappropriate (if not nearly impossible!).

We will therefore demonstrate the effectiveness of the integrated communications model by comparing the success of the UK Lynx Pulse launch described in this study with the effects of the launch in other European markets using more limited channels. We have identified France and Spain as the two key markets to use as benchmarks versus the UK for a number of reasons:

- these three markets (UK, France and Spain) account for the majority (59%) of Lynx's European value sales[5]
- market and brand dynamics are sufficiently similar to allow valid comparisons between the three, e.g. brand perceptions, deo penetration, and young male attitudes and behaviours
- all three markets have managed the Lynx Pulse launch in significantly different ways allowing us to clearly quantify the effect of differing communications approaches.

Differing approaches across Europe

UK

As explained in the first section of this paper, Lynx Pulse was launched in the UK with a fully integrated multimedia campaign.

France

The same advertising was used to launched Lynx Pulse in France, with a significant media budget to support it. However, we were unable to secure exclusive usage of the music track in France and the decision was therefore taken to focus the investment only on advertising, not a multi-channel campaign. France is a good example of a traditional launch using TV and print advertising. It is therefore the most interesting country for our purposes as it allows us to compare an advertising-only model with an integrated multi-channel communication plan.

Spain

Strategic analysis showed that the best way to grow the business in Spain was to focus the bulk of investment behind the core Lynx brand rather than behind individual new variant launches. Lynx Pulse was therefore launched with a lower budget than the UK or France invested in below-the-line activities only. We will use the example of Spain to illustrate what could happen to a new variant launched using only below-the-line channels.

The communications models used in each of the three countries is shown in Figure 29. By analysing these three approaches in detail we will demonstrate that:

- the integrated model deployed in the UK delivered significantly higher sales uplift than either of the alternatives

5. The fourth big country, Germany, was discounted because it used a more general brand advert to launch Lynx Pulse, making its effects incomparable.

	TV	Cinema	Outdoor	Press	Radio	Digital	Local events	Track release
UK	Heavy	Heavy	Heavy	Heavy	Heavy	Heavy	Heavy	Heavy
France	Heavy			Light	Light	Light		
Spain					Light	Light	Light	

■ = Heavy use of the channel ▢ = Light use of the channel

Figure 29: *Summary of communication models used in each country*

- this result cannot be attributed to differences in market size, existing brand size, retail environment or scale of media investment, but is driven primarily by differences in communication planning
- the integrated model is a significantly more effective way of driving sales and return on investment.

The UK delivered better sales results for Lynx Pulse than any of the other countries

In absolute terms, the phenomenon that we created in the UK delivered much higher results for Lynx Pulse than any other country (Figure 30 and 31).

From the data above, the case for integrated communications seems compelling. In the next section we will determine that there are no other variables that have a significant effect.

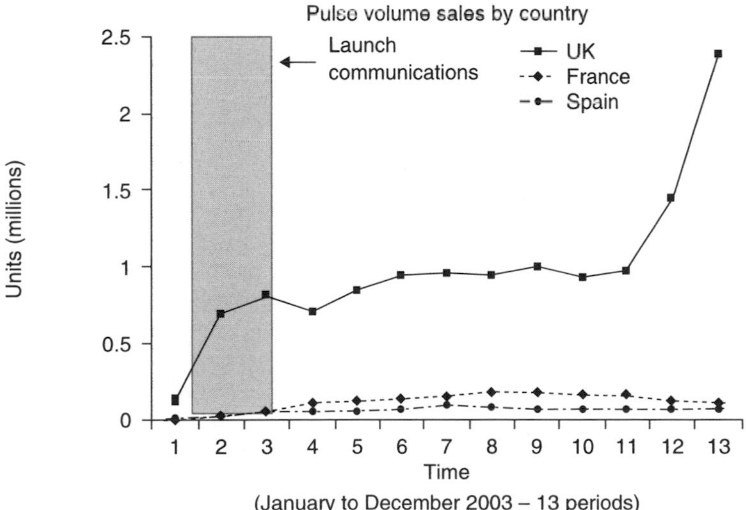

Figure 30: *Lynx Pulse volume sales by country*
Source: IRI/ACNielsen

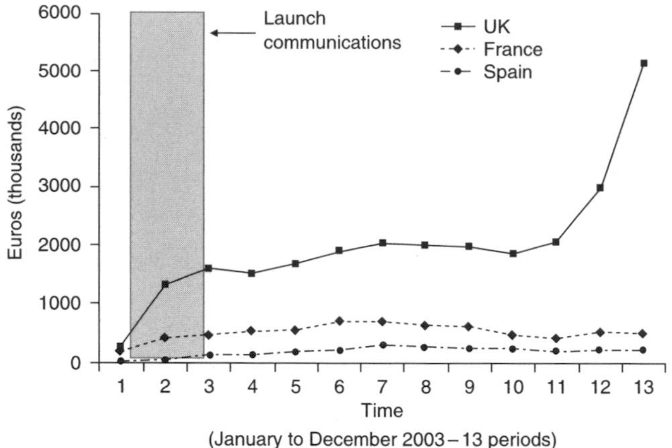

Figure 31: *Lynx Pulse value sales by country*
Source: IRI/ACNielsen

ELIMINATING OTHER VARIABLES

Relative size of the Lynx brand in each country

We will demonstrate in this section that the difference between the results observed in the UK and what we saw elsewhere cannot be explained by the relative size of the Lynx brand in each market.

It is reasonable to assume that the ratio of total Lynx brand sales to Lynx Pulse sales will be the same between markets. For example, total Lynx brand sales in France are 24.2% of Lynx brand sales in the UK. Therefore, all things being equal, Lynx Pulse sales in France can be expected to be 24.2% of Lynx Pulse sales in the UK. Figure 32 shows a summary of these calculations. Any variation from this expected sales figure suggests that something other than market size is driving UK Lynx sales.

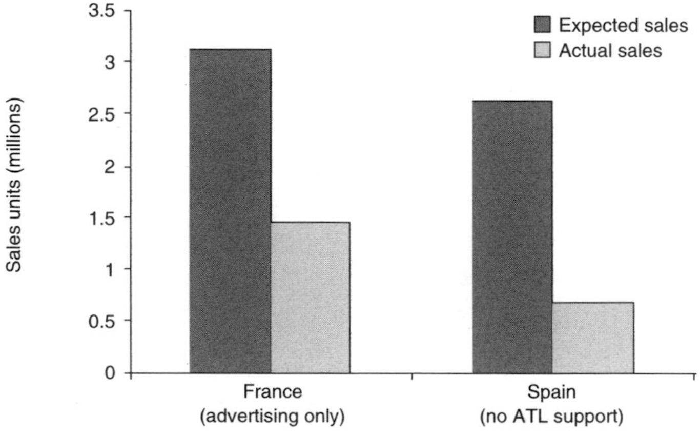

Figure 32: *Lynx Pulse expected volume sales vs actual*
Source: IRI/ACNielsen

The lower than expected sales in both countries show that the UK's performance is clearly not driven by size of market.

Distribution

Different countries built distribution at different speeds and to different levels (Figure 33).[6]

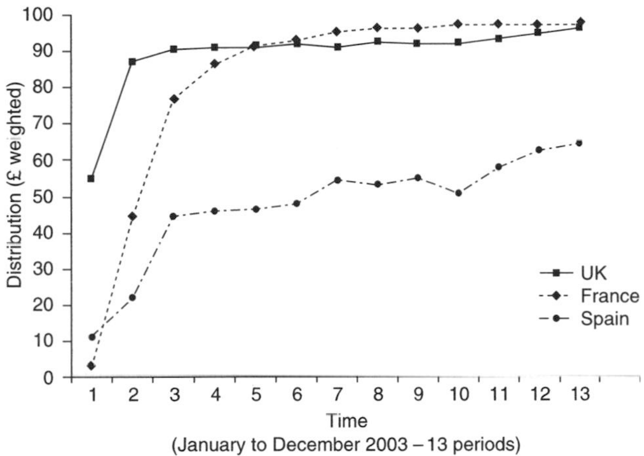

Figure 33: Build-up of distribution of Lynx Pulse
Source: IRI/ACNielsen

To eliminate the effect of distribution we can use calculations of rate of sale (ROS). To make ROS figures comparable for each country we need to, once again, apply the ratios we looked at earlier. This allows us to compare predicted ROS to actual ROS achieved by Lynx Pulse in France and Spain. Again, any deviation from expected ROS figures means that the superior performance of Lynx Pulse in the UK was not driven by distribution (Figures 34 and 35).

This analysis shows lower than expected rate-of-sale figures, thereby eliminating distribution as a driver of Lynx Pulse's relative success in the UK.

Market growth

Clearly, different levels of overall market growth by country could have affected Lynx Pulse sales. We can eliminate the effect of market growth by looking at the market share data (Figures 36 and 37).

The UK shows significantly higher gains in market share proving that UK performance is not driven by total market performance.

6. The data is collected in similar ways in each country, and the distribution levels can therefore be compared.

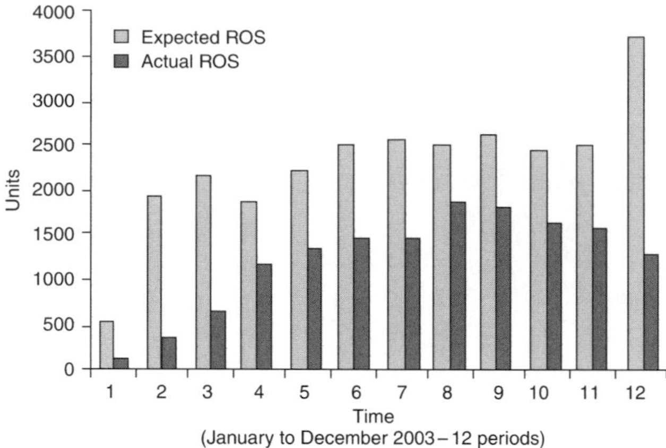

Figure 34: *Expected vs actual ROS in France*
Source: IRI/ACNielsen

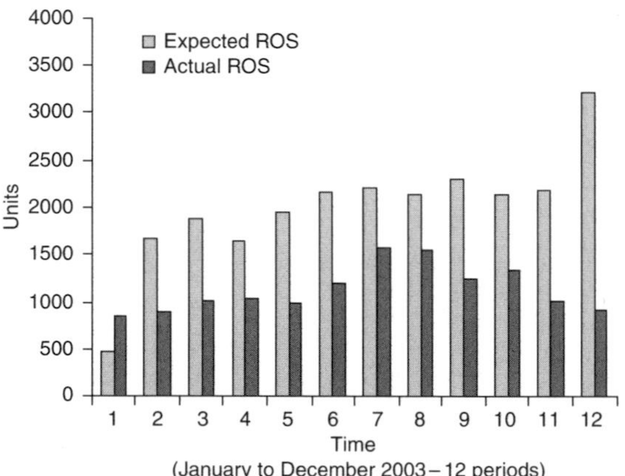

Figure 35: *Expected vs actual ROS in Spain*
Source: IRI/ACNielsen

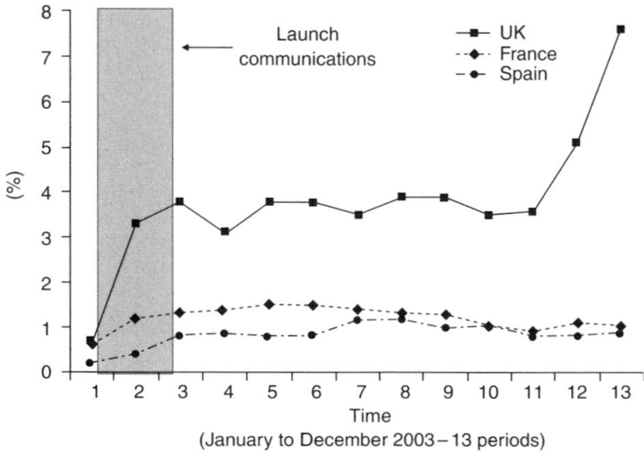

Figure 36: *Lynx Pulse volume share of total deodorant market*
Source: IRI/ACNielsen

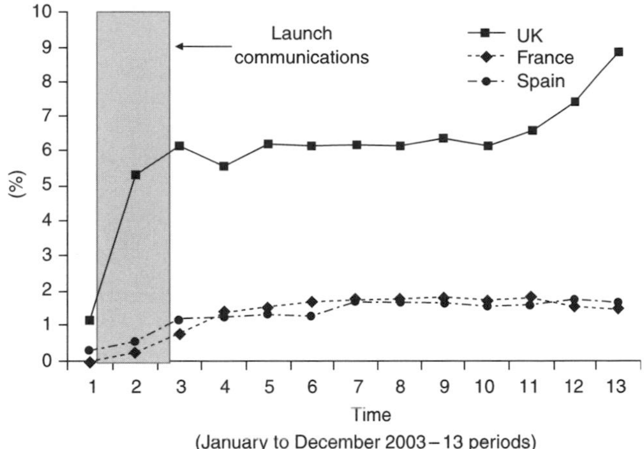

Figure 37: *Lynx Pulse value share by country*
Source: IRI/ACNielsen

Price

The relative price of Lynx Pulse[7] compared to the market in the UK is higher than in France or Spain. This means that the launch of Lynx Pulse in the UK has not been made easier by a lower price relative to market.[8]

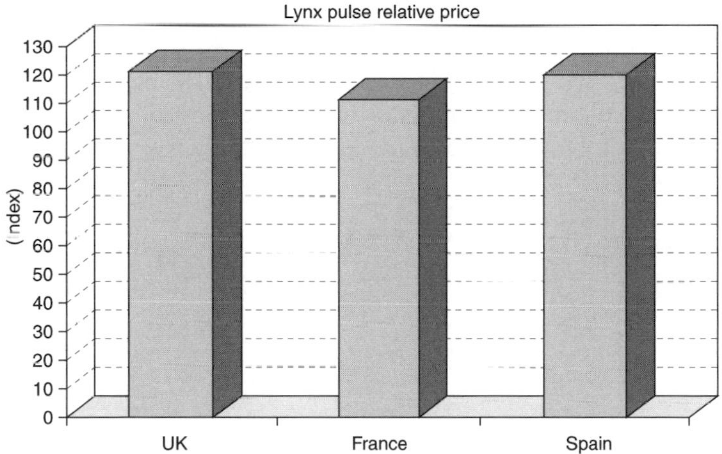

Figure 38: *Lynx prices vs market average*
Source: IRI/Nielsen Price Tracker (price relative to deodorant category average)

Level of communication support

We will demonstrate in this section that the launch of Lynx Pulse in the UK has not been over-supported compared to the launch in France. (Spain will not be part of

7. Given availability of data, we had to look at total Lynx prices in each and assume Lynx Pulse would be sold for the same price as other variants, which is the normal strategy for the brand.
8. The Lynx prices relative to the market have also not changed significantly between 2002 and 2003.

this comparison, as we are using it as a model for what can happen to a new variant launched with very little expenditure.) To do this we will show that the spend per can of Lynx Pulse was actually higher in France than in the UK (Table 5).

TABLE 5: INVESTMENT PER CAN SOLD RATIO

	Lynx Pulse cans sold in 2003	Communication investment[9]	Ratio
UK	12,773,000	€4.71 million	€0.37 per can sold
France	1,457,586	€2.34 million	€1.6 per can sold

Source: IRI/ACNielsen/Initiative Media

This shows that France spent 4.3 times more money per can of Lynx Pulse than the UK, which suggests that it was actually the communication model for the launch rather than the level of investment that made a difference to the sales results.

Competitor activities

Competitor activity in France and Spain is just as intense and competitive as in the UK. The brand faces fierce competition in the three markets and there is no sense in which the launch was easier in the UK.

Different seasonality

Sales peak at Christmas time in the UK, but not in France or Spain. It is just a fact that UK consumers buy deodorants for Christmas when others don't. However, looking at the rest of the year, UK sales still outperform those observed in other countries. It is therefore reasonable to assume that there was a continuation of the effect seen between January and November over the Christmas period.

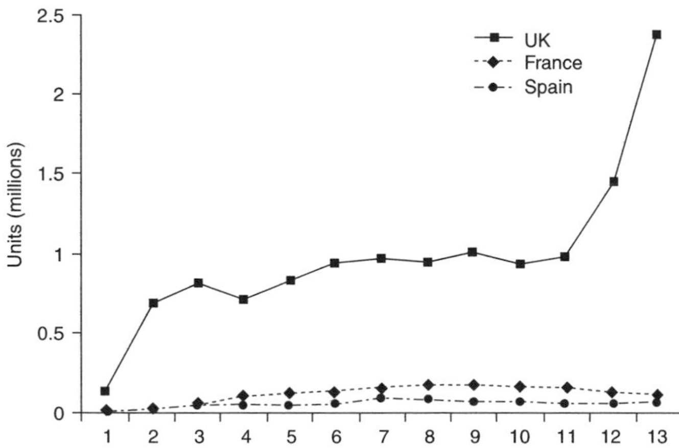

Figure 39: *Volume sales by country*
Source: IRI/ACNielsen

9. Source: Initiative Media/Leader. Gross media data used as a result of Unilever confidentiality policy on net figures.

Summary

We have now taken out all the factors that could have explained the differences between the performance of the Lynx Pulse launch in the UK and in each of the other countries:

- market size
- distribution
- market growth
- price
- level of communication support
- competitor activity
- seasonality.

This means that the difference can only be explained by the way the launch was communicated in these countries. In the following section we will demonstrate the value of integrated communication over advertising on its own.

RETURN ON INVESTMENT

In this section we will demonstrate that launching a new variant by creating a phenomenon around it, with integrated communication, is more efficient than other approaches.[10] For each country, we will look at the ratio between the effect delivered by communication and the budget that was invested to generate it. We will first calculate sales uplift in each individual country and work out the ratio of investment to effect. We will then compare these ratios in order to determine which communication and which level of investment has performed best.

Sales uplift by country

As mentioned at the start of this study, each variant is launched on a 'one in, one out' basis. This means the new variant replaces the least-performing variant from the portfolio. The best way to work out return on investment for the launch of Lynx Pulse is to first isolate the incremental value sales it delivered compared to the variant it replaces. We can then divide these incremental sales by the budget spent to deliver them, and this way work out a ratio of effect to investment.[11]

UK

The total difference between value sales of Lynx Pulse and those of the replaced variant is €20.44m (Figure 40). Total communication support: €4.71m.

10. Confidentiality of profit margin data means that we will have to judge the effect of communication based on the sales uplift that it delivered.

11. This is an acceptable way to assess the relative performances of different communication models as the only difference between the new and the replaced variant, apart from communications, is smell. Both smells have been developed by the same fragrance companies, using the same procedure, the same quality controls, and testing the results with consumers in similar ways.

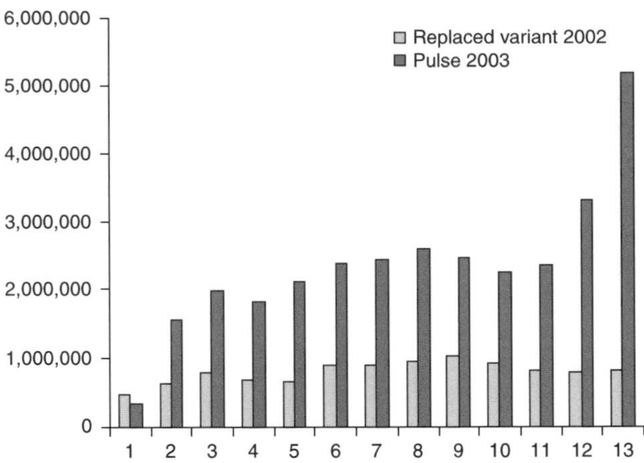

Figure 40: *Difference with replaced variant – UK*
Source: IRI/ACNielsen

The UK ratio of effect to investment is €20.44m/€4.71m = 4.34. The UK model delivered very positive return on investment.

France

The total difference in value sales between Lynx Pulse and the replaced variant was €4.55m. Media spend was €2.34m.

The ratio of effect to investment in France is €4.55m/€2.34m = 1.94. The France model also delivered positive return on investment, at a lower level than the UK.

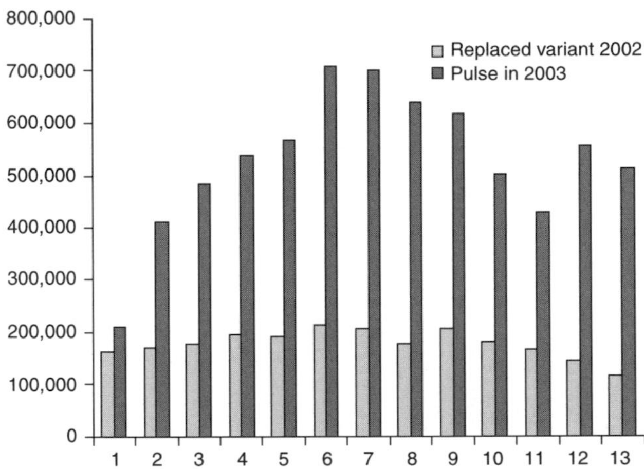

Figure 41: *Difference with replaced variant – France*
Source: IRI/ACNielsen

Spain

In Spain we did not see the same sales success as in France and the UK. The difference compared to replaced variant was negative at around €462,383 (Figure 42). Below-the-line budget was €72,000.

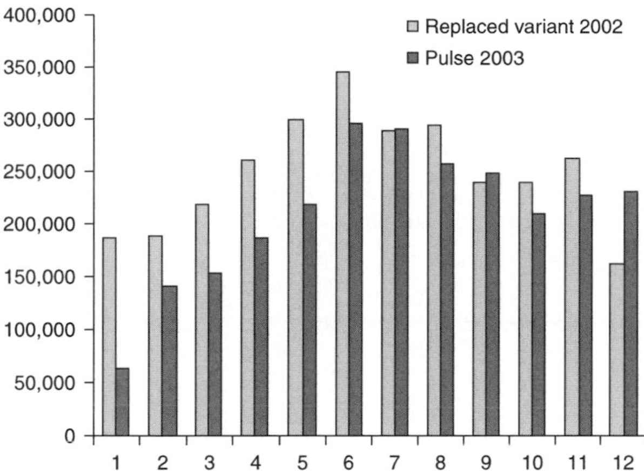

Figure 42: *Difference with replaced variant – Spain*
Source: IRI/ACNielsen

Therefore there was no return on investment in Spain. We cannot, then, calculate a meaningful investment to effect ratio.

Comparing the different models

The ratio of effect to investment is 2.25 times higher for the UK versus France (Table 6). Our integrated, multi-channel campaign for Lynx was more than twice as effective as a traditional advertising-only campaign. The results from Spain illustrate that there is a threshold of investment that one needs to invest to launch a new product successfully.

TABLE 6: SUMMARY OF THE EFFECT TO INVESTMENT RATIO BY COUNTRY

UK	4.34
France	1.94
Spain	–

CONCLUSIONS

We believe this study has demonstrated the value of integration. Integrated multi-channel campaigns can be more than twice as efficient at generating a return than advertising-only solutions. In other words, every euro invested in an integrated campaign should work at least twice as hard as a euro invested in advertising-only campaigns.

Whilst we consider this to be the most significant finding of our work there are also a number of other important lessons.

- In attempting to get people's attention brands must recognise that they compete with popular culture, not just their immediate competitive set of products. Nowadays you need a phenomenon to really get people to sit up and pay attention.

- Brands can learn a lot from understanding how the entertainment industry creates and manipulates culture to gain share of mind.
- Properly integrated campaigns require multiple agencies to work collaboratively towards a common goal.

We believe that all this shows how we have entered a new and different era of communications – an era that demands real consumer engagement, not simply consumer interruption.

14

Marks & Spencer Lingerie

Nice knickers don't sell themselves

How advertising made the difference for Marks & Spencer lingerie

Principal authors: Alice Huntley, Rainey Kelley Campbell Roalfe/Y&R, and Nick Walker, Walker Media

EDITOR'S SUMMARY

This insightful case study supports an important truth about retail: good product doesn't sell itself. Advertising has an important role in shaping perceptions.

The story starts in late 2002 when, while the rest of the M&S brand was recovering nicely after years of decline, its underwear department was being left behind, hampered by a poor image. It was a seller of multipacks and 'granny knickers'. Not good when the boundary between underwear and outerwear was rapidly blurring. M&S was full of practical 'mission shoppers' rather than the more desirable browser fashionistas hunting for something special. Research showed that women's range of lingerie had grown in keeping with their social outlooks and ambitions. They wear different underwear depending on how they feel and what role they want to fill that day.

After identifying that M&S was not tapping in to the way women use lingerie, Rainey Kelley Campbell Roalfe/Y&R developed a campaign to encourage people to buy more than just basic underwear at M&S. The advertising was designed to show off M&S's considerable range of lingerie where women could find something for their every mood, in 'Lingerie Heaven'. Rather than exposing the ads in the traffic-stopping Wonderbra way, media specific to women were chosen, such as women's weeklies *heat* and *Now*. This campaign was mirrored at point of sale.

By understanding how women related to their underwear, 'Lingerie Heaven' delivered sales growth five times ahead of the market and was responsible for a five-fold pay-back in profit.

AN UNTOLD PART OF A FAMOUS STORY

The changing fortunes of Marks & Spencer are arguably Britain's favourite business topic. Everyone, from young to old, from North to South, has an opinion on whether it's getting it right or wrong and, either way, how it could get it 'righter'. More of a British institution than simply a chain of stores, along with fish and chips, and drinking tea, Marks & Spencer is part of what makes Britain, Britain.[1]

Its decline between 1997 and 2001 has been well publicised.[2] Equally well documented is the recovery between 2001 and 2003.[3] That recovery was predicated on the revival of its womenswear business, via a 'back to basics' strategy, exemplified by the Perfect campaign.[4]

Much less well known is the story of its lingerie business. During the decline of Marks & Spencer, the lingerie business, like Marks & Spencer Food, was regarded as a well-child – a solid part of the business with a solid offer and a solid customer base. However, lingerie emerged from the recovery much less powerful than it should have been. This is the story of why that was, and how a single insight-driven idea then took it to five times market growth.

A brief perspective

Marks & Spencer sells an awful lot of lingerie: 45 bras a minute; 25 million pairs of knickers a year.[5] Laid end to end these would stretch from London to the Caribbean.[6] This has led to all sorts of epithets:

> 'The patron saint of women's underwear.'
>
> The *Independent*, 23 March 2000
>
> 'Marks & Spencer is a British knickers institution.'
>
> Serena Rees, co-founder of Agent Provocateur, quoted in the *Guardian*, 29 October 1999

It is no surprise, then, that Marks & Spencer has five times the market share of its biggest competitors, BHS and La Senza.[7] It also follows that with such high sales volumes, small percentage increases are hard to achieve and account for huge sums of money.

---

1. A survey published in April 2004 by TNS on behalf of Tanqueray Gin found Marks & Spencer in the top ten things that define Britain, along with roast beef and Yorkshire pudding, The Beatles and the Queen.
2. See Julie Bevan (2001), *The Rise and Fall of Marks & Spencer*, London, Profile Books.
3. See the amended version of *The Rise and Fall of Marks & Spencer!* At the time of writing, the longevity of the recovery in womenswear was in question. This study focuses on the period between 2001 and 2003.
4. The 'Perfect' campaign, Autumn 2001–02 was a national press and in-store campaign designed to re-establish Marks & Spencer leadership in 'wardrobe essentials', e.g. the Perfect black trouser and polo neck.
5. www2.marks-and-spencer.com.
6. A distance of 4000 miles. Source: www2.marks-and-spencer.com.
7. FashionTrak, 2003. FashionTrak is monitoring service for the clothing and footwear market. It is collected from a nationally representative panel of 10,000 shoppers, who are asked every two weeks to diary what they have bought, from where and for how much.

MARKS & SPENCER LINGERIE: QUIETLY WANING WHEN IT SHOULD HAVE BEEN WAXING

The first full year of the Marks & Spencer recovery, 2002, should have been a bumper year for Marks & Spencer Lingerie. The negative publicity that had dogged Marks & Spencer had begun to wane; perceptions were improving again, and women were returning to Marks & Spencer for their clothing. The lingerie market was very healthy, growing at 7% on the year.

By November 2002, Marks & Spencer Womenswear had gained 1.1 market share percentage points, but Lingerie had only grown by 0.1%, ten times slower than its huge cousin, and 1% behind the market.[8] Marks & Spencer's share of the lingerie market was stuck at 25.5%, a far cry from its 1998 peak of 31%.[9]

Why weren't increased womenswear sales feeding through to sales of lingerie?

DIAGNOSING THE PROBLEM

The problem wasn't a lack of shoppers: 40% of all UK women still shopped for Marks & Spencer lingerie each year, and footfall in Marks & Spencer overall was up 2% on the year.[10] No, the problem was with how much they were buying. Average monthly basket size – i.e. the average number of items bought in a single transaction – was down 0.67% year on year.[11] The average number of transactions per month was down by 2.65%.[12] Women simply weren't buying as much as they used to. Two factors made this worrying.

Marks & Spencer was missing out on fashion-led growth

Blurring boundaries between lingerie and outerwear were fuelling massive growth in the sector. As Kylie, Posh and Britney illustrate (Figure 1), underwear was becoming more and more visible: younger women, happy to display their bra straps under tops, chose bright colours, ribbons, sequins and lace to complement their outfits. Ever-lower waistlines led to the introduction of hipster pants, boy shorts and sequinned thongs.

Marks & Spencer wasn't lacking the right kind of product. It already carried an enormous range of stylish product to please the most gregarious of fashionistas. Besides its celebrated Salon Rose and Wild Hearts ranges,[13] it had over 500 different sorts of knickers (including sequinned thongs).

---

8. FashionTrak 52-week rolling data, November 2001–2002. 52-week rolling data is used throughout unless otherwise specified. It is more robust than 12- or 4-week rolling data and is tougher to affect – a sign of long-term rather than short-term success. 'Lingerie' includes bras, knickers, sleepwear and hosiery.
9. BRC, FashionTrak, 2002.
10. Marks & Spencer internal footfall data July 2002 vs July 2001. 'Footfall' is a retail term used to indicate the number of people passing by a place or entering a store. In Marks & Spencer's case it is gathered automatically by sensors over store doors.
11. Marks & Spencer internal sales data. Annual average monthly basket size in 2001 vs 2002.
12. Marks & Spencer internal sales data. Annual average of transactions per month in 2001 vs 2002.
13. Salon Rose is designed by Agent Provocateur, and Wild Hearts by the Australian fashion designer Collette Dinnigan. Both ranges were launched to significant media acclaim and are amongst Marks & Spencer's fastest-selling lines.

Figure 1: *Fashion trends meant underwear was increasingly being worn as outerwear*

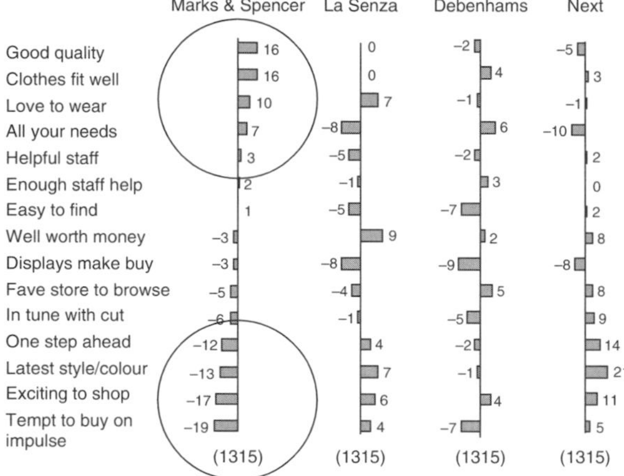

Figure 2: *Perceptually, Marks & Spencer strong on function, weak on fashion*
Source: Millward Brown

The problem was that perceptions of the brand were firmly stuck in ‘functional’ territory: a reliable old fallback for multipacks and ‘granny knickers’, not an exciting destination for the latest styles (Figure 2). Quality – the primary pillar of the brand, and what it is most known and appreciated for,[14] was not translating into style or appeal. The result: a brand that wasn’t browsed.

A closer look at buying behaviour showed that Marks & Spencer lingerie had lots of ‘mission shoppers’ but not a lot of browsers. Women were coming in on a mission to get another version of the bra they bought last year. They weren’t coming in on the off-chance of being surprised or lured into getting something more frivolous.

14. In Y&R’s proprietary brand survey, Brand Asset Valuator, Marks & Spencer ranks in the top 0.7% of 3000+ UK brands for being ‘high quality’.

Figure 3: *The 'Perfect' campaign, 2001–2002, emphasised great wardrobe basics*

> 'I think I am just on auto pilot into that shop.'
>
> Female 35–45

> 'When I went into Marks's I was looking around for a plain white bra ... I definitely wouldn't shop there if I wanted something special.'
>
> Female 45+[15]

The highly successful 'Perfect' campaign, which had powerfully contributed to the increases in womenswear sales,[16] if anything reinforced this behaviour. It featured lingerie in the context of 'perfect wardrobe essentials' – i.e. great basics (Figure 3). This was a sound positioning for the recovery of Marks & Spencer Womenswear, but insufficient for growth in lingerie.

15. Hauck Qualitative Research 2002. The research showed women were much more likely to be browsing and buying 'something special' at places like Next, Debenhams and La Senza.
16. The Perfect campaign case study was finalist in the National Business Awards Advertiser of the Year 2002 and *Retail Week* Campaign of the Year 2002.

Losing out to discounters

But even this functional strength was under threat. Discounters and supermarkets were getting a bigger share of the 'boring basics' – customers picking up a five-pack of knickers with their grocery shop instead of at Marks & Spencer. In the first eight months of 2001, for example, the average competitor lingerie price had fallen from £9.20 to £8.34.[17] The discounters' share of the market was increasing at a frightening rate: growing by a third in just two years.[18]

GETTING MARKS & SPENCER BROWSED AGAIN

Marks & Spencer needed to find a new positioning for lingerie, which could capitalise on its key strengths of quality and range, but which had the power to shift perceptions away from 'good old Marks & Spencer – the reliable fallback' to a place where buying underwear is just as much about what you didn't know you wanted as it is about what you knew you needed – in short, to get Marks & Spencer browsed again.

We knew the range existed – Marks & Spencer had more lines of lingerie than any other retailer[19] – but range on its own was a rather boring proposition. Research showed that browsers have a very different mentality to mission shoppers – the browsing moment is much more emotional, much more engaged:

> 'Browsers are more emotional in their motivations than the more practical searchers.'
>
> Hauck Research

We needed to develop a campaign that was capable of appealing to women on a highly emotional level if we were to succeed.

The targeting challenge

Marks & Spencer particularly wanted to engage with younger customers – especially 35–45s, who were less well represented within Marks & Spencer as a whole. Whatever growth we achieved with under-45s was useless if it alienated the valuable and influential core customer, 45+. Marks & Spencer had had problems in the past with 'going young' at the perceived expense of its most loyal customers.[20] It was critical that older women still felt included.

ROOTING THROUGH THE NATION'S KNICKERS

We asked women to take us on a guided tour of their lingerie drawers, in the privacy of their own homes, explaining why they wore what, and when they wore

17. FashionTrak, 2001.
18. FashionTrak. The total share of the lingerie market accounted for by discounters (defined as Matalan, Primark and factory outlets) grew from 10.9% in 2000 to 14.6% in 2002.
19. Verdict estimates the number of lines Marks & Spencer carries to be double that of BHS or La Senza, the actual proportion is probably treble.
20. 'Going young' was widely held to be the reason for Marks & Spencer loss of sales in 1998–99, e.g. Financial Post, 7 July 1999 'Marks & Spencer goes back to classics to recapture older customer base.'

it. As we suspected, there was something much deeper going on than a passing fashion trend. Two insights emerged that provided a platform for the new idea.

1. *Women are modal and this is beginning to affect the way they wear underwear*
In fact, what lay behind the growth in the lingerie market was an increasing dimensionalisation of mood and mode. Just as women once had three roles as wife, mother and dutiful daughter, and five pairs of knickers, they now had at least 23 roles and at least as many pairs of knickers. Women's lingerie repertoires had expanded in keeping with their social outlooks and ambitions. What they wore underneath their clothes changed the way they felt that day, and helped them to play the part they wanted to play. Without realising it, women were beginning to treat their underwear drawers in the same way they treated their clothing wardrobes. In fact, they were building 'lingerie wardrobes' for themselves.

2. *This 'mood play' is an entirely private form of self-expression*
This language of lingerie is hidden, covert, private, shared only with a privileged intimate few. Lingerie is therefore the ultimate expression of the true nature of femininity: how women see themselves, not how society portrays them. It was clear that for all women, contrary to marketing stereotypes and the popular mythology of the male imagination, pleasing 'him indoors' was only one role that they wanted to play (Figure 4). Lingerie 'for him' was the funny red scratchy thing that he gave

Figure 4: *Two examples of competitors only reflecting 'lingerie for him' – one very familiar and one very recent!*

you on your birthday, which lived buried at the bottom of the drawer. Lingerie 'for me' was a much broader affair, which of course required many more purchases.[21]

THE NEW BRAND IDEA

This was a natural platform for Marks & Spencer to talk about the sides of its range that no one realised it had. If women wanted to be multi-dimensional, then Marks & Spencer's role was to provide them with the opportunity to express this to the full. As Marks & Spencer indisputably had the widest range of lingerie (styles, shapes and sizes) of any retailer, it could feed and inspire women's multi-dimensional inner selves in a way that no one else could.

This thought was encapsulated in a new brand idea: 'Marks & Spencer is Lingerie Heaven.'

Lingerie Heaven is a place where women can be whoever they want to be, and find lingerie to reflect every dimension of their personality and moods. A place where women can find not just 'something for everyone' but 'something for every you'.

THE ROLE FOR ADVERTISING

Advertising was developed from this idea with the following aims:

- to change perceptions so that women expected to find a greater variety of more stylish lingerie in Marks & Spencer
- to legitimise a greater indulgence in modal behaviour – encouraging women to think in terms of lingerie for different moods – and thereby inspire them to buy more kinds of lingerie at Marks & Spencer (Figure 5).

The proposition was: 'In Marks & Spencer's Lingerie Heaven you'll find underwear for every you.'

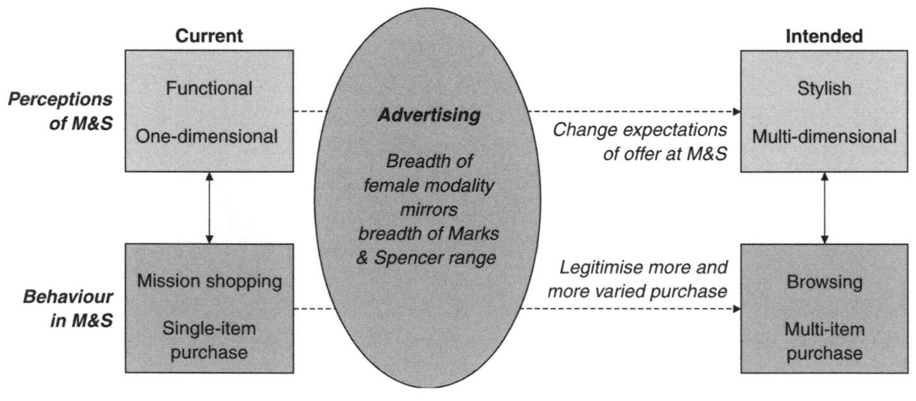

Figure 5: *The advertising model*

21. Without exception, respondents felt that other lingerie brands only reflected the 'for him' mode.

Breaking category conventions

Conventional lingerie advertising imagery focuses on sexual representations of women overtly posing for the camera, primed for public display. Marks & Spencer wanted to capture a more intimate and feminine world – a world where women are relaxed and experimental, happy in their own skin, as if naturally observed in their own female space.

The advertising therefore captured private views of women in their underwear but unconscious of the camera; women who were aspirational, but who had tousled hair, who had natural beauty – who had personalities. It reflected what women really do when they're getting ready. It showed women painting their nails, posing (for themselves!) in front of the mirror, choosing outfits, chatting on the phone, putting on their make-up. The headlines captured the range of different moods and emotions women feel as they decide what kind of 'girl' they are going to be today: from self-indulgent to sporty, fiery to flirty, alluring or playful. Copy lines suggested what it felt like to be in Lingerie Heaven, e.g. for 'self-indulgent girls' the copy reads 'In Lingerie Heaven you can have your cake and eat it'; for 'mischievous girls' it reads 'In Lingerie Heaven you can feel deliciously decadent' (Figure 6).

Creative development research convinced us of the power of this approach across age groups, as evidenced by the following comments.

> 'It's definitely for our age range isn't it?'
>
> (18–24, London)
>
> 'You'd go in to buy something for one occasion and then you would buy something on a whim just because you were in that mood.'
>
> (35–45, lapsed, Manchester)
>
> 'It's Sex and the Cityish, they are of our generation. Not middle aged.'
>
> (25–35, carefree, lapsed, London)
>
> 'Sometimes I shop and I feel like a mum. Other times I feel like a vamp.'
>
> (35–45, Kids R Us, Manchester)
>
> 'I think it's brilliant we could all fit into any one of those roles at some stage.'
>
> (35–45, carefree, lapsed, Manchester)
>
> 'Whatever lifestyle you lead there is something for you.'
>
> (55–65, regular, Manchester)

MAKING MEDIA AND CREATIVE A PERFECT MATCHING SET

It was critical that the media strategy worked to enhance not dilute the creative strategy. This instantly produced a tension.

The creative requirement for intimacy

Client and agencies were all convinced that the media strategy should keep true to the creative sense of a female 'private view'. This was a campaign single-mindedly

Figure 6: *The final creative work showed women getting ready, unaware of the camera*

aimed at women. In total contrast to Wonderbra's traffic-stopping executions,[22] we didn't really want men to see it. This meant that a traditional 'broadcast' campaign was out of the question.[23]

The business requirement for impact

We also needed to generate sufficient frequency and coverage to drive an immediate sales effect in keeping with the expectations of a mass-market retailer like Marks & Spencer.

This meant that obvious 'intimate' media like women's monthlies were also out – they generated too little coverage, too slowly.[24]

The solution was found in women's weeklies.[25] Celebrity magazines such as *Hello!*, *OK!*, *heat* and *Now* offered the best of both worlds, both private and populist.[26] Weeklies provided 60%+ coverage of the core target of 25–45 ABC1 women. Incremental coverage was gained through the *Sunday Times Style* magazine (Figure 7).[27]

Weeklies were perfect for another reason: they quite literally featured what went on 'behind closed doors'. By placing the campaign in a gossip context, we hoped the campaign would get gossiped about too.

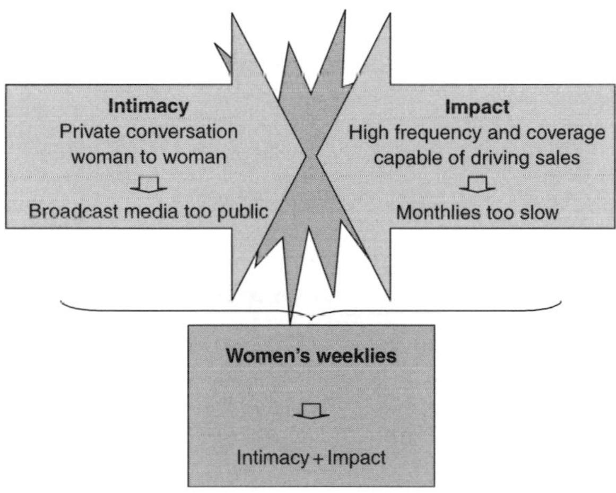

Figure 7: *Women's weeklies delivered both intimacy and impact*

22. See Figure 4. The Wonderbra 'Hello Boys' 48-sheet posters were famously accused of causing car accidents.
23. Most broadcast media hit at least as many men as women. The male:female splits are as follows: national press and outdoor 51:49, TV 56:44.
24. An NRS readership accumulation study in 2003 showed that it takes the average women's monthly 98 days to reach 90% of the total coverage the title is going to achieve.
25. For an average women's weekly, readership accumulation for 90% of coverage is only 25 days. The male:female split is 17:83.
26. And increasingly so – celebrity gossip weeklies grew 195% in circulation between 2000 and 2003: January–June 2000 = 1,434,025 (*heat*, *Hello!*, *Now*, *OK!*), July–December 2003 = 2,799,454 (including *New* and *Closer*).
27. This offered significant numbers of the target audience but still within an intimate environment.

Finding a powerful way to reflect range

The other requirement was that the media should reflect both the multi-dimensional personalities of our modal women and the beauty and breadth of possibilities held within the Marks & Spencer 'lingerie wardrobe'.

We felt the best solution was to buy multiple batches of consecutive right-hand pages. This was a media first – it had never been done before in the weeklies: weeklies typically operate on a very low advertising-to-editorial ratio and rely on cover price to deliver the majority of their income, preferring to maximise yield per page.[28] Weeklies changed their editorial policy in order for this to happen – the owner of *Hello!* in Spain had to approve the change personally.

The resulting campaign ran in April–May and September–October 2003 with multiples of six and then three consecutive pages. Each page expressed a different mood and a different kind of lingerie. During 2003, no fewer than 25 different lingerie moods were featured.

TABLE 1: TOTAL FREQUENCY AND COVERAGE FIGURES

	Coverage	Frequency
ABC1 women 25–40	66.7%	9.7 OTS* (per insertion of 3)[29] 23.3 OTS* (per advert)

* OTS = on-target sales

The strength of media placement added considerably to the campaign's memorability:

> 'This is one of those rare campaigns where the media placement was as much a part of respondents' recall of the advertising as the creative idea. Respondents could remember which magazines they saw the ads in, and how the ads were placed.'
>
> Kirsty Fuller, Flamingo Research

In-store

During the campaign, imagery from the two bursts of advertising was followed through in-store via POS. Promotions were executed in the same style as the advertising.[30]

HOW THE ADVERTISING ACTUALLY WORKED

Advertising tracking measures clearly show the campaign worked in the way we wanted it to, both at a total sample level and amongst the younger target.

28. That is, preferring to sell one page for more money than two pages for half the price, and limiting the total amount of advertising per issue.
29. Because 'range' was such an integral part of the campaign idea, worked for high frequency per set of three rather than per execution. Copy rotation and duplication analysis ensured that not only did we maximise total campaign coverage, but that every execution was seen at least 2.3 times.
30. This study does not attempt to separate the effect of the external advertising from that of the (limited) in-store photography, as this was simply used as extra media space for the same creative executions.

Figure 8: *In-store point of sale and promotions integrated with the campaign*

Getting noticed

The campaign was highly memorable – generating levels of recognition 50% higher than the Millward Brown norm despite lower than average levels of spend for a Marks & Spencer campaign (Table 2).

TABLE 2: HIGHER THAN AVERAGE IMPACT

	Awareness (percentage recognition)	Percentage awareness above MB norm	Media spend	Cost per 1% of awareness
Millward Brown print norm	21%	–	–	–
M&S Perfect campaign (August–September 2002)	27%	29%	£1.5m	£56k
Lingerie campaign (1st burst: April–May 2003)	32%	52%	£700k	£22k
Lingerie campaign (2nd burst: October–November 2003)	28%	33%	£500k	£18k

Source: Millward Brown 2003/Walker Media

As creative development research had predicted, the campaign had above average engagement – scoring highly in terms of being intriguing and striking[31] (Figure 9).

Changing expectations

As intended, the campaign helped to change expectations of what women would find in store. The key perceptual barriers of style – 'offers the latest styles' – and range – 'has a range of lingerie for all your needs' – were communicated through the advertising, without loss of the key Marks & Spencer brand property of quality (Figure 10).

31. Note that the tracking survey is conducted amongst a sample that is 80% female and only 20% male. Analysis of the data showed that impact was higher amongst women than men, discounting the claim that the adverts were only memorable because of greater male interest in lingerie advertising.

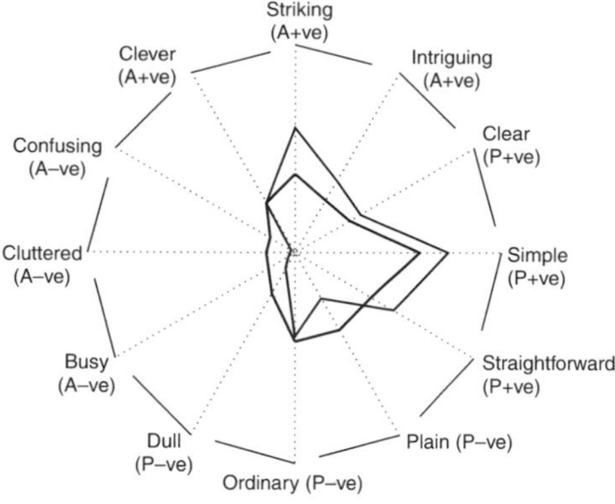

Figure 9: *An impactful campaign*
Source: Millward Brown, 2003

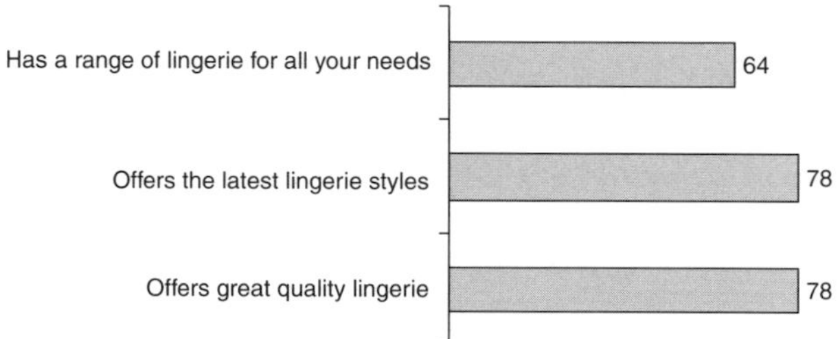

Figure 10: *Advertising communicated stylishness and range: impressions of advertising, percentage agreeing*
Source: Millward Brown

This was matched by changes to the lingerie brand perceptions overall. In keeping with our desire to expand the reputation of Marks & Spencer beyond the purely functional, expectations of range increased across the age groups (Tables 3 and 4).

TABLE 3: RANGE PERCEPTIONS IMPROVED – OFFERS A WIDE RANGE OF LINGERIE FOR ALL YOUR NEEDS

Age	Pre-advertising Agree (%)	Post-advertising (peak) Agree (%)	Difference
16–34	64	72	+8
35–44	72	77	+5
45–54	71	82	+11

Source: Millward Brown, 2003

TABLE 4: STYLE PERCEPTIONS IMPROVED – SELLS THE LATEST STYLES AND COLOURS

Age	Pre-advertising Agree (%)	Post-advertising (peak) Agree (%)	Difference
16–34	50	56	+6
35–44	52	62	+10
45–54	56	63	+7

Source: Millward Brown, 2003

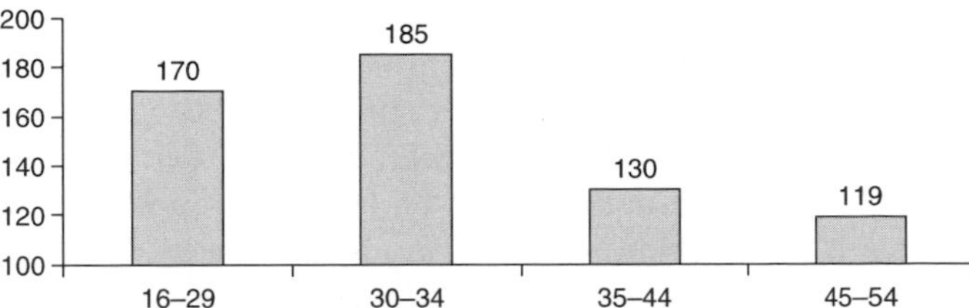

Figure 11: *Advertising was highly persuasive for younger targets: persuasion (made me more likely to visit) indexed vs Millward Brown norm*
Source: Millward Brown, 2003

These shifts in perception also translated into shifts in intention to purchase that were higher than the Millward Brown norm across all ages, but especially amongst the youngest and hardest-to-persuade (Figure 11).

Impact on sales

The campaign generated immediate uplifts in sales. Advertised lines took an average weekly increase of +41% on the base week. Overall, advertised lines saw a total increase of £6.6m during the campaign periods.

This effect was not limited to the advertised lines. During 2003, the whole of Marks & Spencer lingerie business achieved growth in sales of 4% in a market that was shrinking 1% – in effect, growing five times faster than the market it was previously trailing (Figure 12). Market share recovered by 4% (1.3 percentage points). The majority of growth came from the core target of 35–45s, with whom share grew 37% (8.6 percentage points).[32] In a market worth £2.26bn the total share increase represents a basic increase of £29.4m, four and a half times greater than the sales raised from advertised lines alone (Figure 13).

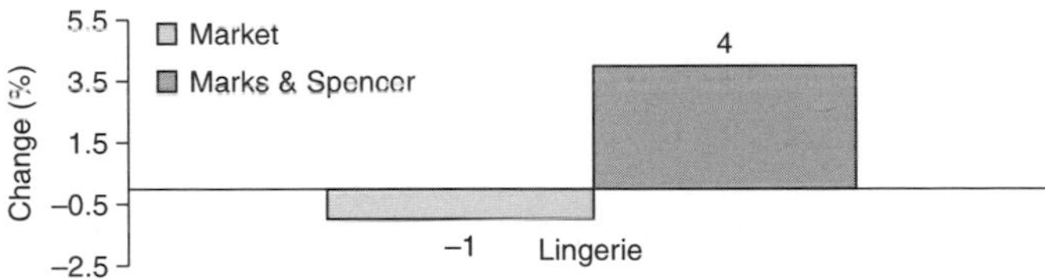

Figure 12: *Marks & Spencer lingerie grew five times faster than the market*
Source: FashionTrak, 2003

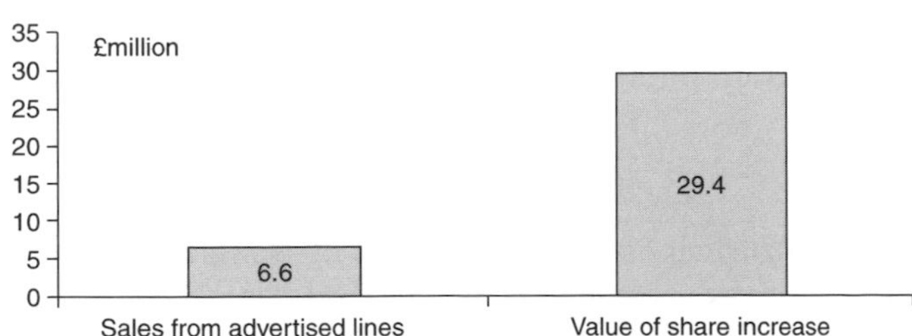

Figure 13: *Overall value of share increase was 4.5 greater than sales from advertised lines*
Source: Marks & Spencer

32. FashionTrak 52, w/e 11 January 2004.

This overall value increase is all the more impressive if we imagine what would have happened if Marks & Spencer hadn't run the 'Lingerie Heaven' campaign. Without 'Lingerie Heaven', Marks & Spencer could have been expected to perform no better than it did in 2002: growing 1% behind the market.

The market in 2003 shrank in value by 1%. Marks & Spencer would therefore have experienced a 2% reduction in value, and a theoretical deficit of £11.5m. If we add this deficit to the £29.4m net value increases, we can assume that the 'Lingerie Heaven' advertising idea actually accounted for £40.9m of additional sales (Table 5).

TABLE 5: WITHOUT ADVERTISING, MARKS & SPENCER WOULD HAVE MADE A £11.5M LOSS

	Year-on-year growth	Net value change
Without advertising	–2%	_£11.5m
With advertising	+4%	+£29.4m
Total value benefit		£40.9m

A five-fold payback

To calculate payback, this paper assumes a commonly accepted average profit margin for clothing retailers of 15%.[33] Taking this as a yardstick, Marks & Spencer made an extra £6.14m of profit out of the additional £40.9m of share increase.

As, in media terms, the Lingerie Heaven campaign only cost £1.2m, Marks & Spencer received five times its original investment (Table 6).[34]

TABLE 6: PAYBACK WAS FIVE TIMES INVESTMENT

Total value benefit	£40.9m
Profit on benefit @ estimated 15%	£6.14m
Cost of campaign	£1.2m
£ profit per £ of campaign spend	£5.12

PROVING IT WAS THE ADVERTISING THAT DID THIS

Advertising can be proved in two ways: by chronological proof (certain things only shifting after advertising starts) and by strategic proof (the way the advertising worked is the reason for the sales increases). It is possible to prove the impact of 'Lingerie Heaven' in both these ways.

Chronological proof

Key business measures such as average number of transactions and weekly sales increased significantly at the same time as the advertising (Figure 14).

33. Based on Marks & Spencer estimate of average retail margins.
34. The exact ratio of additional profit to investment is 1:5.12. In-store signage is effectively free media space.

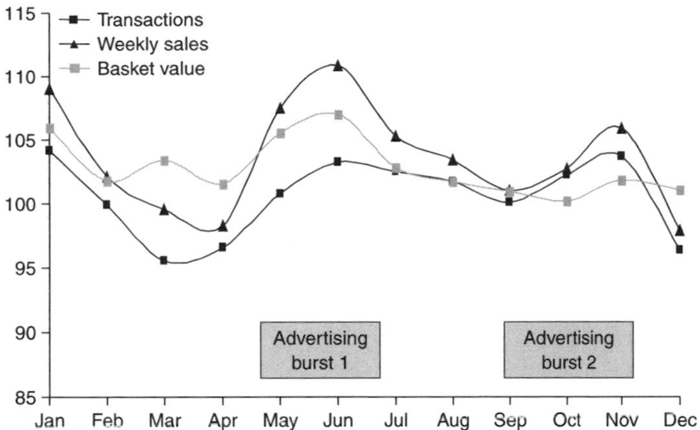

Figure 14: *Key business measures increase during advertised periods: lingerie business performance neasures indexed 2002–2003*

Strategic proof

Let's return to our model. The primary behaviour that the advertising aimed to change was weight of purchase: to turn mission shoppers into browsers and single-item purchasers into multi-item purchasers. This happened: average monthly basket size increased in 2002–2003 by 2% vs a decrease the previous year of 0.67%.[35] The increases only began after the campaign was launched (Figure 15).

Advertising drove increased basket value

Baskets containing advertised lines were 50% more likely to be worth £20 or more, compared to baskets without advertised lines.[36]

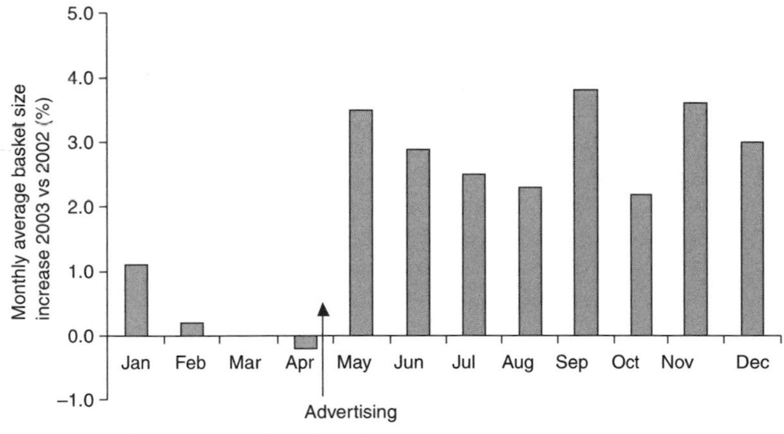

Figure 15: *Basket size increased after launch of campaign*

35. Basket size means average number of items per transaction. While basket size increased, penetration remained almost static at +0.2%, indicating that sales increases were coming as intended from existing shoppers spending more.
36. Source: Marks & Spencer Chargecard analysis, April–June 2003.

Browsing improved

Following the launch of the campaign, perceptions of Marks & Spencer as an enjoyable place to browse increased significantly. Importantly this was done without losing 'ease of shop' – a measure that is particularly important in reflecting the continued loyalty of the older shopper (Figure 16).

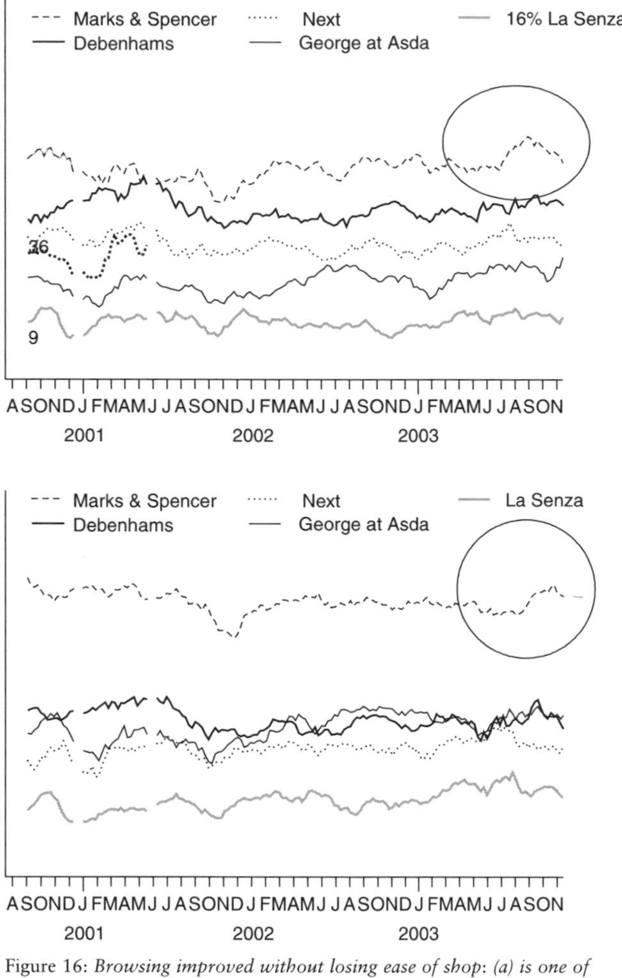

Figure 16: *Browsing improved without losing ease of shop: (a) is one of your favourite stores to browse in; (b) is an easy store to find what you are looking for*

Discounting the other factors

Price

As explained earlier, price was an important driver in the lingerie market. However, price does not explain the increase in basket size or sales. If price reduction was driving the sales, we would have expected average item price to go down. Although

Marks & Spencer reduced its prices by 8% vs the market,[37] it was still able to operate at a 60% premium.[39] In fact, the campaign migrated people on to higher-value items: basket value increased by 2.8% and average item price by 0.7%.[39]

Promotions

Price promotions are a critical weapon in a retailer's arsenal and an important part of the Marks & Spencer lingerie retail calendar. Promotions ran during the campaign as they run every year. However, the promotional mechanics used in 2003 were identical to those used in 2002,[40] and as uplifts were not seen in 2002,[41] promotions cannot account for the increased share.

Product

Product doesn't explain it; Marks & Spencer's most fashionable new ranges, Salon Rose and Wild Hearts,[42] were launched two years prior to the campaign.[43] During the campaign, a new Salon Rose execution was released to replace a Wild Hearts execution that had sold out. Sales on that Salon Rose item rose four-fold the week the advert appeared.

Marks & Spencer didn't need to change its *range* – it was already fantastic – it needed to change *perceptions* about its range.

Place

Marks & Spencer lingerie did not gain footage in 2003, and there was no new distribution. Calculations are therefore all like for like.

The other thing that could have impacted on results was the in-store experience. Although the 'Lingerie Heaven' idea has set a strong direction for how the in-store experience will change in the future, in the timescales there was little room for manoeuvre in 2003 beyond changing the cardboard POS to reflect the advertising.

CONCLUSION

The 'Lingerie Heaven' campaign was responsible for a 1.3 percentage point increase in market share that represented £40.9m in value. It paid for itself five times over. The majority of the growth came from the core target of 35–45s, with whom share is still increasing.[44]

By tapping into a powerful insight about the way that women related to lingerie, 'Lingerie Heaven' gave new breadth to perceptions of Marks & Spencer lingerie and successfully increased the size and value of lingerie baskets bought in Marks & Spencer (Figure 17).

37. Source: FashionTrak 52, w/e 19 November 2003.
38. Source: FashionTrak 52, w/e 19 November 2003.
39. Source: Marks & Spencer sales analysis January–December 2003 vs January–December 2002.
40. The bra promotion ran in April 2002 and 2003, and offered £5 when two bras were purchased from a selected range.
41. As described earlier, basket size decreased during 2002.
42. See note 15.
43. In 2000 and 2001 respectively.
44. Up by 2.8 percentage points at the time of writing (April 2004). Source: FashionTrak, April 2003–April 2004.

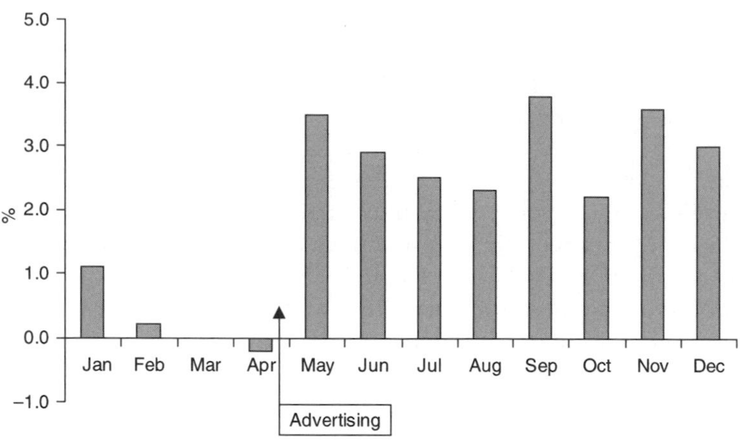

Figure 17: *Monthly average basket size increase 2003 vs 2002 (%)*

It is a powerful example of the role that advertising has to play in fashion retail: a clear demonstration of the fact that good product doesn't just sell itself, and that there is a necessary role for advertising in shifting perceptions of what a retailer has to offer.

SILVER

15

Police Officer Recruitment

How thinking locally put Hertfordshire Constabulary on the national stage

Principal authors: Helen Rosethorn, Marc Rothman, John Wardle, Cathy Reid and Martin Homent, Bernard Hodes Group

EDITOR'S SUMMARY

Public service recruitment is hard, especially in the south-east of England where house prices and salaries are mismatched. The Hertfordshire Constabulary had the further pressure both of boundary changes increasing the size of its constituency and 'competition' from neighbouring forces, especially the Metropolitan Police, for the same candidates.

Casting its net wide in terms of prospects, but narrowly in terms of regionality, the Hertfordshire Constabulary's campaign successfully generated over 2000 local applications (while the national 'Could You?' campaign generated just 61 in Hertfordshire over the same period).

A scale of effect that was rooted in both a more inclusive, less forbidding recruitment message and tone, and media implementation that meant the campaign was quite simply impossible to ignore. The 'For a life less predictable' campaign appeared in libraries, doctors' surgeries and shopping centres as well as traditional media, and grew applications from fewer than 50 a month to a peak of over 300.

Quality of applicant was also enhanced over the period, so that the recruitment target of 400 officers, originally targeted to be reached by 2007, was in fact reached by March 2003.

Specific campaign activity targeted at women, meanwhile, resulted in the growth in numbers of women police officers in Hertfordshire outstripping that of any other region.

Finally, the recent improvement in Hertfordshire's crime statistics (in the form of increased arrests and detections) is related directly to the recruitment of new officers. In all, then, an admirable case of highly localised, creative and effective recruitment campaigning.

INTRODUCTION

By the end of the 1990s police recruitment had become a high-profile national issue in the UK. Fewer and fewer people were coming forward for recruitment and the McPherson Report on the Stephen Lawrence Enquiry had left public confidence in the Police at an all-time low. In 2000 the Home Office launched the Crime Fighting Fund and set itself the target of recruiting an additional 9000 officers nationwide by 2003. A heavy-weight national recruitment initiative was unveiled under the banner of the 'I couldn't, could you?' advertising campaign. The workings and effect of this national campaign are well documented in the 2002 IPA Effectiveness Awards.[1]

This paper focuses on the local situation in Hertfordshire where the recruitment crisis faced by the police was even more acute. A combination of local circumstances meant that the increase in the recruitment rate required was more dramatic and the conditions for recruitment were tougher. As a result, the national recruitment campaign was never going to be sufficient for Hertfordshire's needs and additional local activity was a necessity.

This paper shows that the local campaign led to an extraordinary turnaround in recruitment rates that put Hertfordshire in the national spotlight. The achievements in Hertfordshire have won many awards[2] as well as attracting the attention and praise of the Home Office. The methods used to achieve these results have been deemed best practice by Her Majesty's Inspectorate for the Constabulary and recommended to police forces across the country.

> 'Hertfordshire has a particularly impressive record on recruitment ... particularly for a force of that size.'
>
> John Denham MP, Minister of State for the Home Office,
> House of Common Debate on Law and Order, 24 February 2003

THE BACKGROUND: WHY HERTFORDSHIRE REQUIRED A LOCAL APPROACH TO POLICE RECRUITMENT

The national police recruitment campaign was high profile and highly effective. The 'I couldn't, could you?' campaign worked on the principle that there were sufficient numbers of people interested in the police but that not enough of these people were acting on their interest. In the words of M&C Saatchi, the agency behind the national campaign, the task nationally was not 'more to consider' but 'people to consider more'.[3] In Hertfordshire this approach was not sufficient. Various factors conspired to make the targets for recruitment too high and the conditions for recruitment too tough.

1. 'How thinking negatively ended the negative thinking' won a Silver award in the IPA Effectiveness Awards, 2002. The paper demonstrates the clear and immediate effect of this activity on police officer recruitment across the country.
2. These included in 2003 the CIPD Award for Effectiveness in Recruitment Advertising and the Grand Prix Award for best overall work.
3. The full quote from M&C Saatchi's award-winning IPA police recruitment paper (2002) explains the situation thus: 'The task isn't "more to consider" but people to "consider more" ... Considerers tend to have thought about a career with the police only vaguely and without serious commitment. Typically it is something that they've mooted for a while but done nothing about. Advertising needed to force them to consider the police more actively and in more detail, ultimately making a decision one way or the other.'

Recruitment targets in Hertfordshire

As mentioned above, the Home Office had announced in 2000 that an additional 9000 officers were to be recruited nationwide. This target was allocated across the country with Hertfordshire Constabulary being required to recruit 107 of these officers. However, in Hertfordshire this requirement fell on top of a necessity for incremental recruitment resulting from county border changes.

In 1998 the Home Office had announced border changes that would increase Hertfordshire Constabulary's constituency by 157,000. These changes came into effect in April 2000 requiring the Constabulary to find an additional 294 officers by 2002.[4] In combination this meant that Hertfordshire Constabulary had to recruit more than 400 additional officers within three years.

Recruitment conditions in Hertfordshire

Even in 1999, before new higher targets were introduced, Hertfordshire Constabulary was unable to attract sufficient numbers of recruits. By 2000 actual recruitment was on a marked downward trend (see Figure 1). In order to get to target strength the number of recruits per five-weekly intake needed to be increased to 25 but the actual average intake had dropped to nine. At this run rate the Constabulary estimated that it would take until at least 2007 to reach target strength, a delay that would have unacceptable consequences for local policing.

The situation continued to deteriorate throughout 2000 and did not pick up despite heavy-weight national police recruitment activity from the summer onwards. In fact the situation was so bad that in October 2000 the planned intake had to be cancelled due to a lack of applicants.

Although the police service was experiencing difficulty in maintaining its target strength throughout the country, the particularly tough situation faced by Hertfordshire Constabulary was, in large part, due to its proximity to London and the consequent local labour market conditions.

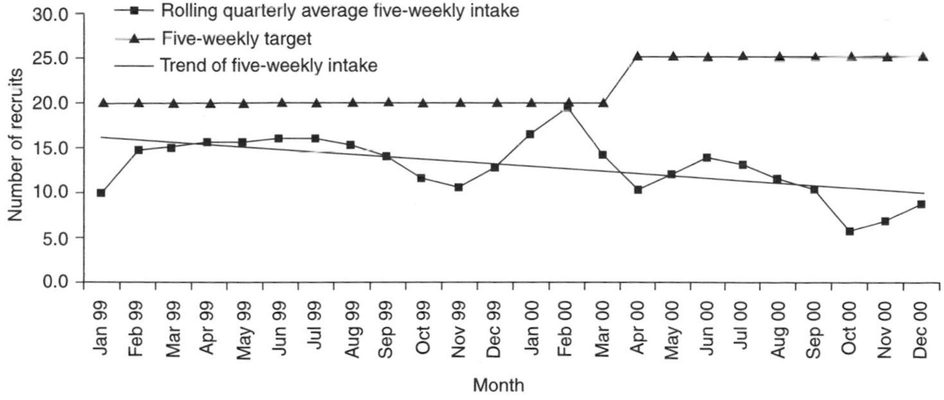

Figure 1: *Five-weekly intakes, January 1999 to December 2000*

4. Hertfordshire Constabulary was offered Metropolitan Police secondees for a two-year period to help cover the target strength shortfall that resulted from border changes. These secondees would be with the force until 2002, after which time the force needed to have recruited the necessary numbers.

Local labour market conditions

Hertfordshire is, on average, a 30-minute commute from central London.[5] As a result, unemployment in the county was amongst the lowest in the country in 2000, while housing costs were amongst the highest. Encouraging people to start a career in policing – or to transfer from other areas – was an uphill struggle given starting salaries in comparison to the cost of living (Table 1).

TABLE 1: HOUSE PRICES FOR NEW OFFICERS, HERTFORDSHIRE AND SURROUNDING COUNTIES, 2000

Policing area	Probationer	New officer	Officer with five years' service	Average house price (Q3, 2000)	Affordable house price* (for a new officer)	Difference (%)
Met						
Basic	16,635	19,713	21,609			
London allowance	4,000	4,000	4,000			
Total	20,635	23,713	25,609	170,485	99,595	171**
Hertfordshire						
Basic	16,635	19,713	21,609	164,689	82,795	199
Bedfordshire						
Basic	16,635	19,713	21,609	100,664	82,795	122
Essex						
Basic	16,635	19,713	21,609	119,538	82,795	144
Cambridgeshire						
Basic	16,635	19,713	21,609	93,441	82,795	113
Buckinghamshire						
Basic	16,635	19,713	21,609	170,758	82,795	206

Notes: house prices from the Halifax Price Index

* Assuming the buyer's borrowing capacity based on an average income multiple of 4 and a deposit of 5%

** For a new officer working for the Met and living in Hertfordshire this differential drops to 165%

Competition from the Metropolitan Police

Even if people were interested in a career in the police service, they were likely to consider the Met rather than their local force due to differences in starting salaries. The salary for a new officer in the Metropolitan Police was £4000 higher than in the Hertfordshire Constabulary and with regional weighting added in April 2000 this differential rose to £6000.

The need for a local approach

With both higher targets and tougher conditions Hertfordshire Constabulary could not rely on merely getting those people who were already interested in the police to 'consider more'. Rather it was going to have to get 'more to consider' – an awful lot more. The Constabulary would have to attract people who had never considered a career in the police. And, it would have to do so without jeopardising the quality of applicants.

5. For example, Welwyn Garden City to London Kings Cross = 30 minutes, while journey times from Potters Bar and Hatfield are even less. Source: National Rail Enquiries.

THE APPROACH: MAKING IT LOCAL

The approach adopted in Hertfordshire was born out of the Constabulary's conviction that policing in its part of the country could be made to appeal to a far wider audience because it was very different to policing in other areas. Hertfordshire did not present the grim inner-city challenge presented by typical police recruitment literature and media stereotypes. Rather it offered a chance to be involved in a genuinely communitarian role with high resulting job satisfaction.

The Constabulary wanted to find a way of expressing the essence and appeal of this role in a language and via media that would get directly to the heart of the community it served. In so doing it wanted to attract members of this community who would never have responded to conventional police recruitment and who would enable the force to be more representative of the population it served.

In 2000 the Constabulary's personnel services manager, Gail Boulter, conducted a review of all previous recruitment marketing materials. Up until 2000 Hertfordshire had used generic, centrally produced recruitment literature provided by the Home Office. While informative, this material was not designed to convey the distinct nature of policing within Hertfordshire. Neither did it do anything to sell the particular benefits of working for the Hertfordshire Constabulary as opposed to any other.

Gail believed that it was vital for new recruitment marketing to reflect this nature and took the decision to appoint a recruitment marketing agency to develop and manage a new, locally developed and driven campaign. Bernard Hodes Group (BHG) was appointed in October 2000 with a brief to maximise the appeal of policing within Hertfordshire and to attract high volumes of high-quality applicants to the Constabulary.

Three elements of BHG's response to this brief were central to its success:

1. A research programme that enabled BHG to identify the essence and appeal of policing in Hertfordshire.
2. Creative thinking that found a way of expressing this essence and appeal in a language that accessed the heart of the Hertfordshire community.
3. Integrated media usage that enabled this language to be heard and acted on by the community.

RESEARCH FEEDBACK

Right from the start it was BHG's aim to build an employer brand for the force, one that conveyed the personality of the organisation and gave potential applicants an idea of what it would be like to work there. In October 2000, consultants from BHG Solutions[6] conducted a large-scale research programme amongst serving officers and external job seekers.[7] The research was designed to investigate the positives and negatives of being a police officer in Hertfordshire and to assess what

6. Solutions is the in-house strategic management consultancy arm of BHG.
7. Solutions interviewed 30 serving officers and 60 external job seekers representing a range of audiences including women, school leavers and people from ethnic minority groups.

job seekers were looking for in a career. Among people from ethnic minorities the research also sought to assess reactions to ethnicity-specific recruitment advertising. The feedback was instrumental in shaping the resulting strategy.

The research showed clearly that both the appeal to potential job seekers and the reward for serving officers of policing in Hertfordshire had very little to do with the grim challenging image presented by typical police recruitment advertising. The themes stressed again and again by officers and job seekers alike were the variety and unpredictability of the role, the satisfaction that came from being able to help the public and the opportunity for real responsibility early on in your career.

> 'You don't know what you will be doing each day.'
> Serving police officer

> 'A varied role, active and challenging, and an opportunity to give more to the county in which I reside.'
> Female job seeker

Importantly, the research also indicated that these themes enabled the Hertfordshire Constabulary to have a broader appeal than the neighbouring Metropolitan Force. In contrast to the Met, Hertfordshire was seen as a very friendly, modern and progressive force to be part of.

> 'Nice area, small constabulary so you would feel a bit closer to the people you work for and the community you work in.'
> Female job seeker

> 'Hertfordshire is well known as an extremely friendly force.'
> Male job seeker

> 'You don't have the extra stress of the Metropolitan Police Force.'
> Female job seeker

CREATIVE STRATEGY

The creative idea arose directly from an observation made by one of the officers in the focus groups that the variety and range of tasks a police officer in Hertfordshire would be expected to fulfil in any one day made the job like no other. The theme of 'No ordinary career' sprang directly from this and shaped all consequent creative thinking.

Individual pieces of communication focused on the specific aspects of Hertfordshire's appeal that had been clear from the research such as the opportunity to contribute to community life, the benefits of a structured career path and the satisfaction of being part of a team, but all within the theme of 'No ordinary career'.

The creative work also sought to challenge the perception that policing is dangerous by portraying officers in everyday situations, thereby reflecting the reality of the role in Hertfordshire. To contrast with the national 'I couldn't, could you?' campaign, the creative aimed to create a 'personality' for the force that was friendly, approachable and (where appropriate) light-hearted. An important part of the strategy was to position the role as an alternative to office work for 'nine to fivers' who may not have considered policing as a career option. Both the brochure and cinema ad helped further this aim (Figures 2–6). From November 2002, the creative was refreshed with a new expression of the core theme: 'A life less predictable' (Figures 7–13).

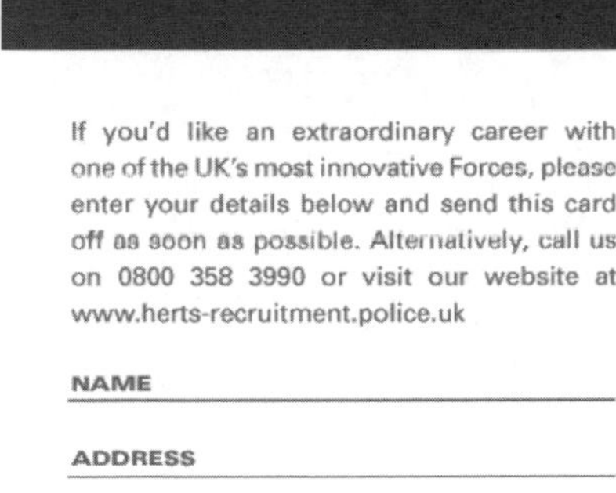

If you'd like an extraordinary career with one of the UK's most innovative Forces, please enter your details below and send this card off as soon as possible. Alternatively, call us on 0800 358 3990 or visit our website at www.herts-recruitment.police.uk

NAME

ADDRESS

Please tick which area you are interested in.

☐ POLICE OFFICER ☐ SPECIAL CONSTABLE

2

Freepost
Recruitment Assessment Unit
Police Headquarters
Stanborough Road
Welwyn Garden City
AL8 6BR

NO ORDINARY CAREER

Figure 2: *No ordinary career: postcard for cinema foyers*

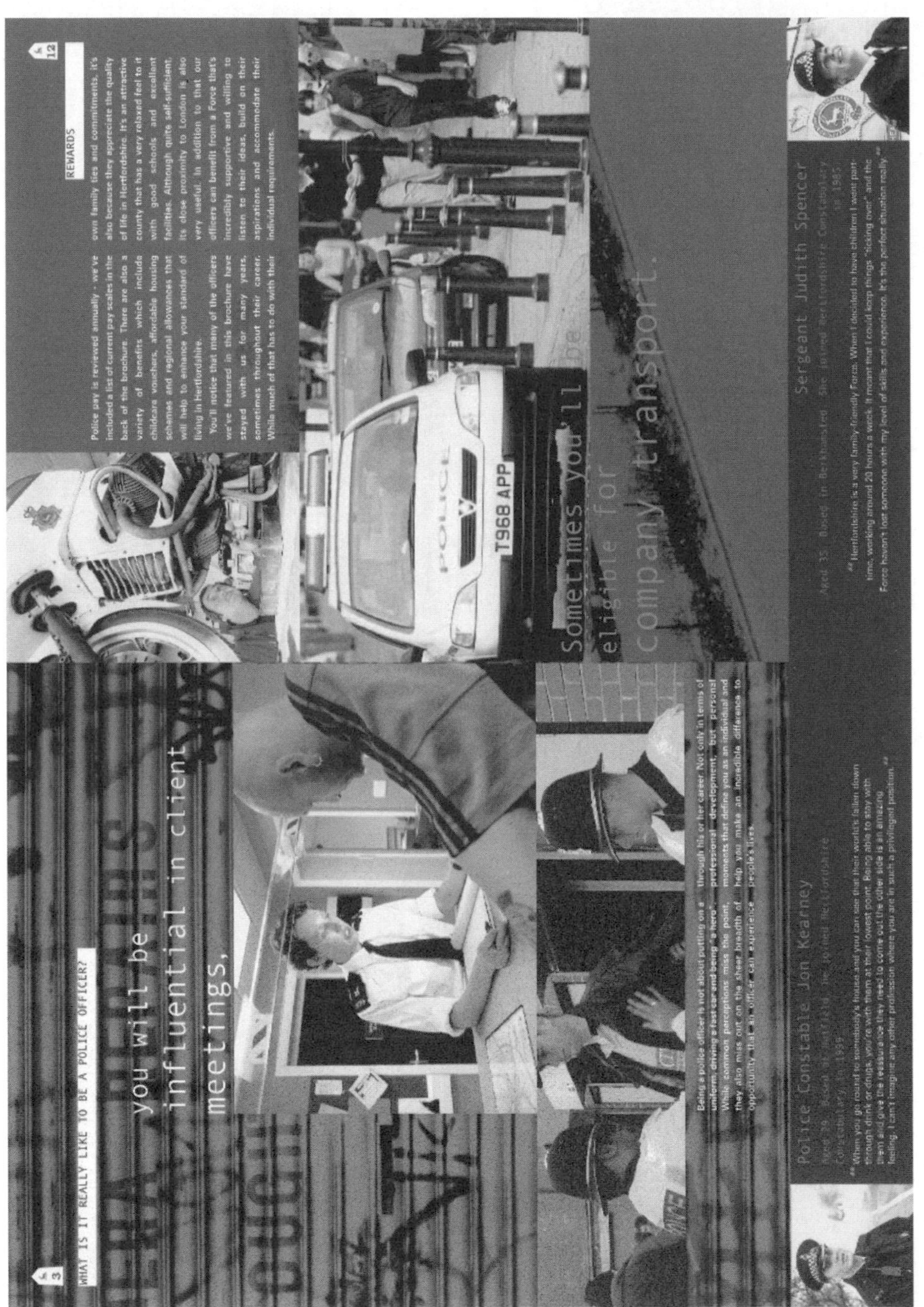

Figure 3: No *ordinary career: recruitment brochure*

SILVER

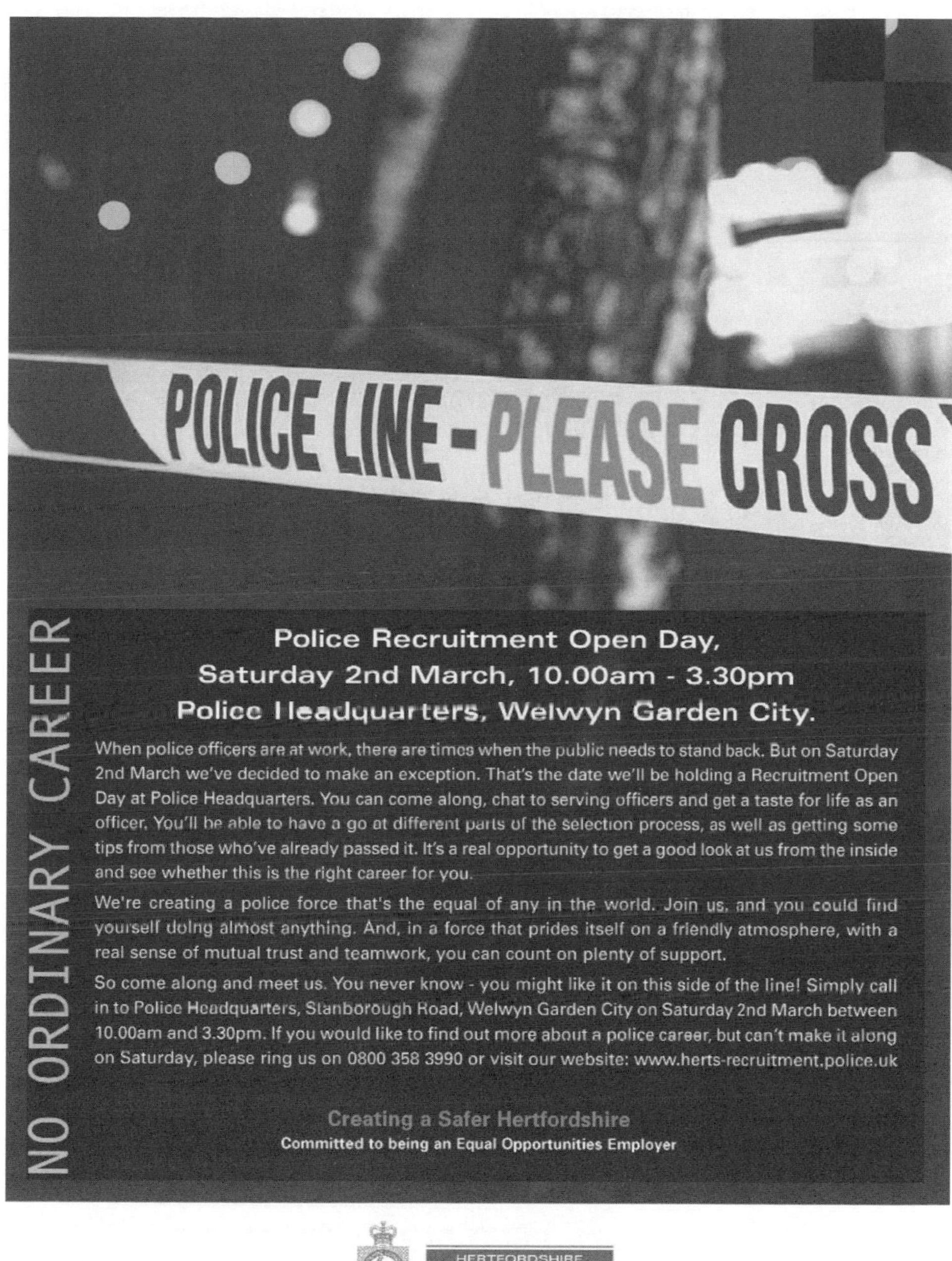

Figure 4: *No ordinary career: poster for open day*

RECRUITMENT OPEN DAY

POLICE HEADQUARTERS, WELWYN GARDEN CITY
Saturday 24th November
10.00am - 3.30pm

It's not difficult to spot police officers. But now you can chat to them and ask questions as well. Hertfordshire Constabulary are holding a Recruitment Open Day where you can meet serving officers to find out whether a career as a police officer might suit you. They'll share their experiences and talk about the qualities that you'll need to make the grade.

It's also a chance to discover what's involved in the recruitment process and even to try out some of the tests we use, such as the grip test, the standing jump or the written assessment. You can also get some top tips from those who've passed the assessment process.

We're one of the friendliest forces around, with a unique sense of mutual trust and teamwork. Come and see for yourself. Our Open Day takes place from 10.00am – 3.30pm on Saturday 24th November at Police Headquarters in Stanborough Road, Welwyn Garden City. Just turn up on the day – we'll look forward to seeing you.

If you can't make it on that date, but would like to know more, call us on 0800 358 3990, e-mail: policerec@herts.police.uk or visit our website: www.herts-recruitment.police.uk

NO ORDINARY CAREER

Creating a safer Hertfordshire

Committed to being an Equal Opportunities Employer

HERTFORDSHIRE CONSTABULARY

Figure 5: *No ordinary career: postcard for open day*

Figure 6: *No ordinary career: poster*

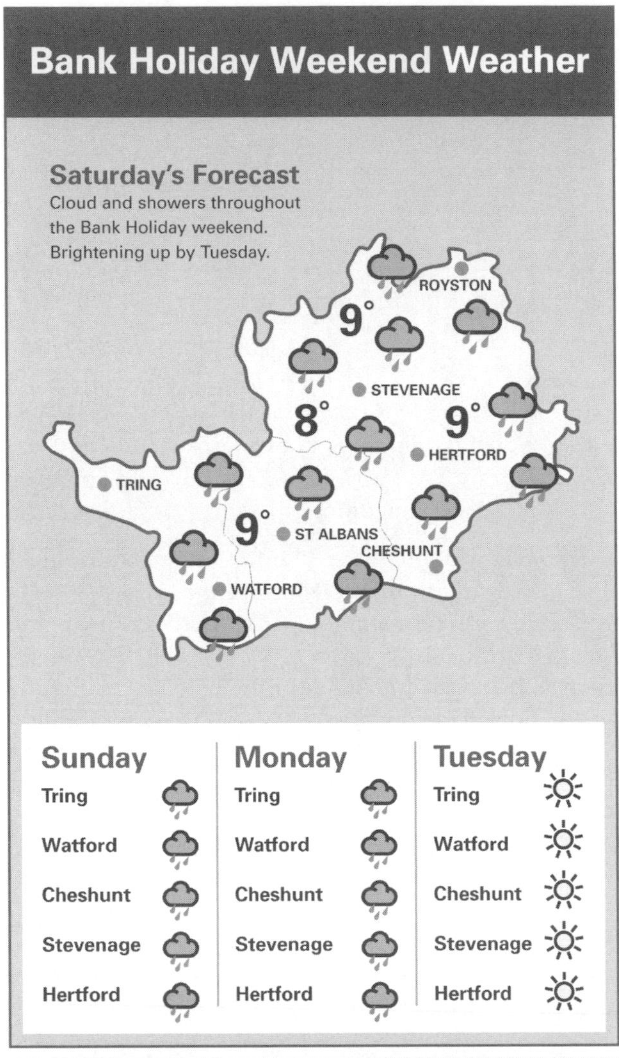

Figure 7: *For a life less predictable: advertisement in local press appearing one day before bank holiday*

Figure 8: *For a life less predictable: local advert*

Figure 9: *For a life less predictable: football stadium steps*

For a life less predictable, become a **POLICE OFFICER.**

Please call **0800 358 3990** or visit www.herts-recruitment.police.uk

Figure 10: *For a life less predictable: mail drop on 14 February 2003*

Figure 11: *For a life less predictable: Christmas giveaway in local shopping centres*

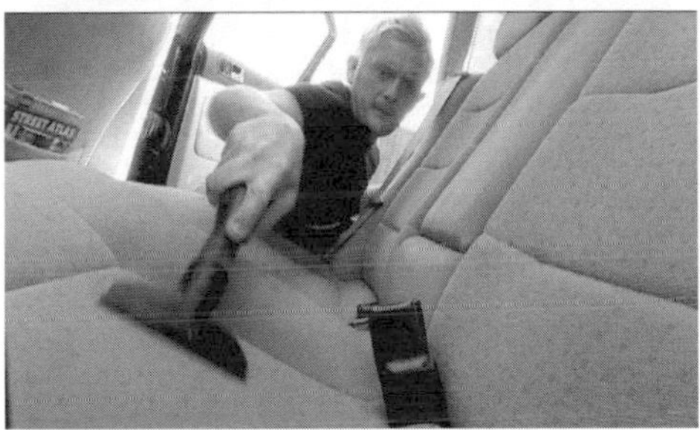

Figure 12: *For a life less predictable: cinema commercial*

HOME | ACCESSIBILITY | APPLY NOW | SITE MAP | CONTACT

Welcome to a life less predictable

ABOUT US | NEWS & EVENTS | POLICE OFFICERS | SPECIAL CONSTABLES | POLICE COMMUNITY SUPPORT OFFICERS | POLICE STAFF | COMMUNITY | DIVERSITY | FUN STUFF

Welcome

On this site, you'll find a wealth of information to help you decide whether you want to apply to join us, either as a **regular police officer**, a **special constable**, a **police community support officer**, or as a member of our **police staff**. If you wish you can even make an application online or request an application pack to be posted to you.

If you're keen to achieve something this worthwhile in an environment that will constantly encourage you to make the most of your abilities, you're looking in the right area.

Jobs

Communications Operator

News Highlights

Police Recruitment Open Days

HOME | ACCESSIBILITY | APPLY NOW | SITE MAP | CONTACT

Police Officers a life less predictable

ABOUT US | NEWS & EVENTS | POLICE OFFICERS | SPECIAL CONSTABLES | POLICE COMMUNITY SUPPORT OFFICERS | POLICE STAFF | COMMUNITY | DIVERSITY | FUN STUFF

Training | Pay | Profiles | Application Process | FAQ | Apply Now | Fitness Test CD-ROM

Home > Police officers > **Apply Now**

Apply Now

You can now complete your application online via the Police Could You website, or request a printed application pack to be posted out to you.

We'll make an initial assessment of your eligibility, and make contact with you soon after.

You can find more information on the application process page. If you require any further help, please telephone our Recruitment team on **01707 354203**. However you decide to apply, we're looking forward to hearing from you. For many applicants it's the first step along the road to a fascinating, rewarding and exceptionally varied career.

Apply online now

Importantly, if you're making your application online be sure to list Hertfordshire Constabulary first as the force you would prefer to apply to. This selection is made in Section 1 About You of the online application.

To receive an application form by post, request an application pack.

Tell a friend about this page

Home > Police officers > **Apply Now**

""I think it would be a good career for anyone""

PC Elvett Phipps

© Hertfordshire Constabulary 2003 | main Herts Police site | Privacy Statement | back to top ^

Figure 13: *For a life less predictable: website*

MEDIA STRATEGY

The message about policing in Hertfordshire had to impact on people who would not normally consider a career in policing. It needed to interrupt people as they were going about their everyday lives in Hertfordshire. The theme of unpredictability therefore extended into the media, with advertising being placed in media where people would not expect to see messages from their local police force.

The consequent media schedule involved a broad use of channels, some expected but many never before used for recruitment advertising. Press adverts appeared in Hertfordshire's local newspapers. Print work has included brochures and direct mail. Posters have appeared in bus shelters, train stations, schools, colleges and other community facilities such as libraries, shopping centres and GPs' surgeries.

Thirty- and 40-second radio adverts (typically in conjunction with open days) have aired on Chiltern FM, Heartbeat FM, Mercury FM and Heart 106.2. A 30-second cinema advert appeared across the county's screens in April 2001, followed by a second execution in summer 2003.

The activity charts (Figure 14) show the spread of media with the notable bursts of activity around open days, which were particularly successful in encouraging people who had not considered policing as a career to find out more in an engaging and exploratory way.

Innovative media use was central to the strategy: the promise of a career full of surprises was strengthened by the appearance of recruitment adverts in unexpected places – on TV pages and the sports section in newspapers, for example. Particularly noteworthy was a small advertisement about the 'predictably bad' bank holiday weather, which appeared in the TV and weather section of local papers (Figure 7). Further executions appeared on football stadium steps at the grounds of Watford FC and Stevenage FC (Figure 9).

	Media Plan 2001												Media Plan 2002												Media Plan 2003		
	Jan	Feb	Mar	Apr	May	Jun	Jul	Aug	Sep	Oct	Nov	Dec	Jan	Feb	Mar	Apr	May	Jun	Jul	Aug	Sep	Oct	Nov	Dec	Jan	Feb	Mar
Local advertising	•	•	•	•	•	•	•	•	•	•	•	•	•	•	•	•	•	•	•	•	•	•	•	•	•	•	•
Specialist advertising	•		•	•	•	•	•	•	•		•	•	•							•	•	•	•		•		•
Diversity advertising			•					•		•	•	•			•	•	•	•	•	•	•	•	•	•	•		
Radio			•		•				•		•			•	•			•			•		•				•
Open Days			•		•				•		•				•			•			•		•				•
Job Fairs									•												•		•		•		
Regional TV and Home TV								•	•																		
Recruitment Web site			•	•	•	•	•	•	•	•	•	•	•	•	•	•	•	•	•	•	•	•	•	•	•	•	•
Fitness CD Rom																						•	•	•	•	•	•
Public Transport advertising					•	•	•	•	•	•	•	•	•	•	•	•	•	•	•	•	•	•	•	•	•	•	•
Local football ground advertising	•	•	•	•	•																						•
Cinema				•	•												•	•									
Posters in libraries, doctors' surgeries etc.	•	•	•	•	•	•	•	•	•	•	•	•	•	•	•	•	•	•	•	•	•	•	•	•	•	•	•

Figure 14: *Media activity*

A bespoke recruitment website, linked to the Hertfordshire Constabulary website, was built and launched in March 2001. All advertisements and materials encouraged people to visit the site: www.herts-recruitment.police.uk (Figure 13).

RESULTS

As set out earlier in this paper, Hertfordshire estimated that it would not be able to recruit the additional 400 officers required until 2007. In fact this target was more than met by March 2003.[8]

Figure 15 shows how recruitment rose rapidly throughout 2001 to reach the required target of 25 recruits every five weeks by the end of that year. The five-weekly intake target was increased to 30 in 2002 in order to reach target strength sooner. Hertfordshire was able to recruit at close to this target throughout the next two years.

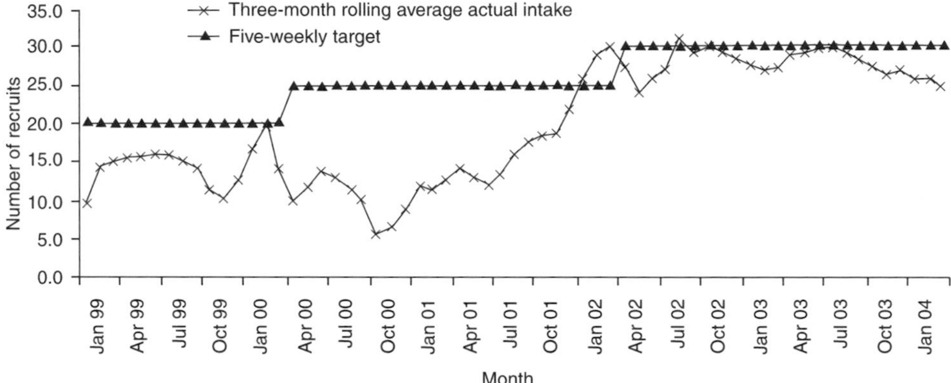

Figure 15: *Number of new recruits per five-weekly intake, January 1999 to March 2003*

HOW CAN WE BE SURE THAT THESE RESULTS ARE DUE TO THE ACTIVITY IN HERTFORDSHIRE?

The use of media with unique response mechanics enables us to point to a clear and direct link between applications and the campaign in Hertfordshire. Response to the campaign could only be effected via two mechanics, a dedicated telephone line or a unique web address. These response mechanics were separate to the mechanics used for the national campaign and were only made known to potential applicants via the local communications activity.

Figure 16 shows the marked upward trend in returned applications via this mechanic. To appear in this data a candidate would have to have called the phone number or visited the website, received the full literature and application pack, completed it and returned it. It shows the quality response to the campaign, not just

8. In actual fact 527 officers were recruited between October 2000 and March 2004 – this figure covered both the additional officer target and recruits to compensate for attrition.

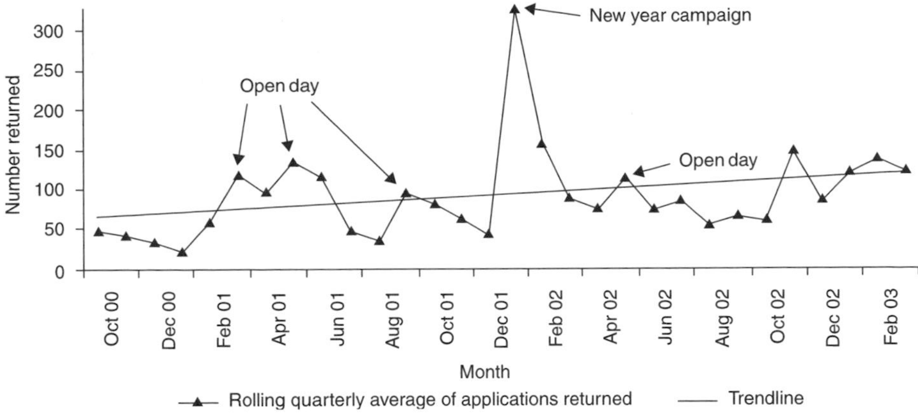

Figure 16: *Number of application packs returned*

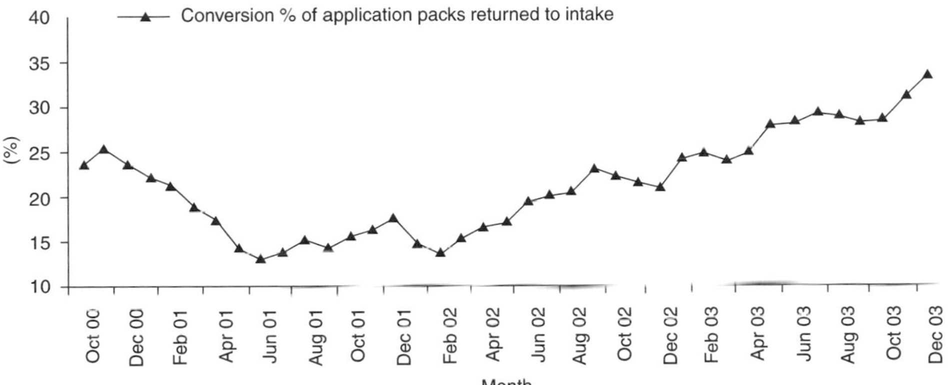

Figure 17: *Conversion rate of application packs returned to intake*

the volume response, and indicates that the campaign was reaching and attracting serious applicants.

Figure 17 shows the conversion rate of application packs returned to intake and illustrates how the campaign gathered strength over its course, attracting increasing numbers of candidates who were able to get through the full application procedure.

Hertfordshire is therefore able to offer clear evidence that its activity was having effect. A cynical reader, however, may argue that increased interest in working for the Hertfordshire Constabulary was the result of the national police recruitment campaign that was running from August 2000 onwards. This view does not stand up to scrutiny.

As highlighted at the start of this study, the national police recruitment campaign has already been the subject of an IPA study. The clear and rapid response to this campaign is well documented. The study draws attention to the immediate turnaround in police recruitment that took place from the summer of 2000 onwards, as set out in Figure 18.[9]

9. This figure is directly reproduced from the 2002 IPA Effectiveness Awards paper. The figures have been double-checked against the original Home Office Police Service Strength figures.

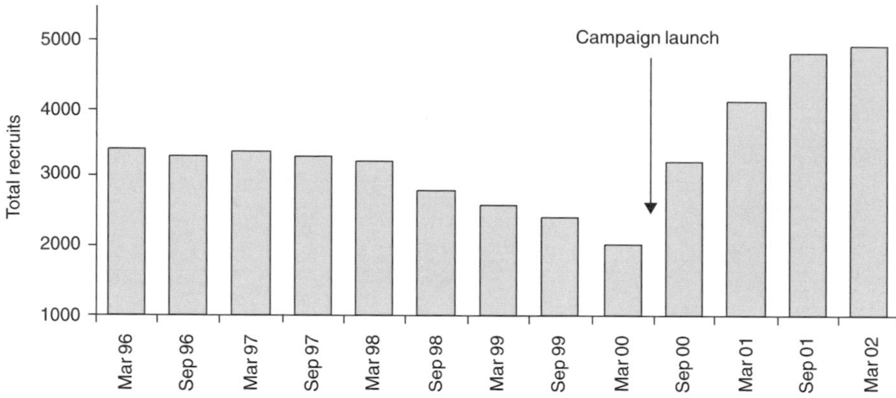

Figure 18: *Reproduction of M&C Saatchi 2002 figure 2: uplift in police recruits graph (six-monthly totals)*
Source: Home Office Police Service Strength

This pattern of response at a national level is in clear contrast to the pattern in Hertfordshire where recruitment stayed at an all-time low throughout the autumn of 2000. In fact the situation was so bad in October 2000 that the planned intake had to be cancelled.[10] It is implausible that the national campaign, which had such an immediate and strong effect, should have been lagged in its effect in Hertfordshire.

However, there is clearer evidence yet that the results in Hertfordshire were attributable to local and not national activity. As set out at the start of this section, the national and the local campaigns had entirely separate response mechanics. If a potential applicant was attracted by the national campaign he or she would apply via the national call centre or website and then be passed on to the Hertfordshire Constabulary if they selected to apply to that force.

Hertfordshire Constabulary kept clear and separate records of the applicants that came to it via this source. This data shows that in 2001 only 11 applications[11] were made to the Hertfordshire Constabulary as a result of the national campaign, increasing to 50 during 2002 (Figure 19). This compares to 932 applications in 2001 and 1355 in 2002 via the local campaign.

HOW CAN WE QUANTIFY THE FINANCIAL VALUE OF HERTFORDSHIRE'S CAMPAIGN?

It is always difficult to quantify truly the financial value of a public-sector recruitment campaign. Previous IPA cases of this nature have compared their costs and results against various assumptions about the costs and likely returns to alternative methods of recruitment such as opening more recruitment centres, paying higher salaries, paying a joining bonus, and so on.[12]

10. Indeed it is not difficult to infer from this that the national campaign may well have had the effect of attracting potential recruits away from Hertfordshire in favour of the Metropolitan Force, which was a prime beneficiary of the national campaign.
11. Note these figures refer to applications *not* recruits. In actual fact the average conversion rate experienced in 2001 and 2002 was one in five, indicating that Hertfordshire would have hired no more than two recruits from the national campaign in 2001 and no more than ten from this campaign in 2002.
12. See, for example, National Police Recruitment campaign 2002, soldier recruitment 1996.

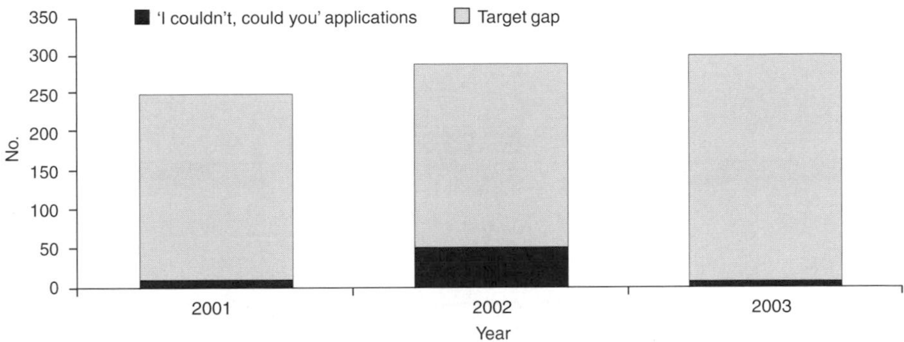

Figure 19: *'I couldn't, could you' applications vs target intake*

The most pertinent comparison to make in this case would be the cost of equalising salaries with the neighbouring Metropolitan Police Force. As set out in the introductory sections of this paper, the fact that a Hertfordshire-based recruit to the police could earn £6000 more by applying to the neighbouring Metropolitan Force was one of the big barriers to recruitment faced by Hertfordshire. Suffice to say that the actual costs of the Hertfordshire recruitment campaign designed, in large part, to overcome this salary discrepancy, were a tiny fraction of the more than £12m per year that it would have cost to ratchet up recruitment by matching London Police salaries.[13]

THE BROADER BENEFITS OF THE CAMPAIGN

Whilst efficiency of public spend is undoubtedly a key objective of any public-sector initiative, the true benefits are much broader and go far beyond financial measures. The full and broader effects of the recruitment campaign in Hertfordshire have been very significant.

Setting the conditions for consensus policing in Hertfordshire

A key objective of Hertfordshire was to recruit candidates who would not have responded to conventional police recruitment advertising and who would enable the force to be more representative of the community they served. Like all police forces, Hertfordshire Constabulary has to reach Home Office set targets for the representation of people from ethnic minority groups. In addition, Hertfordshire sets its own target that 50% of its police officers should ideally be female. The Constabulary saw the achievement of these targets as vital to being able to provide modern, consensus-based community policing.

In addition to adopting a tone that was more welcoming for a more diverse audience, the campaign was able to incorporate specific messages to women and to ethnic minority communities. Adverts written specifically for these audiences appeared in specialist publications such as *Cosmopolitan*, *She*, *Black History*, *KAL* and *The Voice* (Figures 20–23).

13. The total Hertfordshire Constabulary numbers more than 2000, hence the figure of £12m.

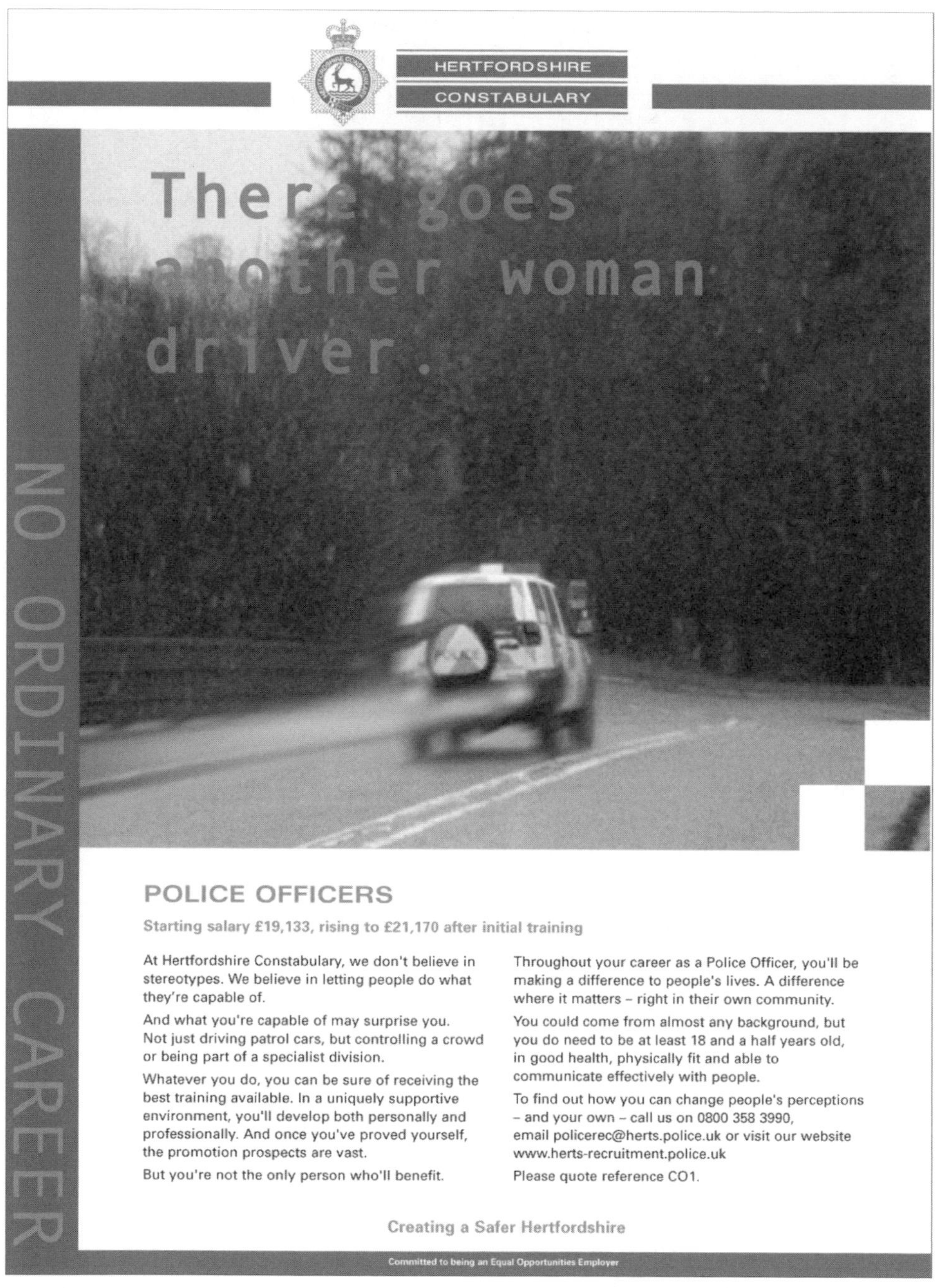

Figure 20: *No ordinary career: advertisement in* Cosmopolitan

THERE'S ONLY ONE THING STOPPING YOU FROM BECOMING A POLICE OFFICER.

PERCEPTIONS.

Policing's not a black or white thing. It's not a male or female thing. It's a community thing.

At Hertfordshire Constabulary, we want our force to be as diverse as the community it serves. Everyone has a contribution to make, regardless of their background.

And there's something else you may not know. It's a great place to build a career.

You could work with the community – with schools or citizens' groups, for example – or specialise in a specific area, like fraud or organised crime.

But it's not just about what you can give us. It's about what we can do for you.

As a police officer, you'll develop skills you never knew you had. Confidence, for example, and the ability to handle yourself in almost any situation. Most of all there's the huge variety. This is the kind of career where you never know what's around the corner. You could be walking the beat one minute, dealing with serious crime the next.

It's not easy. It'll often make demands on your resources, physically, mentally, and sometimes even emotionally. But you'll never have to cope alone. There are support structures in place, both formal and informal, that are there for you whenever you need them.

And Hertfordshire is a uniquely friendly force. Everyone will know your name – from the Chief Superintendent on down – and your ideas will always be listened to. You'll find you make friends for life.

So if you thought being a police officer wasn't for you, is it time to change your perceptions?

For more information about joining Hertfordshire Constabulary, call 0800 358 3990, e-mail policerec@herts.pnn.police.uk or visit our website at www.herts-recruitment.police.uk

Please quote ref: EID1.

Figure 21: *For a life less predictable: advertisement in* Black History

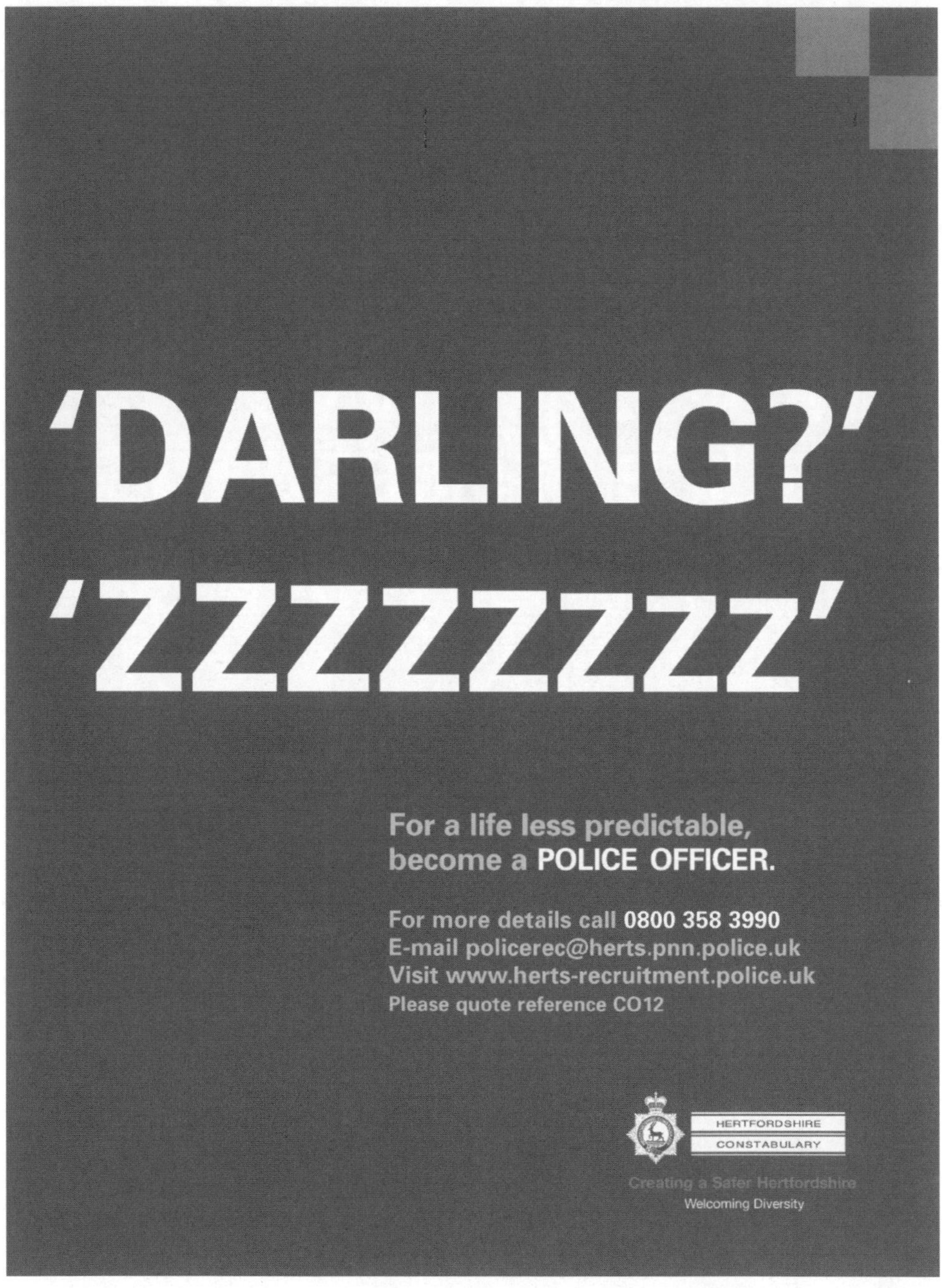

Figure 22: *For a life less predictable: advertisement in* Cosmopolitan

DOCTOR,
LAWYER,
ACCOUNTANT.

For a life less predictable,
become a POLICE OFFICER.

When it comes to career choices, does it sometimes feel as if your mind is being made up for you?
If so, instead of conforming to your family's expectations, why not surprise them – and yourself.
As a police officer, no two days will ever be the same and you'll never know what's around the corner. You could be patrolling the streets one minute, responding to a serious incident the next.
When it comes to training, you'll develop skills you never knew you had. Physical competencies such as self-defence and controlling a suspect will go hand in hand with communication, mediation and self-assertion.
And that will really make your parents proud. To find out more, call 0800 358 3990, e-mail policerec@herts.pnn.police.uk or visit www.herts-recruitment.police.uk
Please quote reference FU02.

HERTFORDSHIRE
CONSTABULARY
Creating a Safer Hertfordshire
Welcoming Diversity

Figure 23: *For a life less predictable: advertisement in* KAL *(targeted at school leavers from ethnic minority groups)*

Over the three-year period of the campaign Hertfordshire Constabulary achieved steady growth in the representation of people from ethnic minority groups and women. In terms of female recruitment in particular, Hertfordshire Police has progressed its ranking and by March 2003 it had the second highest level of female representation amongst police officers of any force in England and Wales (Table 2 and Figures 24 and 25).

TABLE 2: GENDER/FORCE STRENGTH (%)

	2000	2001	2002	2003
West Midlands	21.5	22.2	22.8	24.1
Hertfordshire	19.4	19.6	20.7	22.3
Staffordshire	19.5	19.7	19.6	20.3
England and Wales average	16.5	17.2	17.9	18.7
MPS	15.6	15.8	16.1	17.0

* Forces shown on the basis of top three rankings in 2000 plus comparison to MPS

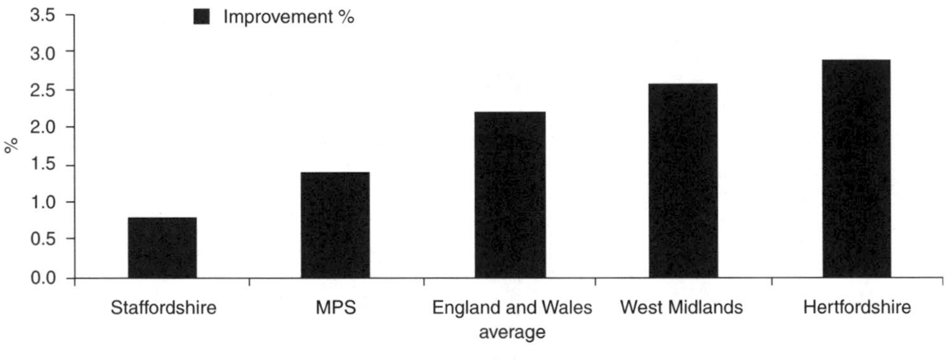

Figure 24: *Improvement in gender/force strength (2000 vs 2003)*

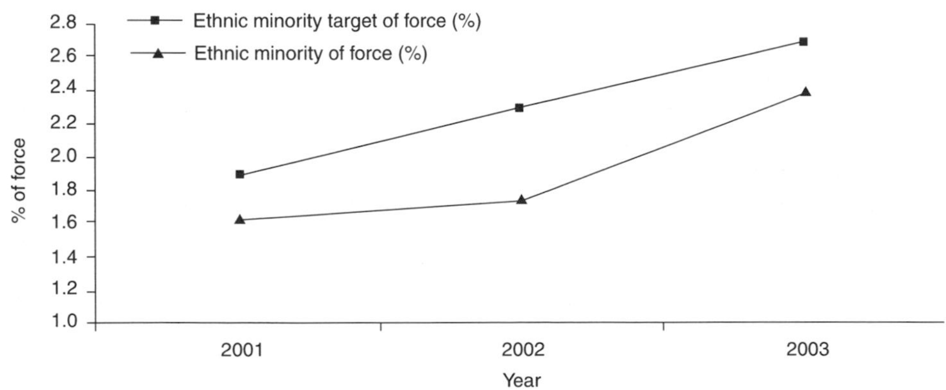

Figure 25: *Ethnic diversity of force*

Improving the fitness levels of candidates

Candidates who meet the entry requirements for new officers must also pass a fitness test. In 2002 a problem with the test started to emerge, one that was a danger to the force's gender representation targets – women were failing the test at a rate considerably higher than men. Prior to 2001 each force in England and Wales had its own fitness test. In Hertfordshire prior to 2001, 90% of male candidates passed at first attempt and 75% of female.

At the end of 2001 a new national test was introduced including elements that women candidates found particularly difficult, e.g. the agility run. The pass rates in Hertfordshire dropped to 87% for men but more worryingly to 41% for women. Hertfordshire Constabulary and BHC worked together to produce a special booklet and CD-ROM to explain to candidates facing the new national fitness test what was involved and how to prepare for it effectively (Figure 26). These materials were introduced in November 2002. Pass rates improved virtually overnight. By the beginning of 2003 they had bounced back up to 97% for men and 82% for women.[14]

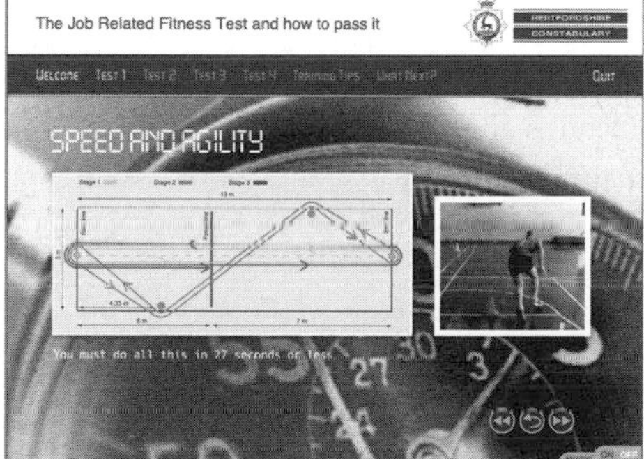

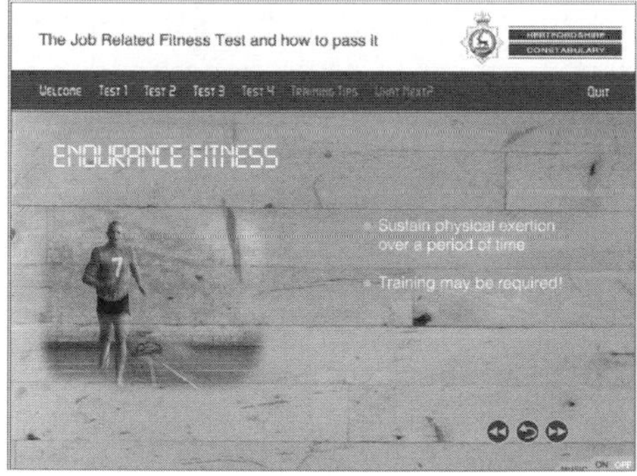

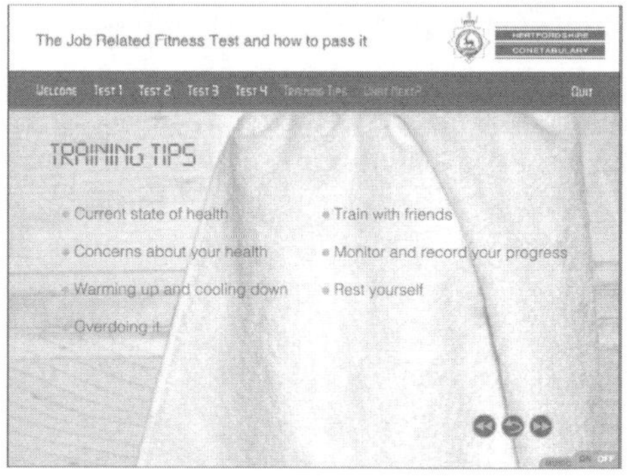

Figure 26: *Fitness test CD-ROM*

14. In April 2003 the Home Office stepped in and revisited the national fitness test as other forces were having problems with falling pass rates. There were concerns that it was operating in a discriminatory fashion and so amendments have been made. As a result both the booklet and CD-ROM were updated and redesigned in January 2004.

Easing the recruitment of support staff

While the bulk of the force's creative advertising has been aimed specifically at police officers, its 'leakage' into other target groups has been significant. Hertfordshire Constabulary has seen applications for police support roles grow significantly – for example, 999 operators and corporate administrators. This in turn has enabled Hertfordshire to improve its service to the community.

Improved service levels

By far the most important effect of the campaign has been that it has enabled Hertfordshire to improve the service levels that it provides to the community. In February 2004 Hertfordshire Constabulary reported to the Police Authority the following improvements: a 9.4% rise in arrests on the preceding year, an 18% increase in crime detection, arrests per officer up by 1.3% and detection per officer up by 9.2%. Such improvements in performance would not have been possible had the force not achieved its target strength.

POSTSCRIPT

Perhaps the most appropriate words to close this paper are those of Her Majesty's Inspectorate of Constabulary. The Inspectorate's 1999 report on Hertfordshire highlighted recruitment as a key concern for the constabulary and noted that 'without large scale transfers from the Metropolitan Police, unlikely with such a differential in salary' it would take five years for Hertfordshire to recruit the numbers necessary given county border changes.[15] And this was of course before the 2001 requirement for further recruits!

By 2002, with Hertfordshire having defied all the odds to recruit on target, the Inspectorate wrote in its report that Hertfordshire had responded to its recruitment challenge with 'a robust recruitment and retention strategy' and noted that 'Her Majesty's Inspector considers that the Force investment in professional marketing and focused recruitment techniques is good practice'. In February 2003 during a House of Commons debate on Law and Order, Home Office Minister John Denham singled out Hertfordshire Police for their achievement: 'Hertfordshire has a particularly impressive record on recruitment,' he said, 'particularly for a force of that size.'

Of course, actions speak louder than words and the postscript to this campaign that is probably the most powerful is that by March 2003 Hertfordshire Constabulary decided to curtail its recruitment advertising. It had reached its target numbers four years early with quality applicants still in the pipeline.

15. Her Majesty's Inspectorate for the Constabulary, report from the 1999 inspection of the Hertfordshire Constabulary.

SILVER
BEST SMALL BUDGET

16

Safer Travel at Night

'Know what you're getting into'

How advertising was the catalyst for a sharp reduction in rapes and sexual assaults by illegal minicab touts

Principal author: Emily James, TBWA\London
Contributing authors: Suzie Shaw, TBWA\London, and
Anni Marjoram and Harry Barlow, Greater London Authority
Media agency: Pawson Media

EDITOR'S SUMMARY

This sensitively written paper demonstrates how advertising truly served to change people's lives for the better. But the people it helped don't even know it, because it is a campaign for crime prevention.

There are an estimated 10,000 illegal minicabs in London. Hidden among this group are an unknown number of sex attackers looking for an easy way to lure vulnerable young women into their cars.

The 'Know what you're getting into' campaign helped change women's attitudes and, more importantly, behaviour in late-night situations. These behavioural shifts importantly took place at a time when people are at their least rational – after a night out, when they want to get home.

It was the catalyst within the broader 'Safer Travel at Night' initiative preventing up to 85 minicab-related rapes and sexual assaults. In effect a 22% reduction in rapes in London.

The idea extended beyond conventional media into 'point of prey' media such as clubs and bars.

While the true impact of this campaign is hard to measure, the financial saving to public services alone is £11m.

This case shows that even on a small budget it is possible to measure effects exceptionally thoroughly, and for this reason it was awarded Best Small Budget.

INTRODUCTION

Advertising is often accused of being a shallow industry. Here is an example of creative thinking in advertising that has had truly life-changing results. The people it has helped don't even know it, because this campaign was about changing the course of events to stop a crime from taking place.

To be effective in this case we needed to influence the behaviour of a specific audience, in a specific location, at a specific moment in time. To add to the difficulty of the task, our advertising had to work on an audience that was not necessarily in a fully rational state of mind.

THE PROBLEM

There are an estimated 10,000 illegal minicabs or 'touts' in London. To most of us, this represents no more than a cheap journey home after a night out, and touting may seem like a relatively harmless offence.

In reality, touting provides cover for some of the most serious crime in London. Hidden amongst this 10,000 are an unquantifiable number of serial rapists and opportunist sex attackers, seeking an easy way to lure vulnerable, young women into their car.

Approximately one-third of all stranger rapes on women in London start with the victim willingly getting into the back of their attacker's car.[1] This is the scale of the threat that illegal minicabs pose. In the year leading up to October 2002, 212 women in London were sexually assaulted by touts. Fifty-four of these women were raped.[2]

Latest Home Office Research estimates that only 13 in every 100 rapes are actually reported. This indicates that there could be more than 400 further minicab-related rapes that we are not aware of.

THE BRIEF

Background

The Mayor of London's Office identified touting as a priority in the drive to make London a safer city. However, it recognised that success would require collaboration between different organisations.

A partnership was orchestrated between key bodies involved in tackling touts. Project Sapphire, the division of the Metropolitan Police responsible for victim care and investigation of sexual assault, had simultaneously been working on a strategy to reduce assaults carried out in this way. Other organisations included Transport for London, the City of London Police and the Public Carriage Office.

The first step in what was termed the 'Safer Travel at Night' campaign centred on providing safer options for women travelling at night.

1. Source: British Crime Survey.
2. Source: Project Sapphire, the Metropolitan Police.

Transport initiatives made between 2000 and 2002 were:

- Transport for London increased the number of night bus routes by 25%
- the night tariff for black taxis was increased to encourage more black taxis to work at night
- the Public Carriage Office started to regulate the London minicab trade by licensing operators
- the Metropolitan Police set up a dedicated police unit, transport operation control unit (TOCU), tasked with tackling touts.

Despite these improvements there was no significant fall in the number of minicab-related sexual assaults (see Figure 1). It was evident that a consumer-facing campaign was required to make women aware of the risks. Effectively, women needed to be made their own protectors.

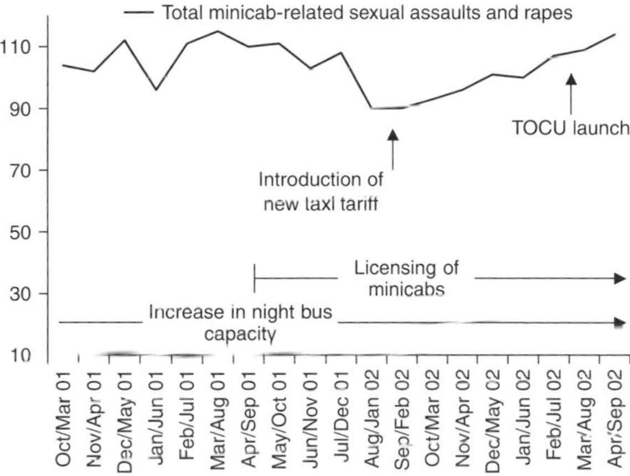

Figure 1: *Development of safe transport alternatives for women and reported illegal minicab-related sexual assaults (six-month rolling data)*
Source: Project Sapphire, the Metropolitan Police, March 2004

Brief

TBWA was approached in June 2002. Our brief was two-fold:

1. To dissuade women from using illegal minicabs by alerting them to the dangers involved.
2. To provide a rallying call for all the parties involved in tackling the crime, including the Metropolitan Police, the Public Carriage Office and Transport for London.

The advertising would carry the Transport for London telephone number, from which a caller would be able to access the phone numbers of licensed minicab offices in their local area, as well as information on night bus routes.

We planned to launch in October 2002, with on-going activity through the winter months. The key period would be in the lead-up to the Christmas party season in November and December.

As this was the first advertising of its kind, no specific targets were set. The key measure of success would be a reduction in minicab-related sexual assaults.

OUR APPROACH

Our first task was to understand why women were risking their safety with illegal minicabs. Budget for formal research was limited and, instinctively, we believed using conventional methods would be misleading. We felt women wouldn't readily admit to putting themselves in danger, even in a one-to-one session. More importantly, we thought attitudes towards illegal minicabs would be considerably different at 2am on a cold and rainy London street than in an early-evening research interview.

We decided that a better way to understand the issues would be to interview key members of the Metropolitan Police and support our findings with observational research.

Police interviews

We held interviews with the two police divisions most closely linked to minicab-related sexual assaults. The first was Project Sapphire – the sexual assault and rape investigation unit of the Metropolitan Police. The second was TOCU – the division tasked with tackling touting in London.

From this research we concluded that there were three main reasons young women risk their safety in illegal minicabs:

1. Lack of viable alternatives.
2. Ignorance – many women seem simply to trust that a man is a legitimate minicab driver just because he says so.
3. Impaired judgement – a combination of alcohol, tiredness and a need to get home can cause women to take risks they wouldn't take under ordinary circumstances.

Observational research

Having had many nights out in central London bars ourselves, it would have been easy to assume that we already knew how women behaved and were familiar with the temptation posed by illegal minicab drivers. However, we felt it important to get a fresh perspective.

We decided to accompany a group of young women from the agency on a night out in Soho and then interview them, along with some of their friends, the following day.

We were struck by the scale of the problem. Touts on the street seemed to be in plentiful supply and frequently propositioned groups of people emerging from bars and clubs.

The insights we gained from talking to the police were fully confirmed. We saw many young women (mostly in groups but occasionally alone) getting into illegal minicabs. It was alarming to observe how willingly they would climb into a stranger's car at 2am, when such behaviour would be unthinkable in daylight hours.

We interviewed our research subjects the following day with two specific objectives. First, to develop an understanding of how people feel at the point they leave a club to go home. Second, to retrace the stages of the evening, with a view to identifying the 'touchpoints' for communicating our message in the relevant environment. These insights were instrumental in developing the strategy.

DEVELOPING THE CREATIVE STRATEGY

The challenge

Through our research we identified the true essence of the challenge we were facing. We had to find a way to persuade women to choose a less convenient form of transport, at a time when they were least likely to make a rational decision.

Creative idea

We had to think creatively about how to communicate our message in a way that would fundamentally change the way women felt about touts and, more importantly, remain effective at the crucial decision-making point.

We based the creative brief on two key insights gained from our research.

1. We needed to alarm women into realising that touts are absolutely not legitimate minicabs and anyone could be behind the wheel.
2. We wanted to make the advertising feel as real as possible. Talking both to the police and the women from the agency, and reading reports from victims of such attacks, there seemed to be an overriding belief that this 'wouldn't happen to me'. Many women felt they'd be OK if they had their mobile phone, or thought they could tell if the driver was trustworthy or not. To be effective we had to make women identify with the risks on a personal level in a way that related to their experiences.

As well as talking to our core audience of women under 30 in London, we felt there was an opportunity to influence the attitudes of other people, such as boyfriends, friends and doormen, who might be in a position to stop a woman from taking an illegal minicab.

The proposition on the creative brief became the campaign line: 'Know what you're getting into' (Figure 2).

We developed a 40-second cinema advert and a complementary print campaign. The commercial was directed by Mike Leigh, who offered his services at a discounted rate (Figure 3).

Figure 2: *Poster*

We open on a harmless-looking minicab driver who talks to camera. He tells us that he has a criminal record, which makes it difficult to get a proper job – 'sexual assault, it doesn't look so good on the old CV'.

He then says, 'but it doesn't stop me picking up women'. At which point he pulls up to the curb and innocently offers a young woman 'Minicab love?' She looks at him, is clearly reassured that taking a ride will be OK, and climbs into the back of the car.

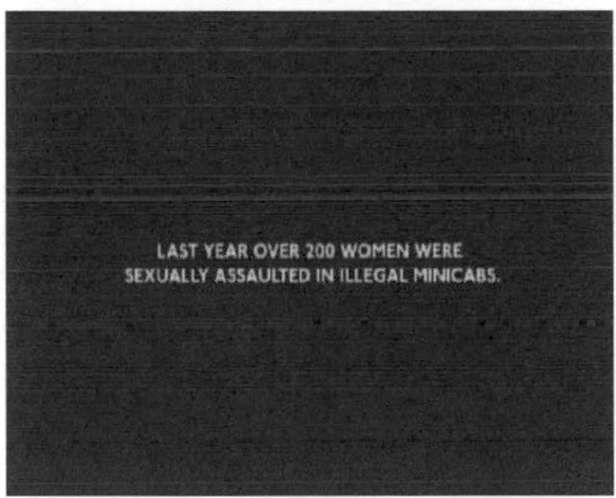

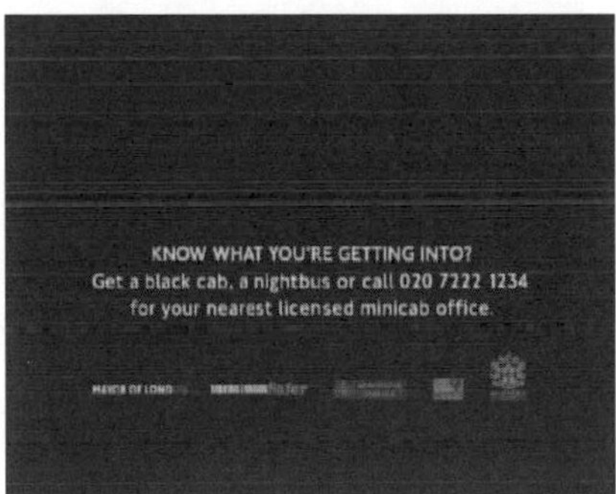

A title then appears to say that 'Last year over 200 women were sexually assaulted in illegal minicabs.' Then the title appears, 'Know what you're getting into?' and direction as to safe travel alternatives.

Figure 3: *Minicab commercial*

MEDIA STRATEGY

A critical element of the campaign was about matching the message to the environment.

We developed a spectrum of communication designed to impact in different ways. Broadcast media targeted women when removed from the situation and in a rational state of mind. More targeted media was used in environments increasingly close to the decision-making point – which we termed 'Point of Prey' – mirroring the progression of a night out (Figure 4).

The role of the broadcast media was to change attitudes towards touts, while the 'Point of Prey' media was designed to offer a practical solution to the problem. Both elements featured the telephone number.

The initial campaign launched in October 2002 with posters and Point of Prey media. Cinema launched in December. Additional budget was then secured to keep the campaign running longer term and into a second year when we ran TV (Figure 5).

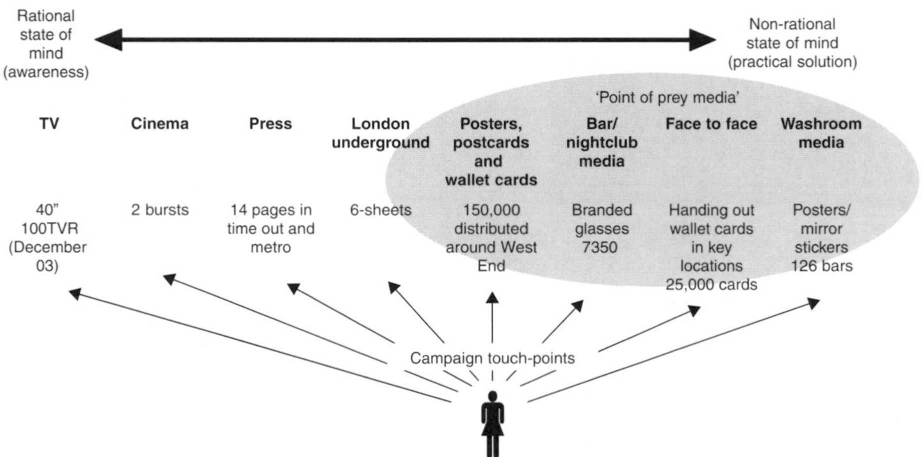

Figure 4: *Media strategy: year 1 and year 2*

Media	Total quantity	Oct 02	Nov 02	Dec 02	Jan 03	Feb 03	Mar 03	Apr 03	May 03	Jun 03	Jul 03	Aug 03	Sep 03	Oct 03	Nov 03	Dec 03	Jan 04	Feb 04	Mar 04
Postcards	62,000																		
A4 posters	31,000																		
Credit card design	50,000																		
A3 posters	5000																		
40" cinema																			
40" TV	100 TVRs																		
Time Out pages																			
Metro	4 × 1/4 pages																		
Double royals	Tube ticket sites																		
6-sheets	Bus and tube																		
Face to face	25,000 cards																		
Washroom panels	Total 126 bars																		
Mirror stickers	550																		
Branded glasses	7350																		

← Year 1 → Start year 2 →

Figure 5: *Campaign timings*

The total media spend in year one was £400K and in year two an additional £300K was allocated. Production costs for the whole campaign totalled £120K.

THE RESULTS

A telling measure of the success of the campaign was the response of those involved. Having initially been developed as a one-off piece of activity, 'Know what you're getting into' has now become the uniting force behind a much larger and longer-term fight against touting.

The Mayor of London's Office worked with partner organisations to secure additional budget to give further support to the campaign. Now in its second year, the campaign has prompted extensive PR and gained widespread support from some valuable sources.

Reduction in minicab-related sexual assaults

The most critical measure of effectiveness is the incidence of minicab-related sexual assaults and rapes. Figure 6 shows what happened.

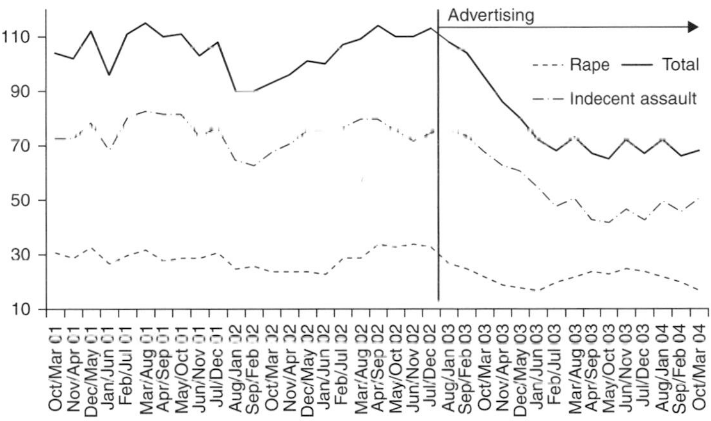

Figure 6: *Minicab-related sexual assaults and rape in London – October 2001 to March 2004 (six-month rolling data)*
Source: Project Sapphire, the Metropolitan Police, April 2004

In the year prior to the advertising, 212 women reported being sexually assaulted by illegal minicab drivers. In the first year of the campaign this dropped to just 155. Over the same period, minicab-related rapes fell from 54 to 42. Total sexual assaults declined by 27% and rapes by 22% in the first 12 months of the campaign, as compared with the previous year. Overall this equates to 85 fewer attacks between October 2002 and March 2004.

Advertising awareness

Following the success of the first year of activity, Transport for London put a tracking study in place to measure the effect of activity in year two.

The pre-wave took place in August/September after year one activity was complete but before any activity commenced for year two. The second wave was in December 2003, following TV and 'Point of Prey' activity.

Table 1 shows the level of recall achieved by the campaign on a media spend of £290K over three months.

TABLE 1: AWARENESS OF THE CAMPAIGN

Recalled 'Safer Travel at Night' campaign	32%
Spontaneously said 'Know what you're getting into'	12%

Source: TfL Tracking, Synovate, December 2003. Sample: 600. Base: 50/50 female/male, all under 45

Attitude shifts

Attitudes changed considerably over a relatively short period (see Table 2).

TABLE 2: ATTITUDES TOWARDS TOUTING

	Pre	Post
Would consider using a tout in the future	39%	27%

Source: TfL Tracking, Synovate, December 2003. Sample: 600. Base: 50/50 female/male, all under 45

Usage shifts

We knew it wasn't enough simply to change attitudes. The critical measure was whether there had been an actual change in behaviour to support the reduction in attacks.

Table 3 shows the change in claimed usage of touts. The number of women using touts reduced by 66% – from 18% in the pre-wave, to 6% post the campaign. The illegal minicab share of the night travel 'market' fell to just 10%.

TABLE 3: ACTUAL USAGE OF ILLEGAL MINICABS

	Pre	Post
Women claiming to use touts	18%	6%
Illegal cab share of market (between 12 and 2am on Saturday)	26%	10%

Source: TfL Tracking, Synovate, December 2003. Sample: 600. Base: 50/50 female/male, all under 45

Calls to the Transport for London (TfL) telephone number

TfL did not start recording call volumes until January 2003. Consequently, we have no year-on-year data from which we can draw comparisons.

One measure we do have is call volumes by day-part. Until the campaign there was limited reason to call the TfL number outside general public transport hours – i.e. when tubes, trains and buses are in full service. Once the campaign launched we were giving women a specific reason to phone late at night, i.e. 11pm to 4am.

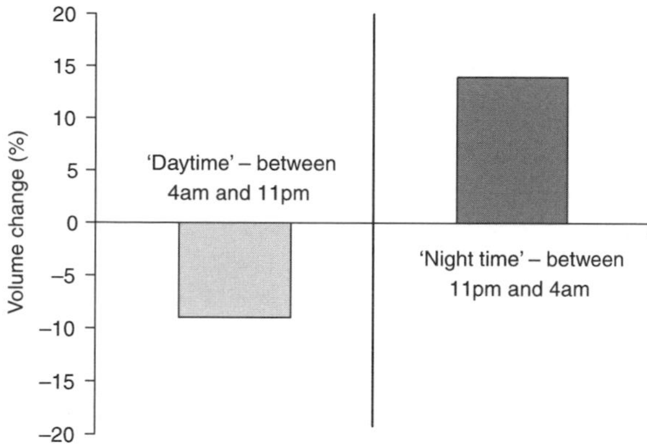

Figure 7: *Percentage change in call volumes to TfL telephone line by day-part between November and December 2003*
Source: Transport for London, March 2004

Figure 7 demonstrates how calls during the late-night hours increased by 14%, while calls during standard public transport hours decreased by 9%.

Anecdotal results

Following the launch, the campaign received widespread support from publications, organisations and high-profile figures. Many theatres, bars, hospitals and nightclubs spontaneously requested publicity material.

The following quote sums up the overwhelming response to the campaign.

> '"Know what you're getting into" has been a significant driving force in effecting change amongst our target audience. ... It has helped direct all parties towards the same goal and has been instrumental in soliciting support from a wide range of organisations all over London.'
>
> Jane Davis, Head of Marketing, GLA

ISOLATING THE EFFECT OF ADVERTISING

In order to determine the contribution advertising made to the reduction in assaults, we need to assess the possible impact of all other factors involved. This analysis falls into two broad areas.

1. Understanding the role and effect of each of the other vital parts of the 'Safer Travel at Night' initiative:
   - improvements to night-time public transport
   - impact of policing
   - regulation of the London minicab trade.
2. Investigating external factors that might explain the results:
   - crime trends
   - lifestyle change
   - other advertising and communication.

Understanding the role and effect of other 'Safer Travel at Night' initiatives

Reducing minicab-related sexual assaults involves seamless collaboration between organisations. Each initiative played a critical role in the broader campaign (Table 4).

TABLE 4: ROLE AND EFFECT OF OTHER INITIATIVES

Initiative	Effect
Transport improvements	Provide safe alternatives for women travelling at night
Policing	Prevent and deter touting
Regulation of minicab trade	Provide safe alternatives and deter touting
Advertising	Build awareness of the risks and effect a behavioural change

By removing any one of the factors mentioned in Table 4 the broader campaign could not have achieved the results it did.

However, we believe it was the advertising that provided the catalyst to change behaviour. While other factors were vital facilitators of change, in giving women safer options and reducing the supply of touts, advertising acted as the driver for change. We seek to demonstrate this below.

Improvements to night-time public transport

Improvements included an increase in night bus routes and greater availability of black taxis with the introduction of the night tariff. These were both critical to ensuring women had safer options for travel at night.

However, one would not expect the improvements to prompt a change in behaviour directly. That was the role for advertising – to make women aware of the risks and direct them towards safer alternatives.

This is demonstrated in Figure 8, which shows how the drop in minicab-related sexual assaults coincided with the advertising campaign.

Supporting this is the evident change in attitudes towards touts amongst young women. Consideration of using a tout dropped from 39% to 27% over a three-month period.[3] Increased availability of alternative forms of transport could not account for this shift.

Reflecting this attitudinal shift amongst women is the change in usage. Figure 9 shows that whilst women's usage of touts reduced by two-thirds following the campaign, men's usage remained constant. Had there been a general shift in response to increased availability, surely this would have been equally evident across both sexes.

Impact of policing

Policing has a crucial role in ensuring the long-term success of this initiative and in June 2002, four months before the advertising launch, the Metropolitan Police set up a specialist division called the Transport Operation Control Unit (TOCU).

3. Synovate Tracking Research, December 2003.

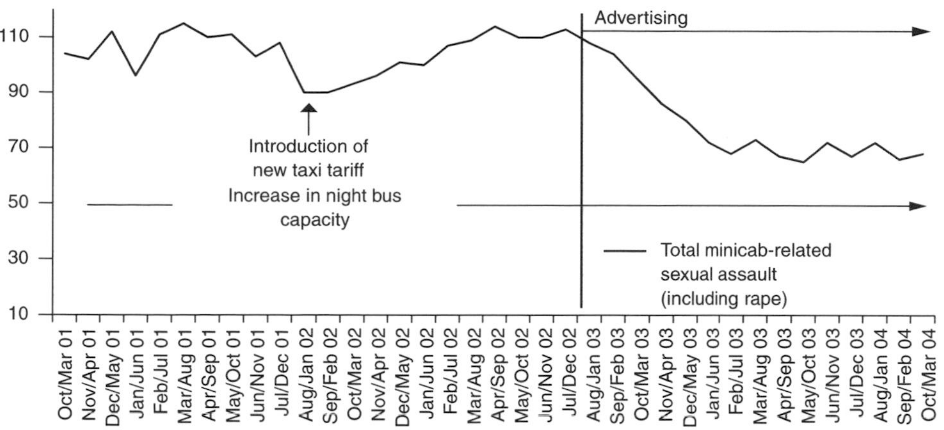

Figure 8: *Total minicab-related sexual assaults (including rape) in London – October 2001 to March 2004 (six-month rolling data)*
Source: Project Sapphire, The Metropolitan Police, April 2004

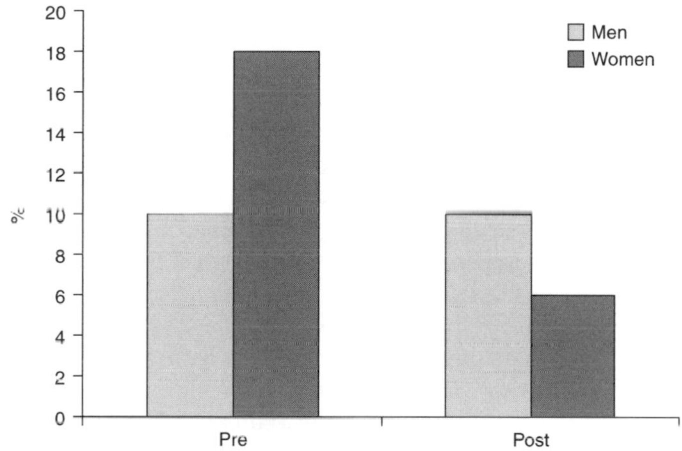

Figure 9: *Male and female usage of touts – pre- and post-advertising*
Source: TfL Tracking, Synovate, December 2003. Sample: 600. Base: 50/50 female/male, all under 45

TOCU tackles touting directly by focusing its operations in known hotspots every Thursday, Friday, Saturday and Sunday night. Despite facing a mammoth task, by December 2003 it had made 650 arrests.[4]

This achievement has undoubtedly had a crucial impact on reducing the availability of illegal minicabs in central London. However, we believe it cannot fully explain the reduction in assaults that occurred.

First, the operations TOCU has undertaken have been focused directly on touts, not their potential victims, so it cannot explain the change in attitudes amongst our audience.

Second, if the reduced availability of illegal minicabs due to policing was the main explanation for the reduction in sexual assaults, we would expect an equal

4. Source: GLA 2004.

decrease in usage between men and women. This is not the case, as is shown in Figure 9.

The true impact of TOCU's operations is yet to be witnessed. In January 2004 touting became a recordable offence. This means DNA samples can be taken from all drivers arrested, and analysed for matches with forensic evidence from past crimes. It is hoped that this will not only directly lead to convictions but will also act as a deterrent to sex attackers continuing to pose as minicab drivers.

Regulation of London minicab trade

The Public Carriage Office is licensing the industry in three phases.

Phase 1: Licensing of minicab offices
(began in June 2001, completed mid-2003)

Phase 2: Licensing of minicab drivers
(began June 2003, completed beginning 2004)

Phase 3: Licensing of cars
(began April 2004 – after the campaign period)

While Phase 1, the licensing of offices, is an important step in the regulation process, it has no specific implications for touting. Illegal minicabs are not connected with minicab offices. Phase 3 commenced after the campaign period we are measuring. Phase 2, the licensing of drivers, is the only element that could have impacted on touting. It coincided with the second year of the campaign. A total of 40,000 drivers in London are now licensed, which means all documentation is verified and every driver is checked for past criminal convictions.

It is improbable that a sexual attacker preying on young women would choose to go through the licensing procedure and with 10,000 non-licensed touts still on the streets providing 'cover' it also seems unnecessary.

Whilst this licensing procedure has been fundamental in providing safer options for women taking legitimate minicabs, one could fairly assume the same number of actual and potential attackers are still at large, but hiding among a smaller mass. This is supported by the fact that the greatest reduction in attacks occurred almost a year prior to the introduction of licensing of drivers.

Explaining what external factors might explain the results

To attribute effectiveness to the advertising it is important to eliminate or quantify the impact of all relevant external factors.

Was the reduction in attacks simply a reflection of a broader crime trend?

In fact the trend is the opposite, as demonstrated by Figures 10 and 11, showing UK and London trends.

Based on this data, one would have expected minicab-related sexual assaults to have increased in line with this general trend. In fact, if they had, they would have been up by around 10%, rather than the 27% decrease we witnessed.

To demonstrate this, Figure 12 shows minicab-related sexual assaults and rapes as a percentage of total sexual assaults and rapes in London, i.e. removing the factor of increased reporting. Minicab-related incidents show a marked reduction relative to attacks in general.

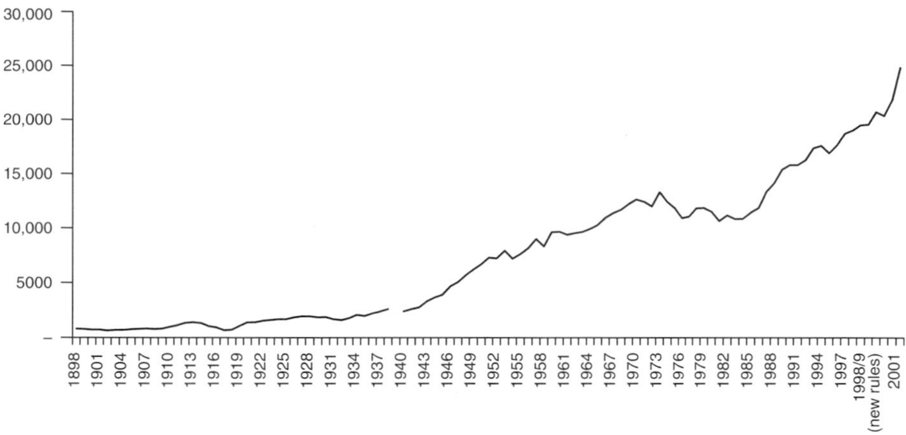

Figure 10: *Recorded sexual assault on females in the UK – 1898 to 2003*
Source: British Crime Survey, 2004

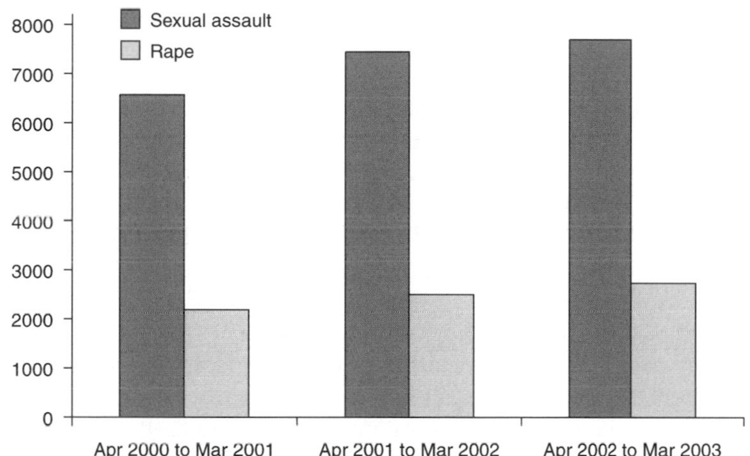

Figure 11: *Reported sexually motivated crime in London – 2000 to 2003*
Source: Metropolitan Police Crime Statistics, February 2004

Obviously all data is based on reported assaults and there is doubt about how well they reflect actual incidents. There is a theory that heightened awareness of specific types of crime increases reporting, thus increasing apparent crime levels.

Indeed, everything else being equal, one would expect a campaign highlighting minicab-related assaults to increase the proportion of actual incidents reported. If this is the case, the real impact of the campaign is greater than observed.

Lifestyle change – were fewer people going out at night?

All evidence indicates the contrary. Approximately half a million people go clubbing in central London every Saturday night and there is no evidence to suggest this figure is decreasing.[5]

5. Source: London's Cultural Capital, 1997.

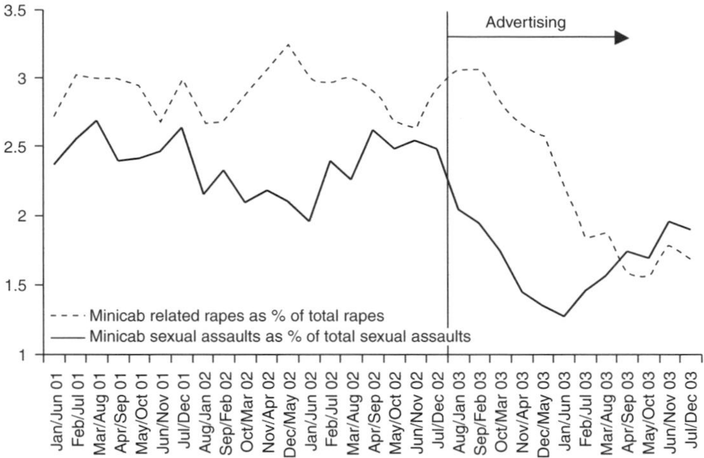

Figure 12: *Minicab-related sexual assaults and rapes as a percentage of total sexual assaults and rapes in London*
Source: Project Sapphire, the Metropolitan Police, March 2004

The population of London has increased at a faster rate than the rest of the country and is projected to grow by an additional 700,000 people by 2016.[6]

Employment in London bars increased 37% between 1995 and 2001, and shows no sign of slowing down.[7]

Usage of night buses has increased consistently since 2000, which again would not suggest a decline in people going out.[8]

Were the results influenced by other communications?

The only other pieces of communication noted were isolated messages on the seat backs of selected black taxis. The activity was somewhat sporadic and to a limited audience so we would argue it did not contribute significantly to the results.

However, there has been extensive PR surrounding the issue. Figure 13 shows some examples of coverage of the campaign in the press.

Before the launch of the campaign, PR was low level and sporadic. With the launch of the advertising PR increased dramatically with the 'Know what you're getting into' campaign being at the source. The increase in PR has been almost solely a result of the campaign and we believe any effect it has had is an additional measure of the success of the advertising.

Figure 14 shows illegal minicab-related PR in the *Evening Standard* prior to and during the campaign period.

6. Source: London's Leisure Economy, 2003.
7. London's Leisure Economy, 2003.
8. Transport for London.

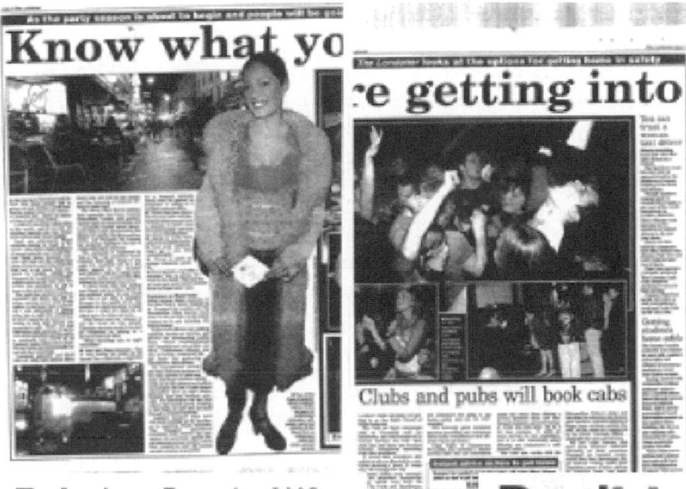

Know what you're getting into

Clubs and pubs will book cabs

The Londoner, December 2003

South London Press, October 2003

Getting home safely

Don't take the risk...

Mayor's plea on illegal minicabs as he launches new campaign to get Londoners home safely

Metro, 2003

Figure 13: *Press coverage*

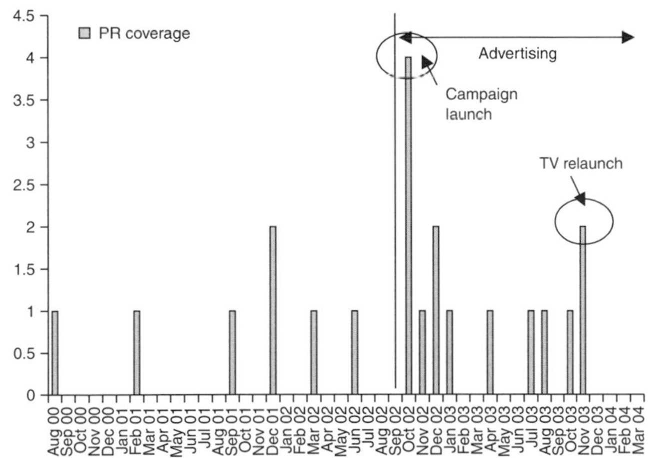

Figure 14: Evening Standard *online – PR coverage of illegal minicab issue, August 2000 to March 2004*
Source: www.thislondon.co.uk

RETURN ON INVESTMENT

How can one quantify the cost of a sexual assault or rape? The cost to the victim and her loved ones goes far beyond anything we could define in this paper. But in order to secure future funds to help fight this crime, it is important to seek to demonstrate that investment in the campaign has been justified on a purely financial basis.

In 2000, the Home Office conducted analysis to try and determine the average cost of crime by category. The figures measure the impact of a series of factors including police investigation time, physical and emotional impact, lost output, health services, legal costs, and so on. Estimated costs are shown in Table 5.

TABLE 5: ESTIMATED COSTS OF CRIMES

Murder	£1,100,000
Serious violence against a person	£130,000

Source: *The Economic and Social Costs of Crime*, Home Office, 2000

Rape is not calculated specifically in the report. However, we believe we can use these figures to benchmark the equivalent effects for rape and sexual assault.

No one rape or sexual assault can be compared with another. Sexual assaults can be of such a serious nature that, with changes to the law, they have now been reclassified as rape. Both crimes are traumatic experiences and victims can require life-long support. The devastation of such attacks suggests that the lifetime cost of a minicab-related sexual assault or rape would at least be equivalent to 'serious violence against another person'.

If one accepts that up to 85 sexual assaults may have been prevented, then the financial saving to public services and private individuals amounts to more than £11m (85 × £130,000). Based on a total investment of £820K, this campaign paid for itself more than 13 times over.

Adding in the value of the PR generated as a direct result of the campaign and the costs saved from winning the support of people such as Mike Leigh, the financial case for investment in the campaign becomes overwhelming.

CONCLUSION

The reduction in minicab-related sexual assaults was the result of collaboration between key organisations.

Evidence suggests that the other initiatives that formed part of the broader 'Safer Travel at Night' campaign, most notably the improvements in night transport, were the vital facilitators of behavioural change. But it was the advertising that was the catalyst to change attitudes and provide the initial impetus to avoid touts.

Through a powerful, simple creative message and an innovative media strategy, our campaign influenced behaviour at a point when our audience was at least in a position to make a considered decision.

What began as a short-term piece of advertising to build awareness of the issue has become the creative idea at the heart of a London-wide campaign to eradicate illegal minicabs.

As a direct result of our activity there are up to 85 women in London who are carrying on their lives normally, unaware of how differently things could have turned out had they chosen to take an illegal minicab to get home.

SILVER

17

The Guardian

A fresh approach to newspaper communications

Principal authors: Alistair Crawford and Andrew Perkins, DDB London, David Bassett, DDB Matrix, Nigel Jones, Claydon Heeley Jones Mason, and Graham Fowles, The *Guardian*

Contributing authors: Les Binet, DDB Matrix, and Matthew Law, Tribal DDB

Media agency: PHD

EDITOR'S SUMMARY

Many advertisers, and most if not all newspaper brands, employ a mix of promotional and brand advertising to grow share and sales. Few do so with a creative campaign that easily accommodates both agendas; fewer still can offer us a rigorous demonstration of effectiveness, both of the constituent parts and the overall whole.

The *Guardian*'s 'Fresh' campaign is one such creative idea, and demonstrably effective at both a micro and macro level. This at a time when the newspaper market was not just in decline but at its most fiercely competitive.

The *Guardian* had consistently been losing readers and share since 1995. A drift due, in part at least, to perceptions of the paper as an overly earnest, heavy read. To correct matters, an emphasis on content rather than brand philosophy was decreed, with Saturday deemed to be the most persuasive shop window on to this new or 'real' *Guardian*. The 'Fresh' campaign was duly conceived to carry both editorial and promotional content.

Share grew immediately, reversing a six-year decline; more surprisingly perhaps, overall sales figures actually grew, and readership likewise bucked the competitive trend. Revenues were enhanced not just by increased sales, but by cover price and display advertising growth coinciding with the paper's revitalised market performance.

Market share projections credit the campaign with generating an additional 20 million sales. More detailed analysis isolates the contribution of promotions, editorial specials and advertising, as well as how they work together.

INTRODUCTION

A new way of thinking about newspaper communications

Between 1995 and 2001, the *Guardian* had been losing share in a declining category. In January 2001, a new marketing and communications strategy was introduced that would not only see share increase swiftly and dramatically, but also grow overall circulation. This study will show how thinking that ignored the conventional wisdom of the category enabled us to reap rich rewards.

Whilst the orthodoxy suggested there should be two tiers to the campaign, one brand-building, the other response-based, we created a campaign that did both jobs at the same time. Our campaign not only serves as a model for newspaper communications but, given the strong similarities to the category, for retail communications in general.

To boldly go ...

Scouring the annals of the IPA, there's a noticeable dearth of papers on daily newspapers. We suspect that's because of the difficulty of putting one together. The hypervolatility of sales, the ever-changing nature of the product and the bewildering variety of short-term, staccato campaigns that go with the territory, ensure the mother of all struggles to disentangle the effects of communications activity.

This paper is, therefore, something of a rarity; only two efforts have preceded us in a very well-established category. On top of that, we're going to break new analytical ground in a notoriously complicated market, establishing both the overall benefit of communications activity, as well as isolating the contribution of its constituent parts, particularly promotions and advertising.

BACKGROUND

A desire for influence before profit

The *Guardian* was founded in 1821 in response to the Peterloo Massacre. Its 11 founders saw it as a much-needed liberal voice against the government injustices meted out that day. Unsurprisingly, it has always had an acute sense of its contribution to the social agenda – what C.P. Scott, one of its editors, described as a 'moral existence'. Indeed, its ultimate goal has been to secure the excellence and independence of its journalistic product and, in turn, to reach as many people as possible with its editorial output.

That it can live up to these ideals has been ensured by the fact that it is owned by a charitable trust, rather than a rapacious press baron. The Scott Trust exists to ensure the paper's success, to the extent that profits from other businesses that it has acquired, such as *Autotrader* and Jazz FM, are used to invest in the paper itself. As the principles of the Trust state, its aim is:

> 'To devote the whole of the surplus profits of the company, which would otherwise have been available for dividends ... towards building up the reserves of the Company and increasing the circulation of, and expanding and improving, the newspaper.'

Ultimately, therefore, this IPA paper is unusual in that it will be about more than how marketing and communications have contributed to profits. The *Guardian* is explicitly not a profit-maximising business: the key criterion against which it measures its success is 'influence', as expressed by sales and readership.[1]

Financial imperatives are not ignored

Whilst not profit-driven, the trust does not represent an opportunity to run the paper in a financially suicidal fashion. The desire for influence must be tethered to the need to generate revenue.

Two sources of revenue represent the lifeblood of the paper:

1. Sales revenue – as generated by the cover price and number of copies sold.
2. Advertising revenue – as derived from the display advertising space sold.[2]

MARKET CONTEXT

The basics

The market we'll be looking at is the quality daily newspaper market. This includes five newspapers, *The Times*, the *Daily Telegraph*, the *Independent*, the *Financial Times* and us. Within this, we have traditionally been the third largest domestic player (Figure 1).

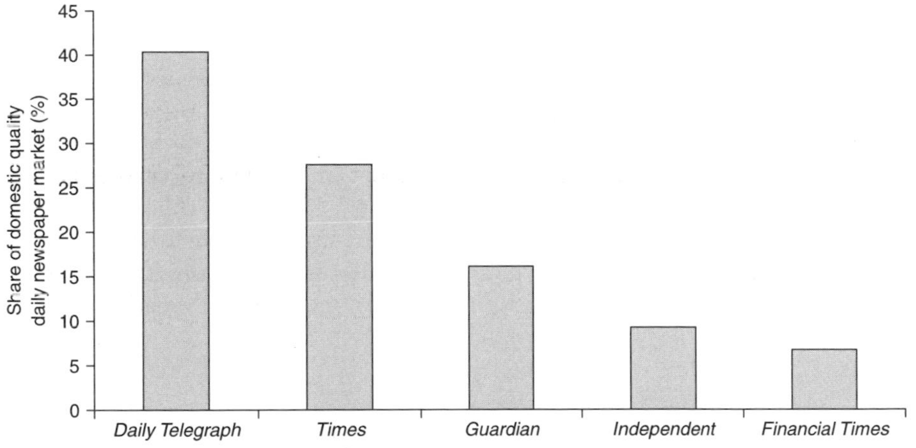

Figure 1: *Share of domestic market, October 2003*
Source: ABC

1. The accepted, industry-wide sources of measurement are: ABCs (Audit Bureau of Circulation) – independently audited sales figures; and NRS (National Readership Survey) – an independent rolling survey of readership habits.
2. Traditionally, advertising revenue comes from two sources, 'classified' and 'display'. Whilst display revenue tends to be a product of *reach*, as expressed by circulation (ABCs) and readership (NRS) figures, classified advertising revenue tends to rise and fall as a result of factors outside our control, particularly the health of the jobs market and the levels of *response* to advertisements. In other words, communications can affect display, but not classified revenue.

The daily market constitutes the Monday to Saturday market. With the exception of the *Financial Times*, all the papers have Sunday sister titles – ours being the *Observer*. However, these tend to be represented by different editorial, marketing and communications staff and the market itself has a different dynamic.

THE NATURE OF THE PROBLEM

A market in steady decline

Achieving influence and revenue within this market is becoming increasingly difficult. Since 1998, there has been a consistent decline in quality newspaper circulation (Figure 2).

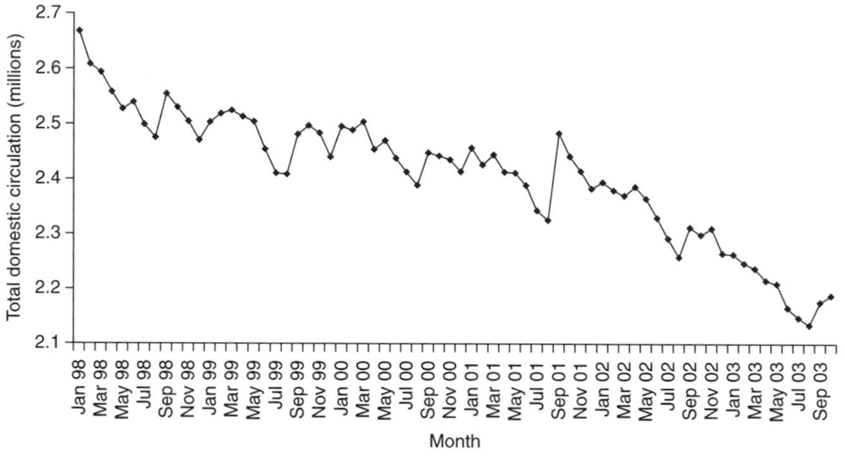

Figure 2: *A declining market: total domestic sales of quality daily newspapers*
Source: ABC

Predominantly, this is down to macro factors about which we can do little. Printed media is a mature category and is suffering from the availability of other information sources, notably the internet, as well as squeeze from other calls on our time. The fight, therefore, is for influence and sales in an ever-diminishing market – at its most basic, to steal *share* from notoriously aggressive competitors.

A downturn in the brand's fortunes

Worse still, within this declining market, the *Guardian* lost share between 1995 and 2000 (Figure 3).

Worryingly, our overall pool of readers had waned, suggesting that the *Guardian* was losing salience and relevance amongst the potential broadsheet-buying public (Figure 4).

And, even within the existing pool of readers, we discovered that a significant number of *Guardian* buyers were of an infrequent or promiscuous bent. This may run counter to expectation. A somewhat old-school image of the quality newspaper market still exists, with most people assuming that individual newspaper's sales are

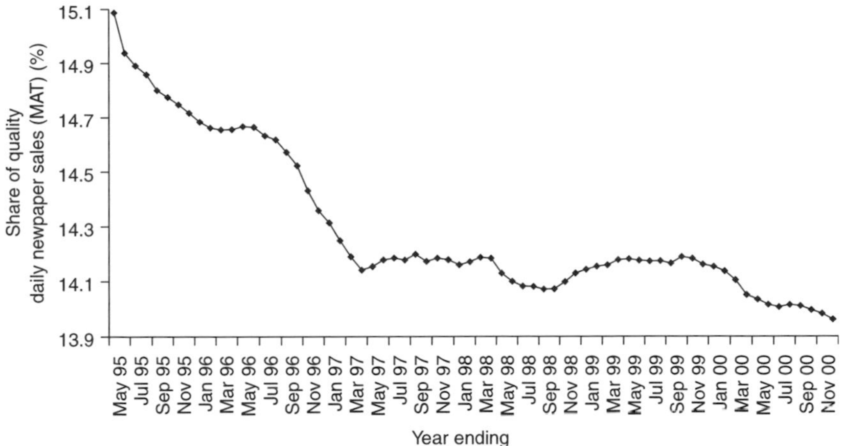

Figure 3: *The* Guardian *was losing market share*
Source: ABC

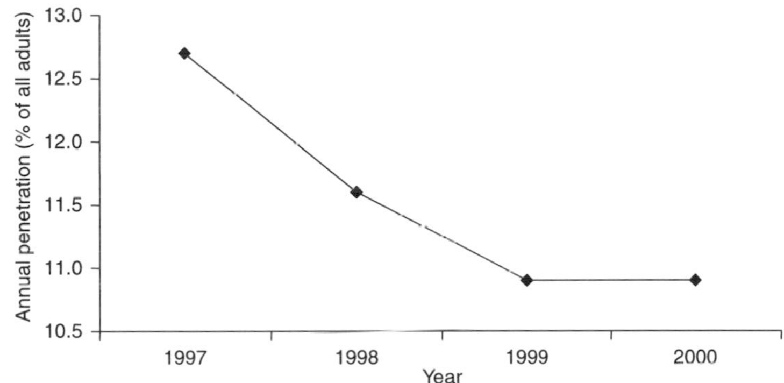

Figure 4: *The* Guardian *readership was falling*
Source: MRS

predominantly generated by a group of habitual purchasers. However, whilst a caucus of day-in and day-outers exists, some 61% of *Guardian* buyers are less frequent purchasers (Figure 5); and a large number of *Guardian* readers also buy other papers (Figure 6).

Whilst we could rely on the fidelity of die-hard fans, it was this vast pool of 'floating voters' whom we needed to convince of our virtues, thus maximising the chances of converting the sale when the mood to buy struck them.

A new team

In 2000, a new marketing director, Marc Sands, was appointed. He, in turn, hired three new communications agencies – DDB London, Claydon Heely Jones Mason (CHJM) and Tribal DDB – from January 2001, to work with existing players PhD and pd3.

DDB London would handle the above-the-line work, whilst pd3 and CHJM would specialise in promotions. Tribal would deal with online responsibilities, with PhD holding sway over media decisions.

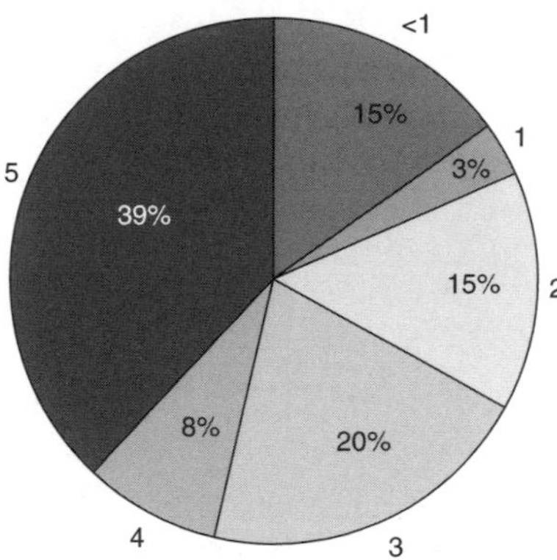

Figure 5: *Most* Guardian *readers don't read it every day: percentage of Monday to Friday readers by frequency of purchase (issues per week)*[3]
Source: The *Guardian*

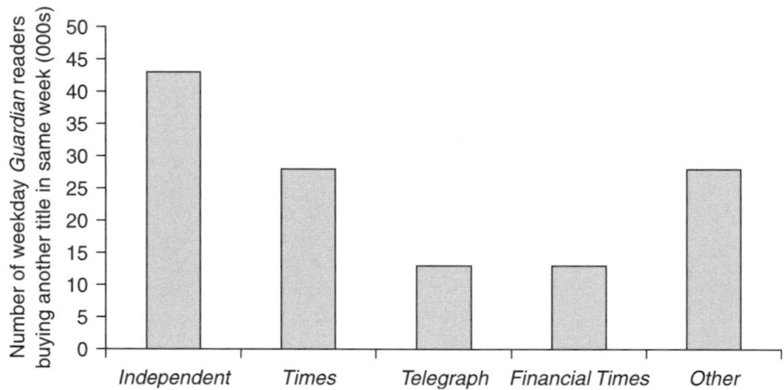

Figure 6: *A large number of repertoire readers*
Source: The *Guardian*

The marketing objectives

These were simple, yet ambitious:

- to maximise 'influence' through readership and circulation; in particular, to reverse the decline in market share
- to maximise incoming revenue from sales and from display advertising.

FINDING A SOLUTION

A gap between perception and reality

Research suggested that the main hurdle to overcome was a long-standing stereotype of the *Guardian* as a dry and earnest paper, dominated by its heavy news

3. We only have frequency of purchase information for Monday to Friday. However, including Saturday would only be likely to accentuate these trends.

reporting. This perception was very strong among non-readers and even repertoire, infrequent readers of the *Guardian*, who had an ingrained view of the brand.

> 'It's mainly for social workers, academics and teachers. I'm not like that.'
>
> 'I always think of it as really heavy going and serious.'
>
> 'It's only for really clever, serious people.'
>
> 'It's mainly for Labour people.'
>
> DDB London pitch research, November 2001

The fact is, this perception was belied by the reality. Whilst its authoritative news coverage was a vital part of the paper, the *Guardian* was a far more vibrant, diverse and accessible newspaper than the stereotype would have had you believe. From an editorial standpoint alone, there was a rich panoply of regular and one-off content that confounded expectation; from *The Guide* to *Weekend* and *Review*, as well as trail-blazing pieces focusing on, for example, the issues of food production and the intrusion of surveillance into ordinary life (Figure 7).

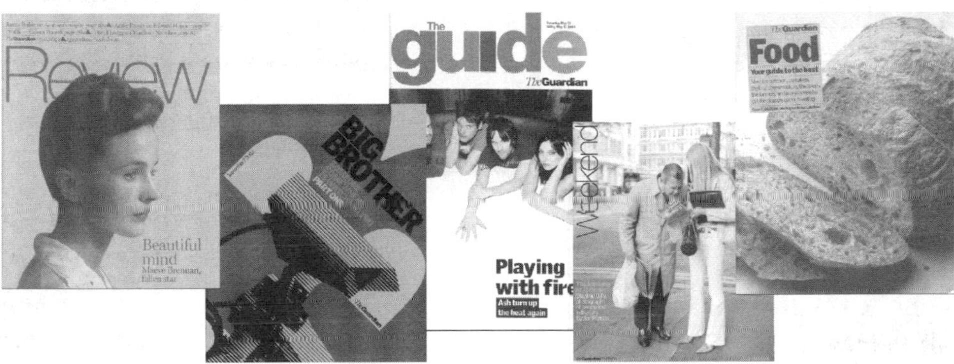

Figure 7

The communications strategy

Demonstration not assertion

Given the lack of understanding of the offering and the variety of supports available to us, we devised a communications strategy that would always give concrete reasons to believe that the *Guardian* was different to the caricature.

Blindingly obvious as this might seem, this went against the conventional wisdom of the category that tended to divide communications up into two tiers: a high-minded brand advert that asserted the paper's values and a suite of communications that did the job of selling papers in the short term.

The communications model for the *Guardian* that had preceded ours, had been an example of this kind of campaign; a brand values advert, 'Free Thinkers Welcome' (Figure 8), composed of a series of vignettes with people asking searching questions, allied to more tactical executions. *The Times*' 'What's Important' campaign (Figure 9) and the *Independent*'s 'It is, are you?' (Figure 10) are other cases in point.

Daddy, where does the water go?
SFX: Sound of bubbling water

Am I a guinea pig?

How do they grow seedless grapes?

If we move to a cheaper area, will it cost the girls their education?

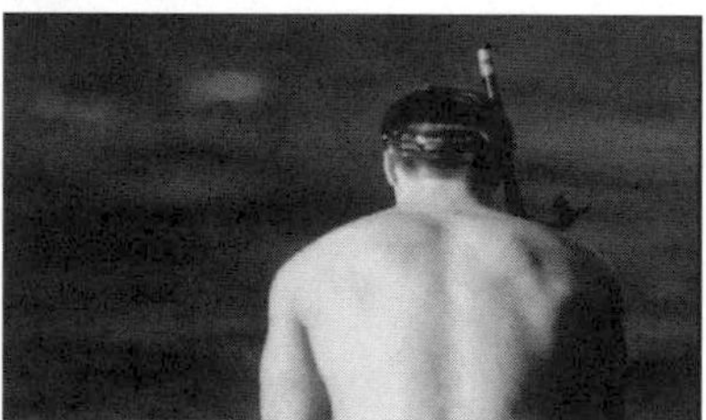

Do sharks know they're not found in these waters?

SFX: Sound of Train
Should trains have seatbelts?

We are all born with a desire to ask questions. Some of us keep asking questions.

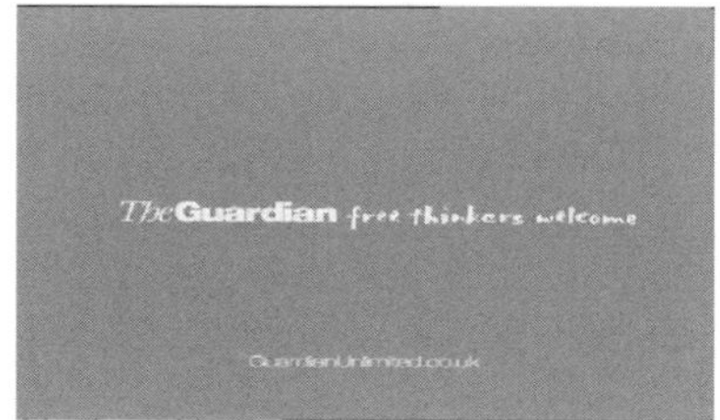

The Guardian. Free Thinkers Welcome

Figure 8: *The* Guardian: *'Free Thinkers Welcome'*

V/O: *The Banana. It's not important really. Or is it?*

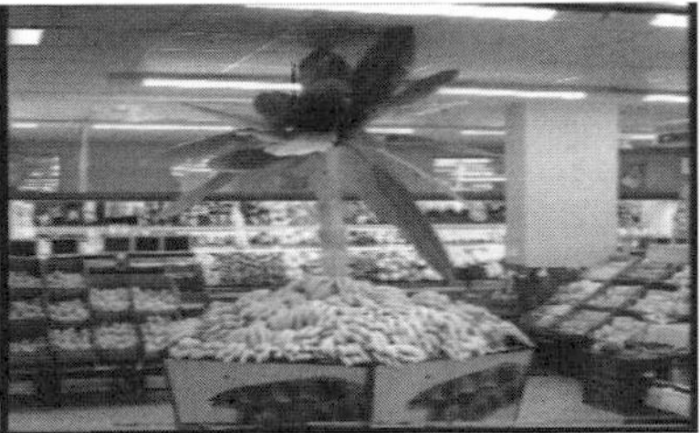

It is to a supermarket. It's their biggest-selling item.

It can inspire a classic comedy moment.

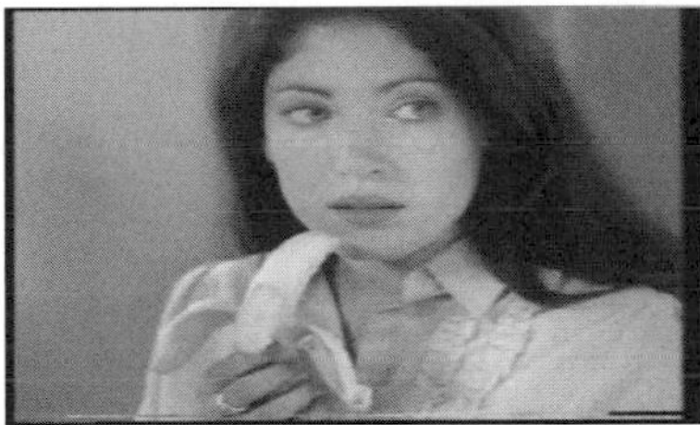

Or a tasteless joke that can go too far and end up with someone losing their job.

In Bristol, a man was jailed for six years for holding up a bank with a banana.

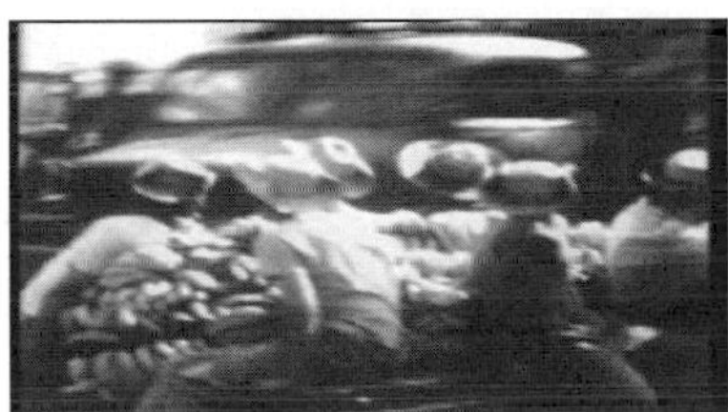

In Guatemala there was a military coup about the banana.

And in the wrong hands it can be a weapon that can wound deeply.

The banana. Are you missing what's important?

Figure 9: The Times: '*Banana*'

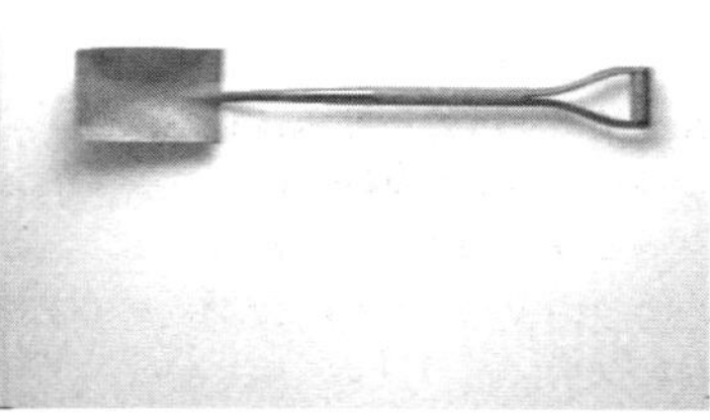

SFX: Classical music

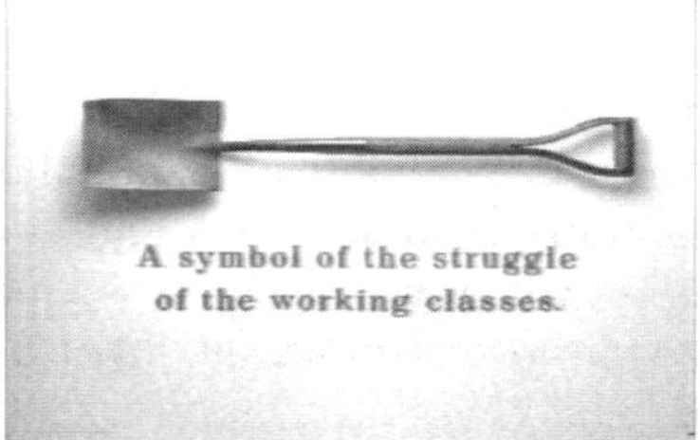

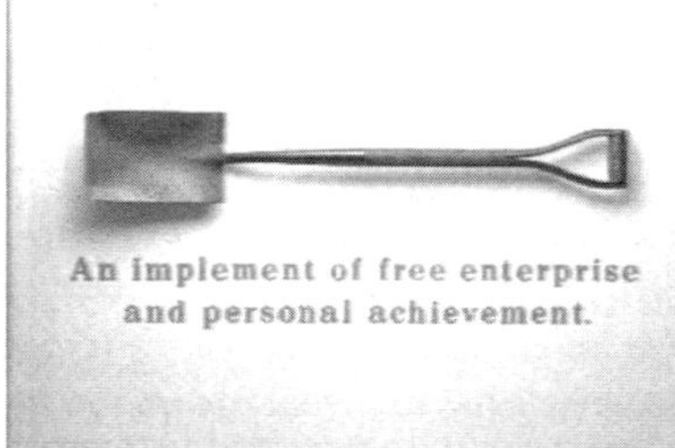

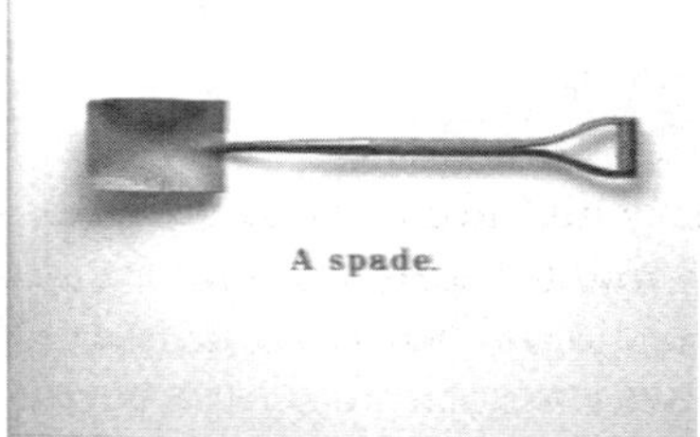

Figure 10: *The* Independent: *Spade*

In the circumstances, we felt we needed to revise this approach and generate a wholly product-focused campaign. A one-off summation wouldn't allow the multi-faceted, diverse depiction of the paper that we sought. Indeed, 'Free Thinkers Welcome' had tended to do the opposite, with its hard-hitting questions reinforcing perceptions of the *Guardian* and its readers, rather than confounding them. We also felt that pure brand adverts would not convince our target audience; doubting Thomases need tangible evidence. Finally, we believed the two-tiered model was inefficient. Pure brand communications tended to take fire-power away from the short-term needs of selling papers on specific days.

Ultimately, our new strategy of building the brand identity purely through demonstration rather than assertion would allow us to do two things at once – meeting both short-term sales needs as well as longer-term brand health.

The creative idea: 'freshness'

The challenge was to find a theme that would glue together very diverse content, from articles on death row, to free CD offers, through to fashion and beauty specials, and to do so in a way that would help with the desired reappraisal. This was particularly difficult given the short time-frames involved – often as little as a week to prepare promotions or produce advertising output.

To give an overall intent and direction to the work, we came up with a brand theme: 'freshness'. Obviously, this represented a challenge to consumers to reappraise; 'freshness' was the antithesis of what they felt about the brand. However, it also provided a clarion call to the agencies to produce work that was dramatically new and different to what had preceded it.

Advertising-wise, every medium used had to be as creative as possible. Even press work, conventionally an 'in tomorrow's paper' panel, needed to exude the values we wanted to communicate.

Press advertising

Figures 11–14 present examples of adverts placed in the press.

TV advertising

Figures 15–18 present examples of TV adverts.

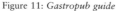

Figure 11: *Gastropub guide*

Figure 12: *Special investigation into AIDS in Africa*

OF LOVE AND WAR: LOST IN LILLE.

By Gustave Clemenceau (1919-1944)

Ah Stella! My Love and Sorrow!
Down in the Rimington's garden
We kissed goodbye my former pain
I stroke your head, your gentle hair
Was made of gold – and then I left:
Milan, for 5 long weeks,
I can reveal so much
Then back to France, all in love for you
And you were gone.
You were gone, the guardian of your house
Said so.
But I'm going to battle this Saturday.
Will I see you again? *Je ne sais pas.*

Translation by Nick Lucas

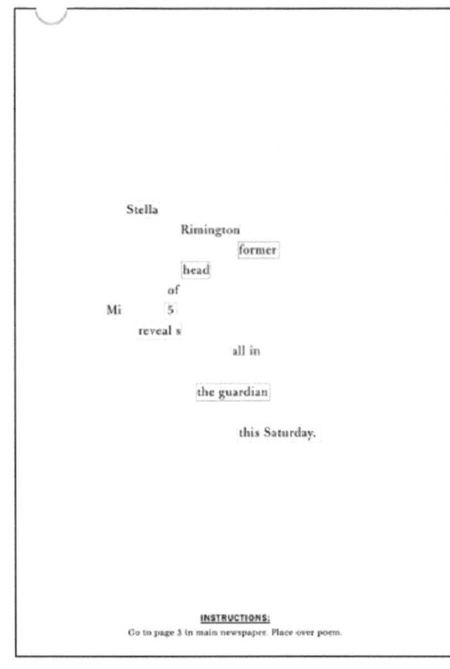

Stella
Rimington
former
head
of
Mi
5
reveal s
all in
the guardian
this Saturday.
INSTRUCTIONS:
Go to page 3 in main newspaper. Place over poem.

Figure 13: *Stella Rimington biography serialisation; press advert and insert to crack code within poem*

Figure 14: *Space handbook*

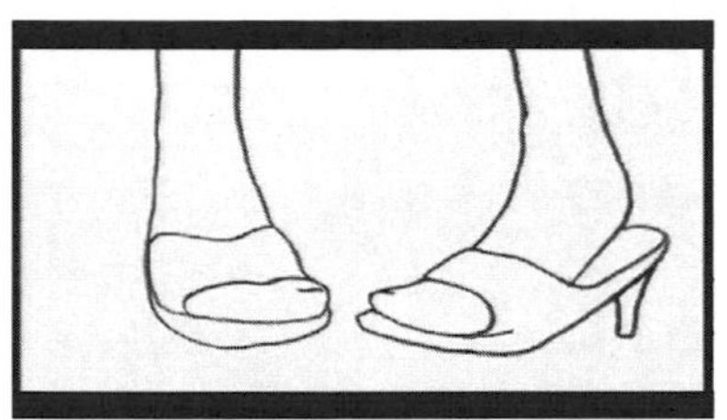

SFX: Music from Badly Drawn Boy album throughout

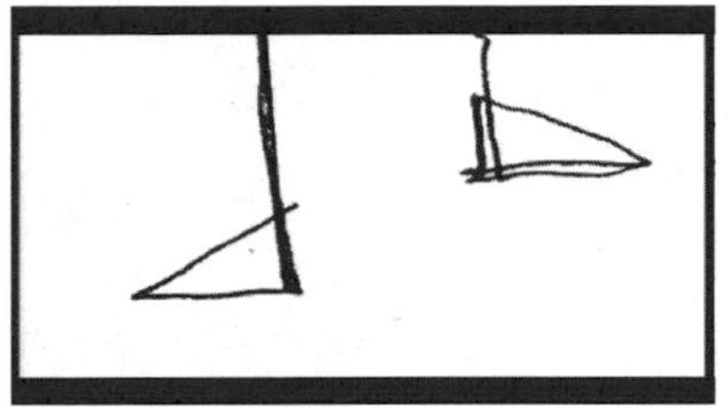

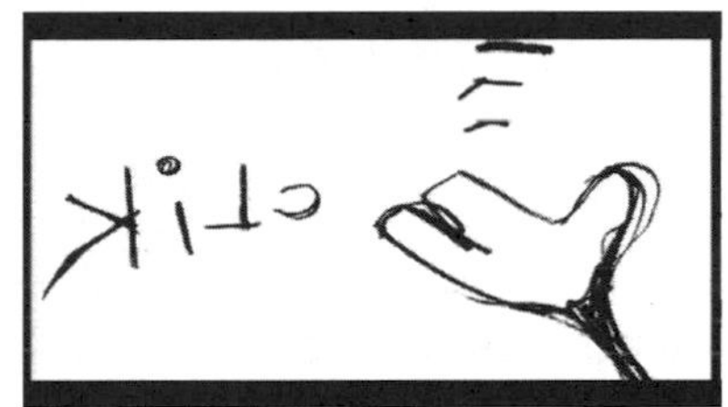

V/O: *Badly Drawn Boy*

Free CD in the Guardian *today*

Figure 15: '*Badly Drawn Boy*' CD

SFX: faint click of the gun

Boy: *Bang!*

SFX: Spud gun blows hole in wall

V/O: *Is our food what it seems …?*

A 32-page supplement on the food industry starts this Saturday in the Guardian

Figure 16: *Food part-work*

A rack of factor 50 sun lotion

Spanish waiter: *'Stacy. That's a very beautiful name'*

Restaurateur replacing glasses with plastic beakers

Pool chair being drilled to floor

V/O: *Collect five tokens*

and you can fly to various European destinations

So get ready, Europe.
The British are coming

Spanish waiter sprays crotch with cologne

Figure 17: *Go flights promotion*

Anxious man on train reading the *Guardian*

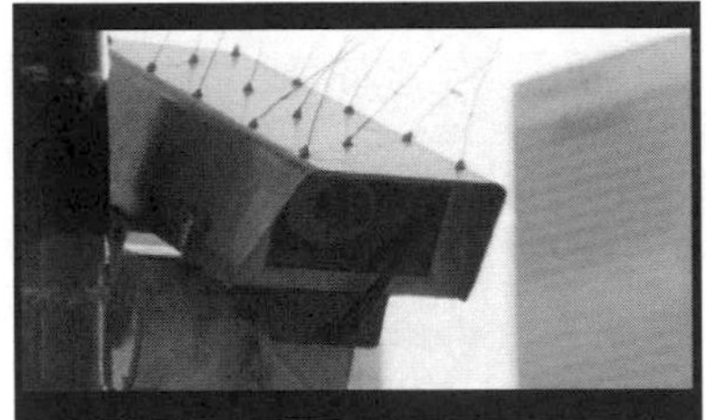

Menacing shot of camera

Phone rings

Man throws away his phone

Man catches his own image in shop CCTV

V/O: Is everything you're doing being monitored?

Big Brother, a three-part special on surveillance starts this Saturday ... you'll wish you'd never read it

Figure 18: *Surveillance part-work*

Online advertising

Figures 19–22 present examples of online advertising.

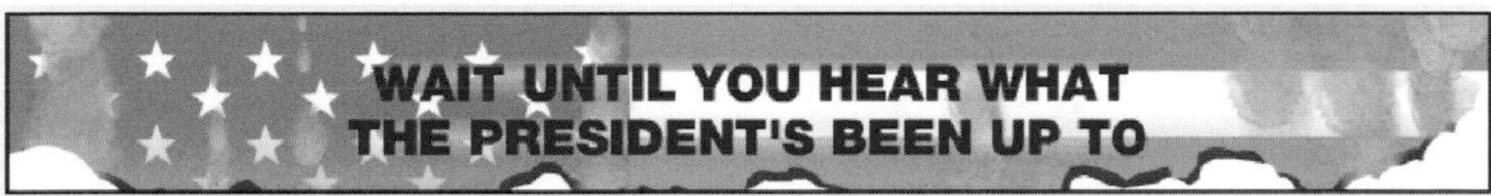

Michael Moore's new book
DUDE, WHERE'S MY COUNTRY?

Exclusive extracts and interview
Guardian Weekend Saturday October 4

Figure 19: *Michael Moore interview and book extracts*

'Big Brother' a 3 part investigation
into the world of surveillance_

Starts Saturday in The Guardian

Figure 20: *Surveillance part-work*

All other channels would have to follow suit. 'Added value' promotions, a vital means of encouraging purchase, had to say something about the brand rather than being purely response based. The 'Big Noise' CD is a case in point, with the CD promoting awareness of the 'Make Trade Fair' cause.

In a different way, the 'Badly Drawn Boy' CD again demonstrated 'freshness' – an unusual choice of artist combined with an interview in *The Guide* with the man himself, encouraging people to read the editorial, rather than simply play the CD (Figure 23).

Figure 21: *Gastropub guide*

Figure 22: *Oxfam 'Big Noise' CD*

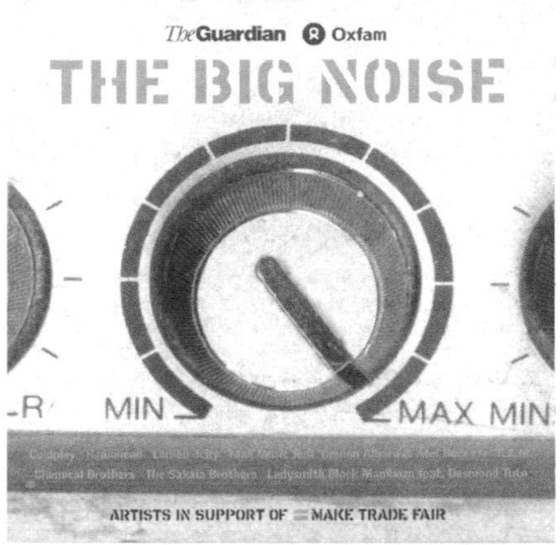

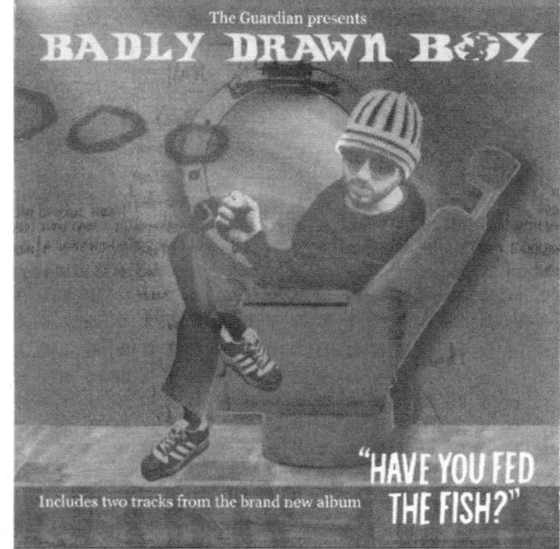

Figure 23: *Oxfam* 'Big Noise' *CD and 'Badly Drawn Boy' CD*

Additional ways of demonstrating 'freshness'

Other channels were also used to express the 'freshness' theme. For the food part-work, CHJM distributed insect lollipops and apples carrying the 'What's really in your food?' message (Figure 24).

Likewise, for *Gastropub* guide, CHJM distributed packets of pork scratchings and scampi fries in London, carrying stickers saying 'Prefer your bar snacks hairless?' and 'Prefer your seafood fresh?' (Figure 25).

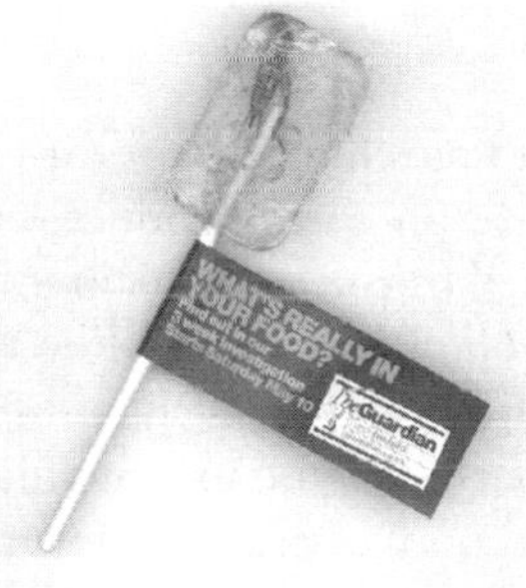

Figure 24: *Food part-works*

Figure 25: *Gastropub guide*

The Saturday push

We put the vast majority of marketing resource behind supporting the Saturday paper. Research had suggested that the Saturday offering would be the most responsive to marketing activity, for the simple reason that people tend to feel that they have more time to read papers at the weekend.[4] From a brand perspective, Saturday was also hugely attractive in that it provided the best shop window for the paper, crammed to the gills as it is with fantastic editorial (Figure 26).

Figure 26

To encourage purchase, two different lures were used: the juicy editorial specials, like those on food production, AIDS in the third world and a guide to gastropubs, as well as promotions involving third parties that should have some fit with the desired *Guardian* brand, like Oxfam's 'Big Noise'.

Overall, we firmly believed that emphasis on Saturday would have a beneficial effect on the paper as a whole: it would be the gateway into the brand, increasing both the potential pool of readers, as well as their predisposition to buy the product more regularly. As a result, we expected to see a turnaround in Saturday share followed by a turnaround in that of weekday sales.

THE MEDIA STRATEGY – AUDIENCE AND CHANNELS

Who we were after

New and infrequent purchasers

The task dictated that we talked to a broad audience. After all, we were looking to ensure salience and relevance amongst the generality of potential broadsheet

4. Source: the Qualitative Consultancy research groups and ICM Telephone Omnibus, March 2001.

purchasers, particularly infrequent and non-purchasers. They tend to be well educated with white-collar jobs and, as a consequence, concentrated in metropolitan areas.

A regional slant

We therefore up-weighted our communications against certain key regions, which had a greater concentration of actual and potential readership. In particular, ITV was bought exclusively in London, North East and West, Yorkshire and the Midlands.

An emphasis on youth

On top of that, we placed an emphasis on 'youth'. In terms of enhancing the *Guardian* 'influence', they represented the best target: as broadsheet greenhorns, they were more likely to respond to our communications, since their brand affiliations were unlikely to be developed or fixed; and they represented an opportunity to sustain that influence in the longer term. From a revenue perspective they were also important, with media buyers paying a premium for this group and their tender years meaning their lifetime value was, potentially, considerable.

Communications activity was angled towards the vital 25–44 ABC1 audience, with ATL media booked against this target, whilst other activity, such as promotions, had the same group in mind.

Media channels

In terms of traditional media, we used three channels for the big Saturday pushes.

Television and radio

Given the need to reach infrequent and non-purchasers, we needed media that maximised reach. On top of that, we had to use channels that could accommodate our desire for advertising within a very specific 48–72-hour window prior to the Saturday. Increasingly, therefore, radio and TV predominated as our channels of choice.

The *Guardian* newspaper itself

Understandably, other press titles were loath to let a competitor appear in their midst, so we were constrained to our own pages. That said, it was a highly efficient way of reaching our infrequent or repertoire readers. Also, using our own medium had a beneficial secondary effect: to convince potential advertisers of our faith in, as well as the creative potential of, the medium.

Online

Alongside that, given the relatively young, upmarket audience, it made sense to use online advertising.

Media plan

On average, we spent about £3.6m per year on communications, deployed as shown in Figure 27.

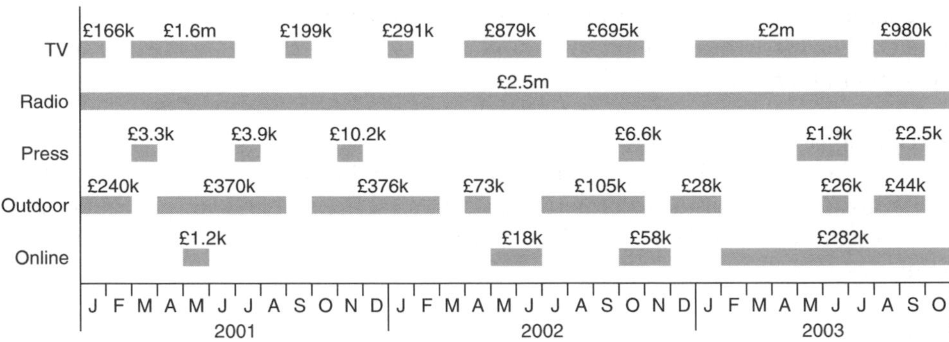

Figure 27: *Media plan*
Source: Ad dynamix

Let's just briefly recap on the strategy (see Figure 28).

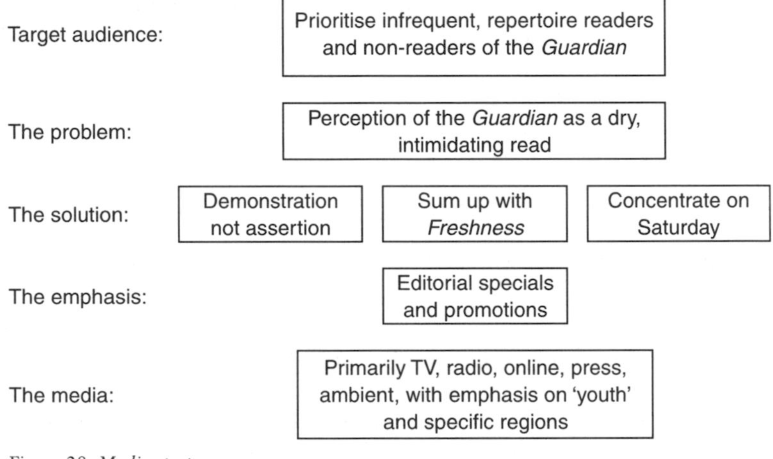

Figure 28: *Media strategy*

With all that in place, let's show you what happened.

RESULTS: A FRESH START FOR THE *GUARDIAN*

What we achieved

Our exclusively content-led strategy worked like a charm. Promotions and editorial initiatives, supported by a whole range of communications, achieved outstanding success against all the objectives set. This created a renaissance in the *Guardian*'s fortunes.

Let's start with market share. A steady six-year decline, dating back to the Murdoch price war of the mid-1990s, was first halted and then reversed. The *Guardian* saw its first significant growth in over ten years, and by October 2003 share had reached its highest levels since spring 1995 (Figure 29).

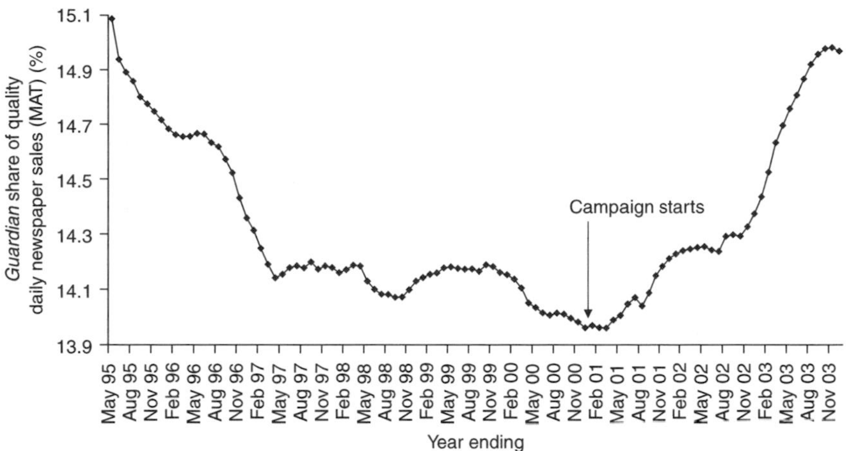

Figure 29: *The* Guardian *market share*
Source: ABC

The tapering off in late 2003 coincided with the launch of tabloid variants by two of our competitors. As you will see later, however, we have strong reason to believe this is a temporary hiccup rather than a permanent state of indigestion.

So, as hoped, we increased market share. But the truly remarkable achievement was that in a rapidly declining market we actually increased sales. What's more, sales grew most where we had focused the majority of our activity: on the Saturday paper (Figure 30).

More evidence for this dramatic turnaround comes from readership figures. Again, we saw an increase in readership of the Saturday paper as the gateway product, which was then followed by an increase in the weekday paper. And again, over the period of the campaign, readership figures for both Saturday and weekday reached their highest levels in eight years (Figure 31).

It wasn't only the Saturday paper that improved its readership levels. In fact, the *Guardian* as a whole was the only one of the five quality newspapers to increase its total average issue readership over the entire period (Figure 32).

Overall, total annual readership of the *Guardian* rose by over 700,000 – increasing the pool of readers that had, previously, been declining (Figure 33).

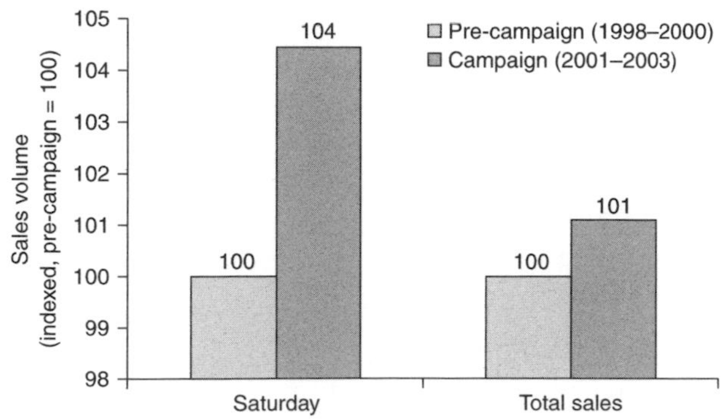

Figure 30: *Sales increased in absolute terms*
Source: The *Guardian*, ABC

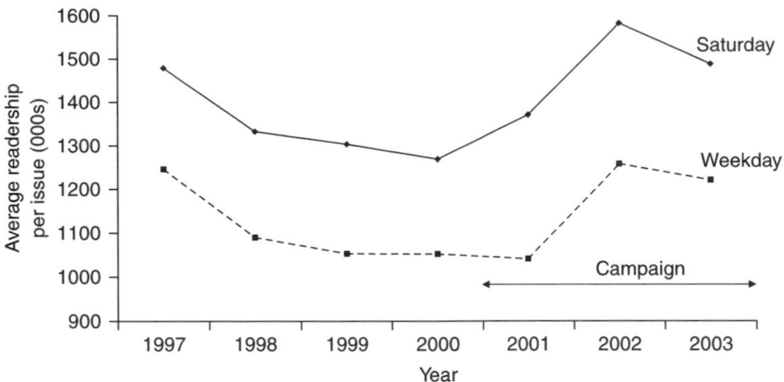

Figure 31: *Saturday readership increased first, weekday readership followed*
Source NRS

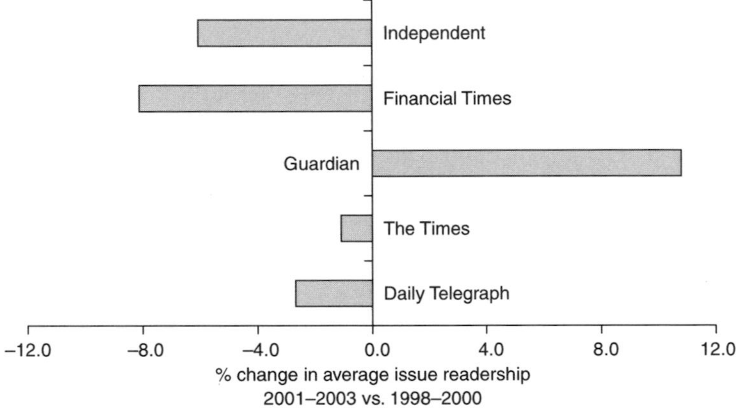

Figure 32: *The* Guardian *was the only quality daily to gain readers*
Source: NRS

A further measure of the *Guardian*'s influence is traffic to the website, Guardian Unlimited. Over the period of the campaign, page impressions quadrupled, outstripping the growth of the medium (see Figures 34 and 49).

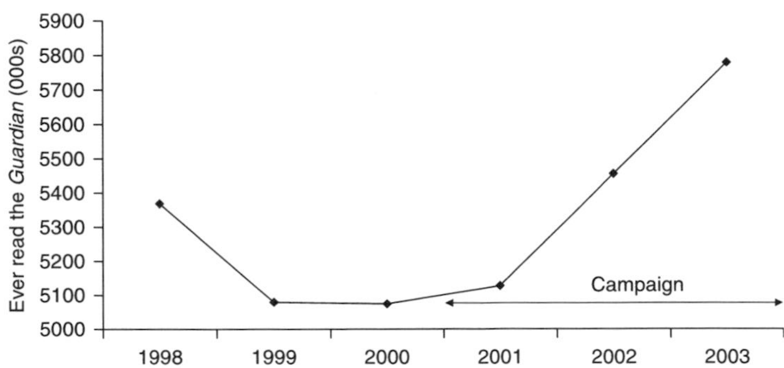

Figure 33: *Readership of the* Guardian *rocketed*
Source: NRS

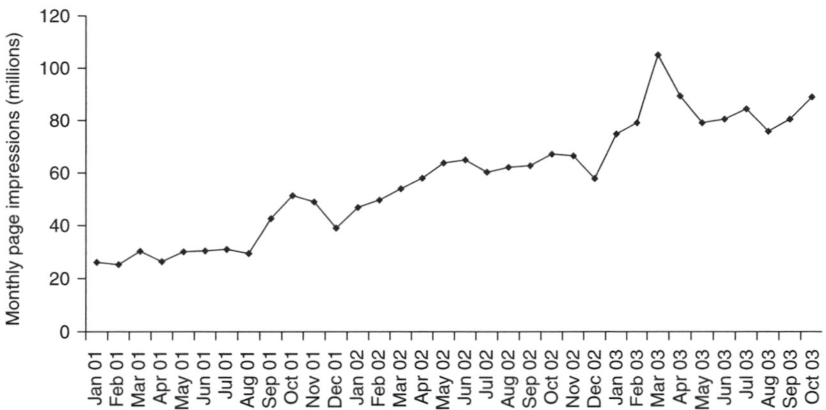

Figure 34: *Guardian Unlimited page impression grew dramatically*
Source: ABCE

Put baldly, the readership, sales and page impressions data show that we achieved our goal of increasing influence of the *Guardian*. And, as a result of this, total revenue from sales and advertising increased (Figure 35).

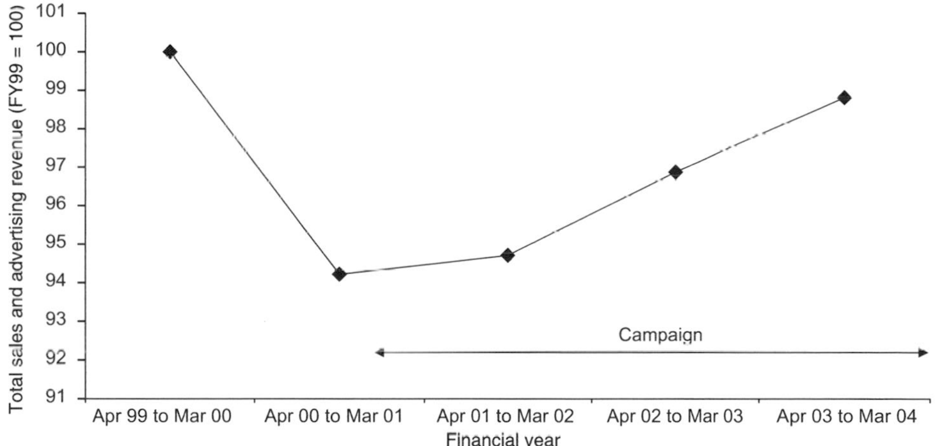

Figure 35: *Total revenue*
Source: The *Guardian*

How that success was achieved and proof it was caused by the communications

So, the *Guardian* enjoyed huge success over the period. We will now prove that it was our communications that caused this, by looking at the details of the turnaround and demonstrating that:

- the *timings* of effects match the timings of our activity
- and when we spent *more*, sales went up more
- and *where* we spent more, sales went up more
- the results were precisely those we had intended.

Saturday sales rose at the same time as our communications in the short term
Our primary aim was to get an immediate uplift in Saturday sales. We have already seen how Saturday sales rose over the whole period, but we can also see that peaks in Saturday sales tend to follow communications against that day (Figure 36).

Overall, those Saturdays supported by communications grew by over 6% during the period, while those Saturdays without support fell (Figure 37).

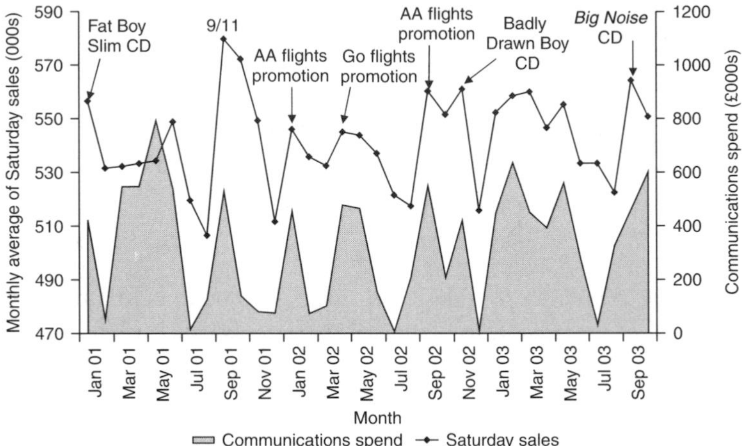

Figure 36: *Saturday sales vs communications spend*
Sources: The *Guardian*, Ad dynamix, CHJM

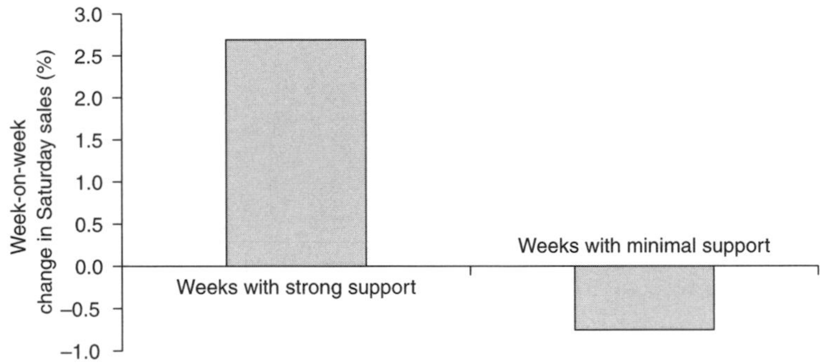

Figure 37: *Saturday sales grew during weeks with communications support*
Source: The *Guardian*

The more we spent on a Saturday, the more immediate sales rose
There was also a significant correlation between the level of communications spend and the change in sales; the more heavily supported Saturdays enjoying greater sales uplifts (Figure 38).

The same thing happens for longer-term Saturday sales
And the uplift was more than just an immediate one. Timings and spend levels of the communication also matched Saturday sales uplifts in the longer term, too (Figure 39).

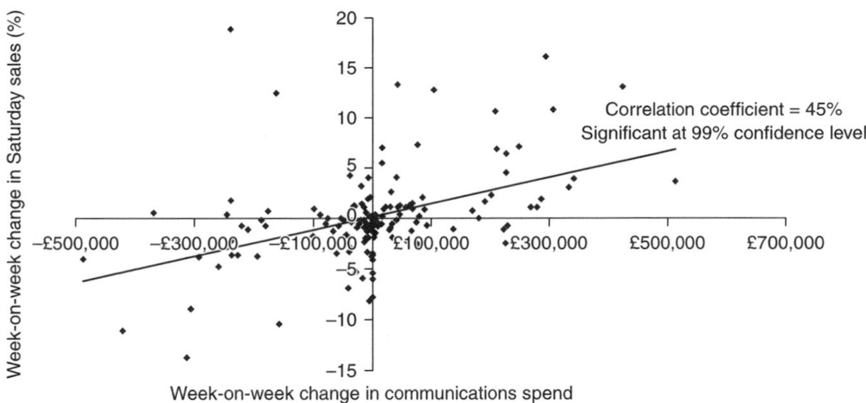

Figure 38: *The more we spent, the faster Saturday sales grew*
Sources: The *Guardian*, Ad dynamix, CHJM

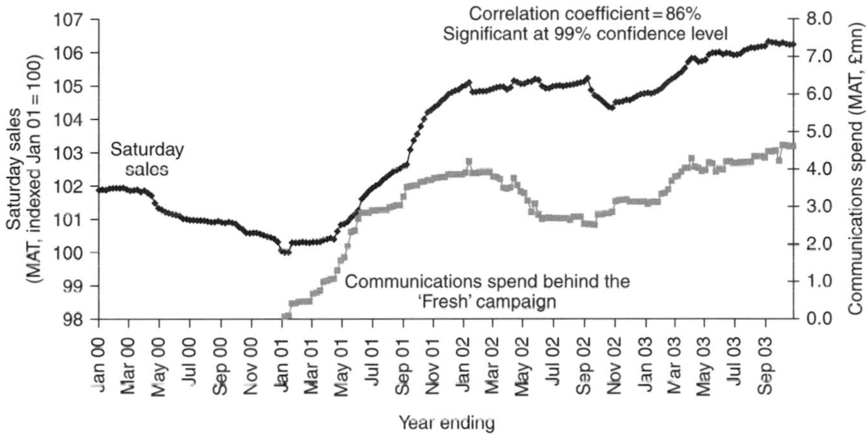

Figure 39: *Long term growth in Saturday sales matches the pattern of spend*
Sources: The *Guardian*, Ad dynamix, CHJM

As per our strategy, Saturday sales grew ahead of weekday sales

If our communications had indeed caused this uplift in sales, we would expect the pattern of uplift to mirror our strategy, Saturday sales growing ahead of the weekday ones. And this is exactly what we did see. We've already shown how readership of the Saturday paper grew most and grew first. We can also show how this followed the timings of our campaign (Figure 40).

We thought that the Saturday paper would act as the gateway product, encouraging people to buy the following weekdays. And this is indeed what happened. There was a strong correlation between Saturday sales and sales over the following week (Figure 41).

What's more, there was a strong correlation between *changes* in Saturday sales and *changes* in the following week. If sales went up on Saturday, they tended to go up for the rest of the week (Figure 42).

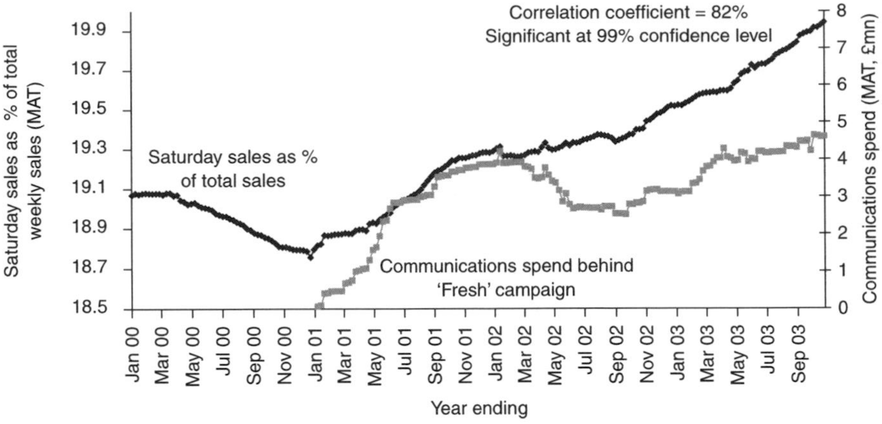

Figure 40: *Changes in the Saturday/weekday mix reflect changes in spend*
Sources: The *Guardian*, Ad dynamix, CHJM

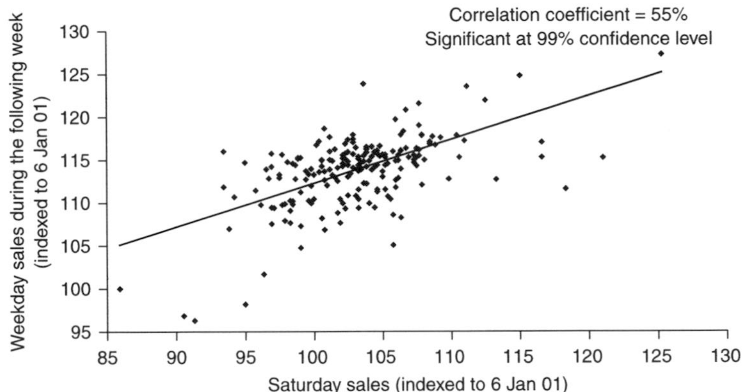

Figure 41: *Weekday sales tend to follow Saturday sales*
Source: The *Guardian*

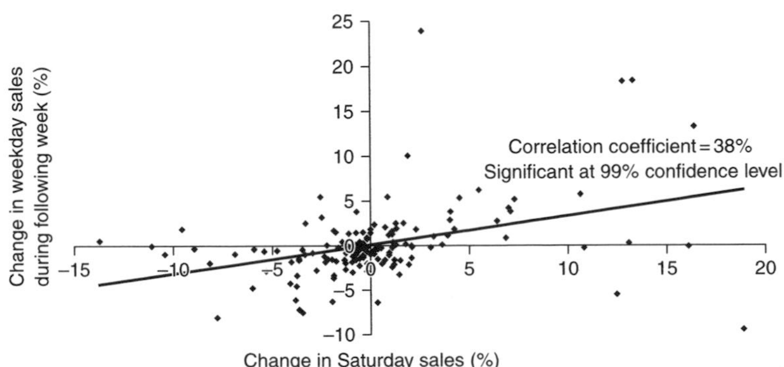

Figure 42: *Changes in weekly sales tend to follow changes in Saturday sales*
Source: The *Guardian*

Our strategy was right. Saturday *did* tend to drive the following weekday sales, as well as being the day most likely to attract that vital wavering buyer. Our decision to concentrate on Saturday was justified.

Total market share growth matches timings and levels of spend
So, communications boosted Saturday sales, which, in turn, boosted sales for the following weekdays. It won't be any great surprise to learn, therefore, that the growth in the *Guardian*'s total market share also matched timings and levels of communications (Figure 43).

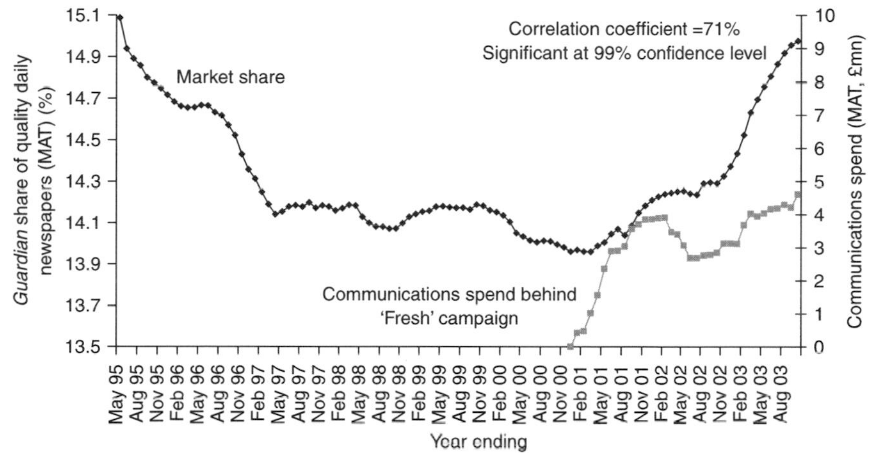

Figure 43: *Market share growth matches communications spend*
Sources: ABC, Ad dynamix, CHJM

The effects of the different communication elements

So how did it all work? We'll now show the individual effect of the different elements of the communications.

Promotions and editorial grandstand caused an uplift in sales
There is clear evidence that promotions and grandstand editorial caused instant uplifts in Saturday sales, and also raised sales for the following weekdays. Promotions tended to have a bigger instant uplift than editorial grandstands, while the editorial tended to have a stronger knock-on effect for the rest of the week (Figure 44).

Looking at individual promotions, we can also see that while CDs produced the most impressive boost to Saturday sales, the other promotions proved more effective at lifting sales in the following week (Figure 45).

The advertising: qualitative proof that it worked
We don't have a tracking study – the short-lived nature of the output militates against on-going awareness and communications diagnostics. However, we do have a series of important, anecdotal measures that suggest its success.

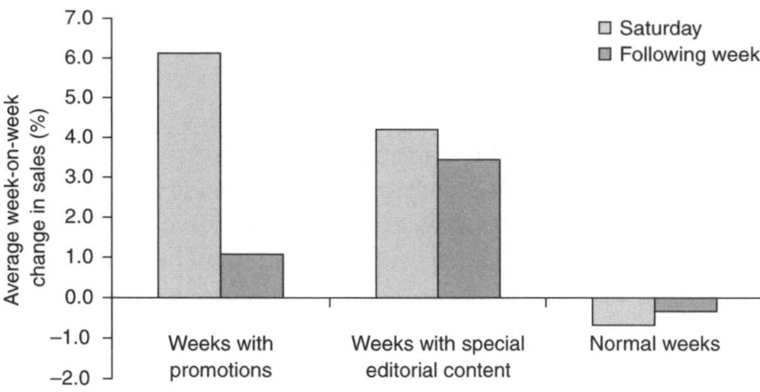

Figure 44: *Average uplift in sales for different types of activity*
Source: The *Guardian*

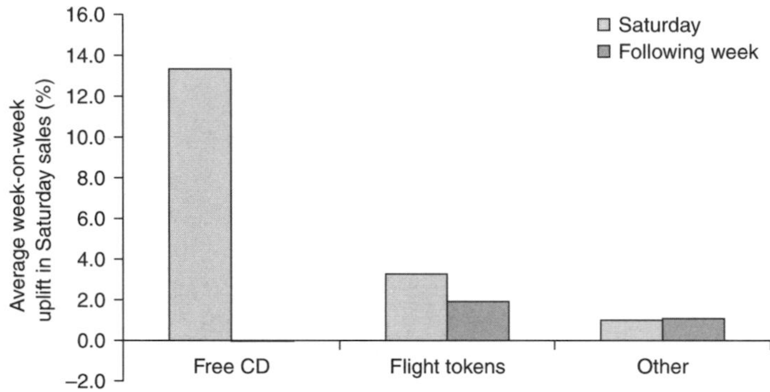

Figure 45: *Average uplift in sales for different kinds of promotion*
Source: The *Guardian*

Qualitative

Recent research demonstrates that our own views of the 'Fresh' output are shared by infrequent and non-purchasers. The following comments come from DDB London qualitative groups and vox pops in May 2004.

> 'They put across a sense of humour that I think the *Guardian* had always previously lacked – I'd always found it really po-faced and preachy. And the current advertising is pretty cool and culturally savvy – unlike my previous image of the paper only being interested in interminable in-depth political analyses and dusty dull exhibitions.'
>
> Male, 35–40, non-purchaser

> 'I'd always had it in my head that it would be read by schoolteachers and civil servants. Those [ads] have a much more youthy feel to them. Makes me feel as though it might, finally, have something relevant to say to me.'
>
> Male, C1, 25–30, non-reader

> 'I'd never picked up the *Guardian* until I saw an ad for *The Guide*, which made me go out and buy the paper. I was really surprised by its contents, especially as I had always thought of the *Guardian* as quite a heavy read. The ads I've seen reflect more of what the paper is actually about today.'
>
> Female, 25–35, infrequent purchaser

Creative awards
The industry itself has recognised the creative power of the advertising, with the campaign winning 56 creative awards since 2001, including:

- Gold campaigns at the *Campaign* press awards 2002, 2003, 2004
- three awards at the British Television Awards 2004
- four awards for TV work at Creative Circle 2002.

Whilst this might be seen simply as vanity, in the *Guardian*'s case, it's hugely important – raising our profile and influence amongst the media community. So the qualitative indications are that the advertising was working. But what about the hard business measures?

Advertising increased sales
We've seen how promotions and special editorial boost sales. The same is also true of advertising. Sales increased during advertised weeks, particularly those with TV, but fell without advertising support (Figure 46).

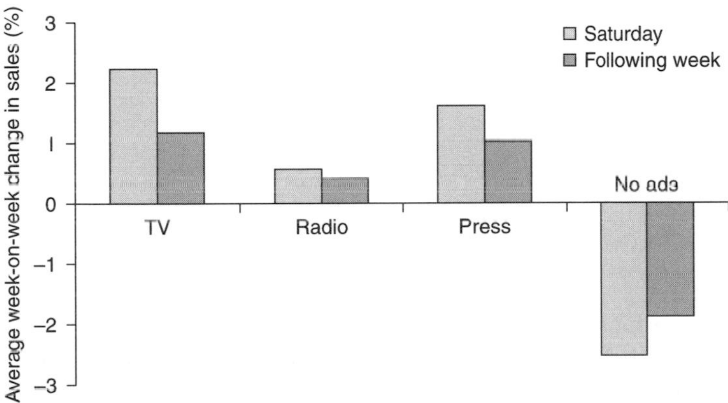

Figure 46: *Average uplift in sales, by different advertising media*
Sources: The *Guardian*, Ad dynamix

Regions with more advertising grew more
Regional data shows the contribution of advertising particularly clearly. As we discussed earlier, some regions received more advertising support than others, and readership increased significantly more in these regions (Figure 47).

This is unequivocal proof of the effect of advertising, because all the other factors that might influence demand – editorial, promotions, price, and so on – were the same everywhere. Only advertising varied by region.

The more we advertised, the more sales increased
Further evidence of the effect of advertising comes from looking at variations in the level of spend. There is a strong correlation between how much we spent on advertising in any given week and the sales uplift that resulted (Figure 48).

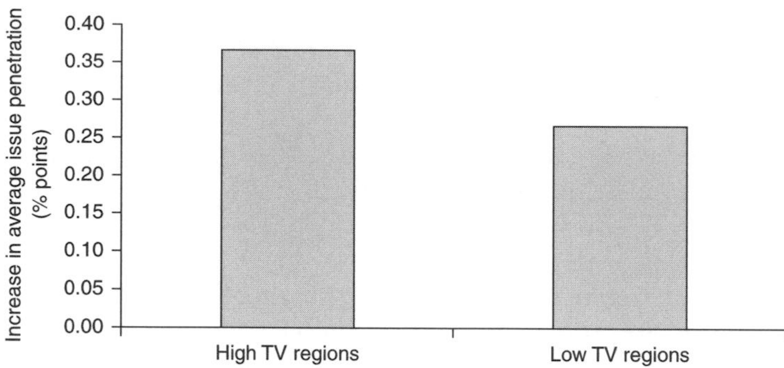

Figure 47: *Saturday readership increased more in upweighted TV regions*
Source: NRS

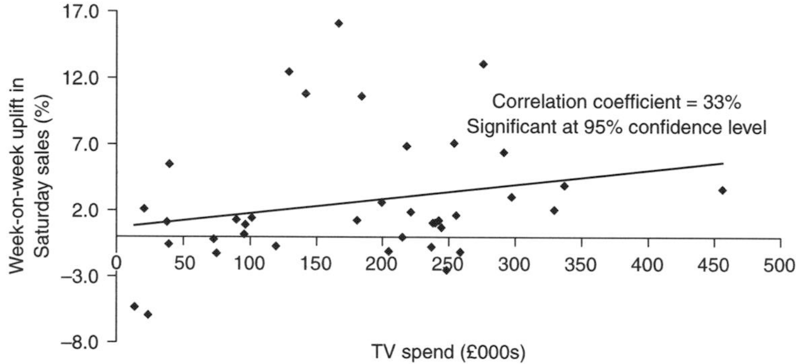

Figure 48: *The more we spent on TV advertising, the faster sales grew*
Sources: The *Guardian*, Ad dynamix

Advertising grew Guardian Unlimited's share

Our final proof of the effect of advertising comes from the online version of the paper. Guardian Unlimited's share of internet traffic, in any given month, clearly correlates with the total level of the *Guardian* adspend. This is a particularly pure

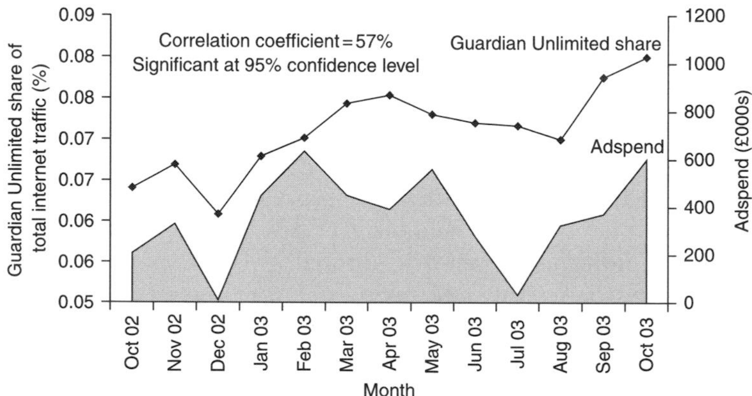

Figure 49: *Share of internet traffic follows adspend*
Sources: ABCE, Ad dynamix

demonstration of the effect of advertising, as there are no promotions online (Figure 49).

So, evidence from levels of spend over time and by region, along with the Guardian Unlimited share, qualitative evidence and industry awards, enable us to see the effect of advertising above and beyond the promotions and editorial specials they supported.

The integrated effects of advertising, promotions and editorial specials

Having isolated the individual effects of the different elements, we can now look at how they worked together. Promotions dramatically enhanced the ability of advertising to uplift sales (Figure 50).

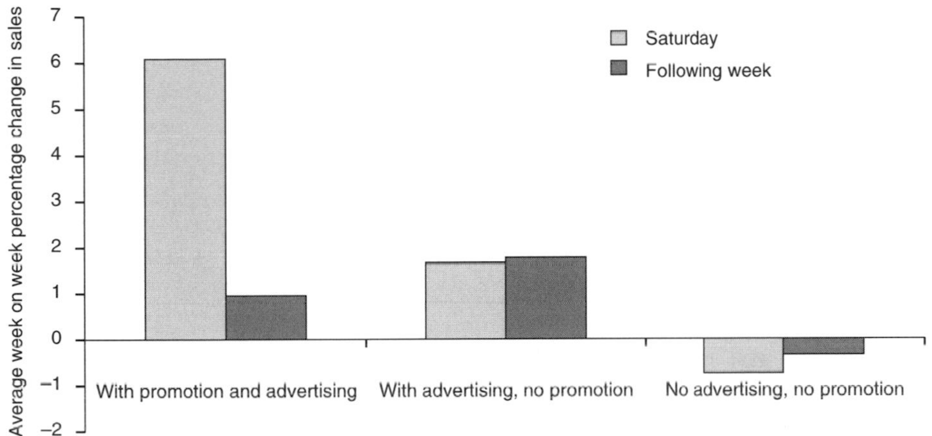

Figure 50: *Average uplift in sales*
Sources: The *Guardian*, Ad dynamix

Again, regional analysis shows that advertising increases the ability of other activity to boost sales; the more advertising support the activity received, the more uplift there was in sales.

This worked for both CD promotions (Figures 51 and 52), for flight promotions (Figure 53) and also held true for editorial specials (Figure 54).

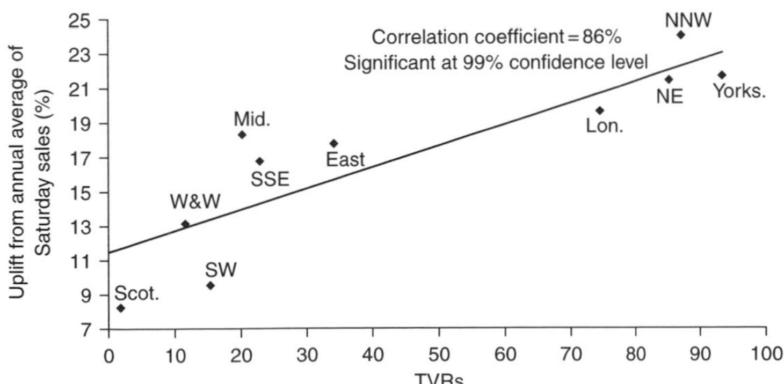

Figure 51: *Fat Boy Slim CD, sales uplift vs TV*
Sources: The *Guardian*, BARB

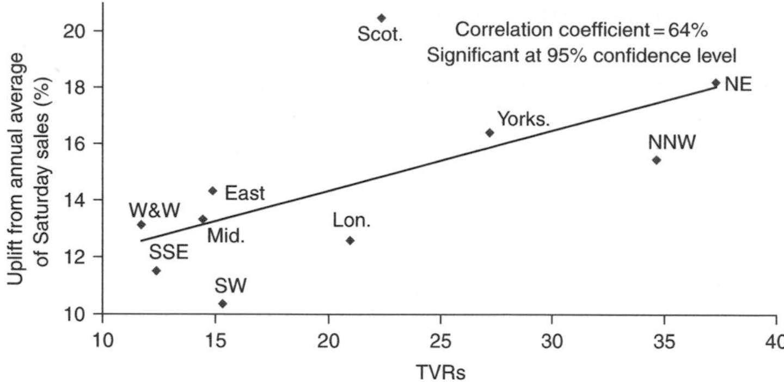

Figure 52: *Badly Drawn Boy CD, sales uplift vs TV*
Sources: The *Guardian*, BARB

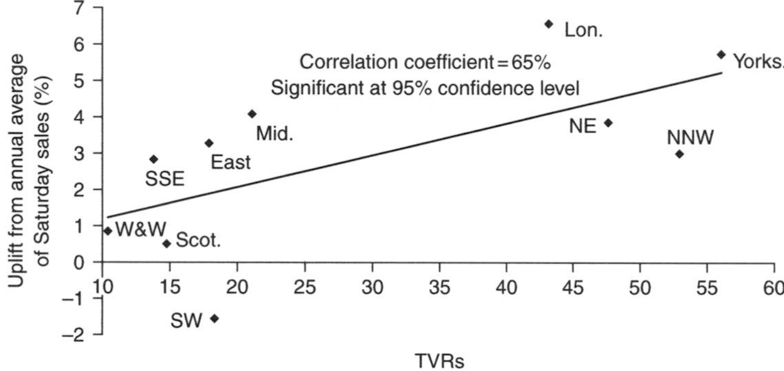

Figure 53: *Go flight offer, sales uplift vs TV*
Sources: The *Guardian*, BARB

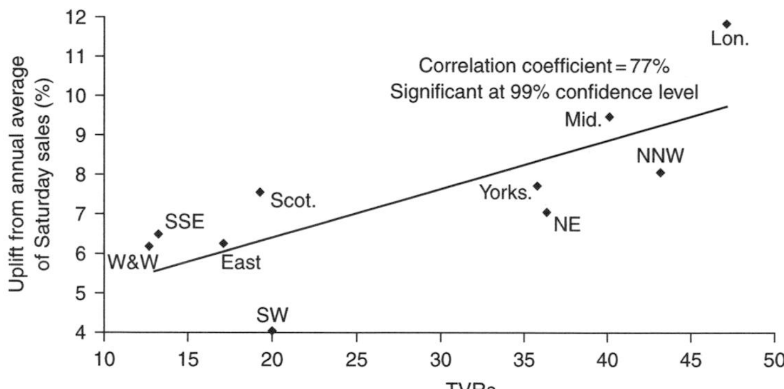

Figure 54: *Definitive food, sales uplift vs TV*
Sources: The *Guardian*, BARB

This is, once again, a vindication of our strategy. We used advertising to demonstrate concrete examples of *Guardian* 'Freshness', whether promotions or content, rather than allowing it to float off into the vacuum of an abstract brand idea. This maximised the power of the promotions and editorial, growing Saturday and weekday sales in both the short and the long term.

The impact on revenue

So, we have shown that by using advertising chiefly to support promotions and content on Saturdays, we increased sales across the whole week in both the short and long term.

We will now demonstrate how our communications generated revenue for the *Guardian*. As we saw earlier, there are two main sources of revenue: sales and advertising. Over the period, the *Guardian* performed strongly in both.

Sales revenue

While the competition were discounting, the increased demand generated by the communications allowed the *Guardian* to actually increase prices, both in absolute and relative terms (Figure 55).

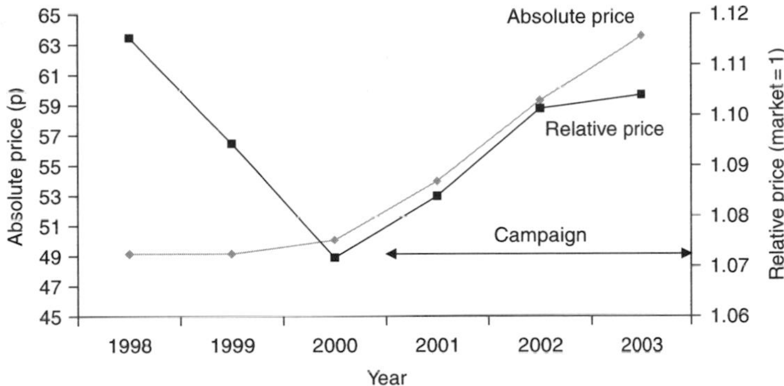

Figure 55: *Price*

With both market share and prices increasing, revenue from full-price sales increased substantially (Figure 56).

And by outperforming the rest of the market, the *Guardian* was therefore able to increase its value share of full-price sales (Figure 57).

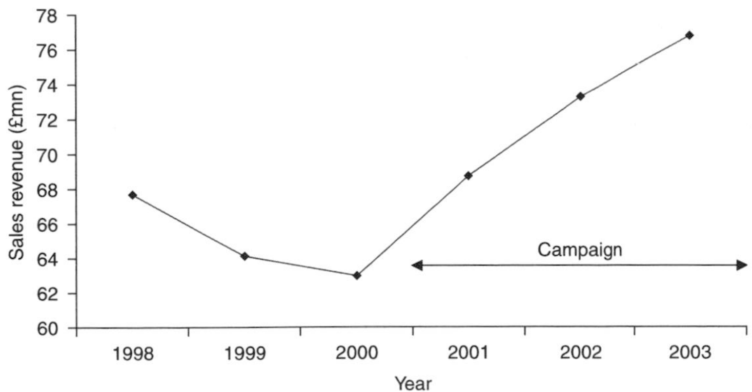

Figure 56: *Value of full-price sales*
Source: ABC

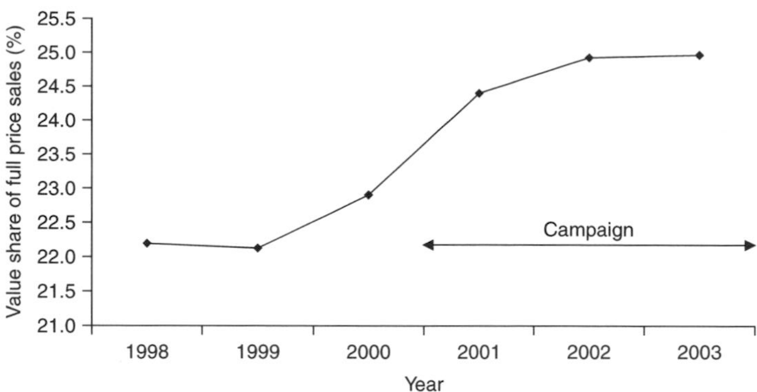

Figure 57: *Value share of full-price sales*
Source: ABC

But there is a further point to make. In order to maintain circulation levels, all the newspapers, to some extent, rely on either discounting (for example, by coupon collection) or bulks (giving away free copies of the paper on trains, for example). But because demand for the *Guardian* remained high, they were able to maintain sales with a far lower level of discounts or bulks than any of their competitors (Figure 58).

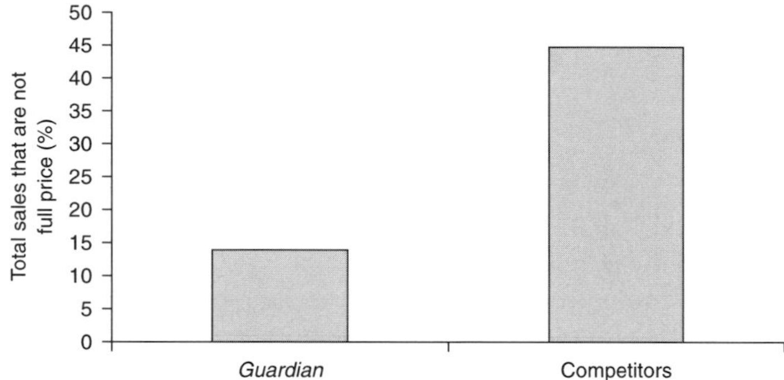

Figure 58: *Percentage of total sales that are not full price*
Source: ABC

And this has not changed significantly over time. Therefore, the *Guardian*'s sales revenue over the period was even better than the full-price sales would at first suggest.

Advertising revenue

Increased display advertising revenue ultimately depends on sales figures and levels and quality of readership. We've already demonstrated that sales and readership rose. In addition, we can see that this was not at the expense of quality. It is vital for the paper to keep as youthful an audience as possible in this ageing sector as advertisers will pay more to reach a younger audience. As can be seen, over the period during which the campaign ran, average reader age for the *Guardian* rose by just 0.7 years, a far smaller rise than the average for the competition (Figure 59).

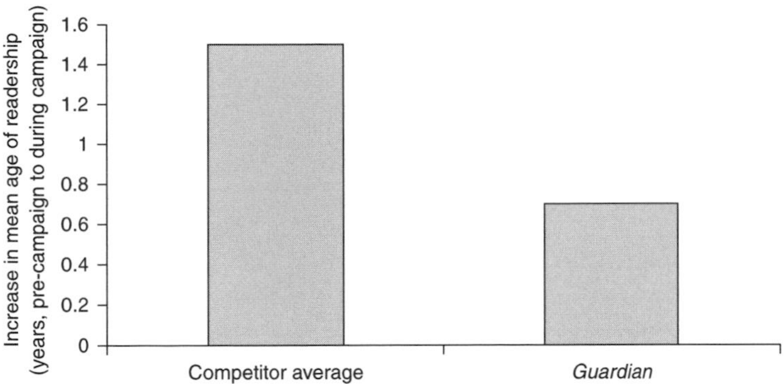

Figure 59: *The Guardian's readership aged less than the competition*
Source: NRS

So, given all that, we would expect to see an uplift in advertising revenue. There is, naturally, a lag here; it takes time for data to be published, and then to be translated into changed behaviour from media buyers. Within a year of the campaign starting, the decline in the *Guardian*'s share of advertising revenue halted and six months later it began to rise steeply, in line with market share (Figure 60). We see the same pattern for absolute advertising revenue (Figure 61).

We've shown how the *Guardian*'s growth in market share, sales and revenue match the timing, levels and intended effects of the communications. Now we'll demonstrate how it could not have been any other factors that were responsible for this remarkable turnaround.

Eliminating other factors

'The news'

Whilst the news agenda certainly has an effect on sales, it can't explain our success. For a start, the vast majority of our results eliminate news as a variable, because

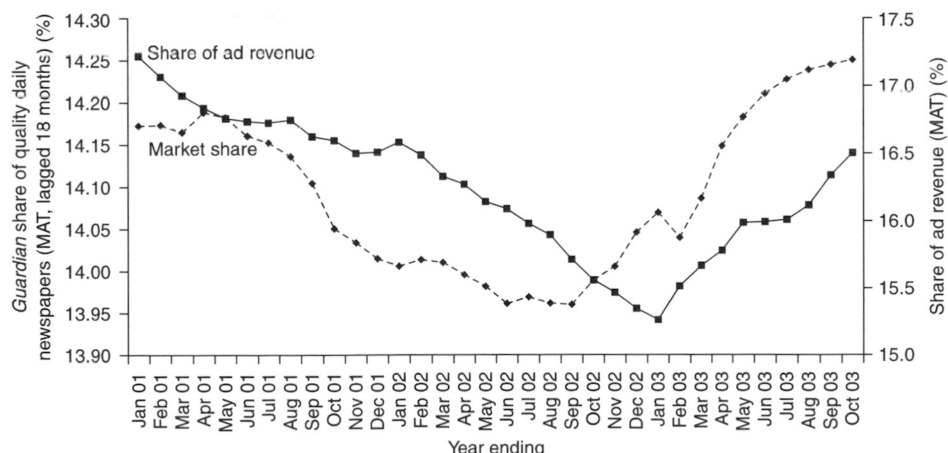

Figure 60: *Share of advertising revenue follows market share with a lag of 18 months*
Sources: ABC, Nielsen

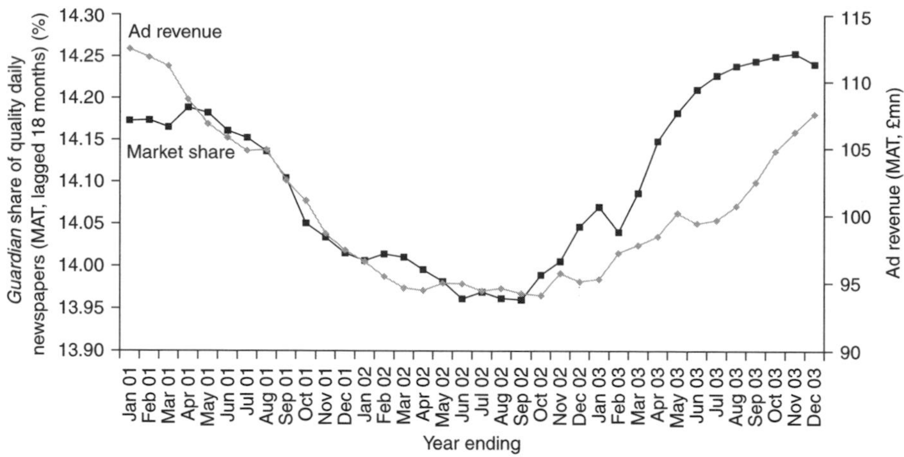

Figure 61: *Advertising revenue follows market share with a lag of 18 months*
Sources: ABC, Nielsen

they concentrate on *share*. The big news stories during this period were common to and covered by all the newspapers, so our relatively greater success can only be explained by marketing activity. Indeed, news stories that have a demonstrable effect on circulation break only rarely. This paper demonstrates that the growth we have achieved is continuous and sustained, rather than down to a few isolated short-term incidents.

A slackening of competition

Nor can the achievement be down to our rivals going to sleep. Although we can't get full marketing spends for our competitors, adspend is a good proxy. In this regard, during the period of the campaign, their adspend actually went up (Figure 62).

NPD

New product development is endemic to this market. There can't be many other categories where a unique version of the product is produced on a daily basis. It would be disingenuous of us to suggest that editorial and marketing innovation

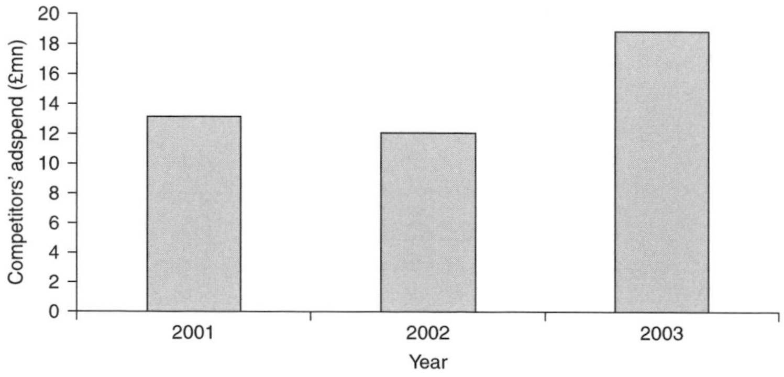

Figure 62: *Our competitors increased their adspend over the period of the campaign*

haven't greatly helped in our task, providing us with a long list of motivating supports for the campaign.

We would, however, suggest that our communications strategy has allowed us to make the greatest capital out of these developments – as we believe we have shown in this paper. After all, it is not as if our competitors have not been hard at it as well, with a vast array of promotional and editorial initiatives of their own.

Distribution

It's almost impossible to gain a competitive advantage here. All national newspapers share one distribution network, through 150 wholesalers who supply to the 55,000 retailers. The only advantages to be gained are through small-scale initiatives, such as non-traditional news retailers and direct distribution, but all evidence suggests that these are of marginal effect.

Supply

That said, it might be possible to flood the market with papers, leading to greater availability and therefore greater overall sales. However, if we had done so, we would have expected to see much greater levels of returns as well; in essence a less efficient ratio of supply to returns. This didn't happen. The proportion of returns remained static during the campaign period.

Price manipulation

We've already shown that frantic discounting was not the key. Price went up both in absolute and relative terms during the campaign. On top of that, our levels of bulks, the only cut-price version of the paper available, remained almost static during this period and at much lower levels than the rest of the market.

POS

Whilst POS forms an important element of the marketing mix within the newspaper segment, achieving sustainable competitive advantage in this area is both difficult and costly. Promotional and display space in the multiples is highly coveted by both newspaper and magazine publishers and is therefore expensive. Coordinating activity across thousands of independent retailers poses significant logistical challenges. Whilst the *Guardian* employs a dynamic and inventive team of retail representatives, the limits of budget and available headcount dictate that we are unable to gain a disproportionate share of voice at the point of purchase.

CONCLUSION

The *Guardian*, and by implication this paper, is about more than profits. Since its founding in 1821, the paper has, above and beyond anything else, aspired to journalistic excellence and influence.

Between 1995 and 2001, that prized influence was being eroded, with market share, sales and readership falling. However the 'fresh' campaign, allied to editorial excellence, enabled the *Guardian* to turn a corner in its fortunes. An approach to communications that put genuine, surprising content before abstract brand sentiments ensured a revitalisation of fortunes.

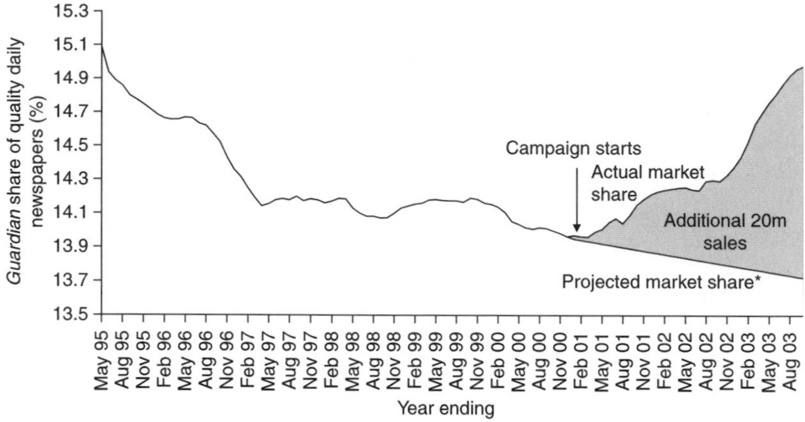

Figure 63: *The* Guardian *market share projection*
Source: ABC
* Forecast based on average monthly share decline for two years prior to start of campaign

Indeed, we can predict what would have happened to the paper's market share without the effect of our communications (Figure 63).

Scary stuff. However, thanks to the 'Fresh' campaign, not only has influence grown again, but so has revenue, putting the paper in a strong position from which to carry on its fight. After almost ten years of decline, the paper is, once again, thriving as a financially viable voice of liberalism and journalistic excellence.

Payback

Issues of confidentiality prevent us from quoting financial information. However the remarkable revenue gains (see Figure 35) more than covered the costs of the campaign.

A postscript on recent months and the future

During the last quarter of 2003, *The Times* and the *Independent* both launched tabloid variants of their papers. This initiative led to a tapering off in the consistent share gains that we'd seen for the *Guardian* over the previous two and half years. We do, however, have every reason to believe that this is a temporary anomaly, rather than the shape of things to come. With market share, readership and the coffers all in a healthy condition, the *Guardian* is in a strong position to fight off these challenges. Indeed, alternative formats had already been under consideration at the time of the tabloid launch and a number of options are currently being assessed. For commercial reasons, we are unable to reveal these, but we're confident that they will represent a different and better option to competitors' offerings and a return to normal proceedings for the *Guardian*.

SILVER
BEST NEW CLIENT

18

Virgin Trains

How a powerful idea fuelled the engine room of Virgin Trains revenue by changing minds and winning hearts

Principal authors: Garbhan O'Bric, Rainey Kelly Campbell Roalfe/Y&R, Lyndsey Jenkins, Manning Gottlieb OMD, and Ioannis Melas, OMD Metrics

EDITOR'S SUMMARY

Train travel isn't an obviously communications-sensitive market. Not least at a time when the market itself is depressed by a succession of tragic crashes and inevitably diminished public perceptions. Not even when the operator in question is Virgin, a legendarily customer-facing and brand-focused company.

Virgin's entry into the market had been stymied initially by poor rolling stock and negative perceptions of the train travel experience. Worryingly for Virgin, these sentiments were increasingly impacting on the broader reputation of the Virgin brand.

For the good of both the Trains subsidiary and its parent, then, the 'new beginning' offered up by the introduction of new Virgin rolling stock in 2002 could not be squandered.

Creative and media worked to engage emotionally and to persuade rationally, to convince local minds and appeal to the nation's hearts. Advertising quickly shifted perceptions and drove consideration of Virgin train travel. Modelling credits the advertising activity with generating £62m of incremental revenue during 2002/3, equivalent to 8.4% of Virgin Trains' total revenue.

Equally telling, albeit of less obvious immediate value commercially, is that Virgin Trains can finally be seen to be making a positive contribution to group brand image.

INTRODUCTION

This paper is the story of a campaign that began to deliver on what Richard Branson called his 'greatest challenge ever': to rekindle the public's enthusiasm for train travel. It is the story of how, in the face of considerable public frustration at the state of train travel in the UK, a communications campaign for Virgin Trains in 2002 worked to overcome people's deeply held negative perceptions in order to create a more positive impression of the company, increase the number willing to consider travelling by train and in turn generate a vastly increased return on advertising investment.

It is the story of a campaign idea that directly accounted for an increase of 12% in revenue across the business periods the advertising ran[1] and over 8% (£62.25m) of total Virgin Trains revenue generated over the period of New Beginning analysis.[2]

BACKGROUND

Close your eyes for a moment and consider the state of train travel in Britain after 30 years of under-investment; the endless delays endured, the cramped conditions on board dated carriages. Consider also the hefty price increases; the leaf-strewn lines that managed to instantly cripple services and the tales of travellers stranded late at night.

This gives you a taste of the prevailing public sentiment towards rail travel when Virgin Trains acquired the UK's two biggest rail franchises, the Cross Country (XC) and West Coast (WC) networks in 1997 (Figure 1).

Overnight, Virgin Trains took control of 400 trains a day carrying 31 million passengers a year.[3] As the sole operator on these two lines, it inherited not only a legacy of under-funding and poor rolling stock, but also all the negative perceptions that went with it.

> 'I am surprised they could find anyone to sell this railway to.'
>
> *Independent On Sunday*, 1997

Furthermore, in light of previous Virgin successes in other consumer markets, expectations were running high.

> 'Mr Branson's success in restoring the glitz and glamour to air travel [is] sorely needed in the rail sector if it is to undergo the renaissance many have said it needs.'
>
> *Financial Times*, 1997

1. OMD Metrics 2004/Virgin Train Business Periods 03/08–03/09 (15 September 2002–9 November 2002).
2. OMD Metrics 2004/Virgin Trains Business Periods 03/02–04/05 (April 2002–June 2003).
3. Virgin Trains internal data.

Figure 1: *Virgin Trains network map*

FAR FROM A SMOOTH RIDE

However, rather than the rapid improvement initially hoped for in 1997, things only got worse and the initial air of optimism was quickly dispelled by a succession of tragic rail crashes.[4]

The Hatfield crash in particular resulted in widespread service disruptions for Virgin Trains, causing continued delays and dropping levels of punctuality.[5] It emerged through the subsequent investigation that the general condition of the track and track bed 'were immensely worse than expected'[6] and the related investment that followed necessitated hefty fare hikes.[7]

By 2002 'the public's verdict on the performance of Britain's railways could scarcely be more damning',[8] as the proportion of respondents who believed Britain's railways had deteriorated in recent years exceeded the proportion that believed they had improved by a ratio of 13 to one.[9]

4. Southall (1997), Ladbroke Grove (1999), Hatfield (2000), Potters Bar (2002).
5. The average numbers of trains arriving on time dropped to 71% on WC and just 62.4% on XC in the last quarter of 2001 (Virgin Trains internal data).
6. Director General of the Association of Train Operators.
7. Leisure tickets on Virgin Trains' Cross Country network rose by 5%, almost double the rate of inflation and business tickets increased by 7%.
8. YouGov special survey for the *Daily Telegraph*, 2002.
9. YouGov special survey for the *Daily Telegraph*, 2002.

> 'Passengers are at best jaded and at worst angry. They feel a sense of despair because the railways are now in such a mess.'
>
> Rail Passengers Council

Indeed, the state of the railways was having an impact across *all* aspects of British life. A survey conducted by the British Chamber of Commerce in 2002 found that the cost of time and productivity lost as a result of rail delays was £21,000 to the average firm, equivalent to 'losing a member of staff for nearly two months'.

> 'Businesses have experienced at first hand the impact of decades of decay and decline on the UK rail network. Unreliable services, poor timetabling and inadequate infrastructure are a continual drain on resources and willpower.'
>
> British Chamber of Commerce, 2002

Understandably these developments served to fuel the criticism that had now become an everyday occurrence across the media. The BBC created a 'Railways in Crisis' site dedicated to coverage of the trials and tribulations of the industry, even appointing a BBC News Online 'Rail Commuters Champion'. Classic tabloid journalism prevailed when the *Sun* wryly observed that 'Passengers wasted 8000 years waiting for delayed trains in the past year' (Figure 2).

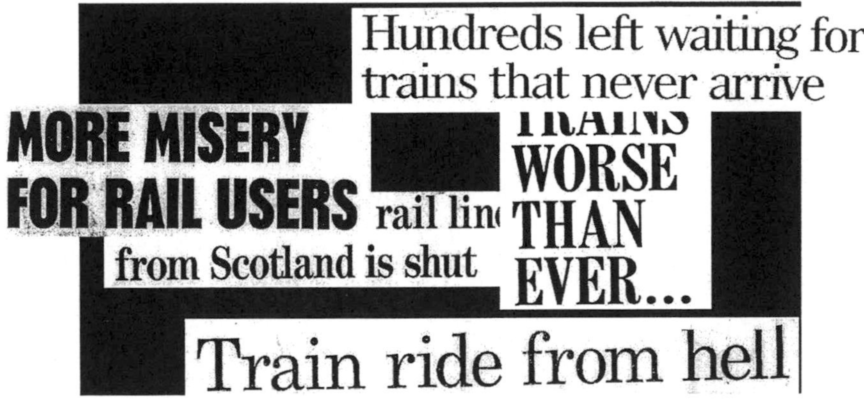

Figure 2: *Railway misery – a focus for considerable media attention*

POINTING THE FINGER

The sheer number of different key stakeholders, regulators, authorities and operators provoked considerable public confusion as to who was accountable. Blame was spread widely and no one emerged unscathed, from the Government – whom a vast majority (eight to one) believed had done a bad job – to the rail operators themselves, where every aspect of the rail companies' service was rated either 'poor' or 'dreadful'.[10]

10. YouGov special survey for the *Daily Telegraph*, 2002.

Such was the extent of the public's dissatisfaction, nearly two in five passengers in 2002 were willing to support a boycott of the railways organised by the Better Rail Advisory Group.[11]

VIRGIN TRAINS GETS SINGLED OUT

It was tough enough being a rail operator at such times but a number of factors resulted in Virgin Trains being singled out for particular attention. First, as part of the Virgin Group, with a proven track record of success in other markets and a celebrated chairman, people's expectations had been high.

> 'Since government has abdicated any responsibility for the national train set, perhaps it is only an entrepreneur who can save our railways. Over to you Mr Branson!'
>
> *Financial Times*, 1997

The subsequent disappointment was palpable:

> 'When Branson bought the trains, he promised airline-style travel, but it isn't there yet.'
>
> Virgin Trains qualitative research, 2001

Second, as the operator of the UK's two biggest rail franchises it was understandable that the company would receive the lion's share of attention. Virgin Trains service delays received national press coverage, reviews of the company's revenue performance were not limited to the business pages and it often found itself being the focus of consumer anger at pan-industry price increases.[12]

This had a profound effect on perceptions of the brand. Compared with other companies in the group, Virgin Trains found it neither enjoyed the respect or emotional affinity that the other Virgin brands commanded nor was it seen to exhibit the traditional characteristics that defined its sister brands (Figure 3).

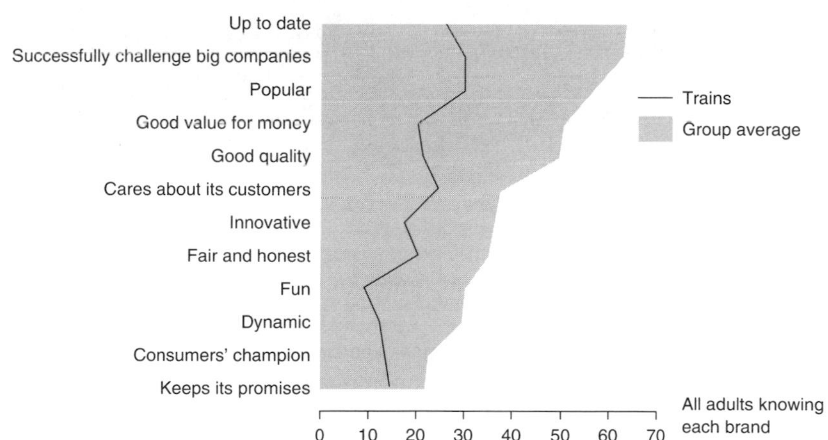

Figure 3: *Virgin Trains underperforming on all criteria that define Virgin Group brands*
Source: HPI, Virgin Brand Tracking Study, 2002

11. The *Express* newspaper, January 2002.
12. 'Virgin Trains arrive 6 hours late'/'Passengers hit out at Virgin Fares' – BBC Railways in Crisis.

Virgin Trains was increasingly perceived as an unsuccessful brand that delivered poor service and one that was not consumer conscious.[13] For a brand group that defined itself as a consumer champion, this was increasingly having a negative effect on the Virgin group at large.[14]

Virgin's mission of rekindling the public's enthusiasm for train travel had 'yet to leave the station'.

GETTING BACK ON TRACK

By 2002 the company was in desperate need to inform the public of real progress and that Virgin would meet the public expectation and keep its promise of an improved rail service.

The eventual delivery of a whole new fleet of state-of-the-art trains, consisting of 78 'Voyager' trains and 53 'Pendolino' trains, as part of an on-going £2bn investment in new rolling stock, and the improved higher-frequency timetable this facilitated, would provide that opportunity (Figure 4).

Figure 4: *The new Pendolino and Voyager trains*

The related marketing objective was quite simple:

- raise awareness of the arrival of the new trains and higher-frequency timetable
- fuel perceptions of Virgin Trains as an innovative and dynamic modern rail operator
- leverage the occasion to drive brand reappraisal and affinity.

13. HPI Brand Tracking Study 2002/TRBI Brand & Advertising Tracking Study.
14. HPI Brand Tracking Study. In 2000 Virgin Trains scored -1 on the contribution to the Virgin brand image balance. By April 2002 this had declined to -9.

However, in attempting to achieve this, there were two reasons why the advertising idea developed was unlike anything Virgin had done before.

1. The replacement of the old rolling stock would be slow and staggered. Initially, new trains and a new timetable would appear only on the Cross Country network and it would be approximately two years before the West Coast network had received full delivery of all new Pendolino trains.[15]
2. The degree of public agitation meant that confidence could not be won overnight. We needed to be conscious of the need not to appear brash or self-congratulatory for risk of underestimating public sentiment and provoking further scorn.

The significance of these two factors meant that expectations needed to be managed carefully, and simply celebrating the new rail fleet as an end in itself would be insufficient.

NOT THE LAUNCH OF A NEW PRODUCT, BUT THE BEGINNING OF A NEW ERA

We needed to present the new fleet and new timetable in the context of a bigger brand idea. The solution was to celebrate not the launch of a train but the beginning of a new era. The brand idea was 'A New Beginning'.

The focus lay not in dramatising the death of the old rail service, but rather in the spirit, determination and labour of love demanded to deliver a brighter future. Such an idea would work not only to reassure the public that Virgin Trains was now starting to deliver on its promises, but would also signal the brand's intent for future improvement.

However, any execution would have to steer clear of the overtly irreverent and brash advertising that defined other Virgin brands (Figures 5 and 6). Such an approach would risk being seen as treating a subject of national importance in a flippant manner and underestimating the seriousness with which the public viewed the issue.

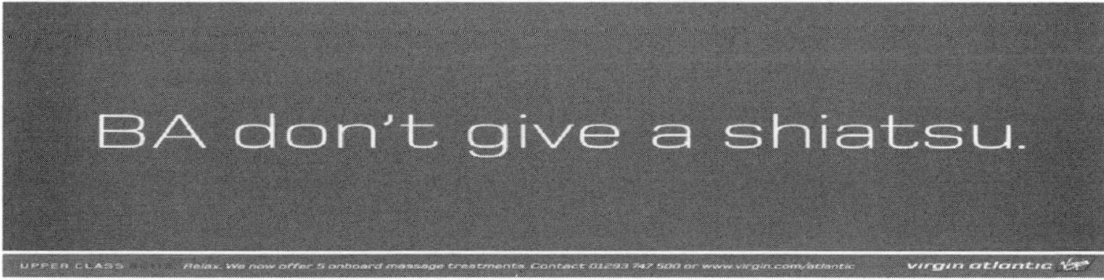

Figure 5: *Taking a dig at the competition – Virgin Atlantic 48-sheet poster*
Source: Rainey Kelly Campbell Roalfe/Y&R

15. Voyager rollout began early 2002 reaching critical mass (over 50% of XC network trains) by September 2002. Pendolino fleet would not be fully operational until the end of 2004.

Figure 6: *Celebrities in compromising positions – Virgin Mobile TV advert featuring 'Wyclef'*
Source: Rainey Kelly Campbell Roalfe/Y&R

COMMUNICATIONS STRATEGY

In order to credibly inform the public of a 'New Beginning', transform their perceptions of train travel and encourage a reappraisal of Virgin Trains it became apparent from consumer segmentation that the communications would need to work at two levels (Figure 7).

Band C audiences displayed such a low disposition and antipathy towards trains that no communication could shift perceptions and behaviours in the short term. However, in direct contrast, Band A exhibited a positive disposition to train travel but was an audience for whom the pleasure and passion of train travel had waned recently. For such a target the challenge was to re-engage them in the experience of rail travel, to make them feel good again about trains. An involvement model-based communication strand to 'New Beginning', celebrating the emotional and experimental advantages of the new trains, was required.

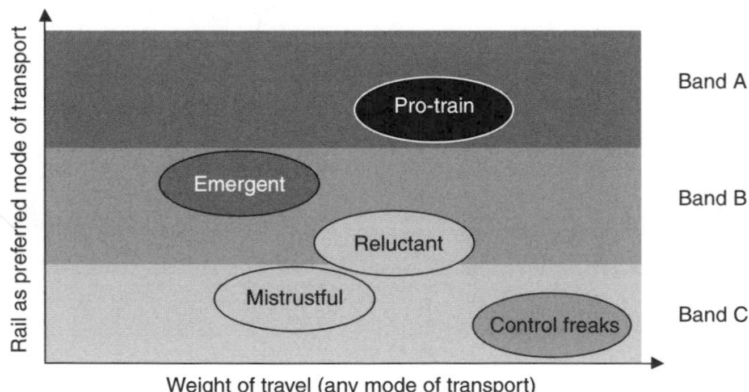

Figure 7: *Segmentation identified distinct cluster groups within the travel market*
Source: Pegram Walters Travel Segmentation Study for Virgin Trains, 2001

Band B consisted of a collection of individuals who had become cautious and cynical about train travel. Many of these were business travellers for whom the Cross Country network simply did not fulfil their main priority of providing convenient travel opportunities, especially compared to the current motorway network that virtually mirrored this line. For this group, feel-good advertising alone would prove insufficient. These were doubters who would demand factual, logical advantages to rail travel and proof of change. A rational, persuasive form of communications highlighting the new timetable and product benefits would help to convince them.

Thus, segmentation revealed there were some people we couldn't reach at all, some we needed to reach rationally and some we needed to reach emotionally. The 'New Beginning' campaign was structured to win hearts and convince minds.

MEDIA STRATEGY

The staggered roll-out of new trains across the Cross Country network and the new timetable had a profound effect on the media strategy and delivery of the 'hearts and minds' messages.

The need to ensure that the public felt well informed of any changes to their local service at all times, demanded a media strategy that would start educating and informing minds at a local level, before inspiring the country's hearts at a national level (Figure 8).

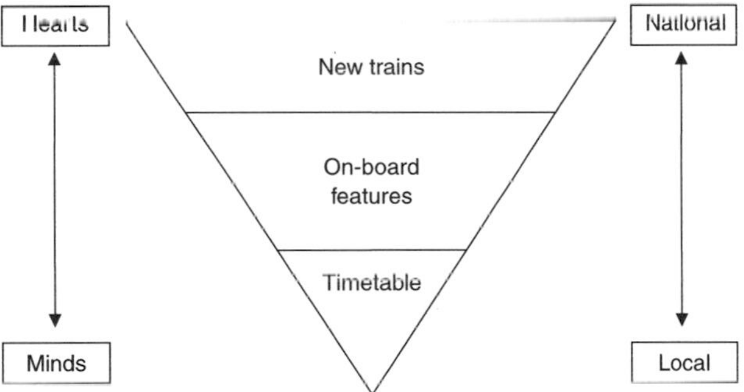

Figure 8: *'New Beginning' communications hierarchy*

CONVINCING LOCAL MINDS

A total of 115 towns and cities were targeted with messages customised locally. In planning the level of marketing activity, each location was categorised in terms of marketing communications priority. This prioritisation was achieved by calculating:

- expected revenue growth following the new trains
- the daily and peak-time service increases by location
- the size of the primary audiences in each location.

Media was then selected according to its ability to:

- deliver communications to a controlled locality ensuring minimal overspill into unrelated areas;[16] to this end, detailed mapping and location analysis was carried out[17]
- drive home the improved service frequency message that was the real, hard benefit to the Cross Country network.

Consistent with the staggered roll-out, media began with low-level radio and local press activity from April. In September, when the new timetable then came into existence and the presence of new trains reached critical mass, we built a local crescendo of activity with:

- a high-frequency local radio campaign[18]
- multiple-format outdoor activity (Figures 9 and 10)[19]
- high-impact colour executions in daily, evening local press[20]
- banner sites in the two biggest Cross Country network towns of Birmingham and Manchester.

Figure 9: *Example of local bus-side creative*

Figure 10: *Example of local 48-sheet creative*

16. Each town would experience varied frequency of new train service and timetable changes.
17. RAB Radio Mapping Tool, JICREG Regional Press Mapping and Posterscope Local Buying Knowledge.
18. Two radio executions with 54 adaptations for 27 regional radio stations.
19. Three street liners and superside executions with 54 adaptations across 1500 buses and three 48-sheet executions with 51 adaptations across 700 posted sites.
20. Five executions across 42 local press titles.

APPEALING TO THE NATION'S HEARTS

With minds engaged in the rational dimensions of the 'New Beginning' campaign, the second aspect was to celebrate the emotion and experience of train travel at the dawn of this new era. In other words, to make people feel good again about train travel.

Generating the feel-good factor

The need for an emotive means of parading the sleek design, innovative product features and exciting travel experience necessitated media of scale and warmth. The solution was a 60-second, high-quality piece of film that could be used across both cinema and TV (Figure 11).

Figure 11: *'New Beginning' TV/cinema advert stills*

From the nation's pop-wannabes battling it out live on Saturday night to the search for the Philosopher's Stone, programming and film selection criteria were based on their ability to facilitate the critical feel-good factor and thus enable people to enjoy the Virgin Trains advertising experience in greater depth.[21]

21. Example TV programming, *Pop Stars: The Rivals*; example cinema exhibition, *Harry Potter and The Philosopher's Stone*. Delivered 325 network TVRs; 11.5m adult cinema admissions.

Pulling no punches

On a national level, we still appreciated that there would be consumers who not having been exposed to the local rational activity would feel that this new dawn was unduly founded and had little back-up unless we added some weight and credibility to the claims of the TV and cinema activity.

A heavy national press campaign featuring quality and mid-market papers, and a bold, half-page double-page spread creative gave us this added weight and purposely placed us in an environment that had traditionally been one of our most critical. The adverts in the national press gave us factual evidence and an explanation to the 60-second hearts message (Figure 12).

WORLD

Earth Summit » Britain takes leading role in initiative to stop multinationals' corrupt practices in the Third World

Blair promises to crack down on corruption

Failure means disaster for our planet. But does the PM begin to understand?

Whatever deal comes out of the summit will not be enough. But failure could sink hopes of international co-operation for years to come, writes Geoffrey Lean

WORLD 17

Children killed in Israeli helicopter strike

Argentine settlers breathe life into dying rural Spain

Figure 12: *National press half-page double spread*

Up close and personal

As a personal medium in which the user is actively involved and choosing content, online enabled us to create an intimate connection with the consumer and yet deliver a mixture of practical, rational content in relevant city-based sites or large-format images. Keywords, screensavers, roadblocks and banners were all employed across a wide range of sites targeting the active travel seeker.

Figure 13 shows an overview of the 'hearts and minds' spend and usage.

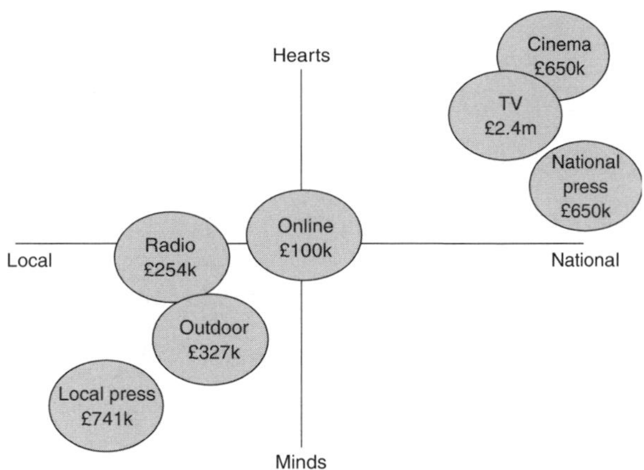

Figure 13: *Overview of media role and total spend of £5.16m April-December 2002*[22]

DID IT WORK?

Post-campaign advertising tracking measures[23] clearly show the campaign worked as intended and proved highly effective.

Getting noticed

The television advertising campaign generated a 57% increase in spontaneous advertising awareness. It proved highly memorable, achieving very high levels of recognition, far beyond category norms, outperforming campaigns with a bigger spend from high-profile categories traditionally considered more emotionally engaging (Figure 14).

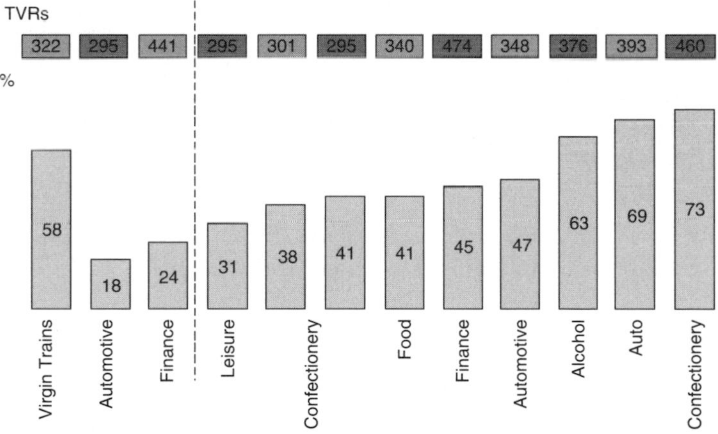

Figure 14: *Punching above its weight (advertising recognition, peak first-burst benchmarks)*
Base: all respondents
Source: TRBI – Virgin Trains Brand & Advertising Tracking, December 2002

22. Total 'New Beginning' period analysed by OMD Metrics as April 2002–June 2003 with added activity, total spend £10.84m.
23. The Research Business International – Brand & Advertising Tracking Study, Wave 11, December 2002.

Changing perceptions

For both leisure and business travellers, the advertising had a profound effect on people's perception of Virgin Trains. As intended, the campaign helped to generate positive brand image shifts of Virgin Trains as a more dynamic, innovative and progressive rail operator (Figure 15).

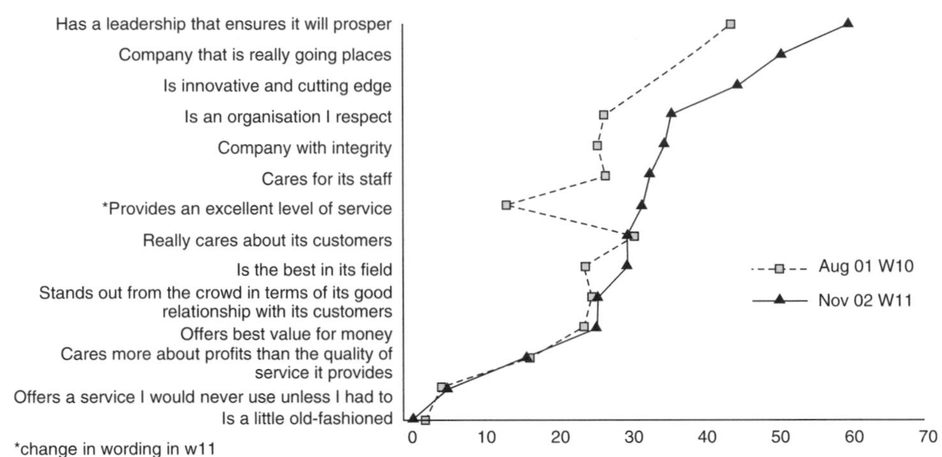

Figure 15: *Considerable positive shift across numerous brand perceptions*
Source: TRBI – Virgin Trains Brand & Advertising Tracking, December 2002

The number of travellers for whom advertising created a more positive perception of Virgin Trains increased dramatically (Table 1).

TABLE 1: NUMBER OF RESPONDENTS WHO AGREED THE ADVERTISING 'MADE ME THINK ABOUT VIRGIN TRAINS IN A MORE POSITIVE LIGHT'

Type of traveller	Pre-advertising Agree (%)	Post-advertising Agree (%)	Increase (%)
Leisure	23	44	90
Business	19	28	47

Source: TRBI, December 2002

Critically, as a direct result of the advertising the number of people who had a more positive impression of train travel in general rose by 38%.[24]

Advertising affected choice of travel

Importantly, the advertising not only shifted brand perceptions but also led to a dramatic increase in the number of travellers who agreed they were 'very likely to choose Virgin Trains' (Table 2).

24. TRBI – Virgin Trains Brand & Advertising Tracking Study, December 2002. The number of respondents who agreed with the statement 'The advertising made me think about train travel in general in a more positive light' rose from 16% to 22%. An increase of 38%.

TABLE 2: CONSIDERABLE SHIFT IN THE NUMBER OF PEOPLE WHO AGREED THEY WERE 'VERY LIKELY TO CHOOSE VIRGIN TRAINS'

Type of traveller	Pre-advertising Agree (%)	Post-advertising Agree (%)	Change (%)
Leisure	18	30	66
Business	27	34	26

Source: TRBI, December 2002

In an era when word of mouth and personal recommendations are such a potent force in product choice, a testament to the effectiveness of the advertising is evident in the considerable increase in the number of respondents who said they were 'very likely' to recommend Virgin Trains (Table 3).

TABLE 3: CONSIDERABLE SHIFT IN THE NUMBER OF PEOPLE 'VERY LIKELY TO RECOMMEND VIRGIN TRAINS'

Type of traveller	Pre-advertising Agree (%)	Post-advertising Agree (%)	Change (%)
Leisure	25	44	76
Business	27	33	22

Source: TRBI, December 2002

The conversion of Virgin Trains from a negative to a positive contributor to total Virgin Group brand equity

Perhaps one of the most illustrative examples of the impact of the advertising is the related knock-on effect Virgin Trains now had on the Virgin Group at large. Prior to the 'New Beginning' campaign the brand was perceived so poorly it was damaging perceptions of the overall Virgin Group. Following the advertising campaign Virgin Trains made, for the first time, a positive contribution to the group's brand image.[25] Indeed, such was the scale of the turnaround, it was the single largest positive swing recorded in the history of the Virgin Group (Figure 16).

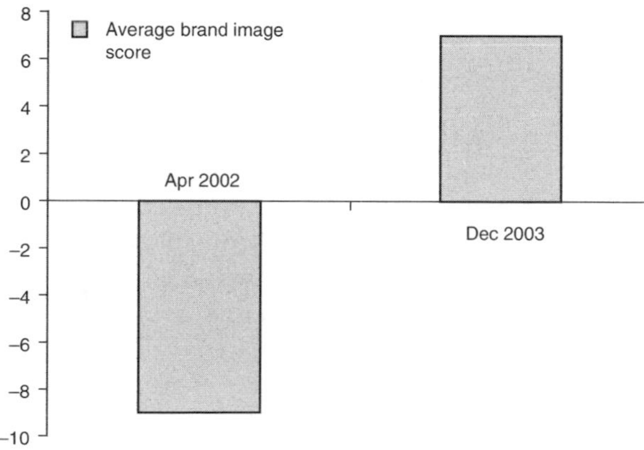

Figure 16: *Virgin Trains improves brand imagery performance by +16*

25. HPI Brand Tracking Study, 2003. In December 2003 Virgin Trains scored 7 on the contribution to the Virgin Brand Image Balance, an increase of 16 points since April 2002.

DID IT MAKE A POSITIVE CONTRIBUTION TO THE BOTTOM LINE?

Recognising the immediate objective of the advertising campaign was to leverage the launch of the new trains to drive reappraisal of Virgin Trains, the ultimate intention was to have a positive impact on revenue.

Revenue figures saw a massive uplift during, and for some time after, the campaign. The rate of total revenue growth on the Cross Country network alone almost doubled, rising from 15% to 27%.[26] We must bear in mind that this uplift was caused by a number of factors, not least the presence of the new trains and increased service frequency, and so extra analysis has been carried out to separate the numerous revenue drivers.

Advertising delivers an immediate effect

OMD Metrics have been conducting econometric analysis of Virgin Trains revenue variation since October 2000 identifying all drivers of revenue. The model has allowed us to isolate the direct impact of the 'New Beginning' advertising on total Virgin Trains revenue across the period the campaign ran, from September through to November.

We can accurately calculate that the 'New Beginning' advertising directly contributed 11.78% of total Virgin Trains revenue across the business periods it ran.[27] The significance of this contribution can be seen in the light of previous advertising revenue returns (Table 4).

TABLE 4: MASSIVELY INCREASED CONTRIBUTIONS FROM ADVERTISING

	1999–2001 average	'New Beginning' campaign
Percentage of revenue driven by advertising	5.3%	11.78%

Source: OMD Metrics, 2004

Considerable impact beyond the short term[28]

Proof of just how impactful the 'New Beginning' campaign was is that it was extremely well remembered and acted upon by passengers for a considerable period after the campaign. As a result, Virgin Trains revenue continued to be driven by the advertising for much longer than it was actually on air. Across all models the advert stock rates[29] of the 'New Beginning' TV were very high at 90% – not a surprising result for a 60-second TV spot. The true value created by the TV campaign,

26. Virgin Trains Revenue Management, 2004.
27. Virgin Trains business periods 03–08 to 03–09 (15 September–9 November 2002) equates to £10.14m in revenue uplift.
28. Total 'New Beginning' spend analysed from April 2002 to June 2003 is £10.84m.
29. As part of our on-going econometric analysis for Virgin Trains we report the carryover/tail effect of advertising by using advert stock rates. For every campaign, we test all possible advert stock rates from 90% (remembered well – revenue effect diminishes by 10% each month) to 0% (not remembered – only direct revenue effect) and let the models determine the length of time each campaign was remembered and produced revenue.

however, only becomes apparent when we calculate the halo effect it had on other media. Comparing the results with the previous wave of models, we find the advert stock rates of press and radio advertising improved with the 'New Beginning' campaign (Table 5).

TABLE 5: THE TV CAMPAIGN SEEMED TO MAKE THE AUDIENCE MORE PERCEPTIVE ABOUT OTHER MEDIA USED, MAGNIFYING THEIR REVENUE-GENERATING CAPABILITY

	Average pre-'New Beginning' advert stock (%)	Average 'New Beginning' advert stock (%)
Press	30	70
Radio	25	60

Source: OMD Metrics, 2004

Cracking the difficult business market

As segmentation identified, the business traveller proved reluctant to consider travelling by train, particularly on the Cross Country network. Testament to the effectiveness of the 'New Beginning' campaign is the considerable increase in business travel revenue generated directly as a result of the advertising (Table 6).

TABLE 6: GREATER RETURNS FROM 'NEW BEGINNING' ADVERTISING THAN PREVIOUS CAMPAIGNS

	Pre-'New Beginning' advertising	'New Beginning' advertising
Percentage of XC business revenue driven by advertising	9.2%	13.9%

Source: OMD Metrics, 2004

By June 2003, the cumulative effect of the 'New Beginning' advertising was an increase in revenue of £62.25m, or 8.4% of total Virgin Trains 2002/2003 revenue. This represents a £5.74 return for every pound spent on advertising.

Reversing declining returns

Furthermore, the 'New Beginning' campaign not only reversed a downward year-on-year trend in average return per advertising pound spent, but actually delivered the highest average return ever achieved by the brand – an increase of 64% when compared to the average pre-'New Beginning' return (Table 7).[30]

If Virgin Trains had not instigated the successful 'New Beginning' advertising campaign, then Virgin Train's fortunes would have been very different (Figure 17).

30. 2002–03 refers to period April 2002 to June 2003 where total 'New Beginning' advertising spend and effect was analysed by OMD Metrics.

TABLE 7: ADVERTISING RETURNS PER £ SPENT WERE IN DECLINE UNTIL 'NEW BEGINNING'

	Revenue return per advertising £ spent			
	1999	2000	2001	2002–03 'New Beginning'
Total VT return	£3.64	£3.50	£3.36	£5.74

Source: OMD Metrics, 2004

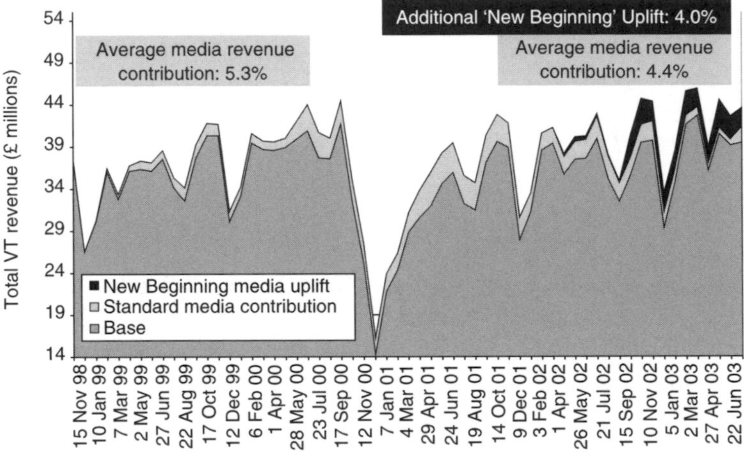

Figure 17: *The revenue effect of media over time if Virgin Trains advertising had not happened*
Source: OMD Metrics, 2004

PROVING THE ADVERTISING DID THIS

One challenge in proving the effectiveness of this campaign was to separate the revenue boost driven by the advertising from that caused by the appearance of the new trains. After all, the trains and higher-frequency timetable themselves attracted passengers and therefore raised Virgin Trains revenue independently of the advertising.

Econometric modelling proved crucial in achieving the above because it allowed us to separate the discrete effect of each major revenue driver and quantify the revenue effect (Figure 18).

Therefore, we are extremely confident that the media returns only represent the pure revenue boost of the advertising, 'cleansed' of the natural revenue boost that occurred due to the attraction of the new rolling stock and the increased Virgin Trains timetable.

The ultimate proof of the power of the idea

By comparing results on the West Coast network (where no new trains or increased frequency of service took place) with the Cross Country network, we effectively had a 'test area vs control area' for advertising evaluation. We can identify the direct effect of the advertising campaign on the West Coast network by using the

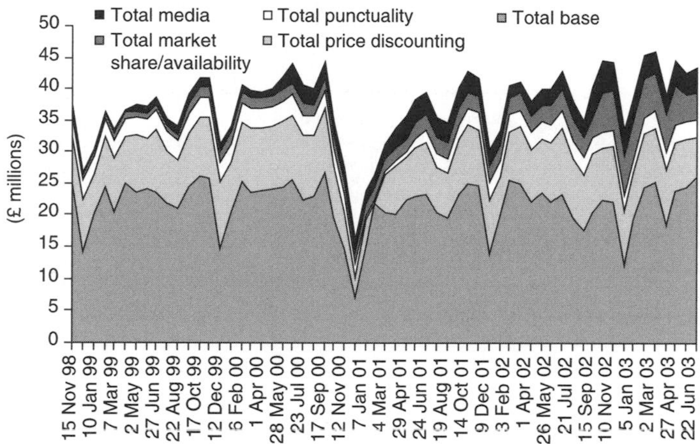

Figure 18: *The revenue effect of seasonality and brand equity (base), availability*[31] *(which includes new product), pricing and punctuality*
Source: OMD Metrics, 2004

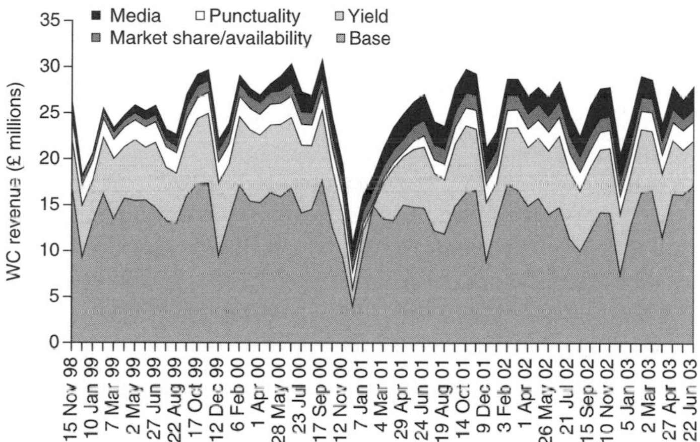

Figure 19: *In effect, the communications idea increased West Coast revenue even where no new trains or increased frequency of service was available*
Source: OMD Metrics, 2004

models to again isolate the individual revenue drivers. This amounts to £42.15m, an increase in revenue of 2.6% from before the advertising aired (Figure 19 and Table 8).

31. The availability factor is the industry measure of the share of trains running on the network per train operating company at any given time. Virgin Trains availability increased significantly in the Cross Country franchise at the time of the new train's roll-out, so this factor captures the boosting revenue effect of the roll-out of the new trains in the models.

TABLE 8: QUANTIFYING THE COMPARATIVE MEDIA REVENUE EFFECT BY FRANCHISE

	Pre-'New Beginning' advertising contribution to revenue (%)	'New Beginning' advertising contribution to revenue (%)	Increase (%)	Pound value of 'New Beginning' advertising to revenue
West Coast	6.2	8.8	41.9	£42.15m
Cross Country	2.9	7.3	251.7	£18.95m

Source: OMD Metrics, 2004

CONCLUSION

'New Beginning' was a campaign idea that leveraged, but was not dependent upon, the launch of a new fleet of trains to tackle head-on the negative perceptions Virgin Trains had encountered. It was an idea that provoked the travelling public to re-evaluate their understanding of the brand and encouraged a significantly increased number of people to consider travelling with Virgin Trains, many of whom would not have an opportunity to experience the new trains for some time to come. It was a campaign idea that contributed £62.25m to Virgin Trains revenues, a more than five-fold return on investment.

Above all, 'New Beginning' demonstrates the power of a creative idea to transform the very basis of a brand's relationship with its consumer and place it in a very strong position to enjoy long-term growth and prosperity.

We began the paper by citing Richard Branson's belief that rekindling the public's enthusiasm for train travel would be his 'greatest ever challenge'. The 'New Beginning' advertising campaign has lit the touch paper.

> 'To all those responsible for the current campaign for Virgin Trains, I do believe that it's one of the best campaigns that any Virgin company has ever launched and would like to congratulate everyone involved in it.'
>
> Richard Branson

SILVER
BEST IDEA

19

Volkswagen Diesel

Don't forget it's a diesel

How making it OK to drive a diesel proved highly profitable for Volkswagen UK

Principal authors: Ben Malbon, DDB London, and Sara Donoghugh, DDB Matrix
Contributing authors: Sarah Carter and Richard Butterworth, DDB London, and Les Binet, DDB Matrix
Media agency: MediaCom
Digital agency: Tribal DDB
DM agency: Proximity London

EDITOR'S SUMMARY

This was a good paper, which was awarded the Best Idea prize – for its bravery, its originality and its breadth of media. It tells the story of how making it OK to drive a diesel proved to be profitable for Volkswagen.

Diesels have long been seen as boring, dull, noisy, smelly and sluggish. But since 2001, Volkswagen's campaign has helped radically change perceptions. Its diesel sales have increased dramatically in terms of both volume and value, the Golf has become the UK's best-selling diesel car and people are buying more powerful and more expensive Volkswagen diesels then ever before.

Fronted by the high-powered Golf GTi, Volkswagen's diesel marques were given a new sense of style and desirability with communications that were intelligent and witty in tone – a break from typically apologetic diesel ads. Volkswagen showed its confidence in its diesel range by becoming the first car advertiser to go on TV with a brand-led diesel message: 'Don't forget it's a diesel'.

The campaign saw diesel sales revenues grow by 60%, sales revenues grow by 60% and sales of high-powered diesels rise from 33 to 53% of Volkswagen's diesel mix.

This campaign led to £180.2m in additional revenue for Volkswagen UK.

INTRODUCTION

In 2001 people thought diesels were boring, dull, noisy, smelly and sluggish. Less than a year later, people's perceptions had been changed radically. Volkswagen's diesel sales had increased dramatically in terms of both volume and value, Golf was the UK's best-selling diesel car, and people were buying more powerful and more expensive Volkswagen diesels than ever before. It had become OK to drive a diesel. This paper will show how communications contributed to this remarkable story. The audacity and scale of Volkswagen's campaign was unprecedented in the diesel sector. It altered people's perceptions of diesel for ever.

MARKETING OPPORTUNITY

Market background

Rudolf Diesel patented his diesel engine technology in 1892. Though a technological miracle at the time, for over 100 years diesels had been viewed as a poor second to their petrol cousins. In 2001, strong perceptions of diesel engines being dirty, sluggish and underpowered still persisted.[1] Diesel-powered cars were driven by 'alternative types' – Greens, teachers and *Guardian* readers; if you were a man and you wore sandals in the summer, you probably drove a diesel. They were not aspirational; they were a million miles away from 0–60 claims and the world of the GTi. In short, diesel was shorthand for everything most car drivers did not want to be.

While petrol has thus traditionally dominated the UK car market (see Table 1),[2] during 2001 it became clear that the near future would provide a window of opportunity for dramatic and sustained growth in the diesel sector. Legislative changes due to come into effect in April 2002 meant that company car drivers were now to be taxed on the CO_2 emissions of their engines rather than the miles driven per annum. This would clearly favour diesel cars – they generally have lower CO_2 emissions than petrol cars.

Volkswagen opportunity

Volkswagen had historically been a significant player within the diesel sector of the UK market, punching above its 'market share' weight, but it had tended to trail Peugeot. In 2001, Volkswagen had a 13% share of the UK diesel market, compared to Ford's 12% and Peugeot's 14% (see Table 1). This contrasted with Volkswagen's 5.8% share of the petrol car market.[3]

Volkswagen has offered diesel cars as part of its range for nearly three decades. In 2001 Turbodiesel (or TDI) engines were available across the range of cars offered by Volkswagen in the UK, from the entry-level Lupo up to the Passat.

1. DDB qualitative research, 2001.
2. In 2001, petrol had an 82.2% share of the car market in the UK, with diesel (17.7%) making up almost all the remaining share (source: SMMT).
3. Source: SMMT.

TABLE 1: PEUGEOT WAS MARKET LEADER IN 2001

Peugeot	1
Volkswagen	2
Ford	3
Vauxhall	4
Citroën	5
Renault	6
Audi	7
Rover	8
Skoda	9
Mercedes	10

Source: SMMT

Volkswagen had launched new 130bhp TDI and 150bhp TDI engines in July and November 2001 respectively, and sales of these were going well. Their extra power and frugal fuel consumption figures clearly provided the potential to radically change people's perceptions of diesel engine performance. Volkswagen was rightly very proud of them.

Late in 2001, Volkswagen decided that 2002 and the accompanying legislative changes provided a massive opportunity not simply to sell more diesel cars than before but also to increase the value extracted from the UK diesel market in the form of revenue sales. There were two reasons for this decision.

1. Unit-for-unit, Volkswagen UK makes more in revenue terms from diesel than it does for petrol. The average amount paid for a Volkswagen diesel in 2001 was 18% higher than for a Volkswagen petrol.[4]
2. The introduction in mid-2001 of the two more highly powered and higher-priced diesel engines (the 130bhp and 150bhp TDIs) represented an excellent opportunity to persuade current petrol drivers who would never *normally* consider diesel to purchase these particular Volkswagen diesels. These engines would be available in higher-specified variants of individual models (more akin to the GTi end of the market), and this would provide Volkswagen with opportunities to add yet further to value sales.

Volkswagen threats

However, as well as these opportunities, there were two threats to Volkswagen's existing enviable share of the market for diesels.

1. All of Volkswagen's major mainstream competitors were developing and planning to introduce impressive new and powerful diesel engines of their own. This suggests, *ceteris paribus*, that Volkswagen might expect to lose market share, as competitors caught up with its leading technologies. Volkswagen would need to work hard to protect its strong existing position in the diesel market.
2. The dominant motivation for buying into the diesel market had conventionally been an economic one. Diesel is a sector where miles per gallon tend to take priority over miles per hour. The new 130bhp and 150bhp engines delivered

4. Source: NCBS.

more power and admirably frugal fuel consumption figures, but they were also more expensive to start with. Customers might well be surprised to learn that the diesel cars they'd find in retailers were even more expensive than the petrol ones.

Both of these threats would have to be addressed.

Primary business objective

With all this in mind, Volkswagen UK set a simple but ambitious business objective of maximising value sales of diesel whilst minimising volume lost in doing so.

Marketing objectives

The marketing objectives developed to achieve this were also simple but necessarily ambitious:

- to increase the diesel share of total Volkswagen sales
- to dramatically increase the sales mix of higher-variant diesels.

The models selected as priorities were Golf and Passat. These models are Volkswagen's representatives within the two most important car sectors (by volume) for diesel. Golf was also important for more than simply volume opportunity reasons. Golf was the most popular and iconic model in the Volkswagen range, with a reputation for stylishness, performance and driver enjoyment. If Volkswagen could persuade people that it was now possible to drive an impressively powerful diesel Golf, it was hoped that the positive PR and word of mouth would help gild less iconic and less stylish models with the sheen of desirability and acceptability.

COMMUNICATIONS

Research had shown that there was a large group of diesel-considering petrol drivers who were persuaded of the rational merits of diesel (in the form of lower lifetime ownership costs, due to lower fuel bills and higher resale values), but who could not bring themselves to make the switch.[5] Their heads saw the sense, but their hearts remained unconvinced.

Research found that there were three key barriers in the way.

1. Diesel cars were thought to be sluggish and dirty (despite general awareness of improvements in diesel technology):

   'Taxis don't really accelerate very well do they?'[6]

---

5. Research commissioned by Volkswagen in October 2001 found that over half (54%) of drivers aged 17+ would consider a model with a diesel engine next time they bought a car (NOP, 2001), yet only 17.7% of new car buyers were buying diesels (SMMT).
6. The driver quotes in this section are from DDB qualitative research conducted in 2001.

'You have to put on gloves at the petrol stations.'

'Diesels are like cars with square wheels.'

2. Diesel cars were thought to be unstylish cars driven by unstylish people:

'My Dad's a taxi driver – so that's what I think of when I think of diesel.'

3. Diesels were seen as a niche sector, not taken seriously by the manufacturers:

'You get the feeling that car makers aren't particularly proud of their diesel cars – all the adverts you see are about their petrol cars. It seems it's these that they want to push.'

A three-pronged marketing and communications strategy was devised that confronted each of these barriers head on.

1. *Message*: to combat the perception of diesels being sluggish, a campaign was developed that single-mindedly set out to persuade people that Volkswagen diesels were just as good as petrol. The role for the advertising was to inject the Volkswagen diesel brand with sexiness and a sense of desire. The campaign would, where possible, feature the most impressively powerful of Volkswagen's range of diesels – the new 150bhp Golf GTi – as evidence of exceptional performance.
2. *Tone and style*: to combat the perception that diesels were unstylish, all communications would be intelligent and witty in tone, and have extremely high production values (in contrast to the usual, almost apologetic, diesel communications).
3. *Media strategy*: to combat the perception that diesels were a niche that didn't matter to Volkswagen, a substantial and integrated campaign was planned.

   The scale of the campaign was important (see Figure 1). Volkswagen wanted its target audience to see Volkswagen talking confidently and publicly about its diesel offering. The bulk of the budget was put behind broadcast media (Volkswagen was the first car advertiser to go on television with a brand diesel message).

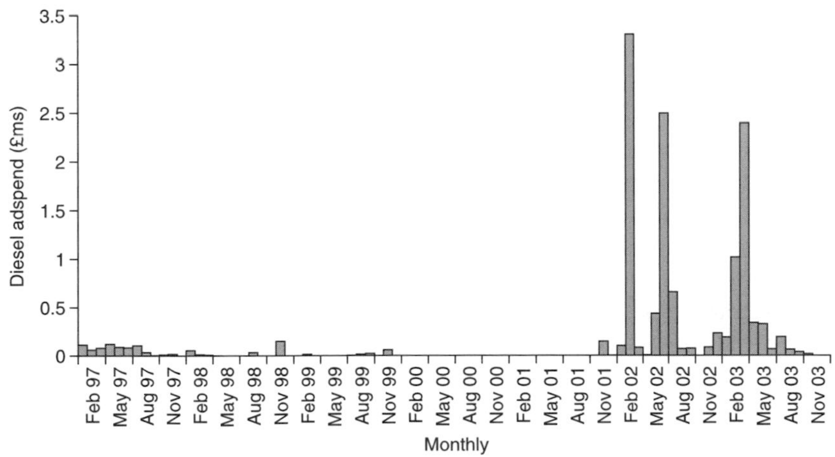

Figure 1: *Volkswagen increased its diesel adspend dramatically*
Source: MMS

A carefully integrated campaign was equally important. Volkswagen wanted its diesel message to feel ubiquitous. Multiple touchpoints would add weight to the perception that Volkswagen took diesels very seriously indeed, acting as a continual reminder of the desirability of Volkswagen diesels.

The media strategy, developed with Volkswagen's media partner MediaCom, was to make Volkswagen diesels synonymous with 'performance'. Performance car titles such as *EVO* and *CAR* magazine were used. TV spots were bought in sports and performance-related programming – the FA Cup, Grand Prix and Rugby. Press adverts were placed in sports sections of newspapers, and the sports results section of the *Mail on Sunday* was sponsored by Volkswagen diesel. Communications spend for 2002 and 2003 totalled £12.3m.

CREATIVE SOLUTION

Creative work

Qualitative research had discovered how petrol drivers feared that if they bought a diesel they would be constantly reminded they were driving a diesel – it would be noisy, smelly and sluggish. The creative challenge was to convince potential diesel drivers that they'd be able to forget they were driving a diesel. A fully integrated campaign was developed around the message that Volkswagen diesels are just as good as Volkswagen petrols. The overall creative idea, 'Don't forget it's a diesel', dramatised the difficulty that drivers of Volkswagen diesels had in remembering their car was not petrol.

This was a genuinely powerful creative idea, and had the flexibility to work across a broad range of channels, with each channel performing a distinct and well-defined role within the overall campaign.

- Television, three radio adverts, and posters were used to drive mass awareness of Volkswagen diesels' performance, and reinforce the overall stature of the campaign. National and specialist motoring press were used to provide further substantiation. TV, in particular, was intended to provoke people's interest in Volkswagen diesels so that they would seek further information (for example, online or at retailers) (Figures 2–5).
- Petrol pump nozzle adverts and 6-sheet posters near petrol stations were used to prompt awareness of Volkswagen diesels' performance at the very point of fuel purchase (Figures 6 and 7).
- Volkswagen's online agency, Tribal DDB, built a diesel microsite, designed to provide more information than could be presented through ATL channels (Figure 8).
- An online advertising campaign for the Golf and the Passat ran on websites such as Men's Health, Reuters and Times Online. This ran later in 2002 to sustain the campaign throughout that year (Figure 9).
- Direct mail, created by Volkswagen's direct marketing agency, Proximity London, was used to target key people in the fleet market. A self-inking rubber stamp with 'Don't forget it's a diesel' on it was sent to 15,000 fleet managers (Figure 10).

TV script

Client	Volkswagen
Product	Diesel
Title	Reminders
Length	50″
Creative	Dylan & Feargal

Music: **Mike Oldfield's 'Tubular Bells'**

We see a woman in a car park writing something in the dirt on the side of her car. We can't read the word from our perspective.

We cut to another guy opening his garage door to reveal the word 'DIE' spray-painted on one door, with a Passat revealed behind.

We see a woman rearranging fridge magnet letters to make a word, starting with 'D'.

We cut to a guy in his dressing gown putting a post-it note on the inside of his Passat windscreen at night.

We cut to a woman finding lots of pieces of paper in her husband's clothes, but the word on them is not fully revealed.

We see a man pulling off the diesel pump from his son's toy garage, much to the boy's bemusement.

We cut to a man pulling into a petrol station in a Golf GTi. He looks at his hand, to reveal the word 'Diesel' written on it, before he fills up.

We then see reveals of the word 'DIESEL', as written on the car in dirt and with fridge magnets.

Super: Volkswagen diesel.

Super: It's easy to forget.

Figure 2: *Script for Volkswagen diesel TV advert – 'Reminders'*

Figure 3: *Stills from the Volkswagen diesel TV advert – 'Reminders'*

Figure 4: *Volkswagen diesel 48-sheet poster/press ad – 'Stretched Pump'*

- Innovative ambient media were used to provide a further reminder of Volkswagen's diesel performance. Packets of 'forget-me-not' seeds were subtly altered to feature a diesel message and Volkswagen branding. These were tipped-on in motoring titles (Figure 11).
- Further press and poster executions were developed as the campaign unfolded. Later executions featured the Passat Sport TDI 130bhp in place of the Golf (Figures 12 and 13).
- A viral film, called 'Bollocks', was developed and distributed to carefully selected recipients via e-mail (Figures 14 and 15).

The campaign media plans are shown in Figure 16.

Radio script

Client	Volkswagen
Product	Passat
Title	Weasel
Length	30″
Creative	Matt & Pete

This advert takes the form of one of those 'teach yourself' tapes.

The voice is very calm, slow and considered.

MVO: A few simple reminders for drivers of the new Passat 130bhp TDI Sport.

Dogs In Equador Sniff Elephant's Legs.

Derek Is Easily Spotted Eating Lettuce.

Do Italians Eat Spaghetti Every Lunchtime?

The new Volkswagen Passat 130bhp TDI Sport.

Don't forget it's a Do Italians Eat Spaghetti Every Lunchtime

Figure 5: *Volkswagen diesel radio script – 'Weasel'*

Figure 6: *Volkswagen diesel petrol pump nozzle cover*

Figure 7: *Volkswagen diesel six-sheet poster (bought near petrol stations) – 'Post-it'*

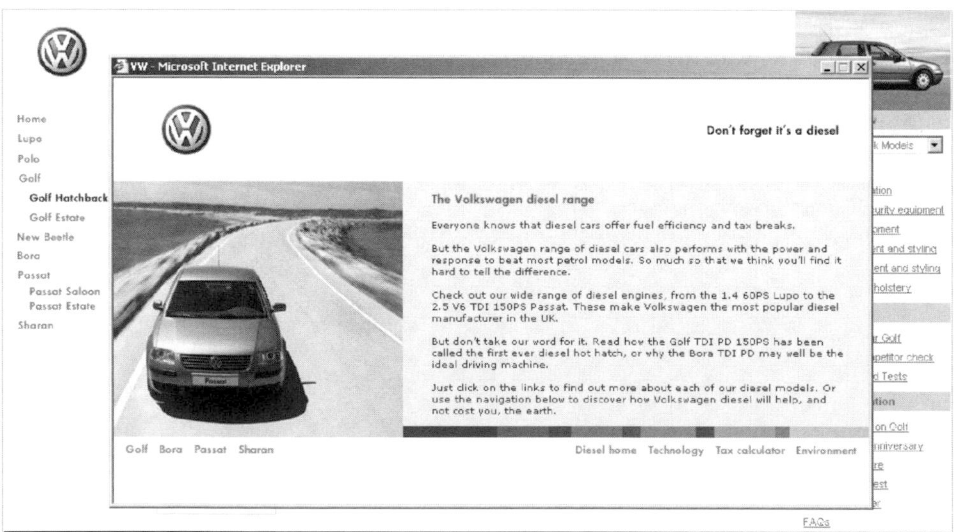

Figure 8: *Screen grabs from the Volkswagen diesel microsite*

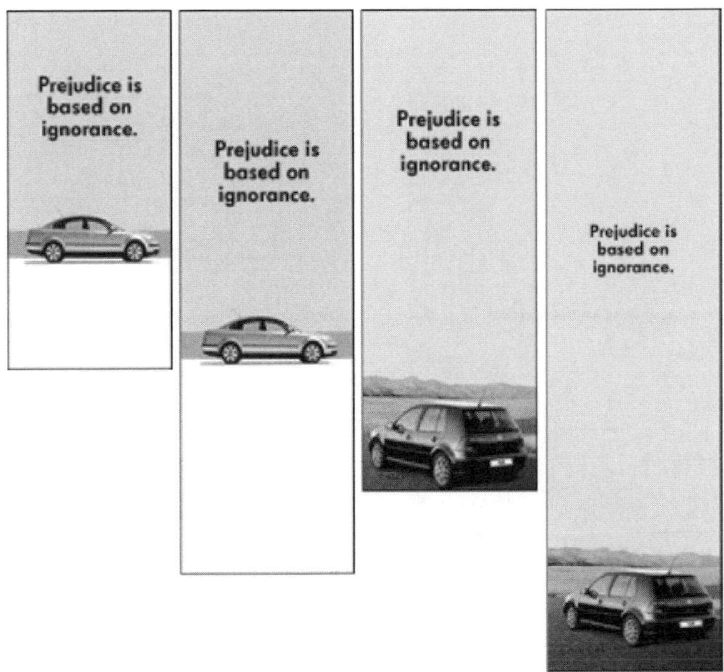

Figure 9: *Volkswagen diesel online advertising for Golf and Passat*

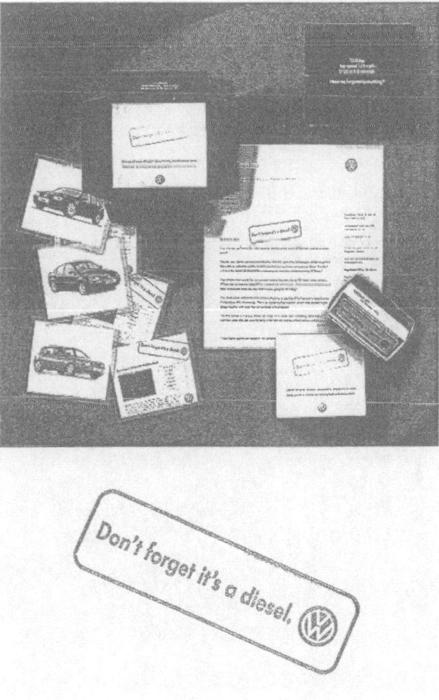

Figure 10: *Volkswagen diesel mailer to fleet customers – 'Don't Forget' stamp*

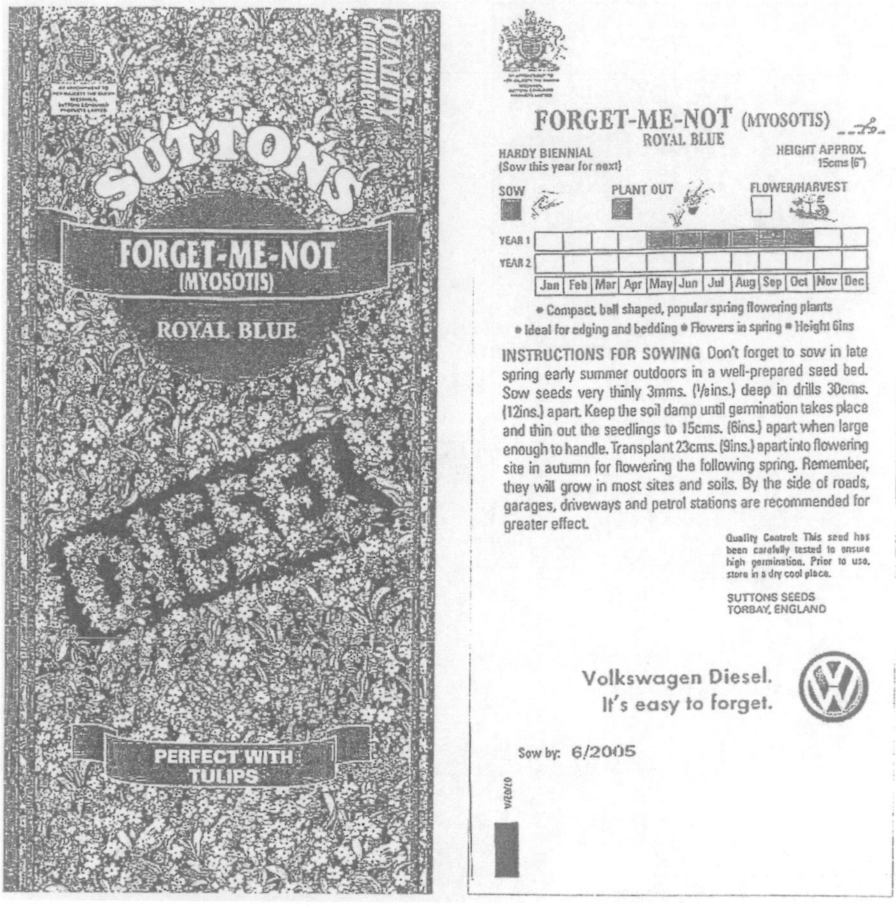

Figure 11: *Volkswagen diesel tip-on for motoring titles – 'Seed Packet'*

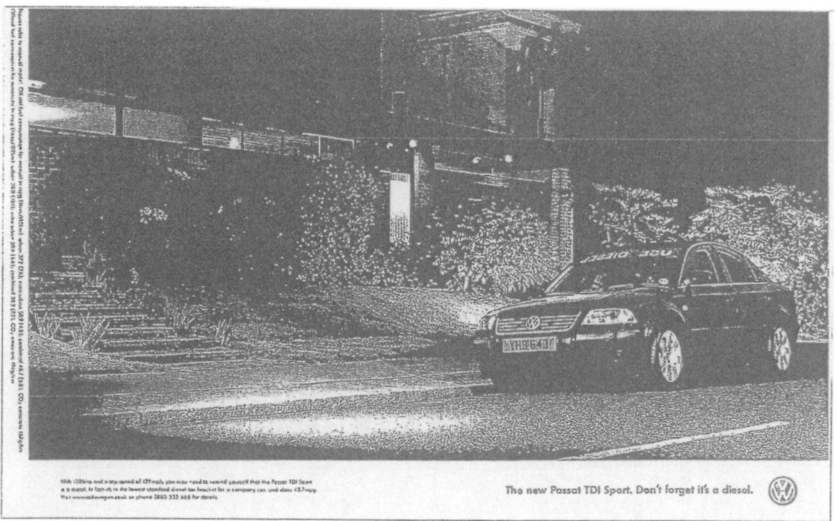

Figure 12: *Volkswagen diesel press advert – 'Visor'*

Figure 13: *Volkswagen diesel poster – 'Elepump'*

Figure 14: *Stills from Volkswagen diesel viral advert – 'Bollocks!'*

TV script

Client	Volkswagen
Product	Diesel
Title	Bollocks!
Length	40″
Creative	Dan & Amber

The main character of this advert would be an angelic four-year-old girl. It could be shot from her eye level with the adults cropped at the waist. We see the girl walk with her nanny up to a sweet shop. As they reach the door, the sign in the door reads 'Closed'.

Girl: (Annoyed) Bollocks!

She gets slightly tugged at the arm.

We then see the girl perched on the toilet. She looks over to see there is no toilet roll left.

Girl: (Annoyed) Bollocks!

The little friend's face looks shocked. We see the girl on tiptoes reaching for a biscuit jar in the kitchen. Her fingertip brushes the jar pushing it away.

Girl: (Annoyed) Bollocks!

We see the girl eating an ice cream. She's walking along a beachfront holding her mum's hand. As she takes a bite of the ice cream it drops on to the dirty floor.

Girl: (Annoyed) Bollocks!

Her mum stops dead. We then see her in the parents' bedroom playing fancy dress with a friend. The mum's clothes are all over the floor and she is walking around in her mother's high-heel shoes. As she shuffles along one of the shoes slips off.

Girl: (Annoyed) Bollocks!

We see the little girl painting outside. As she rinses her paintbrush in a glass of water she accidentally tips it over on to her painting.

Girl: (Annoyed) Bollocks!

We then cut to a petrol station where the little girl's dad is filling up his Passat TDI. The mum is sitting in the front gazing out of the window while the little girl sits in the back looking at her dad. Suddenly the dad looks down, then in a panic pulls the pump nozzle out. He looks very annoyed.

Dad: Bollocks!!

Super: Volkswagen diesels. It's easy to forget.

Figure 15: *Script for Volkswagen diesel viral advert – 'Bollocks!'*

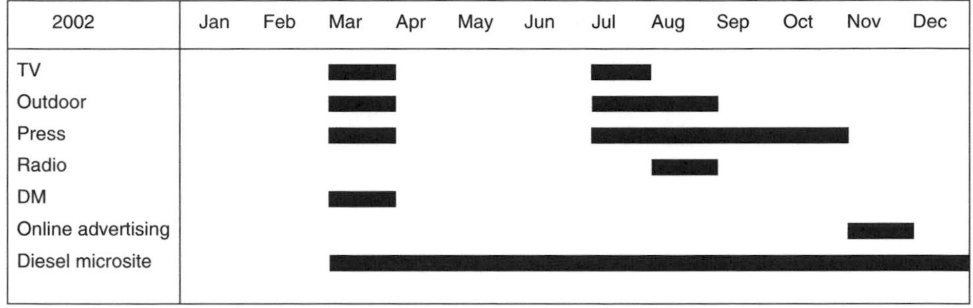

2003

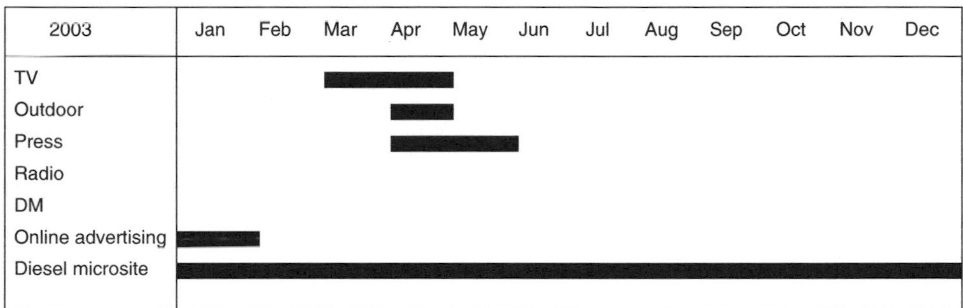

Figure 16: *Campaign media plans*

Retailer network and POS

The integrated approach extended to Volkswagen's retailer network. At least one diesel car was to be available for test driving at all times, and the diesel cars were given prominent position and lighting in the showroom. The point of sale in retailers was consistent with the national campaign. No customer would walk out of a retailer without feeling that Volkswagen was taking its diesels very seriously indeed.

CAMPAIGN RESULTS

The campaign produced impressive results. Volkswagen achieved everything it set out to. Diesel sales became a larger percentage of Volkswagen sales, sales of higher-powered diesels increased, people paid more for Volkswagen diesels, diesel sales revenues increased, and while Volkswagen became market leader in diesel, the Golf became the UK's best-selling diesel car. From the end of 2001 to the end of 2003 total revenues from diesel sales increased by £485m.[7]

7. Value sales are indexed throughout the paper for reasons of commercial confidentiality.

Volkswagen's sales mix changed

The diesel share of total Volkswagen sales volume increased dramatically from 32% in 2001 (pre-campaign) to 46% in 2003 (Figure 17).

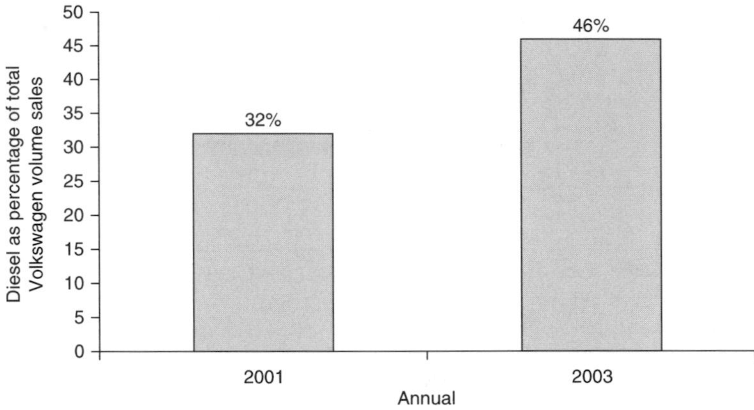

Figure 17: *Diesel became a larger percentage of Volkswagen sales*
Source: SMMT

Sales of higher-powered diesels increased

The proportion of diesels sold with more powerful engines increased from 33% in 2001 to 53% in 2003 (Figure 18).

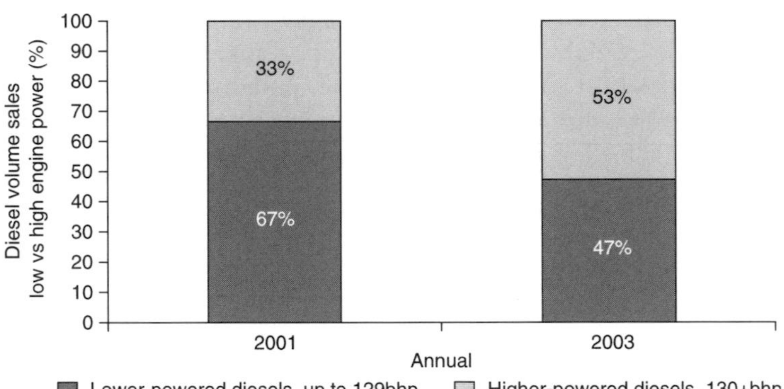

Figure 18: *Sales of higher-powered Volkswagen diesels increased*
Source: Volkswagen

People were prepared to pay more for Volkswagen diesels

People were prepared to pay more for their Volkswagen diesels after the advertising started: (a) in absolute terms, (b) relative to Volkswagen petrols and (c) relative to diesel competitors (Figure 19).

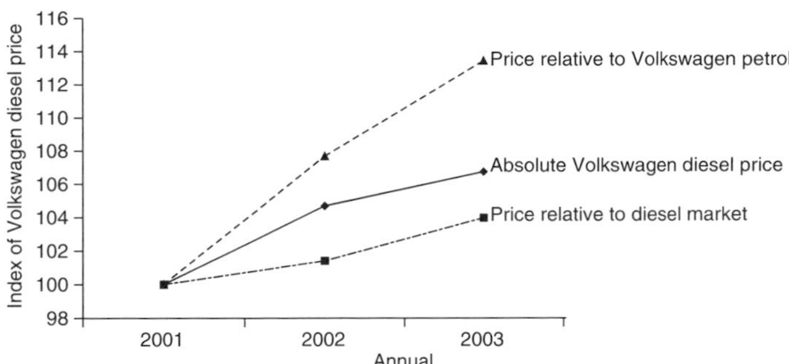

Figure 19: *The amount paid for a Volkswagen diesel went up*
Source: NCBS

Diesel sales revenues increased

As a result of these extra sales of more highly powered and more expensive diesels, sales revenues from diesel increased (Figure 20).

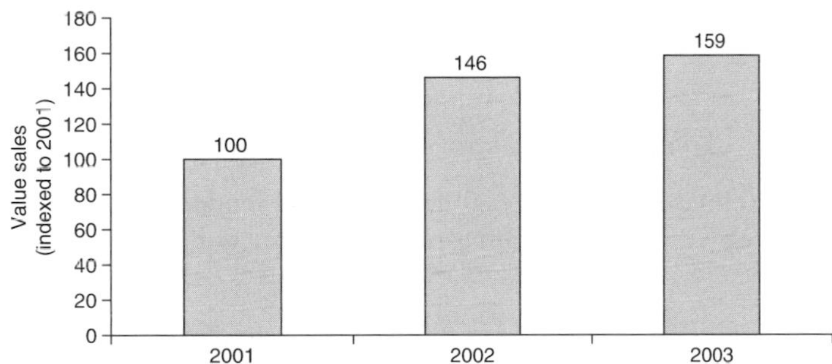

Figure 20: *Sales revenue rose by 60%*
Sources: SMMT, NCBS

Sales revenues increased more than for any other marque

In fact, Volkswagen's value sales increased between 2001 and 2003 by more than any other marque (Figure 21).

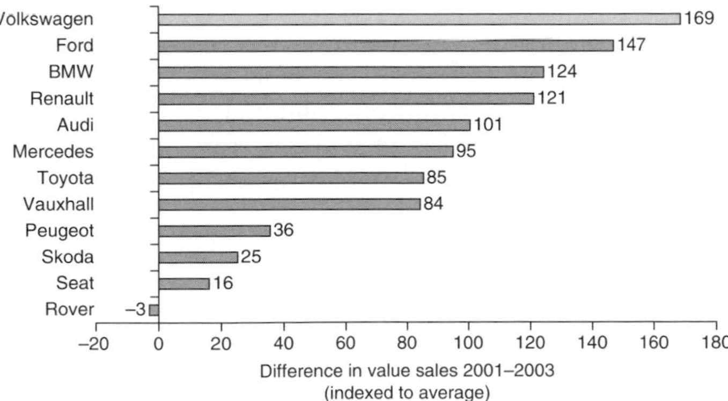

Figure 21: *Volkswagen revenue increased more than other marques*
Sources: SMMT, NCBS

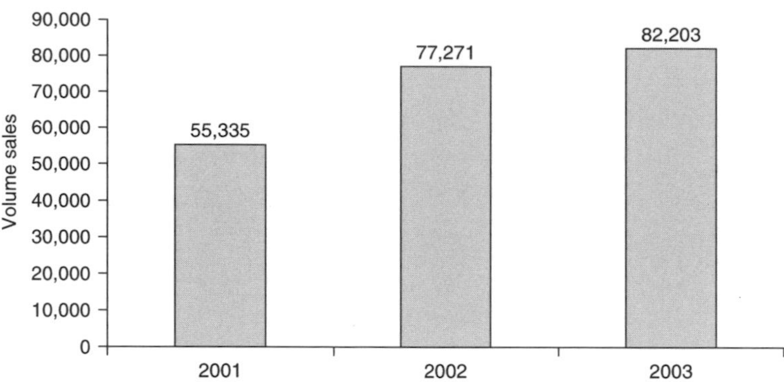

Figure 22: *Volkswagen increased revenue without losing volume*
Source: SMMT

What's more, while (as explained above) one might have presumed the strategy of introducing and advertising costlier higher-performing diesel models could have led to a reduction in volume sales, Volkswagen achieved this increase in value sales without sacrificing volume (Figure 22).

Volkswagen became market leader in diesel

By the end of 2002 Volkswagen diesel had achieved leadership of the diesel sector in market share terms, overtaking long-time rival Peugeot.

Golf became the UK's biggest-selling diesel car

The Volkswagen Golf became the biggest-selling diesel car in the UK in 2002, overtaking the Ford Focus. This was particularly important. If Golfs powered by diesel were becoming so much more popular and acceptable, then (so the logic went) some of the other cars in the range would be more easily accepted in their diesel guise.

Summary of results

- Volkswagen increased the diesel share of its overall product mix.
- Volkswagen increased the richness of its diesel mix, with increasing share of diesel sales coming from higher-powered and higher-priced variants.
- Volkswagen persuaded people to pay more for Volkswagen diesels – an impressive feat given that the primary motivation for people to enter the diesel market is to save money.
- Value sales increased between 2001 and 2003 more for Volkswagen than for any other mainstream marque.
- Volkswagen achieved this without losing its position in the market – by the end of 2002 Volkswagen had established itself as diesel market leader for the first time.
- Golf – more usually associated with the high performance GTi – became the UK's best-selling diesel car in 2002.

PROVING COMMUNICATIONS WERE RESPONSIBLE FOR THESE EFFECTS

There are six main strands of proof that together comprise compelling evidence of the central role that communications played in the impressive performance of Volkswagen's diesel range in 2002 and 2003.

1. Communications worked exactly as planned.
2. Growth of advertised models outstripped that for non-advertised models.
3. The timings of communications correlate with the timings of key changes in business performance.
4. Levels of spend correlate with changes in sales mix.
5. An identical Volkswagen diesel range in European markets did not enjoy the levels of performance enjoyed by Volkswagen in the UK.
6. Nothing else can explain this impressive performance.

Each of these points is now explained in detail.

Communications worked exactly as planned

As we now go on to outline, the evidence suggests that communications were memorable, well liked, shifted perceptions and drove consideration.

The television advertising was seen and remembered
The above-the-line advertising created an impact, with 59% of the audience recalling the television advert – very impressive for an ad about engines, especially diesels.

The television advertising was liked and made relevant points
People who saw the advert felt it 'made the point in a clever way' and left them 'feeling good' to a significantly greater extent than the average for non-Volkswagen car adverts.

Thinking back to the original objectives, the advertising performed well on scores for 'made the car seem appealing', helping to overturn preconceptions of diesel as downmarket and lacking style or sophistication (Figure 23).[8]

The television advert communicated the intended message
The advertising clearly communicated the intended message about Volkswagen diesels (Table 2).

TABLE 2: THE INTENDED MESSAGE

Statement	Percentage agreeing
Volkswagen's diesel cars are as good as petrol cars	84
You can't tell Volkswagen diesels are diesel cars	80
As good performance as a petrol car	68

Base: recognised description of TV advert
Source: Millward Brown (fieldwork 18 March–15 April 2002)

8. The advertising also scored significantly above the average on every other diagnostic measure, including 'stylish'.

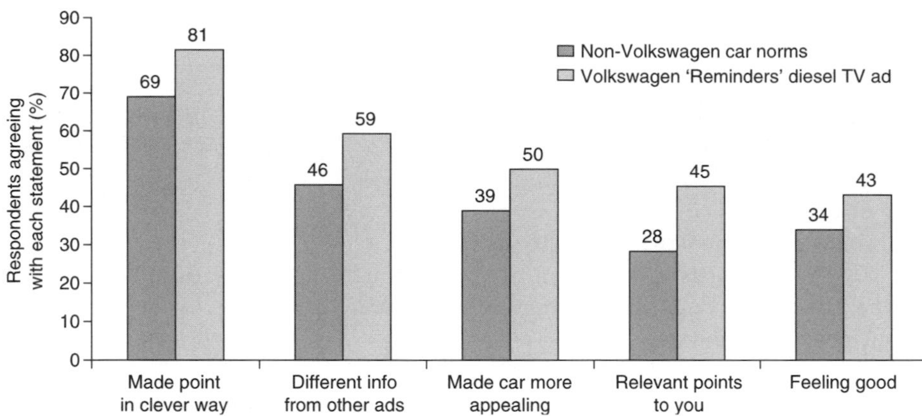

Figure 23: *Volkswagen diesel adverts score higher than norm*
All differences are significant at the 95% confidence level
Base: respondents who recognised description of TV advert
Source: Millward Brown (fieldwork 18 March–14 April 2002 and 15 April–12 May 2002)

Communications helped change perceptions of Volkswagen diesels
Following each of the two communication bursts, more people agreed with the statement 'Volkswagen makes cars with impressive diesel technology'.

What's more, changes in levels of agreement corresponded exactly with the time that communications ran (Figure 24).

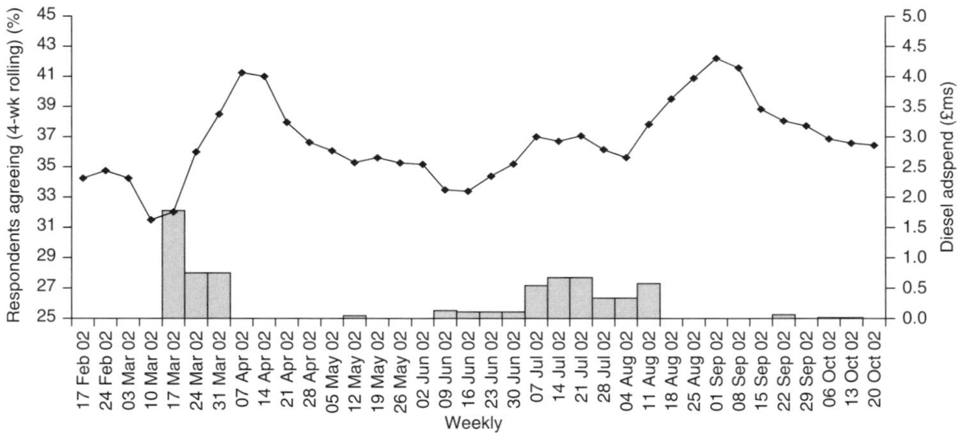

Figure 24: *Adverts changed people's perception of the Volkswagen offering*
Base: all respondents; respondents agreeing with statement 'Volkswagen makes impressive diesel technology'
Source: Millward Brown, MMS

The television advertising helped boost consideration for diesels
Following each burst of communication the percentage of diesel considerers who would definitely consider buying a Volkswagen increased (Figure 25). Again, the noticeable uplifts in consideration occurred at precisely the time that communications were on air.

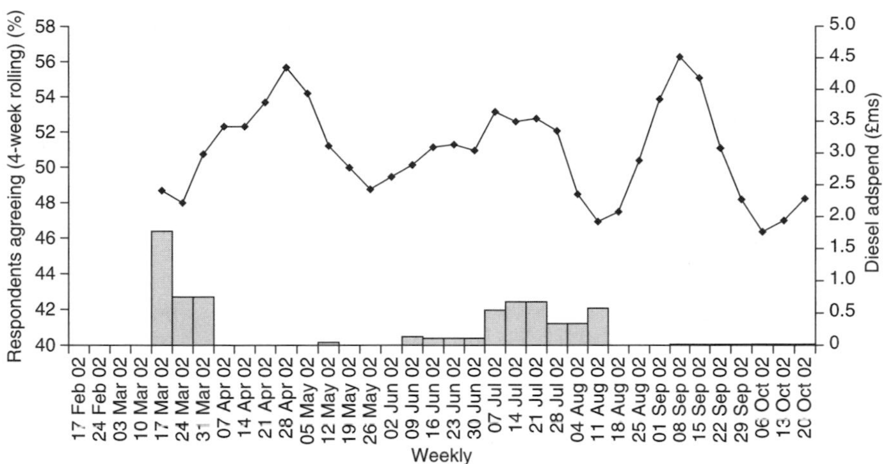

Figure 25: *Volkswagen gets shortlisted more often amongst diesel considerers*
Base: respondents that would consider buying a diesel car next time; respondents agreeing with statement 'I would shortlist a Volkswagen'
Source: Millward Brown, MMS

Website traffic on the diesel microsite increased

A significant increase in traffic on the diesel microsite was recorded in the days immediately following the TV advertising. The share of total visitors to the Volkswagen website who visited the diesel microsite whilst they were there increased markedly (Figure 26).

Absolute numbers increased from 4000 per week to 8000 per week. The TV had achieved one of its main objectives – prompting people's interest in Volkswagen diesel to the extent that they sought more information.

The timing of the uplifts in visitor numbers to the diesel microsite coincided with the periods that the communications ran.

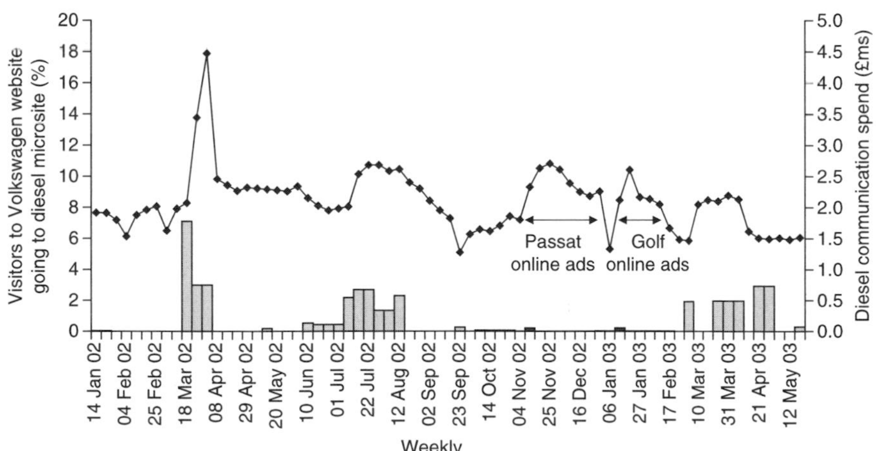

Figure 26: *Share of visitors to the diesel site rose*
Source: Tribal DDB, MMS

Online advertising campaigns for Passat and Golf, timed for late 2002 and early 2003, also coincided with noticeable and significant uplifts in numbers of visitors to the site.

The extraordinary efficiency of the online advertising in driving visitors to the microsite is noteworthy. These peaks in site visitors around Q4 2002 and Q1 2003 were achieved by spending just £12,500 per week.

Direct mail (DM) worked

The effectiveness of the diesel DM is one of the areas in which we're admittedly less well furnished with hard data than we'd like. There are gaps in our knowledge that make in-depth evaluation impossible. We've not got information on response rates, for example.

However, post-campaign quantitative research found that the fleet mail pack (featuring a 'Don't Forget It's a Diesel' rubber stamp) was remembered by nearly all respondents (93%) who'd received it. Furthermore, the pack left a favourable impression on most (67%) of these recipients.[9]

Summary – communications worked as planned

Overall, it is fair to say that communications worked exactly as planned. They were memorable, well-liked, shifted perceptions and drove consideration.

Growth of advertised models outstripped that for non-advertised models

The second strand of evidence supporting communications' central role in Volkswagen's diesel performance in 2002 and 2003 relates to the performance of the advertised models versus the non-advertised models. At a general level, the shift to diesel was much greater for advertised models than it was for non-advertised models (Figure 27).

Diesel sales revenues for the two advertised models increased significantly more than for non-advertised models (Figure 28).

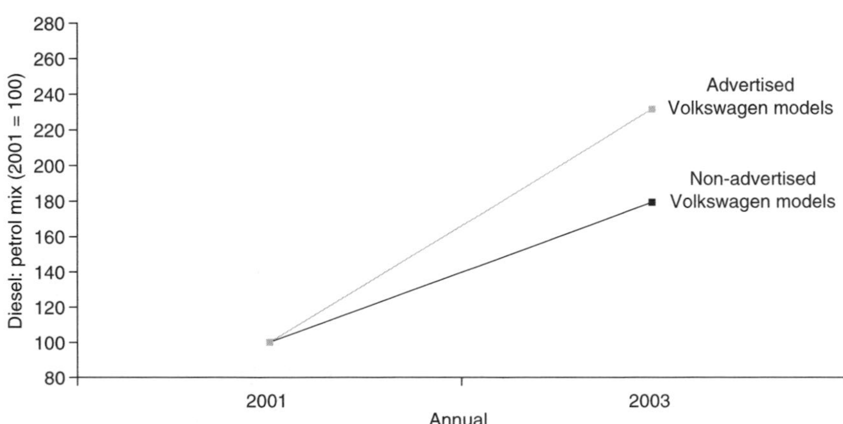

Figure 27: *Shift from petrol to diesel was much bigger for advertised models*
Note: chart shows diesel/petrol mix of advertised models vs non-advertised models
Sources: NCBS, SMMT

9. Source: Proximity London.

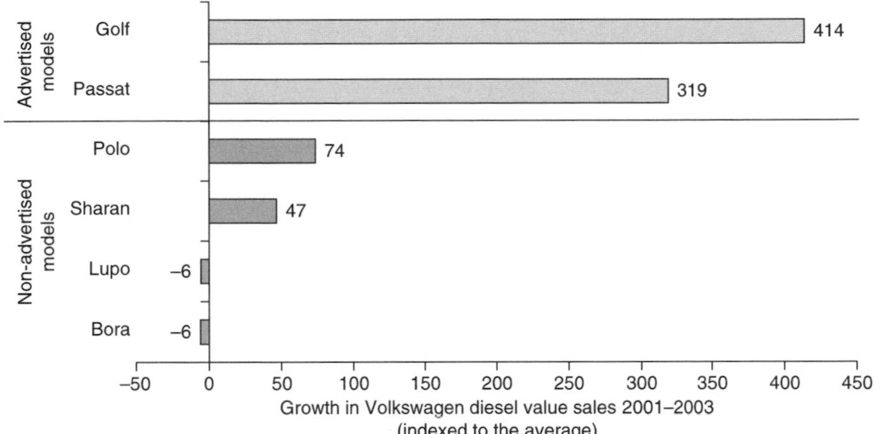

Figure 28: *Sales revenue of the advertised models grew the most*
Source: Volkswagen

The timings of key changes correlate with the timings of key changes in business performance

A third strand of evidence is based around the timings of a range of changes in performance. As discussed above, increases in consideration of diesel and perceptions that 'Volkswagen make impressive diesel technology' coincide exactly with communications. Huge increases in visitors to the diesel microsite also occur at precisely the time communications ran. In addition, the diesel share of total Volkswagen sales shows noticeable uplifts during and immediately after communications ran (Figure 29).

The average price paid for a Volkswagen diesel increased sharply at the time that the main 'Don't forget' TV campaign first broke (Figure 30).

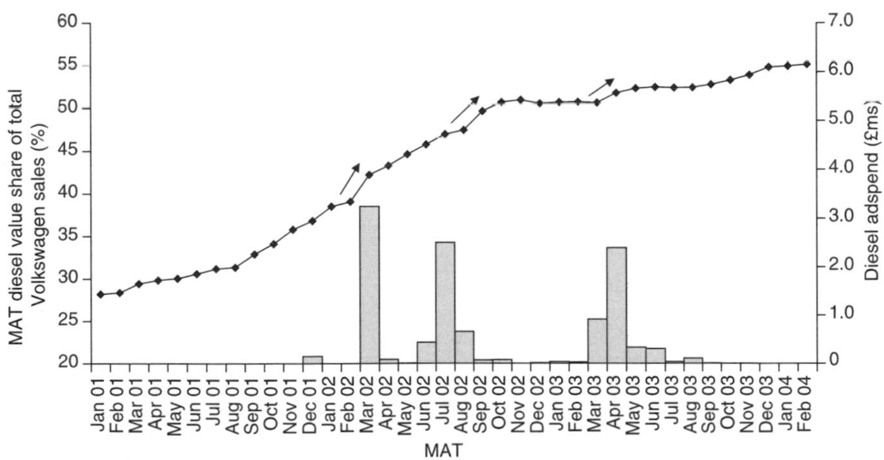

Figure 29: *The timing of the adverts corresponds to the change in the sales mix*
Sources: SMMT, NCBS

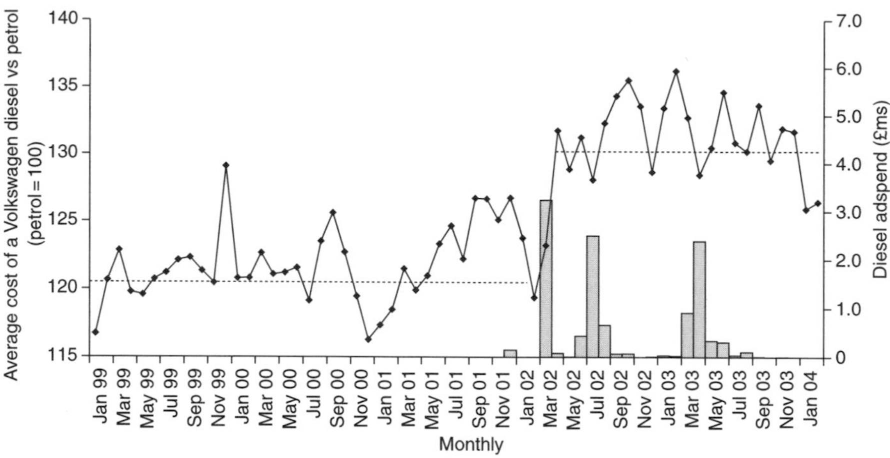

Figure 30: *People started paying more for their diesels at the start of the adverts*
Source: Volkswagen, MMS

Levels of spend correlate with changes in sales mix

Not only do the timings of significant effects match communications, but as spend increases, the relative levels of sales mix show corresponding changes as well (Figure 31).

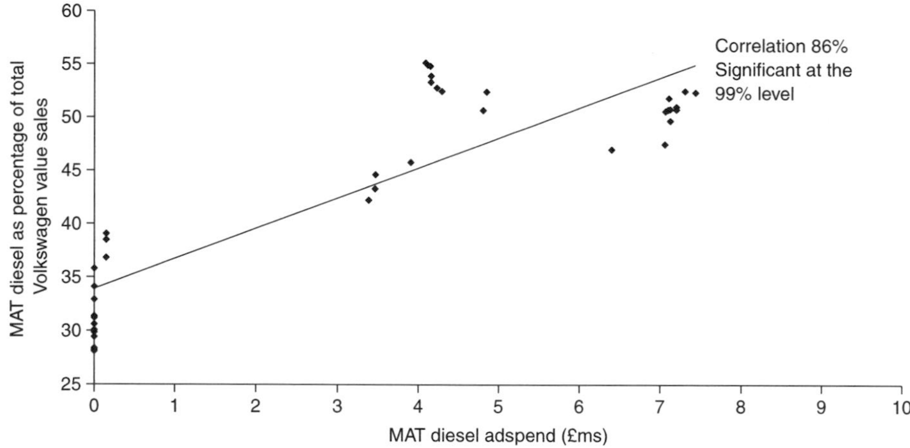

Figure 31: *Sales performance matched the level of diesel advertising*
Source: Volkswagen, MMS

An identical Volkswagen diesel range in European markets did not enjoy the levels of performance enjoyed by Volkswagen in the UK

In other European markets where Volkswagen did not run such large-scale campaigns for diesels, Volkswagen experienced significantly reduced volume share compared to the UK. Opportunities for increased diesel penetration were,

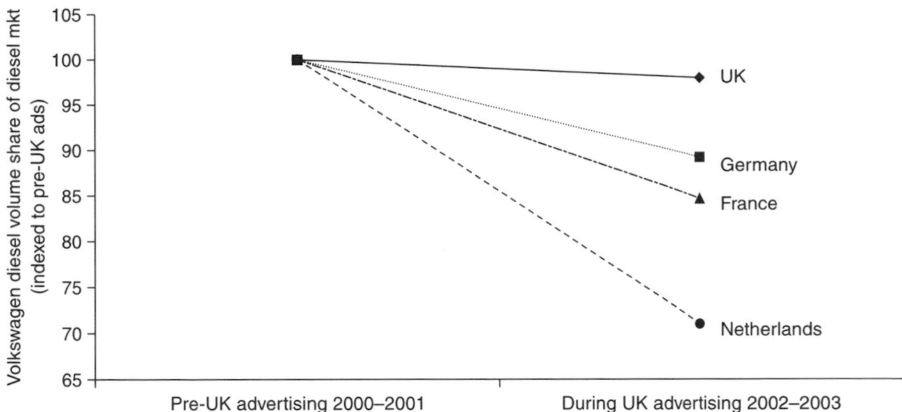

Figure 32: *Volkswagen diesel share in the UK should have fallen*
Source: SMMT, KBA, VDA, CCFA, RAI

admittedly, more limited in European markets, where diesels are more popular. But as Figure 32 shows, this can't explain why *Volkswagen*'s relative diesel volume share declined much more in Germany, Italy and the Netherlands.[10]

Nothing else can explain this impressive performance

Outlined above is a wide array of evidence supporting the assertion that the Volkswagen diesel 'Don't forget' campaign had a significant effect on Volkswagen UK's sales of diesel cars in 2002 and 2003. But what else might have explained this?

Was it price?
Prices were not cut during 2002. In fact, the average price paid for a Volkswagen diesel increased versus 2001 in absolute terms, relative to Volkswagen petrol and relative to competitors, as outlined above (Figure 18).

Was it the engine technology?
Volkswagen's diesel engines are highly regarded, and undoubtedly played a vital role in driving sales. They were the foundation for the growth that was enjoyed by Volkswagen. It would be doing a disservice to the 14,000 Volkswagen engineers working on developing and improving Volkswagen's cars and engines to suggest their efforts were not a critical ingredient. However, we would suggest that the engines alone were not enough to explain the impressive performance of Volkswagen's diesels during 2002 and 2003; the rational and emotional benefits of these engines had to be convincingly communicated to potential diesel purchasers.

- The introduction of the new more powerful diesel engines (the 130bhp and the 150bhp) pre-dates the timing of the main diesel communications by some seven months.[11] During those seven months, whilst sales are impressive, they are not nearly as impressive as after the communications had started.

10. Frustratingly, it was not possible to obtain accurate market share data for Spain and Italy.
11. The 130bhp was introduced in July 2001; the 150bhp was introduced in November 2001.

- Exactly the same diesel engines were available across Europe as in the UK from 2001 through to 2003. Yet, as has already been seen (Figure 32), Volkswagen's diesel performance in other markets was not as impressive as that of the UK.
- Bora is broadly mid-way between Golf and Passat in terms of size and was available with exactly the same engines and technology. Yet, Bora diesel value sales did not increase at all over this period (see Figure 28).

Could changes to models (excluding engines) or new models be a factor?
The nature of the diesel product, and in particular Golf and Passat (the two cars at the heart of the campaign) did not change during this period. In fact, both the Passat and the Golf were past the halfway point of their lifespan. If anything, in product life-cycle terms they were seen as ageing models compared to their main competitors.

Volkswagen did launch a number of impressive new models in 2002 – the New Polo, and the '25th Anniversary' Golf GTi. In addition, the high-performance Passat W8 was launched in June 2001. Yet these launches cannot account for the increase in Volkswagen diesel sales in 2002. First, only a relatively small percentage of Polo sales are diesels compared to Golf and Passat. Second, the Anniversary GTi and the Passat W8 are low-volume high-performance petrol-engined cars; if anything, they would have taken sales away from Volkswagen's performance diesels.

Could the changing legislation itself be a factor?
In 2002, all UK manufacturers were subject to exactly the same changes in company car taxation legislation as Volkswagen.

Could distribution be a factor?
Diesel cars were available in all retailers before and after the campaign first went on air. The number of retailers did not change significantly over this period.[12]

Could placement in retailers be a factor?
The honest answer is that we have no real way of knowing for sure what role the improved placement of diesel cars in retailers might have played. There was no retailer-based evaluation of what effect this had, and Volkswagen's on-going tracking study does not probe for retailer-focused image measures.

The enhancements within retailers were focused at people who had already made the decision to find out more about Volkswagen diesel. Whilst improved retailer position undoubtedly added to the sense that Volkswagen took diesel seriously once these prospects arrived at retailers, we suspect that this would have had little or no effect in getting people to the retailers in the first place.

Could changes in the strategy for Volkswagen fleet be a factor?
Volkswagen's relative share of the diesel fleet market did not show signs of great change during 2002 or 2003 (see Figure 33).

---

12. Source: Volkswagen.

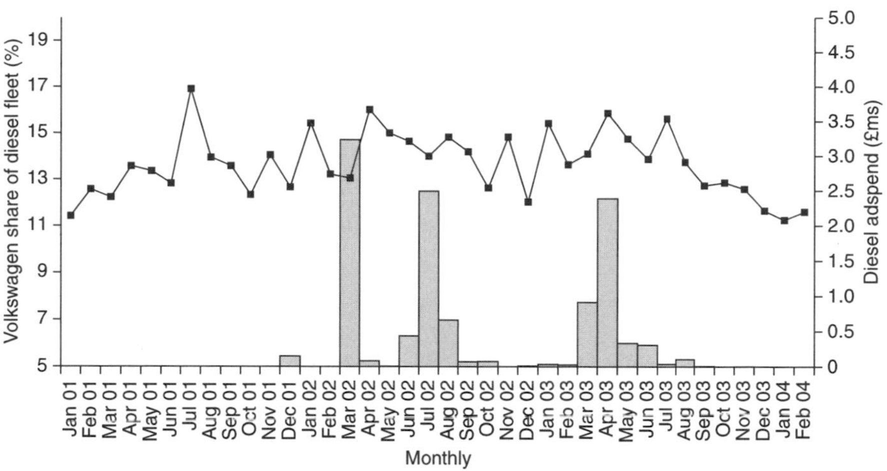

Figure 33: *Fleet sales were not responsible for Volkswagen's success*
Source: SMMT, MMS

Could poor competition be a factor?

Throughout 2001 and 2002 numerous competitors introduced a wide range of impressive new diesel engines for their model line-ups. These offerings were heavily lauded in the influential motoring press:

> 'Dynamically, the Ford Focus is the car to beat in this sector, but it lacked a quality diesel. This has all changed with the TDCi engine.'
>
> *Auto Express*, 2 January 2002 (the Ford Focus is one of Golf's main competitors)

> 'Until recently ... the ageing TDdi engine did not do proper justice to the Focus. However, that changed with the launch of the all-new 1.8-litre Duratorq TDCi at the start of the year ... the TDCi is easily the smoothest and quietest diesel the class has ever seen ... at times you could be fooled into thinking you've got petrol power underfoot.'
>
> *Auto Express*, 12 June 2002

> 'With impressive vehicles such as the [Peugeot] 307 HDi available, the days of petrol dominance are clearly coming to an end.'
>
> *Auto Express*, 2 January 2002 (the Peugeot 307 is a core competitor to Golf)

> 'This second-generation common rail turbo-diesel is one of the best around ... right up there at the top. The TDCi engine really does make Britain's best-selling car even better.'
>
> *Top Gear Magazine*, February 2002 (the Mondeo is a main competitor to Passat)

> 'There's no hint that [the Vectra 2.2 DTi] is an oil burner ... [it's] impressively refined.'
>
> *What Car?*, July 2002 (the Vauxhall Vectra is a main competitor to Passat)

> 'The Ford [Focus 1.8 TDCi] is still the best to drive and its engine is impressively refined. Quickest by some margin is Volkswagen's Golf [1.9 GT TDi PD 130], but it's the least rewarding to drive and has the noisiest engine.'
>
> *What Car?*, November 2002, competitive road test

Summary

A broad spectrum of potential factors that might have played a role in Volkswagen's impressive diesel performance in 2002 and 2003 has been eliminated. The price of Volkswagen diesels, the engine technology on its own, changes to Passat or Golf, the changing company car legislation, increases in distribution, improvements in retailer display, increases in Volkswagen's fleet share of diesel sales, and poor competition have all been discounted as potential driving factors behind Volkswagen's performance.

WHAT WOULD HAVE HAPPENED TO VOLKSWAGEN WITHOUT THE 'DON'T FORGET' CAMPAIGN?

With increased competition and a strategy that was consciously focusing on the more premium end of the diesel market, one might expect Volkswagen to lose market share. This did not happen. Two strands of evidence suggest that if the campaign had not run then Volkswagen would have lost volume sales within the diesel market.

The Peugeot example as a benchmark

Peugeot has been the traditional and undisputed champion of diesel technology. It was the market leader up to 2002, offering a range of models in the same car sectors as Volkswagen and at similar price points. Its existing competitors to Passat and Golf (the 406 and 306, respectively) were broadly the same age as Passat and Golf during the campaign. What's more, in June 2001 Peugeot launched its 306 replacement, the brand new 307, with the high-performance HDi diesel engine arriving in October 2001. It was designed to go head to head with Golf. Yet despite all this, Peugeot's diesel volume sales declined between 2001 and 2003 (Figure 34).

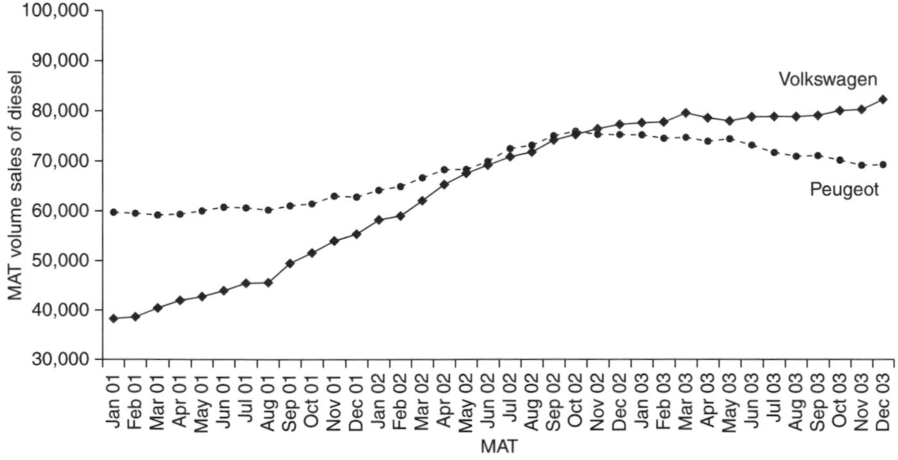

Figure 34: *Volkswagen could have lost sales like Peugeot*
Source: SMMT

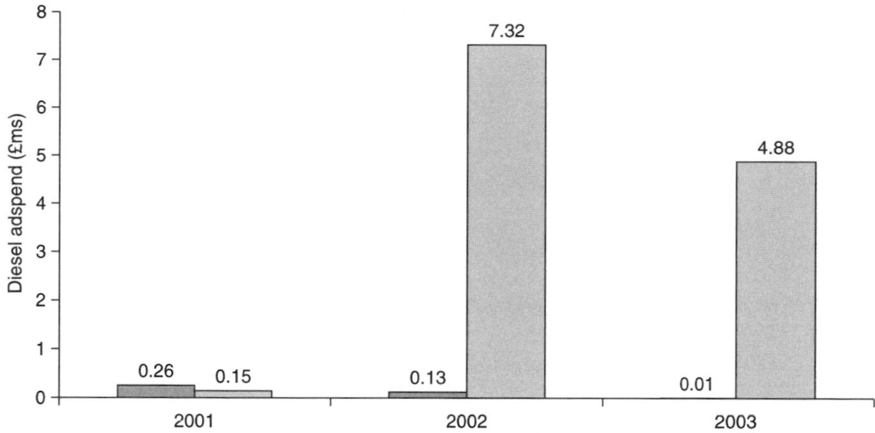

Figure 35: *Volkswagen outspent Peugeot*
Source: MMS

A significant difference between the two manufacturers can be found in their relative spends on diesel. During 2002 Volkswagen spent over 56 times more than Peugeot on diesel advertising: £7.32m versus £130,000 (Figure 35).

Peugeot provides a real-life example of what could well have happened to Volkswagen's fortunes in diesel had the 'Don't forget' campaign not run.

Econometric modelling as comparative evidence

The contribution of communications towards the business success of Volkswagen's diesels can be calculated using Volkswagen's econometric model. This model suggests that diesel volume sales would have been approximately 5.2% lower had Volkswagen not run the 'Don't forget' campaign (Figure 36).

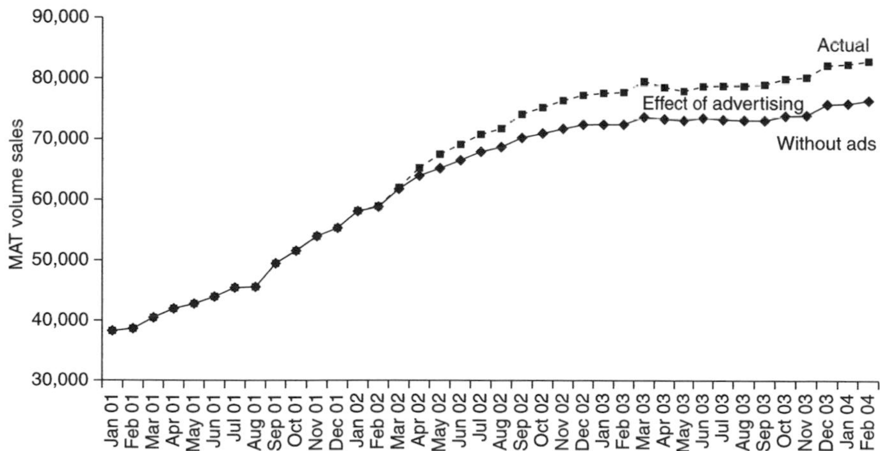

Figure 36: *The effect of the Volkswagen diesel campaign*
Source: Econometric model

PAYBACK FOR VOLKSWAGEN

It is not possible to disclose Volkswagen's profit levels here. However, by increasing diesel's share of total marque sales, and by persuading people to buy more powerful and more expensive diesel variants, the 'Don't forget' campaign contributed significantly to increasing Volkswagen's profitability.

Short-term payback

Although it is somewhat shortsighted to look at communications in such a way in the car market (with its three-year purchase cycle), we have been able to show through econometric modelling that this investment in communications paid for itself in the short term.

Modelling of UK performance suggests an incremental revenue return for Volkswagen during the period 2002–2003 of between £180.2m, against a communications investment of £12.3m (Table 3).

Interestingly, a European comparison using the 'least worst case scenario' of the European markets' experiences for Volkswagen – Germany – provides an incremental revenue return for Volkswagen UK of £224m (see Figure 32 for the European comparison).

TABLE 3: REVENUE VERSUS ADSPEND

	Incremental revenue (£m)	Diesel adspend (£m)
Euro comparison	224.0	12.3
Econometric model	180.2	12.3

Source: SMMT, VDA, CCFA, RAI, econometric model, MMS

Taking the more conservative of these two figures, based upon Volkswagen's econometric model, we'd suggest that the communications investment provided a more modest but still highly impressive incremental revenue return for 2002–2003 of £180.2m.

Longer-term payback

The real profit gains for Volkswagen, however, will be made over the long term. The diesel sector has continued to grow in importance in the UK every year since 2001, and this growth shows few signs of slowing. Because of the three-year buying cycle, the ultimate return on investment for Volkswagen will extend for some years into the future, with positive impacts upon Volkswagen's volumes, revenues and profits for at least three years from 2003, when the campaign came to an end.

CONCLUSIONS

Before the 'Don't forget it's a diesel' campaign ran, diesels were tainted with perceptions of sluggishness, smelliness and noisiness. A diesel was something slightly embarrassing that you were probably driving to save money. The 'Don't forget' campaign persuaded new car buyers that driving Volkswagen diesels could be sexy and could be aspirational. The campaign generated substantial short-term additional revenues for Volkswagen UK, and it did so profitably. More significantly, the campaign elevated Volkswagen to a position of long-term strength in this increasingly important sector of the UK car market.

The power of ideas

In 2001, Volkswagen was already in a strong position in the diesel market. It had an impressive product, and it was selling well. All the signs were that it was well placed to enjoy a successful 2002 and 2003.

Volkswagen could have rested on its laurels and simply waited for orders. It did not. It would have been foolish to do so, anyway, with the twin threats of improving competition and some more expensive diesels to sell looming large. Instead of being satisfied with volume sales increases alone, Volkswagen had spotted the opportunity to extract further additional value from the rapidly evolving diesel market. Volkswagen identified the potential to enrich its relative diesel sales mix to deliver increased revenue per diesel unit sold.

Volkswagen wasn't the only car manufacturer in the UK to spot the opportunity for growth in the diesel market. Yet only Volkswagen acted so decisively. Volkswagen wasn't the only car manufacturer in the UK to have ambitions for growth in diesel value sales in 2002. Yet only Volkswagen matched its ambition with a strategy of equal audacity.

This is important. It's the main lesson we've learned from our experiences of creating and developing the 'Don't forget' campaign. This paper shows how a genuinely powerful creative idea can deliver against a bold business strategy. It shows how a genuinely powerful creative idea has the potential to overturn prejudices, change behaviours, and ultimately transform business fortunes.

Section 3

Bronze Winners (summaries)

For full case histories please contact the IPA Information Centre by emailing info@ipa.co.uk

AA Loans

Those 'very nice' AA men now fix loans too

Getting to the top of shopping lists in this highly commoditised market

Principal authors: Max Wright, Rapier, and Stuart Garvie, Manning Gottlieb OMD

SUMMARY

This case study demonstrates how to take a well-established brand from one commoditised market into another and get it moving right to the top of shopping lists within two years.

BACKGROUND

In 1999, Centrica became the new owner of the AA, a non-profit-making mutual society with over 150 products and services. The AA found itself facing the challenge of meeting shareholder expectations to increase revenues and profits.

One product to be chosen to deliver greater returns was the AA's loans business. This small business was created as a joint venture with Capital Bank (now HBoS) in 1984 to provide unsecured general loans for AA breakdown members.

Using only direct selling through AA internal channels such as direct mail, and test media such as the motoring press, the business was worth almost £300m in loans advances in 2001.[1]

TIME FOR A STEP-CHANGE

In January 2002, the AA appointed Rapier to its agency roster with the task of working alongside Manning Gottlieb OMD, to help create a 'step-change' in the AA's loans business.

Our brief was to double both loan volumes and loans advances within two years[2] despite limited market growth in previous years.[3]

This task was made more difficult because of consumers' apathy surrounding borrowing. They simply arranged loans with the high-street banks that they banked with. This behaviour accounted for 62% of unsecured loans in 2001.[4]

1. CPFL monthly accounts, December 2001.
2. CPFL targets.
3. Finance and Leasing Association (FLA) monthly statistics, December 1999–December 2001.
4. National Opinion Polls Financial Research Survey (NOP FRS), 2001.

A TRULY INTEGRATED SOLUTION

Our solution was to build the business from the bottom up. First, we changed our focus to concentrate solely on car loans for used car buyers rather than to target more broadly with a general loans message. This meant that we could leverage the AA's motoring-centric brand.

Creatively, we kept things simple in order to stand out. We put consumers straight into each execution, and let them highlight the array of potential uncertainties that used car buyers might experience. This positioned AA Loans as a problem-solver.

Second, we changed our media approach so that we could target both those currently 'in market' and those that would be in market in the future. We rationalised our existing 'in market' response activity to improve efficiency and increase frequency. We then introduced new test response media such as radio, interactive TV, regional motoring press and door-drops to further increase responses.

Once we had rationalised these and reached saturation levels, we broadened our activity to increase brand consideration amongst future car loans customers. TV, tube panels, roadside posters and drive-time radio were added to the campaign.

Over the next two years, there were 34 different press executions in 67 titles, three inserts, four online executions, four posters, two radio commercials and two TV executions. Each was based on one of our identified uncertainties.

THE RESULTS

Between 2001 and 2003, AA Loans outperformed the market and grew its share of advances by 150%.[5] This meant that although we fell slightly short of doubling AA Loans volume, our newly recruited customers were more valuable than we had planned for and we exceeded our value target, which increased by 134%.[6] In turn, profit increased by 37%.[7]

This business success was directly related to our communications activity, as these communications were our only source of sales.

Not only did we increase spontaneous average brand awareness by ten points between 2001 and 2003,[8] the AA also became the most spontaneously considered car loans brand in the market bar one by November 2003, ahead of Barclays and Direct Line.[9]

Econometric modelling has shown that return on investment grew significantly: 21% more than that achieved prior to the campaign.[10]

CONCLUSION

Only a few years ago, when drivers found themselves stranded in their cars in the middle of nowhere, they would only have wanted the AA to fix their car. Now, when in the same situation, they increasingly want the AA to help them buy a better one.

5. FLA monthly statistics, December 2001–December 2003.
6. CPFL monthly accounts, December 2001–December 2003.
7. CPFL monthly accounts, December 2001 and 2003.
8. TNS Tracking, December 2003.
9. TNS Tracking, December 2003.
10. Manning Gottlieb OMD econometrics.

Army Recruitment

Up and over the 'wall of fear'

How advertising is helping the Army meet its manning obligations

Principal authors: Mark Tomblin and Mark Pihlens, Publicis
Contributing author: Adrian Marks, ZenithOptimedia

SUMMARY

During the mid-late 1990s the Army consistently failed to meet its establishment targets – the number of soldiers it needs to do its job properly.

This paper tells the story of how – in one of the most daunting recruiting environments imaginable – the Army set about addressing that problem, and of the crucial role that advertising played in helping to solve it.

THE ESSENCE OF THE TASK

To meet its overall manning and skills objectives, the Army felt that it needed to reach beyond its traditional recruiting pools to another group entirely: young people who might not have previously considered a job in the Army but had the right qualities to thrive in the modern service. An additional challenge was how to interest such people in the Army in the most difficult recruiting environment for a generation.

FIRST STEP: REPACKAGING THE ARMY

The Army is one of the best places to learn skills that are transferable to civilian life and valued by future employers. The problem is that there are currently an off-puttingly complex 1400 different training options in the Army. So these were packaged into nine 'career groups' (CGs) based on broad analogies with jobs in civilian life, so as to make it easier for potential recruits to engage with the organisation.

SECOND STEP: SCALING THE 'WALL OF FEAR'

Joining the Army engenders 'getting in' fears and 'getting out' fears in prospective soldiers (Figure 1).

The role of advertising was thus to manage these fears, by opening up the secret, somewhat alien, world of the Army and revealing recognisable individuals with

Figure 1: *A daunting metaphorical wall*

recognisable skills. To this end a CG-based testimonial television advertising campaign was developed around the line 'Not your basic training' which reflected our chosen positioning of the Army as *the ultimate skills provider*. This went on air in September 2000.

THE RESULTS

Intermediate measures and responses

Given that we were communicating a complex and information-rich message to a diverse group of people, the movement in measures which reflected the levels of fear that young people felt about the prospects offered by Army life was excellent, as was the uplift in actual responses.

The enlistment story

Of course, the acid test of the new campaign is whether it helped the Army achieve its objectives in terms of people joining up. In fact, recruitment targets have been hit in each of the last two fiscal years and the Army's manning deficit is shrinking for the first time in a decade or more. Figure 2 shows that while the gap is not yet closed, it has been very nearly halved in a little under two years.

While it would be idle to pretend that the new advertising approach has caused this closure entirely on its own, we believe that we have proved that it has played a crucial role in helping many young people over the wall of fear that stands between them and a job in the Army.

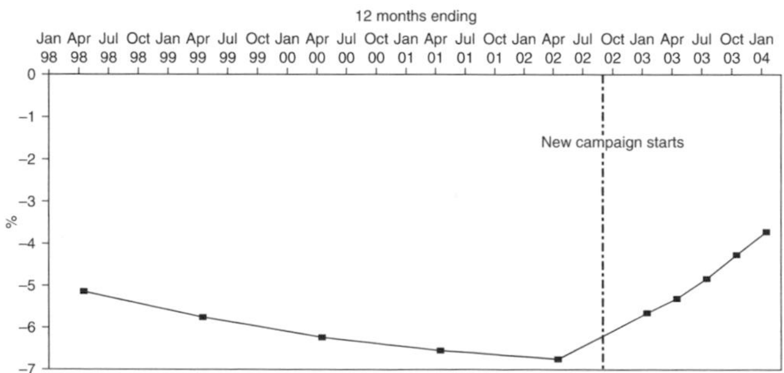

Figure 2: *Army manning deficit: 1998–2004 (%)*

BMW Films

'The Hire'

Film it and they will come. How internet films acted like a magnet for BMW prospects and set a new economic standard for marketing efficiency

Principal authors: Lachlan Badenoch, Adrian Ho and Rob White, Fallon
Media agency: Zenith Optimedia

SUMMARY

At a time of falling TV ratings, lost generations of audiences, and the rise of ad-skipping personal video recorders, BMW's internet film series *The Hire* represents a bold step for a marketer into the world of branded entertainment, a world where much had been theorised but no benchmarks existed to give confidence of economic pay-off.

It was a risk, but a highly calculated one. This paper demonstrates the economic rewards BMW has been able to enjoy for its marketing courage, and for its belief in an idea.

MAKING THE CASE FOR INNOVATION

In 2000, facing a year with no significant product introductions to drive showroom traffic, BMW North America set a high marketing bar, bought an 'impossible' idea, and never wavered in its belief that it would work.

After several years of competition-leading marketing efficiency, BMW faced larger spending competitors like Lexus and Mercedes starting to over take its sales. Despite this and a lack of new products, sales growth had to be maintained.

Developing a radical solution seemed complex, but the tools were simple: great cars that could win over drivers through *experience*. The task was to get people more excited about that prospect, turning desire for the car into going to drive one themselves.

Showcasing the cars in a short internet-based film series (named *The Hire*) evolved organically from this core challenge and, most importantly, belief in the *positive* possibilities of the new media paradigm.

REVERSING THE MODEL

The 'impossible' idea of using *The Hire* as the cornerstone of the year's marketing programme required reversing the normal content-to-distribution ratio: shifting significant money to production. To make the model work, production values (for which read A-list Hollywood talent) had to be high enough that viewers would actively seek out these films, and value what they found.

It transformed a marketing idea into a brand property.

SUCCESS

In all, eight films were produced and launched in 2001 and 2002. They are still being downloaded and viewed today.

The economic rewards enjoyed by BMW came in two forms: as a more efficient replacement to a traditional media campaign, and as an on-going annuity contributing to the brand's perceptual and financial income.

An incredibly efficient marketing tool

This case shows that *The Hire*:

- attracted a huge audience of the right profile
- cost only 56% of BMW's traditional advertising (brand exposure gained per dollar spent)
- attracted $26 million equivalent of exposure in additional free publicity
- drove up a host of key brand attributes and measures among viewers
- increased planned dealer visits among target viewers by factors of 400% to 550%
- over 2001 and 2002, reduced the cost per unit sale of BMW's marketing effort to 65% and 77% of its 1998 levels, while growing sales at a higher rate than the competition.

The annuity effect

The Hire has not required further investment since 2002, yet is still working to build the brand. At the time of writing in 2004, total film views on the internet had passed the 64 million mark and were continuing to climb.

Furthermore *The Hire*'s value as a BMW property created demand for future expressions. The films are now available on DVD via the web, dealers and owners' clubs, even trading at good prices on eBay; and a profit-producing venture publishing a comic-book series of *The Hire* is the latest project to hit the public eye.

The crux of the ROI argument is marketing efficiency. However, this paper suggests that the annuity effects represent incremental value that no traditional ad campaign could hope to generate.

It is this increasing, not decreasing, value from the time of investment that justifies and will ultimately reward further development of this type of marketing model.

We have only just begun to scratch the surface.

BT Broadband

Broadband has landed

How a rampaging rhino and a three-headed dragon helped BT create widespread public demand for Broadband

Principal authors: Phil Teer, Michele Danan, Dan Goldstein, St Luke's, and David Blackwell, BT
Media agency: PHD

SUMMARY

'I think the fact that BT's really swung behind Broadband is phenomenally important, and I thank you for that.'

Tony Blair, Prime Minister, 2003

Within BT it had long been acknowledged that the deregulation of the UK telecommunications market would erode its core revenue stream derived from voice communications. BT's survival relied upon developing future streams of revenue outside of voice telephony; the most critical of these future markets was internet-based telecommunications.

By 2002 internet penetration in the UK was amongst the highest in the world, around 55% of all households had internet access. But, with the market nearing saturation, BT's revenue growth from this source was slowing down. Nearly all internet-enabled households used 56k dial-up modems to access the internet. BT knew that Broadband was the next major opportunity for its business. Broadband represented a significant price premium on dial-up in the form of monthly subscription fees.

It wasn't just BT that was keen to see Broadband take off in the UK. The Government had seen its potential too: widespread adoption of Broadband was deemed crucial to our standing as a global e-economy. But, despite the best efforts of the Government and other Broadband players to stimulate demand, Broadband adoption in the UK was dismally slow. In October 2001 there were only 250,000 Broadband subscribers, less than 0.5% of the population. This contrasted with the situation in other countries, indeed the UK had the lowest Broadband penetration in Europe, despite it being available to over two-thirds of the population for some 18 months.

Oftel was looking to BT to take responsibility for stimulating widespread national demand for Broadband. BT decided that in order to create such a demand it needed to employ a national advertising campaign. It decided to ignore the fact that Broadband had been available in the UK for some time; it felt it crucial to give the UK's 'twenty-first-century data highways' a proper launch of mass appeal and popular importance. The launch of Broadband had to be nothing short of A National Event.

The advertising campaign developed in partnership with St Luke's was as intense and exciting as the best Hollywood action movie, but was set within a quiet street in British suburbia. It depicted Broadband as an exciting public network lying beneath every street and accessible by every household. The campaign very quickly created a mass awareness, a mass excitement and a mass understanding of Broadband and the possibilities it presented. By doing so the advertising created a massive increase in people's intention to sign up to Broadband: within two months of the advertising launch over 50% of those people that could get Broadband intended to do so or had already signed up to get it. This intention translated into action: monthly acquisitions to BT Broadband increased by 200% within five months of launch and the market as a whole experienced an increase in subscription rates of some 60%.

In order to isolate advertising's effect we constructed two econometric models: one to isolate the effects of the advertising on BT's acquisition of Broadband customers and one to isolate the effects of the advertising on growing the Broadband market as a whole. We demonstrate that the advertising generated 119,332 new subscribers to BT Broadband between September 2002 and September 2003. This represents 37% of all BT Broadband subscribers attained during this period. The value of these subscribers in their first year of subscription is £61,097,984, or a return of £2.40 on every advertising £1 invested. We calculate that the value of these subscribers over a six-year period is £193,448,181, or a return of £6.60 per advertising £1 invested.

In addition to BT's subscription gain and true to its secondary objective of growing the Broadband category as a whole, the advertising generated a total of 213,753 subscribers to Broadband – representing a market growth of some 15% with a first-year value of £85,287,447 in subscription fees.

We wished to demonstrate the extent to which the uptake of Broadband contributes to the UK's GDP. Using a model pioneered in the United States we were able to apply a series of projections on the UK's economic growth due to an increased Broadband adoption amongst the population. We isolated just the 213,753 Broadband subscribers generated by the advertising and projected their impact on the UK economy over time. We conservatively calculate that over a period of 15 years the total contribution of this group to UK GDP will amount to over £500m.

BRONZE

BUPA

The personal health service

How a big idea made a big difference to a big brand and a big business

Principal authors: Jo Reid and David Golding, WCRS
Media agency: Starcom MediaVest

SUMMARY

This paper tells how Britain's biggest private health insurer, through advertising, repositioned itself in the public imagination as a health and care company that anyone can use and, in doing so, delivered significant returns to BUPA.

The private medical insurance (PMI) market had been in decline since 1996 and BUPA forced to defend its share from encroachment by new low-cost competitors. In 1998, WCRS was briefed to 'Make BUPA more relevant to more people by showing them other points, beyond PMI, through which they can access BUPA and the benefits of private healthcare'. Broadening the appeal of the brand would make it less reliant on PMI and allow it to capitalise further on other elements in this massive 40,000-employee health and care organisation (e.g. hospitals, residential care homes and health assessment centres). Doing this would necessitate bringing these elements together into a meaningful whole, making it famous and doing this in a way that reflected the intrinsic existing strengths of BUPA.

'The Personal Health Service' refocuses on the *total* BUPA offering including care and wellness products, and it reframes BUPA as offering a personal and individual, rather than private, service. From being a private illness business 'The Personal Health Service' suggests that BUPA is a tailored personal wellness business and a complement to the comprehensive, mass service offered by the NHS.

The repositioning of BUPA as 'The Personal Health Service' has had many strengths. It has become a common orientation point and service mission for five different Business Units and contributed to higher morale and concomitant decrease in turnover amongst staff. It has generated a philosophy that puts the customer at the heart of all new product, service and marketing initiatives such as individually tailored pricing and the use of customer satisfaction as the key performance indicator for managers across the business. It has also led to a change in BUPA's call-handling process, which has empowered handlers to handle calls as they see fit and thus to build personal member rapport: this has contributed to a reduction in member lapse rates and therefore retention of their potential lifetime value.

Advertising has carried a variety of messages in support of 'The Personal Health Service', some focusing on products and services and some on it as an ethos. It has achieved consistently high levels of awareness but more importantly has led to significant increases in awareness of advertised products and services beyond PMI. Furthermore, consideration of the brand and of these products and services has risen, with consequent positive revenue effects. Since 2000, we have seen increased *private* occupancy in BUPA care homes (i.e. occupancy by those who choose and pay for their own accommodation), and from 2000 to 2002 a 16% increase in health screenings and 18% increase in self-pay treatments, higher than for the market as a whole.

Although features of BUPA such as personal pricing have made econometric modelling impossible, we have attempted to assess the extent to which other factors beyond advertising could have influenced these increases. If attitudes to and beliefs about the NHS had worsened, BUPA's services would be obvious beneficiaries. However, we have evidence that shows simultaneous improvements in perceptions of the NHS. Neither has there been a marked improvement in perceptions of private health per se, which could also explain BUPA's gains. A heightened public interest in managing health could also have had a positive effect, particularly on health assessments, but actually there was little change here between 2000 and 2002. And demographic shifts do not explain an increase in private care home residency as the number of people in the appropriate age bracket diminished over the period. In terms of marketing activity for care homes, health assessments and self-pay there is no significant competitor to BUPA to examine, and BUPA's share of voice has declined so individual parts of BUPA could not have benefited from any enhancement in the prominence of the brand as a whole. And below the line, BUPA spent no more in the relevant areas over the period in question. We therefore state with confidence that communication of BUPA's repositioning as 'The Personal Health Service' in advertising has been instrumental in effecting an increased interest in and take-up of products and services beyond PMI, making a contribution to revenue in excess of the advertising investment made.

BRONZE

Children's Hearings

How Scotland's revolutionary Children's Hearings system has used advertising to inspire and motivate local people in local communities

Principal author: Michael Kemsley, Barkers
Media agency: Feather Brooksbank

SUMMARY

Scotland's Children's Hearings system works with children and young people who may have offended, been neglected or abused. Its unique structure and remit allow it to concentrate on the welfare of the child rather than retribution, and it puts the decisions into the hands of everyday people – peers who bring their unique, local insight to each case.

For several years numbers of applicants to the panel had been in desperate decline. An urgent call to action was required that would resonate with people from all walks of life. We can prove that a new advertising strategy led to a dramatic change in fortunes for the Children's Hearings system.

THE PROBLEM

The role of a panel member entails exposure to highly traumatic cases, weekend work, time off for training courses and a general demand on free time. It is also unpaid. It requires a high level of dedication, and although training and support is given, these demands should not be underestimated. There are 30 Children's Panels operating throughout Scotland, each dependent on the commitment of local volunteers for its ability to function.

Our initial objective was to reverse the decline in respondents. A secondary objective was to attract a broader cross-section of the community to the panel.

Attracting newcomers to the panel is crucial and an annual recruitment campaign is held every September. This consisted of a small media campaign, which had performed adequately until 1998 when response levels reached a critical level. Evidence also showed the majority of applicants to be female, older people and those from higher socio-economic groups, leaving a substantial and vital section of the community under-represented, contrary to the ethos and requirement of the panel.

Through extensive research we discovered that the main motivations to joining the panel were clear, strong and personal drivers such as a desire to help children – especially in a local context – and an aim to give something back to society. There was a requirement for more detail about the system, its successes and capabilities.

THE SOLUTION

To succeed we needed less of a traditional recruitment focus and more of a product-based advertising campaign. A new set of brand values would have to be associated with Children's Hearings, engaging a wider audience and emphasising the positives that membership could bring. We would have to appeal to a new audience and we had to engage them in a deeply emotive, positive way.

The new campaign was developed. It stood for 'my local area and the kids that live here', it was 'for people like me' and it showed a true philanthropic value.

To ensure maximum success and synergy the panel management was given guidance on preparing more positive and welcoming recruitment packs, engaging local politicians and media, and developing public information points in libraries and supermarkets. The new optimism about Children's Hearings would permeate at all levels and create a new wave of applicants, vying for recognition as one of society's enablers.

OUTCOME

The overall number of respondents in 2000 was 1460, and 1105 in 2001. Following the change in strategy promoting the more positive and personal aspects of the work, this rose to 4133 in 2002 and 3816 in 2003. This can be translated as an overall increase of 374% from 2001 to 2002.

The 2003 results also show that the number of male applicants has reached a high of 30%, which we can relate to the media targeting of sports pages used in this campaign.

We have proved successful in meeting the objective of attracting applicants from the lower socio-economic groupings, with 38% of applicants in 2002 coming from C2DEF groups compared to 32% in 2001 and 34% in 2000.

We can also show a cost per respondent of £41.05 for 2002/3 and £75.66 for 2000/1 – a reduction of 45.74%.

These figures demonstrate the level and type of respondents contacting the response centre. With the exception of the aforementioned local authority collateral, there has been no other promotional work to which we could attribute such a massive increase.

Additionally, there has been no significant change to length or composition of media type used throughout the recorded period.

CLOSE

Inviting people to sacrifice free time and expose themselves to potentially upsetting situations without pay is no mean feat. However, we have seen a response growth of 374%. We have proven that small budget doesn't necessarily equate to small campaign, and we can clearly demonstrate that advertising has achieved goals and revolutionised recruitment to the Children's Hearings system.

BRONZE

Imperial Leather

Imperial Leather sponsorship wins the 2002 Commonwealth Games

Principal author: Lorna Hawtin, BDH\TBWA

SUMMARY

In the summer of 2002, Manchester hosted the Commonwealth Games and PZ Cussons' Imperial Leather was one of the major sponsors.

This is the story of how Imperial Leather (IL) was able to win the sponsorship game for PZ Cussons: by being true to its own unique perspective, rather than to corporate sponsorship norms, it was able to dominate and put its own stamp on the Games – achieving all its objectives.

- The new brand identity would become accepted and established – at home and abroad.
- The reputation of the company and the brand amongst all key stakeholders, including consumers, employees, trade partners and journalists, would be enhanced.
- The brand's vision would be underlined.

THE CHALLENGE

On first examination, a significant opportunity was presented by the Games. There was a natural geographical fit with PZ Cussons' international businesses and the event coincided with the roll-out of the new Imperial Leather brand identity worldwide. Plus an association with the biggest ever sporting event to be held in the UK could only help to enhance PZ Cussons' corporate stature at home.

From a communications perspective we were more cautious. We feared such a major diversion of resources into sponsorship on the tail end of an important relaunch, and we were not looking to build an association with sporting performance, adrenalin and machismo. We were struggling to see how a sporting event could fit with our fmcg female target audience.

In some quarters, there were even doubts over the calibre of the event itself. The Olympics was seen as the 'big brother' of athletics occasions – we didn't want to tie ourselves to an event that was seen as second best. Plus, negative media speculation threatening a repeat of the Millennium Dome debacle was affecting confidence.

Finally, we had a tiny ten-day window in a busy year that was to include the Football World Cup and the Queen's Golden Jubilee Celebrations.

Our challenge therefore became to unite a diverse audience of trade buyers, UK and City journalists, PZ Cussons' UK staff and PZ Cussons' international businesses under a single campaign that could work for PZ Cussons, as much as for IL.

COMMUNICATIONS STRATEGY

As newcomers to the field, our first port of call was to understand the conventions of corporate sports sponsorships.

It seemed that a brand's involvement in sport was frequently viewed as a demonstration of its support for a 'worthwhile cause' complete with a very worthy tone of voice. We saw how IL with its informal, engaging and cheeky personality could adopt a much more disruptive tone of voice to create real impact across the board.

Our strategy was to become the least 'official' of the official sponsors of the 2002 Commonwealth Games.

Integration was to become a critical foundation stone of the Connections strategy. A low-weight national TV burst spearheaded the campaign. This was supported by a range of other activities including an on-pack promotion, stadium hoardings and bibs, local press activity, affinity tie-ups with local radio stations, competitions, posters, PR, staff events and activities, consumer sampling events, hospitality and a 'fun and games' roadshow.

COMMUNICATIONS EFFECTS

We have evidenced that during the period of the Games, IL branding dominated press and TV coverage in the UK and around the Commonwealth. The brand's PR coverage was impressive across both trade, City and consumer titles, and the campaign has subsequently won several major awards and made a substantial contribution to staff morale and trade relationships, all contributing to raising the profile of the company and the IL brand.

Tracking amongst all adult consumers measured a spontaneous sponsorship awareness level over 50% higher than the nearest rival sponsor, and brand health showed sustained improvements for over six months following the campaign.

In the four-week data period of the games, IL's value sales across all washing and bathing categories increased by 30% versus the four weeks prior to the games. A strong performance, when the rest of the market saw a 5% value decline in the same period. A comparison of IL sales in the six months prior to the games versus the six months immediately following, has shown an incremental £3.7m turnover.

Given the UK media and production budget of £1.6m and without exposing profit margins, we can safely suggest that the campaign paid back in full in the UK within the first six months.

It was an exhilarating and an exhausting experience and with a creative approach, ruthless consistency, passion and commitment, your brand could also become a sponsorship winner.

Lamb

'We love our lamb'

How staying true to a long-term strategy in tough market conditions delivered a seventy-fold return on investment

Principal authors: Samantha Reading, BMF Advertising (Australia), and Karen Judson, Meat & Livestock Australia

SUMMARY

In 2001/02, Meat & Livestock Australia (MLA) and its agency BMF delivered a significant return on a modest advertising investment from lamb producers. This year's campaign enabled the value of the industry to grow 17.4% by driving consumer demand at a time of serious drought, when supply was down. The $2.4m marketing budget delivered a remarkable seventy-fold return on investment to the Australian lamb industry.

THE CHALLENGE

Lamb operates in a true marketplace, where there is no marketing 'control' over supply or price. Marketing is essentially the only variable. The effectiveness of lamb marketing programmes has to be measured by examining predicted and actual lamb prices using an economic model called the 'Demand Index'. This Index is a price elasticity model that measures consumer demand. It was developed specifically and independently for the meat industry and can be used to predict price, consumption or demand.

In 2001/02 the Index predicted that with expected reduced supply and no change to consumer demand, retail prices would rise by 9.7%.

While it was vital to continue to drive demand, especially given higher prices, we needed to consider how far prices could be pushed up before Australian families would restrict their lamb consumption and turn toward substitutes. Historically lamb has been a relatively price-sensitive product.

THE CAMPAIGN

2001/02 was the third year of the 'We love our lamb' campaign, a successful long-term marketing strategy of brand and tactical activity. This was not about a one-off TV campaign, but rather a fully integrated programme of highly creative communications targeting young parents and families through cost-efficient media.

While expectations for the advertising were high, there was a budget of only $2.4m for marketing activity (including media, advertising production, PR and POS). Lamb producers contributed 24c per lamb towards marketing for the year 2001/02.

Our 2001/02 campaign was based on the six 'Lamb principles' that have proved effective over time. These are:

1. Sales volume can only be generated by demand from contemporary families.
2. Mainstream cuts (chops and roasts) provide the greatest volume opportunity.
3. Lamb needs to be supported by year round activity, not just in the traditional spring.
4. All activity should be integrated and touch consumers in many different ways.
5. Lamb communications need to have a distinctive voice to stand out and be noticed.
6. Passion and energy must drive the entire agency and client team!

The significant difference was that research for 2001/02 gave us some key insights:

- kids love the sweet taste and tenderness of lamb
- developmentally it is important for 6- to 12-year-old children to express their independence – and their favourite meals are those they can eat with their fingers.

So we identified lamb chops as nature's perfect finger food, already complete with their very own 'handle'.

Further investigation revealed that certain annual events were seen as 'rituals' – important opportunities for family togetherness, be it around a BBQ or over a lamb roast. It was important to have distinctive activity around these rituals, to reinforce the connections they had with lamb.

Following on from these insights, the lamb campaign for 2001/02 consisted of a two-fold approach.

1. Brand activity to modify the young parents' mindset and influence the positioning of lamb. The 'Kids love things with handles' campaign spanned TV, POS, print, guerrilla marketing and online media.
2. Tactical activity spikes to increase lamb usage and add interest to a broader target market at key times in the year. Activity was based around the footy finals, Australia Day and Mother's Day, across TV, print, POS, promotions, radio and online.

THE RESULTS

The marketing programme stimulated consumer demand and delivered the following outstanding results.

- Retail prices (adjusted for inflation) were pushed up by 20.7%, well above the predicted 9.7%. This was 12.8% higher than the biggest price increase ever seen.
- Consumer expenditure on lamb rose 17.4% from $1.262bn to $1.482bn, an increase of $220m ($173m over the predicted increase).
- The domestic saleyard value of lamb rose by 48%.
- Saleyard prices rose an incredible 56%, encouraging more sheep farmers to switch from wool production to lamb production.
- The 24c per lamb marketing expenditure resulted in a $17.30 return for each lamb sold.
- The $2.4m marketing budget delivered a remarkable seventy-fold return on investment to the Australian lamb industry.

BRONZE

Rainbow

How a clever communication strategy led to an international campaign for Rainbow evaporated milk, taking it to the number one slot in three years

Principal author: Inder Bangari, TDA DDB
Media agency: OMD

SUMMARY

Historically, fresh milk supply was limited in the Gulf region. In the 1960s, Friesland introduced the category of evaporated milk in the region with the launch of Rainbow. It was packed in a tin can and was easy to store and transport. It was promoted as a brand for tea whitening, drinking and cooking, and for making desserts. In the late 1980s, dairy farms emerged in the region and dramatically increased the supply of fresh milk.

The greater availability of fresh milk and the aggressive support behind both fresh milk and IMP (instant milk powder) brands, cannabalised evaporated milk volumes.

The category started stagnating with flat growth rates in the early 1990s. By the mid-1990s, the category volumes started declining.

With the decline of the category, Rainbow (the number two brand in the category) also started losing volumes. Besides, Rainbow commanded a price premium over other brands and hence was the most susceptible to volume loss.

The challenge was to identify a clear *raison d'être* for Rainbow.

Friesland appointed TDA DDB as its advertising agency and briefed it to take action and turn the brand around. The first thing the agency did was to commission research.

Category adoption analysis indicated the prime motivator for first time purchase was prompted by its usage in tea whitening. Retention of a brand in a household primarily depended upon its performance in tea whitening.

The next logical research requirement was to identify the key criteria for selecting an evaporated milk brand and assess Rainbow's relative position versus the competition.

The category was perceived to be primarily for tea whitening and, within that, Rainbow emerged as a clear leader: a trusted brand that imparted a rich/creamy taste and flavour to tea/coffee.

Although the tea consumption habit is well ingrained amongst all nationalities, three key nationality groups were identified that contributed to more than 95% of all evaporated milk consumed.

Most brands resorted to the easy route of addressing Arabs in Arabic and everyone else in English.

TDA DDB, on the other hand, realised that the different ethnic groups needed slightly different messages, and would respond more warmly if they were spoken to in their own language. This approach would be more expensive in terms of production, but more effective in building brand empathy.

Consumer research indicated that Rainbow was held in high esteem and enjoyed the status of a 'saviour', a messiah, that brought joy and delight in the harsh, arid conditions. It was always served to family and friends as a sign of good hospitality. Rainbow was not merely perceived to be 'milk in a can'. The brand name and pack graphics are recognised icons that signal a brand that imparts a unique taste and flavour to tea, coffee and food preparations, and conjure up images of spreading happiness and joy.

It was crucial to build strong brand values amongst the youth while strengthening Rainbow's emotional connection with the older generation.

After gaining consumer and business learnings, a long-term plan was formulated that clearly identified business objectives and strategy for distinct markets. Also, a strategic long-term communication plan was agreed upon.

A regional media support plan across six markets was developed on a tight budget to break in March 1998. In order to maximise the use of the budgets, higher media weights were planned for priority markets and maintenance support for remaining countries to ensure dominant SOV within category and a significant SOV versus fresh milk and IMP.

The strategically developed campaign based on thorough analysis of consumer understanding and category dynamics resulted in advertising that rejuvenated Rainbow, strengthening emotional bonding with consumers, building volumes and shares for six successive years, reversing a trend of four years of flat/declining volumes and shares.

During the four-year period from 1998, Rainbow's household penetration increased by 34% in the lead market, UAE. Besides, there was a 33% increased 'share of usage' in tea whitening for Rainbow in 2001 versus 1999.

Also, Rainbow did not gain share by cutting price – in fact, the competition cut prices while Rainbow maintained its premium pricing. By increasing the price gap between Rainbow and the competition, the quality perception of the brand was further enhanced, while protecting brand profitability.

Implementation of solid strategic thinking and smart media targeting resulted in stimulating a declining brand by clearly establishing its 'reason for existence'. Advertising investment over six years for Rainbow paid for itself 2.8 times over.

By virtue of the Rainbow advertising, the entire category was positioned as a tea whitener and started gaining volumes.

Road Safety

How a nine-year investment of £8.68m in road safety advertising made a leading contribution to a £704m economic payback

Principal authors: David Lyle, Julie Anne Bailie, Dawn Reid, Robert Lyle and Pauline Kerr, LyleBailie International

SUMMARY

Road deaths grab headlines every day. Journalists often ask, is the advertising working?

This case study explores how a £8.68m investment in coordinated road safety advertising made a significant contribution to an economic payback of £704.35m, over a nine-year period, 1995 to 2003.

The human payback was in the 2774 lives saved from death and serious injury, compared to the previous nine years.

While previous case studies have examined the effectiveness of behaviour-specific campaigns (such as drink driving, seatbelts, speeding) over shorter time-spans, the difference in this study is that it probes the cumulative effect of a series of road safety advertising campaigns, over the longer term.

THE DOE'S OBJECTIVE

The Government's committed objective since 1995 has been:

> 'to reduce the number of killed or seriously injured on Northern Ireland's roads by one-third'
>
> Source: DoE 1995 Road Safety Plan; NI Road Safety Strategy, 2002–2012

The current target is to achieve this reduction by 2012, lowering killed/serious injuries (KSIs) to under 1200 per year.

THE STRATEGIC SOLUTION

To help achieve the objective, the campaign had to *disrupt* the road user's escapist mindset and make road safety a front-of-mind issue. To do this, the agency introduced a new methodology to road safety advertising, which was:

- data led
- research led
- psychology led.

This data-led approach led to a tight definition of target audiences.

The data-led foundations of the strategy fed directly into the research-led interrogation of the problem, ensuring that we probed the precise target audiences. From 1994 to 2003 the agency engaged with 81,328 research subjects on road safety.

The findings of this research, from its inception in 1994, led directly to the application of ?SYCHOLOGICAL ©REATIVITY™ to road safety education campaigns.

Shock alone is not enough. This strategy insists on a persuasive moral argument in each advertisement, disrupting the road user's comfortable self-deception, dramatising the consequences of human error on the road with raw realism, conveyed with clarity of culpability.

COMMUNICATIONS ACTIVITY

From 1995 to 2003, the total expenditure was £8.68m, with 75.4% of the budget being spent on TV. The decision to major on TV was research led. No other channel of communication could compare with TV's speed in achieving 90% coverage.

RESULTS

During the nine years from the launch of the new advertising strategy, total KSIs fell by 2774, compared to the previous nine years. The economic saving of £704.35m is based upon government figures: £1.25m per death and £0.140m per serious injury.

When the KSI data is linked to the growth of licensed vehicles, we find that KSIs per 10,000 vehicles have fallen by 42.32%.

The stark reality is that the 33% growth in licensed vehicles for 1995–2003, compared to 1986–1994, could have produced a 33% increase in moving metal killing and maiming people.

But how do we know that the advertising contributed to these results?

A series of surveys, independently conducted, confirms the role of the advertising, proving that:

- the new advertising strategy produced a dramatic increase in the awareness of road safety advertising
- the TV advertising was the most important factor in creating an awareness of road safety
- the DoE TV campaigns emerged as the most influential, according to the public
- the road safety TV ads were massively influential compared to all other sources, including TV reports and press articles about road safety.

A Millward Brown survey into the public's perception of which factors were most influential in saving lives on Northern Ireland's roads isolates the advertising effect, as compared to other possible factors. The DoE's TV ads emerge as the most influential, in the public perception.

CONCLUSION

DoE's road safety advertising has worked alongside enforcement, engineering and other educational measures in reducing road carnage in Northern Ireland. The evidence isolates the advertising effect and proves it has made a major and influential contribution to the reduction in overall deaths and serious injuries. A £8.68m investment in advertising played a leading role in achieving a £704.35m economic saving. Today, 2774 people, who would have been killed or maimed, enjoy life.

> 'It is rare to conduct advertising research nowadays without the public's reference to the Road Safety Campaign and its success, not only in changing attitudes, but, importantly, in encouraging people to reassess and shift their behaviour as well. In short, the campaign has infiltrated the lives of people in Northern Ireland and become part of current folklore.'
>
> Millward Brown Ulster, 17 May 2004

BRONZE

Sony Ericsson T610

Redrawing the adoption curve

Principal author: Martin Smith, Bartle Bogle Hegarty
Contributing author: Heather Alderson, Bartle Bogle Hegarty

SUMMARY

Rapid advances in technology have created a proliferation of new technology products, making successful launches difficult and rare. This paper demonstrates a new and more effective way of launching technology products.

It shows how the combination of advertising's timing and targeting in six major markets made a big difference to its effectiveness.

By bravely advertising significantly after the launch of its T610 camera phone, Sony Ericsson created the must-have phone of 2003. It challenged traditional handset launch advertising by ignoring early adopters and instead targeting mainstream consumers.

This approach didn't just pay back the investment – it was more than twice as effective as the traditional mobile launch model.

THE TRADITIONAL LAUNCH MODEL

The traditional model when launching a new mobile phone (or any other piece of new technology for that matter) is to target early adopters with feature-rich broadcast advertising because there is a belief that their recommendation (either verbally or tacitly through visibility of use) will in turn influence the early majority/ more mainstream consumers.

New thinking

We challenged this approach. We felt that the influence of early adopters on mainstream consumers was over-estimated. It was based on the assumption that early adopters mix and discuss mobile phones, and desire similar things from them.

All our evidence suggested that this was not the case. Both groups seek exclusivity, however an early adopter's definition of exclusivity was, in part, the exclusion of the mainstream.

We found that early adopters are very focused on what they can *do* with phones. In focus groups they eagerly discuss the more advanced applications and compare performance credentials. Mainstream consumers, on the other hand, tend to focus on the appearance of the phone and look for obvious clues that something is new, different and better.

OUR STRATEGY

The T610 launch strategy was to speed up the pace at which consumers adopt new technology, in order to create more sales, more quickly. Essentially, this meant changing the targeting, message and timing of launch communications.

We changed the targeting, to focus on mainstream consumers, not the traditional new technology target of early adopters.

This meant that we had to change the message. Mainstream consumers are more interested in the appearance and social status of a mobile handset and less interested in its technological features. The advertising strategy focused on the T610's aesthetic, in order to create social cachet, whilst communicating the social importance of the in-built camera.

TV advertising introduces people to the stylish world of the T610. In the 'Pass it on' commercial everything is choreographed around the process of sharing an image. In print, we celebrated the visual contrast of the T610's two-tone design style in a confident understated manner.

Media placement reinforced this. Our simple, iconic product statements were placed in more style-driven magazines and arresting outdoor locations than the traditional 'gadget magazines' media strategy.

Lastly, we changed the timing. Product ubiquity is important to mainstream consumers, so advertising was delayed until four months *after* the launch of the handset itself. This was incredibly brave, since the average lifespan for any new mobile handset is under one year. The T610 therefore had less time in which to generate more sales than its competitors.

ADVERTISING PAYBACK

Comparing the growth in T610 sales with that of other camera phones, we can determine that a traditional approach would have generated 241,353 sales for the T610.

However, our new mainstream approach generated an additional 377,213 sales, making the total sales generated by advertising 618,566 T610 handsets.

Based on an industry average profit margin, a traditional launch approach would have generated €11,440,127 profit. However, our mainstream approach generated an additional €17,879,908 profit, making the total payback from advertising €29,320,035.

Total media and production spend for the T610 was €22m. Therefore, the total advertising return exceeded the investment by more than 30%.

CONCLUSION

Sony Ericsson's unusual timing, targeting and creative strategy paid off. By delaying advertising and targeting mainstream consumers instead of early adopters, its advertising accelerated the speed of adoption of the T610 and made it the best-selling camera phone of 2003.

Virgin Mobile Australia

Winning big with a loser called Warren

Principal authors: Olly Taylor, Host, and
George Monical, Virgin Mobile Australia
Media agency: Mitchell and Partners (Qld)

SUMMARY

This is a story about one three-month campaign that featured a remarkably unattractive, single and desperate young man called Warren, and the stir it caused in the Australian market.

The Warren campaign delivered Virgin Mobile Australia (VMA) the most significant results in its history and put the brand back on track at a time when it needed it most.

Warren helped propel VMA to its highest ever market placing, helped acquire valuable groups of young text messagers, lowered the average age of the user base, reduced churn, increased usage and attracted new users.

This paper charts the effects of the campaign and demonstrates, using deliberately conservative criteria, its value. It will show that based upon increased acquisition and decreased customer churn, the Warren campaign was worth approximately 9.7m AUD (approx £3.8m), on a total media and production cost of 2.5m AUD (approx £976,000).

THE CREATIVE BRIEF

By the beginning of 2003 steady share growth was faltering. The beginning of quarter 2, 2003, saw a decline in market share for the first time since launch. This was tangible evidence that despite a growing market VMA was underperforming. This was a critical time for VMA and a turning point for the brand. At this time the new Virgin To Virgin 5 cent text rate was introduced.

The leap in the creative brief was to dramatise the benefit of the 5 cent text rate in a distinctive way. Instead of seeing the lowered price as a reason to send more texts, the brief emphasised that as a result of the 5 cent rate people with Virgin might receive lots more texts.

CREATIVE IDEA

The idea was Warren. A lovable loser in desperate need of a girlfriend. He made his own dating ads encouraging people to text him to strike up a relationship. The ads all featured a phone number, 0403 WARREN, that people could text or call.

MEDIA STRATEGY AND IMPLEMENTATION

Youth focus: the media strategy exploited the broadly targeted media plans of the other telcos to specifically focus on the 16–24 age group only. This focus allowed the share of voice to be maximized from 3% share to a 15% share of exposure against 16–24s in TV alone.

Social focus: this audience is difficult to target with single (broadcast) media, especially during the 'outdoorsy' Australian summer. The multimedia strategy was designed to make use of media in 'social interaction' and 'out and about' media such as, public transport, taxi backs, street press, pizza boxes and cinema/bar washrooms. The aim was two-fold: to get them in 'mobile heavy' scenarios and in times of social interaction where Warren could spark discussion.

Effect 1: Warren cut-through

Overall 74% of respondents claimed to have seen the 'Warren' campaign across all media. This figure rises to 85% amongst 18–24s. The recall figure should be compared to Nielsen's benchmark recall figure for all TV campaigns in Australia of 50%. A significant result on a share of voice of under 3%.

Effect 2: overwhelming response

Warren received over 600,000 calls and texts during the campaign period. Put in context this represents a call or text from over 4% of the entire Australian mobile-owning population.

Effect 3: increased text usage

Existing customers upped their average monthly text count and those recruited during this campaign were higher-volume texters and younger users than the average for VMA.

Effect 4: increased acquisition

We have estimated that Warren accounted for 49% of the gross additions over the campaign period (October to February). Adhering to the conservative assumptions of 18-month customer tenure, margin not revenue and 20% value discount, this is valued at 7.5m AUD in incremental gross margin.

Effect 5: increased retention

Warren also had a significant impact on customer loyalty and retention. As a result of the campaign, churn was 21% lower in 2003 than the same time period in the previous year. It has been calculated that this reduction in attrition has a value of 2.2m AUD.

TOTAL COMMUNICATION VALUE

The two factors of significant value are:

1. 49% increase in acquisition – value 7.5m AUD.
2. 21% reduction in churn – value 2.2m AUD.

Total: 9.7m AUD (approx £3.8m).

Total investment: 2.5m AUD (approx £976,000).

Weetabix

How Weetabix profited from energetic brand advertising to become the best-selling cereal in the UK

Principal authors: Kit Fordham, Justin Pahl, Louise Burrows and Nick Alford, FCB London

SUMMARY

This paper demonstrates how a change in brand and advertising strategy helped establish Weetabix as the number one in value sales for the first time in its illustrious 70-year history; and, in so doing, will have generated an estimated £10.52m in extra revenues by the end of July 2005.

It shows that this was no 'natural progression' from the number two breakfast cereal brand. Fundamental changes in consumer attitudes and behaviour were threatening the long-term commercial value of family staple breakfast cereals and ushering in dramatic growth for so-called 'repertoire brands'. The Weetabix brand faced a very real challenge in sustaining its longer-term commercial value, let alone moving ahead to become market leader.

Rather than find a way to ring-fence the Weetabix brand, FCB London's task was to find a strategic solution that would capitalise on these consumer trends. FCB London's scoop was to identify a means of actually strengthening on-going brand loyalty, and, therefore, the long-term commercial value of Weetabix. The best form of defence was, as ever, attack.

The success of the brand solution for Weetabix was in large part due to the fact that the creative idea could be articulated in all conceivable forms of communication, thereby maximising the effect on brand loyalty. Such was the clarity of the strategy that a focus would be provided for Weetabix internally, in particular in terms of future NPD. Fundamentally, this is the story of how creativity transformed potential adversity into lasting prosperity for the Weetabix brand and Weetabix Limited.

The paper uses recently published thinking on the long-term effects of advertising to demonstrate the payback that comes from full-value, ad-driven sales. It scales short-term sales uplifts year on year to provide a demonstration of the 'lifetime' value of advertising on consumers' brand relationship. As such, it demonstrates a model of advertising payback that prompts a radical upward revision of existing theories of advertising's contribution to revenue.

THE STRATEGIC AND CREATIVE SOLUTION

In our investigation of the brand and its recent advertising, it became clear that Weetabix could not rely on the involvement framework of advertising, where advertising's emotional values are transferred to the brand, leading in turn to greater brand commitment. Qualitative research undertaken by FCB London revealed that Withabix/Withoutabix advertising (the previous campaign) was broadly enjoyed but did little to drive commitment to the Weetabix brand. It was intrusive and likeable but failed to substantiate the brand's reason for being. It provided a tonal blueprint for future advertising development but little more.

The fulcrum of FCB London's strategic solution for the Weetabix brand lay in the nutritional properties of whole wheat: energy release over a sustained period. This was a product benefit relevant to all ages and stages, from the very youngest through to the eldest, and something that worked strongly with mothers, still the gatekeeper to most purchases in the sector. 'Energy release' was the product truth of Weetabix that could drive brand loyalty through reaffirming the brand's role at breakfast and its ultimate benefit to a diverse body of consumers.

The communications objective was clear: to position Weetabix as a wholesome source of energy. This led to the following brand proposition: 'Weetabix: Power Packs For People'; and this to the idea: 'Weetabix. Generating Energy For Everyone'.

Apart from TV, posters and press, which launched in June 2002, the campaign extended into sponsorship, crop circles, actors on the Underground and schools sports days.

THE RESULTS

The 'Energy' campaign re-energised the Weetabix brand. In terms of advertising response, the campaign registered strongly in relation to Millward Brown norms, was well liked and crucially got across the message that 'Weetabix gives you steady-release energy'. In turn this strengthened the brand relationship both on the rational dimensions of Weetabix providing energy and helping you feel good, as well as the emotional aspect (i.e. the brand affinity with Weetabix). As the advertising re-built the brand this in turn led to greater brand loyalty, especially amongst mothers. As a result, Weetabix volume sales rose in year one and stayed higher in year two. Weetabix value sales continued to grow in year two.

The econometrics demonstrates that 6.3% of Weetabix's total volume sale was attributable to the 'Energy' campaign in the 12 months to 31 July 2003. Taking this 6.3% figure and applying it to Weetabix's total value sales of £86.1m it can be calculated that the 'Energy' campaign generated £5.42m of revenue in one year alone.

However, using recently available thinking, the long-term payback of the 'Energy' campaign can be calculated, not just the one-year snapshot established by the econometrics. The paper presented by JB Kazmierczak, 'Long-term Effects of Advertising and Promotion', at the European Advertising Effectiveness Symposium, Copenhagen, in June 2001, demonstrates using IRI data that advertising has a carry-over effect in years two and three. Further, consumers who purchase on the basis of advertising versus promotional effects have been proven to be more likely to repeat purchase, and these additional purchases are more likely to be full-value sales.

These factors prove that effective advertising has an effect over a three-year period, not just one year.

Therefore the amount of total Weetabix value sales attributable to the 'Energy' campaign becomes £10.52m by the end of 31 July 2005. Given that the initial advertising investment behind the 'Energy' campaign between June 2002 and July 2003 was £5.5m, it can be seen that this cost was outweighed by total value sales generated even before pure profit is calculated.

How to Access the IPA dataBANK

The IPA Effectiveness dataBANK represents the most rigorous and comprehensive examination of marketing communications working in the marketplace, in the world. Over the 25 years of the IPA Effectiveness Awards competition (1979 to 2004), the IPA has collected over 1000 examples of best practice in advertising development and results across a wide spectrum of marketing sectors and expenditures. Each case history contains up to 4000 words of text and is illustrated in full by market, research, sales and profit data.

ACCESS

The dataBANK is held in the IPA Information Centre for access by IPA members only. Simply contact the Centre by emailing *info@ipa.co.uk*. Simple or more sophisticated searches can be run, free of charge, by qualified, professional knowledge executives across a range of parameters including brand, advertiser, agency, target market (by age, sex, class, and so on), medium and length of activity, which can be specified by the user and the results supplied by email or other means as required.

PURCHASING IPA CASE STUDIES

Member agencies will be allowed a maximum number of 25 case studies for download in any given calendar year, after which they will be charged at £17 each. Alternatively, members can sign up to WARC (see overleaf) at a beneficial IPA rate and can then download case studies as part of that subscription.

FURTHER INFORMATION

For further information, please contact the Information Centre at the IPA, 44 Belgrave Square, London SWIX 8QS.
Telephone: +44 (0)20 7235 7020
Fax: 020 7245 9904
Website: *www.ipa.co.uk*
Email: *info@ipa.co.uk*.

www.WARC.com

The IPA case histories dataBANK can also be accessed through the World Advertising Research Center (WARC). Reached by logging on to *www.warc.com*, the world's most comprehensive advertising database enables readers to search all the IPA case histories, over 2000 case histories from similar award schemes around the world, including the Advertising Federation of Australia and the Institute of Communications and Advertising in Canada, plus thousands of 'how to' articles on all areas of communication activity. Sources include the Journal of Advertising Research, Canadian Congress of Advertising, *Admap*, and the American Association of Advertising Agencies, as well as the IPA.

IPA dataBANK Case Availability

* Denotes publication in the relevant *Advertising Works* volume

NEW ENTRIES 2004

2004 AA Loans*
2004 Ackermans (SA)
2004 Army Recruitment*
2004 B&Q
2004 Beck's Bier (Australia)
2004 BMW Films – The Hire*
2004 Bounty (Paper Towels)*
2004 British Airways*
2004 BT Broadband*
2004 BUPA*
2004 Cadbury's Dream (SA)
2004 Central London Congestion Charge*
2004 Children's Hearings (Scottish Executive)*
2004 Co-op Food Retail
2004 Cravendale (Milk)*
2004 Crown Paints
2004 Direct Line*
2004 East of England Development Agency (Broadband)*
2004 Electoral Commission (Northern Ireland)
2004 Eurostar*
2004 Evergood Coffee (Norway)
2004 First Direct
2004 Garnier
2004 Guardian, The*
2004 Honda*
2004 Imperial Leather*
2004 Kiwi (SA)
2004 Lamb (Meat & Livestock Australia)*
2004 Lego Bionicle
2004 Listerine
2004 Lynx Pulse*
2004 M&G
2004 Magnum
2004 Marks & Spencer Lingerie*
2004 McVities Jaffa Cakes
2004 Northern Ireland Tourist Board
2004 O_2*
2004 Police Officer Recruitment (Hertfordshire Constabulary)*
2004 Postbank (Post Office SA)
2004 Rainbow (Evaporated Milk)*
2004 Road Safety (DoE Northern Ireland)*
2004 Roundup
2004 s1jobs
2004 Safer Travel at Night (GLA)*
2004 Sony Ericsson T610*
2004 Standard Bank (SA)
2004 The Number 118 118*
2004 Tobacco Control (DH)*
2004 Toyota Corolla
2004 Tritace
2004 TUI (Germany)
2004 Vehicle Crime Reduction (Home Office)
2004 Virgin Mobile Australia*
2004 Virgin Mobile*
2004 Virgin Trains*
2004 Volkswagen Diesel*
2004 Weetabix*

2000 1001 Mousse*

A

1982 Abbey Crunch
1990 Abbey National Building Society
1990 Abbey National Building Society (plc)
1980 Abbey National Building Society Open Bondshares
1990 Aberlour Malt Whisky*
1996 Adult Literacy *
2002 Aerogard Mosquito Repellent (Australia)
1986 AGS Home Improvements*
1988 AIDS
1994 AIDS*
1986 Air Call
1990 Alex Lawrie Factors
1980 All Clear Shampoo*
1992 Alliance & Leicester Building Society*
1990 Alliance & Leicester Building Society*
1988 Alliance & Leicester Building Society*
1984 Alliance Building Society
1990 Allied Dunbar
1984 Allinson's Bread
1984 Alpen
1990 Alton Towers
1992 Amnesty International
1990 Amnesty International*
1990 Anchor Aerosol Cream
1994 Anchor Butter
1988 Anchor Butter
1992 Andrex
1994 Andrex Ultra
1986 Andrex*

1986 Anglia Building Society
1996 Anglian Water
2002 Anti-Drink Driving*
1990 Anti-NHS Reform Campaign (BMA)
1994 Anti-Smoking
2000 Archers*
1998 Army Recruitment*
1996 Arrol's 80
1994 Arthur's (Cat food)
1988 Audi
1990 Audi*
1998 Audi*
1982 Austin Metro*
1980 Austin Mini*
1990 Auto Express
1996 Automobile Association*

B

2002 B&Q
1988 Babycham
1988 Baby Fresh
1998 Bacardi Breezer
1996 Bacardi Breezer
2000 Bahlsen Biscuits
1992 Bailey's
2002 Bakers Complete*
1988 Barbican
1990 Barbican Health & Fitness Centre
1996 Barclaycard*
1992 Barclaycard
1998 Barclays Bank Current Account
2002 Barnardo's*
1994 Batchelors
1998 Batchelors Supernoodles*
1998 Bell's Whisky
2002 Benadryl*
1986 Benylin*
1990 Billy Graham's Mission 89
1986 Birds Eye Alphabites*
1992 Birds Eye Country Club Cuisine
1994 Birds Eye Crispy Chicken
1982 Birds Eye Oven Crispy Cod Steaks in Batter*
1988 Birmingham Executive Airways
1990 Black Tower
1996 Blockbuster Video
1982 Blue Riband
2000 Bluewater*
1994 BMW*
1994 Boddington's*
1990 Bodyform
1994 Book Club Associates
1998 Boots Advantage Card
1988 Boots Brand Medicines
1998 Boursin
1994 Boursin
1986 Bovril
2000 Bowmore
1990 Bradford & Bingley Building Society
1986 Bradford & Bingley Building Society*
1980 Braun Shavers
1982 Bread Advisory Council*
1982 Breville Toasted Sandwichmaker
2002 Britannia Building Society*
1996 British Airways
1994 British Airways*
1984 British Airways Shuttle Service
1994 British Diabetic Association*
1980 British Film Institute*
1994 British Gas Central Heating
1988 British Gas Flotation*
1988 British Nuclear Fuels
1988 British Rail Young Person's Railcard
1982 British Sugar Corporation
1980 British Turkey Federation
2000 BT Business
1992 BT
1996 BT Business*
1994 BT Business
1992 BT Call Waiting*
2002 BT Cellnet*
1986 BT Consumer*
1986 BT Privatisation*
2002 BT Retail*
1998 Bud Ice
2002 Budweiser*
1988 Budweiser
2002 BUPA
2000 BUPA
1980 BUPA
1996 Butter Council

C

1996 Cable Television
1994 Cadbury's Boost*
1992 Cadbury's Caramel
1998 Cadbury's Creme Eggs
1988 Cadbury's Creme Eggs
1984 Cadbury's Creme Eggs
1992 Cadbury's Crunchie
1984 Cadbury's Curly Wurly*
1980 Cadbury's Dairy Box
1982 Cadbury's Flake
1984 Cadbury's Fudge*
1994 Cadbury's Highlights
1990 Cadbury's Mini Eggs
1994 Cadbury's Roses*
1986 Cadbury's Wispa
1988 Café Hag
1996 Californian Raisins
1980 Campari*
1992 Campbell's Condensed Soup
1988 Campbell's Meatballs*
1994 Campbell's Soup
1996 Cancer Relief Macmillan Fund
1984 Canderel

1992 Caramac
1994 Car Crime Prevention
1998 Carex
1996 Carling Black Label
1994 Carling Black Label
1984 Carousel
1998 Carrick Jewellery
1986 Castlemaine XXXX*
1992 Cellnet Callback
1988 Center-Parcs
1992 Central Television Licence Renewal
2000 Channel 5
1990 Charlton Athletic Supporters Club*
1980 Cheese Information Service
1996 Cheltenham & Gloucester Building Society
1988 Chessington World of Adventures
2002 Chicago Town Pizza
1998 Chicago Town Pizza
1994 Chicken Tonight
2000 Chicken Tonight Sizzle and Stir*
1994 Child Road Safety
1992 Childhood Diseases Immunisation
1990 Children's World
1984 Chip Pan Fires Prevention*
1990 Choosy Catfood*
1998 Christian Aid*
1992 Christian Aid
1994 CICA (Trainers)*
1992 Citroën Diesel Range
1988 Clairol Nice n' Easy
1988 Clarks Desert Boots*
1996 Classic Combination Catalogue
1994 Clerical Medical
1992 Clorets
1988 Clover
1984 Clover
1980 Cointreau
1998 Colgate Toothpaste*
1990 Colman's Wholegrain Mustard
2000 Confetti.co.uk*
2000 Co-op*
1996 Cooperative Bank
1994 Cooperative Bank*
1990 Copperhead Cider
1982 Country Manor (Alcoholic Drink)
1986 Country Manor (Cakes)
1984 Cow & Gate Babymeals*
1982 Cracottes*
2000 Crime Prevention
1990 Croft Original*
1982 Croft Original
1980 Croft Original
2002 Crown Paint
2000 Crown Paints*
1990 Crown Solo*
1984 Cuprinol*
1986 Cyclamon*

D

1996 Daewoo*
1982 Daily Mail*
2002 Dairy Council (Milk)*
2000 Dairylea*
1992 Danish Bacon & Meat Council
1980 Danum Taps
1990 Data Protection Registrar
1980 Day Nurse
1994 Daz
1996 De Beers Diamonds*
2002 Debenhams
1980 Deep Clean*
2000 Degree
1980 Dettol*
2002 DfES Higher Education
1984 DHL Worldwide Carrier
1998 Direct Debit
1992 Direct Line Insurance*
1990 Dog Registration
2000 Domestic Abuse*
2002 Domino's Pizza*
2002 Dr Beckmann Rescue*
1980 Dream Topping
1988 Drinking & Driving
1998 Drugs Education*
1994 Dunfermline Building Society
1980 Dunlop Floor Tiles
1990 Duracell Batteries
1980 Dynatron Music Suite

E

1988 E & P Loans*
2000 easyJet*
2002 Economist, The*
1992 Economist, The*
1994 Edinburgh Club*
1990 Edinburgh Zoo
1980 Eggs Authority
1992 Electricity Privatisation
1980 Ellerman Travel & Leisure
1996 Emergency Contraception
1986 EMI Virgin (records)*
1980 English Butter Marketing Company
1986 English Country Cottages
1992 Enterprise Initiative
1992 Equity & Law
1990 Eurax (Anti-Itch Cream)
1994 Evening Standard Classified Recruitment
1984 Exbury Gardens

F

1990 Family Credit
1998 Famous Grouse
1982 Farmer's Table Chicken
2000 Felix*
1996 Felix*

K

1992 K Shoes*
1996 Kaliber
1992 Kaliber
1990 Karvol
1980 Kays Catalogue
1992 Kellogg's All Bran*
1984 Kellogg's Bran Flakes*
2000 Kellogg's Coco Pops*
1994 Kellogg's Coco Pops
1984 Kellogg's Coco Pops*
1982 Kellogg's Cornflakes
1980 Kellogg's Frozen Waffles
2000 Kellogg's Nutri-Grain*
2002 Kellogg's Real Fruit Winders*
1980 Kellogg's Rice Crispies*
1982 Kellogg's Super Noodles*
1998 Kenco
1986 Kensington Palace*
1998 KFC
1984 KFC
2000 KFC USA
1988 Kia Ora*
1984 Kleenex Velvet
1990 Knorr Stock Cubes*
1988 Kodak Colour Print Film
1994 Kraft Dairylea
1984 Kraft Dairylea*
1980 Krona Margarine*
1986 Kronenbourg 1664

L

1990 Lada
1992 Ladybird
1990 Lanson Champagne*
1992 Le Creuset
1982 Le Crunch
1990 Le Piat D'or
1986 Le Piat D'or
1996 Le Shuttle
1990 Lea & Perrin's Worcestershire Sauce*
1980 Lea & Perrin's Worcestershire Sauce
1988 Leeds Permanent Building Society
1988 Lego
1984 Leicester Building Society
1996 Lenor
2002 Levi Strauss Engineered Jeans (Japan)
1992 Levi Strauss UK*
1980 Levi Strauss UK
1988 Levi's 501s*
1996 Lil-lets
1990 Lil-lets*
1996 Lilt
1992 Limelite*
1980 Limmits
2000 Lincoln Insurance
2000 Lincoln USA
1980 Lion Bar
1992 Liquorice Allsorts
1988 Liquorice Allsorts
1988 Listerine*
1980 Listerine
1998 Littlewoods Pools
1992 Lloyds Bank
1984 Lloyds Bank*
1990 London Buses Driver Recruitment
1984 London Docklands*
1982 London Docklands
1990 London Philharmonic
1992 London Transport Fare Evasion
1986 London Weekend Television
1980 Lucas Aerospace*
1996 Lucky Lottery
1992 Lucozade
1980 Lucozade*
2000 Lurpak*
1988 Lurpak
2002 Lynx*
1994 Lyon's Maid Fab
1988 Lyon's Maid Favourite Centres

M

1988 Maclaren Prams
1990 Malibu
2002 Manchester Evening News (Job Section)*
1982 Manger's Sugar Soap*
1988 Manpower Services Commission
1994 Marks & Spencer
2002 Marmite*
1998 Marmite*
1998 Marmoleum
1988 Marshall Cavendish Discovery
1994 Marston Pedigree*
1986 Mazda*
1986 Mazola*
1998 McDonald's
1996 McDonald's
1980 McDougall's Saucy Sponge
1990 Mcpherson's Paints
1988 Mcpherson's Paints
2000 McVitie's Jaffa Cakes
1992 Mercury Communications
1988 Metropolitan Police Recruitment*
1990 Midland Bank
1988 Midland Bank
1992 Miele
1988 Miller Lite*
2000 Moneyextra*
1988 Mortgage Corporation*
2002 Mr Kipling*
1984 Mr Muscle
1994 Multiple Sclerosis Society
1996 Murphy's Irish Stout*
2000 Myk Menthol Norway*

N

2000 National Code and Number Change
1996 National Dairy Council – Milk*
1992 National Dairy Council – Milk
1980 National Dairy Council – Milk
1992 National Dairy Council – Milkman*
1996 National Lottery (Camelot)
1996 National Savings
1984 National Savings: Income Bonds
1982 National Savings: Save by Post*
1986 National Westminster Bank Loans
1982 Nationwide Building Society
1990 Nationwide Flex Account
1988 Nationwide Flex Account
1990 Navy Recruitment
1988 Nefax
1982 Negas Cookers
1982 Nescafé
2000 Network Q
1992 Neutrogena
1982 New Man Clothes
1994 New Zealand Lamb
1980 New Zealand Meat Producers Board
1996 Nike
1994 Nike
1994 Nissan Micra*
2000 No More Nails*
1986 No.7
1988 Norsk Data
1998 North West Water
1998 North West Water – Drought
2002 Norwich Union Pensions
1998 Norwich Union
1990 Nouvelle Toilet Paper
2000 NSPCC*
1990 Nurofen
1986 Nursing Recruitment
1994 Nytol

O

1980 Observer, The – French Cookery School Campaign
2002 Ocean Spray*
1988 Oddbins*
1998 Olivio*
2002 Olivio/Bertolli*
1998 Olympus
1982 Omega Chewing Gum
1998 One2One*
1992 Optrex*
1998 Orange*
1996 Orange*
2000 Orange International
2000 Orange Just Talk*
1984 Oranjeboom
1990 Otrivine
1992 Oxo*
1990 Oxo
1988 Oxo
1998 Oxo Lamb Cubes
1988 Oxy 10

P

1986 Paignton Zoo
2000 Pampers South Africa*
1988 Paracodol*
1984 Paul Masson California Carafes
1982 Pedal Cycle Casualties*
1998 Penguin
1994 Peperami*
1994 Pepsi Max
1990 Perrier
1986 Perrier
2000 Persil*
2000 PG Tips*
1990 PG Tips*
1996 Philadelphia*
1994 Philadelphia
1994 Phileas Fogg
1988 Phileas Fogg
1988 Phileas Fogg
1980 Philips Cooktronic
1980 Philips Video
1998 Physical Activity Campaign (HEB Scotland)
1990 Pilkington Glass
1992 Pilsner
1986 Pink Lady
1998 Pizza Hut*
1996 Pizza Hut
1994 Pizza Hut
1996 Pirelli
1990 Pirelli
1986 Pirelli
1984 Pirelli
1990 Plax
1980 Plessey Communications & Data Systems
1998 Polaroid*
1994 Police Federation of England and Wales
2002 Police Recruitment*
2002 Police Recruitment (Could You?)
2002 Police Recruitment Northern Ireland
1996 Polo Mints
1984 Polyfoam
1986 Portsmouth News
2002 Post Office*
1980 Post Office Mis-sorts
1986 Post Office Special Issue Stamps
1996 Potato Marketing Board
1998 Pot Noodle
1984 Presto
1980 Pretty Polly*
1990 Price Waterhouse
1992 Prudential

Q
1984 QE2
1988 Quaker Harvest Chewy Bars*
1982 Qualcast Concorde Lawn Mower*
1984 Qualcast Mow-n-trim and Rotasafe
1986 Quatro
1986 Quickstart
1996 Quorn Burgers

R
1982 Racal Redec Cadet
1990 Radion Automatic*
1994 Radio Rentals
1990 Radio Rentals
1996 RAF Recruitment
1980 RAF Recruitment*
1994 Range Rover
2000 Reading and Literacy*
1992 Real McCoys
2000 Rear Seatbelts*
1998 Red Meat Market*
1984 Red Meat Consumption
1988 Red Mountain*
1996 Reebok*
1992 Reebok
1990 Reliant Metrocabs
1994 Remegel
1998 Renault
1986 Renault 5
1990 Renault 19*
1996 Renault Clio*
1992 Renault Clio*
1984 Renault Trafic & Master
1996 Ribena
1982 Ribena*
2002 Rimmel*
1986 Rimmel Cosmetics
1996 Rocky (Fox's Biscuits)
1988 Rolls Royce Privatisation*
1996 Ross Harper*
1988 Rover 200
1982 Rowenta
1990 Rowntree's Fruit Gums
1992 Royal Bank of Scotland
1986 Royal College of Nursing
2002 Royal Mail
1986 Royal Mail Business Economy
1990 Royal National Institute for the Deaf
1996 RSPCA
1988 Rumbelows

S
1994 S4C
1988 Saab*
1996 Safeway
2002 Sainsbury's* (Jamie Oliver)
2002 Sainsbury's* (Promotion)
1996 Samaritans
1986 Sanatogen
1980 Sanatogen
1988 Sandplate*
1986 Sapur (Carpet Cleaner)
1992 Save the Children*
1988 Schering Greene Science
2000 scoot.com*
1980 Scotcade
1984 Scotch Video Cassettes
1998 Scotland on Sunday
1992 Scotrail
1992 Scottish Amicable*
1998 Scottish Prison Service
2002 Seafish Industry Authority
2002 Seatbelts*
1980 Seiko
1992 Sellafield Visitors Centre
2002 Senokot
1980 Shake 'n' Vac
1984 Shakers Cocktails*
2002 Shell Corporate
2002 Shell Optimax
1980 Shloer*
1986 Shredded Wheat
1990 Silent Night Beds*
2002 Skoda*
1992 Skol
1982 Skol
1980 Slumberdown Quilts
1990 Smarties
1980 Smirnoff Vodka
1980 Smith's Monster Munch
1982 Smith's Square Crisps
1992 Smith's Tudor Specials
1994 Smoke Alarms*
1992 Smoke Alarms
1996 So ...? (Fragrance)
1986 Soft & Gentle
1996 Soldier Recruitment
1994 Solvent Abuse
2000 Solvite*
1996 Solvite
1992 Sony
1988 Sony
1992 Sony Camcorders
1996 Springers by K (Shoes)
1984 St Ivel Gold*
2000 Standard Life
2000 Star Alliance
2002 Stella Artois*
2000 Stella Artois*
1998 Stella Artois
1996 Stella Artois*
1992 Stella Artois*
2002 Strathclyde Police
1994 Strepsils*
1990 Strongbow
1982 Summers the Plumbers

1980 Sunblest Sunbran
1990 Supasnaps
2000 Surf*
1980 Swan Vestas*
1984 SWEB Security Systems
1992 Swinton Insurance
1998 Switch
1996 Switch

T
1992 Tandon Computers
1990 Tango
1986 TCP*
1986 Teletext
1986 Territorial Army Recruitment
2000 Terry's Chocolate Orange*
2002 Tesco*
2000 Tesco*
1980 Tesco
1990 Tetley Tea Bags
1984 Thomas Cook
1992 Tia Maria
1990 Tia Maria
1990 Times, The
1994 Tizer
1980 Tjaereborg Rejser*
1980 Tolly's Original
2002 Tommy's: The Baby Charity*
1984 Torbay Tourist Board*
1986 Toshiba*
1986 Touche Remnant Unit Trusts
1992 Tower of London
1996 Toyota RAV4
1982 Trans World Airlines
1984 Tri-ac (Skincare)
1980 Triumph Dolomite
1994 TSB
1988 TSB*
1986 TSB*
1982 Turkish Delight*
1986 TV Licence Evasion*
2000 Twix Denmark

U
1984 UK Canned Salmon
1986 Umbongo Tropical Juice Drink
1998 UPS
1990 Uvistat*

V
1988 Varilux lenses
1994 Vauxhall Astra
1996 Vauxhall Cavalier
1990 Vauxhall Cavalier
1996 Vegetarian Society
1986 Virgin Atlantic
1994 Visa
1986 Vodafone
1998 Volkswagen*
2002 Volkswagen (Brand)*
2002 Volkswagen Passat*
1992 VW Golf*

W
1980 Waistline
2002 Waitrose*
1992 Wales Tourist Board
2002 Walkers Crisps*
1996 Walkers Crisps*
1998 Wallis
1980 Wall's Cornetto
1996 Wall's Viennetta
1984 Wall's Viennetta*
1984 Walnut Whips
1990 Warburtons Bread*
1984 Websters Yorkshire Bitter
1988 Weight Watchers Slimming Clubs
2002 West End Quay
1990 Westwood Tractors
1992 Whipsnade Wild Animal Park*
1980 Whitegate's Estate Agents*
1990 Wilson's Ultra Golf Balls
1988 Winalot Prime*
1994 Wonderbra*

Y
2000 Yellow Pages Norway
1980 Yeoman Pie Fillings
1980 Yorkie
1982 Yorkshire Bank
2002 Yorkshire Forward/Yorkshire Tourist Board

Z
1984 Zanussi*
1994 Zovirax

Index